Mortgage Lending

principles & practices

4th edition

HONDROS LEARNING™
4140 Executive Parkway
Westerville, Ohio 43081
www.hondroslearning.com

Published 2012. Printed in the United States of America

16 15 14 13 12 1 2 3 4 5

ISBN: 978-1-59844-159-8

Table of Contents

Table of Contents

Table of Contents

Foreword

For the last decade, the world of the mortgage broker has been a never-ending and exhilarating roller coaster ride. Between the drastic drops in interest rates and the dramatic rise in refinancing opportunities, many people have flocked to the mortgage industry. But huge curves are now ahead as the industry has been rocked with the issue of predatory lending and the nationwide downturn in the housing market.

Fortunately, opportunities still abound in the mortgage broker industry. Borrowers—many making the biggest purchasing decision of their life—now realize more choices in lenders can mean significant cost reduction for them. More than ever, consumers are comparison shopping and considering options other than traditional bank lenders. Customer service now plays a major role in borrowers' decisions on who will help them through the lending process.

You cannot ignore, however, the dramatically rising foreclosure rates across the country. Government is looking far beyond the down economy to identify the causes of these high rates. Many legislators and regulators blame the mortgage broker industry. As a result, mortgage brokers are more heavily regulated than ever before, at both the state and federal levels—and even local municipal levels. Additionally, brokers are finding themselves regulated not only as part of the lending process by federal and state banking regulators, but also in areas such as general consumer protection laws—an area from which they have historically been exempt.

Thus, it is more important than ever to arm yourself with knowledge of the industry and the ethical dilemmas that may arise. This text provides a comprehensive outline of all of the regulations that surround the mortgage industry. It alerts you to scenarios where compliance issues arise and helps provide solutions to them. It also provides a background of the industry's history that helps explain how and why today's complex regulatory scheme evolved.

As customer service becomes even more important, mortgage professionals can distinguish themselves as leaders in the industry by being most knowledgeable in the applicable laws and consummate professionals who transverse the ethical industry pitfalls with grace and honor.

—Helen Mac Murray

Partner, Mac Murray, Cook, Petersen, & Shuster

New Albany, Ohio

Preface

A mortgage loan is one of the biggest commitments a person will make in his or her lifetime. Because of this, mortgage professionals must be knowledgeable, ethical, and customer focused when it comes to providing home loans.

As a mortgage professional, you will guide consumers through the process of applying for a loan, facilitating this by seeking potential clients and assisting them in the application process. Steps involved include:

- Gathering and evaluating information about a customer's financial status for informed decision making
- Explaining the features and benefits of the different loan programs available
- Ensuring consumers select the program that is right for them
- Preparing the loan closing package
- Closing the loan

Not only do mortgage loan originators facilitate first mortgages, they can also help consumers refinance loans and obtain second mortgages. The steps involved in both of these processes closely match those listed above.

Mortgage loan originators also develop relationships with commercial and residential real estate agencies as well as with other mortgage professionals as a way of developing business by referral. Referral sources may come from a wide variety of places—satisfied customers, mortgage industry professionals, and also your own personal associations.

This textbook will provide you an overview in the mortgage industry, but not everything will be contained within these pages. It is common for a MLO still to be learning after years of experience. Federal and state laws, products, guidelines, and procedures will change, and you will be expected to keep current with what is going on in the mortgage industry. We would encourage and challenge you to become a true mortgage professional through not only doing the job listed in a job description, but also going above and beyond with your knowledge, customer service, and ethical behavior.

Using this Text

Mortgage Lending Principles and Practices was designed to give you the information you need to successfully enter the mortgage sales field. Contained here is a ***primer on the primary and secondary mortgage markets,*** as well as a complete ***review of the economic, legal,*** and ***valuation aspects of the real estate market.*** In addition, a thorough ***overview of federal lending legislation***—including amendments to the Truth in Lending Act and RESPA—is presented. This text also details the types of ***loan products and finance instruments***—including conventional and alternative financing tools—available today. You will also learn the fundamentals of the residential ***mortgage lending process***—from pre-qualifying potential borrowers to closing a loan. The important topic of ***ethical issues*** is also covered.

Whether used in the classroom or for self-study, you will find the information presented in a clear and concise manner. The authors have provided key terms, examples, chapter summaries and quizzes, as well as mortgage exercises and case studies to reinforce the concepts presented. Once you have completed your pre-licensing course or self-study program, keep this book handy as a valuable reference tool in your new mortgage career.

Hondros Learning™

Hondros Learning™ is a leading provider of classroom materials for mortgage pre-licensing and continuing education. Together with Hondros College, we have provided training and educational products for more than one million students.

Our *National Mortgage Lending CompuCram®* exam prep software is the perfect companion to this book. The software is a self-paced question and answer application designed to help you study for the national mortgage lending exam. For more information about CompuCram or any of our other products, please visit www.hondroslearning.com, www.compucram.com.

Reviewer Acknowledgments

Hondros Learning™ thanks the following expert reviewers for their valuable contributions and assistance in developing this text:

Edward C. Davies
Director of Operations, American School of Business

Lisa M. Durand
President, Albany Funding, Inc.

Linda Heninger
Mortgage Instructor, Hondros Learning

Helen Mac Murray
Partner, Mac Murray, Cook, Petersen, & Shuster

J. Thad McIntyre, CRMS
President, Nationwide Home Loans

Bob Niemi
Executive Director, Ohio Mortgage Bankers Association

James F. O'Hagan
Instructor, American School of Business

Graham Montigny
Adjunct Faculty Instructor, Hondros College

Britt Scearce
Senior Loan Advisor; Adjunct Faculty Instructor, Hondros College

Debbie Sousa
Director of Education and Event Planning, Massachusetts Mortgage Bankers Association

Marv Stockert
EVP, Falcon Innovations

1

Chapter 1

An Overview of Mortgage Lending

In This Chapter

Mortgage lending is a profession that requires knowledge of many disciplines, including real estate, finance, appraisal, and others to be effective. This chapter provides an overview of the mortgage lending industry, beginning with a brief history of mortgage lending in the United States. Federal legislation transformed a period of uncertainty into the thriving mortgage industry we have today. The role of the primary mortgage market and how it is sustained and renewed by the secondary mortgage market is reviewed.

At the end of this chapter, you will be able to:

- Identify historical events affecting today's mortgage industry.
- Contrast the primary mortgage market and secondary mortgage market.
- Identify entities involved in the primary mortgage market and the secondary market.
- Identify the regulatory agencies involved in mortgage lending.
- Discuss the seeds of the subprime mortgage crisis.

Key Terms

Demand Deposits
Disintermediation
Federal Home Loan Mortgage Corporation (Freddie Mac)
Federal Housing Finance Agency (FHFA)
Federal National Mortgage Association (Fannie Mae)
Government National Mortgage Association (Ginnie Mae)
Government-Sponsored Enterprise (GSE)
Mortgage
Mortgage-Backed Securities (MBS)
Mortgage Banker
Mortgage Broker
Mortgage Loan Originator (MLO)
Primary Mortgage Market
Secondary Mortgage Markets
Securitization

A Brief History of Mortgage Lending

Real estate cycles are part of the mortgage industry. However, in the past few years we have experienced an unprecedented economic and real estate crisis, and the outcome is still uncertain. Economists and industry experts continue to analyze, asking: What caused this crisis? Whose fault was it? What could we have done differently to avoid this? What can we do to make sure this never happens again? All of these questions will be answered in time. For now, we can provide some background on these issues, with the understanding that almost every aspect of the mortgage industry has influenced the current state of affairs:

- Political leaders and housing advocates felt it was everyone's right to own a home, even when perhaps not everyone was ready for the commitment of homeownership.
- Wall Street and investors paid higher priced incentives for subprime loans.
- Government-sponsored enterprises (GSEs) relaxed underwriting standards for conventional mortgage guidelines through automation.
- Unethical appraisers inflated values under pressure from clients.
- Unethical mortgage loan originators placed borrowers in loan programs based upon personal profit and not suitability.
- Consumers purchased homes they could not realistically afford.
- Mortgage products allowed financing with no loan documentation.

The Seeds of Today's Mortgage Industry

In the United States from the 1900s through the 1930s, buying a home was a much different process than it is today. When banks first started making home mortgage loans, a purchaser would typically have to make a large down payment (as much as 50% of the purchase price) and accept a loan that had a balloon payment due after a very short term (as short as a year or two, but almost never more than five years). This meant that borrowers were forced into a constant cycle of refinancing, with no interest rate security.

Several events led to the mortgage industry we have today. First, the Federal Reserve Act of 1913 created the **Federal Reserve System**. This Act established a federal charter for banks that permitted them to make real estate loans. Although these loans were initially the short-term, high down payment loans just referenced, the Act established the framework for government involvement with mortgage lending. Furthermore, the Federal Reserve Act was instrumental in implementing a system for the government to influence interest rates. Other significant banking legislation followed:

- The **Federal Home Loan Bank Act of 1932,** passed during the height of the Great Depression, established **Federal Home Loan Banks**, which had the authority to lend money to thrifts—savings and loan associations (S & Ls), credit unions, and savings banks—so that they could finance home mortgages in their neighborhoods.
- The **Banking Act of 1933**, also known as the Glass-Steagall Act, created the **Federal Deposit Insurance Corporation** (FDIC) to insure depositors against bank default. This was an important step in enticing people to, once again, save their money in banks. This allowed the banks to have a continued source of funds to make more home mortgage loans.
- The **National Housing Act of 1934** extended this protection to savings and loan depositors with the creation of the **Federal Savings and Loan Insurance Corporation** (FSLIC). After the savings and loans crisis of the 1980s exhausted FSLIC reserves, it was abolished by the federal **Financial Institutions Reform Recovery and Enforcement Act** (FIRREA) in 1989. FIRREA transferred all assets previously held by FSLIC to the Savings Association Insurance Fund (SAIF), a division of the FDIC.

Federal Home Loan Banks

Federal Home Loan Banks (FHL Banks), established in 1932 by the Federal Home Loan Banking Act, are 12 regional cooperative banks that U.S. lending institutions use to finance housing and economic development in their communities. FHL Banks have been the largest source of funding for community lending for eight decades. The purpose of the 12 FHL Banks is to use their collective resources to expand credit opportunities throughout all markets. More than 8,000 lenders are members of the FHL Bank System, representing approximately 80% of the insured lending institutions in the country. Community banks, thrifts, commercial banks, credit unions, community development financial institutions, insurance companies, and state housing finance agencies are all eligible for membership through the purchase of stock. As the FHL Banks are entirely privately owned by these member-owners, they do not have the pressure for high rates of return required by publicly traded companies. As cooperatives, the FHL Banks pass their government-sponsored enterprise (GSE) benefits to their members in the form of lower borrowing costs, which are passed on to consumers.

Today, FHL Banks contribute 10% of their net income to the **Affordable Housing Program** (AHP). This grant program is the largest source of private sector grants for housing and community development in the country. They also play a part in the funds available for "jumbo loans," which are those not meeting conforming loan limit guidelines set by secondary market leaders Fannie Mae and Freddie Mac.

Federal Housing Administration (FHA)

The **Federal Housing Administration** (FHA) was created by the National Housing Act of 1934 with the intent of helping the housing industry recover from the Great Depression. The FHA was not intended to fund loans; instead, the FHA provided **mortgage insurance** so banks would not have to incur losses for defaults on home loans. The creation of the FHA allowed banks to commit more of their funds to home mortgage loans, while at the same time improving the quality of those loans by requiring them to conform to FHA standards. Banks that followed FHA guidelines would be reimbursed for the insured amount of any borrower's default.

Under the FHA program, there are no income limits on borrowers who can take advantage of the program, although the government does limit the mortgage amount that can be insured, based on a sound appraisal and the median price of homes in a particular area.

Because banks are not at risk for borrower default, the FHA was able to create innovative programs and terms over the years for the mortgages they insure. For example, when mortgages required as much as 50% down, the FHA introduced loans that required only a 20% down payment. When short maturities were the norm, the FHA created loan programs with 20-year maturities. This eventually grew to 30 years as the market changed (with 40-year loans not uncommon in some high-cost areas). Finally, the FHA innovated amortizing loans, where the monthly payments would retire the debt over the life of the loan instead of leaving the borrower with a large balloon payment due at the end.

In 1965, the Federal Housing Administration became part of the Department of Housing and Urban Development (HUD). Today, the FHA is the largest insurer of mortgages in the world, insuring over 34 million properties since its inception.

Government-Sponsored Enterprises (GSEs)

GSEs are entities established by Congress to improve the efficiency of markets and enhance the flow of credit to targeted sectors of the economy. GSEs may serve as financial intermediaries to assist lenders and borrowers, primarily in housing and agriculture, or create a secondary market where loans may be sold. The Federal Home Loan Banks are government-sponsored enterprises, as are secondary market leaders Fannie Mae and Freddie Mac. The federal government has issued recommendations for reform that include the winding down GSEs Fannie Mae and Freddie Mac with a goal of bringing more private capital back into the housing market. Reform of the industry is likely to continue for some time, thought the impact of such reforms remains uncertain. Every mortgage loan originator has an obligation to stay current with the changes in the mortgage industry.

Primary Mortgage Market Lenders

Mortgages are *written instruments using real property to secure repayment of a debt.* The process of originating, processing, underwriting, closing, and funding a mortgage occurs in the **primary mortgage market** (or simply, primary markets). This is where borrowers and mortgage loan originators come together to negotiate terms and effectuate mortgage transactions. The primary market is comprised of various lending institutions; for example, commercial banks, savings and loan associations (S & Ls), credit unions, mutual savings banks, mortgage bankers, and mortgage brokers.

Commercial Banks

Commercial banks are *financial institutions that provide a variety of financial services, including loans.* Although banks remain the largest source of investment funds in the country today, until recently, their activities were focused on relatively short-term commercial and consumer loans. Residential mortgages were not a significant part of their business, primarily due to government regulations that limited the amount of long-term investments they could make. These limitations were imposed on commercial banks because the vast majority of the deposits they hold are demand deposits—money that a customer may withdraw from the bank at any time. Demand deposits that are immediately accessible—such as consumer checking accounts—are considered less reliable for reinvesting in long-term real estate loans than other types of bank deposits, such as savings accounts or certificates of deposit (CDs), which customers are expected or required to leave in the bank for longer periods of time.

Recently, commercial banks have increased their participation in home mortgage lending for several reasons:

- Banks want to take advantage of existing customer relationships built through checking accounts and other traditional services.
- Banks anticipate that mortgage borrowers will become bank customers for other services.
- There have been important changes in state and federal banking regulations that require banks to hold different percentages of funds on reserve for different types of loans, based on the perceived risk of those loans. First lien home mortgages with loan-to-value less than 80% are in the lowest risk category. Thus, banks need to maintain fewer funds on reserve to cover losses for home mortgage loans than for other types of loans, leaving more funds available for other loans or investments.

Savings and Loan Associations

Savings and loan associations (S & Ls) —sometimes called **thrifts**—are *financial institutions that specialize in taking savings deposits and making mortgage loans.* Traditionally, S & Ls were the major real estate lending institutions, able to dominate local mortgage markets—even though commercial banks had more assets to invest—mainly because deposits placed with S & Ls were savings deposits less frequently subject to immediate withdrawal than demand deposits (checking) held by banks.

When interest rates surged in the late 1970s and early 1980s, S & Ls, which were limited by law as to how much interest they could pay on savings deposits, were unable to offer attractive returns to depositors. This resulted in widespread **disintermediation**, which is the *loss of deposits to competing investments (e.g., money market funds and government bonds) that offered much higher returns.* Worse, S & Ls were saddled with long-term, non-liquid mortgages at low interest rates (by 1980s standards) that they were unable to sell to the secondary market since, at that time, S & Ls were not using the uniform qualifying standards set by major secondary market investors.

Management mistakes, risky investments, economic slumps—and sometimes fraud—resulted in a dramatic increase in the failure rate of S & Ls, which cost the federal government and taxpayers billions of dollars, leading to a massive restructuring of the industry. Despite this crisis, S & Ls continue to participate as home mortgage lenders, and now follow secondary market qualifying standards. While perhaps a smaller player in the mortgage industry than in the past, S & Ls are required to keep 65% of their assets in mortgage-related activities or it will be required to change its charter.

Mortgage Banking Companies

Mortgage banking companies are institutions that *specialize in making only mortgage loans to consumers.* Unlike banks and other financial institutions, they do not take deposits from customers. They are regulated by federal regulations and the state banking laws applicable to each state in which they do business. There are two types: Mortgage bankers and mortgage brokers.

Mortgage Banker

A **mortgage banker** is a *company, individual, or entity that originates, processes, underwrites, closes/funds, and services mortgage loans.* While mortgage bankers close loans in their own name, they may fund loans with the company's own capital or through a **warehouse line of credit** until it is sold in the secondary market, often immediately.

Even if loans are sold on the secondary market, mortgage bankers may continue to act as agents and service the loans for a fee. Alternatively, they can sell the servicing rights and earn a **service release premium** (SRP), which is the payment received by a lending institution, such as a bank or retail mortgage lender, on the sale of the right to service a closed mortgage loan. to the secondary mortgage market.

Mortgage Brokers

A **mortgage broker** is a *company or individual who, for a fee, places loans with wholesale lenders, but does not service such loans.* Nor do mortgage brokers underwrite or fund their loans, but, rather, act as a conduit in residential mortgages. Among the services that a mortgage broker typically provides are:

- Collecting financial and other required information from borrowers,
- Analyzing income and debt to determine maximum mortgage amounts the borrower can afford,
- Advising borrowers on available loan programs,
- Explaining the loan process,
- Filling out a loan application,
- Providing required disclosures,
- Processing the loan file and submitting it to lenders,
- Assisting borrowers to understand and respond to lender decisions, and
- Participating in the loan closing process.

Brokers often have knowledge of and access to nontraditional lenders who are able to supply a particular type of loan needed to purchase a property, for example, a loan from an investor for a buyer who was turned down by a traditional mortgage lender. However, mortgage brokers do *not* make underwriting decisions.

Other Primary Residential Mortgage Lenders

Among the other types of financial institutions that make originate, process, underwrite, close/fund loans for residential first or second mortgages are credit unions, finance companies, and mutual savings banks.

Credit Unions

Credit unions are *cooperative financial institutions owned and controlled by their members in order to pool their deposits, receive better interest rates, and loan money to fellow members.* Traditionally, credit unions only made home improvement loans and other types of consumer loans. More recently, some credit unions have begun making mortgage loans, both second mortgages, such as home equity loans, and even first mortgages since credit unions can sell secondary market-qualified loans.

Finance Companies

Finance companies are *organizations that specialize in making higher-risk loans at higher interest rates.* Finance companies are sources of second mortgages and home equity loans made directly to borrowers. Although banks and other lenders also make these types of loans, finance companies are often in a position to loan higher percentages of the borrower's equity and work with borrowers who have blemished credit, pricing loans accordingly.

Mutual Savings Banks

Mutual savings banks are *state- or federal-chartered banks that are owned by depositors and operate for their benefit.* They are conservative by nature, and often hold a large portion of their assets in home mortgages. Their activities are usually oriented toward the communities they serve to maintain close supervision of their loans, but modern economic realities have forced mutual savings banks to increase their pool of funds and diversify their mortgage holdings via the secondary market. While they are found mostly in the northeastern United States, there are a number of savings institutions in other areas that continue to operate as mutuals. Like S & Ls, mutual savings banks are known as **thrifts**.

Portfolio Lending

Portfolio lending is a term to describe the strategy where *financial institutions that make real estate loans keep and service those loans in-house as part of their investment portfolios, instead of selling on the secondary market.* Portfolio lending may be practiced by major financial institutions, smaller community banks, or other types of nontraditional lenders or investors. Portfolio lenders can make lending decisions based on many factors. For example, they may choose to make these types of loans as a service to customers who may need a loan amount larger than can be sold to the secondary market or as an investment because the lender likes the project, rate of return, or possible future profit sharing in a particular real estate venture.

Secondary Mortgage Markets

Originally, banks and other lenders made home mortgage loans to borrowers from deposits they collected directly from other customers. As more people saved more money, the lender could make more loans. But if depositors were not saving money, funds for mortgage loans were not available. This, along with a desire to maximize returns on investment dollars and shift credit risk, led to the creation of the **secondary mortgage markets** (or simply, secondary markets). Secondary markets are *private investors or government agencies that buy and sell real estate mortgages.*

The first secondary mortgage markets were established by the federal government in an attempt to moderate local real estate cycles:

- When the secondary market players buy mortgages from local banks, those local banks then have more money to lend again to other potential homeowners in their area.
- When local banks invest surplus funds in real estate investments from other regions of the country, the effects of local real estate cycles can be moderated as the banks also have stable investments from other areas that may be going through different phases of the real estate cycle.

An important by-product of secondary mortgage markets is the **standardization** of loan criteria. Any changes implemented by secondary mortgage markets become requirements around the country for those wanting to sell mortgages in the secondary market.

Case in Point

Example A: Tenth Bank is in an area that's booming right now. Businesses are coming to the area and lots of people are moving there. Many of these people are looking to purchase a home and have come to Tenth Bank to borrow money. The trouble is, most of Tenth Bank's deposits are already tied up in real estate loans. But, by selling its current home mortgage loans on the secondary market, Tenth Bank can get more money to make new loans. Tenth Bank and its customers are happy, and the effects of a potential credit crunch in the local real estate market are moderated because Tenth Bank can acquire additional funds from national secondary mortgage markets.

Case in Point (continued)

Example B: Later, Tenth Bank finds itself in a different situation. The local community is still doing well, so Tenth Bank has lots of people depositing money in the bank, but there's little activity in the real estate market. With this surplus of deposits, Tenth Bank may have trouble finding enough local investments with a high enough return to purchase. In this case, Tenth Bank could buy real estate mortgage loans on the secondary market. Tenth Bank would also then hold real estate investments from across the country and would not need to worry as much about a down turn in the local real estate market.

Example C: Tenth Bank is considering some new home mortgage loan requests. The loans seem to be riskier for several reasons relating to the borrowers and the property. Tenth Bank is not so quick to approve these loans because, if they don't meet the criteria of the secondary markets, Tenth Bank must hold the loans and cannot sell them to the secondary market. This helps stabilize the local real estate market as it discourages banks from making too many risky loans. Furthermore, the standardized criteria help Tenth Bank feel secure in the mortgage investments it buys on the secondary market from other areas of the country, even though it may never see the actual borrowers and properties it is helping to finance.

Mortgage-Backed Securities

Mortgage-backed securities (MBSs) are *debt obligations that represent claims to the cash flows from pools of mortgage loans.* Mortgage loans purchased from the primary mortgage market are assembled into pools by a government/quasi-governmental entity or a private investor who operates in the secondary mortgage market. Securities are then issued that represent claims on the principal and interest payments made by borrowers on the loans in the pool; a process known as **securitization**. Any asset may be securitized as long as it is cash-flowing. The term mortgage-backed security, therefore, is reflective of the underlying asset in the security.

Common types of mortgage-backed securities include:

- **Pass-through securities**, which are most common, pay interest and principal payments on a monthly basis. Some types pay even if payments aren't collected from the borrower. The investor does not own any particular mortgage, but instead, a proportionate interest in the cash flow generated by the entire pool. The payments of interest, principal, and sometimes prepayment, penalties are passed through to the investor.
- **Stripped mortgage-backed securities** (SMBS) are pass-through securities that are created by separating—or stripping apart—the principal and interest payments from the underlying mortgages that back standard mortgage-backed securities.
- **Collaterized mortgage obligations** (CMOs) are bonds that represent claims to specific cash flows from large pools of home mortgages. The streams of principal and interest payments on the mortgages are distributed to the different classes of CMO interests, known as tranches, according to a complicated deal structure. Each tranche may have different principal balances, coupon rates, prepayment risks, and maturity dates. CMOs may be highly sensitive to changes in interest rates and any resulting change in the rate at which homeowners sell their properties, refinance, or otherwise prepay their loans. Investors in these securities may not only be subjected to this prepayment risk, but also exposed to significant market and liquidity risks.

Secondary Market Participants

Secondary markets are generally defined as private investors and government agencies that buy and sell real estate mortgages, although private investors tend to be a much smaller percentage of the secondary markets. These private investors can be Wall Street or investment brokers, high-risk investors, insurance companies, or pension plans, for example. This discussion will focus on three organizations responsible for the vast majority of the secondary mortgage market activity:

- Federal National Mortgage Association (FNMA or Fannie Mae)

- Government National Mortgage Association (GNMA or Ginnie Mae)
- Federal Home Loan Mortgage Corporation (FHLMC or Freddie Mac)

Fannie Mae and Freddie Mac, both government-sponsored enterprises, securitize and keep loans and mortgage-backed securities in their portfolios. They both have substantially similar charters and regulatory structures. Ginne Mae, on the other hand, is a wholly-owned government corporation, not a GSE. Also, unlike Freddie Mac and Fannie Mae, Ginnie Mae does not purchase mortgages from lenders, nor does it buy, sell, or issue securities.

Federal National Mortgage Association

The **Federal National Mortgage Association** is the nation's largest investor in residential mortgages. Fannie Mae was originally chartered as a GSE by Congress in 1938 to provide liquidity and stability to the U.S. housing and mortgage markets, primarily as a place for lenders to sell their FHA-insured loans. In 1968, Fannie Mae was made a private shareholder-owned company and remains in that structure today, though in 2008, it was placed in conservatorship under the Federal Housing Finance Agency because of severe financial and cash flow problems resulting from the declining real estate market and mortgage foreclosure epidemic.

Fannie Mae buys mortgages (conventional, FHA, or VA) or interests in pools of mortgages from lenders. The lender, who must own a certain amount of stock in Fannie Mae, assembles a pool of loans, and then a participation interest in that pool (usually 50% to 95%) is sold to Fannie Mae. Loans sold to Fannie Mae are usually serviced by the originating lender or another mortgage servicing company (called a subservicer), for which Fannie Mae pays a service fee.

Fannie Mae pools loans that generally conform to its standards and converts them into mortgage-backed securities, which it guarantees as to timely payment of principal and interest. In this way, both the lender and Fannie Mae own an interest in the loans.

Government National Mortgage Association

The **Government National Mortgage Association** was created in 1968 as a government-owned corporation, operating under the Department of Housing and Urban Development (HUD). A primary function of Ginnie Mae is to promote investment by guaranteeing the payment of principal and interest on FHA, VA, Rural Housing Service, or HUD's Office of Public and Indian Housing federally insured or guaranteed mortgages through its mortgage-backed securities program. Ginnie Mae's mortgage-backed securities are the only ones that carry the full faith and credit guarantee of the United States government. Therefore, regardless of whether the mortgage payment is made, investors will receive payments.

Federal Home Loan Mortgage Corporation

The **Federal Home Loan Mortgage Corporation** was created in 1970 as a nonprofit, federally chartered institution controlled by the Federal Home Loan Bank System. Like Fannie Mae, Freddie Mac buys mortgages on the secondary market, pools them, and sells them as a mortgage-backed security to investors on the open market. Also like Fannie Mae, Freddie Mac was converted to a privately held stock corporation and is currently under the conservatorship of the Federal Housing Finance Agency.

Freddie Mac actively sells the mortgage loans from its portfolio to investors throughout the world by issuing its own mortgage-backed securities, thus acting as a conduit for mortgage investments. The funds generated by the sale of the mortgages are then used to purchase more mortgages. While its MBSs are not backed by the full faith and credit of the federal government, Freddie Mac, like Fannie Mae, has special authority to borrow from the U.S. Treasury in order to continuing operating in the secondary market.

Secondary Market Standards

An important reason why the secondary market is able to function as it does is that standardized underwriting criteria are used to qualify borrowers and property. Once lenders realized the advantages of selling their home mortgages in the secondary market, they were quick to conform to the underwriting guidelines—such as loan-to-value and income expense ratios—established by Fannie Mae and Freddie Mac, along with other secondary market agencies. Furthermore, both Fannie Mae and Freddie Mac rely on automated underwriting systems (AUS) that they have developed to further streamline and standardize the underwriting process. Fannie Mae uses Desktop Underwriter® (DU®) and Freddie Mac uses Loan Prospector® (LP®).

Because the secondary market performs such an important function in providing liquidity of mortgage funds, the standards set by the secondary market have a great influence on lending activities in the primary market. For example, once secondary agencies began accepting adjustable rate mortgages (ARMs), 15-year fixed rate mortgages, and convertible ARMs, these types of financing became more readily available in the primary market. Lenders were more willing to make these kinds of loans when they knew the loans could be sold to the secondary market. In contrast, option ARMs and no documentation/no qualification loans are not being purchased by the secondary market today; therefore, these types of financing are virtually nonexistent, although FHA may allow no income, no asset verification refinance loans on existing FHA loans.

While the agencies may relax or tighten their standards in response to current economic or market factors, this standardization of loan qualifications and other lending procedures helped reduce or eliminate much of the variation in loan quality, types of loan programs offered, and aspects of home loans that were made in different parts of the country. These underwriting standards also create some degree of confidence in purchasers of the mortgage-backed securities. The purchasers know that the mortgages backing the securities must be of a minimum quality, lessening their risk in investing in properties they can't view or assess.

Oversight of Financial Institutions

Several federal agencies, including HUD and FDIC, as well as state agencies regulate financial institutions, in addition to the Federal Reserve.

Federal Deposit Insurance Corporation

The **Federal Deposit Insurance Corporation** (FDIC) is an independent agency created by the Congress in 1933 to maintain stability and public confidence in the nation's financial system by insuring deposits in banks and thrift institutions; examining and supervising financial institutions for safety, soundness, and consumer protection; and managing receiverships. As of May, 2010, the FDIC insured deposits for nearly 8,000 institutions. The FDIC insures deposits only. It does not insure securities, mutual funds, or similar types of investments that banks and thrift institutions may offer.

The FDIC directly examines and supervises more than half of the banks and savings banks in the banking system for operational safety and soundness. Banks can be chartered by the states or by the federal government. Banks chartered by states also have the choice of whether to join the Federal Reserve System. The FDIC is the primary federal regulator of banks that are chartered by the states that do not join the Federal Reserve System. In addition, the FDIC is the back-up supervisor for the remaining insured banks and thrift institutions.

Office of Thrift Supervision

The **Office of Thrift Supervision** (OTS), a division of the U.S. Department of the Treasury, was established in 1989 to supervise, charter, and regulate federal thrift institutions. Savings banks, savings and loans, cooperative banks, and credit unions classify as thrift institutions (the word "Federal" or the initials "F.S.B." appear in the federal institution's name).

Office of Comptroller of Currency

The **Office of Comptroller of Currency** (OCC) charters, regulates, and supervises all National banks and federal branches/agencies of foreign banks (the word "National" or the initials "N.A." appear in or after the bank's name). It is headed by the Comptroller, who is appointed by the President and is also a director of the FDIC.

National Credit Union Administration

The **National Credit Union Administration** (NCUA) is the independent federal agency that charters and supervises federal credit unions. NCUA, backed by the full faith and credit of the U.S. government, operates the National Credit Union Share Insurance Fund (NCUSIF) which insures the savings of 80 million account holders in all federal credit unions and many state-chartered credit unions.

Federal Financial Institutions Examination Council

The **Federal Financial Institutions Examination Council (FFIEC)** is a formal interagency body empowered to proscribe uniform principles, standards, and report forms for the federal examination of financial institutions by the Board of Governors of the Federal Reserve System (FRB), the Federal Deposit Insurance Corporation (FDIC), the National Credit Union Administration (NCUA), the Office of the Comptroller of the Currency (OCC), and the Office of Thrift Supervision (OTS), and to make recommendations to promote uniformity in the supervision of financial institutions.

Federal Housing Finance Agency (FHFA)

The Federal Housing Finance Agency is an independent federal agency created by the **Federal Housing Finance Regulatory Reform Act of 2008** (Division A of the larger Housing and Economic Recovery Act of 2008). The purpose of the FHFA is to promote a stronger, safer U.S. housing finance system. To that end, the FHFA has broad powers similar in function and structure to federal banking regulators, including expanded legal and regulatory authority over the secondary mortgage markets and oversight of the 14 housing-related government-sponsored enterprises—including Fannie Mae and Freddie Mac—and oversight of the 12 Federal Home Loan Banks (FHL Banks).

The creation of the FHFA merged the powers and regulatory authority of the former **Federal Housing Finance Board** (FHFB) and the **Office of Federal Housing Enterprise Oversight** (OFHEO), as well as the GSE mission office at the Department of Housing and Urban Development (HUD). The Federal Housing Finance Board was originally established to regulate the Federal Home Loan Banks that were created in 1932. The Office of Federal Housing Enterprise Oversight was originally established as an independent entity within the Department of Housing and Urban Development by the Federal Housing Enterprises Financial Safety and Soundness Act of 1992.

Real Success

State banking authorities also regulate financial institutions that operate in their states. Regulations, laws, and procedures for mortgage bankers and mortgage brokers may vary from state to state. Also, it is important to understand the differences in any state, county, or municipal jurisdiction in which you are doing business.

Present Day Mortgage Lending

The creation of Fannie Mae was really the birth of the mortgage industry that we have today. Over the years, changes in the industry, along with rising interest rates and a desire to shift credit risk, caused lenders to place even greater emphasis on the ability to sell their loans. As more and more options became available, the secondary mortgage market, led by Fannie Mae, grew in importance as a source of funds for lenders and a means of readily available capital for potential homeowners at attractive interest rates.

However, the demand for safe, mortgage-backed securities is considered one of the factors that led to the subprime crisis that has caused such upheaval in the global financial world. In order to make more and more residential loans, lenders created many new loan programs that the secondary market players were willing to purchase, some of which had relaxed qualifying standards, such as:

- Requiring little or no income or asset documentation.
- Not considering a borrower's impaired credit or ability to repay the loan.
- Waiving the need for an appraisal to verify value of the property being financed.
- Requiring minimum or no down payment.
- Allowing borrowers to avoid mortgage insurance with a first and second mortgage combined for up to 100% of the value of the property.

In addition, some lenders would offer adjustable rate mortgages (ARMs) that had negative amortization, rate adjustments occurring as often as every six months, and exorbitant interest rate caps. These risky loan programs may have been offered to "subprime" borrowers, those who may have poor credit history, higher debt, lower income, previous bankruptcy, short employment history, and other less than ideal characteristics. While most of these loan programs are no longer offered today, such loans frequently resulted in a high rate of delinquency and foreclosure. When mortgaged-backed securities declined in value, investors quit purchasing them, tightening credit around the world. The impact of such a credit crunch on the current market is significant. For example:

- Available financing for jumbo loans is limited.
- Most high-risk loan programs are no longer available.
- Risk-based pricing continues to be a factor.
- Underwriting guidelines are tightened up.
- Mortgage insurance availability may be restricted.

Dodd-Frank Wall Street Reform and Consumer Protection Act of 2010

The industry continues to evolve. The comprehensive H.R. 4173 was signed into law as the Dodd-Frank Wall Street Reform and Consumer Protection Act of 2010 in July, 2010. It will have significant impact on nearly every aspect of mortgage lending. Of most interest to mortgage loan originators are Title X, designated as the Consumer Financial Protection Act, and Title XIV, designated as the Mortgage Reform and Anti-Predatory Lending Act. The Dodd-Frank Act is expected to change the landscape of the mortgage industry forever. While most of the changes will be phased in over the next few years as rules and regulations are promulgated—and our understanding of these changes will evolve over time—it's important to introduce this legislation here. Mortgage loan originators are responsible for understanding and complying with the new rules and regulations as they are implemented.

Title X: Consumer Financial Protection Act

Title X of the Dodd-Frank Wall Street Reform and Consumer Protection Act of 2010, designated as the **Consumer Financial Protection Act,** provides broad authority related to rules and enforcement in order to address and prevent what it defines as "abusive" financial practices. It also:

- Provides states with more regulatory authority over federally chartered institutions.
- Imposes additional requirements related to data collection and reporting.
- Mandates studies on certain mortgage-related issues that will likely result in additional legislation.

Section 1011 of Subtitle A of Title X creates a new **Consumer Financial Protection Bureau** (CFPB) whose task is to enforce consumer financial protection laws. While the Bureau is within the Federal Reserve, it is intended to function independently as an Executive agency. The Bureau is charged with supervision, examination, and enforcement over all insured depository institutions and credit unions with assets over $10 billion; all non-depository institutions that broker, originate, or service mortgage loans; as well as any other provider(s) of consumer services at its discretion, with some exceptions such as auto dealers, attorneys, accountants and tax preparers, and real estate brokerage activities.

Regulatory Authority and Enforcement

The Act consolidates consumer protection responsibilities currently handled by the Office of the Comptroller of the Currency, Office of Thrift Supervision, Federal Deposit Insurance Corporation, Federal Reserve, National Credit Union Administration, the Department of Housing and Urban Development, and Federal Trade Commission under the Consumer Financial Protection Bureau.

The Bureau also has the authority to investigate and conduct hearings on violations of most consumer protection laws. If it determines a violation occurred, the Bureau may issue a cease and desist order or pursue civil action. It has no authority to bring criminal charges, but could refer cases to the Department of Justice and must refer potential tax law violations to the Internal Revenue Service.

Structure of the Bureau

Section 1013 (c)(d)(e)(g) of Subtitle A of Title X creates a number of offices within the Bureau:

- Office of Fair Lending and Equal Opportunity
- Office of Financial Education
- Office of Service Member Affairs
- Office of Financial Protection for Older Americans

As discussed in Section 1013 (b) of Subtitle A of Title X, the Bureau also supports three functional units: Research Unit that provides analysis of trends in consumer financial products, Community Affairs Unit tasked with consumer education and access, and Complaints Unit that will provide website and phone access for collecting and monitoring consumer complaints.

Consumer Advisory Board

Section 1014 of Subtitle A of Title X creates the **Consumer Advisory Board**, which is tasked with advising and consulting with the Bureau in the exercise of its functions under the Federal consumer financial laws, and to provide information on emerging practices in the consumer financial products or services industry, including regional trends, concerns, and other relevant information.

Title XIV: Mortgage Reform and Anti-Predatory Lending Act

Title XIV of the Dodd-Frank Wall Street Reform and Consumer Protection Act of 2010 is designated as the **Mortgage Reform and Anti-Predatory Lending Act**. It takes several steps to address what Congress considers to be abusive or predatory lending practices in the mortgage industry. For example, Subtitle B of Title XIV:

- Requires mortgage loan originators to apply new minimum qualifying standards and defines a new category of "qualified" loans.
- Requires verification/documentation of the borrower's ability to repay the loan.
- Establishes penalties for irresponsible lending, including extended foreclosure defense for borrowers.

Subtitle C of Title XIV expands consumer protection for high cost mortgages.

Some key provisions of Titles X and XIV are discussed below and in later chapters.

Qualified Residential Mortgage (QRM)

The Mortgage Reform and Anti-Predatory Lending Act contains provisions in § 1412 that require financial institutions that securitize mortgages loans to retain an economic interest of at least 5%, although securities backed by loans that meet the criteria of a **qualified residential mortgage (QRM)** will be exempt once final rules are implemented.

The proposed rule—issued by the Federal Deposit Insurance Corporation (FDIC), Department of the Treasury, Federal Reserve System, U.S. Securities and Exchange Commission (SEC) and Department of Housing and Urban Development in March of 2011—defines a qualified residential mortgage as one with the following characteristics:

- 20% down payment required (LTV no greater than 80%)
- Qualifying standards of 28% housing expense ratio and 36% total debt-to-income ratio
- Borrower cannot currently be 30 or more days past due on any debt obligation, regardless of credit score
- Borrower cannot have been 60 or more days past due on any debt obligation in the past 24 months
- Borrower cannot have been through bankruptcy, foreclosure, engaged in short sale or deed in lieu of foreclosure, or subject to federal or state debt judgment in the past 36 month

The Consumer Financial Protection Bureau has 18 months after the transfer of rulemaking authority to promulgate final rules.

Chapter 1 Summary

1. **Mortgages** are written instruments using real property to secure repayment of a debt. Their use in the home purchasing process continues to evolve. The Federal Reserve Act of 1913 created the Federal Reserve, established a federal charter for banks to make real estate loans, and set up a way to influence interest rates. The National Housing Act of 1934 created the **Federal Housing Administration** (FHA) to insure banks against losses for defaults on home loans. The 12 **Federal Home Loan Banks** (FHL Banks) were established in 1932 as regional cooperative banks that U.S. lending institutions use to finance housing and economic development in their communities. The **Federal National Mortgage Association** (Fannie Mae) was created in 1938 as the first secondary market to address the problem of uneven supply of money for mortgage loans.

2. The **primary market** consists of lenders making mortgage loans directly to borrowers. Primary lenders include commercial banks, savings and loans (S & Ls), savings and mutual savings banks, and mortgage companies, which includes mortgage bankers who may originate/fund/service loans, and mortgage brokers who place loans with lenders. S & Ls were once the largest provider of home mortgage loans, but regulation and risky investments left many savings and loans insolvent.

3. The **secondary market** consists of private investors and government entitites that buy and sell home mortgages; created to moderate local real estate cycles, give lenders new money to lend again, and standardize loan criteria. The **Federal National Mortgage Association** (Fannie Mae) is the largest investor in residential mortgages, buying and selling **mortgage-backed securities**. The **Federal Home Loan Mortgage Corporation** (Freddie Mac) also issues mortgage-backed securities. The **Government National Mortgage Association** (Ginnie Mae) is government-owned and managed by HUD. Ginnie Mae guarantees payment of principal and interest on government insured or guaranteed loans (such as FHA and VA) for its mortgage-backed securities.

4. In addition to the Federal Reserve, oversight of the mortgage industry includes: **Federal Deposit Insurance Corporation** (FDIC)—insures deposits and examines and supervises financial institutions; **Office of Thrift Supervision** (OTS)—supervises, charters, and regulates federal thrift institutions; **Office of Comptroller of Currency** (OCC)—charters, regulates, and supervises all National banks; the **National Credit Union Administration** (NCUA)—charters and supervises federal credit unions; **Federal Financial Institutions Examination Council (FFIEC)**—formal interagency body empowered to prescribe uniform principles, standards, and make recommendations; **Federal Housing Finance Agency** (FHFA)—legal and regulatory authority over the secondary mortgage markets, Fannie Mae/ Freddie Mac, and the Federal Home Loan Banks (FHL Banks).

5. Looser qualifications for home mortgages led to significant increases in borrower default on risky loans, resulting in the so-called **subprime mortgage crisis**. As a consequence, qualification standards are tightening, many laws have been passed related to predatory lending, higher risk loan programs are unavailable, and financing is more difficult to obtain.

6. The **Dodd-Frank Wall Street Reform and Consumer Protection Act of 2010** is a significant overhaul of the nation's financial laws, including those that affect the mortgage industry. Title X of Dodd-Frank, Consumer Financial Protection Act, creates a new **Consumer Financial Protection Bureau** (CFPB) within the Federal Reserve that consolidates broad regulatory authority. Title XIV of Dodd-Frank, Mortgage Reform and Anti-Predatory Lending Act, addresses abusive lending practices. Consumer protection responsibilities currently handled by the Office of the Comptroller of the Currency, Office of Thrift Supervision, Federal Deposit Insurance Corporation, Federal Reserve, National Credit Union Administration, the Department of Housing and Urban Development, and Federal Trade Commission will be consolidated under the CFPB when fully implemented.

Chapter 1 Quiz

1. ***Which is NOT a function of the secondary markets?***
   A. moderate effects of local real estate cycles
   B. provide lenders with money to make more loans
   C. serve as a depository for consumer assets
   D. standardize underwriting guidelines

2. ***The Consumer Financial Protection Bureau was created by the***
   A. Federal Reserve Act.
   B. Federal Home Loan Bank Act.
   C. National Housing Act.
   D. Dodd-Frank Wall Street Reform and Consumer Protection Act.

3. ***Which agency is conservator of Fannie Mae and Freddie Mac?***
   A. Department of Housing and Urban Development
   B. Federal Housing Administration
   C. Federal Housing Finance Agency
   D. Office of Federal Housing Enterprise Oversight

4. ***Which is the largest secondary market participant?***
   A. Federal Home Loan Mortgage Corporation
   B. Federal Housing Administration
   C. Federal National Mortgage Association
   D. Government National Mortgage Association

5. ***Mortgage brokers***
   A. act as intermediaries between borrowers and lenders.
   B. originate and service mortgage loans.
   C. provide funding for mortgage loans.
   D. underwrite mortgage loans.

6. ***What was established in 1932 as a cooperative to finance housing in local communities?***
   A. Federal Home Loan Mortgage Corporation
   B. Federal Home Loan Banks 12
   C. Federal Housing Finance Agency
   D. Government National Mortgage Association

7. ***Which is NOT a primary lender for residential properties?***
   A. commercial banks
   B. insurance companies
   C. mortgage companies
   D. savings and loan associations

8. ***Which statement about Ginnie Mae is TRUE?***
   A. Ginnie Mae buys loans from commercial banks and mortgage companies.
   B. Ginnie Mae is a private corporation.
   C. Ginnie Mae is a participant in the primary market.
   D. Ginnie Mae guarantees mortgage-backed securities.

2

Chapter 2

The Business of Real Estate

In This Chapter

Business and real estate cycles are influenced by many factors. They both respond to supply and demand, inflation, and interest rates. Real estate markets and the mortgage industry are interrelated. Real estate can be affected positively or negatively by interest rates; interest rates depend on supply and demand for money; loan activity depends on availability of money; and property values depend on the health of the economy. This chapter looks at the four broad forces influencing real estate cycles: Physical, economic, governmental, and social. Following that is a look at some government influences on real estate finance, focusing on fiscal policy and taxation, and monetary policy. We'll also look at how the actions of the Federal Reserve affect interest rates.

At the end of this chapter, you will be able to:

- Identify broad influences on the real estate market.
- Discuss how fiscal policy and monetary policy are made.
- Explain the role of the Federal Reserve System.
- Identify tax laws affecting real estate.

Key Terms

Business Cycles
Discount Rate
Economic Base
Fed Funds Rate
Federal Open Market Committee (FOMC)
Federal Reserve Board (the Fed)
Fiscal Policy
Inflation
Interest Rate
Monetary Policy
Moral Suasion
Open Market Operations
Real Estate Cycles
Reserve Requirements
Supply and Demand

Factors Affecting Real Estate

To be an effective mortgage professional, it is important to have some understanding of how the real estate industry functions as a whole. Economic factors have a broad influence on the real estate market, such as business and real estate cycles. As you will see, there are many forces that affect those cycles.

Business Cycles

Business cycles are *general swings in the economy over a period of time* which may be broadly categorized as periods of economic growth and expansion or stagnation and decline. These periods can last an unpredictable amount of time, depending on a number of different economic factors, such as inflation and the job market.

Many of these business cycle activities and factors are so interrelated that they increase and deflate other businesses along with them. It's difficult to stabilize these cycles as it's hard to know when they will begin or what's causing them (although the government does try). Most of the time, though, a cycle must ride itself out, either to a point where interest rates or other costs become so high that purchasing slows and prices begin to fall, or to a point where interest rates or costs are so low that even those people previously reluctant to spend can't pass up such low rates or prices and spending increases.

The economic factors that influence business cycles also influence real estate cycles, for example, supply and demand, inflation, and interest rates.

Supply and Demand

The concept of **supply and demand** says that *for all products, goods, and services, when supply exceeds demand, prices will fall, and when demand exceeds supply, prices will rise.* This economic theory says that supply and demand seek to balance each other and, thus, the market responds. When demand for a product (such as housing) exceeds supply, the price for that product will rise, stimulating more production. As production increases, more of the demand is satisfied until, eventually, the supply outstrips demand and a buyer's market is created. At that point, prices will fall and production will slow until demand catches up with supply, then the cycle starts over. In a healthy economy, supply and demand are more or less in balance, but the forces affecting supply and demand are constantly changing, thereby shifting the balance.

Inflation

Inflation is an *increase in the cost of goods or services over a period of time, which impacts a buyer's purchasing power.* This may be **cost inflation**, which mostly affects new home prices as builders pass on to buyers their increased costs of labor and building materials. Or it could be **demand inflation**, which mostly affects existing home prices as too many people seek to live in an area with a limited supply of housing. High inflation could affect a real estate cycle more than a business cycle because the actual costs are so much higher. A person usually thinks twice about buying a $100,000 house that has increased in price by $10,000, but is more likely to shrug off a $5 rise in a $50 pair of shoes, even though both prices rose by the same percentage.

Interest Rates

The **interest rate** is the *amount charged by a lender to a borrower for the use of assets, expressed as a percentage of principal.* This is the **cost of money** that people or businesses must pay to use another person's money for their own purposes. Inflation is one factor that can cause interest rates to rise or fall. And while most big-ticket items are affected by high interest rates, they hinder real estate more than other goods because mortgages are long-term, high-dollar commitments. In fact, the single most important factor in determining demand in the real estate market is interest rates. Low interest rates tend to increase demand for property; high interest rates tend to decrease demand. All other things being equal, a drop in interest rates can spur activity in the real estate market for home purchasing or refinancing.

Real Estate Cycles

Real estate cycles are *general swings in real estate resulting in increasing or decreasing activity and property values during different phases of the cycle.* Real estate cycles last for varying lengths of time. They are the response of the real estate and mortgage markets to the forces of supply and demand, but there are two factors that separate the housing market from other supply and demand models.

First, with real estate there's a **lag time** that exists for market forces to respond to perceived changes in supply and demand. This lag time is the result of the time it takes for a house to be bought, sold, or built. If people lose their job today, they can't expect to sell their homes tomorrow. Or if construction companies see a need for housing, it takes time for them to build houses; and when they see that there's no longer a need for housing, they often have some houses started that still must be finished. Because of this, real estate cycles generally take longer to respond to upturns and downturns than other businesses. When the real estate market is in balance, there will be slightly more properties available than there are buyers.

The second factor that makes the real estate market different is the **limited supply** of land in any given area. This constraint will surface again when value is discussed.

Broad Forces Influencing Real Estate Cycles

Imbalances in supply and demand may be short-term or long-term, depending on the causes. Some of the causes of real estate cycles are supply of land, inflation, cost of money, availability of credit, construction costs, and health of the economy. Important factors can include fiscal and monetary policies. Other influences on real estate cycles are demographics, population shifts, and growth. All of these factors can be divided into the four broad forces that affect real estate (remembered easily as the acronym P E G S):

- Physical
- Economic
- Governmental
- Social

Physical

Physical forces that affect real estate cycles can be on a property or external to it, natural or man-made. Physical forces can include location and popularity, as areas within a city or entire regions go in and out of favor with the public because of location, jobs, climate, or other reasons. Land availability and desirability are important factors in real estate cycles, as well as overall supply and demand. The environment can also have an impact on real estate cycles, sometimes in a positive way as from a natural waterway or man-made lake, or in a negative way as from pollution that affects an entire area.

Economic

Local economic trends have a big impact on real estate cycles. This is best understood by the concept of economic base. The **economic base** of an area is *the main business or industry that a community uses to support and sustain itself.* While the presence of a good economic base is important for all businesses in an area, it's critical to maintain home values in real estate markets. This is due to the immobility of real estate and customers. Houses can't be moved to where there are buyers and, usually, buyers can't just move their jobs to where a specific house is.

The economic base of an area is a primary factor in determining the supply of housing. In prosperous areas, there should be funds available to finance the purchase and construction of housing and, in theory, the marketplace will function smoothly.

The past several years have shown that national economic factors are increasingly important. Although local economic health is still a major factor, it is being influenced more and more by the national economic picture where inflation, cost of money (interest rates), and availability of credit are also considerations.

Governmental

Government activities affecting real estate can be divided nationally and locally. National government influences include taxation, fiscal and monetary policies, secondary markets, government financing programs, and federal regulations. The federal government also influences interest rates via the Federal Reserve Board. And since the federal government is the largest borrower in the country, its spending has a huge influence on the national economy.

Local government activities are also having a greater effect on the real estate market. State and local governments have two types of laws that influence real estate: Revenue-generating laws and right-to-regulate laws.

Revenue-generating laws deal with taxes, and although they're passed primarily to raise revenue, they can have other effects on real estate. **Right-to-regulate laws** deal with the police power that governments reserve for themselves. These laws can take the form of land use controls, zoning laws, environmental protection laws, eminent domain, and escheat—all of which can affect real estate by limiting land usage. Furthermore, in many areas of the U.S., overcrowded cities are beginning to enact no-growth policies, which limit the number of new houses. If no-growth becomes widespread, the housing supply will be squeezed more and lead to price increases.

Social

Social forces also have an interrelated effect on real estate cycles. These factors include demographics, migrations, family size, population shifts, growth, and age. As populations grow and change, so do their housing needs. Social behavior patterns and population distribution can have major effects on supply and demand in the real estate market. For example, an increase in the number of people in their prime home buying years can push up housing prices and supply. Smaller families, high divorce rates, and a trend toward later marriages also stimulate demand, because there are fewer persons per household. Finally, the general aging of the population means that more changes are likely on the horizon.

Migrations of the population are also powerful forces. This social factor may actually be the result of an economic factor (e.g., a factory moving into or out of an area) or a governmental factor (e.g., higher or lower state/local tax rates). Housing values can benefit from an influx of people, or be devastated by an exodus.

Government Influence on Real Estate and Mortgages

Government has a large influence on many aspects of real estate markets and the mortgage industry. This was seen in the discussion of the creation and oversight of the secondary market and the creation of the Federal Housing Finance Agency (FHFA) in Chapter 1. It will be seen again in later discussions regarding the impact of federal legislation and regulations as well as government loan programs. The mechanisms used to affect interest rates in the United States also have a significant influence. The next few topics focus on the federal government's fiscal and monetary policies, as well as the actions of the Federal Reserve Board. These are important means of control and influence over the supply and cost of money.

As we examine the federal government's use of fiscal policy through the U.S. Treasury Department (including taxation) and monetary policy through the Federal Reserve Board (which affects interest rates), keep in mind what we have just learned about business and real estate cycles. As we shall see, fiscal and monetary policies have direct and indirect influences on real estate, including interest rates charged by lenders for all types of loans, including mortgages. This is because, to a large degree, the supply of money in the United States is controlled by the federal government, and interest rates, like the cost of most things in a market economy, are controlled primarily by the law of supply and demand.

Remember, the law of supply and demand says that for all products, goods, and services, when supply exceeds demand, prices will fall, and when demand exceeds supply, prices will rise. This is true for real estate, for houses, and for money itself. If the supply of something is large—in this case, if there is a large amount of money in circulation—then the price will fall, so interest rates will tend to fall. Falling interest rates tend to increase business activity, real estate activity, and borrowing activity. Conversely, if the supply of money is small, then the price of borrowing money will tend to rise and be reflected in higher interest rates. Of course, there are other factors that affect interest rates, but the forces of supply and demand have the greatest effect. This leads us back to how the federal government uses fiscal and monetary policy via the United States Treasury and Federal Reserve Board to control the supply of money and influence interest rates in the U.S. economy.

Fiscal Policy and the U.S. Treasury Department

Fiscal policy is the *government's plan for spending, taxation, and debt management.* The legislative and executive branches of government enact fiscal policy by passing legislation that sets the government's priorities for how much money will be collected, from whom it will be collected, and how it will be spent. The ultimate goals of fiscal and monetary policies are supposed to be economic growth, full employment, and international balance of payments. Unfortunately, there's much debate over which policies actually promote those results. Worse yet, the government's fiscal policy is subject to tremendous political pressure.

The United States Treasury Department is part of the executive branch of the federal government. The Treasury Department, as fiscal manager of the nation, is responsible for carrying out the nation's fiscal policy by doing the actual spending, taxing, and debt financing through an account it keeps with the Federal Reserve. Treasury funds come from a number of sources, but the largest source is personal and business income taxes. The Treasury Department issues all government checks, uses the Internal Revenue Service to collect taxes and enforce tax laws, and issues interest-bearing notes (called securities) to cover any spending deficits. Deficit spending and taxation are the two main policy tools that the Treasury Department can and does use to implement fiscal policy. Both of these policies are a means of controlling the supply of money in circulation and thus, also indirectly affect interest rates.

Deficit Spending

Deficit spending occurs when the *government spends more money than it takes in from tax revenue.* When federal income is less than federal expenditures, a shortfall called a federal budget deficit results. When a deficit occurs, the Treasury obtains funds to cover the shortfall by issuing interest-bearing securities to investors. Depending on their term, these securities are referred to as Treasury Bills or T-Bills (less than one year), Treasury Notes (one to ten years), or Treasury Bonds (30 years). In issuing these securities, the federal government is borrowing from the private sector and accumulating debt. When the government borrows money to cover deficits or debt, less money is available for private borrowers.

While some economists believe that federal deficits and debt have little impact on interest rates, others believe that large-scale federal borrowing can have a dramatic effect on interest rates as private borrowers compete for limited funds remaining. Government borrowing (whether through deficits or debt), as well as the compounding effect of interest that is paid on the bonds or debt instruments. is the single largest drain on the supply of mortgage loan funds.

Taxation

The second tool of fiscal policy is taxation. Taxes directly impact the spending habits and abilities of all businesses and individuals. Lower taxes mean taxpayers have more funds for lending or investing. Higher taxes mean they not only have fewer funds to lend or invest, but will also be more likely to invest in tax-exempt securities instead of taxable investments, like mortgages. While some would argue that government spending is necessary and has the same net result on economic activity, higher taxes result in people having less money to buy homes.

Taxation can also have direct and deliberate secondary effects on real estate and mortgage financing. Along with raising revenue, tax provisions are used to implement social policies by encouraging or discouraging certain behaviors or activities. This is done through tax deductions and exemptions. For example, the deduction for mortgage interest from taxable income effectively stimulates housing and encourages home ownership. Tax code changes beginning in 1988 have limited the deductibility of home mortgage interest, which was previously fully deductible. If the money is used to buy or improve a primary residence, then mortgage interest is deductible for loans up to $1,000,000. Interest on home loans for purposes other than buying or improving a home is deductible to a much lesser extent, depending on filing status.

Provisions of the **Tax Reform Act of 1986** also limited or eliminated tax benefits previously available for real property owners. The capital gains exclusion for long-term capital gains was eliminated, as were accelerated cost recovery methods, while straight line cost recovery periods for income and investment property were increased. The ability to offset losses from income property (termed "passive losses") against income from wages and salaries was restricted for many taxpayers. All of these served to make real estate investing less attractive.

Still, investors can deduct expenses and depreciation for commercial and investment properties. **Depreciation** is *expensing of the cost of business or investment property over a set number of years, determined by the IRS to be the asset's useful life.* For example, the cost of a residential building is divided by a depreciation life of 27.5 years, whereas the cost of a commercial building is divided by a depreciation life of 39 years. For a property to be depreciable, it must be used in a trade or business. Thus, a house rented to tenants is a depreciable asset, whereas your personal residence is not (even if you use part of it for a home office). Only buildings and improvements are depreciable; land is not. Repairs are expensed in the year they are incurred. Rules are complicated, though, so professional tax advice is always encouraged.

The **Taxpayer Relief Act of 1997** added some beneficial tax treatment for homeowners, by adding a new tax exclusion on the sale of a principal residence. The exclusion is $500,000 for married couples filing jointly and $250,000 for single taxpayers. Anyone selling a home can claim the exclusion as often as every two years—without having to buy another home of equal or greater value—as long as three conditions are met:

1. The seller must have owned the home for at least two of the five years preceding the sale,
2. The seller must have used the property as a principal residence for at least two of the five years preceding the sale, and
3. The seller must not have used the exclusion for a sale during the prior two years.

The IRS has clarified these rules such that in certain circumstances (such as a job relocation), if the person did not own or use the home for the entire two-year period, the exclusion amount may be prorated.

Real Success

Other tax-related programs come and go. For example, with the **American Recovery and Reinvestment Act of 2009**, Congress authorized a tax credit of up to $8,000 for qualified first-time home buyers purchasing homes on or after January 1, 2009 and before December 1, 2009.

These tax laws are mentioned here simply to make you aware that fiscal policy and tax laws can affect real estate, and you should make a point of **staying current**. However, you should never give tax advice to anyone. Refer people to tax professionals because tax laws are complicated and change frequently.

Monetary Policy and the Federal Reserve

Monetary policy is the *government's mechanism through which it can exert control over the performance of the economy, primarily through the supply and cost of money.* Monetary policy is conducted by the Federal Reserve System—the Fed for short—and it influences demand mainly by raising and lowering short-term interest rates.

The **Federal Reserve Act of 1913** established the **Federal Reserve System** as the nation's central bank with 12 regional Federal Reserve Banks (FRBs). The FRBs serve as lenders of last resort to provide funds to banks to avoid the bank panics that were common in the late 1800s and early 1900s.

Federal Reserve System

The Federal Reserve and state and federal agencies supervise and regulate the nation's financial institutions to ensure their financial soundness and compliance with banking, consumer, and other applicable laws. The Fed is made up of the Board of Governors (Federal Reserve Board), Federal Open Market Committee (FOMC), Federal Advisory Council, Federal Reserve Banks, and more than 5,000 member banks.

The **Board of Governors**, called the **Federal Reserve Board**, is a seven-member committee that controls the Federal Reserve System. The governors are appointed by the President and confirmed by the Senate for 14-year terms. The Board members control the Fed's monetary policy by implementing various policy tools. The Board also has substantial control over regulations affecting the activities of financial institutions and oversees federal regulations dealing with money.

The **Federal Open Market Committee (FOMC)** controls the Fed's open market operations—the sale and purchase of government securities. The FOMC consists of the seven members of the Federal Reserve Board, plus the President of the Federal Reserve Bank of New York, and four other Federal Reserve Bank Presidents. FOMC actions are a very important way of controlling the money supply.

The **Federal Advisory Council** consists of 12 members, one elected by each of the 12 Federal Reserve Banks, as district representatives. They meet quarterly with the Board of Governors to discuss business conditions and make policy recommendations.

Figure 2.1: Federal Reserve Map of the United States.

Federal Reserve Banks

Federal Reserve Banks have one main office located in each of the 12 Federal Reserve districts. In addition, there are 25 branches and 12 offices. FRBs provide services to all financial institutions and are referred to as "the bankers' banks," storing currency and coin, processing checks and electronic payments. All national banks chartered by the federal government are required to join the Federal Reserve and purchase stock in its district reserve bank, making each Federal Reserve Bank technically owned by the member banks in that district. Each Reserve Bank has a nine-member board of directors. State-chartered banks and other depository institutions may join if they meet certain requirements.

Each member bank has some input into the Fed's policies via the election of six directors to its district Federal Reserve Bank. All member and non-member banks are subject to the rules and policies implemented by the Fed—such as maintaining required reserves of depositors' funds.

Monetary Policy

The goal of any central bank is to stabilize the economy. The Fed's primary mission is to ensure that enough money and credit are available to sustain economic growth without inflation. These are the tools used by the Fed to implement its monetary policy:

- Open market operations
- Discount rates
- Reserve requirements

Open Market Operations

The major tool used by the Fed to affect the supply of reserves in the banking system is **open market operations**, which is the *buying and selling of U.S. government securities (bonds) on the open market.* The **Federal Open Market Committee** (FOMC) is responsible for open market operations. The FOMC meets eight times each year to discuss the present and future state of the economy, including where interest rates should ideally be to accomplish the Fed's long-term objectives of economic growth and stability with minimal inflation.

One of the things the Fed does at its FOMC meeting is try to exert indirect influence over long-term interest rates by establishing a target **federal funds rate**. The federal funds rate affects the short-term interest rate that banks charge when they borrow money in the Fed funds market (usually very short-term loans for a day or two to help banks cover reserve requirements caused by the normal daily fluctuations in their deposits).

To hit its target federal funds rate, the Fed will sell or buy **securities** (also called bonds). When the Fed *sells* federal fund securities, it is *increasing* its stockpile of cash and taking money out of circulation. Since the banks have less money available to lend, the federal funds rate rises. Conversely, when the Fed *buys* securities, it is *decreasing* its stockpile of cash and putting more money into circulation. Since the banks that sold the security (or the banks of the customers that sold the security) have more money available, the banks want to quickly re-lend the money to earn interest on it instead of just letting it sit in their banks. Since the banks have more money to lend, the federal funds rate falls.

Keep in mind, though, that other factors, such as inflation, may be applying upward pressure on interest rates at the same time that an increase in money supply is exerting downward pressure. And the Fed can only exert influence on short-term federal funds interest rates. The Fed does *not* set the prime rate, but while the Fed's actions have no direct effect on the prime rate, long-term rates do usually follow the lead established by the federal funds rate movement.

Discount Rates

The **discount rate** is the interest rate the Federal Reserve Banks (FRBs) charge financial institutions for short-term loans of reserves, although the Fed discourages banks from borrowing funds from them directly unless the bank is in financial trouble and not able to borrow from other banks on the open Fed funds market. The FRBs offer three discount window programs:

- **Primary credit.** Under the primary credit program, loans are extended for a very short term (usually overnight) to depository institutions in sound condition. The primary credit rate is set above the usual level of short-term market interest rates.
- **Secondary credit.** Institutions that are not eligible for primary credit may apply for secondary credit to meet short-term liquidity needs, but at a higher rate than the primary credit rates and with more restrictions.
- **Seasonal credit.** This is extended to small depository institutions in agricultural or seasonal resort communities with the interest rate being an average of selected market rates.

Even though each of the discount windows have their own interest rate, note that the generic term "discount rate" may sometimes be used to describe the primary credit rate.

Unlike open market operations, which interact with financial market forces to influence short-term interest rates, the discount rate is set by the Boards of Directors of the Federal Reserve Banks, and it is subject to approval by the Board of Governors. The discount rate is, therefore, less of a policy tool. Changes in the discount rate, however, can cause financial markets to respond to a potential change in the direction of monetary policy. A higher discount rate can indicate a more restrictive policy, while a lower rate may be used to signal a more expansive policy.

Reserve Requirements

Reserve requirements are the *percentage of funds that depository institutions must hold in reserve against specified deposit liabilities in the form of cash or in an account at a Federal Reserve Bank.* The original purpose of reserve requirements was to help avert financial panic by giving depositors some confidence that their deposits were safe and accessible. The Federal Reserve sets reserve requirements for all commercial banks, savings banks, savings and loans, credit unions, and U.S. branches and agencies of foreign banks.

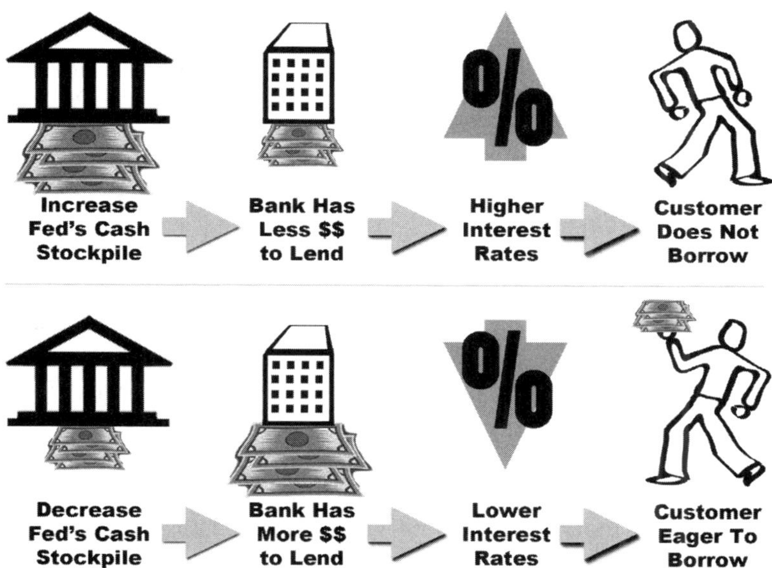

Figure 2.2 How Federal Reserve Actions Affect Interest Rates.

By raising or lowering reserve requirements, the Fed controls the supply of money, which then affects the cost of money. For example, if the Federal Reserve Board wanted to raise interest rates or make credit tougher to get, it would raise the reserve requirements, which decreases the money supply available for banks to loan. When there's a smaller supply of money, higher interest rates should decrease demand. (See Part A in Figure 2.2.)

Conversely, if the Fed wanted to lower interest rates or make credit easier to get, then it would lower the reserve requirements. Lowering the reserve requirements increases the money supply available for banks to loan out. When there's a larger supply of money, lower interest rates will result, increasing demand. (See Part B in Figure 2.2.)

So even though the Fed does not directly set long-term interest rates, changing the supply of money through reserve requirements does have that effect. Using this strategy to adjust interest rates and control inflation, however, has become a less important near-term Fed tool because it has a large effect on the money supply by affecting all of the deposit assets of banks. Instead, the Fed is able to have a similar outcome on a smaller, more manageable scale with FOMC open market operations.

Adjusting Interest Rates

The balancing efforts of the Fed are directed at managing the growth of the money supply to allow adequate growth of the economy at reasonable interest rates, without fueling inflation or fears of inflation that could lead to higher interest rates. Prior to 1979, the Federal Reserve attempted to moderate interest rates by increasing the money supply when interest rates started to rise, with the intent of causing rates to fall. This policy led to high inflation as more and more money was pumped into the economy to satisfy borrowers' demands.

In October of 1979, the Fed adopted a different approach. Rather than try to control interest rates by adjusting the money supply, the Fed instituted a policy of controlling the money supply (and inflation) by adjusting interest rates. The discount rate reached as high as 14% in 1981. The result was a much tighter credit market, since the only way to slow the rampant growth of the money supply was to discourage borrowing by raising interest rates. As inflation was brought under control, the Fed was able to lower the discount rate.

Part of the Fed's role in managing interest rates is not only to deal with actual inflation, but also with anticipated inflation. In recent years, the Fed has adopted a policy of trying to anticipate future economic conditions rather than simply reacting to them as it had in the past. This has also involved trying to further reduce the size and impact of swings in the business cycle. Most economists and businesses watch the Fed's actions when the FOMC meets to see if they will raise the discount rate to reduce growth and head off inflation, or lower rates in an effort to spur economic growth and head off recession. Although many believe that inflation is less of a threat in our current global economy, the Fed still plays an important role in managing economic growth and interest rates. Even though the Fed does not directly raise long term interest rates, by changing the supply of money, the Fed is causing the price of money (interest rates) to rise. This change affects the cost of money to the bank; the bank then passes that increased cost on to the customer.

Moral Suasion

Moral suasion is *using persuasive influences of authorities on the public so that they will behave in a certain way*. For example, a mayor appeals to community spirit as a way of increasing voluntary participation in a recycling program. Within financial markets, moral suasion is often a factor in how the public perceives credit. For example, the Chairman of the Federal Reserve Board may make a speech stating that the Fed is concerned about rising stock prices fueling inflation. Even though there may not be any intention of actually raising interest rates, the Chairman's statement may, nevertheless, still produce the desired effect of having the public and financial markets do less speculating in the market for fear of higher interest rates without actually having to raise interest rates to achieve this result.

Chapter 2 Summary

1. **Business cycles** are general swings in business activity. Real estate lags behind business cycles. The law of **supply and demand** says that for all products, goods, and services when supply exceeds demand, prices will fall and when demand exceeds supply, prices will rise.
2. **Inflation** is an increase in the cost of goods or services; cost inflation is when manufacturers pass along increased costs; demand inflation is when too many people with money want to buy the same thing. **Interest rates** are fees people or businesses must pay to use another's money for their own purposes. Interest rates are a primary factor in determining demand for real estate.
3. **Real estate cycles** are the response of real estate and mortgage markets to the forces of supply and demand. Two things separate the housing markets from other supply and demand models: The lag time for construction industry response and limited supply of land.
4. **Physical, economic, government**, and **social** forces (P E G S) affect real estate cycles. **Physical:** Location, popularity, climate, environment, internal or external. **Economic:** Economic base of an area (critical for home values), cost of money. **Government:** Federal includes fiscal policy (taxes), monetary policy (interest rates), regulation; state/local government includes revenue-generating (taxes) and regulating (police power, which addresses land use controls, zoning, environment, eminent domain, escheat). **Social:** Demographics, migration, family size, population shift, growth, age.
5. **Fiscal policy** is the government's plan for spending, taxing, and managing debt. The Treasury Department carries out fiscal policy by issuing checks, collecting taxes, and issuing notes to cover deficits. Tools of fiscal policy are deficit spending and taxation. Deficit spending occurs when expenditures exceed revenues. Taxation is a way to collect revenue and implement social policies, such as giving tax deductions for mortgage interest to promote home ownership.
6. **Monetary policy** is government's way to control supply and cost of money. The Federal Reserve Board (the Fed) is responsible for monetary policy, maintaining economic stability, and regulating banks. Policy tools include: **Open market operation** (Fed sells/buys bonds to adjust money supply and demand); **discount rate** (interest rate charged to member banks on overnight loans); **reserve requirements** (banks must keep money on deposit—can't lend it out).
7. **Moral suasion** is using persuasive influences on public and financial markets.

Chapter 2 Quiz

1. ***The cost of money***
   - A. does not affect demand for real estate.
   - B. greatly influences a homebuyer's decision.
   - C. has no influence on a homebuyer's decision.
   - D. is not the same as interest rates.

2. ***The economic base of an area***
   - A. creates buyer's markets but not seller's markets.
   - B. does not influence the local housing market.
   - C. gives stability to a region, supports real estate values, and determines housing supply in an area.
   - D. is responsible for government money coming in to support an area.

3. ***In a healthy economy, supply***
   - A. fluctuates significantly.
   - B. is in balance with demand.
   - C. is less than demand.
   - D. significantly outweighs demand.

4. ***The law of supply and demand says that***
   - A. for all products, goods, and services when demand exceeds supply, prices will fall and when supply exceeds demand, prices will rise.
   - B. for all products, goods, and services when supply exceeds demand, prices will fall and when demand exceeds supply, prices will rise.
   - C. real estate doesn't respond at all.
   - D. there will always be a shortage of houses due to population growth.

5. ***The United State Treasury***
   - A. gets most of its funds from federal income taxes.
   - B. is considered the nation's fiscal manager.
   - C. manages the government's finances.
   - D. all of the above

6. ***The interest rate charged by the Fed to member banks that borrow money against their deposits is called the***
   - A. deposit insurance.
   - B. discount rate.
   - C. prime rate.
   - D. reserve requirement.

7. ***The percentage of deposits that banks are required to maintain on deposit with the Federal Reserve System is called the***
   - A. deposit insurance.
   - B. discount rate.
   - C. prime rate.
   - D. reserve requirement.

8. ***Excessively high levels of government borrowing could lead to***
   - A. excess funds for real estate investment.
   - B. government securities disappearing from the open marketplace.
   - C. high interest rates.
   - D. low interest rates.

9. ***The agency responsible for supervising the growth of the nation's money and credit supply and regulating banks is the***
   - A. FDIC.
   - B. Federal Reserve Board.
   - C. Office of Thrift Supervision.
   - D. U.S. Treasury.

10. ***The Federal Reserve Board influences interest rates with***
    - A. federal discount rates.
    - B. open market operations.
    - C. reserve requirements.
    - D. all of the above

3

Chapter 3

The Mortgage Lending Process

In This Chapter

This chapter introduces you to the many roles played by the mortgage professional. It then walks you through the loan process and discusses the important differences between pre-qualification and pre-approval. It provides an overview of the tasks of the mortgage loan originator, qualifying buyers, and documenting mortgage files. Standards relating to income, credit history, and net worth are also discussed. You will also calculate housing expense ratios and total debt-to-income ratios using secondary market guidelines.

At the end of this chapter, you will be able to:

- Define the various roles that mortgage professionals play.
- Distinguish between pre-approval and pre-qualification.
- Identify the steps in the loan process.
- Discuss the information necessary to complete a standard loan application.
- Identify criteria for evaluating borrowers.
- Calculate income and debt ratios.
- Explain credit scoring.
- Discuss the settlement process, including reconciliation.

Key Terms

Assets
Bankruptcy
Credit History
Credit Scoring
Debts
Debt-to-Income Ratio
Discount Points
Float
Housing Expense Ratio
Liabilities
Loan Processor
Mortgage Loan Originator
PITI
Point
Pre-Approval
Pre-Qualification
Rate Lock
Reserves
Servicer
Stable Income
Underwriter
Yield Spread Premium

Role of the Mortgage Professional

Mortgage professionals can work for any bank, credit union, mortgage lender, mortgage investor, or mortgage broker. Depending upon the size of the company, one may need to wear many different hats in the organization. With a large company, duties may lie in just one area, such as taking loan applications from prospective borrowers. In other situations, one might perform any number of functions, and may even be responsible for guiding borrowers through much of the mortgage process. This chapter is designed to give you an overview of the various roles in the mortgage industry. It's important to understand the basics of mortgage lending, and what the duties may be, regardless of who you work for.

Functions of Mortgage Professionals

In addition to the typical duties and paperwork performed in most office jobs, there are specific functions for mortgage professionals, depending on the needs of the company. The terms origination, underwriting, and servicing may seem foreign now, but they have specific definitions that will mean more as you study the mortgage profession.

Origination

Origination is *the process of making or initiating a new loan.* Origination involves being the initial contact to a consumer and taking a loan application. It can also involve ordering a credit report and assembling all of the other forms and documents required by the person or company who is underwriting the loan.

Loan Processing

A loan processor works on the file assembled by the originator. The **processor** is typically *responsible for verification of the information contained in the file* (such as sending out employment verification forms) and also coordination of the various aspects of the loan (such as working with the title company).

Underwriting

Underwriting is *the process of evaluating and deciding whether to make a new loan and, if yes, on what terms.* This is done by the funding source—usually an investor, depository, or mortgage lender, but never by a mortgage broker, who only originates loans for lenders. Underwriting involves evaluating credit scores, credit history, appraisals, job history, and other measures of strength or weakness in the borrower and the collateral. There are specific skills and expertise required for this function that go beyond simply evaluating numbers produced by a computer. Additional experience and training are required in this area.

Servicing

Servicing is *the continued maintenance of a loan after the loan has closed.* This can be done, for example, by a lender, a servicing company set up solely to perform this function, or some other acceptable entity. Servicing involves maintaining direct contact with borrowers, sending mortgage and escrow analysis statements, collecting payments, and pursuing late payments. Often, a primary lender will sell a mortgage to the secondary market, but still service the loan for a fee.

Many mortgage companies offer a combination of these functions to their clients. For one loan, they may provide all of the services: Originate the loan (find the borrower), underwrite the loan (evaluate the borrower), and service the loan (continue to interact with the borrower). If the lender is not able to provide a loan product that meets the needs of a particular borrower, the lender may simply act as a broker and assist in finding another lender in order to earn an origination fee.

The Loan Process

Generally speaking, with today's federal disclosure requirements, borrowers should complete a loan application only when they are ready to buy a particular home. Even if the borrower is *not* ready to make an offer on the house, the borrower may be pre-qualified. This is ***not*** the same as pre-approving buyers. The two terms are not interchangeable, so it is important to thoroughly understand the differences between them.

Pre-Qualification

Pre-qualification is *the process of pre-determining how much a potential borrower* ***might*** *be eligible to borrow.* This may be done by any mortgage loan originator, but it **does not guarantee approval**. Pre-qualification of a buyer is *not* binding on the mortgage broker or lender—which is why the distinction is important. It is a free "test run" of the loan application process that usually takes only a few hours. The mortgage broker or lender is only saying that it looks *favorable* that the borrower will be approved. Often there's more background research, documentation, and information that the mortgage broker or lender must obtain, but won't until the borrower has actually applied for the loan. However, if the lender renders a credit decision, the pre-qualification becomes an application and the required disclosures will need to be delivered.

The pre-qualification process involves asking prospective borrowers questions about income and debts. A credit report may be pulled by a MLO, or the borrower may just be asked questions about his or her financial situation. A mortgage loan originator's pre-qualification of a prospective borrower may be as simple as making sure that the borrower has a steady job and no glaring credit report problems, like a recent bankruptcy. Often, a MLO will compute the borrower's income and debt ratios to get an idea of how much house a prospective buyer may be able to afford.

Some lenders or mortgage brokers offer a loan pre-qualification certificate form, which is not binding. Assuming a credit decision is not anticipated as a result of this, it does not trigger required disclosures. MLOs may also provide a closing cost worksheet while the loan is still in the pre-qualification state. If such a worksheet is provided, however, it must become a part of the loan file once it becomes a formal application.

Pre-Approval

Pre-approval is *the process by which a lender determines if potential borrowers can be financed through the lender, and for what amount of money.* They are rendering a credit decision. Generally speaking, a mortgage broker *cannot* give a borrower a pre-approval; only the lender can pre-approve. For a pre-approval, a borrower goes through most of the same steps in the loan process, such as completing an application and providing documentation of income and assets. With a pre-approval, a lender is stating that the prospective borrower's situation has been investigated and, provided all circumstances stay the same, the lender is willing to loan a certain amount of money to purchase a house. This is especially helpful when working with buyers because it is a powerful negotiation tool in getting an offer accepted by a seller and, in most cases, is a requirement of contract acceptance.

Of course, a borrower's circumstances can and do change which is why there are always conditions listed on a pre-approval. Depending upon internal pre-approval procedures, some pre-approvals are more specific and binding. This is where experience is helpful, and where you should take advantage of the wisdom and experience your employer and other senior mortgage professionals can offer. Pre-approvals are always in writing and always follow the policies and procedures established by your employer or mortgage lender.

Completing an application in anticipation of a credit decision triggers federally mandated disclosures, which includes a Good Faith Estimate of closing costs (GFE) and a Truth in Lending Statement (both of which will be discussed in detail in the next chapter). In order to submit a loan application for pre-approval, the borrower must be given a GFE, which binds the MLO to its terms. While the Department of Housing and Urban Development (HUD) allows a borrower to be pre-approved without identifying a specific property address, mortgage loan originators are *not* required to provide a GFE under such circumstances.

Information related to a loan application must also be reported on the Loan/Application Register (LAR) to comply with the **Home Mortgage Disclosure Act** (which is covered in the next chapter).

Traditional Steps

The real estate loan approval process traditionally consists of four steps, including:

1. Consulting with the mortgage loan originator
2. Completing a loan application
3. Processing a loan application
4. Analyzing the borrower and property

Real Success

Traditionally, borrowers went to a mortgage loan originator's office for face-to-face meetings. These days, though, with busy schedules and a competitive environment, many MLOs will visit prospective borrowers at home or at work. The Internet has changed this process as well—many of these steps can now be done quickly and conveniently online or by other electronic means. Answering initial questions, completing a loan application, getting final approval, and closing the loan can all be done electronically. Most of this chapter looks at the process from the traditional approach of meeting with the borrower face-to-face. Keep in mind that regardless of how the application is obtained, the mechanics of the loan process, the steps taken, information needed, and end result are still the same.

Consulting with the Mortgage Loan Originator

Whether a prospective borrower wishes to consult with a mortgage loan originator in person or online, the first step to choose the right one. If a borrower already has a relationship with a MLO, this may be a good place to start. On the other hand, if a borrower has past credit problems, it may be helpful to use a mortgage company that deals with many different lenders, although in today's tight market and stringent credit score qualifying standards, this is not the fix for credit issues it once was. As borrowers decide how to proceed with applying for their loan, remember these points:

- Do not interject your opinion into the situation. Let the person's job history and credit dictate the course of action you suggest. This is especially important if you are a MLO representing many different lenders and loan programs.
- Always let clients or customers have the final say as to how they apply for a loan and with whom.
- If you work with more than one investor or company program, always consult with your mortgage company or employer regarding the policies in all areas before giving any type of advice or recommendation.

After the lender is selected, initial discussions usually involve the various types of mortgages it offers (e.g., 30-year, 15-year, fixed rate, ARM) so the borrower can decide which loan best suits his or her needs. A borrower will need to give the lender a good deal of personal and financial data on which the lender will base the lending decision. Providing the borrower with a complete list of required documents and reviewing these documents early in the application will help speed up the approval process.

When the goal is an actual loan approval (not pre-approval) for a purchase, the **sales contract** will be examined as well. The MLO wants to ensure that it's possible to comply with the terms of the agreement. Of particular concern are the **financing commitment date** and the **closing date**. Often a contract calls for a closing date that is too early to be realistic. If it's impossible for the lender to meet the closing date, a more feasible date can be agreed upon by all parties to the contract to avoid frustration. Loan fees and pricing adjustments may also be listed in the sales agreement.

Interest Rates

One topic that inevitably arises very early in a borrower's conversations with a MLO is the interest rate that may be available. The **interest rate** is the *amount charged by a lender to a borrower for the use of assets, expressed as a percentage of the loan amount (the principal).* When considering interest rates, you may hear the term **basis point**, which is 1/100th of a percentage point. For example, 325 basis points equal 3.25% or 3 1/4%.

A couple of other terms to keep in mind when discussing interest with borrowers:

- **Par rate** is a term that describes the rate without discounts or points that lenders offer only to mortgage brokers, also known as the "wholesale" rate, that does not create an additional charge or provide for a credit for the borrower.
- **Rate Lock.** This is a commitment guaranteed by a lender that an interest rate will not change on a specific loan for a specific period of time. Since a **lock-in agreement** generally requires that the loan close

by a specific date, the anticipated close date should be carefully considered. If a loan closes after the rate lock expires, the lender may choose to offer the market rate current at that time or the original lock-in rate.

- **Float.** Between the time of application and closing, a borrower may choose to bet on interest rates decreasing by electing to float. Floating is essentially choosing not to lock the interest rate. Since it is the borrower's responsibility to lock his or her rate before closing, choosing to float is considered risky and may result in a higher interest rate.

Common Fees Associated with Real Estate Loans

In addition to the **interest**, there are other fees associated with processing a real estate loan, for example, fees for pulling a borrower's credit bureau report, securing a property appraisal report, and for completing inspections. Other items like title insurance and recording fees are paid if and when a loan closes. Fees that occur only when a loan closes are likely to be paid out of closing funds, but other early expenses incurred must be paid, even if the loan doesn't close.

A prior relationship with a mortgage loan originator can help when discussing fees, because the MLO may agree to absorb some smaller costs, such as for the credit report. More costly items, such as a property appraisal, may have to be paid for by the borrower before a final underwriting decision is made.

Lender's return—which you may see referenced as **lender's yield**—is essentially the *total amount of money the lender can make from a loan in relation to the amount invested.* Most of the lender's return is accounted for as a result of interest paid by the borrower. Another opportunity for a lender to recognize return is at closing when the fees are collected from the borrower. A lender could also recognize a return during the loan term through servicing fees or by collecting a fee for those loans that allow a prepayment penalty if the borrower pays off the loan before the end of its term. A lender is generally only interested in the total amount of money it will make from the loan, not necessarily its source.

Title XIV of the Dodd-Frank Wall Street Reform and Consumer Protection Act (Pub.L. 111-203, H.R. 4173), which is designated as the Mortgage Reform and Anti-Predatory Lending Act, prohibits any direct or indirect compensation to a mortgage loan originator that varies based on the terms of the loan, other than the amount of principal (§ 1403 (c)(1)). Final rules that address this provision are covered in more detail in the next chapter.

Loan Origination Fees

For loans that actually close, lenders charge a loan **origination fee** to *cover the administrative costs of making and processing the loan*, including setting up the loan on the lender's books. Such fees may be referred to collectively as **points**. A point is simply *one percent of the loan amount.* So, on a $120,000 loan, the borrower would have to pay an additional $1,200 for every point the lender charged as an origination fee. Points can be charged for many reasons, such as closing fees, underwriting fees, documentation fees, etc., but all points serve to help increase the lender's return. Mortgage loan originators base loan fees on what the market will bear.

Another factor the lender considers when determining the number of points charged on a loan is the sale of the loan on the secondary market. For example, a lender may need to sell a loan at a discount to compensate that secondary market buyer for the time value of money. The lender can attempt to make up some of any loss by charging the borrower points. Alternatively, in a competitive environment, some of those fees may even be waived as the lender can sell the loan in the secondary market at a premium. It all depends on the current market and rate of the loan.

A MLO must set the fees to offset the **actual costs and expenses** incurred in the origination of the loan. If not, they can be fined for **upcharging** the borrower, which is *profiting from a third party or lender fee.* For example, on VA loans, this loan fee/origination can be no higher than one point. For FHA and conventional loans, the loan fee/origination varies, but is often in the one- to four-point range.

Origination fees must be disclosed to the borrower on the Good Faith Estimate (GFE) of closing costs within three business days of the MLO's receipt of a completed loan application.

Real Success

MLOs can collect a credit report fee at application, but no other fees may be collected until a **Truth in Lending Statement** (TIL) and a **Good Faith Estimate** (GFE)—as required by the Truth in Lending Act and the Real Estate Settlement Procedures Act (RESPA)—are delivered to the borrower and the borrower indicates his or her intention to proceed with the transaction. At that point, other transaction fees—such as for an appraisal—may be charged. Furthermore, RESPA prohibits the collection of any fee unless it was properly disclosed to the borrower on the Good Faith Estimate. In order to keep borrowers satisfied with the mortgage application process and performance of the mortgage loan originator, it is crucial that their expectations are met as to what closing costs are and what they will need to bring to closing.

Discount Points

Discount points represent a ***pre-payment of interest*** *at the beginning of a loan for the purpose of* ***reducing the note interest rate*** *charged for some defined period of the life of the loan.* This essentially shifts the timing of when the lender collects its fees for making the loan. With discount points, the borrower pays *more* out-of-pocket upfront in order to pay *less* out-of-pocket later. Discount points, especially if paid by the seller, could allow the borrower to qualify for a loan that would otherwise be impossible to get.

By charging discount points up front, the lender is able to make up the required return on investment that is lost by making the loan **below par rate**. However, it's important to know that to be legitimate, the discount points must reflect a **bona fide reduction** to the market or par rate that is reasonably consistent with established industry norms and practices for secondary market transactions. In other words, a lender could not quote a higher interest rate than the borrower would qualify for, then offer discount points to lower it.

Discount points have traditionally been associated with FHA and VA purchase loans, but points for conventional loans are common in some areas. Although paying discount points to get a lower interest rate would seem to be of benefit primarily to the buyer, discount points can also benefit the seller. Who pays the points is open to negotiation; a seller or builder may be willing to pay discount points to make the property more marketable.

How the discount is priced, in other words, how many points it takes to buy the rate down, is based on many assumptions and calculations by the lender, primary of which is an assumption as to how long the loan might last and where the interest rates are headed. Generally, lenders assume that the typical 30-year loan is either paid off when property is sold or refinanced within eight to 12 years, and will price its discount points with that in mind.

The difference between origination "points" and discount points is apparent on the Good Faith Estimate. All origination points must be lumped together as the origination fee on the GFE, while discount points used to buy down the rate must be indicated as a **charge** the borrower incurs for the interest rate selected. This allows the borrower to make an informed decision about the rate options available and the impact on the loan.

Yield Spread Premium

Yield spread premium (YSP) is *a tool that MLOs can use to* ***lower the upfront cash out-of-pocket expenses at closing*** for a borrower in exchange for **higher monthly out-of-pocket payments** required by a higher interest rate. Like discount points, YSP also shifts the timing of the out-of-pocket fees that a borrower pays to a lender for the privilege of getting a loan, but with YSP, the borrower pays *less* out-of-pocket upfront, but pays *more* out-of-pocket later.

Yield spread premium must be disclosed to the borrower on the GFE as a **credit** the borrower receives for the interest rate selected. This allows the borrower to make an informed decision about the rate options available and the impact on the loan.

Qualifying Standards

When mortgage loan originators first meet with a potential borrower—either for pre-qualification or pre-approval—they will likely perform an analysis of the current or allowable monthly housing expense based on the borrower's gross income and debt. This provides the MLO—and the borrower—with a realistic understanding of what mortgage payment the borrower may be able to afford.

There are two qualifying standards:

- Housing expense ratio
- Total debt-to-income ratio (sometimes called total expense debt ratio or total debt service ratio)

Both ratios may be considered in the underwriting analysis, although some automated underwriting systems (AUS) rely only the debt-to-income ratio. Underwriting is addressed in more detail later in this chapter. Besides gross income, the key element needed to determine these ratios is **PITI**, which is an acronym for a mortgage payment that is the sum of monthly **P**rincipal, **I**nterest, **T**axes (property taxes and perhaps mandatory special assessments, if applicable), and **I**nsurance (homeowners hazard/flood insurance and mortgage insurance, if applicable). When the collateral property requires **association fees** as a condition of ownership, for example as with a condominium, the association fees must be taken into consideration and PITI adjusted to get the complete housing expense.

Qualifying standards may vary from lender to lender, but with increased lender dependence on the national secondary market, the majority of lenders throughout the country have incorporated into their own conventional loan underwriting procedures the standards set by the major secondary market investors, specifically Fannie Mae and Freddie Mac. Of course, if the loan being contemplated is to be made in conjunction with the FHA or VA, those underwriting standards must be applied (underwriting standards for conventional loans and FHA and VA loans will be discussed in more detail in later chapters).

Housing Expense Ratio

A borrower's housing expense ratio, also called the **front end ratio**, is the relationship of the borrower's total monthly housing expense to gross income, expressed as a percentage:

Total Housing Expense ÷ Gross Income = Ratio %

Conventional lenders consider a borrower's income adequate for a loan if the proposed total mortgage payment of PITI does not exceed **28%** of stable monthly gross income. **Stable monthly income**, which is covered in more detail later, is *a borrower's monthly income that can reasonably be expected to continue in the future.* This is usually a borrower's **gross monthly income** from primary employment and any other acceptable income.

Case in Point

Mark has a stable monthly gross income of $2,900 and the house he wants to buy would have a monthly mortgage payment of $700:

$2,900 **Stable Monthly Gross Income**

$ 700 **Proposed Mortgage Payment (PITI + association fees, if required)**

$700 ÷ $2,900 = 0.24 or 24%

His housing expense ratio in this example is 24%, which is acceptable for a conventional loan since it's below 28%.

Total Debt-to-Income Ratio

A borrower's total debt-to-income ratio (DTI), also known as the **back end ratio**, is the relationship of the borrower's total monthly debt obligations (including PITI housing and long-term debts) to gross income, expressed as a percentage.

Total Debt ÷ Gross Income = Ratio %

Conventional lenders want to be sure the borrower's housing expenses (as explained previously), plus any installment debts with 10 or more payments left or other debt that will not be cancelled, do not exceed **36% of stable monthly gross income**. Here, alimony, child support, or any other court-ordered obligations the borrower has must count as debt against this ratio. Debts with fewer than ten payments remaining may still be counted against the borrower if payments are high (e.g., $600 car payment). If there are student loans currently in deferment, these need to be calculated as debt regardless of how soon the loans will be repaid.

Case in Point

$2,900	**Stable Monthly Gross Income**
$700	**Proposed Mortgage Payment (PITI + association fees, if required)**
$225	**Auto Payment (18 payments left)**
+ $100	**Child Support**
$1,025	**Total**

$1,025 ÷ $2,900 = 0.35 or 35%

The borrower's total DTI ratio in this example is 35%, which is acceptable for a conventional loan since it's below 36%.

When the underwriter considers both ratios, the borrower must generally qualify under **both**.

Using Ratios to Determine Maximum Mortgage Payment

Using the housing expense ratio and debt-to-income ratio, it's easy to determine the maximum mortgage payment for which a borrower should qualify. To determine the maximum mortgage payment allowable under the first ratio, take the borrower's stable monthly income and multiply that by the maximum housing expense ratio (28% or 0.28 for conventional loans).

To determine the figure that represents the largest mortgage payment allowed under the second ratio, take the borrower's stable monthly income and multiply it by the maximum total debt-to-income ratio (36% or 0.36 for conventional loans). This provides the amount of total long-term debts the borrower is permitted to have. Take this total and subtract the monthly long-term obligations the borrower has already (not including mortgage PITI payments) and this provides a figure that represents the largest mortgage payment allowed under the second ratio.

The total debt-to-income ratio is a more realistic measure of the borrower's ability to support the loan payments because it considers *all* of the borrower's recurring financial obligations, which means that the maximum mortgage payment allowed is likely to be smaller than if only the housing ratio were considered. When the underwriter considers both ratios, the **smaller of the two** would be the maximum mortgage payment allowable.

Case in Point

Mary Smith has a stable monthly gross income of $3,200. She has three long-term monthly debt obligations: A $220 car payment, a $75 personal loan payment, and a $50 revolving charge card payment. What's the maximum monthly mortgage payment for which she can qualify?

Housing expense ratio: 28%

	$3,200	**Monthly Gross Income**
x	**0.28**	**Income Ratio**
	$ 896	**Maximum Mortgage PITI Payment**

Total debt-to-income ratio: 36%

	$3,200	**Monthly Gross Income**
x	**0.36**	**Income Ratio**
	$1,152	**Maximum Debt**
-	**$220**	**Car Payment**
-	**$ 75**	**Personal Loan Payment**
-	**$ 50**	**Revolving Charge Card Payment**
	$807	**Maximum Mortgage PITI Payment**

The maximum monthly mortgage payment Mary can qualify for is $807. Remember, when both ratios are used, Mary must qualify under both ratios, so the lower figure is the most she can afford. Of course, if she could pay off some of her debts and reduce her total long-term monthly obligations, she would be able to qualify for a larger mortgage payment.

Completing the Uniform Residential Loan Application

Lenders expect the loans they make to be repaid in a timely manner without collection or foreclosure. Thus, employment stability, income potential, history of debt management, and assets are important considerations. A loan application is designed to elicit responses that detail the borrower's history, trends, and attitude as a means of trying to predict future loan repayment behavior.

The uniform residential loan application (Fannie Mae **Form 1003** or Freddie Mac **Form 65**) is a form lenders require potential borrowers to complete that allows them to collect pertinent information about the borrower and the property. An application may either be in writing or electronically submitted, including a written record of an oral application. The borrower typically completes a loan application during the initial consultation with the mortgage loan originator. There's a great deal of information asked; therefore, attention to detail when completing the application is advised. If the borrower doesn't provide all necessary data during the initial consultation, the missing information must be provided at a later date, which will delay the loan process.

When is an Application an "Application"?

According to **§ 3500.2 (b) of** the Real Estate Settlement Procedures Act (24 C.F.R. Part 3500.2), an **application** is defined as the ***submission of a borrower's financial information in anticipation of a credit decision*** relating to a federally related mortgage loan that includes:

- Borrower's name, monthly income, and Social Security number to obtain a credit report
- Property address and an estimate of the value of the property
- Mortgage loan amount sought
- Any other information deemed necessary by the MLO

This triggers federal disclosure requirements, which are discussed in detail in the next chapter.

Uniform Residential Loan Application

This application is designed to be completed by the applicant(s) with the Lender's assistance. Applicants should complete this form as "Borrower" or "Co-Borrower," as applicable. Co-Borrower information must also be provided (and the appropriate box checked) when ☐ the income or assets of a person other than the Borrower (including the Borrower's spouse) will be used as a basis for loan qualification or ☐ the income or assets of the Borrower's spouse or other person who has community property rights pursuant to state law will not be used as a basis for loan qualification, but his or her liabilities must be considered because the spouse or other person has community property rights pursuant to applicable law and Borrower resides in a community property state, the security property is located in a community property state, or the Borrower is relying on other property located in a community property state as a basis for repayment of the loan.

If this is an application for joint credit, Borrower and Co-Borrower each agree that we intend to apply for joint credit (sign below):

Borrower ______________________ Co-Borrower ______________________

I. TYPE OF MORTGAGE AND TERMS OF LOAN

Mortgage Applied for:	☐ VA ☐ FHA	☐ Conventional ☐ USDA/Rural Housing Service	☐ Other (explain):	Agency Case Number	Lender Case Number

Amount $	Interest Rate %	No. of Months	**Amortization Type:**	☐ Fixed Rate ☐ GPM	☐ Other (explain): ☐ ARM (type):

II. PROPERTY INFORMATION AND PURPOSE OF LOAN

Subject Property Address (street, city, state & ZIP)	No. of Units
Legal Description of Subject Property (attach description if necessary)	Year Built

Purpose of Loan ☐ Purchase ☐ Refinance ☐ Construction ☐ Construction-Permanent ☐ Other (explain):

Property will be: ☐ Primary Residence ☐ Secondary Residence ☐ Investment

Complete this line if construction or construction-permanent loan.

Year Lot Acquired	Original Cost	Amount Existing Liens	(a) Present Value of Lot	(b) Cost of Improvements	Total (a + b)
	$	$	$	$	$

Complete this line if this is a refinance loan.

Year Acquired	Original Cost	Amount Existing Liens	Purpose of Refinance	Describe Improvements ☐ made ☐ to be made
	$	$		Cost: $

Title will be held in what Name(s)	Manner in which Title will be held	Estate will be held in: ☐ Fee Simple ☐ Leasehold (show expiration date)
Source of Down Payment, Settlement Charges, and/or Subordinate Financing (explain)		

III. BORROWER INFORMATION

Borrower				Co-Borrower			
Borrower's Name (include Jr. or Sr. if applicable)				Co-Borrower's Name (include Jr. or Sr. if applicable)			
Social Security Number	Home Phone (incl. area code)	DOB (mm/dd/yyyy)	Yrs. School	Social Security Number	Home Phone (incl. area code)	DOB (mm/dd/yyyy)	Yrs. School
☐ Married ☐ Separated	☐ Unmarried (include single, divorced, widowed)	Dependents (not listed by Co-Borrower) no.	ages	☐ Married ☐ Separated	☐ Unmarried (include single, divorced, widowed)	Dependents (not listed by Borrower) no.	ages
Present Address (street, city, state, ZIP)	☐ Own ☐ Rent ____No. Yrs.			Present Address (street, city, state, ZIP)	☐ Own ☐ Rent ____No. Yrs.		
Mailing Address, if different from Present Address				Mailing Address, if different from Present Address			

If residing at present address for less than two years, complete the following:

Former Address (street, city, state, ZIP)	☐ Own ☐ Rent ____No. Yrs.	Former Address (street, city, state, ZIP)	☐ Own ☐ Rent ____No. Yrs.

IV. EMPLOYMENT INFORMATION

Borrower			Co-Borrower		
Name & Address of Employer	☐ Self Employed	Yrs. on this job Yrs. employed in this line of work/profession	Name & Address of Employer	☐ Self Employed	Yrs. on this job Yrs. employed in this line of work/profession
Position/Title/Type of Business	Business Phone (incl. area code)		Position/Title/Type of Business	Business Phone (incl. area code)	

If employed in current position for less than two years or if currently employed in more than one position, complete the following:

Freddie Mac Form 65 6/09 Page 1 of 5 Fannie Mae Form 1003 6/09

Uniform Residential Loan Application. Source: www.eFannieMae.com.

Borrower			IV. EMPLOYMENT INFORMATION (cont'd)		Co-Borrower
Name & Address of Employer	☐ Self Employed	Dates (from – to) Monthly Income $	Name & Address of Employer	☐ Self Employed	Dates (from – to) Monthly Income $
Position/Title/Type of Business		Business Phone (incl. area code)	Position/Title/Type of Business		Business Phone (incl. area code)
Name & Address of Employer	☐ Self Employed	Dates (from – to) Monthly Income $	Name & Address of Employer	☐ Self Employed	Dates (from – to) Monthly Income $
Position/Title/Type of Business		Business Phone (incl. area code)	Position/Title/Type of Business		Business Phone (incl. area code)

V. MONTHLY INCOME AND COMBINED HOUSING EXPENSE INFORMATION

Gross Monthly Income	Borrower	Co-Borrower	Total	Combined Monthly Housing Expense	Present	Proposed
Base Empl. Income*	$	$	$	Rent	$	
Overtime				First Mortgage (P&I)		$
Bonuses				Other Financing (P&I)		
Commissions				Hazard Insurance		
Dividends/Interest				Real Estate Taxes		
Net Rental Income				Mortgage Insurance		
Other (before completing, see the notice in "describe other income," below)				Homeowner Assn. Dues		
				Other:		
Total	$	$	$	**Total**	$	$

* **Self Employed Borrower(s) may be required to provide additional documentation such as tax returns and financial statements.**

Describe Other Income *Notice:* **Alimony, child support, or separate maintenance income need not be revealed if the Borrower (B) or Co-Borrower (C) does not choose to have it considered for repaying this loan.**

B/C		Monthly Amount
		$

VI. ASSETS AND LIABILITIES

This Statement and any applicable supporting schedules may be completed jointly by both married and unmarried Co-Borrowers if their assets and liabilities are sufficiently joined so that the Statement can be meaningfully and fairly presented on a combined basis; otherwise, separate Statements and Schedules are required. If the Co-Borrower section was completed about a non-applicant spouse or other person, this Statement and supporting schedules must be completed about that spouse or other person also.

Completed ☐ Jointly ☐ Not Jointly

ASSETS Description		Cash or Market Value	Liabilities and Pledged Assets. List the creditor's name, address, and account number for all outstanding debts, including automobile loans, revolving charge accounts, real estate loans, alimony, child support, stock pledges, etc. Use continuation sheet, if necessary. Indicate by (*) those liabilities, which will be satisfied upon sale of real estate owned or upon refinancing of the subject property.		
Cash deposit toward purchase held by		$			
List checking and savings accounts below			LIABILITIES	Monthly Payment & Months Left to Pay	Unpaid Balance
Name and address of Bank, S&L, or Credit Union			Name and address of Company	$ Payment/Months	$
Acct. no.	$		Acct. no.		
Name and address of Bank, S&L, or Credit Union			Name and address of Company	$ Payment/Months	$
Acct. no.	$		Acct. no.		
Name and address of Bank, S&L, or Credit Union			Name and address of Company	$ Payment/Months	$
Acct. no.	$		Acct. no.		

Freddie Mac Form 65 6/09 Page 2 of 5 Fannie Mae Form 1003 6/09

Uniform Residential Loan Application. Source: www.eFannieMae.com.

VI. ASSETS AND LIABILITIES (cont'd)

Name and address of Bank, S&L, or Credit Union		Name and address of Company	$ Payment/Months	$
Acct. no.	$	Acct. no.		
Stocks & Bonds (Company name/ number & description)	$	Name and address of Company	$ Payment/Months	$
		Acct. no.		
Life insurance net cash value Face amount: $	$	Name and address of Company	$ Payment/Months	$
Subtotal Liquid Assets	$			
Real estate owned (enter market value from schedule of real estate owned)	$			
Vested interest in retirement fund	$			
Net worth of business(es) owned (attach financial statement)	$	Acct. no.		
Automobiles owned (make and year)	$	Alimony/Child Support/Separate Maintenance Payments Owed to:	$	
Other Assets (itemize)	$	Job-Related Expense (child care, union dues, etc.)	$	
		Total Monthly Payments	$	
Total Assets a.	$	Net Worth (a minus b) ▸ $	**Total Liabilities b.**	$

Schedule of Real Estate Owned (If additional properties are owned, use continuation sheet.)

Property Address (enter S if sold, PS if pending sale or R if rental being held for income) ▼		Type of Property	Present Market Value	Amount of Mortgages & Liens	Gross Rental Income	Mortgage Payments	Insurance, Maintenance, Taxes & Misc.	Net Rental Income
			$	$	$	$	$	$
		Totals	$	$	$	$	$	$

List any additional names under which credit has previously been received and indicate appropriate creditor name(s) and account number(s):

Alternate Name	Creditor Name	Account Number

VII. DETAILS OF TRANSACTION

a.	Purchase price	$
b.	Alterations, improvements, repairs	
c.	Land (if acquired separately)	
d.	Refinance (incl. debts to be paid off)	
e.	Estimated prepaid items	
f.	Estimated closing costs	
g.	PMI, MIP, Funding Fee	
h.	Discount (if Borrower will pay)	
i.	Total costs (add items a through h)	

VIII. DECLARATIONS

If you answer "Yes" to any questions a through i, please use continuation sheet for explanation.	**Borrower** Yes	No	**Co-Borrower** Yes	No
a. Are there any outstanding judgments against you?	☐	☐	☐	☐
b. Have you been declared bankrupt within the past 7 years?	☐	☐	☐	☐
c. Have you had property foreclosed upon or given title or deed in lieu thereof in the last 7 years?	☐	☐	☐	☐
d. Are you a party to a lawsuit?	☐	☐	☐	☐
e. Have you directly or indirectly been obligated on any loan which resulted in foreclosure, transfer of title in lieu of foreclosure, or judgment? (This would include such loans as home mortgage loans, SBA loans, home improvement loans, educational loans, manufactured (mobile) home loans, any mortgage, financial obligation, bond, or loan guarantee. If "Yes," provide details, including date, name, and address of Lender, FHA or VA case number, if any, and reasons for the action.)	☐	☐	☐	☐

Freddie Mac Form 65 6/09 **Page 3 of 5** **Fannie Mae Form 1003 6/09**

Uniform Residential Loan Application. Source: www.eFannieMae.com.

VII. DETAILS OF TRANSACTION		
j.	Subordinate financing	
k.	Borrower's closing costs paid by Seller	
l.	Other Credits (explain)	
m.	Loan amount (exclude PMI, MIP, Funding Fee financed)	
n.	PMI, MIP, Funding Fee financed	
o.	Loan amount (add m & n)	
p.	Cash from/to Borrower (subtract j, k, l & o from i)	

VIII. DECLARATIONS

If you answer "Yes" to any question a through l, please use continuation sheet for explanation.	Borrower Yes	Borrower No	Co-Borrower Yes	Co-Borrower No
f. Are you presently delinquent or in default on any Federal debt or any other loan, mortgage, financial obligation, bond, or loan guarantee?	☐	☐	☐	☐
g. Are you obligated to pay alimony, child support, or separate maintenance?	☐	☐	☐	☐
h. Is any part of the down payment borrowed?	☐	☐	☐	☐
i. Are you a co-maker or endorser on a note?	☐	☐	☐	☐
---				
j. Are you a U.S. citizen?	☐	☐	☐	☐
k. Are you a permanent resident alien?	☐	☐	☐	☐
l. Do you intend to occupy the property as your primary residence?	☐	☐	☐	☐
If "Yes," complete question m below.				
m. Have you had an ownership interest in a property in the last three years?	☐	☐	☐	☐
(1) What type of property did you own—principal residence (PR), second home (SH), or investment property (IP)?	______		______	
(2) How did you hold title to the home— by yourself (S), jointly with your spouse or jointly with another person (O)?	______		______	

IX. ACKNOWLEDGEMENT AND AGREEMENT

Each of the undersigned specifically represents to Lender and to Lender's actual or potential agents, brokers, processors, attorneys, insurers, servicers, successors and assigns and agrees and acknowledges that: (1) the information provided in this application is true and correct as of the date set forth opposite my signature and that any intentional or negligent misrepresentation of this information contained in this application may result in civil liability, including monetary damages, to any person who may suffer any loss due to reliance upon any misrepresentation that I have made on this application, and/or in criminal penalties including, but not limited to, fine or imprisonment or both under the provisions of Title 18, United States Code, Sec. 1001, et seq.; (2) the loan requested pursuant to this application (the "Loan") will be secured by a mortgage or deed of trust on the property described in this application; (3) the property will not be used for any illegal or prohibited purpose or use; (4) all statements made in this application are made for the purpose of obtaining a residential mortgage loan; (5) the property will be occupied as indicated in this application; (6) the Lender, its servicers, successors or assigns may retain the original and/or an electronic record of this application, whether or not the Loan is approved; (7) the Lender and its agents, brokers, insurers, servicers, successors, and assigns may continuously rely on the information contained in the application, and I am obligated to amend and/or supplement the information provided in this application if any of the material facts that I have represented herein should change prior to closing of the Loan; (8) in the event that my payments on the Loan become delinquent, the Lender, its servicers, successors or assigns may, in addition to any other rights and remedies that it may have relating to such delinquency, report my name and account information to one or more consumer reporting agencies; (9) ownership of the Loan and/or administration of the Loan account may be transferred with such notice as may be required by law; (10) neither Lender nor its agents, brokers, insurers, servicers, successors or assigns has made any representation or warranty, express or implied, to me regarding the property or the condition or value of the property; and (11) my transmission of this application as an "electronic record" containing my "electronic signature," as those terms are defined in applicable federal and/or state laws (excluding audio and video recordings), or my facsimile transmission of this application containing a facsimile of my signature, shall be as effective, enforceable and valid as if a paper version of this application were delivered containing my original written signature.

Acknowledgement. Each of the undersigned hereby acknowledges that any owner of the Loan, its servicers, successors and assigns, may verify or reverify any information contained in this application or obtain any information or data relating to the Loan, for any legitimate business purpose through any source, including a source named in this application or a consumer reporting agency.

Borrower's Signature X	Date	Co-Borrower's Signature X	Date

X. INFORMATION FOR GOVERNMENT MONITORING PURPOSES

The following information is requested by the Federal Government for certain types of loans related to a dwelling in order to monitor the lender's compliance with equal credit opportunity, fair housing and home mortgage disclosure laws. You are not required to furnish this information, but are encouraged to do so. The law provides that a lender may not discriminate either on the basis of this information, or on whether you choose to furnish it. If you furnish the information, please provide both ethnicity and race. For race, you may check more than one designation. If you do not furnish ethnicity, race, or sex, under Federal regulations, this lender is required to note the information on the basis of visual observation and surname if you have made this application in person. If you do not wish to furnish the information, please check the box below. (Lender must review the above material to assure that the disclosures satisfy all requirements to which the lender is subject under applicable state law for the particular type of loan applied for.)

BORROWER ☐ I do not wish to furnish this information	**CO-BORROWER** ☐ I do not wish to furnish this information
Ethnicity: ☐ Hispanic or Latino ☐ Not Hispanic or Latino	**Ethnicity:** ☐ Hispanic or Latino ☐ Not Hispanic or Latino
Race: ☐ American Indian or Alaska Native ☐ Asian ☐ Black or African American ☐ Native Hawaiian or Other Pacific Islander ☐ White	**Race:** ☐ American Indian or Alaska Native ☐ Asian ☐ Black or African American ☐ Native Hawaiian or Other Pacific Islander ☐ White
Sex: ☐ Female ☐ Male	**Sex:** ☐ Female ☐ Male

To be Completed by Loan Originator:
This information was provided:
- ☐ In a face-to-face interview
- ☐ In a telephone interview
- ☐ By the applicant and submitted by fax or mail
- ☐ By the applicant and submitted via e-mail or the Internet

Loan Originator's Signature X		Date
Loan Originator's Name (print or type)	Loan Originator Identifier	Loan Originator's Phone Number (including area code)
Loan Origination Company's Name	Loan Origination Company Identifier	Loan Origination Company's Address

Freddie Mac Form 65 6/09 — Page 4 of 5 — Fannie Mae Form 1003 6/09

Uniform Residential Loan Application. Source: www.eFannieMae.com.

CONTINUATION SHEET/RESIDENTIAL LOAN APPLICATION		
Use this continuation sheet if you need more space to complete the Residential Loan Application. Mark **B** f or Borrower or **C** for Co-Borrower.	Borrower:	Agency Case Number:
	Co-Borrower:	Lender Case Number:

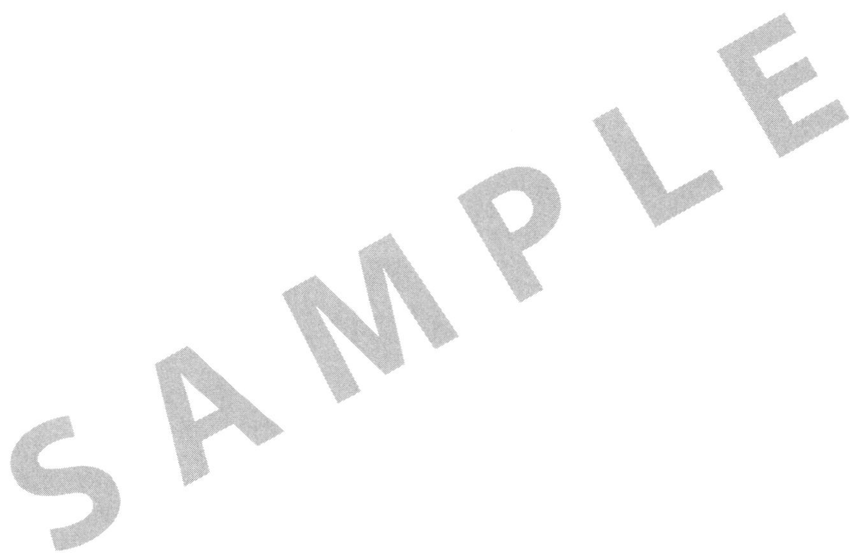

I/We fully understand that it is a Federal crime punishable by fine or imprisonment, or both, to knowingly make any false statements concerning any of the above facts as applicable under the provisions of Title 18, United States Code, Section 1001, et seq.

Borrower's Signature X	Date	Co-Borrower's Signature X	Date

Freddie Mac Form 65 6/09 | Page 5 of 5 | Fannie Mae Form 1003 6/09

Uniform Residential Loan Application. Source: www.eFannieMae.com.

*Co-Borrowers

The first part of Form 1003 discusses requirements for borrowers and co-borrowers. A **co-borrower** is simply a person who signs a note along with another primary borrower and accepts a joint obligation to repay the loan. Co-borrowers have joint ownership interest in the security property as indicated on the title. A **co-signor**, on the other hand, is a credit applicant who does *not* have ownership interest in the security property as indicated on the title, but signs the note. The most common co-borrower is a spouse. Non-occupant parents may also be co-borrowers or co-signors, as they lend an established earnings pattern and financial status to their children who otherwise would be unable to purchase a home.

Co-borrowers must have credit history and assets acceptable to the underwriter. Furthermore, if the co-borrower does not reside in the collateral property, he or she must be able to support both his or her own housing expense *plus* a proportionate share, if not all, of the proposed housing expense for the applicant. Marginal co-borrowers, therefore, should not be relied on heavily, and may do more harm than good.

If there is a co-borrower, applicants must indicate whether the co-borrower's income or assets will be used for qualifying, in which case, the co-borrower's information must be included on the application. Generally, spouses have merged assets and credit and so would be able to use the same application. When you have two unmarried adults on a mortgage application, you need to determine whether their assets and liabilities are sufficiently joined so that the information can be meaningfully and fairly presented on a combined basis. If so, they too can complete a single application. If the co-borrowers do not have joint assets and liabilities, separate applications should be used. For privacy purposes, credit reports and information disclosed on the mortgage application should be handled separately in such cases.

Section I: Type of Mortgage and Terms of Loan

This section details the specific **mortgage option** that a borrower has chosen from among those offered by the lender, including loan amount, rate, and term. (Mortgage types and loan terms are covered in later chapters.)

Section II: Property Information and Purpose of Loan

This section asks for detailed information about the **subject property**. For a **purchase**, the MLO needs to see the sales contract for the home the borrower wants to buy. It's critical to complete as much information on this section as possible, paying particular attention to property address (to confirm that it agrees with the sales agreement/tax bill), number of units, and property type (owner occupied or investment). Also, it's necessary to document the source of the down payment, including any secondary financing being used to purchase the property. If this is a **refinance**, as much of the existing information as possible about the property must be completed to provide the lender with an idea of improvements that have been made which may increase value.

Title. Borrowers should indicate the manner in which title will be held and what name(s) will hold the title to the property. If unsure, they may need to ask an attorney. **Do not assume or advise.** (Ownership options are covered in a later chapter.)

Occupancy. Occupancy of the property will determine the interest rate, available programs, and overall risk of the loan. Generally, investment loans are a higher risk than owner-occupied loans.

Note: Loans insured by the Federal Housing Administration require that borrowers establish bona fide occupancy of the home as the borrower's principal residence within **60 days** of signing the security instrument, with continued occupancy for at least one year.

Section III: Borrower Information

This section requests **personal information** about the borrower and, if applicable, co-borrower: Name, address, phone number, Social Security number, age, schooling, marital status, etc. When inquiring about a borrower's marital status, MLOs must comply with the Equal Credit Opportunity Act (12 C.F.R. § 202.2(u)) definitions:

- Married
- Unmarried (which includes persons who are single, divorced, or widowed)
- Separated

The application also asks how many dependents the borrower must support. If there are co-borrowers with joint dependents, it's necessary to indicate the number of dependents only for the primary borrower.

If the borrower has resided at his or her present address for two years or less, previous address information—and whether the borrower owned or rented—must also be provided. This information is also required from the co-borrower, if applicable. MLOs may ask for contact information for lenders, landlords, or rental agents.

Section IV: Employment Information

Borrowers must provide details about all current and previous **employment** over a **two-year period**, including years on the job, position, type of business, and contact information. Frequent job changes within the same field and with consistent or increasing income are *not* detrimental to the mortgage decision. Borrowers must be able to explain any gaps of employment over one month.

Borrowers must indicate if they are **self-employed**, which is defined as owning **25%** or more of the business. Employment information is also required from the co-borrower, if applicable.

Section V: Monthly Income and Combined Housing Expense Information

This section provides spaces for base **employment gross income**, overtime, bonuses, commissions, dividends, interest, net rental income, and income from any other sources. Income derived from alimony or child support does *not* need to be disclosed unless the borrower wants this considered as income to help qualify for a larger loan. Also, note that those who are self-employed may need to supply additional supporting documents, such as personal tax returns, corporate tax returns, or financial statements, to show income.

Monthly housing expenses, such as rent, mortgage payments, secondary financing, insurance, real estate taxes, etc., are included as well. The lender wants to see what the borrower is currently paying and what the proposed total payment would be for the new mortgage to gauge the potential extra burden of the new loan. This allows underwriters to evaluate the possibility that payment shock could result from a large increase in housing without accumulated assets to support it.

Section VI: Assets and Liabilities

Borrowers must list all assets and liabilities to determine net worth. **Assets** are *items of value*, such as cash on hand, checking or savings accounts, stocks, bonds, cash value of insurance policies, equity in real estate, retirement funds, automobiles, and personal property.

Liabilities are *financial obligations owed by a borrower.* Liabilities include the following:

- **Debts** are *any recurring monetary obligation that will not be cancelled* (e.g., monthly bills). Borrowers must list all debts—installment loans, credit cards, mortgages, collections, slow pays, judgments, student loans (even if currently deferred), etc. The lender generally will not consider installment loan debt with **less than ten monthly payments** remaining (except for leases, which always count regardless of how few payments remain) or unless the payments on those installment loans significantly affect the borrower's ability to meet credit obligations.
- While any equity in a pledged asset that may be collateral on another loan, such as real estate, would be considered an asset, the **amount owed** on the asset would be considered a liability against the borrower's net worth.

- Borrowers must also reveal **alimony** or **child support** required to be paid as a liability and should be prepared to produce a copy of a divorce decree for verification.

Lenders obtain a credit bureau report and compare liabilities listed on the application. If a liability is not listed on the credit report, the payment information needs to be verified.

Net worth is determined by *subtracting liabilities from total assets*. Most lenders feel that a borrower's net worth is a good indicator of credit worthiness. A high net worth shows an ability to manage money, and may help offset other marginal items on an application. Furthermore, liquid assets that can be sold in an emergency to make payments can give a lender an added feeling of security in making a loan.

Section VII: Details of the Transaction

Here the MLO estimates what **funds** are required by the borrower at closing by adding and subtracting items such as purchase price, prepaid items (e.g., escrows for taxes, insurance, etc.), estimated closing costs, mortgage insurance, loan amount, etc. The borrower also needs to reveal secondary financing, closing costs to be paid by the seller, and any other credits, such as equity from selling his or her current home and deposits being held by a broker or title company.

Section VIII: Declarations

The borrower (and any co-borrower) must respond to critical questions about:• Outstanding judgments, bankruptcies, foreclosures, lawsuits, etc.

- Delinquency or defaults on any federal debt or other loan.
- Obligations to pay alimony or child support.
- Borrowed funds used for any part of the down payment.
- Co-signers on any other debts.
- Citizenship or permanent residency status.
- Intentions to occupy the property as a primary residence.
- Ownership interest in other properties in the past three years.

Section IX: Acknowledgment and Agreement

The borrower and co-borrower, if applicable, must date and sign the application to acknowledge that they have answered everything truthfully. By signing the application, borrowers are acknowledging 11 disclosures, so they should take the time to read and understand this section. Both the MLO and the applicant(s) are responsible for ensuring the information contained in the application is truthful, accurate, and complete.

Section X: Information for Government Monitoring Purposes

This section is used by the government to monitor lender compliance with equal credit and equal housing laws. The Equal Credit Opportunity Act (ECOA) prohibits discrimination in granting credit based on age, sex, race, marital status, color, religion, national origin, and receipt of public assistance. When meeting with a borrower face-to-face, the MLO must complete this section if the applicant declines to supply the requested information. The MLO must note the applicant's ethnicity, race, and sex on the basis of visual observation and surname, to the extent possible.

The mortgage loan originator is required to sign the application. Contact information, as well as the MLO's NMLS unique identifier, must also be included.

Special Notice for Balloon Mortgages

A balloon mortgage is a loan that has level monthly payments that would fully amortize over a stated term, but which provides for a lump-sum payment to be due at the end of an earlier specified term. Fannie Mae requires MLOs using the 1003 Uniform Residential Loan Application to insert a special notice regarding the nature of the balloon features on Form 1003 or in a separate attachment to the form if the loan includes this feature. If an attachment is used, the borrower(s) must sign the attachment. The following language must be inserted, using capital letters:

> "THIS LOAN MUST EITHER BE PAID IN FULL AT MATURITY OR REFINANCED TO A MARKET LEVEL FIXED-RATE MORTGAGE. YOU MUST REPAY THE ENTIRE PRINCIPAL BALANCE OF THE LOAN AND UNPAID INTEREST THEN DUE IF YOU DO NOT QUALIFY FOR THE CONDITIONAL RIGHT TO REFINANCE AS SPECIFIED IN THE NOTE ADDENDUM AND MORTGAGE RIDER. THE LENDER IS UNDER NO OBLIGATION TO REFINANCE THE LOAN IF QUALIFICATION CONDITIONS ARE NOT MET. YOU WILL, THEREFORE, BE REQUIRED TO MAKE PAYMENT OUT OF OTHER ASSETS THAT YOU MAY OWN, OR YOU WILL HAVE TO FIND A LENDER, WHICH MAY BE THE LENDER YOU HAVE THIS LOAN WITH, WILLING TO LEND YOU THE MONEY. IF YOU REFINANCE THIS LOAN AT MATURITY, YOU MAY HAVE TO PAY SOME OR ALL OF THE CLOSING COSTS NORMALLY ASSOCIATED WITH A NEW LOAN EVEN IF YOU OBTAIN REFINANCING FROM THE SAME LENDER."

See: https://www.efanniemae.com/sf/formsdocs/forms/1003.jsp

Processing the Loan Application

Once the application has been properly completed and the required Truth in Lending Statement and Good Faith Estimate disclosures have been delivered to and accepted by the borrower, the mortgage loan originator can begin gathering other pertinent information to validate the data. Some MLOs accept a borrower's check stubs or W-2 forms, copies of bank statements, and other documents; others use verification forms that are sent out to the borrower's employer, banks, other creditors, and any previous mortgage lender. A credit report is ordered and a preliminary title report prepared. An approved appraiser is also contacted to appraise the property.

A borrower's ability to qualify for a real estate loan depends on many factors related to income, credit history, and assets. There are guidelines for determining what sufficient income for a given housing expense is, but it would be wrong to apply these figures too rigidly. *All* aspects of the borrower's financial situation must be considered before a loan decision is made. Quality, quantity, and durability of income are important, but a borrower with a marginal income may still qualify for a loan if the borrower has substantial assets, indicating an ability to manage financial affairs.

Conversely, strong earnings and substantial assets may not be enough to offset the damage caused by poor credit paying habits. A borrower must be both able and willing to pay the housing expense.

Finally, keep in mind that a good property with a large down payment can offset marginal credit or income as well. Borrowers who make large investments in their property are far less likely to default than those with little or no equity.

Income

Before deciding if a borrower has sufficient income to qualify for a loan, the underwriter must decide what portion of the borrower's total verified earnings are acceptable as a part of the total monthly income. This is accomplished by studying the dependability of the income source(s) and the probability that the income will continue.

Stable monthly income, the *monthly income that can reasonably be expected to continue in the future*, is generally meant to include the **gross** base income of the borrower(s) from **primary** jobs.

Secondary Sources of Income

Predictable earnings from acceptable secondary sources are considered if a lender's thorough analysis determines they can be substantiated and are durable. Secondary sources of income include, but are not limited to, the following:

- Bonuses
- Commissions above base salary
- Part-time earnings
- Overtime
- Disability payments
- Social Security
- Pensions
- Retirement payments
- Interest-yielding investments
- Rental income
- Alimony
- Child support
- Maintenance
- Unemployment and welfare (if verifiable, continuous, and ongoing)

A **quality** source of income is one that is *reasonably reliable,* such as income from an established employer, government agency, interest-yielding investment account, etc. A **durable** source of income can be *expected to continue for a sustained period.* Permanent disability, retirement earnings, and interest on established investments clearly are enduring types of income. Temporary unemployment benefits are unlikely to be counted.

Bonuses, Commissions, and Part-Time Earnings

To be considered durable, these types of income must be shown to have been a consistent part of the borrower's earnings for two years. Less than two years is considered unstable, but may be used to justify a higher qualifying ratio. Proof of such consistency can be shown by submitting copies of W-2 forms, pay stubs, or federal income tax returns. Tax returns are reviewed for unreimbursed business expenses which is deducted from income. The lender may send the employer a request for verification of employment earnings and the likelihood of continuance for **at least three years**. If durable, a **two-year average** of these earnings is used.

Overtime

Overtime earnings technically are eligible to count as part of a borrower's qualifying monthly gross income, but many underwriters are reluctant to rely on such earnings because their durability is uncertain. When qualifying buyers, overtime earnings should not be counted unless they show a consistent pattern. If substantiated, a **two-year** average is used.

Disability Payments

Disability payments count as income if they are a permanent source of income, but the lender will use caution if they are only for a limited time. If the benefits have a defined expiration date, the remaining term should be at least **three years** from the date of the mortgage application.

Social Security

Social Security income counts as permanent income for a borrower who's reached retirement age. If these payments are the result of a disability or some other condition, the lender treats them like other disability payments and verifies a **three year** continuance.

Pensions and Retirement Benefits

Lenders generally consider pension and retirement benefits as stable income, although they may investigate the source to determine solvency.

Interest-Yielding Investments

If the investments are sound and interest payments have been consistent, lenders will consider this durable income. If investments are a source of down payment, income must be deducted in proportion to what is used for the loan closing.

Rental Income

Income from rental properties can be counted if a stable pattern of positive **cash flow** can be verified. Cash flow is money available to an individual on a regular basis after subtracting all expenses. Rents must cover all expenses and mortgage payments, while still leaving excess cash for the owner. Tax returns are used for verifying rental income and expenses. If rental income is not reported on current tax returns, rental leases and PITI documentation must be obtained.

To determine the amount of rental income that may be counted, deduct PITI from gross rental income then multiply by **75%** to reach **net income**.

Alimony, Child Support, and Maintenance

These sources of income can be considered part of the borrower's monthly qualifying income if it's determined they are likely to be made on a consistent basis. Such a determination is dependent on whether the payments are required by written agreement or court decree, the length of time the payments have been received, the age of the child (child support payments generally stop at age 18), the overall financial and credit status of the payer, and the ability of the borrower to compel payment if necessary (e.g., through a court order). Alimony, child support, and/or maintenance should be expected to continue for a **minimum of three years** in order to be used in income calculations. They do *not* need to be listed as sources of income if a borrower does not want them considered as income for the loan.

A copy of the **divorce decree** is generally sufficient to establish the amount and the enforceability of the required payments. To verify receipt of income, the borrower must verify child support payments either by 12 months of cancelled checks or bank statements showing deposits.

Child support income for dependent children is *not* taxed and, therefore, is not included on tax returns. Such non-taxable income may be grossed up by **125%.** Child support for non-dependent children *is* listed on tax returns, as is alimony income.

Unemployment and Welfare

When considering whether income from unemployment or welfare can be counted as stable income, you should ask these questions:

- Is it verifiable—can it proven that the income was received?
- Is it continuous—has this income stream been regular for two years?
- Is it ongoing—is this income stream likely to continue for at least three more years?

Case in Point

Here are some examples. Borrower A has worked as a greens keeper for five years at a golf course. Every winter, he is laid off and receives unemployment, and he gets a W-2 from the unemployment office each year. His unemployment income should be considered. Borrower B has a six-year-old son and receives Aid for Dependent Children. This, too, should be considered if the borrower chooses to include it on the application.

Remember: MLOs may not discriminate against a borrower on the basis of receipt of public assistance.

Self-Employment Income

To be classified as self-employment income, the borrower must own **at least 25% of the business**. For this income to be used for qualifying, self-employed borrowers need to provide personal and entity (corporation, partnership, sole proprietorship) **tax returns** (all schedules) for a **minimum of two years**. The lender may also ask to see **financial statements,** which are *documents that show assets and liabilities for an individual or an entity, such as a company for a specific period or point in time.* Profit and loss statements and/or balance sheets may also be required.

Secondary market guidelines generally require a self-employed borrower to have operated the business profitably for at least **two years**. If a borrower has been self-employed for *less* than two years, it is difficult to qualify for a loan. However, someone with a shorter history of self-employment, one to two years, may be considered if the borrower's most recent signed federal income tax returns reflect income:

- At the same (or greater) level in a field providing the same products or services as the current business, or
- In an occupation in which the borrower had similar responsibilities to those undertaken in connection with the current business.

In such cases, the lender must give careful consideration to the nature of the borrower's level of experience and the amount of debt the business has.

Considering Nontaxable Income

If lenders can verify that a regular source of a borrower's income is nontaxable—such as child support payments, Social Security benefits, disability retirement payments, workers' compensation benefits, certain types of public assistance payments, and food stamps—and is likely to continue, they may develop an **adjusted gross income** for the borrower by **adding 25%** of the nontaxable income to the borrower's income, according to the Fannie Mae Selling Guide (Chapter B3-3.1-04). You may hear this process described as "grossing up." The Selling Guide goes on to indicate the following:

> *If the actual amount of federal and state taxes that would generally be paid by a wage earner in a similar tax bracket is more than 25% of the borrower's nontaxable income, the lender may use that amount to develop the adjusted gross income, which should be used in calculating the borrower's qualifying ratio.*

Evaluating Income

Keeping in mind a lender's general guidelines toward certain kinds of income, it's still important to remember that each type of income is evaluated *separately* by the underwriter. When deciding which income counts toward a home mortgage, the underwriter takes each income source and looks at employment history, advancement, and education/training in deciding the strength of each position—particularly for the borrower's primary job.

Employment History

When evaluating the elements of a borrower's income (quantity, quality, and durability), the underwriter analyzes the individual's employment **stability**. A borrower with a history of steady, full-time employment is given more favorable consideration than one who has changed employers frequently, unless the changes are properly explained.

As a general rule, a borrower should have continuous employment for at least **two years** in the same field. However, every borrower is unique and if there is not an established two-year work history, there may be explainable circumstances that would warrant loan approval, such as having recently finished college or being discharged from military service.

Advancement. Even if the borrower has changed employers frequently, if it was for the sake of advancement and/or the borrower can show a stable and reliable flow of predictable income, the underwriter will not likely view the changes negatively. On the other hand, persistent job hopping without maintaining income flow or showing some advancement usually signifies a problem of some kind, and an underwriter will tend to regard the individual's earnings as unstable.

Education and Training. Special education or training that prepares a person for a specific kind of work can strengthen a loan application. Such education or training can offset minor weaknesses with respect to earnings or job tenure, especially if the underwriter is convinced there's a continuing demand for people in this line of work, there's job stability in that particular field, or there's opportunity for advancement.

Computing Monthly Income

After deciding which income counts, all gross monthly income from those sources is added together to arrive at a total gross monthly income figure. If a borrower earns an hourly wage, it must be converted to a monthly figure. To convert a person's hourly wages to monthly earnings:

1. Multiply the hourly wage by the number of hours worked in a week
2. Multiply by 52 (weeks in a year)
3. Divide by 12 (months in a year)

Case in Point

Our borrower makes $19.50 per hour. Assuming the borrower works 40 hours a week, to compute the monthly gross income:

Hourly Wage:	**$19.50**
Weekly Income:	**$19.50 x 40 hours = $780**
Annual Income:	**$780 x 52 weeks = $40,560**
Monthly Income:	**$40,560 ÷ 12 months = $3,380**

Verifying Income

The borrower can substantiate employment and income by providing:

- **W-2 forms** for the previous **two years.**
- **Payroll stubs** for the previous **30-day** period.

Since federal labor regulations promulgated by the Department of Labor (29 C.F.R. § 516.5) and the Equal Employment Opportunity Commission (29 C.F.R. § 1627.3) require employers to keep payroll records for **three years**, if the borrower cannot locate pay stubs or W-2's, it may be possible to get copies directly from the employer.

Pay stubs must identify the borrower, employer, and the borrower's gross earnings for both the current pay period and year-to-date. Pay stubs may reveal other factors that could impact the mortgage application, such as garnishments or 401K loans.

Verbal employment confirmations are normally done on each borrower prior to closing. **Verification of Employment (VOE)** forms may also be used to verify income and employment history.

IRS Form 4506-T

Underwriters generally require the lender to obtain a completed and signed **Form 4506-T** from all borrowers at application. This form gives the lender permission to request electronic transcripts of federal tax returns from the IRS when documenting the borrower's income. Under current requirements, the lender determines if and when to submit the form to the IRS (or designee) to obtain the tax information. These transcripts are used to validate the borrower's income against their W-2s with the intention of helping to reduce instances of mortgage fraud. Many lenders have some level of quality control audit procedures where a random number of loan files are pulled for review; sometimes this is done prior to close, and sometimes after close. Since the 4506-T form is valid for only 90 days, some MLOs also ask borrowers to sign a second form prior to closing so that tax information may be accessed as part of the quality assurance process if necessary.

Reasonable Ability to Repay

The Dodd-Frank Wall Street Reform and Consumer Protection Act (Pub.L. 111-203, H.R. 4173) includes provisions in §§ 1411, 1412, 1414 of Title XIV—designated as the Mortgage Reform and Anti-Predatory Lending Act—that amend the Truth in Lending Act (15 U.S.C. 1631 et seq.) by inserting a new § 129C. One provision requires mortgage lenders to determine—based on "verified and documented information"—that the borrower has a "reasonable ability to repay" the loan according to its terms (including all applicable taxes, insurance, and assessments). The Board of Governors of the Federal Reserve System promulgated a rule to amend Regulation Z (12 C.F.R. Part 226) to implement this provision, effective as of April, 1, 2011. The proposed rule applies to any consumer credit transaction secured by a dwelling (whether or not it is owner-occupied), with the following exceptions:

- Open-end credit plan
- Timeshare plan
- Reverse mortgage
- Temporary loan

The proposal establishes multiple options for complying with the ability-to-repay mandate. One option is to require a creditor to consider and verify the following information about the borrower:

- Current or reasonably expected income or assets,
- Current employment status,
- Monthly payment on the mortgage (with the calculation based on the fully indexed rate),
- Monthly payment on any simultaneous loan,
- Monthly payment for mortgage-related obligations,
- Current debt obligations,
- Monthly debt-to-income ratio, or residual income, and
- Credit history.

Qualified Mortgages

Another option for compliance with the ability-to-repay requirement, according to the proposed rule, is for the creditor to originate a "qualified mortgage." The following alternative operates a legal safe harbor and defines a qualified mortgage as one for which:

- The loan does not contain negative amortization, interest-only payments, balloon payments, or a loan term exceeding 30 years.
- Total points and fees do not exceed 3% of the total loan amount.
- The borrower's income or assets are verified and documented.
- The underwriting is based on the maximum interest rate in the first five years, uses a payment that fully amortizes the loan over its term, and considers any mortgage-related obligations.

A second alternative to defining a qualified mortgage includes the criteria listed above as well as these additional underwriting requirements: Consumer's employment status, monthly payment for any simultaneous loan, consumer's current debt obligations, total debt-to-income ratio or residual income, and consumer's credit history.

Other Provisions of the Proposed Rule

The proposal also implements provisions of the Dodd-Frank Act that:

- Limits prepayment penalties to prime qualified mortgages with a fixed rate, and also limits the amount.
- Lengthens the time creditors must retain records that evidence compliance with the ability-to-repay and prepayment penalty provisions (three years).
- Prohibits evasion of the rule by structuring a closed-end extension of credit as an open-end plan.

The rulemaking will become a proposal of the Consumer Financial Protection Bureau and will not be finalized by the Board of Governors of the Federal Reserve System. All mortgage loan originators have a legal and ethical obligation to stay current with the applicable laws and regulations as they are implemented.

Mortgage Exercise 3-1

Two months ago, Lisa Zorn was honorably discharged from the Air Force, where she spent four years training as an airplane mechanic. After discharge, she moved to take a 40 hour/week apprentice mechanic job with a major airline company where she earns $18/hour. Last month, her husband Dave, who has worked the past two years as registered nurse, found a nursing job with a local hospital making $625 per week. They just bought a new car and pay $400 each month on that loan. *See the Appendix for answers to check your work.*

1. What is the maximum mortgage payment (PITI) a lender would allow for a conventional loan based on the housing expense ratio?

2. What is their total debt-to-income? What is the maximum mortgage amount (PITI) a lender would likely approve?

3. Can the Zorns get approved for a loan even though they've only been at their jobs a short time? Explain.

Credit History

Credit history is a *record of debt repayment, detailing how a person paid credit accounts in the past as a guide to whether he or she is likely to pay accounts on time and as agreed in the future.* A **debt** is simply money owed. When evaluating a borrower's credit history, however, a debt is generally considered *any secured or unsecured recurring monetary obligation that will not be cancelled until paid in full.* A car lease is considered a debt; so is a student loan or court-ordered child support. Utilities and insurance premiums are *not* considered debts because they can, in theory, be cancelled. Lenders assume borrowers would turn off their phones or cable service before losing their houses. Gray areas can include such things as doctor bills. These are generally not considered to be debt unless there is a payment schedule (e.g., for braces). Borrowers must inform a lender of *all* debts—even things that may not show up on a credit report.

As part of the loan evaluation, the underwriter analyzes the borrower's and any co-borrower's credit history by obtaining a credit report from a national credit reporting company—e.g., Experian (formerly TRW), Equifax, and TransUnion. If the credit history shows a slow payment record or other derogatory credit information (suit, judgment, repossession, collection, foreclosure, or bankruptcy), a loan application could be declined or the borrower put into a **high-risk** (B-C credit) category.

In some cases, derogatory ratings don't prevent a borrower from obtaining a loan if the credit problems can be explained. The underwriter must be satisfied that these problems don't represent the borrower's overall attitude toward credit obligations, and the circumstances were temporary and no longer exist.

Real Success

If a borrower's credit report is laced with derogatory ratings over a period of years, there's probably little hope for loan approval through a traditional lender. Perpetual credit problems more likely reflect an attitude instead of a circumstance, and it's reasonable for lenders to presume that pattern will continue. All credit problems can be resolved with time, however, so never assume a borrower can't qualify for a loan eventually.

When evaluating a borrower's credit history, lenders use a number of methods, including objective evaluation methods, to ensure compliance with the **Equal Credit Opportunity Act** (ECOA). This Act prohibits discrimination in lending based on age (except minors under 18), sex, race, marital status, color, religion, national origin, or receipt of public assistance.

You must never discourage an applicant from submitting a mortgage application because of his or her membership in a protected class under ECOA.

Credit Scoring

Credit scoring is an *objective means of determining creditworthiness of potential borrowers based on a number system.* A credit score is a numeric representation of the borrower's credit profile compiled by assigning specified numerical values to different aspects of the borrower. These numbers are adjusted up and down based on the strengths and weaknesses of particular qualifications.

For example, a person with a large line of available credit that is hardly used would likely score higher than a person with lower credit limits but whose credit cards are all maxed out. The numbers are added from all the categories and a credit score based on these various criteria is assigned.

Credit scores also play an important role in automated underwriting since Fannie Mae and Freddie Mac have identified a strong correlation between mortgage performance and credit scores. The higher the credit score, the better credit risk a borrower is; the lower the score, the higher the risk of default.

Credit Scoring Systems

Credit scores are the result of very complex calculations carried out by a computer that takes into account every aspect of the borrower's credit file. There are many different names for credit scoring systems. The system that most consumers are likely to be familiar with is **FICO**, which was developed by Fair, Isaac & Co. Other common names for credit scoring systems include BEACON (used by Equifax) and EMPERICA (used by TransUnion). Items considered by a credit scoring system include the following:

- Number of open accounts
- Total credit limit
- Types of credit (e.g., credit cards, installment loans)
- Length of credit history (e.g., when opened, latest activity)
- Total amount of debt outstanding
- Number of late payments in the past 30-60-90 days
- Presence of adverse public records (e.g., liens, judgments, or bankruptcies)
- Number of recent credit inquiries
- Re-establishment of positive credit history after past payment problems

Credit scoring systems do not consider items such as a consumer's race, sex, age, marital status, religion, national origin, salary, or employment history.

Each of these three main credit bureau scores is calculated a little differently. For example, FICO weighs payment history as 35% of the total score, amounts owed as 30%, length of credit history as 15%, and new credit and types of credit used as 10% each. Regardless of the actual calculation, all credit bureaus produce similar credit scores, which range from about **300 to 850**. While lenders can't tell you exactly how each credit score is computed, they will disclose what cutoff scores they use in qualifying borrowers for various mortgage loan programs.

Secondary Market

The secondary market has pricing adjustments to the interest rate depending upon credit score and LTV. Fannie Mae and Freddie Mac guidelines generally consider those with credit scores **above 720** to be an *acceptable* credit risk and therefore have little interest rate adjustment. Those with scores **between 620 and 660** are considered *marginal* and are held to a more comprehensive review. Fannie Mae and Freddie Mac do *not* accept loans with credit scores **below 620** except for certain products and programs. Before making decisions regarding qualification, lenders are encouraged to check the accuracy of credit information.

Real Success

Credit scores also come into play with FHA loans. For example, in 2010, the Federal Housing Administration changed its policy so that the standard 3.5% down payment on an FHA-insured loan applies only to those borrowers who have a credit score of 580 or above. Other borrowers need to put at least 10% down, or may not qualify at all. Even so, it's important to understand that most lenders impose even stricter guidelines than these when underwriting an FHA-insured loan. Make sure that you stay current with the program guidelines of the loan products with which you deal, for example, by reading FHA's Mortgagee Letters.

Explaining Derogatory Credit

Most people try to meet credit obligations on time; when they don't, there's usually a reason. Job loss, hospitalization, prolonged illness, death in the family, or divorce can create financial pressures that affect debt-paying habits. If a few derogatory items appear on a credit report, it may be possible to show that the problems occurred during a specific period of time for understandable reasons, and that prior and subsequent credit ratings have been good.

If borrowers refuse to accept responsibility by explaining credit difficulties based on misunderstandings or on the creditors themselves, underwriters may not look favorably upon such explanations. Underwriters reason that a borrower's reluctance to take responsibility for prior credit problems is an indication of what can be expected in the future.

Borrowers may have questions regarding credit scores. The Fair Credit Reporting Act, as amended by Section 212(c) of the Fair and Accurate Credit Transactions Act of 2003 (16 C.F.R. Part 602), requires that a **Notice to the Home Loan Applicant Credit Score Information Disclosure** be provided to borrowers. This disclosure must include the score that a credit reporting agency distributed to the lender used in connection with a home loan and the key factors affecting the credit scores. This disclosure must include contact information for any credit agency used.

Bankruptcy

Bankruptcy, as established by Title 11 of the United States Code, is a court process that cancels debt and provides some relief for creditors. There are two basic proceedings for individuals:

- **Chapter 7.** Sometimes called a straight bankruptcy, it is a *liquidation proceeding.* The debtor turns over all non-exempt property to the bankruptcy trustee, who then converts it to cash for distribution to the creditors. The debtor receives a discharge of all dischargeable debts, usually within four months. Someone wishing to file Chapter 7 must meet certain tests related to income and debt.
- **Chapter 13.** This is filed by individuals who want to pay off their debts over a period of three to five years. This is preferable to those who have non-exempt property that they want to keep. It is only an option for individuals who have predictable income and whose income is sufficient to pay their reasonable expenses with some amount left over to pay off their debts.

According to the Fair Credit Reporting Act (15 U.S.C. 1681c § 605 (a)(1)), consumer reporting agencies may maintain bankruptcy information on a consumer's credit report for no more than 10 years from the date of entry of the order for relief or the date of adjudication, whichever the case may be. While credit reporting agencies do keep completed Chapter 7 bankruptcies on the credit report for the maximum 10 years, they often keep Chapter 13 bankruptcies on the credit report only for seven years after discharge date. This is an incentive for consumers to file under Chapter 13 and repay their debts.

Other Negative Information

According to FICO, in addition to Chapter 13 bankruptcies, the other types of negative information that remains on a consumer's credit report for **seven years** includes:

- Late payments
- Foreclosures
- Collections (generally, depending on the age of the debt being collected)

Also, information that is part of the public record may show for seven years, although unpaid tax liens can remain indefinitely.

Bill Consolidation and Refinancing

Even without derogatory ratings, lenders may find other concerns in a credit report that might indicate the borrower is a marginal credit risk. If an individual's credit pattern is one of continually increasing liabilities and periodically bailing out through bill consolidation (borrowing a larger sum of money to pay off many smaller debts) and refinancing, he or she may be classified as a marginal risk. This pattern suggests a tendency to live beyond a prudent level. It is a subjective consideration likely to influence the lender's decision if a borrower is weak in other areas, such as income or net worth.

Real Success

Creditors who have a legitimate business need to access a potential borrower's credit report when a business transaction is initiated by the consumer may do so, as long as they have authorization from the borrower. While some MLOs require separate written consent from the borrower before obtaining a credit report, Block IX, the Acknowledgment and Agreement section of the Uniform Residential Loan Application, includes language that authorizes the creditor to access the borrower's credit information from any source named in the application or from a consumer reporting agency.

Although credit reports presented by borrowers would not likely be acceptable to lenders, the Fair Credit Reporting Act (15 U.S.C. 1681b § 604 (b) (2) (B) (IV)) does allow consumers to request one free credit report per year from each of the national credit bureaus—Experian, Equifax, and TransUnion—by visiting www.annualcreditreport.com. Borrowers should be encouraged to take advantage of this annually. They are also entitled to a free report if information in a credit report resulted in some sort of adverse action, if the consumer was a victim of identity theft and a fraud alert was inserted in a credit file, if the credit file contains inaccurate information as a result of fraud, or if the consumer is on public assistance or is unemployed.

Assets

Assets are simply *items of value.* The underwriter takes the necessary steps to verify the nature and value of assets held by a borrower. If a borrower has a marginal total debt-to-income ratio, above average assets can offset this deficiency. Underwriters know that assets, especially in liquid form such as savings or stocks and bonds, can be used to pay unexpected bills or to support a borrower when there's a temporary interruption in income.

Liquid versus Non-Liquid Assets

Liquid assets are cash and any other assets—such as stocks or bonds—that can *quickly be converted to cash.* Automated underwriting systems generally consider the following assets liquid and include their value when evaluating borrowers:

- Checking and savings accounts
- Gift funds
- Certificates of deposit
- Money market funds
- Mutual funds
- Stocks and bonds
- Secured borrowed funds
- Retirement accounts
- Trust funds, if the borrower is the beneficiary or settlor and the trust is irrevocable
- Expected cash from properties pending sale

Non-liquid assets include:

- Cash deposits on the sales contract
- Cash value of life insurance policies
- Net worth of businesses owned
- Automobiles

Evaluating Assets

There are three aspects of a borrower's assets in which lenders and underwriters are interested: Down payment, reserves, and other assets.

Down Payment

It must be determined that the borrower has **sufficient liquid assets** to make the cash down payment and pay the closing costs and other expenses incidental to the purchase of the property. Most loan programs require the borrowers to bring at least 5% of the down payment from their own personal savings history into the transaction. There are some programs that allow a smaller down payment—mostly government programs or those geared to first time home buyers. The lender also wants to know the **source** of the borrower's down payment. Savings or sale of a prior home are both acceptable sources of down payment.

Borrowed Funds. Borrowed funds must be secured and the debt considered in the total debt-to-income ratio.

Gifts. If an applicant lacks the necessary funds to close a transaction, a gift of the required amount is usually acceptable to the underwriter. The gift should be confirmed by means of a **gift letter** signed by the donor. The letter should clearly state that the money represents a gift and *does not have to be repaid.* The gift usually must be from an immediate family member, although rules can vary. In addition to the gift letter, lenders want to verify that the donor has the funds available to provide the gift by seeing a copy of the gift check and a copy of the deposit receipt showing funds have been deposited and are available for closing. In the past this has been an area of mortgage fraud, so it is important to validate the funds came from the account verified on the gift letter and bank statement provided by the donor.

Fannie Mae and Freddie Mac require borrowers to make at least a 5% down payment from their own funds in addition to the gift, unless the gift equals 20% or more of the purchase price. On conventional loans, borrowers can't use borrowed funds or gifts for the first 5%.

Reserves

Reserves are *cash on deposit or other highly liquid assets a borrower will have available after the loan funds.* Lenders would like to see enough to cover two months' PITI mortgage payments of principal, interest, taxes, and insurance (and assessments such as condominium association fees, if applicable) after the borrower makes the down payment and pays all closing costs, but in most cases this is not required. For investment properties, six months' PITI payments must be verified for loans on non-owner-occupied property. When borrowers convert a primary residence that they have occupied during the past 12 months into investment property, if the equity in the property is less than 30%, they are required to have six months reserves for **both properties**—the investment property and their own principal residence—for conventional loans.

Other Assets

Having assets in addition to cash and other liquid assets shows that the borrower is able to manage money and has resources, if needed, to handle emergencies and make mortgage payments.

Real estate equity is an important asset to consider. Equity is *the difference between the market value of the property and the sum of the mortgages and other liens against the property.* Equity, less all selling expenses, is what a buyer should receive from the sale of property. If the equity from the sale of a home is the source of money for the purchase of the subject property, the underwriter might require evidence that the sale closed and the borrower received the proceeds before making the new loan. If the loan is a construction loan and the borrower owns the lot, the underwriter treats the borrower's equity in that lot as cash or its equivalent when determining the down payment needed.

Other real estate also counts as an asset. But only the equity in the property—and not its total value—contributes to net worth, since only the equity can be converted to cash by selling an interest in or mortgaging the property. Real estate with little or no equity, or investment property with income that's equal to or below expenses, hurts a loan application more than it helps because the property may require cash from the borrower. Of course, a lender must be told of any financial obligations or expense shortfalls not covered by property rents.

Verifying Deposits for Down Payment/Reserves

Documentation of assets includes **one to two months of bank statements** (all pages) to verify available funds. A **Verification of Deposit (VOD)** form may also be used to verify bank statement balances, both current balance and average balance. When the underwriter reviews the bank statements or receives the completed Verification of Deposit forms, four questions are considered:

- Does the verified information conform to statements in the loan application?
- Is there enough money in the bank to pay costs of buying the property?
- Has the bank account been opened recently (within the last few months)?
- Is the present balance notably higher than the average balance?

Lenders prefer to see **seasoned funds**, which means they have been in the account for the entire period covered by the bank statements. Recently opened accounts or higher-than-normal balances must be explained as these are strong indications the applicant may have borrowed the funds. Also, the source of any large and unusual deposit will need to be documented.

Insurance and Escrow Requirements

Providing funds to a borrower to purchase or refinance a home carries with it a great deal of financial risk for the lender, who is said to have an **insurable interest** in the property. To protect that collateral, therefore, lenders normally require insurance.

Homeowner's Hazard Insurance. A policy that covers loss or damage to the home or property in the event of fire or other disaster such as tornado, snow, and hail damage. Lenders generally:

- Require the policy to be sufficient to replace the home or reimburse the mortgage amount with the lender being named on the actual policy.
- Have the right to place insurance on the property to cover its interest (the loan value) in the event of a loss if the borrower does not comply with the lender's insurance requirements.
- Require borrowers to pay the first year's insurance premium in full ***prior*** to closing.
- Incorporate the annual insurance cost (along with current property taxes) into an **escrow account,** which is prorated over the next 12 months to determine a monthly insurance and property tax payment amount. This is added to the monthly principal and interest due for loan repayment. Upon payment each month, the insurance and taxes are deposited into the borrower's escrow account. When property taxes and insurance become due, the lender/servicer forwards the payment to the respective recipients on behalf of the property owner.

Flood Insurance. Homeowner's hazard insurance does **not** cover damage caused by the peril of flood. When a property is located in a federally designated special flood hazard area (SFHA), the lender for federal loans will require a flood insurance policy for the life of the loan in addition to homeowner's hazard insurance. Flood insurance must be purchased from the **National Flood Insurance Program (NFIP)** or from an insurer participating in the Write Your Own program. In order to buy federal flood insurance, the property must be in a community that is voluntarily participating in the NFIP.

Mortgage Exercise 3-2

Sam Able wants to buy a home, and it's estimated that an 80% conventional loan will have a mortgage payment of $878. He has an automobile payment of $212 a month with 14 installments remaining. He earns $700 per week. His down payment and closing costs are estimated at $18,400. Sam is selling a home with equity of $14,000. He has a checking and savings account with a local bank, and plans to draw on that account to close the transaction. The Verification of Deposit came back showing that Sam's savings account has an average monthly balance of $1,000 and a current balance of $3,600. *See the Appendix for answers to check your work.*

1. What is Sam's housing expense ratio?

2. What is Sam's total debt-to-income ratio?

3. Will Sam have any problems closing this transaction? Explain.

4. Do you see any problems with Sam's Verification of Deposit? Explain.

Underwriting

There are general steps all lenders take before deciding whether or not to make a real estate loan and on what terms. This evaluation process is called **loan underwriting**, where an underwriter evaluates the documentation, borrower information, and various risk factors associated with a loan in order to make a decision. According to Freddie Mac, "Underwriting mortgage loans is an art, not a science." The underwriting process can be automated, where all information is fed into an automated underwriting system (AUS), or manual, which is done by an individual who works for the lender. Both processes have various qualifying standards applied to the loan information. Regardless or whether underwriting process is manual or automated, the resulting final decision will be one of these three options:

1. Reject the loan as applied for (which may be because the borrower or collateral was not a good risk or because the loan application file was incomplete)
2. Make the loan on the terms applied for
3. Make the loan on different terms (for example, a higher interest rate, a different loan program, additional collateral, etc.)

Putting Together a Loan File

In order to make any decision, however, the underwriter must have all of the relevant data. Before submitting a loan file to underwriting, MLOs should review the application one last time before shipping it for the underwriter's review. A good mortgage loan originator takes ownership of the loan file, ensuring that the information in the submitted application is accurate, that all required documentation in the loan file is included and complete, and that all readily identifiable issues that an underwriter might raise have been addressed. If a loan processor misses something, it's the MLO's job to figure it out and fix it before it goes to the underwriter. The goal of the MLO should be to never have a loan file rejected as "incomplete."

When evaluating a loan file, the primary concern throughout the loan underwriting process is determining the degree of **risk** a loan represents. The underwriter attempts to answer two fundamental questions:

- Is there sufficient value in the property pledged as collateral to assure recovery of the loan amount in the event of default?
- Does the borrower's overall financial situation, which is comprised of credit, income, and assets, indicate a reasonable expectation of making the proposed monthly loan payments in a timely manner?

A complete and accurate loan file, therefore, allows the underwriter to make an informed decision.

Automated Underwriting Systems (AUS)

Automation is used in all facets of the lending process. The purpose of automated underwriting is to reduce the cost of examining a loan application and speed up mortgage approvals. An AUS is able to provide consistent underwriting decisions using statistical computer models based on traditional underwriting factors, and never considers factors such as race, ethnicity, age, or any other characteristic prohibited by law. And with large databases of statistics and information available, the secondary market has increased efforts to manage credit risk by improving loan criteria.

The AUS makes a recommendation to accept a loan for delivery, or refers it for an underwriter for further manual review and analysis. Even with an automated approval, an underwriter still must validate the information entered into the AUS, along with the supporting documentation. While lenders may rely on automated underwriting systems for a preliminary decision, it generally comes down to a human underwriter to make the final decision.

Both Fannie Mae and Freddie Mac have proprietary automated underwriting systems, and they charge lenders for the privilege of using them. Fannie Mae's automated underwriting system is **Desktop Underwriter®** (DU®). Freddie Mac has a similar direct AUS called **Loan Prospector®** (LP®).

Real Success

There's no standardized order in which to assemble the loan file, although particular lenders may have a preference. Submitting the loan file for final underwriting can usually be accomplished in an email or FAX. If it is an especially large loan file, you may choose to send it through the mail or overnight it. Also, it is a good practice to include a "Dear underwriter" letter on the top of the stack. If the loan application has some potential issues—for example, unusual circumstances, odd letters of explanation, strange income—use the letter to prepare the underwriter for what's coming. Let the underwriter know that you know where the issues are; if he finds something strange on his own, he may start doubting the whole package. Do anything you can do to make the process go smoothly.

Also, for the sake of your borrowers, find out how long the file will sit in the review queue and when they can expect a decision. It's stressful waiting to hear—keep them informed to alleviate their worry. Share with your borrowers that during busy times, it might take the underwriter several weeks to finish. The **Equal Credit Opportunity Act** (12 C.F.R. § 202.9 (a)(i)), however, requires a lender to communicate a credit decision (approval, counteroffer to, or adverse action) within **30 days** of receiving a completed application.

Closing

After the loan is approved and all "prior to doc" conditions are met—for example, the lender may request to see a closing statement from the sale of the borrower's previous home, a final inspection report, or property insurance policy—the lender issues a **clear to close** the loan and the necessary documents are prepared for closing. **Closing**, or **funding**, completes the process of granting a loan as funds are disbursed in accordance with the settlement statement. If the transaction involves the **sale** of real property, closing also involves *transfer of ownership of real property from seller to buyer, according to the terms and conditions in the sales contract or escrow agreement.* This is the final stage in a real estate transaction, when the seller receives value for property (cash, mortgage, etc.) and the buyer receives title.

Closing Procedures

You may also hear the closing process referred to as **settlement** or **loan consummation**. Generally speaking, the mechanics of closing are the responsibility of either an escrow/title agent or an attorney. This escrow agent may be the lender's in-house escrow department, an independent escrow company, or a title insurance company.

With a sales transaction, the escrow agent simultaneously follows the instructions of both the borrower and seller, as per the sales contract, agreement, or a separate set of escrow instructions. A copy of the sales contract or escrow instructions must be provided to the escrow agent, the title company, and the lender.

The title agent gathers all necessary documents, calculates the various prorations, adjustments, and fees charged to each party, and also compares the Good Faith Estimate of closing costs to the HUD-1 settlement statement to verify the proper tolerance with disclosed fees. Each party receives a HUD-1 settlement statement that complies with the Real Estate Settlement Procedures Act (RESPA).

The lender wants to ensure that there are no unforeseen problems during closing, see that the loan papers (e.g., promissory note, mortgage, deed, etc.) are signed, and be available to make one final check to be sure that everything is in order. Once the necessary documents have been recorded, loan funds may then be disbursed to the proper parties, according to the sales contract or escrow instructions.

Real Success

Closing procedures may be different from state to state—or even from one part of a state to another. For example, in some states, an attorney is required to close the loan. Other states allow a title agent to perform the loan closing. Closings may be conducted in escrow, which means they are handled by a disinterested third party, or roundtable, where all parties are present. A borrower who cannot attend a closing may be able to use a power of attorney if one exists specific to the property being transferred.

Another important thing to keep in mind is that settlement costs may also differ from region to region. For example, in some areas, the seller traditionally pays fees related to title, while in other areas, the buyer pays title fees. Regardless of local practices, however, the determination of who pays certain fees may be negotiated during the sales process and documented in the purchase contract.

If you are taking an application from a state with which you are unfamiliar, research the mortgage regulations and laws from that state. Licensing requirements may also be different; however, note that not only must an individual MLO be licensed to do business in that state, but the MLO's employing company must also generally be licensed in that state.

Settlement Statement Reconciliation

The **Real Estate Settlement Procedures Act (RESPA)** is the federal law dealing with real estate closings that sets forth procedures and guidelines for disclosing settlement costs using a standard settlement statement. Provisions of RESPA, including a look at the HUD-1 settlement statement, are covered in detail in the following chapter.

To understand the final distribution of money involved in a transaction as detailed on the settlement statement, however, one must be familiar with the concept of **debits** and **credits**.

- **Debits** (like debts) are *sums of money owed.* A debit is charged to a particular party on a balance sheet to represent money that must be paid out. The settlement statement reflects the total costs the seller and the buyer must pay.
- **Credits** are *sums of money received.* A credit is given to a particular party on a balance sheet to represent money that is paid by another party or that has already been paid. The settlement statement also reflects the total amounts credited to the seller and the buyer.

Debits and credits work together when **reconciling** the settlement statement. All debits owed by the borrower are totaled and added to the loan amount/purchase price. Then the credits are totaled and subtracted from the total debits to determine *how much money the borrower must bring to closing*. The mortgage amount shows up as a **credit** to the borrower, since it is the lender who brings that money to closing. The details on a settlement statement allow a buyer to see the **acquisition cost**, which is a total of the amount of money necessary to purchase the property, since it shows the sales price as well as the charges necessary to close the loan.

A similar process occurs on the seller's side. All credits due to the seller are totaled and added to the purchase price. All debits owed are totaled and subtracted from the total money due to determine how much money the seller receives at closing.

Proration

Proration is *the division of expenses between buyer and seller in proportion to the actual usage of the item* represented by a particular expense as of the **day the loan is funded.** In order to adjust a cost shared by both buyer and seller, it's necessary to determine whether the expense is accrued or prepaid. **Accrued expenses** are the items on a settlement statement for which *the cost has been incurred, but the expense has not yet been paid;* for example, mortgage interest. Accrued expenses are prorated on the settlement statement as a debit to the seller and a credit to the buyer. **Prepaid expenses** are the *items on a settlement statement the seller has already paid;* for example, condominium association fees or property tax in counties where it is paid in advance. Prepaid expenses are prorated on the settlement statement as a credit to the seller and a debit to the buyer.

When performing proration calculations, expenses may be prorated using:

- A 360-day year, 12 months of 30 days each.
- A 365-day year, counting the exact number of days in each month (taking leap years into account).

Often, local custom dictates which factor is used. Either way, the steps to calculate the adjustment are similar:

1. Determine if the expense is accrued or prepaid.
2. Divide the expense by the appropriate period to find a monthly (daily) rate.
3. Determine how many months (days) are affected by the expense.
4. Multiply the monthly (daily) rate by the number of affected months (days).
5. Determine which party is credited and which is debited.

Chapter 3 Summary

1. The common areas of work for a mortgage professional are mortgage loan originator, loan processor, underwriter, and servicer. A mortgage loan **originator** takes applications, pulls credit reports, orders appraisals, and assembles documents for mortgage loans. A loan **processor** works on the file assembled by the originator, verifying the information in the file and coordinating other aspects of the loan and closing. The **underwriter** is responsible for reviewing the file and arriving at a credit decision for the lender or investor, based on the credit risk associated with a particular loan. If there are conditions on the loan, they must be satisfied prior to closing. A **servicer** oversees the collection of mortgage payments and pursues late payments on behalf of the mortgagee.

2. **Lender's return** is the total amount a lender or broker makes on a loan, such as from loan fees, discount points. **Points** are 1% of loan amount; increase lender's yield, and are paid for many reasons. **Discount points** are used to buy down the interest rate. **Yield spread premium** is a tool mortgage loan originators can use to reduce a borrower's settlement costs.

3. Borrowers can get pre-qualified or pre-approved. **Pre-qualification** is when a mortgage broker or lender reviews a borrower's history to determine if they're likely to get approved for a loan, and the approximate amount. Pre-qualification is *not* binding on the lender. **Pre-approval** is when a lender uses an application to determine that potential borrowers can be financed for a certain amount for a specific property. A mortgage broker cannot give a borrower a pre-approval; only a lender can.

4. The loan process consists of four steps: 1. **Consulting** with a MLO; 2. Completing the **application**; 3. **Processing** the application; 4. **Analyzing** the borrower and the property. Common fees include credit report, appraisal, title work, inspections, etc. The loan application asks a number of personal and financial questions, along with information about the property the borrower wishes to purchase. MLO must document that a borrower is reasonably able to repay the loan.

5. Address and **employment** information must go back two to three years. **Income** should be stable and verifiable. Alimony/child support may be excluded as income if borrower chooses (if included, may be grossed up 125%). Those who are self-employed (at least 25% ownership) may need personal and company tax returns and financial statements. **Assets** and **liabilities** must all be disclosed, including alimony and child support, if it's an obligation. **Liquid assets** can be quickly and easily converted to cash. **Net worth** is assets minus liabilities. Borrowers must answer all declarations truthfully.

6. **Bankruptcy** is a court process that cancels debt and provides some relief for creditors. Chapter 7 bankruptcy is a liquidation proceeding where the debtor receives a discharge of all dischargeable debts. Chapter 13 bankruptcy is filed by individuals who want to pay off their debts over a period of three to five years. Chapter 13 bankruptcy usually appears on a credit report for 7 years.

7. The **underwriting** process may evaluate: Capacity (ability to pay), collateral (down payment, home value), credit (good payment history), character (job stability, reserves), and conditions (health of job market, economy). Some elements of the mortgage process may be automated to reduce time and costs for lenders. Automated underwriting systems (AUSs) offer computerized analysis to recommend accepting the loan or refer it to a human underwriter for further consideration. Fannie Mae's AUS is **Desktop Underwriter**® (DU®); Freddie Mac's system is called Loan Prospector®.

8. Monthly **income** must show stability, quality, and durability. Bonuses, commission, part-time earnings, and overtime all count if shown to be a consistent part of the borrower's income for the past few years. Lenders do not usually count temporary unemployment, welfare, and other income. **Credit history** is a record of debt repayment. **Credit scoring** is an objective means of evaluating credit. Lenders verify assets and may require financial statements. The three main credit bureaus produce similar credit scores, which range from about **300 to 850.** A **gift letter** can show part of the down payment/closing costs are a non-repayable gift.

9. Conforming loans sold on the secondary market (e.g., Fannie Mae and Freddie Mac) require income ratios of **28%** for housing expense and **36%** for debt-to-income (DTI). The housing expense ratio is the relationship of the borrower's total monthly housing expense, or PITI (Principal, Interest, Taxes, Insurance or PITI), to gross monthly income (stable), expressed as a percentage. PITI must also consider required homeowners association fees. Total debt-to-income ratio is the relationship of the borrower's total monthly debt obligations (including housing and debts that will not be cancelled and that have ten or more payments remaining) to gross monthly income, expressed as a percentage. A borrower must qualify under **both** ratios. Fannie Mae, however, focuses on the back-end ratio (DTI).

10. **Closing**, also called settlement, is the culmination of the loan process where papers are signed and funds disbursed. In a real estate sales transaction, it's also the transfer of ownership of real estate from a seller to a buyer, per terms of the sales contract (seller receives value for property—cash, mortgage, etc.—and buyer gets title). **Proration** is the division of expenses between buyer and seller in proportion to the actual usage of the item represented by a particular expense as of the day the loan is funded.

Chapter 3 Quiz

1. ***Bob is buying a house. It was appraised at $236,000, the sales price is $228,000, and the loan amount is $216,800. In order to buy down his interest rate, Bob is willing to pay 2 points in addition to the 1 point in loan origination fees. What is the price of Bob's discount points?***
   A. $4,336
   B. $4,720
   C. $6,840
   D. $7,080

2. ***Non-taxable child support income***
   A. cannot be considered as stable income.
   B. may be counted at 75%.
   C. may be counted at 100%.
   D. may be counted at 125%.

3. ***If the borrower is self-employed, he or she should provide***
   A. average monthly income amount earned over the previous two years.
   B. employment verification from the last employer.
   C. profit and loss statements for the previous six years.
   D. tax returns for the previous two or three years.

4. ***A gift letter***
   A. can come from a borrower's parent or guardian only.
   B. cannot be used for part of the down payment.
   C. must be signed by the donor.
   D. must state when the gift is to be repaid.

5. ***To be classified as self-employment income, the borrower must own at least what percent of the business used for qualifying?***
   A. 5%
   B. 10%
   C. 25%
   D. 50%

6. ***Conforming loans follow guidelines of***
   A. ECOA.
   B. Fannie Mae and Freddie Mac.
   C. the FHA.
   D. RESPA.

7. ***When qualifying for a conventional loan, stable gross monthly income can include***
   A. alimony received (that a borrower chooses to reveal).
   B. bonus received for the first time last year.
   C. erratic unemployment earnings.
   D. income from other family members.

8. ***If the lender wants the borrower's permission to get copies of his income tax returns, the borrower must sign what form?***
   A. 1003
   B. 4506-T
   C. 95-IRS
   D. URAR

9. ***Joe wants to get a loan to buy a house. When evaluating his credit obligations, which would LEAST LIKELY be considered as debt?***
   A. car loan payment
   B. cell phone service payment
   C. child support payments
   D. credit card payments

10. ***A borrower has a stable monthly gross income of $3,200 and recurring monthly debts of $370. What is the maximum amount of money available to him for monthly housing expenses in order to qualify for a conforming loan?***
   A. $782
   B. $896
   C. $928
   D. $1,152

4

Chapter 4

Federal Lending Legislation

In This Chapter

The federal government and all state governments have enacted numerous laws that affect various aspects of the real estate industry. As a mortgage professional, not only are you obligated to know and understand the law, you have a duty to stay current with changes to the law. In this chapter, we'll examine the following federal laws, grouped into three broad categories:

- Laws requiring financial disclosures in real estate transactions: Truth in Lending Act and the Mortgage Disclosure Improvement Act, Real Estate Settlement Procedures Act, Homeowner's Protection Act, Equal Credit Opportunity Act
- Laws protecting privacy and consumer identification: Fair Credit Reporting Act, Fair and Accurate Credit Transactions Act Red Flag Rules, Gramm-Leach-Bliley Act, U.S. Patriot Act, National Do Not Call Registry
- Laws prohibiting predatory lending: Home Ownership Equity Protection Act, Federal Reserve Mortgage Loan Originator Compensation Rule

We will also review provisions of Title V of the Housing and Economic Recovery Act of 2008 (Pub.L. 110-289), which is designated the Secure and Fair Enforcement Mortgage Licensing Act, more commonly known as the SAFE Act.

In Chapter 13 Ethics, you will have the opportunity to learn about federal laws **prohibiting illegal discrimination**: Civil Rights Act, Fair Housing Act, Equal Credit Opportunity Act, Community Reinvestment Act, and the Home Mortgage Disclosure Act.

At the end of this chapter, you will be able to:

- Discuss disclosure provisions of federal laws related to mortgage lending.
- Identify procedures to protect the privacy of consumers.
- Describe regulations put in place to address predatory lending.
- Define education requirements for mortgage loan originators.

Key Terms

3/7/3 Rule

Affiliated Business Arrangement (AfBA)

Annual Percentage Rate (APR)

Equal Credit Opportunity Act (ECOA) / Regulation B

Fair and Accurate Credit Transactions Act (FACT Act)

Fair Credit Reporting Act (FCRA) / Regulation V

Good Faith Estimate (GFE)

Gramm-Leach-Bliley Act

Home Ownership and Equity Protection Act (HOEPA)

Homeowners Protection Act (HPA)

Housing and Economic Recovery Act of 2008 (HERA)

HUD Uniform Settlement Statement (HUD-1)

Mortgage Disclosure Improvement Act (MDIA)

Real Estate Settlement Procedures Act (RESPA) / Regulation X

Red Flag Rules

Rescind

Secure and Fair Enforcement for Mortgage Licensing Act (SAFE Act)

Truth in Lending Act (TILA) / Regulation Z

Truth in Lending Statement (TIL)

U.S. Patriot Act

Dodd-Frank Wall Street Reform and Consumer Protection Act of 2010

In July, 2010, the United States Congress passed the **Dodd-Frank Wall Street Reform and Consumer Protection Act** (Pub.L. 111-203, H.R. 4173). The stated purpose of this far-reaching financial legislation is "to promote the financial stability of the United States by improving accountability and transparency in the financial system, to end 'too big to fail', to protect the American taxpayer by ending bailouts, to protect consumers from abusive financial services practices, and for other purposes."

The two titles of the Dodd-Frank Wall Street Reform and Consumer Protection Act of 2010 with the greatest impact on the mortgage industry are Title X, designated as the **Consumer Financial Protection Act**, and Title XIV, designated as the **Mortgage Reform and Anti-Predatory Lending Act**. Title X creates the **Consumer Financial Protection Bureau** as an independent entity within the Federal Reserve and transfers to it the rulemaking and enforcement authority over many consumer financial laws, including:

- Truth in Lending Act (TILA)
- Real Estate Settlement Procedures Act (RESPA)
- Homeowners Protection Act (HPA)
- Fair Credit Reporting Act (FCRA)
- Fair and Accurate Credit Transactions Act (FACTA)
- Portions of the Gramm-Leach Bliley Act related to information privacy
- Equal Credit Opportunity Act (ECOA)
- Home Mortgage Disclosure Act (HMDA)
- Home Ownership and Equity Protection Act (HOEPA)
- Secure and Fair Enforcement for Mortgage Licensing Act (SAFE Act)

While Dodd-Frank indicates that final regulations for most of the mortgage provisions are required within 18 months of its enactment, actual implementation depends on the transfer of responsibility to the Consumer Financial Protection Bureau and the issuing of final rules and regulations. The expected timeline for complete implementation of Dodd-Frank may be as much as three and half years from the passage of the Act. Even so, it is possible that some provisions may never be implemented exactly as proposed in the Act. Every mortgage loan originator is responsible for staying current with the regulations as they are implemented.

Laws Requiring Financial Disclosures

A mortgage loan originator, mortgage broker, mortgage banker, or any other agent of the lender should be aware of the various disclosure requirements when making real estate loans. Some of the disclosures that must be made by the lender include the total costs involved in the transaction. The lender or lender's agent must also disclose whether there is any relationship with service companies that the lender, lender's agent, or mortgage loan originator suggests that a buyer or seller use when the mortgage is for a purchase, and if any compensation is being paid (but not necessarily the amount). Of course, there are many disclosure duties real estate agents, lenders, and even sellers have. The source of the duty to disclose varies according to which disclosures are involved.

Some disclosures are imposed by federal (or state) law, and others are imposed by one's responsibilities to an employer or lender. Here, we'll focus on federal disclosure requirements relating to real estate finance and mortgage loans:

- Truth in Lending Act (TILA)
- Mortgage Disclosure Improvement Act (MDIA) amending TILA
- Real Estate Settlement Procedures Act (RESPA)
- Homeowners Protection Act (HPA)
- Equal Credit Opportunity Act (ECOA)

Truth in Lending Act (TILA)

Prior to the 1968 passage of the **Truth in Lending Act**, or TILA, there were no federal laws requiring the disclosure of consumer credit costs. The findings and declaration of purpose for the passage of TILA (15 U.S.C. 1601 § 102 (a)) follows:

> *The Congress finds that economic stabilization would be enhanced and the competition among the various financial institutions and other firms engaged in the extension of consumer credit would be strengthened by the informed use of credit. The informed use of credit results from an awareness of the cost thereof by consumers. It is the purpose of this title to assure a meaningful disclosure of credit terms so that the consumer will be able to compare more readily the various credit terms available to him and avoid the uninformed use of credit, and to protect the consumer against inaccurate and unfair credit billing and credit card practices.*

The Truth in Lending Act is administered by the **Board of Governors of the Federal Reserve System**, although administration will transfer to the Consumer Financial Protection Bureau (CFPB). The specific provisions of the Act, which is contained in Title I of the Consumer Credit Protection Act as amended (15 U.S.C. 1601 et seq.) are implemented by **Regulation Z.** TILA has been amended numerous times, most recently with the Housing and Economic Recovery Act of 2008, the Mortgage Disclosure Improvement Act (MDIA), which went into effect in 2009, and the Dodd-Frank Wall Street Reform and Consumer Protection Act of 2010.

While Regulation Z does not set limits on interest rates or other finance charges imposed by lenders, it does regulate the disclosure of these items. Specifically, the Act requires all creditors who deal with consumers to make certain disclosures concerning all finance charges and related aspects of credit transactions (including disclosing finance charges expressed as an annual percentage rate). The Act also establishes a three-business day right of rescission in certain transactions.

These provisions apply to each creditor who offers or extends credit to consumers (people, not companies) in the ordinary course of business, primarily for personal, family, or household purposes. The credit offered must be subject to a finance charge or payable by written agreement in **more than four installments**. Under the Act, the definition of **credit** includes all real estate loans made to consumers—no matter what the amount—if the loan is for *other than business or commercial purposes*. (One exemption from coverage is credit of more than $25,000 that is not secured by real property.)

Disclosures

Disclosures are required in two general areas:

- **When creditors offer credit but before the transaction is consummated.** Regulation Z requires disclosures be made clearly, conspicuously, in writing, and in a form the consumer may keep and read prior to the loan closing. If the disclosures are incorporated into the loan agreement, they must be separated from all other loan details; for example, they may be placed in a boxed section on the form or be separated by bold print dividing lines.
- **When credit terms are advertised to potential customers.** Advertisers of consumer credit must clearly and conspicuously provide certain information if they use specific triggering terms in their credit ads. The credit terms advertised must actually be available.

The following are the specific disclosures required by Regulation Z:

- Truth in Lending Statement (TIL) and a guide on how to read the TIL
- Consumer Handbook on Adjustable Rate Mortgages (CHARM booklet) and adjustable rate mortgage (ARM) loan program details *(only for all ARM loans)*
- When Your Home is on the Line Disclosure *(only for home equity installment loans and home equity lines of credit)*

A creditor must retain evidence of compliance with these disclosure requirements for at least **two years** after the disclosures were required to be made.

Annual Percentage Rate (APR)

For residential mortgages, disclosure of the **annual percentage rate** (APR) is very important. The APR tells a borrower *the total cost of financing a loan in percentage terms, as a relationship of the total finance charges to the total amount financed.* The APR is *not* simply the interest rate that appears in the promissory note, known as the **note rate**. Rather, it reflects certain **finance charges** associated with the loan, spread out over the life of the loan. Therefore, the APR is generally higher than the note rate.

It can be a challenge to explain closing costs and fees to consumers, especially to define those fees that are considered finance charges for the purpose of calculating the APR. Regulation Z defines the **finance charge** (12 C.F.R. § 226.4) as the *cost of consumer credit as a dollar amount.* It includes any charge payable directly or indirectly by the consumer and imposed directly or indirectly by the creditor as an incident to or a condition of the extension of credit. It does not include any charge of a type payable in a comparable cash transaction.

The finance charge includes fees and amounts charged by someone other than the creditor, (unless otherwise excluded) if the creditor:

- Requires the use of a third party as a condition of or an incident to the extension of credit, even if the consumer can choose the third party; or
- Retains a portion of the third-party charge, to the extent of the portion retained.

Fees charged by a third party that conducts the loan closing (such as a settlement agent, attorney, or escrow or title company) are finance charges only if the creditor:

- Requires the particular services for which the consumer is charged;
- Requires the imposition of the charge; or
- Retains a portion of the third-party charge, to the extent of the portion retained.

Fees charged by a mortgage broker (including fees paid by the consumer directly to the broker or to the creditor for delivery to the broker) are finance charges even if the creditor does not require the consumer to use a mortgage broker and even if the creditor does not retain any portion of the charge.

Charges Included in the Finance Charge

According to Regulation Z § 226.4 (b), the following are examples of finance charges:

- Interest, time price differential, and any amount payable under an add-on or discount system of additional charges
- Service, transaction, activity, and carrying charges, including any charge imposed on a checking or other transaction account to the extent that the charge exceeds the charge for a similar account without a credit feature
- Points, loan fees, assumption fees, finder's fees, and similar charges
- Premiums or other charges for:
    - Any guarantee or insurance protecting the creditor against the consumer's default or other credit loss
    - Credit life, accident, health, or loss-of-income insurance, written in connection with a credit transaction
    - Insurance against loss of or damage to property, or against liability arising out of the ownership or use of property, written in connection with a credit transaction
- Charges imposed on a creditor by another person for purchasing or accepting a consumer's obligation, if the consumer is required to pay the charges in cash, as an addition to the obligation, or as a deduction from the proceeds of the obligation
- Discounts for the purpose of inducing payment by a means other than the use of credit
- Debt cancellation fee, including charges or premiums paid for debt cancellation coverage written in connection with a credit transaction, whether or not the debt cancellation coverage is insurance under applicable law

Additional considerations related to what is included as finance charges for the purpose of determining APR are discussed later in this chapter in connection with high cost and higher-priced loans.

Charges Excluded from the Finance Charge

According to Regulation Z § 226.4 (c)(d)(e), the following are excluded from the finance charge:

- Application fees charged to all applicants for credit, whether or not credit is actually extended
- Charges for actual unanticipated late payment, for exceeding a credit limit or for delinquency, default, or a similar occurrence
- Charges imposed by a financial institution for paying items that overdraw an account, unless the payment of such items and the imposition of the charge were previously agreed upon in writing
- Fees charged for participation in a credit plan, whether assessed on an annual or other periodic basis
- Seller's points
- Interest forfeited as a result of an interest reduction required by law on a time deposit used as security for an extension of credit
- These fees in a transaction secured by real property or in a residential mortgage transaction, if bona fide and a reasonable amount:
    - Fees for title examination, abstract of title, title insurance, property survey, and similar purposes
    - Fees for preparing loan-related documents, such as deeds, mortgages, and reconveyance or settlement documents
    - Notary and credit report fees
    - Property appraisal fees or fees for inspections to assess the value or condition of the property if the service is performed prior to closing, including fees related to pest infestation or flood hazard determinations
    - Amounts required to be paid into escrow or trustee accounts if the amounts would not otherwise be included in the finance charge
- Discounts offered to induce payment for a purchase by cash, check, or other means
- Premiums for voluntary credit life, accident, health, loss-of-income insurance, or debt cancellation coverage if the following conditions are met:
    - The insurance coverage or debt cancellation agreement or coverage is not required by the creditor, and this fact is disclosed in writing
    - The fee or premium for the initial term of insurance coverage or debt cancellation coverage is disclosed, as well as the term of insurance or coverage when less than the term of the transaction
    - Any consumer in the transaction signs or initials an affirmative written request for the insurance or debt cancellation coverage after receiving the specified disclosures
- Premiums for insurance against loss of or damage to property, or against liability arising out of the ownership or use of property when the following conditions are met:
    - The insurance coverage may be obtained from a person of the consumer's choice, and this fact is disclosed
    - When the coverage is obtained from or through the creditor, the premium for the initial term of insurance coverage is disclosed, as well as the term of the insurance if less than the term of the transaction
- If itemized and disclosed, the following security interest charges may be excluded:
    - Taxes and fees prescribed by law that actually are or will be paid to public officials for determining the existence of or for perfecting, releasing, or satisfying a security interest
    - The premium for insurance in lieu of perfecting a security interest to the extent that the premium does not exceed fees described above that otherwise would be payable

- Taxes on security instruments or on documents evidencing indebtedness if the payment of such taxes is a requirement for recording the instrument

√ **Note:** These prohibited offsets—interest, dividends, or other income received or to be received by the consumer on deposits or investments—shall not be deducted in computing the finance charge.

Real Success

Whenever you quote an interest rate to a consumer—including advertisements, websites, etc.—the APR must also be disclosed. When a potential borrower inquires about the cost of credit orally, only the annual percentage rate is required to be stated. If you cannot determine the APR in advance, other cost information for the consumer's specific transaction may be given, as well as:

- For open-end credit, the corresponding annual percentage rate must be stated.
- For closed-end credit, the APR for a sample transaction must be stated.

As a general rule to assist you with determining what closing costs are included in the APR, consider this: If a borrower was purchasing a home for cash, there would be certain closing costs that he would ***not*** incur, such as an application fee, credit report fee, underwriting fee, mortgage insurance, and interest. These are generally the same costs that ***are*** included in the APR calculation.

Truth in Lending Statement (TIL)

According to Regulation Z (12 C.F.R. § 226.19), in a mortgage transaction subject to the Real Estate Settlement Procedures Act that is secured by the consumer's dwelling, other than a home equity line of credit, creditors must provide the Truth in Lending Statement (TIL)—along with other required disclosures—at application or placed in the mail **no later than the third business day after the creditor receives the consumer's written application or no later than the seventh business day before consummation of the transaction.** This means that in order to comply with the Mortgage Disclosure Improvement Act, the earliest a loan may close is the **seventh business day** after the initial disclosures are delivered or placed in the mail (§ 226.19 (a)(2)(i)).

The only fee that may be collected prior to these mandated disclosures is a fee for a **credit report**, assuming the fee is bona fide and reasonable in amount. Other loan origination fees may be collected after these disclosures are hand-delivered to the borrower or three (3) business days after they are mailed (§ 226.19 (a)(1)(ii)(iii)).

Note that mortgage loan originators and servicers are prohibited from charging a fee for the preparation of the Truth in Lending Statement (TIL) or other disclosures required by the Truth in Lending Act or the Real Estate Settlement Procedures Act (24 C.F.R. § 3500.12).

As with other disclosures required by the Truth in Lending Act, the TIL may be made available in a language other than English at the consumer's request.

Data in the "Federal Box"

- Finance charge expressed as an **annual percentage rate** (the APR is labeled with a phrase such as "The cost of your credit as a yearly rate"); not the note rate
- Total **finance charges**—the amount of money paid toward interest over the life of the loan, plus the upfront fees (e.g., origination fee, loan fee, commitment fee, assumption fee, prepaid interest, prepaid PMI, prepaid credit life insurane

- **Amount financed**—the total amount of credit the lender extends to the borrower, reflecting the subtraction of any prepaid finance charges the borrower paid and the addition of other amounts financed
- **Total of payments** paid at the end of the loan term

Both the initial and final Truth in Lending Statements must also include the following language:

> *You are not required to complete this agreement merely because you have received these disclosures or signed a loan application.*

Other Data Included for Closed-End Transactions

- Name of the lender/creditor
- Notice of a right to receive an itemization of the amount financed, including the principal amount, all finance charges detailed, and any discounts, points, fees, mortgage insurance premiums, etc., that are financed (this can be satisfied by a Good Faith Estimate)
- Number, amount, and timing of payments scheduled to repay the obligation
- New payment, late payment, and prepayment provisions
- Description and identification of the security (there will be a phrase such as "There is a security interest in the property purchased")
- Whether the loan may be assumed by a subsequent buyer
- Notice that consumers may not be able to refinance to a lower rate in the future (previously required only for adjustable rate loans)
- Payment summary table indicating initial interest rate and corresponding monthly payment

In addition, for adjustable or step-rate mortgages, the payment summary table must include the maximum interest rate and payment that can occur during the first five years and a "worst case" example showing the maximum rate and payment possible over the life of the loan, for example:

	Introductory Rate and Monthly Payment (first period)	Maximum During First Five Years (date)	Maximum Ever as early as (date)
Interest Rate	______ %	______ %	______ %
Principal + Interest Payment	$ ______	$ ______	$ ______
Est. Taxes + Insurance (Escrow) [Includes Private Mortgage Insurance]	$ ______	$ ______	$ ______
Total Est. Monthly Payment	$ ______	$ ______	$ ______

New Disclosure Form on the Horizon

In response to provisions in the Dodd-Frank Wall Street Reform and Consumer Protection Act of 2010 (Pub.L. 111-203, H.R. 4173), the Consumer Financial Protection Bureau has tested multiple iterations of a proposed single integrated disclosure that combines the disclosure requirements in the Truth in Lending Act (currently provided for by the Truth in Lending Statement) and the Real Estate Settlement Procedures Act (currently provided for by the Good Faith Estimate), revising its samples in response to comments from consumers and mortgage professionals. A final round of testing was expected to be conducted in February 2012, after which the accompanying federal rules related to the new disclosures are expected to be explained. The actual date for final implementation of any revised form and accompanying rules was unknown at the time of this printing, although the Dodd-Frank Act requires the CFPB to issue the combined model disclosures and implementing rules by July 21, 2012. Every MLO has an obligation to stay current with provisions of the Dodd-Frank Act as they are implemented via rules and regulations. For the most current information, see the mortgages section on the Consumer Financial Protection Bureau website: http://www.consumerfinance.gov/knowbeforeyouowe/

FEDERAL TRUTH IN LENDING STATEMENT

(This is neither a contract nor a commitment to loan)

Applicant(s):	JOE BUYER	**Prepared By:**	FIRST BANK
Applicant Address:	123 Market Ave, Anytown US 10001		111 1st St, Anytown US 10001
Property Address:	9876 Oak St, Anytown US 10001	**Date Prepared:**	4/17/11
Application Number:	123456789	**Loan Type:**	Conventional Fixed

ANNUAL PERCENTAGE RATE The cost of your credit as a yearly rate.	**FINANCE CHARGE** The dollar amount the credit will cost you.	**Amount Financed** The amount of credit provided to you or on your behalf.	**Total of Payments** The amount you will have paid after you have made all payments as scheduled.
5.325	**$244,714.53**	**$242,865.02**	**$487,579.55**

INTEREST AND PAYMENT SUMMARY

	Rate and Monthly Payment
Interest Rate	**5.2500%**
Principal + Interest Payment	**$1,354.38**
Est. Taxes + Insurance (Escrow)	**$ 255.00**
Includes Private Mortgage Insurance	
Total Est. Monthly Payment	**$1,609.38**

THERE IS NO GUARANTEE THAT YOU WILL BE ABLE TO REFINANCE TO LOWER YOUR RATE AND PAYMENTS.

☐ **This loan has a Variable Rate Feature. Variable Rate Disclosures have been provided to you earlier.**
☐ **This loan has a Demand Feature.**
☐ **Filing/Recording Fee: $ 0**

Late Charge: If your payment is delinquent for **15** days or more, you will pay a late charge of **5** % of the payment in accordance with the terms of your note.

Prepayment: If you pay off your loan early: **You will not have to pay a penalty.**

Assumption: Someone buying your home **will not** be allowed to assume the remainder of the mortgage on its original terms.

See your Note and Mortgage for any additional information about nonpayment, default, and required repayment in full before the scheduled date, prepayment penalties, and assumption of the obligation.

Insurance: You may obtain hazard and flood insurance from any company you choose that is acceptable to the lender.

YOU ARE NOT REQUIRED TO COMPLETE THIS AGREEMENT MERELY BECAUSE YOU HAVE RECEIVED THESE DISCLOSURES OR SIGNED A LOAN APPLICATION.

I/We hereby acknowledge receipt of copies of this Truth in Lending Statement:

Applicant	***Date***	***Applicant***	***Date***

APR Accuracy and Redisclosure

According to Regulation Z (§ 226.22), the annual percentage rate is generally considered accurate if it does not vary above or below the APR initially disclosed by more than:

- 1/8% (.125) for a regular transaction.
- 1/4% (.25) for an irregular transaction.

An "irregular" transaction is defined as one that includes one or more of the following features:

- Multiple advances
- Irregular payment periods
- Irregular payment amounts (other than an irregular first period or irregular first and final payment)

If a change renders the APR inaccurate prior to loan consummation, the Mortgage Disclosure Improvement Act requires that the borrower be given corrected disclosure of all terms. The consumer must receive the corrected disclosures no later **three (3) business days** prior to loan consummation. If the corrected disclosures are mailed or delivered by some method other than in person, the consumer is considered to have received them three (3) business days after they were mailed (§ 226.19 (a)(2)(ii)).

The loan generally cannot be consummated until both waiting periods have expired. However, a borrower *may* be able to **waive** the waiting periods and expedite the closing if there's a **bona fide personal financial emergency**, such as to avoid foreclosure. This requires a dated written statement from the borrower with the details of the emergency (§ 226.19 (a)(3)).

Also, remember that consumers are NOT required to continue with the loan during these waiting periods simply because the creditor provided these disclosures.

3/7/3 Rule

You can remember these disclosure requirements as the 3/7/3 Rule:

- Initial disclosure must be given (or placed in the mail) within **three (3) business days** of receipt of a completed application.
- The earliest a loan may be consummated is on the **seventh (7th) business day** after disclosures are delivered/mailed.
- Any corrected disclosures must be received by the consumer at least **three (3) business days** before the loan is consummated.

When considering these waiting periods, Regulation Z defines a **business day** to be all calendar days **except** Sundays and the legal public holidays specified in 5 U.S.C. 6103(a), such as New Year's Day, the birthday of Martin Luther King, Jr., Washington's Birthday, Memorial Day, Independence Day, Labor Day, Columbus Day, Veterans Day, Thanksgiving Day, and Christmas Day (§ 226.2 (a)(6)). Note the difference between how these waiting periods are defined:

> **Example 1:** The creditor takes an application for a fixed rate loan on Tuesday, May 1, and mails the initial TIL the next day, Wednesday, May 2. The earliest the loan can close—assuming the APR on the final TIL is within the tolerance—is the following Thursday, May 10, the seventh business day after mailing the initial disclosure (assuming no legal federal holidays occur during the waiting period).
>
> **Example 2:** Same situation as above, but on Friday, May 4, the interest rate goes up, causing the APR to increase by more than .125 percent. The creditor mails a revised TIL on Saturday, May 5. The consumer is assumed to have received it three business days later (Wednesday, May 9). The three business-day waiting period then begins Thursday. Since the next day after the three business-day waiting period is a Sunday, the earliest this loan will close is Monday, May 14 (assuming no legal federal holidays occur during the waiting period).

Right of Rescission

Under Regulation Z (§§ 226.15 and 226.23), consumers have the right to rescind certain credit transactions. **Rescind** means to *take back or withdraw an offer or contract.* The right of rescission as discussed in these sections of Regulation Z applies to any credit transaction involving the establishment of a security interest (for example, a mortgage or deed of trust) in their **principal residence**, such as:

- Home equity loans
- Home improvement loans
- Refinances
- Home equity lines of credit

There are additional rescission rights associated with high cost and higher-priced loans, which are discussed later in this chapter.

This right of rescission does **not** apply to the following:

- Purchase loans (which protects sellers who may have entered into another contract or purchased a home contingent on the buyers purchasing their present home)
- Construction loans (which protects builders who may have performed services based on the buyer's commitment)
- Commercial loans
- Loans on vacation or second homes
- A refinancing or consolidation by the same creditor of an extension of credit already secured by the consumer's principal dwelling unless the new amount financed exceeds the unpaid principal balance, any earned unpaid finance charge on the existing debt, and amounts attributed solely to the costs of the refinancing or consolidation
- A transaction in which a state agency is a creditor

Some points to remember:

- When more than one consumer has the right to rescind, the **exercise of the right by one consumer is effective for all consumers.**
- If a consumer does choose to exercise the right to rescind, the mortgage is void and the creditor must return any money it collected related to the loan **within 20 calendar days.** The consumer has no liability for the loan, including finance charges.
- Consumers may exercise the right to rescind the credit transaction until midnight of the **third business day** following loan consummation, delivery of the required rescission notice, or delivery of all material disclosures, **whichever occurs last.**

Note that for the purposes of rescission, the term **consumer** is expanded to include any "natural person in whose principal dwelling a security interest is or will be retained or acquired, if that person's ownership interest in the dwelling is or will be subject to the security interest" (§ 226.2 (a)(11)).

Case in Point

Loan papers for a refinance are signed on Wednesday. The consumer can consider and think about the mortgage closing on Thursday (Day 1), Friday (Day 2) and Saturday (Day 3). Under Regulation Z's provisions for rescission, Saturdays are included in the rescission period, but Sundays and federal holidays are not included in the three business-day calculation. The mortgage can be recorded and money disbursed the next business day, Monday (assuming Monday is not a legal federal holiday).

Wednesday	Thursday	Friday	Saturday	Sunday	Monday
Loan Consummation	Day 1	Day 2	Day 3	--	$$ Disbursed

Notice of Right to Rescind

Creditors must inform consumers of their right to rescind by providing **two copies** of a **Notice of Right to Rescind** document to *each consumer entitled to rescind.* The notice of the right to rescind must be in a separate document from the sale or credit document, and must identify the transaction or occurrence and conspicuously disclose the following:

- The retention or acquisition of a security interest in the consumer's principal dwelling
- The consumer's right to rescind
- How to exercise the right of rescission, with a form to use that designates the address of the creditor's place of business
- The effects of rescission
- The date on which the rescission period ends

Extended Right of Rescission

Consumers may have the right to an extended rescission period of up to **three years** under these circumstances:

- The creditor fails to properly notify consumers of the right to rescind.
- The creditor does not provide the consumer with the required material disclosures (or the required corrected redisclosures). "Material" refers to annual percentage rate, finance charge, amount financed, total payments, or payment schedule within the acceptable tolerances.

For the purposes of extended rescission, the acceptable **tolerances** for accuracy include:

1/2 of 1 percent tolerance. The finance charge and other disclosures affected by the finance charge (such as the amount financed and the annual percentage rate) shall be considered accurate if the disclosed finance charge is:

- Understated by no more than **0.5%** of the face amount of the note or **$100**, whichever is greater, or
- Greater than the amount required to be disclosed.

1 percent tolerance. In a refinancing of a residential mortgage transaction with a new creditor if there is no new advance and no consolidation of existing loans, the finance charge and other disclosures affected by the finance charge (such as the amount financed and the annual percentage rate) is considered accurate if the disclosed finance charge is:

- Understated by no more than **1%** of the face amount of the note or **$100**, whichever is greater, or
- Greater than the amount required to be disclosed.

The extended right to rescind expires **three years** after the occurrence giving rise to the right of rescission, upon transfer of all of the consumer's interest in the property, or upon sale of the property, whichever occurs first.

Additional Rescission Considerations for Foreclosures

After the initiation of foreclosure on the consumer's principal dwelling that secures the credit obligation, the consumer shall have the right to rescind the transaction if:

- A mortgage broker fee that should have been included in the finance charge was not included.
- The creditor did not provide the properly completed Notice of Rescission.

Tolerance for disclosures. After the initiation of foreclosure on the consumer's principal dwelling that secures the credit obligation, the finance charge and other disclosures affected by the finance charge (such as the amount financed and the annual percentage rate) shall be considered accurate if the disclosed finance charge is:

- Understated by no more than $35; or
- Greater than the amount required to be disclosed.

Advertising Disclosures

Prior to the passage of the Truth in Lending Act, an advertiser might have disclosed only the most attractive credit terms, distorting the true cost of financing. For example, the ad could have included the low monthly payments (e.g., $275 a month) without indicating the large down payment necessary to qualify for that payment level. Advertisers did not have to disclose the APR or whether the transaction was a credit sale or lease. The Act requires the advertiser to tell the whole story, and tell it **clearly** and **conspicuously**. Here's a critical example: If discussing an adjustable rate mortgage that has a fixed term, the word "**fixed**" must be accompanied by an equally prominent and closely proximate statement of the fixed time period and the fact that the rate may vary or the payment may increase after that period.

Anyone who places advertising that references consumer credit is required to follow the advertising provisions of the Truth in Lending Act. Also, if specific loan terms are shown in an ad, those terms must be **actually available**.

Triggering Terms Requiring Disclosure

If an advertisement is for credit secured by a dwelling, the advertisement may not state any other rate, except that a simple annual rate that is applied to an unpaid balance may be stated in conjunction with, but not more conspicuously than, the annual percentage rate. If an advertisement contains any one of the triggering terms about the loan as specified in the Truth in Lending Act, that advertisement must also include the required disclosures. Examples of triggering terms in advertisements include:

- The amount of the down payment (e.g., "20% down")
- The amount of any payment (e.g., "Pay only $700 per month")
- The number of payments (e.g., "Only 360 monthly payments")
- The period of repayment (e.g., "30-year financing available")
- The amount of any finance charge (e.g., "1% finance charge")

Required Advertising Disclosures

If any triggering terms are used in an ad, *all* of these disclosures must be made:

- Amount or percentage of down payment
- Terms of repayment, e.g., payment schedule, including any balloon payments
- Annual percentage rate, using that term spelled out in full or APR; if the rate may increase (e.g., for ARMs), that fact must also be disclosed

If an ad discloses only the APR, the additional disclosures are *not* required.

Terms That Do NOT Trigger Disclosure

Examples of terms that do *not* trigger required disclosures include:

- "5% Annual Percentage Rate loan available here."
- "Easy monthly payments."
- "FHA financing available." or "100% VA financing available."
- "Terms to fit your budget."

Advertising Closed-End Credit

A **closed-end** credit transaction is one in which the balance is expected to be repaid—along with any interest and finance changes—by a specified future date. Most real estate loans are closed-end. Additional advertising provisions in Regulation Z (§ 226.24) related to these loans include:

Rate. If an advertisement states a simple annual rate of interest and more than one rate applies over the term of the loan, the advertisement must also disclose—with equal prominence and in close proximity to the advertised rate—this information:

- Each simple annual rate of interest that will apply; if a variable-rate, a reasonably current index and margin must be used

- The period of time during which each simple annual rate of interest applies
- The APR for the loan

Payment Amount. If the advertisement states the amount of any payment, it must also disclose—with equal prominence and in close proximity to the payment—this information:

- The amount of each payment that applies over the term of the loan, including any balloon payment; if a variable-rate, a reasonably current index and margin must be used
- The period of time during which each payment applies

√ ***Note:*** When the ad for a first lien mortgage loan states the amount of any payment, it must also state prominently (but not with equal prominence) and in close proximity to the advertised payment that the payments do ***not*** include amounts for taxes and insurance, if applicable, and that the actual payment amount will be higher.

Payment and Rate Comparisons. Advertisements may not compare actual or hypothetical payments or rates and a "teaser" payment or simple annual rate available for the advertised product unless the ad includes a clear and conspicuous comparison to the terms required to be disclosed (APR, term, payments, etc.). If it's a variable rate transaction where the advertised payment or simple annual rate is based on the index and margin used to make subsequent rate or payment adjustments, the advertisement must include an equally prominent statement in close proximity that the payment or rate is subject to adjustment as well as the time period when the first adjustment will occur.

Use of the Term "Fixed." If an advertisement references **both variable and non-variable rate** loans, the terms "adjustable rate mortgage," "variable rate mortgage," or "ARM" must appear with equal prominence as any use of the term "fixed" or "fixed rate mortgage." Also, the term "fixed" must clearly refer *only* to the transactions with fixed rates. If referring to a payment or to a variable rate, it must also include the time period for which the rate or payment is fixed and a statement that the rate can vary and the payment can increase after that.

If an advertisement references a **variable rate** loan, the phrase "adjustable rate mortgage," "variable rate mortgage," or "ARM" must appear before the first use of the term "fixed" and must be at least as conspicuous as the word "fixed." In addition, the ad must clearly indicate the time period for which the rate or payment is fixed, and the fact that the rate may vary or the payment may increase after that period.

If the ad references a **non-variable rate** loan where the payment amount increases, the use of the word "fixed" must state the fact that the rate may vary or the payment may increase after that period.

Catalogs, Multiple-Page Ads, Electronic Ads. If a catalog or other multiple-page advertisement, or an electronic advertisement (such as an advertisement appearing on an Internet web site) gives information in a table or schedule in sufficient detail that includes triggering terms requiring additional disclosure, it would be considered a single advertisement under the following circumstances:

- The table or schedule is clearly and conspicuously set forth; and
- Any statement of the triggering credit terms appearing anywhere else in the catalog or advertisement clearly refers to the page or location where the table or schedule begins.

The table or schedule of terms must include all appropriate disclosures for a representative scale of amounts up to the level of the more commonly sold higher-priced property or services offered.

Advertising Open-End Credit

Regulation Z was amended to comply with the Mortgage Disclosure Improvement Act of 2009 (§ 226.16) to address the unique challenges in advertising open-end credit plans secured by the borrower's dwelling. Remember, **open-end** credit refers to loan where credit is extended to the borrower during the term and the creditor may impose a finance charge on the outstanding unpaid balance, such as a home equity line of credit (HELOC). It's critical that ads for these loans not use misleading terms, such as "free money." These loans are also subject to the disclosure provisions previously discussed as well these additional provisions:

Additional Disclosures. If any of the triggering terms are used or the payment terms of the plan are set forth, affirmatively or negatively, in an advertisement, the ad must also clearly and conspicuously state the following:

- Any **loan fee** that is a percentage of the credit limit under the plan and an estimate of any other fees imposed for opening the plan expressed as a single dollar amount or a reasonable range
- Any **periodic rate** used to compute the finance charge expressed as an annual percentage rate
- The **maximum annual percentage rate** that may be imposed in a variable-rate plan

Further, if an advertisement states an initial annual percentage rate that is *not* based on the index and margin used to make later rate adjustments in a variable-rate plan, the ad must also clearly indicate the period of time such initial rate is in effect and a reasonably current APR that would have been in effect using the index and margin.

Balloon Payments. In an ad that states a minimum payment, if it's possible that a balloon payment would result if only that minimum periodic payment is made, that fact must be stated with equal prominence and close proximity.

Promotional Rates and Payment. If a HELOC advertisement states a promotional rate and/or a promotional payment, the ad must disclose—in a clear and conspicuous manner and with equal prominence and in close proximity to each listing of the promotional rate or payment—each of these facts:

- The period of time during which the promotional rate or payment applies
- If a promotional rate, any APR that applies (if a variable rate, the APR must be disclosed within established accuracy standards)
- If a promotional payment, the amounts and time periods of any payments that will apply under the plan (if the payment is based on the application of a variable index and margin, it must be disclosed based on a reasonable current index and margin)

If an ad stating a promotional rate is broadcast on radio or television, in lieu of stating these disclosures, a toll-free telephone number (or one that allows consumers to reverse charges) from which to get additional cost information must be indicated.

√ ***Note:*** These provisions do ***not*** apply to an envelope in which an application or solicitation is mailed, nor to a banner advertisement or pop-up advertisement linked to an application or solicitation provided electronically.

Other General Provisions

Tax Implications. Care must be taken to ensure that an advertisement that states any tax implications—such as whether or not interest is tax-deductible—is not misleading. There are additional requirements imposed on ads distributed in paper form or through the Internet rather than broadcast on radio or television. If the ad states the advertised extension of credit may exceed the fair market value of the dwelling, is must also clearly and conspicuously state that the interest on that portion of the loan is not tax deductible for Federal income tax purposes. Furthermore, the consumer must be advised to consult a tax adviser about the deductibility of interest and charges.

Misrepresentations. Regulation Z prohibits misrepresentations about a loan product being government endorsed, as well as any misleading use of the current lender's name in the advertisement or claims of debt elimination. It also prohibits using the term "counselor" in any advertisement to refer to a for-profit mortgage broker or lender. In a foreign language advertisement, providing information about some trigger terms or required disclosures in a foreign language, while providing information about other trigger terms or required disclosures only in English, is also prohibited.

Clear and Conspicuous Standard. When considering **oral advertisements** for credit secured by a dwelling, including alternative disclosures as provided for by § 226.24(g), a clear and conspicuous disclosure, whether by radio, television, or other medium, means that the required disclosures are given at a speed and volume sufficient for a consumer to hear and comprehend them. For example, information stated very rapidly at a low volume in a radio or television advertisement would not meet the clear and conspicuous standard if consumers cannot hear and comprehend the information required to be disclosed.

Other Prohibited Practices

Regulation Z was amended to comply with the Mortgage Disclosure Improvement Act of 2009 (§ 226.42) to specifically address perceived abuses in the mortgage industry. The following prohibitions apply to any **closed-end mortgage** loan that is subject to TILA and secured by the consumer's **principal dwelling**, regardless of pricing or loan purpose.

Appraisal

Creditors, mortgage brokers, and their affiliates are prohibited from coercing, influencing, or encouraging an appraiser to misstate the value of the dwelling. For example, the law specifically prohibits these practices:

- Implying to an appraiser that current or future retention of the appraiser depends on the amount at which the appraiser values a consumer's principal dwelling
- Excluding an appraiser from consideration for future engagement because the appraiser reports a value of a consumer's principal dwelling that does not meet or exceed a minimum threshold
- Telling an appraiser a minimum reported value of a consumer's principal dwelling that is needed to approve the loan
- Failing to compensate an appraiser because the appraiser does not value a consumer's principal dwelling at or above a certain amount
- Conditioning an appraiser's compensation on loan consummation

In addition, a creditor cannot extend credit if the creditor knows, at or before closing, that improper coercion has occurred by anyone unless the creditor can document that it has acted with reasonable diligence to determine that the appraisal does not materially misstate or misrepresent the dwelling's value. It is not a violation to ask an appraiser to consider additional information about the dwelling or comparable properties or to ask an appraiser to correct factual errors. In addition, the following practices are *not* prohibited:

- Obtaining multiple appraisals of a consumer's principal dwelling, so long as the creditor adheres to a policy of selecting the most reliable appraisal, rather than the appraisal that states the highest value
- Withholding compensation from an appraiser for breach of contract or substandard performance of services as provided by contract

Servicing

Servicing may be defined as receiving any scheduled periodic payments from a borrower according to the terms of any mortgage loan—including amounts for escrow accounts—and making the payments to the owner of the loan or other third parties of principal and interest and such other payments. The following servicing practices would be a violation of Regulation Z:

- Failing to credit a payment as of the date of receipt (unless the delay results in no adverse consequences to the borrower) when the payment complies with the terms of the legal contract between the lender and the borrower. However, if a servicer accepts a payment that does not conform to the written requirements, the servicer shall credit the payment no later than five days after receipt.
- Imposing any late fee or delinquency charge in connection with a payment, when the only delinquency is attributable to late fees or delinquency charges assessed on an earlier payment, and the payment is otherwise a full payment for the applicable period and is paid on its due date or within any applicable grace period. This prohibited practice may be referred to as "pyramiding" late fees.
- Failing to provide, within a reasonable period of time, statements showing the payoff amounts as of a specified date in time.

Real Estate Settlement Procedures Act (RESPA)

The **Real Estate Settlement Procedures Act of 1974** (RESPA) became effective on June 20, 1975. The U. S. Department of Housing and Urban Development (HUD) promulgated **Regulation X**, which implements RESPA. With the passage of the Dodd-Frank Wall Street Reform and Consumer Protection Act of 2010, RESPA will be under the regulatory authority of the new Consumer Financial Protection Bureau. The purposes of RESPA are to help consumers become better shoppers for settlement services and to eliminate unnecessary increases in the costs of certain settlement services due to kickbacks and referral fees.

Settlement Services

Regulation X (24 C.F.R. § 3500.2) defines settlement services as any service provided in connection with a prospective or actual settlement, including, but not limited to, any one or more of the following:

- Origination of a federally related mortgage loan (including, but not limited to, the taking of loan applications, loan processing, and the underwriting and funding of such loans)
- Services by a mortgage broker (including counseling, taking of applications, obtaining verifications and appraisals, and other loan processing and origination services, and communicating with the borrower and lender)
- Any services related to the origination, processing, or funding of a federally related mortgage loan
- Title services, including title searches, title examinations, abstract preparation, insurability determinations, and the issuance of title commitments and title insurance policies
- Services by an attorney
- Preparation of documents, including notarization, delivery, and recordation
- Rendering of credit reports and appraisals
- Inspections, including inspections required by applicable law or any inspections required by the sales contract or mortgage documents prior to transfer of title
- Conducting of settlement by a settlement agent and any related services
- Services involving mortgage insurance
- Services involving hazard, flood, or other casualty insurance or homeowner's warranties
- Services involving mortgage life, disability, or similar insurance designed to pay a mortgage loan upon disability or death of a borrower, but only if such insurance is required by the lender as a condition of the loan
- Services involving real property taxes or any other assessments or charges on the real property
- Services by a real estate agent or real estate broker
- Any other services for which a settlement service provider requires a borrower or seller to pay

Covered Transactions

Regulation X (§ 3500.05) covers loans secured with a mortgage placed on **residential properties** designed for occupancy of from **one to four families**—most conventional loans and government agency loans such as FHA, VA, and USDA—including most purchase loans, assumptions, refinances, property improvement loans, home equity lines of credit, and some construction loans.

The following types of transactions are *not* covered:

- An all-cash sale
- A sale where the individual home seller takes back the mortgage
- A rental property transaction
- Temporary construction loans
- Other business purpose transaction
- Property of 25 acres or more
- Vacant or unimproved property unless a dwelling will be constructed or moved onto the property within two years

RESPA Provisions

The Real Estate Settlement and Procedures Act is a consumer protection law that includes provisions to mandate specific disclosures and prohibit certain practices.

Kickbacks, Fee-Splitting and Unearned Fees

Section 8 of the Real Estate Settlement and Procedures Act (12 U.S.C. 2607):

- Prohibits giving or accepting a fee, kickback, or anything of value in exchange for referrals of settlement service business involving a federally related mortgage loan (allows a thing **of minimal value** used for promotional purposes, such as pens, mementos, coffee cups, hats, etc.)
- Defines prohibited **thing of value** to include, without limitation, monies, things, discounts, salaries, commissions, fees, duplicate payments of a charge, stock, dividends, distributions of partnership profits, franchise royalties, credits representing monies that may be paid at a future date, the opportunity to participate in a money-making program, retained or increased earnings, increased equity in a parent or subsidiary entity, special bank deposits or accounts, special or unusual banking terms, services of all types at special or free rates, sales or rentals at special prices or rates, lease or rental payments based in whole or in part on the amount of business referred, trips and payment of another person's expenses, or reduction in credit against an existing obligation
- Prohibits fee-splitting and receiving unearned fees or a percentage of any charge made or received for services not actually performed
- Prohibits a "required use" of specific settlement service providers, except in cases where a lender refers a borrower to an attorney, credit reporting agency, or real estate appraiser to represent the lender's interest in the transaction
- Does **not** prohibit the payment of fees to attorneys, title companies, or agents for service actually performed, the payment of a bona fide salary or compensation to a person for goods or products actually furnished or services actually performed in the making of a loan, and payments pursuant to cooperative brokerage and referral arrangements or agreements between real estate agents and brokers
- Allows legitimate discounts on services to consumers if a combination of settlement services is offered at a total price lower than the sum of the individual settlement services, as long as:
    - The use of any such combination is optional to the purchaser, and
    - The lower price for the combination is not made up by higher costs elsewhere in the settlement process.
- Subjects violators to criminal and civil penalties, including:
    - Fines up to $10,000
    - Imprisonment up to one year
    - Liability up to three times the amount of the charge paid for the service (civil lawsuit)

Affiliated Business Arrangements (AfBAs)

While kickbacks from referrals are prohibited, RESPA does recognize the legitimacy of affiliated business arrangements involving real estate settlement services for federally related mortgage loans (Regulation X § 3500.15). An affiliated business arrangement is a situation where a person in a position to refer settlement services—or an associate of that person—has either an affiliate relationship with or a direct or beneficial ownership interest of more than **1%** in a provider of settlement services and who then refers business to that provider or in some way influences the selection of that provider. Within the scope of this definition, a "person" could be an individual or a corporation, association, partnership, or trust. The term "associate" refers to someone who has one or more of the following relationships with a person in a position to refer settlement business:

- A spouse, parent, or child of that person
- A corporation or business entity that controls, is controlled by, or is under common control with such person

- An employer, officer, director, partner, franchisor, or franchisee of that person
- Anyone who has an agreement, arrangement, or understanding with that person when the purpose or substantial effect of which is to enable that person to benefit financially from the referrals

How someone with ownership interest receives compensation for settlement services is important under RESPA. Legitimate fees or wages for **services actually rendered** or hours worked are permissible. Additionally it is permissible to accept **bona fide compensation** from the ownership interest or franchise relationship between entities in an affiliate relationship, as long as it is for ordinary business purposes and is not a fee for the referral of settlement service business or an unearned fee. That compensation could include dividends, capital or equity distributions, business loans, advances, and capital or equity contributions.

Seller Required Title Insurance

Section 9 of RESPA (12 U.S.C. 2608) prohibits a seller from requiring the home buyer to use a particular title insurance company, either directly or indirectly, as a condition of sale. Buyers may sue a seller who violates this provision for an amount equal to **three times** all charges made for the title insurance.

Limits on Escrow Accounts

Section 10 of RESPA (12 U.S.C. 2609) sets limits on the amounts a lender may require a borrower to put into an escrow account for purposes of paying taxes, hazard insurance, and other charges related to the property. RESPA does *not* require lenders to impose an escrow account on borrowers; however, certain government loan programs or lenders may require escrow accounts as a condition of the loan, for example, a mortgage loan that includes mortgage insurance MUST have an escrow account. In addition, a loan that meets the TILA definition of a "higher-priced" loan is required to have a lender-imposed escrow account for at least 12 months.

During the course of the loan, RESPA prohibits a lender from charging excessive amounts for the escrow account. Each month, the lender may require a borrower to pay into the escrow account no more than **1/12 of the total of all disbursements payable during the year** (one month), plus an amount necessary to pay for any shortage in the account. In addition, the lender may require a cushion, not to exceed an amount equal to **1/6 of the total disbursements for the year** (two months).

The lender must perform an escrow account analysis once during the year and notify borrowers of any shortage. Any **excess of $50 or more** in the escrow account must be returned to the borrower, assuming that the borrower is not delinquent with payments. In that case, the lender is not required to return any excess escrow.

Prohibition on Certain Fees

Federal law requires that consumers of credit be given specific disclosures. The Real Estate Settlement Procedures Act prohibits lenders and servicers from charging a fee for the preparation of the Truth in Lending Statement (TIL) or other disclosures required by the Truth in Lending Act, or the disclosures and statements required by RESPA, such as the Good Faith Estimate, HUD-1 Settlement Statement, or annual escrow account statements.

Required Disclosures

RESPA requires that borrowers receive disclosures at various times throughout the loan process. Some disclosures spell out the costs associated with the settlement/closing, outline lender servicing and escrow account practices, and describe business relationships between settlement service providers. RESPA mandates different disclosures when the loan application is made, prior to settlement, at settlement, and after settlement.

Disclosures Within 3 Business Days of Completed Application

Application is defined by RESPA (Regulation X § 3500.2) as the submission of a borrower's financial information in anticipation of a credit decision relating to a federally related mortgage loan which includes:

- Borrower's name
- Borrower's monthly income
- Borrower's Social Security number to obtain a credit report
- Property address
- Estimate of value of the property
- Loan amount
- Any other information deemed necessary by the mortgage loan originator

When consumers complete an application—or provide the information sufficient to complete an application—mortgage loan originators must give them certain disclosures. If a borrower does not get these disclosures at the time of application, the MLO must provide them **within three (3) business days** of receiving the completed application.

If the applicant withdraws the application or the lender turns down the loan before the end of the three business-day period, RESPA does **not** require the mortgage loan originator to provide these documents.

HUD's Settlement Costs Booklet. Contains clear and concise consumer information regarding various real estate settlement services including:

- Description and explanation of the nature and purpose of each cost
- Description and explanation of the nature and purpose of escrow accounts
- Explanation of consumer's options to select settlement service providers
- Explanation of unfair practices and unreasonable or unnecessary chargers the borrower should avoid

The Dodd-Frank Act gives the Director of the Consumer Financial Protection Bureau the authority to prepare and revise this booklet every five years (§ 1450). Although required for **purchase transactions only** under RESPA as originally enacted, the scope of this requirement may become broader to include refinances, reverse mortgages, and other loans as provisions of the Act are implemented via regulations.

Good Faith Estimate (GFE) of Settlement Costs. Provides a summary of the borrower's settlement charges. Some of the charges are fixed, and some could change at settlement. While a Good Faith Estimate is not a loan commitment, the charges listed on the GFE must be good for at least 10 business days.

Recall that prior to delivery of the mandated disclosures, the only fee that may be charged to a borrower is the credit report fee. Once the borrower receives the GFE and other mandated disclosures and the borrower indicates an intention to proceed, the mortgage loan originator may collect other loan origination fees.

After the TIL and GFE are...	And borrower has indicated the intent to proceed, other fees may be collected ...
Hand-delivered to the borrower	That day
Emailed to the borrower with the borrower's permission	The next day after a send receipt is returned as evidence that the email was received
Faxed to the borrower	The next day after a signed TIL and GFE are faxed back
Mailed to the borrower	Three (3) business days after the TIL and GFE are mailed

Mortgage Servicing Disclosure Statement. Discloses to the borrower whether the lender intends to service the loan or transfer servicing to another lender. It also provides information about complaint resolution, for example, if the borrower wishes to challenge any late charges or penalties.

Mortgage Servicing Disclosure Statement

NOTICE TO FIRST LIEN MORTGAGE LOAN APPLICANTS: THE RIGHT TO COLLECT YOUR MORTGAGE LOAN PAYMENTS MAY BE TRANSFERRED. FEDERAL LAW GIVES YOU CERTAIN RELATED RIGHTS. IF YOUR LOAN IS MADE, SAVE THIS STATEMENT WITH YOUR LOAN DOCUMENTS, SIGN THE ACKNOWLEDGMENT AT THE END OF THIS STATEMENT ONLY IF YOU UNDERSTAND ITS CONTENTS.

You are applying for a mortgage loan covered by the Real Estate Settlement Procedures Act (RESPA) (12 U.S.C. 2601 et seq.). RESPA gives you certain rights under Federal law. This statement describes whether the servicing for this loan may be transferred to a different loan servicer. "Servicing" refers to collecting your principal, interest, and escrow payments, if any, as well as sending any monthly or annual statements, tracking account balances, and handling other aspects of your loan. You will be given advance notice before a transfer occurs.

Check the appropriate box under "Servicing Transfer Information."

Servicing Transfer Information

☐ We may assign, sell, or transfer the servicing of your loan while the loan is outstanding.

or

☐ We do not service mortgage loans of the type for which you applied. We intend to assign, sell, or transfer the servicing of your mortgage loan before the first payment is due.

or

☐ The loan for which you have applied will be serviced at this financial institution and we do not intend to sell, transfer, or assign the servicing of the loan.

Acknowledgment of Mortgage Loan Applicant

I/we have read this disclosure form, and understand its contents, as evidenced by my/our signature(s) below. I/we understand that this acknowledgment is a required part of the mortgage loan application.

____________________________ Applicant's Signature / Date

____________________________ Co-Applicant's Signature / Date

Mortgage Servicing Disclosure Statement

Disclosures Before Settlement Occurs

RESPA mandates additional disclosures before settlement—or closing—occurs:

Affiliated Business Arrangement (AfBA or ABA) Disclosure. Required whenever a settlement service provider involved in a RESPA covered transaction refers the consumer to a provider with whom the referring party has an ownership or other beneficial interest. The referring party must give the AfBA disclosure to the consumer at or prior to the time of referral. The disclosure must describe the business arrangement that exists between the two providers and give the borrower an estimate of the second provider's charges. Except in cases where a lender refers a borrower to an attorney, credit reporting agency, or real estate appraiser to represent the lender's interest in the transaction, the referring party may not require the consumer to use the particular provider being referred.

HUD-1 Settlement Statement. A standard form that clearly shows all charges imposed on borrowers and sellers in connection with the settlement. RESPA allows the borrower to request to see the HUD-1 Settlement Statement **one (1) business day before the actual settlement.** The settlement agent must then provide the borrowers with a completed HUD-1 Settlement Statement based on information known to the agent at that time.

Disclosures At Settlement

HUD-1 Settlement Statement. Shows the actual settlement costs of the loan transaction. Separate forms may be prepared for the borrower and the seller. Where it is not the practice that the borrower and the seller both attend the settlement, the HUD-1 should be mailed or delivered as soon as practicable after settlement.

Initial Escrow Statement. Itemizes the estimated taxes, insurance premiums, and other charges anticipated to be paid from the escrow account during the first 12 months of the loan. It lists the escrow payment amount and any required cushion. Although the statement is usually given at settlement, the lender has 45 days from settlement to deliver it.

Disclosures After Settlement

RESPA requirements continue even after the loan closes:

Annual Escrow Statement. Must be delivered to borrowers by loan servicers once a year. This statement summarizes all escrow account deposits and payments during the servicer's 12-month computation year. It also notifies the borrower of any shortages or surpluses in the account and advises the borrower about the course of action being taken.

Servicing Transfer Statement. Required if the loan servicer sells or assigns the **servicing rights** to a borrower's loan to another loan servicer. Generally, the loan servicer must notify the borrower **15 days** before the effective date of a servicing transfer. As long the borrower makes a timely payment to the old servicer within 60 days of the servicing transfer, the borrower cannot be penalized. The notice must include the name and address of the new servicer, toll-free telephone numbers, and the date the new servicer will begin accepting payments.

Note that a bona fide transfer of ownership of a loan into the secondary market without a corresponding transfer of servicing rights is **not** covered under this provision of RESPA and, therefore, does not require a servicing transfer statement to the borrower.

Good Faith Estimate (GFE)

RESPA requires mortgage loan originators to provide the borrower, without charge, a Good Faith Estimate (GFE) of the dollar amount of settlement charges no later than three (3) business days of the receipt of a completed application. It can be provided by a lender or a mortgage broker, although RESPA indicates that the lender is ultimately responsible for ascertaining whether the GFE has been provided. If the mortgage broker has provided a GFE, the lender is not required to provide an additional GFE. RESPA requires the use of HUD's three-page, standardized Good Faith Estimate, until such time as the Consumer Financial Protection Bureau replaces it with an integrated form that combines the disclosure requirements on the Truth in Lending Statement with those on the GFE.

Affiliated Business Arrangement Disclosure Statement Format

Notice
To: ______________________ **Property:** ______________________
From: ______________________ **Date:** ______________________
(Entity Making Statement)

This is to give you notice that [referring party] has a business relationship with [settlement services provider(s)]. [Describe the nature of the relationship between the referring party and the provider(s), including percentage of ownership interest, if applicable.] Because of this relationship, this referral may provide [referring party] a financial or other benefit.

[A.]Set forth below is the estimated charge or range of charges for the settlement services listed. You are NOT required to use the listed provider(s) as a condition for [settlement of your loan on] [or] [purchase, sale, or refinance of] the subject property. THERE ARE FREQUENTLY OTHER SETTLEMENT SERVICE PROVIDERS AVAILABLE WITH SIMILAR SERVICES. YOU ARE FREE TO SHOP AROUND TO DETERMINE THAT YOU ARE RECEIVING THE BEST SERVICES AND THE BEST RATE FOR THESE SERVICES.

[provider and settlement service]	**[charge or range of charges]**
______________________	______________________
______________________	______________________

[B.]Set forth below is the estimated charge or range of charges for the settlement services of an attorney, credit reporting agency, or real estate appraiser that we, as your lender, will require you to use, as a condition of your loan on this property, to represent our interests in the transaction.

[provider and settlement service]	**[charge or range of charges]**
______________________	______________________
______________________	______________________

ACKNOWLEDGEMENT

I/we have read this disclosure form, and understand that [referring party] is referring me/us to purchase the above-described settlement service(s) and may receive a financial or other benefit as the result of this referral.

______________________ **Signature**

Affiliated Business Disclosusre

OMB Approval No. 2502-0265

U.S. DEPARTMENT OF HOUSING AND URBAN DEVELOPMENT

Good Faith Estimate (GFE)

Name of Originator	Borrower
Originator Address	Property Address
Originator Phone Number	
Originator Email	Date of GFE

Purpose

This GFE gives you an estimate of your settlement charges and loan terms if you are approved for this loan. For more information, see HUD's *Special Information Booklet* on settlement charges, your *Truth-in-Lending Disclosures*, and other consumer information at www.hud.gov/respa. If you decide you would like to proceed with this loan, contact us.

Shopping for your loan

Only you can shop for the best loan for you. Compare this GFE with other loan offers, so you can find the best loan. Use the shopping chart on page 3 to compare all the offers you receive.

Important dates

1. The interest rate for this GFE is available through ☐. After this time, the interest rate, some of your loan Origination Charges, and the monthly payment shown below can change until you lock your interest rate.
2. This estimate for all other settlement charges is available through ☐.
3. After you lock your interest rate, you must go to settlement within ☐ days (your rate lock period) to receive the locked interest rate.
4. You must lock the interest rate at least ☐ days before settlement.

Summary of your loan

Your initial loan amount is	$
Your loan term is	years
Your initial interest rate is	%
Your initial monthly amount owed for principal, interest, and any mortgage insurance is	$ per month
Can your interest rate rise?	☐ No ☐ Yes, it can rise to a maximum of %. The first change will be in .
Even if you make payments on time, can your loan balance rise?	☐ No ☐ Yes, it can rise to a maximum of $
Even if you make payments on time, can your monthly amount owed for principal, interest, and any mortgage insurance rise?	☐ No ☐ Yes, the first increase can be in and the monthly amount owed can rise to $. The maximum it can ever rise to is $.
Does your loan have a prepayment penalty?	☐ No ☐ Yes, your maximum prepayment penalty is $.
Does your loan have a balloon payment?	☐ No ☐ Yes, you have a balloon payment of $ due in years.

Escrow account information

Some lenders require an escrow account to hold funds for paying property taxes or other property-related charges in addition to your monthly amount owed of $☐.
Do we require you to have an escrow account for your loan?
☐ No, you do not have an escrow account. You must pay these charges directly when due.
☐ Yes, you have an escrow account. It may or may not cover all of these charges. Ask us.

Summary of your settlement charges

A	Your Adjusted Origination Charges *(See page 2.)*	$
B	Your Charges for All Other Settlement Services *(See page 2.)*	$
A + B	Total Estimated Settlement Charges	$

Good Faith Estimate (HUD-GFE) 1

2010 GFE Sample

Understanding your estimated settlement charges

Your Adjusted Origination Charges	
1. Our origination charge This charge is for getting this loan for you.	
2. Your credit or charge (points) for the specific interest rate chosen ☐ The credit or charge for the interest rate of [ ] % is included in "Our origination charge." (See item 1 above.) ☐ You receive a credit of $ [ ] for this interest rate of [ ] %. This credit **reduces** your settlement charges. ☐ You pay a charge of $ [ ] for this interest rate of [ ] %. This charge (points) **increases** your total settlement charges. The tradeoff table on page 3 shows that you can change your total settlement charges by choosing a different interest rate for this loan.	
A Your Adjusted Origination Charges	$

Some of these charges can change at settlement. See the top of page 3 for more information.

Your Charges for All Other Settlement Services	
3. Required services that we select These charges are for services we require to complete your settlement. We will choose the providers of these services. *Service* *Charge*	
4. Title services and lender's title insurance This charge includes the services of a title or settlement agent, for example, and title insurance to protect the lender, if required.	
5. Owner's title insurance You may purchase an owner's title insurance policy to protect your interest in the property.	
6. Required services that you can shop for These charges are for other services that are required to complete your settlement. We can identify providers of these services or you can shop for them yourself. Our estimates for providing these services are below. *Service* *Charge*	
7. Government recording charges These charges are for state and local fees to record your loan and title documents.	
8. Transfer taxes These charges are for state and local fees on mortgages and home sales.	
9. Initial deposit for your escrow account This charge is held in an escrow account to pay future recurring charges on your property and includes ☐ all property taxes, ☐ all insurance, and ☐ other [ ].	
10. Daily interest charges This charge is for the daily interest on your loan from the day of your settlement until the first day of the next month or the first day of your normal mortgage payment cycle. This amount is $[ ] per day for [ ] days (if your settlement is [ ]).	
11. Homeowner's insurance This charge is for the insurance you must buy for the property to protect from a loss, such as fire. *Policy* *Charge*	
B Your Charges for All Other Settlement Services	$
A + B Total Estimated Settlement Charges	$

Good Faith Estimate (HUD-GFE) 2

2010 GFE Sample

Instructions

Understanding which charges can change at settlement

This GFE estimates your settlement charges. At your settlement, you will receive a HUD-1, a form that lists your actual costs. Compare the charges on the HUD-1 with the charges on this GFE. Charges can change if you select your own provider and do not use the companies we identify. (See below for details.)

These charges **cannot increase** at settlement:	The total of these charges **can increase up to 10%** at settlement:	These charges **can change** at settlement:
▪ Our origination charge ▪ Your credit or charge (points) for the specific interest rate chosen *(after you lock in your interest rate)* ▪ Your adjusted origination charges *(after you lock in your interest rate)* ▪ Transfer taxes	▪ Required services that we select ▪ Title services and lender's title insurance *(if we select them or you use companies we identify)* ▪ Owner's title insurance *(if you use companies we identify)* ▪ Required services that you can shop for *(if you use companies we identify)* ▪ Government recording charges	▪ Required services that you can shop for *(if you do not use companies we identify)* ▪ Title services and lender's title insurance *(if you do not use companies we identify)* ▪ Owner's title insurance *(if you do not use companies we identify)* ▪ Initial deposit for your escrow account ▪ Daily interest charges ▪ Homeowner's insurance

Using the tradeoff table

In this GFE, we offered you this loan with a particular interest rate and estimated settlement charges. However:

- If you want to choose this same loan with **lower settlement charges,** then you will have a **higher interest rate.**
- If you want to choose this same loan with a **lower interest rate,** then you will have **higher settlement charges.**

If you would like to choose an available option, you must ask us for a new GFE.

Loan originators have the option to complete this table. Please ask for additional information if the table is not completed.

	The loan in this GFE	The same loan with lower settlement charges	The same loan with a lower interest rate
Your initial loan amount	$	$	$
Your initial interest rate[1]	%	%	%
Your initial monthly amount owed	$	$	$
Change in the monthly amount owed from this GFE	No change	You will pay $ **more** every month	You will pay $ **less** every month
Change in the amount you will pay at settlement with this interest rate	No change	Your settlement charges will be **reduced** by $	Your settlement charges will **increase** by $
How much your total estimated settlement charges will be	$	$	$

[1] *For an adjustable rate loan, the comparisons above are for the initial interest rate before adjustments are made.*

Using the shopping chart

Use this chart to compare GFEs from different loan originators. Fill in the information by using a different column for each GFE you receive. By comparing loan offers, you can shop for the best loan.

	This loan	Loan 2	Loan 3	Loan 4
Loan originator name				
Initial loan amount				
Loan term				
Initial interest rate				
Initial monthly amount owed				
Rate lock period				
Can interest rate rise?				
Can loan balance rise?				
Can monthly amount owed rise?				
Prepayment penalty?				
Balloon payment?				
Total Estimated Settlement Charges				

If your loan is sold in the future

Some lenders may sell your loan after settlement. Any fees lenders receive in the future cannot change the loan you receive or the charges you paid at settlement.

Good Faith Estimate (HUD-GFE) 3

2010 GFE Sample

GFE Page 1

Page 1 of the GFE explains the purpose of the disclosure and summarizes the critical data a borrower needs in order to "shop" for settlement services and determine the best loan. The name of the borrower and of the mortgage loan originator's entity must go in the top of page 1, and the name of the individual MLO may also be added. The remaining data is organized into sections:

Important Dates

This indicates the date through which the specific interest rate for the loan is and informs the borrower that changes in the rate can result in changes to origination charges and the indicated monthly payment. While there are no restrictions on the amount of time an interest rate must remain available, the estimate for all other settlement charges—as shown in Line 2 of this section—must be available for **at least ten (10) business days**. Since rates can change daily, by locking the rate a certain number of days prior to settlement, the mortgage loan originator can lessen the possibility of having to redisclose. The Regulation X definition of a "business day" includes "any day on which the business entity is open to the public for carrying on substantially all of the entity's business functions" (§ 3500.2 (b)).

Loan Summary

This gives a concise summary of terms of the loan, including the amount, term, initial interest rate, initial monthly payment of principal and interest (as well as any mortgage insurance), whether the rate can rise under certain circumstances, and if the loan has a prepayment penalty or requires a balloon payment. Note that "initial" loan amount refers to the amount of the principal loan balance on the date of closing. "Initial" interest rate is the rate applicable on the date of closing.

Escrow Account Information

This indicates whether the lender requires an escrow account for taxes or other charges such as hazard insurance.

Summary of Settlement Charges

This shows the bottom line that most consumers are interested in—the total estimated settlement charges. For a borrower, this number is generally the amount of money he needs to bring to settlement in addition to funds for the down payment.

GFE Page 2

The settlement charges for the loan are documented on page 2. The amounts shown in Blocks 1, 2, and 8 cannot increase at settlement. There is a 10% tolerance applied to the sum of the prices of each service listed in Blocks 3, 4, 5, 6, and 7, where the mortgage loan originator requires the use of a particular provider or the borrower uses a provider selected or identified by the mortgage loan originator. Any services in Blocks 4, 5, or 6 for which the borrower selects a provider other than one identified by the mortgage loan originator are not subject to any tolerance and, at settlement, would not be included in the sum of the charges on which the 10% tolerance is based. Where a mortgage loan originator permits a borrower to shop for third party settlement services, the mortgage loan originator must provide the borrower with a written list of settlement services providers at the time of the GFE, on a separate sheet of paper.

Block 1 Origination Charges

Here the mortgage loan originator must specify a lump-sum origination charge. It must include any amounts received for origination services, including administrative and processing services, performed by or on behalf of the mortgage loan originator. No fees may be itemized separately. If there is a lender and a mortgage broker in the same transaction, the total charges for both must be contained in Block 1. This does not include any charge for the specific interest rate chosen (points). This fee cannot change unless there is a changed circumstance.

Block 2 Your Credit or Charge (Points) for the Specific Interest Rate Chosen

This block states the charge (points) or credit adjustment as applied for the specific interest rate chosen, if applicable. For transactions involving mortgage brokers, the mortgage broker must indicate through check boxes whether there is a credit to the borrower for the interest rate chosen on the loan, the interest rate, and the amount of the credit, or whether there is an additional charge (points) to the borrower for the interest rate chosen on the loan, the interest rate, and the amount of that charge. Only one of the boxes may be checked; a credit and charge cannot occur together in the same transaction.

For a mortgage broker, the credit or charge for the specific interest rate chosen is the net payment to the mortgage broker from the lender. This is the sum of all payments to the mortgage broker from the lender, including payments based on the loan amount, a flat rate, or any other computation, and in a table funded transaction, the loan amount less the price paid for the loan by the lender. When the net payment to the mortgage broker from the lender is positive, there is a credit to the borrower and it is entered as a negative amount in Block 2 of the GFE. When the net payment to the mortgage broker from the lender is negative, there is a charge to the borrower and it is entered as a positive amount in Block 2 of the GFE. If there is no net payment (i.e., the credit or charge for the specific interest rate chosen is zero), the mortgage broker must insert "0" in Block 2 and may check either the box indicating there is a credit of "0" or the box indicating there is a charge of "0."

For transactions without a mortgage broker, the lender may choose not to separately disclose in this block any credit or charge for the interest rate chosen on the loan; however, if this block does not include any positive or negative figure, the lender must check the first box, insert the interest rate, and must also insert "0" in Block 2.

The amount stated in Block 2 is subject to **zero tolerance** while the interest rate is locked, i.e., any credit for the interest rate chosen cannot decrease in absolute value terms and any charge for the interest rate chosen cannot increase.

√ **Note:** An increase in the credit is allowed since this increase is a reduction in cost to the borrower. A decrease in the credit is not allowed since it is an increase in cost to the borrower.

Line A Your Adjusted Origination Charges

The mortgage loan originator must add the numbers in Blocks 1 and 2 and enter this subtotal at highlighted Line A. The subtotal at Line A is a negative number if there is a credit in Block 2 that exceeds the charge in Block 1. The amount stated in Line A is subject to zero tolerance while the interest rate is locked. In the case of "no cost" loans, where "no cost" refers only to the mortgage loan originator's fees, Line A must show a zero charge as the adjusted origination charge. In the case of "no cost" loans where "no cost" encompasses third party fees as well as the upfront payment to the mortgage loan originator, all of the third party fees listed in Block 3 through Block 11 to be paid for by the mortgage loan originator (or borrower, if any) must be itemized and listed on the GFE. The credit for the interest rate chosen must be large enough that the total for Line A results in a negative number to cover the third party fees.

Block 3 Required Services that We Select

The mortgage loan originator must identify each third party settlement service required and selected by the mortgage loan originator (excluding title services), along with the estimated price to be paid to the provider of each service. Examples of such third party settlement services might include provision of credit reports, appraisals, flood checks, tax services, and any upfront mortgage insurance premium. The mortgage loan originator must identify the specific required services and provide an estimate of the price of each service. Mortgage loan originators are also required to add the individual charges disclosed in this block and place that total in the column of this block. The charge shown in this block is subject to an overall **10% tolerance**.

Block 4 Title Services and Lender's Title Insurance

The mortgage loan originator must state the estimated total charge for third party settlement service providers for all closing services, regardless of whether the providers are selected or paid for by the borrower, seller, or mortgage loan originator. The MLO must also include any lender's title insurance premiums, when required, regardless of whether the provider is selected or paid for by the borrower, seller, or MLO. All fees for title searches, examinations, and endorsements, for example, would be included in this total. The charge shown in this block is subject to an overall **10% tolerance**.

Block 5 Owner's Title Insurance

For all purchase transactions the mortgage loan originator must provide an estimate of the charge for the owner's title insurance and related endorsements, regardless of whether the providers are selected or paid for by the borrower, seller, or mortgage loan originator. For non-purchase transactions, the MLO may enter "NA" or "Not Applicable" in this Block. The charge shown in this block is subject to an overall **10% tolerance**.

Block 6 Required Services that You Can Shop For

The mortgage loan originator must identify each third party settlement service required by the mortgage loan originator where the borrower is permitted to shop for and select the settlement service provider (excluding title services), along with the estimated charge to be paid to the provider of each service. The MLO must identify the specific required services (e.g., survey, pest inspection) and provide an estimate of the charge of each service. The MLO must also add the individual charges disclosed in this block and place the total in the column of this block. The charge shown in this block is subject to an overall **10% tolerance**.

Block 7 Government Recording Charges

The mortgage loan originator must estimate the state and local government fees for recording the loan and title documents that can be expected to be charged at settlement. Since the charge shown in this block is subject to an overall **10% tolerance**, it's important to have a good idea of how many pages the mortgage will be as that affects the recording charges. Remember that an ARM or a condominium loan, for example, usually has extra pages.

Block 8 Transfer Taxes

The mortgage loan originator must estimate the sum of all state and local government fees on mortgages and home sales that can be expected to be charged at settlement, based upon the proposed loan amount or sales price and on the property address. A **zero tolerance** applies to the sum of these estimated fees.

Block 9 Initial Deposit for Your Escrow Account

The mortgage loan originator must estimate the amount that it will require the borrower to place into a reserve or escrow account at settlement to be applied to recurring charges for property taxes, homeowner's and other similar insurance, mortgage insurance, and other periodic charges. The mortgage loan originator must indicate through check boxes if the reserve or escrow account will cover future payments for all tax, all hazard insurance, and other obligations that the mortgage loan originator requires to be paid as they fall due. If the reserve or escrow account includes some, but not all, property taxes or hazard insurance, or if it includes mortgage insurance, the mortgage loan originator should check "other" and then list the items included.

Block 10 Daily Interest Charges

The mortgage loan originator must estimate the total amount that will be due at settlement for the daily interest on the loan from the date of settlement until the first day of the first period covered by scheduled mortgage payments. The mortgage loan originator must also indicate how this total amount is calculated by providing the amount of the interest charges per day and the number of days used in the calculation, based on a stated projected closing date.

Block 11 Homeowner's Insurance

The mortgage loan originator must estimate the total amount of the premiums for any hazard insurance policy and other similar insurance, such as fire or flood insurance that must be purchased at or before settlement to meet the mortgage loan originator's requirements. The mortgage loan originator must also separately indicate the nature of each type of insurance required along with the charges. To the extent a mortgage loan originator requires that such insurance be part of an escrow account, the amount of the initial escrow deposit must be included in Block 9.

Line B Your Charges for All Other Settlement Services

The mortgage loan originator must add the numbers in Blocks 3 through 11 and enter this subtotal in the column at highlighted Line B.

Line A+B Total Estimated Settlement Charges

The mortgage loan originator must add the subtotals in the right-hand column at highlighted Lines A and B and enter this total in the column at highlighted Line A+B.

"Average Charges" Permitted

A settlement service provider that obtains a service from a third party on behalf of a borrower or seller is allowed to disclose an "average charge" on the Good Faith Estimate. Typically, these permitted third party services include, but are not limited to, appraisals, credit reports, flood certificates, tax services, and recording documents. Settlement service providers determine classifications of transactions to determine the average cost, based on the period of time (between 30 days and six months), the type of loan, and the geographic area. Average charge calculations are not permitted for services where the cost is based on the price of the loan or property value, for example, transfer taxes, interest charges, escrow reserves, and insurances.

The total amount charged to a specific borrower cannot exceed the charges for a specific class of transaction, and the same average charge must be used for all loans within that classification. A provider must retain all documentation used to calculate the average charge for three years after a settlement for which the average charge was used.

When the use of average charges is prohibited by state law, HUD's RESPA rule would not preempt it.

GFE Page 3

The last page of the GFE summarizes the categories of charges, grouping them according to whether or not they can increase at settlement and, if so, to what degree. This also introduces the borrower to the HUD-1 Settlement Statement and makes the connection between that and the amounts that appear on the GFE. Page 3 also provides consumer tools for comparison, as well as a notice to the borrower that any fees related to selling the loan will not affect the loan or charges at settlement.

Tradeoff Table

The tradeoff table allows borrowers to see the relationship between their total estimated settlement charges and the interest rate and resulting monthly payment (which includes the payment of principal and interest as well as escrows for property taxes and insurance, mortgage insurance and any other items that may be included). The mortgage loan originator must complete the left hand column using the loan amount, interest rate, monthly payment figure, and the total estimated settlement charges from page 1 of the GFE. Then, the MLO may choose to provide the borrower with the same information for two available alternative loans for which the borrower would be eligible, one with a higher interest rate and one with a lower interest rate. The alternative loans must use the same loan amount and be otherwise identical to the loan in the GFE, for example, the identical number of payment periods; the same margin, index, and adjustment schedule if the loans are adjustable rate mortgages; and the same requirements for prepayment penalty and balloon paymentIf the MLO fills in the tradeoff table, he or she must show the borrower the loan amount, alternative interest rate, alternative monthly payment, the change in the monthly payment from the loan in this GFE to the alternative loan, the change in the total settlement charges from the loan in this GFE to the alternative loan, and the total settlement charges for the alternative loan. If these options are available, an applicant may request a new GFE, which the MLO must provide.

Shopping Cart

This chart is a shopping tool to be provided by the mortgage loan originator for the **borrower** to complete, in order to compare GFEs.

Provisions Related to the GFE

Section 3500.7 of Regulation X identifies specific provisions related to the terms expressed in a Good Faith Estimate.

Availability of Terms

The estimate of the charges and terms for all settlement services must be available for at least **10 business days** (recall that the Regulation X definition of a "business day" includes "any day on which the business entity is open to the public for carrying on substantially all of the entity's business functions" (§ 3500.2 (b)) from when the GFE is provided, but it may remain available longer, if the mortgage loan originator extends the period of availability. This 10-business day provision, however, does **not** apply to the interest rate, charges and terms dependent upon the interest rate—which includes the charge or credit for the interest rate chosen—the adjusted origination charges, and per diem interest. Because of this, borrowers and lenders frequently agree to a **rate lock** for a pre-determined period of time.

Tolerances of Amounts in the GFE

The actual charges at settlement **may not exceed** the amounts included on the GFE for these charges:

- The origination charge, which may be for any service involved in the creation of a mortgage loan, including but not limited to the taking of the loan application, loan processing, and the underwriting and funding of loan, and the processing and administrative services required to perform these functions
- The credit or charge for the interest rate chosen or the adjusted origination charge while the borrower's interest rate is locked
- Transfer taxes

Additionally, the sum of these charges at settlement for the following services **may not be greater than 10% above** the sum of the amounts included on the GFE:

- Lender-required settlement services, where the lender selects the third party settlement service provider
- Lender-required services, title services and required title insurance, and owner's title insurance, when the borrower uses a settlement service provider identified by the mortgage loan originator
- Government recording charges

The amounts charged for all other settlement services included on the GFE may change at settlement.

Curing Tolerance Violations

If any charges at settlement exceed the charges listed on the GFE by more than the permitted tolerances, the only way the mortgage loan originator can cure the tolerance violation is by reimbursing the borrower the amount by which the tolerance was exceeded, **at settlement or within thirty (30) calendar days** after settlement.

Binding GFE

The mortgage loan originator is bound, within the tolerances indicated above, to the settlement charges and terms listed on the GFE provided to the borrower, unless a new GFE is provided prior to settlement. When it is necessary to provide a revised GFE, MLOs must do so within **three (3) business days** of receiving information sufficient to establish changed circumstances. Also, mortgage loan originators must document the reason for the revised GFE and then retain that documentation for no less than **three (3) years** after settlement.

Reasons for providing a revised a GFE to a borrower include:

- Changed circumstances that **increase settlement costs** to the point of exceeding the tolerances
- Changed circumstances affecting the borrower's **eligibility for the specific loan terms** identified in the GFE
- **Borrower-requested changes** to the mortgage loan identified in the GFE that change the settlement charges or the terms of the loan
- Changes to the charge or credit for the interest rate chosen, the adjusted origination charges, per diem interest, and loan terms related to the interest rate if the interest rate has **not been locked** by the borrower or if a locked interest rate has **expired**

Note that for **new home purchases** where settlement is anticipated to occur more than 60 calendar days from the time a GFE is provided, the mortgage loan originator may provide the GFE to the borrower with a clear and conspicuous disclosure stating that at any time up until 60 calendar days prior to closing, the MLO may issue a revised GFE. If no such separate disclosure is provided, the MLO cannot issue a revised GFE unless under the circumstances indicated above.

Changed Circumstances

Regulation X (§ 3500.7 (f)(i)) defines "changed circumstances" as:

- Acts of God, war, disaster, or other emergency.
- Information particular to the borrower or transaction that was relied on in providing the GFE—such as credit quality of the borrower, the amount of the loan, value of the property, etc.—that changes or is found to be inaccurate after the GFE has been provided.
- New information particular to the borrower or transaction that was not relied on in providing the GFE.
- Other circumstances that are particular to the borrower or transaction—such as boundary disputes, the need for flood insurance, or environmental problems.

The mortgage loan originator is presumed to have relied on the borrower's name, the borrower's monthly income, the property address, an estimate of the value of the property, the mortgage loan amount sought, and any information contained in any credit report obtained by the mortgage loan originator before providing the GFE. None of this information collected by the MLO prior to issuing the GFE may later become the basis for a changed circumstance requiring a revised GFE, unless the MLO can demonstrate that:

- There was a change in the particular information or that it was inaccurate.
- The mortgage loan originator did not rely on that particular information in issuing the GFE.

Also, market fluctuations by themselves are *not* considered to be changed circumstances.

Expiration of the Original GFE

If a borrower does not express an intent to continue with an application **within ten (10) business days** after the Good Faith Estimate is provided, or such longer time specified by the mortgage loan originator, the MLO is no longer bound by the GFE.

HUD-1 Settlement Statement

refi

The **HUD-1 Settlement Statement** used for RESPA compliance (Regulation X § 3500.8) must be completed by the person conducting the closing (settlement agent) and must clearly itemize all charges imposed upon the borrower and the seller by the mortgage loan originator, all sales commissions—whether to be paid at settlement or outside of settlement—and any other charges which either the borrower or the seller will pay at settlement. For each separately identified settlement service in connection with the transaction, the name of the person ultimately receiving the payment must be shown together with the total amount paid to such person.

The HUD-1 is used for transactions with a borrower and seller. A HUD-1 must be prepared for both the borrower and for the seller, although it is permissible for the borrower's HUD-1 to show only his information and the seller's to show only his. For transactions with a borrower and *no seller*—for example, refinancing and subordinate lien loans—the HUD-1 may be completed by using only the borrower's side of the settlement statement, or the **HUD-1A** may be used.

The HUD-1 Settlement Statement is **not** required for open-end home equity loans subject to the Truth in Lending Act and Regulation Z. However, the HUD-1 form may be used for loans not subject to RESPA without subjecting the transaction to the provisions of RESPA.

The lender must retain each completed HUD-1 or HUD-1A and related documents for **five years** after settlement, unless the lender disposes of its interest in the mortgage and does not service the mortgage. In that case, the lender shall provide its copy of the HUD-1 or HUD-1A to the owner or servicer of the mortgage as a part of the transfer of the loan file. Such owner or servicer shall retain the HUD-1 or HUD-1A for the remainder of the five-year period.

Compatibility with the GFE

In order to promote comparability between the charges on the Good Faith Estimate and the charges on the HUD-1, if a seller pays for a charge that was included on the GFE, the charge should be:

- Listed in the borrower's column on page 2 of the HUD-1.
- Offset by listing a credit in that amount to the borrower on lines 204-209 on page 1 of the HUD-1, and by a charge to the seller in lines 506-509 on page 1 of the HUD-1.

If a mortgage loan originator (other than for no-cost loans), real estate agent, other settlement service provider, or other person pays for a charge that was included on the GFE, the charge should be listed in the borrower's column on page 2 of the HUD-1, with an offsetting credit reported on page 1 of the HUD-1, identifying the party paying the charge.

Charges Paid Outside of Closing (P.O.C.)

Charges paid outside of settlement by the borrower, seller, mortgage loan originator, real estate agent, or any other person, must be included on the HUD-1 but marked "P.O.C." for "Paid Outside of Closing" (settlement) and must not be included in computing totals. However, indirect payments from a lender to a mortgage broker may **not** be disclosed as P.O.C., and must be included as a credit on Line 802. P.O.C. items must not be placed in the Borrower or Seller columns, but rather on the appropriate line outside the columns. The settlement agent must indicate whether P.O.C. items are paid by the borrower, seller, or some other party by marking the items paid by whoever made the payment as "P.O.C." with the party making the payment identified in parentheses, such as "P.O.C. (borrower)" or "P.O.C. (seller)".

In the case of "no cost" loans where "no cost" encompasses third party fees as well as the upfront payment to the mortgage loan originator, the third party services covered by the "no cost" provisions must be itemized and listed in the borrower's column on the HUD-1/1A with the charge for the third party service. These itemized charges must be offset with a negative adjusted origination charge on Line 803 and recorded in the columns.

HUD-1 Page 1

Page 1 contains identification such as the borrower's name and address, the address or other location information on the property, the lender's identifying loan number, the settlement date, the name and address of the lender. This page also provides a notice related to charges paid outside of closing (P.O.C.).

Section J Summary of Borrower's Transaction. Indicates the details of the borrower's transaction, including the gross amount due from the borrower, adjustments for items paid by the seller in advance, amounts paid by or on behalf of the borrower, adjustments for items unpaid by the seller, and the cash at settlement paid by—or in some cases, to—the borrower.

- Lines 101 and 102—Contract sales price of the property being sold and the sale price of any items of tangible personal property.

OMB Approval No. 2502-0265

A. Settlement Statement (HUD-1)

B. Type of Loan

1. ☐ FHA 2. ☐ RHS 3. ☐ Conv. Unins. 4. ☐ VA 5. ☐ Conv. Ins.	6. File Number:	7. Loan Number:	8. Mortgage Insurance Case Number:

C. Note: This form is furnished to give you a statement of actual settlement costs. Amounts paid to and by the settlement agent are shown. Items marked "(p.o.c.)" were paid outside the closing; they are shown here for informational purposes and are not included in the totals.

D. Name & Address of Borrower:	E. Name & Address of Seller:	F. Name & Address of Lender:
G. Property Location:	H. Settlement Agent:	I. Settlement Date:
	Place of Settlement:	

J. Summary of Borrower's Transaction		K. Summary of Seller's Transaction	
100. Gross Amount Due from Borrower		**400. Gross Amount Due to Seller**	
101. Contract sales price		401. Contract sales price	
102. Personal property		402. Personal property	
103. Settlement charges to borrower (line 1400)		403.	
104.		404.	
105.		405.	
Adjustment for items paid by seller in advance		**Adjustments for items paid by seller in advance**	
106. City/town taxes to		406. City/town taxes to	
107. County taxes to		407. County taxes to	
108. Assessments to		408. Assessments to	
109.		409.	
110.		410.	
111.		411.	
112.		412.	
120. Gross Amount Due from Borrower		**420. Gross Amount Due to Seller**	
200. Amounts Paid by or in Behalf of Borrower		**500. Reductions In Amount Due to Seller**	
201. Deposit or earnest money		501. Excess deposit (see instructions)	
202. Principal amount of new loan(s)		502. Settlement charges to seller (line 1400)	
203. Existing loan(s) taken subject to		503. Existing loan(s) taken subject to	
204.		504. Payoff of first mortgage loan	
205.		505. Payoff of second mortgage loan	
206.		506.	
207.		507.	
208.		508.	
209.		509.	
Adjustments for items unpaid by seller		**Adjustments for items unpaid by seller**	
210. City/town taxes to		510. City/town taxes to	
211. County taxes to		511. County taxes to	
212. Assessments to		512. Assessments to	
213.		513.	
214.		514.	
215.		515.	
216.		516.	
217.		517.	
218.		518.	
219.		519.	
220. Total Paid by/for Borrower		**520. Total Reduction Amount Due Seller**	
300. Cash at Settlement from/to Borrower		**600. Cash at Settlement to/from Seller**	
301. Gross amount due from borrower (line 120)		601. Gross amount due to seller (line 420)	
302. Less amounts paid by/for borrower (line 220)	( )	602. Less reductions in amount due seller (line 520)	( )
303. Cash ☐ From ☐ To Borrower		**603. Cash ☐ To ☐ From Seller**	

The Public Reporting Burden for this collection of information is estimated at 35 minutes per response for collecting, reviewing, and reporting the data. This agency may not collect this information, and you are not required to complete this form, unless it displays a currently valid OMB control number. No confidentiality is assured; this disclosure is mandatory. This is designed to provide the parties to a RESPA covered transaction with information during the settlement process.

Previous editions are obsolete | Page 1 of 3 | HUD-1

2010 HUD1 Sample

L. Settlement Charges			Paid From Borrower's Funds at Settlement	Paid From Seller's Funds at Settlement
700. Total Real Estate Broker Fees				
Division of commission (line 700) as follows:				
701. $	to			
702. $	to			
703. Commission paid at settlement				
704.				
800. Items Payable in Connection with Loan				
801. Our origination charge	$	(from GFE #1)		
802. Your credit or charge (points) for the specific interest rate chosen	$	(from GFE #2)		
803. Your adjusted origination charges		(from GFE A)		
804. Appraisal fee to		(from GFE #3)		
805. Credit report to		(from GFE #3)		
806. Tax service to		(from GFE #3)		
807. Flood certification		(from GFE #3)		
808.				
900. Items Required by Lender to Be Paid in Advance				
901. Daily interest charges from to @ $ /day		(from GFE #10)		
902. Mortgage insurance premium for months to		(from GFE #3)		
903. Homeowner's insurance for years to		(from GFE #11)		
904.				
1000. Reserves Deposited with Lender				
1001. Initial deposit for your escrow account		(from GFE #9)		
1002. Homeowner's insurance months @ $ per month	$			
1003. Mortgage insurance months @ $ per month	$			
1004. Property taxes months @ $ per month	$			
1005. months @ $ per month	$			
1006. months @ $ per month	$			
1007. Aggregate Adjustment	-$			
1100. Title Charges				
1101. Title services and lender's title insurance		(from GFE #4)		
1102. Settlement or closing fee	$			
1103. Owner's title insurance		(from GFE #5)		
1104. Lender's title insurance	$			
1105. Lender's title policy limit $				
1106. Owner's title policy limit $				
1107. Agent's portion of the total title insurance premium	$			
1108. Underwriter's portion of the total title insurance premium	$			
1200. Government Recording and Transfer Charges				
1201. Government recording charges		(from GFE #7)		
1202. Deed $ Mortgage $ Releases	$			
1203. Transfer taxes		(from GFE #8)		
1204. City/County tax/stamps Deed $ Mortgage $				
1205. State tax/stamps Deed $ Mortgage $				
1206.				
1300. Additional Settlement Charges				
1301. Required services that you can shop for		(from GFE #6)		
1302.	$			
1303.	$			
1304.				
1305.				
1400. Total Settlement Charges (enter on lines 103, Section J and 502, Section K)				

Previous editions are obsolete Page 2 of 3 HUD-1

2010 HUD1 Sample

Comparison of Good Faith Estimate (GFE) and HUD-1 Charges		Good Faith Estimate	HUD-1
Charges That Cannot Increase	**HUD-1 Line Number**		
Our origination charge	# 801		
Your credit or charge (points) for the specific interest rate chosen	# 802		
Your adjusted origination charges	# 803		
Transfer taxes	#1203		

Charges That in Total Cannot Increase More Than 10%		Good Faith Estimate	HUD-1
Government recording charges	# 1201		
	#		
	#		
	#		
	#		
	#		
	#		
	#		
Total			
Increase between GFE and HUD-1 Charges		$ or	%

Charges That Can Change		Good Faith Estimate	HUD-1
Initial deposit for your escrow account	#1001		
Daily interest charges	# 901 $ /day		
Homeowner's insurance	# 903		
	#		
	#		
	#		

Loan Terms

Your initial loan amount is	$
Your loan term is	years
Your initial interest rate is	%
Your initial monthly amount owed for principal, interest, and and any mortgage insurance is	$ includes ☐ Principal ☐ Interest ☐ Mortgage Insurance
Can your interest rate rise?	☐ No. ☐ Yes, it can rise to a maximum of %. The first change will be on and can change again every after . Every change date, your interest rate can increase or decrease by %. Over the life of the loan, your interest rate is guaranteed to never be **lower** than % or **higher** than %.
Even if you make payments on time, can your loan balance rise?	☐ No. ☐ Yes, it can rise to a maximum of $.
Even if you make payments on time, can your monthly amount owed for principal, interest, and mortgage insurance rise?	☐ No. ☐ Yes, the first increase can be on and the monthly amount owed can rise to $. The maximum it can ever rise to is $.
Does your loan have a prepayment penalty?	☐ No. ☐ Yes, your maximum prepayment penalty is $.
Does your loan have a balloon payment?	☐ No. ☐ Yes, you have a balloon payment of $ due in years on .
Total monthly amount owed including escrow account payments	☐ You do not have a monthly escrow payment for items, such as property taxes and homeowner's insurance. You must pay these items directly yourself. ☐ You have an additional monthly escrow payment of $ that results in a total initial monthly amount owed of $. This includes principal, interest, any mortgage insurance and any items checked below: ☐ Property taxes ☐ Homeowner's insurance ☐ Flood insurance ☐ ☐ ☐

Note: If you have any questions about the Settlement Charges and Loan Terms listed on this form, please contact your lender.

Previous editions are obsolete Page 3 of 3 HUD-1

2010 HUD1 Sample

- Line 103—Total charges to borrower detailed in Section L and totaled on Line 1400 (page 2).
- Lines 104 and 105—Additional amounts owed by the borrower, such as charges that were not listed on the GFE or items paid by the seller prior to settlement but reimbursed by the borrower at settlement.
- Lines 106 through 112—Items which the seller had paid in advance, and for which the borrower must therefore reimburse the seller, for example, taxes and assessments paid in advance, flood and hazard insurance premiums if the borrower is being substituted as an insured under the same policy, planned unit development or condominium association assessments paid in advance.
- Line 120—Total of Lines 101 through 112.
- Line 201—Any amount paid against the sales price prior to settlement.
- Line 202—Amount of the new loan made by lender when a loan to finance construction of a new structure constructed for sale is used as or converted to a loan to finance purchase; also used for the amount of the first user loan, when a loan to purchase a manufactured home for resale is converted to a loan to finance purchase by the first user. For other loans covered by 24 C.F.R. part 3500 (Regulation X) which finance construction of a new structure or purchase of a manufactured home, list the sales price of the land on Line 104, the construction cost or purchase price of manufactured home on Line 105 (Line 101 would be left blank in this instance) and amount of the loan on Line 202. The remainder of the form should be completed taking into account adjustments and charges related to the temporary financing and permanent financing and which are known at the date of settlement.
- Line 203—Used when borrower is assuming or taking title subject to an existing loan or lien on the property.
- Lines 204-209—Used for other items paid by or on behalf of the borrower to indicate any financing arrangements or other new loan not listed in Line 202, for example, if the borrower is using a second mortgage or note to finance part of the purchase price, the borrower receives a credit from the seller for closing costs, or a seller (typically a builder) makes an "allowance" to the borrower for items that the borrower is to purchase separately.
- Lines 210 through 219—Items not yet paid that the borrower is expected to pay, but which are attributable in part to a period of time prior to the settlement, for example, taxes paid in arrears, utilities used but not yet paid by seller.
- Line 220—Total of Lines 201 through 219.
- Lines 301 and 302—Summary lines for the borrower.
- Line 303—Indicates either the cash required from the borrower at settlement or cash payable to the borrower at settlement with the appropriate box checked (if the borrower's earnest money is applied toward the charge for a settlement service, the amount applied should not be included on Line 303 but instead should be shown on the appropriate line for the settlement service, marked "P.O.C. (Borrower)", and must not be included in computing totals).

Section K, Summary of Seller's Transaction. Indicates the details of the seller's transaction, including the gross amount due to the seller, adjustments for items paid by the seller in advance, reductions in amount due to the seller, adjustments for items unpaid by the seller, and the cash at settlement paid to—or in some cases, by—the seller. Instructions for the use of Lines 101 and 102 and 104-112 and Lines 210-219 in Section J apply also to Lines 401-412 and 510-519 in Section K.

- Line 501—Used if the seller's real estate broker or other party who is not the settlement agent has received and holds a deposit against the sales price (earnest money) which exceeds the fee or commission owed to that party; if that party will render the excess deposit directly to the seller, rather than through the settlement agent, the amount of excess deposit should be entered on Line 501 and the amount of the total deposit (including commissions) should be entered on Line 201.
- Line 502—Used to record the total charges to the seller detailed in section L, and totaled on Line 1400 (page 2).
- Line 503—Used if the borrower is assuming or taking title subject to existing liens which are to be deducted from sales price.
- Lines 504 and 505—Used for the amounts (including any accrued interest) of any first and/or second loans which will be paid as part of the settlement.

- Line 506—Used for deposits paid by the borrower to the seller or other party who is not the settlement agent; amount of the deposit in Line 201 is entered on Line 506 unless Line 501 is used or the party who is not the settlement agent transfers all or part of the deposit to the settlement agent, in which case the settlement agent will note in parentheses on Line 507 the amount of the deposit that is being disbursed as proceeds and enter in the column for Line 506 the amount retained by the above-described party for settlement services; if the settlement agent holds the deposit, a note should be inserted in Line 507 indicating that the deposit is being disbursed as proceeds.
- Lines 506-509—May be used to list additional liens/seller obligations which must be paid off through the settlement to clear title to the property, including charges that were disclosed on the GFE but that are actually being paid for by the seller; may also be used to indicate funds to be held by the settlement agent for the payment of either repairs, or water, fuel, or other utility bills that cannot be prorated between the parties at settlement because the amounts used by the seller prior to settlement are not yet known (subsequent disclosure of the actual amount of these post-settlement items to be paid from settlement funds is optional); any amounts entered on Line 204--209 including seller financing arrangements should also be entered on Lines 506-509.
- Instructions for the use of Lines 510 through 519 are the same as those for Lines 210 to 219 above.
- Line 520—Total of Lines 501 through 519.
- Lines 601 and 602—Summary lines for the seller.
- Line 603—Indicates either the cash required to be paid to the seller at settlement or the cash payable by the seller at settlement, with the appropriate box checked.

HUD-1 Page 2

Page 2 itemizes the settlement charges paid by both the borrower and the seller, including items paid in connection with the loan, items required by the lender to be paid in advance, reserves deposited with the lender, title charges, government recording and transfer charges, and any additional settlement charges.

- Lines 700-704—Indicates any real estate broker commissions—including any commission splits where the settlement agent disburses portions of the commission to two or more sales agents or real estate brokers—disbursed at settlement. If the sales agent or real estate broker retains part of the deposit against the sales price (earnest money) to apply towards commission, only that part of the commission being disbursed at settlement should be shown on Line 703 with a note on Line 704 indicating the amount to be retained as a "P.O.C." item. Line 704 may also be used for additional charges made by the sales agent or real estate broker, or for a sales commission charged to the borrower, which will be disbursed by the settlement agent.
- Line 801—Records "Our origination charge," which includes all charges received by the mortgage loan originator—except any charge for the specific interest rate chosen (points)—including administrative and processing services, performed by or on behalf of the mortgage loan originator. This number must not be listed in either the buyer's or seller's column.
- Line 802—Records "Your credit or charge (points) for the specific interest rate chosen," which states the charge or credit adjustment as applied to "Our origination charge," if applicable. This number must not be listed in either column or shown on page one of the HUD-1. For a mortgage broker originating a loan in its own name, the amount shown on Line 802 is the difference between the initial loan amount and the total payment to the mortgage broker from the lender (the sum of the price paid for the loan by the lender and any other payments to the mortgage broker from the lender, including any payments based on the loan amount or loan terms, and any flat rate payments). For a mortgage broker originating a loan in another entity's name, the amount shown on Line 802 is the sum of all payments to this mortgage broker from the lender, including any payments based on the loan amount or loan terms, and any flat rate payments. In either case, when the amount paid to the mortgage broker exceeds the initial loan amount, there is a credit to the borrower and it is entered as a negative amount. When the initial loan amount exceeds the amount paid to the mortgage broker, there is a charge to the borrower and it is entered as a positive amount. For a lender, the amount shown on Line 802 may include any credit or charge (points) to the borrower.
- Line 803—Records "Your adjusted origination charges," which states the net amount of the loan origination charges, the sum of the amounts shown in Lines 801 and 802. This amount is listed as either

a positive number (for example, where the origination charge shown in Line 801 exceeds any credit for the interest rate shown in Line 802 or where there is an origination charge in Line 801 and a charge for the interest rate (points) is shown on Line 802) or as a negative number (for example, where the credit for the interest rate shown in Line 802 exceeds the origination charges shown in Line 801). In the case of "no cost" loans, where "no cost" refers only to the mortgage loan originator's fees, the amounts shown in Lines 801 and 802 should offset, so that the charge shown on Line 803 is zero. Where "no cost" includes third party settlement services, the credit shown in Line 802 will more than offset the amount shown in Line 801. The amount shown in Line 803 will be a negative number to offset the settlement charges paid indirectly through the mortgage loan originator.

- Lines 804-808—Records each of the "Required services that we select" identifying each settlement service provider by name and the amount paid recorded either inside the columns or as paid to the provider outside closing ("P.O.C.").
- Lines 804-807—Records specific fees as indicated.
- Lines 808 (and additional sequentially numbered lines, as needed)—Records other third party services required by the mortgage loan originator or other required disclosures from the mortgage loan originator (which must be listed outside the columns).
- Lines 901-903—Records specific items the lender requires to be paid at the time of settlement, but which are not necessarily paid to the lender (e.g., FHA mortgage insurance premium), other than reserves collected by the lender and recorded in the 1000-series.
- Lines 904 (and additional sequentially numbered lines)—Used to list additional items required by the lender (except for reserves collected by the lender and recorded in the 1000-series), including premiums for flood or other insurance; also used to list amounts paid at settlement for insurance not required by the lender.
- Lines 1000-1007—Used for amounts collected by the lender from the borrower and held in an account for the future payment of the obligations listed as they fall due; include the time period (number of months) and the monthly assessment. In many jurisdictions this is referred to as an "escrow," "impound," or "trust" account. In addition to the property taxes and insurance listed, some lenders may require reserves for flood insurance, condominium owners' association assessments, etc. The amount in line 1001 is listed in the columns, and the itemizations in lines 1002 through 1007 are listed outside the columns. After itemizing individual deposits in the 1000 series, the servicer makes an adjustment based on aggregate accounting.
- Lines 1100-1108—Covers title charges and charges by attorneys and closing or settlement agents as specified. The title charges include a variety of services performed by title companies or others and include fees directly related to the transfer of title (title examination, title search, document preparation), fees for title insurance, and fees for conducting the closing. The legal charges include fees for attorneys representing the lender, seller, or borrower, and any attorney preparing title work. The series also includes any settlement, notary, and delivery fees related to the services covered in this series. Disbursements to third parties must be broken out in the appropriate lines or in blank lines in the series, and amounts paid to these third parties must be shown outside of the columns if included in Line 1101. Charges not included in Line 1101 must be listed in the columns. Additional sequentially numbered lines in the 1100-series may be used to itemize title charges paid to other third parties, as identified by name and type of service provided.
- Lines 1200-1205—Covers specific government-recording and transfer charges. Charges paid by the borrower must be listed in the columns as described for lines 1201 and 1203, with itemizations shown outside the columns. Any amounts that are charged to the seller and that were not included on the Good Faith Estimate must be listed in the columns.
- Line 1206 (and additional sequentially numbered lines)—Used to record specific itemized third party charges for government recording and transfer services, but the amounts must be listed outside the columns.

- Line 1301 (and additional sequentially numbered lines)—Used to record required services that the borrower can shop for, such as fees for survey, pest inspection, or other similar inspections. These lines may also be used to record additional itemized settlement charges that are not included in a specific category, such as fees for structural and environmental inspections; pre-sale inspections of heating, plumbing or electrical equipment; or insurance or warranty coverage. The amounts must be listed in either the borrower's or seller's column.
- Line 1400—States the total settlement charges as calculated by adding the amounts within each column.

HUD-1 Page 3

The last page of the HUD-1 offers a comparison of the exact amounts from the Good Faith Estimate (GFE) and the actual settlement charges indicated on the HUD–1 or HUD-1A Settlement Statement.

Charges That Cannot Increase. The amounts shown in Blocks 1 and 2, in Line A, and in Block 8 on the borrower's GFE are entered in the appropriate line in the Good Faith Estimate column. The amounts shown on Lines 801, 802, 803, and 1203 of the HUD-1/1A are entered in the corresponding line in that column, which must include any amounts shown on page 2 of the HUD-1 in the column as paid for by the borrower, plus any amounts that are shown as P.O.C. by or on behalf of the borrower. If there is a credit in Block 2 of the GFE or Line 802 of the HUD-1/1A, the credit is entered as a negative number.

Charges That Cannot Increase More Than 10%. A description of each charge included in Blocks 3 and 7 on the borrower's GFE is entered on separate lines in this section, with the amount shown on the borrower's GFE for each charge entered in the corresponding line in the Good Faith Estimate column. For each charge included in Blocks 4, 5, and 6 on the borrower's GFE for which the mortgage loan originator selected the provider or for which the borrower selected a provider identified by the mortgage loan originator, a description is entered on a separate line in this section, with the amount shown on the borrower's GFE for each charge entered in the corresponding line in the Good Faith Estimate column. The mortgage loan originator must identify any third party settlement services for which the borrower selected a provider other than one identified by the mortgage loan originator so that the settlement agent can include those charges in the appropriate category. Additional lines may be added if necessary. The amounts shown on the HUD-1/1A for each line is entered in the HUD-1/1A column next to the corresponding charge from the GFE, along with the appropriate HUD-1/1A line number. The HUD-1/1A column includes any amounts shown on page 2 of the HUD-1 in the column as paid for by the borrower, plus any amounts that are shown as P.O.C. by or on behalf of the borrower. The amounts shown in the Good Faith Estimate and HUD-1/1A columns for this section are separately totaled and entered in the designated line. If the total for the HUD-1/1A column is greater than the total for the Good Faith Estimate column, then the amount of the increase must be entered both as a dollar amount and as a percentage increase in the appropriate line.

Charges That Can Change. The amounts shown in Blocks 9, 10, and 11 on the borrower's GFE are entered in the appropriate line in the Good Faith Estimate column. Any third party settlement services for which the borrower selected a provider other than one identified by the mortgage loan originator is also included in this section. The amounts shown on the HUD-1/1A for each charge in this section are entered in the corresponding line in the HUD-1/1A column, along with the appropriate HUD-1/1A line number. The HUD-1/1A column includes any amounts shown on page 2 of the HUD-1 in the column as paid for the borrower, plus any amounts that are shown as P.O.C. by or on behalf of the borrower. Additional lines may be added if necessary.

Loan Terms. This section is completed in accordance with the information and instructions provided by the lender in a format that permits the settlement agent to simply enter the necessary information in the appropriate spaces, without the settlement agent having to refer to the loan documents themselves.

Homeowners Protection Act (HPA)

The federal **Homeowners Protection Act** of 1998, or HPA, (Pub. L. No. 105-216, 112 Stat. 897) requires lenders or servicers to provide certain disclosures and notifications concerning **private mortgage insurance** (PMI) on residential mortgage transactions. Most provisions of the Act do *not* apply to home loans made before July 29, 1999. This Act covers lenders that grant **residential mortgages**, defined as a *mortgage, loan,* *or other evidence of a security interest created with respect to a single-family dwelling that is the primary residence of the borrower.* A **single-family dwelling** is defined as a *residence consisting of one family dwelling unit.* The Homeowners Protection Act also requires lenders that refinance or service home mortgages to comply with its terms.

Exclusions

The HPA does *not* cover loans that do not have private mortgage insurance or loans secured by second or multi-family homes. Nor does it apply to:

- Veterans Affairs (VA) or Federal Housing Administration (FHA) loans.
- Loans with lender-paid PMI, although these loans do require an upfront disclosure to the borrower.

Disclosure Provisions of the HPA

The HPA requires that lenders provide an **initial written disclosure** regarding PMI cancellation—and **annual reminders** of this right—to residential mortgage borrowers. The written notice must include these disclosures:

- **Borrower Cancellation.** The borrower's right to request cancellation of PMI when a mortgage has been paid down to **80%** of its original appraised value or purchase price, whichever is less. Additionally, a borrower requesting PMI cancellation must have:
  - A good history of payment,
  - Not taken out any other loans on the property, and
  - Not experienced a decline in the value of the home.
- **Automatic Termination.** The automatic cancellation of PMI by the lender when a mortgage has been paid down to **78%** of the property's original value, assuming the borrower is current with payments.
- **Prepayment.** The borrower's right to accelerate the cancellation date by making additional payments that bring the loan-to-value ratio to 80%.

The Act requires written disclosure for both adjustable rate and fixed rate home mortgages on primary residences. Disclosure requirements, however, vary depending on how the mortgage accrues interest:

- **Fixed Rate Mortgages.** At the loan closing for a fixed rate mortgage, lenders must provide an initial amortization schedule with a written notice stating both the cancellation date that the borrower may seek to cancel PMI based on the amortization schedule and the automatic termination date.
- **Adjustable Rate Mortgages (ARMs).** For ARMs, an amortization schedule would not be provided at closing, but the lender must inform the borrower when the LTV reaches 80%.

A **final disclosure** must be sent to the borrower after the PMI coverage has been terminated or cancelled to notify the borrower that the borrower is no longer covered by PMI and that the borrower is not required to pay PMI premiums any longer. Additional disclosures are required for so-called high-risk loans.

High-Risk Loans

The borrower-requested cancellation of PMI at 80% LTV and the automatic termination at 78% LTV requirements do not apply to high-risk loans. However, high-risk loans are subject to final termination and are divided into two categories: Conforming and nonconforming:

- **Conforming.** Conforming loans are loans that have an original principal balance not exceeding Fannie Mae and Freddie Mac's limit for conforming loans. PMI on a conforming high-risk loan must be terminated by the first day of the month following the date that is **the midpoint of the loan's initial amortization schedule** (in the case of a fixed rate loan) or amortization schedules (in the case of an adjustable rate loan) if, on that date, the borrower is current on the loan. If the borrower is not current on that date, PMI must be terminated when the borrower becomes current.
- **Nonconforming.** Nonconforming loans are residential mortgage transactions that have an original principal balance exceeding Freddie Mac's and Fannie Mae's conforming loan limit. If a residential mortgage transaction is a lender-defined high-risk loan, PMI must be terminated on the date on which

the principal balance of the mortgage—based solely on the initial amortization schedule (in the case of a fixed rate loan) or the amortization schedules (in the case of an adjustable rate loan) for that mortgage—is first scheduled to reach 77% of the original value of the property securing the loan, regardless of the outstanding balance for that mortgage on that date.

Disclosure

When PMI is required for high-risk residential mortgage transactions, the lender must provide to the borrower a written notice stating that PMI will not be required beyond the date that is the midpoint of the loan's amortization schedule if, on that date, the borrower is current on the payments as required by the terms of the loan. The lender must provide this notice at consummation.

The lender need not provide disclosure of the termination at 77% LTV for lender-defined high-risk mortgages.

Real Success

Property values can change over time for a variety of reasons—for example, an overall increase in a neighborhood's property values or significant home improvements. Borrowers whose PMI payments are included in their mortgage may assume that the equity in their homes should trigger the automatic cancellation of PMI. Although the Homeowners Protection Act does not require a mortgage servicer to consider the current property value, borrowers may contact the lender or servicer to determine if they have internal policies and procedures for the early cancellation of PMI because of increased values. For example, a servicer might consider:

- A minimum amount of time (years) before a borrower can request cancellation.
- A good payment history for at least a minimum amount of years.
- Documentation of home improvements to demonstrate the higher property value, which could include a new appraisal.

Equal Credit Opportunity Act

The **Equal Credit Opportunity Act** (15 U.S.C. § 1691) is a federal law that *ensures that all consumers are given an equal chance to obtain credit.* The illegal discrimination provisions of ECOA are covered in Chapter 13 Ethics. The law, implemented by **Regulation B,** also contains disclosure provisions, the primary one being the creditor's lending decision. Generally, creditors must notify applicants of their **lending decision**—whether credit was extended or rejected—**within 30 days** of the filing of a complete application.

- If the application is approved, the creditor may provide a **Commitment Letter** to the borrower.
- If an incomplete application is submitted, creditors must send the applicant a **Notice of Incomplete Application.**
- When **adverse action** is taken—an application has been denied, the applicant was offered less favorable terms than those applied for, or there was a change in terms of an existing credit agreement—the creditor must either provide notice of the *specific reasons* for the decision or inform the applicant of his right to request specific reasons for the decision within 60 days. This notice, called a **Statement of Adverse Action,** must be in writing.

Creditors must also disclose to consumers what their rights are under ECOA, including a notice to the applicant of their right to receive a copy of any **appraisal report** on the property (one- to four-family dwelling) that was used in the decision-making process if they make a request **within ninety (90) days** of a credit decision.

Title XIV of the Dodd-Frank Wall Street Reform and Consumer Protection Act of 2010, which is designated the Mortgage Reform and Anti-Predatory Lending Act, amends the Equal Credit Opportunity Act (§ 1474) to require a creditor to furnish a copy of any and all written appraisals developed in connection with an application for a first lien loan on a dwelling promptly upon completion, but in no case later than three business days prior to the closing of the loan, whether the creditor grants or denies the applicant's request for credit or the application is incomplete or withdrawn.

Record Retention

After a creditor notifies an applicant of an action taken, the creditor is required to maintain the following for **25 months** (12 months for business credit):

- Any application that it receives
- Any information required to be obtained concerning characteristics of the applicant to monitor compliance
- Any other written or recorded information used in evaluating the application and not returned to the applicant at the applicant's request
- The notification of action taken and the statement of specific reasons for adverse action
- Any written statement submitted by the applicant alleging a violation of ECOA

NOTICE TO APPLICANT OF RIGHT TO RECEIVE COPY OF APPRAISAL REPORT

APPLICATION NO:

PROPERTY ADDRESS:

You have the right to receive a copy of the appraisal report to be obtained in connection with the loan for which you are applying, provided that you have paid for the appraisal. We must receive your written request no later than **90** days after we notify you about the action taken on your application or you withdraw your application. If you would like a copy of the appraisal report, contact :

(Applicant) (Date)	(Applicant) (Date)
(Applicant) (Date)	(Applicant) (Date)

Calyx Form rra.frm 12/96

Sample Notice of Applicant Right to Receive Copy of Appraisal Report

Laws Related To Privacy and Consumer Identification

To keep from destroying the integrity of a relationship with a customer, financial information gathered as part of the loan process must be kept confidential. It should never be revealed to unauthorized people nor taken advantage of for personal benefit. Various laws have passed that address the disclosure and protection of private information. This section discusses the following federal laws:

- Fair Credit Reporting Act (FCRA)
- Fair and Accurate Credit Transactions Act (FACT Act)
- Gramm-Leach-Bliley Act
- U.S. Patriot Act
- National Do Not Call Registry

Fair Credit Reporting Act (FCRA)

Regulation V implements the **Fair Credit Reporting Act** (15 U.S.C. § 1681), a *federal law dealing with the granting of credit, access to credit information, the rights of debtors, and the responsibilities of creditors.* In brief, FCRA gives consumers access to the same information about themselves that lenders use when making credit decisions. The Federal Trade Commission publishes guides for consumers that explain all of their rights under FCRA, including the ability to seek damages for violations of their rights. Identity theft victims and active duty military personnel have additional rights.

Consumer Rights

The Fair Credit Reporting Act provides consumers with the following rights:

Adverse Action

Anyone who uses a credit report or another type of consumer report to deny an application for credit, insurance, or employment—or to take another adverse action—must provide the consumer with the name, address, and phone number of the agency that provided the information. The requirements under FCRA differ somewhat from those under the Equal Credit Opportunity Act, although both laws can be satisfied with a single adverse action notice.

Copy of Consumer Credit File

Consumers are entitled to a free copy of their credit file from a consumer credit reporting agency under these circumstances:

- Information in a credit report resulted in adverse action.
- The consumer was a victim of identify theft and a fraud alert was inserted in credit file.
- The credit file contains inaccurate information as a result of fraud.
- The consumer is on public assistance or is unemployed.

Additionally, all consumers are entitled to one free disclosure every 12 months upon request from each of the three nationwide credit bureaus.

Request a Credit Score

Although it is not free, consumers have the right to ask for a credit score from any consumer reporting agencies that create or distribute scores used in residential real property loans.

Title X of the Dodd-Frank Wall Street Reform and Consumer Protection Act of 2010, § 1100F, amends the Fair Credit Reporting Act to require a creditor to provide a consumer with a written or electronic disclosure of the numeric credit score used in taking any adverse action, including a risk-based pricing notice.

Adverse Action Notice

Applicant(s): William A Sample
Loan Amount: $ 150,000
Interest Rate: 6.000 %
Term: 360 months

Date Denied: May 1, 2009
Noticed Mailed: May 5, 2009

In compliance with Regulation B (Equal Credit Opportunity Act), you are advised that your recent application for an extension of credit has been declined. The decision to deny your application was based on the following reason(s):

- Delinquent credit obligations
- Temporary employment
- Insufficient stability of income
- Stable monthly income insufficient to make monthly mortgage payments

Our decision was based in whole or in part on information that has been obtained from the consumer reporting agency checked below. You have a right under the Fair Credit Reporting Act to know the information contained in your credit file at the consumer reporting agency. The reporting agency played no part in our decision and is therefore unable to supply specific reasons for the credit decision.

☐ Agency #1: Experian, Toll Free: 888-397-3742, P.O. Box 2002, Allen, TX 75013

☐ Agency #2: Equifax, Toll Free: 800-685-1111, P.O. Box 740241, Atlanta, GA 30374

☒ Agency #3: TransUnion, Toll Free: 800-888-4213, P.O. Box 1000, Chester, PA 19022

You also have a right to a free copy of your report from the reporting agency, if you request it no later than 60 days after you receive this notice. If you find that any information contained in the report you receive is inaccurate or incomplete, you have the right to dispute the matter with the reporting agency.

If you have any questions regarding this notice or if you have additional information that might assist us in further evaluating your loan application, please contact:

ABC SAVINGS AND LOAN
123 Main Street
Anytown, USA 00011
1-800-555-9999

NOTICE
The Federal Equal Credit Opportunity Act prohibits creditors from discrimination against credit applicants on the basis of race, color, religion, national origin, sex, marital status, or age (provided the applicant has the capacity to enter into a binding contract); because all or part of the applicant's income derives from any public assistance program; or because the applicant has in good faith exercised any right under the Consumer Credit Protection Act. The Federal Agency that administers compliance with this law concerning this creditor is the Office of Thrift Supervision.

Sample Adverse Action Notice

Dispute Incomplete or Inaccurate Information

Consumers have the right to dispute any incomplete or inaccurate information they find in their credit report. The consumer reporting agency must correct or delete inaccurate, incomplete, or unverifiable information.

Limit Prescreened Offers

Consumers may choose to limit "prescreened" offers of credit and insurance based on information in their credit report. Unsolicited prescreened offers for credit and insurance must include a toll-free phone number to call to be removed from the lists on which these offers are based.

Consumer Reporting Agency Obligations

Under the Fair Credit Reporting Act, consumer reporting agencies:

- May **not report outdated negative** information. In most cases, a consumer reporting agency may not report negative credit information that is more than **seven years old** or bankruptcies that are more than ten years old. There is no time limit on the reporting of criminal convictions.
- Must **limit access** to a credit file. A consumer reporting agency may provide information to people with a legitimate business need—usually to consider an application with a creditor, insurer, employer, landlord, or other business. FCRA specifies those with a valid need for access.
- May not give out consumer credit information to an employer, or a potential employer, without written consent given to the employer by the consumer.

Fair and Accurate Credit Transaction Act (FACT Act)

The **Fair and Accurate Credit Transaction Act** of 2003 (Pub.L. 108-159), sometimes referred to as either the FACT Act or simply FACTA, amended the federal Fair Credit Reporting Act and is intended primarily to *help consumers fight the growing crime of identity theft.* Accuracy, privacy, limits on information sharing, and new consumer rights to disclosure are included in the FACT Act.

Provisions of the FACT Act

The FACT Act actually contains seven major titles: Identity Theft Prevention and Credit History Restoration, Improvements in Use of and Consumer Access to Credit Information, Enhancing the Accuracy of Consumer Report Information, Limiting the Use and Sharing of Medical Information in the Financial System, Financial Literacy and Education Improvement, Protecting Employee Misconduct Investigations, and Relation to State Laws.

Access to Credit Reports

One of the major provisions of the FACT Act is to allow consumers easier **access to their credit reports** as a way to *spot possible identity theft* and to *allow dispute of inaccurate information.* The FACT Act requires that consumers applying for home loans receive the **Home Loan Applicant Credit Score Information Disclosure** notice, which explains their rights. Prior to the passage of the FACT Act, consumers had to pay to get a copy of their report from each of the three national credit bureaus: Equifax, Experian, and TransUnion. The FACT Act allows consumers to request and obtain a free copy of their credit report **once every 12 months** from each of these credit bureaus by contacting a centralized website, maintained in cooperation with the Federal Trade Commission—www.annualcreditreport.com—or by calling 877-322-8228.

To protect sensitive data, the FACT Act allows consumers who request a copy of their credit report to also request that the first five digits of their Social Security number (or similar identification number) not be *included* in the file.

Para informacion en espanol, visite www.ftc.gov/credit o escribe a la FTC Consumer Response Center, Room 130-A 600 Pennsylvania Ave. N.W., Washington, D.C. 20580.

A Summary of Your Rights Under the Fair Credit Reporting Act

The federal Fair Credit Reporting Act (FCRA) promotes the accuracy, fairness, and privacy of information in the files of consumer reporting agencies. There are many types of consumer reporting agencies, including credit bureaus and specialty agencies (such as agencies that sell information about check writing histories, medical records, and rental history records). Here is a summary of your major rights under the FCRA. **For more information, including information about additional rights, go to www.ftc.gov/credit or write to: Consumer Response Center, Room 130-A, Federal Trade Commission, 600 Pennsylvania Ave. N.W., Washington, D.C. 20580.**

- **You must be told if information in your file has been used against you.** Anyone who uses a credit report or another type of consumer report to deny your application for credit, insurance, or employment – or to take another adverse action against you – must tell you, and must give you the name, address, and phone number of the agency that provided the information.
- **You have the right to know what is in your file.** You may request and obtain all the information about you in the files of a consumer reporting agency (your "file disclosure"). You will be required to provide proper identification, which may include your Social Security number. In many cases, the disclosure will be free. You are entitled to a free file disclosure if:
    - a person has taken adverse action against you because of information in your credit report;
    - you are the victim of identify theft and place a fraud alert in your file;
    - your file contains inaccurate information as a result of fraud;
    - you are on public assistance;
    - you are unemployed but expect to apply for employment within 60 days.

  In addition, by September 2005 all consumers will be entitled to one free disclosure every 12 months upon request from each nationwide credit bureau and from nationwide specialty consumer reporting agencies. See www.ftc.gov/credit for additional information.
- **You have the right to ask for a credit score.** Credit scores are numerical summaries of your credit-worthiness based on information from credit bureaus. You may request a credit score from consumer reporting agencies that create scores or distribute scores used in residential real property loans, but you will have to pay for it. In some mortgage transactions, you will receive credit score information for free from the mortgage lender.
- **You have the right to dispute incomplete or inaccurate information.** If you identify information in your file that is incomplete or inaccurate, and report it to the consumer reporting agency, the agency must investigate unless your dispute is frivolous. See www.ftc.gov/credit for an explanation of dispute procedures.
- **Consumer reporting agencies must correct or delete inaccurate, incomplete, or unverifiable information.** Inaccurate, incomplete or unverifiable information must be removed or corrected, usually within 30 days. However, a consumer reporting agency may continue to report information it has verified as accurate.

Sample Fair Credit Reporting Act Summary

- **Consumer reporting agencies may not report outdated negative information.** In most cases, a consumer reporting agency may not report negative information that is more than seven years old, or bankruptcies that are more than 10 years old.
- **Access to your file is limited.** A consumer reporting agency may provide information about you only to people with a valid need -- usually to consider an application with a creditor, insurer, employer, landlord, or other business. The FCRA specifies those with a valid need for access.
- **You must give your consent for reports to be provided to employers.** A consumer reporting agency may not give out information about you to your employer, or a potential employer, without your written consent given to the employer. Written consent generally is not required in the trucking industry. For more information, go to www.ftc.gov/credit.
- **You may limit "prescreened" offers of credit and insurance you get based on information in your credit report.** Unsolicited "prescreened" offers for credit and insurance must include a toll-free phone number you can call if you choose to remove your name and address from the lists these offers are based on. You may opt-out with the nationwide credit bureaus at 1-888-5-OPTOUT (1-888-567-8688).
- **You may seek damages from violators.** If a consumer reporting agency, or, in some cases, a user of consumer reports or a furnisher of information to a consumer reporting agency violates the FCRA, you may be able to sue in state or federal court.
- **Identity theft victims and active duty military personnel have additional rights.** For more information, visit www.ftc.gov/credit.

States may enforce the FCRA, and many states have their own consumer reporting laws. In some cases, you may have more rights under state law. For more information, contact your state or local consumer protection agency or your state Attorney General. Federal enforcers are:

TYPE OF BUSINESS:	CONTACT:
Consumer reporting agencies, creditors and others not listed below	Federal Trade Commission: Consumer Response Center - FCRA Washington, DC 20580 1-877-382-4357
National banks, federal branches/agencies of foreign banks (word "National" or initials "N.A." appear in or after bank's name)	Office of the Comptroller of the Currency Compliance Management, Mail Stop 6-6 Washington, DC 20219 800-613-6743
Federal Reserve System member banks (except national banks, and federal branches/agencies of foreign banks)	Federal Reserve Board Division of Consumer & Community Affairs Washington, DC 20551 202-452-3693
Savings associations and federally chartered savings banks (word "Federal" or initials "F.S.B." appear in federal institution's name)	Office of Thrift Supervision Consumer Complaints Washington, DC 20552 800-842-6929
Federal credit unions (words "Federal Credit Union" appear in institution's name)	National Credit Union Administration 1775 Duke Street Alexandria, VA 22314 703-519-4600
State-chartered banks that are not members of the Federal Reserve System	Federal Deposit Insurance Corporation Consumer Response Center, 2345 Grand Avenue, Suite 100 Kansas City, Missouri 64108-2638 1-877-275-3342
Air, surface, or rail common carriers regulated by former Civil Aeronautics Board or Interstate Commerce Commission	Department of Transportation , Office of Financial Management Washington, DC 20590 202-366-1306
Activities subject to the Packers and Stockyards Act, 1921	Department of Agriculture Office of Deputy Administrator - GIPSA Washington, DC 20250 202-720-7051

Sample Fair Credit Reporting Act Summary

National Credit Score Disclosure

Applicant Loan #
Applicant
Address

In evaluating your application for a home mortgage loan, one factor your lender will consider is one or more of your credit scores because they assist the lender in evaluating your credit history in a faster, more objective manner. Your credit scores are found on your credit report, **a copy of which was provided to you with this disclosure.** The range of possible scores is from 300 to 850. Your lender may also obtain and consider other credit scores in making its decision on your application from the consumer reporting agencies listed below.

In addition to the credit scores, your credit report lists the key reasons why your scores were less than the maximum possible scores. Please keep in mind that these reasons are provided based on variables, where you received less than the maximum number of points possible. The listing of these reasons does not by itself indicate that you would not be approved for the loan you have requested. The lender considers many factors in addition to your credit score in making a decision on your application. If your application is not approved, you will receive a separate notice stating the specific reasons for that action which may or may not relate to your credit scores.

The originator or lender did not calculate your credit scores, nor did they develop the scoring models. If you have any questions about your credit scores or the information in the credit report from which the credit scores were computed, you can contact the consumer reporting agencies at the addresses listed below:

Equifax	**TransUnion**	**Experian**
PO Box 740258	PO Box 1000	PO Box 2104
Atlanta, GA 30374-0258	Chester, PA 19016-4000	Allen, TX 75013
Phone: 800) 685-1111	**Phone: 800) 888-4213**	**Phone: 888) 397-3742**
Website: www.equifax.com	www.transunion.com/direct	www.experian.com

Notice to Home Applicant

(Pursuant to the Fair Credit Report Act [15 U.S.C. 1681g Sec 609(g)(1)(D)] as amended 12/4/03)

In connection with your application for a home loan, the lender must disclose to you the score that a consumer reporting agency distributed to users and the lender used in connection with your home loan, and the key factors affecting your scores.

The credit score is a computer-generated summary calculated at the time of the request and based on the information a consumer reporting agency or lender has on file. The scores are based on data about your credit history and payment patterns. Credit scores are important because they are used to assist the lender in determining whether you will obtain a loan. They may also be used to determine what interest rate you may be offered on the mortgage. Credit scores can change over time, depending on your conduct, how your credit history and payment patterns change, and how credit scoring technologies change.

Because the score is based on information in your credit history, it is very important that you review the credit-related information that is being furnished to make sure it is accurate. Credit records may vary from one company to another.

If you have questions about your credit score or the credit information that is furnished to you, contact the consumer reporting agency at the address and telephone number provided with this notice, or contact the lender, if the lender developed or generated the credit score. The consumer reporting agency plays no part in the decision to take any action on the loan application and is unable to provide you with specific reasons for the decisions on a loan application. If you have any questions concerning the terms of the loan, contact the lender.

This acknowledges that this Disclosure, along with a copy of my/our credit report, has been provided to each applicant/client pursuant to 15 U.S.C. 1681g Sec 609(g)(1)(D) as amended 12/4/03 and effective 12/4/04.

_______________________ _______________________
Applicant Date Applicant Date

____
Originator Date

Rev12/1/04

Sample National Credit Score Disclosure

Fraud Alerts and Freezes

If a consumer believes he or she has been a victim of identity theft, the FACT Act allows the consumer to contact the credit bureau and place a **fraud alert**. If you are running a credit report and you see a fraud alert, you must contact the person whose name is on the account at the number provided to the credit bureau or take other reasonable steps to ensure that the person applying for a mortgage loan is not really an identity thief. The FACT Act also allows consumers to place a **credit freeze** in order to prevent the information from showing on a credit report. The consumer may then "thaw" the credit report when they apply for a loan.

The Act also allows members of the military who are deploying overseas to place a credit freeze, thereby making fraudulent applications for credit more difficult.

Truncation of Credit and Debit Card Numbers

The FACT Act also prohibits businesses from printing more than five digits of any customer's credit/debit card number or expiration date on any receipt provided to the cardholder at the point of sale or transaction. The provision excludes handwritten or imprinted receipts if that is the only method of recording the card number.

Security and Disposal

To further protect the privacy of consumer financial information, the FACT Act requires businesses to take measures to responsibly **secure and dispose** of sensitive personal information found in a consumer's credit report. Reasonable methods for security and disposal include:

- Burning or shredding papers that contain consumer report information so that information cannot be reconstructed.
- Destroying or erasing electronic files or media so that information cannot be recovered or reconstructed.
- Placing all pending loan documents in locked desks, cabinets, or storage rooms at the end of the work day.

Red Flags Rules

Several widely reported surveys on the number of identity theft victims were released as Congress went into final hearings on FCRA amendments. One report released by the Federal Trade Commission in September 2003 estimated that approximately 10 million people were victims of identity theft in 2002 alone. This resulted in **Section 114** of the FACT Act, known as the **Red Flags Rules**, which requires:

- Financial institutions and creditors to implement a written identity theft prevention program.
- Card issuers to assess the validity of change of address requests.
- Users of consumer reports to reasonably verify the identity of the subject of a consumer report in the event of a notice of address discrepancy.

Section 114 applies to federal and state-chartered banks and credit unions, non-bank lenders, mortgage brokers, any person that regularly participates in a credit decision—including setting the terms of credit, and any person who requests a consumer report. Every organization has the flexibility to define a program that is appropriate to the size and operation of their particular business.

Red Flags

According to the FTC, red flags generally fall into these categories:

- Alerts, notifications, or warnings from a consumer reporting agency
- Suspicious documents
- Suspicious personally identifying information, such as a suspicious address
- Unusual use of—or suspicious activity relating to—a covered account
- Notices from customers, victims of identity theft, law enforcement authorities, or other businesses about possible identity theft in connection with covered accounts

Gramm-Leach-Bliley Act (GLB Act)

The **Financial Services Modernization Act of 1999**, also known as the **Gramm-Leach-Bliley Act** (Pub.L. 106-102), includes provisions in **Title V - Privacy** to *protect and regulate the disclosure of consumers' personal financial information.* There are three principal parts to the privacy requirements: The Financial Privacy Rule, Safeguards Rule, and Pretexting Provisions.

The GLB Act gives authority to eight federal agencies and the states to administer and enforce Title V - Privacy. These regulations apply to financial institutions, which include not only banks, securities firms, and insurance companies, but also companies providing many other types of financial products and services to consumers, such as:

- Lending, brokering, or servicing any type of consumer loan.
- Transferring or safeguarding money.
- Preparing individual tax returns.

- Providing financial advice or credit counseling.
- Providing residential real estate settlement services.
- Collecting consumer debts.

Financial Privacy Rule

Information that many would consider private—including bank balances and account numbers—is regularly bought and sold by banks, credit card companies, and other financial institutions. The **Privacy Rule** (15 U.S.C. §§ 6801–6809) governs the collection and disclosure of customers' personal financial information—known as **nonpublic personal information**—restricting when and under what circumstances such information may be disclosed to affiliates and to nonaffiliated third parties. Nonpublic personal information could include the following types of information:

- What a consumer or customer puts on an application
- Data about the individual from another source, such as a credit bureau
- Transactions between the individual and the company, such as an account balance, payment history, or credit/debit card purchase information
- Whether or not an individual is a consumer or customer of a particular financial institution

These restrictions are based on a required **Consumer Privacy Policy** notice provided to the consumer, explaining the lender's information collection and information sharing and transfer practices, and giving the consumer instructions on how to **opt out** of having this information shared. A financial institution must disclose its policy to consumers before they disclose personal information, as well as **annually** for customers during the financial relationship.

Even if a consumer does *not* opt-out, financial institutions are prohibited from disclosing—other than to a consumer reporting agency—access codes or account numbers to any nonaffiliated third party for use in telemarketing, direct mail marketing, or other marketing through electronic mail. Creditors are responsible for validating any other entity to which they transfer custody of a private consumer data.

Consumer or Customer?

A company's obligations under the GLB Act depend on whether the company has consumers or customers who obtain its services:

- A **consumer** is *an individual who obtains or has obtained a financial product or service from a financial institution for personal, family or household reasons.*
- A **customer** is a *consumer with a continuing relationship with a financial institution.* Generally, if the relationship between the financial institution and the individual is significant and/or long-term, the individual is a customer of the institution.

For example, a person who gets a mortgage from a lender or hires a broker to get a personal loan is considered a customer of the lender or the broker, while a person who uses a check-cashing service is a consumer of that service.

Under the GLB Act, **customers** must receive a financial institution's privacy notice **every year** for as long as the customer relationship lasts. **Consumers**, on the other hand, are entitled to receive a privacy notice from a financial institution *only if the company shares the consumers' information with companies not affiliated with it*, with some exceptions.

Safeguards Rule

The **Safeguards Rule** (15 U.S.C. §§ 6801–6809) requires all financial institutions to design, implement, and maintain safeguards to protect customer information while it is in the custody and control of the institution and its agents. This rule applies not only to financial institutions that collect information from their own customers, but also to any institution—such as a credit reporting agency or even an educational institution—that receives customer information from other financial institutions. A written Safeguards Policy must include provisions that:

- Ensure the security and confidentiality of customer records.

- Protect against any anticipated threats or hazards to the security of such records.
- Protect against the unauthorized access or use of such records or information in ways that could result in substantial harm or inconvenience to customers.

Pretexting Provisions

This provision (15 U.S.C. §§ 6821–6827) protects consumers from individuals and companies that obtain their personal financial information under false, fictitious, or fraudulent pretenses.

U.S. Patriot Act

The Uniting and Strengthening America by Providing Appropriate Tools Required to Intercept and Obstruct Terrorism Act (Pub.L. 107-56), more commonly known as the Patriot Act, was signed in October 2001 in response to the September 11, 2001, terrorist attacks, The Act increases the ability of law enforcement agencies to search telephone, e-mail, medical, financial, and other records; eases restrictions on foreign intelligence gathering within the United States; expands the Secretary of the Treasury's authority to regulate financial transactions, particularly those involving foreign individuals and entities; and enhances the discretion of law enforcement and immigration authorities in detaining and deporting immigrants suspected of terrorism-related acts.

Title III of the Patriot Act, designated the International Money Laundering Abatement and Financial Anti-Terrorism Act of 2001, requires lenders and banks to create and maintain **customer identification programs** (CIPs) to prevent financing of terrorist operations and money laundering (§ 326). CIPs require covered institutions to verify the identity for customers who are entering into a "formal relationship," such as taking out a loan or a credit account.

Minimum Data Required

A covered institution must obtain, at a minimum, the following information from all customers opening a new account:

- Name
- Date of birth
- Residential or work address for individuals, or physical location address for legal entities
- A tax identification number (TIN) for U.S. citizens or legal entities organized under state law
- For lawful permanent residents or non-immigrants, a TIN, passport number and country of issuance, alien identification card number, or number and country of issuance of any other government-issued document evidencing nationality or residence and bearing a photo
- For non-U.S. legal entities with no TIN, a government-issued certificate of existence or good standing

If a lender is extending credit to the borrower using a mortgage broker as its agent, then it must ensure the broker is performing the bank's CIP.

The National Do Not Call Registry

A provision of the federal Telemarketing Sales Rule (16 C.F.R. Part 310), the Do Not Call (DNC) Registry is managed by the **Federal Trade Commission** (FTC), the nation's consumer protection agency and enforced by the FTC, the Federal Communications Commission (FCC), and state law enforcement officials.

The National Do Not Call Registry applies to any plan, program, or campaign to sell goods or services through interstate phone calls. This includes telemarketers who solicit consumers, often on behalf of third party sellers. It also includes sellers who provide, offer to provide, or arrange to provide goods or services to consumers in exchange for payment. The National Do Not Call Registry does *not* limit calls by political organizations, charities, or telephone surveyors. To keep from violating Do Not Call regulations, a company must maintain national and internal lists of customers and prospects and keep them updated regularly. The federal DNC list must be updated every three months, and the internal DNC list must be updated every 30 days.

A consumer who receives a telemarketing call despite being on the registry is able to file a complaint with the FTC. Violators could be fined up to **$16,000 per incident.**

PATRIOT ACT
INFORMATION DISCLOSURE

Applicant Name ______________________
Co-Applicant Name ______________________
Present Address ______________________
Mailing Address ______________________

To help the government fight the funding of terrorism and money laundering activities, Federal law requires all financial institutions to obtain, verify, and record information that identifies each person who opens an account.

What this means for you: When you open an account, we will ask for your name, address, date of birth, and other information that will allow us to identify you. We may also ask to see your driver's license or other identifying documents.

I/we acknowledge that I/we received a copy of this disclosure.

SAMPLE

______________________ ______________________
Applicant Date

______________________ ______________________
Applicant Date

Calyx Form patriotinfo.frm 04/04

Sample Patriot Act Information Disclosure

Established Business Relationship

A telemarketer or seller may call a consumer with whom it has an **established business relationship** (EBR) for up to **18 months** after the consumer's last purchase, delivery, or payment, even if the consumer's number is on the National Do Not Call Registry. In addition, a company may call a consumer for up to **three months** after the consumer makes an inquiry or submits an application to the company. Obtaining the name, phone number, and **signature** from a consumer provides written consent that does not expire until rescinded. One warning: If a consumer has asked to be put on the company's internal do not call list, the company may not call, even if there is an EBR. This prohibition is only against solicitation of new business. Calls may be made to consumers in reference to a current relationship, such as a creditor making a collection call.

Laws Against Predatory Lending

Predatory lending involves loans that *take advantage of ill-informed consumers through excessively high fees, misrepresented loan terms, frequent refinancing that does not benefit the borrower, and other prohibited acts.* Predatory lending targets borrowers with little knowledge of, or defense against, these practices. To combat predatory lending, federal and state regulations require that complete and clear disclosures be made to borrowers. This section focuses on the federal **Home Ownership and Equity Protection Act** of 1994 (HOEPA) and on **higher-priced loans** as defined by amendments to the Truth in Lending Act. It will also examine some provisions of Title XIV of the Dodd-Frank Wall Street Reform and Consumer Protection Act of 2010, designated as the Mortgage Reform and Anti-Predatory Lending Act.

Home Ownership and Equity Protection Act (HOEPA)

The **Home Ownership and Equity Protection Act** (HOEPA), a 1994 amendment to the Truth in Lending Act, *establishes disclosure requirements and prohibits deceptive and unfair practices in lending.* HOEPA also establishes requirements for certain loans with high interest rates and/or fees. The rules for these loans are contained in **Section 32 of Regulation Z**, which implements the Truth in Lending Act.

This Act is enforced by the Federal Trade Commission for non-depository lenders and by each state's attorney general. HOEPA also gives the Federal Reserve Board broad regulatory authority to prohibit additional practices it finds to be unfair or deceptive, not just for HOEPA loans but all consumer mortgage loans. A lender who violates HOEPA may be sued by the consumer, who may be able to recover statutory and actual damages, court costs, and attorney's fees. In addition, a violation of HOEPA may enable a consumer to rescind the loan for up to **three years**.

High Cost Loan Triggers

HOEPA provisions must be complied with once the triggers for a "high cost loan" have been met. A high cost loan, according to HOEPA, is closed-end loan secured by a borrower's principal residence. The rules primarily affect **refinancing** and **home equity installment loans** that also meet the definition of a high-rate or high-fee loan. The rules do *not* cover loans to buy a home (although purchase loans *are* included in the definition of "higher-priced" loans that are discussed later) or loans to build a home, reverse mortgages, or home equity lines of credit. A HOEPA loan is further defined by either the annual percentage rate (APR) or the total amount of finance charges.

Annual Percentage Rate Trigger

A loan with an APR that exceeds the limits indicated below would be considered a HOEPA loan:

- For a first mortgage, the APR exceeds by **more than eight percentage points** the yield on Treasury securities of comparable maturity.
- For a second mortgage, the APR exceeds by **more than ten percentage points** the yield on Treasury securities of comparable maturity.

Creditors should use the **15th of the month before the month** in which the application was received to identify the appropriate Treasury security yield. The selection of the Treasury index for purposes of calculating HOEPA loans is completely unrelated to the index selection and use for adjustable rate mortgages. Setting the rate for an ARM and determining HOEPA coverage are two separate and distinct exercises. This provides one more important reason to document when applications are received.

Total Finance Charge Trigger

The last HOEPA trigger is based on total finance charges and fees. A loan must comply with HOEPA requirements if the total points and fees paid by the consumer exceeds the larger of **eight percent of the loan amount** or a specific dollar amount that is adjusted annually by the Federal Reserve Board based on the Consumer Price Index. For example, the total dollar fee trigger for 2012 is $611.

The calculation of total finance charges for HOEPA is **not** the same as the standard Regulation Z calculation of finance charges. In addition to the fees and charges typically considered, some of the non-finance charges normally exempt by Regulation Z from the finance charge calculation—such as application fees paid by the borrower to the lender—must be considered for HOEPA. Another charge that *must be included* in the points/fee trigger is the amount of any optional credit, life, accident, or loss of income **insurance**, even if the cost of insurance may have been disclosed. Because voluntary credit insurance *is included* in the HOEPA calculation, a loan that did not meet the HOEPA triggers when considering APR for the Truth in Lending statement may become a HOEPA loan at closing when the borrower decides to make the purchase. If this happens, the lender must prepare HOEPA disclosures and delay the closing for the mandatory HOEPA **three business-day waiting period**.

Impact of the Dodd-Frank Act

Title XIV of the Dodd-Frank Wall Street Reform and Consumer Protection Act of 2010, designated as the Mortgage Reform and Anti-Predatory Lending Act (§ 1431), amends the Truth in Lending Act so that, when implemented via regulation, the triggers that define a high cost loan are lowered to:

- Total points and fees exceeding **5%** on mortgage loan of at least $20,000 or 8% or a certain dollar amount on loans below $20,000
- APR exceeding average prime offer rate (APOR) by **6.5%** on first lien loans for $50,000 or more or 8.5% on smaller and second lien loans
- Prepayment penalty applicable for more than three years after closing or that exceed 2% of the prepayment

The Act also expands the definition of points and fee used for calculating the HOPEA loan trigger and requires the borrower to present certification from an approved loan counselor.

Note: The daily Treasury Yield rates can be accessed from the online **Resource Center of the U.S. Department of the Treasury**:

http://www.treasury.gov/resource-center/data-chart-center/Pages/index.aspx

Prohibited Loan Terms

A loan that is subject to the Home Ownership and Equity Protection Act may not include the following terms (12 C.F.R. § 226.34):

- A payment schedule that provides for regular periodic payments that do not fully amortize and result in a **balloon payment** on HOEPA loans having terms of **less than five years**, unless it is a bridge loan of less than one year used by consumers to buy or build a home.
- **Negative amortization**—monthly payments that do not fully pay the interest due on the loan and that cause an increase in the borrower's total principal debt are prohibited. Any interest rate changes and payment schedule caps must be coordinated to avoid this situation.
- A **repayment schedule** that consolidates more than two periodic payments that are to be paid in advance from the proceeds of the loan. The borrower should get the maximum use of the funds and have a legitimate opportunity to use the loan proceeds.
- **Default interest rates** higher than pre-default rates.
- **Rebates**—a refund calculated by a method less favorable than the actuarial method for rebates of interest arising from a loan acceleration due to default.
- **Prepayment penalties** are generally prohibited, although there are exceptions. Prepayment penalties are allowed if limited to the first two years of the loan or if the source of the prepayment funds is a refinancing by the lender or lender affiliate. They're also allowed if the amount of the periodic payment of principal, interest, or both will not change at any time during the first four years of the loan. Prepayment penalties may also be allowed in cases where the borrower's debt-to-income ratio does not exceed 50%.
- **Demand clauses**, including any provision that enables the creditor to call the loan before maturity, are strictly prohibited. Only certain behavior of the consumer would permit the lender to call the loan; for example, fraud, material misrepresentation, default, or damage to the security property.

Prohibited Acts and Practices

Additionally, according to Regulation Z (§ 226.34), creditors granting loans meeting HOEPA criteria may **not**:

- Grant loans solely on the collateral value of the borrower's property without regard to the borrower's ability to repay the loan.
- Disburse proceeds from home improvement loans to anyone other than the borrower, jointly to the borrower and the home improvement contractor, or, in some instances, to a third-party escrow agent, as established by written agreement between the borrower, the creditor, and the contractor.
- Sell or otherwise assign the loan without furnishing the following statement to the purchaser or assignee: "Notice: This is a mortgage subject to special rules under the federal Truth in Lending Act. Purchasers or assignees of this mortgage could be liable for all claims and defenses with respect to the mortgage that the borrower could assert against the creditor."
- Refinance a HOEPA loan into another HOEPA loan within the first 12 months of origination, unless the new loan is in the borrower's best interest. The prohibition also applies to assignees holding or servicing the loan.

Verifying Repayment Ability

Creditors may not grant loans solely based on the collateral value of the borrower's property without regard to the borrower's ability to repay the loan, including the consumer's current and reasonably expected income, employment, assets other than the collateral, current obligations, and mortgage-related obligations, which include expected property taxes, premiums for mortgage-related insurance required by the creditor, and similar expenses. Income and assets can include:

- Expected income or assets,
- Tax returns and W-2s,
- Payroll receipts,
- Financial institution records, or
- Other third-party documents that provide reasonably reliable evidence of the consumer's income or assets.

The amounts the creditor uses to verify the repayment ability cannot be materially greater than the amounts the creditor could have verified when the loan was consummated.

Furthermore, the lender must determine the borrower's repayment ability using the largest payment of principal and interest scheduled in the first seven years following consummation. The creditor must also consider the current obligations and mortgage-related obligations and assess the borrower's repayment ability taking into account at least one of the following:

- The ratio of total debt obligations to income
- The income the consumer will have after paying debt obligations

A creditor is not presumed to be in compliance if the regular periodic payments for the first seven years of the transaction would cause the principal balance to increase or if the term of the loan is less than seven years and the regular periodic payments when aggregated do not fully amortize the outstanding principal balance.

The requirement to prove ability to repay does not apply to temporary or "bridge" loans with terms of 12 months or less, such as a loan to purchase a new dwelling where the borrower plans to sell a current dwelling within 12 months.

Required Disclosures

Creditors granting loans meeting HOEPA criteria must disclose certain facts about the loan as part of the loan package at least **three business days** prior to consummation of a mortgage transaction.

This notice is intended to protect consumers from pressure tactics that imply the consumer is already locked into the agreement, or that canceling will be prohibitively complex or expensive.

In addition, the creditor must disclose:

- The annual percentage rate (APR).
- The regular payment amount (including any balloon payment where the law permits balloon payments).
- The loan amount; when the amount borrowed includes credit insurance premiums, that fact must be stated.
- For variable rate loans, the amount of the maximum monthly payment and the fact that the rate and monthly payment may increase.
- For a mortgage refinancing, the total amount borrowed, as reflected by the face amount of the note must be disclosed. Where the amount borrowed includes premiums or other charges for optional credit insurance or debt-cancellation coverage, that fact must also be stated. To be considered accurate, the amount disclosed cannot vary by more than $100 above or below the amount required to be disclosed.

These disclosures are in addition to the other required Truth in Lending disclosures. A sample of the required HOEPA disclosure language is shown (the disclosure statements in brackets are provided to the consumer only when applicable):

Disclosure Form

You are not required to complete this agreement merely because you have received these disclosures or signed a loan application.

If you obtain this loan, the lender will have a mortgage on your home.

You could lose your home, and any money you have put into it, if you do not meet your obligations under the loan.

You are borrowing $ __________ . [Optional credit insurance ☐ is ☐ is not included in this amount.]

The annual percentage rate on your loan will be

_________ %.

Your regular frequency payment will be $_________ .

[At the end of the loan, you will still owe us

$ balloon amount .]

[Your interest rate may rise. Increases in the interest rate could raise your payment. The highest amount your payment could increase is to $ ___________ .]

Higher-Priced Mortgage Loans

With the passage of the Housing and Economic Recovery Act of 2008, amending Regulation Z and the Truth in Lending Act, a new category of loans was defined: **Higher-priced mortgage loans**. While the high cost loans defined and regulated by HOEPA are less common in today's credit market, the federal government recognized there was still a segment of the loan market between average rate, or prime, loans and loans that do not meet the fee or APR trigger requirements of HOEPA. In order to further protect consumers, Regulation Z (§ 226.35) sets forth specific requirements for handling these higher-priced loans.

Defining Higher-Priced Loans

Higher-priced loans are closed-end mortgage loans secured by the borrower's principal dwelling where the APR **exceeds the applicable average prime offer rate** by at least:

- 1.5 percentage points for first lien loans, or
- 3.5 percentage points for junior lien loans.

This definition *does* include **home purchase** loans, but does *not* include loans to finance:

- The initial construction of a dwelling.
- A temporary or "bridge" loan with a term of 12 months or less, such as a loan to purchase a new dwelling where the consumer plans to sell a current dwelling within 12 months.

- A reverse mortgage transaction.
- A home equity line of credit.

Unlike the HOEPA APR test, a higher-priced loan's APR is measured against the **applicable average prime offer rate**, which is an annual percentage rate derived from average interest rates, points, and other loan pricing terms currently offered to consumers by a representative sample of lenders for mortgage transactions that have low-risk pricing characteristics. The average prime offer rate for both fixed and adjustable rate loans is published in a table and updated at least weekly.

Restrictions

Regulation Z imposes the following restrictions on loans that meet the definition of a higher-priced mortgage loan:

- **Repayment Ability**. Creditors are obligated to verify the repayment ability of the borrower.
- **Prepayment Penalties**. These are generally prohibited unless it is limited to the first two years of the loan. A prepayment penalty is prohibited if the amount of the periodic payment of principal, interest, or both can change at any time during the first four years of the loan. It is also prohibited if the source of the prepayment funds is a refinance by the creditor or its affiliate.
- **Escrow Accounts**. An escrow account must be established for property taxes and premiums for mortgage-related insurance required by the creditor when the loan is a first lien that secures the borrower's principal dwelling. This is not required for loans on cooperatives or on condominium units where the condo association maintains a master policy to insure all units.

Escrow Requirements on Jumbo Loans

In response to the Dodd-Frank Wall Street Reform and Consumer Protection Act of 2010 (Pub.L. 111-203, H.R. 4173), the Federal Reserve Board adopted a final rule related to escrow requirements on higher-priced first lien loans that exceed Freddie Mac's conforming loan limit (jumbo loans). The rule relates to a 2008 rule implementing the Home Ownership and Equity Protection Act (HOEPA) which prohibits a creditor from extending such a higher-priced mortgage loan unless an escrow account is established for payment of required property taxes and premiums for related insurance, including any required mortgage insurance premiums and homeowners hazard insurance. If property hazard insurance is paid through a homeowners association, as may be the case with a condominium, it would be excluded from the escrow requirement. Similarly, if the property taxes for a cooperative are paid by the corporation and collected through cooperative association fees, property taxes would be excluded from these escrow requirements.

This rule, which became effective April 1, 2011, revised § Sec. 226.35(b)(3) of Regulation Z, as proposed, to provide a higher APR threshold for determining whether jumbo mortgage loans secured by a first lien on a consumer's principal dwelling are higher-priced mortgage loans for which an escrow account must be established.

As revised, the threshold for coverage of the escrow requirement for jumbo loans is 2.5 percentage points (rather than 1.5 percentage points) in excess of the average prime offer rate for a comparable transaction, as of the date the transaction's rate is set. Raising the APR threshold applicable to jumbo loans eliminates the mandatory escrow requirement for loans with an APR above the existing threshold but below the new threshold. Creditors may, at their option, elect to continue to use the 1.5 percentage point threshold for these loans.

Federal Reserve Mortgage Loan Originator Compensation Rule

One of the objectives of the Dodd-Frank Wall Street Reform and Consumer Protection Act of 2010 (Pub.L. 111-203, H.R. 4173) was to address perceived unfair practices by mortgage loan originators related to **compensation** paid by consumers. The Federal Reserve Board, anticipating the Dodd-Frank amendments to the Truth in Lending Act, promulgated a final rule—which became effective April 2011—as an amendment to Regulation Z, found in Part 226, Subpart E, Special Rules for Certain Home Mortgage Transactions, that addresses compensation consistent with Dodd-Frank. According to the Compliance Guide prepared by the staff of the Board of Governors of the Federal Reserve System, this rule applies to transactions involving closed-end extensions of credit secured by a consumer's principal dwelling and must be followed by all persons who originate loans, including mortgage brokers and their employees, as well as mortgage loan officers employed by depository institutions and other lenders. For the purposes of this rule, **loan originator** is defined in Regulation Z § 226.36 (a) as:

> *... a person who for compensation or other monetary gain, or in expectation of compensation or other monetary gain, arranges, negotiates, or otherwise obtains an extension of consumer credit for another person. The term "loan originator" includes an employee of the creditor if the employee meets this definition. The term "loan originator" includes the creditor only if the creditor does not provide the funds for the transaction at consummation out of the creditor's own resources, including drawing on a bona fide warehouse line of credit, or out of deposits held by the creditor.*

The rule prohibits creditors from compensating MLOs based on the loan's interest rate or other terms or conditions—such as the APR, loan-to-value, loan program or provisions (such as a prepayment penalty) selected. This prohibition also applies to compensation from a mortgage broker to an employee who originates loans: A mortgage broker cannot pay an employee more for a transaction with a 6% interest rate than a 5% interest rate, for example. Compensation can be based on any of the following triggers:

- Flat fee fixed in advance
- Hourly rate for time worked
- Overall loan volume
- Long-term loan performance
- Existing/new customer
- "Pull-through" rate, i.e., quality of loan files

Creditors can also set a minimum and a maximum compensation—such as paying 1% for **all loans** the MLO originates, with a minimum of $1,000 and a maximum of $5,000—as long as the amount is the same for every transaction.

Note that "compensation" does not include any amounts a mortgage loan originator receives as payment for bona fide and reasonable non-affiliated third party charges, such as an appraisal fee, escrow fees, or insurance premiums. However, fees that are paid to affiliated third parties would be considered part of MLO compensation.

Dual Compensation

If a MLO receives compensation for a transaction directly from a consumer, no one else may compensate the MLO for that transaction, either directly or indirectly (§ 226.36 (d)(2)). All compensation to a MLO must be either what is called **borrower paid origination** (BPO) or **lender paid origination** (LPO), such as when the consumer pays points to the lender/creditor who then compensates the MLO. A MLO who receives compensation from the lender/creditor in this manner cannot also receive compensation from the consumer.

The rule does not prohibit a consumer from accepting a higher interest rate in return for reducing closing costs, known as **yield spread premium** (YSP). This shows as a credit to the borrower on the Good Faith Estimate and is not considered to be compensation paid by the consumer to the MLO.

Steering and Safe Harbor

To further protect the interests of the consumer, Regulation Z § 226.36 (e) prohibits mortgage loan originators from "steering"—influencing, advising, counseling, directing—consumers to accept the terms offered by a particular creditor in order to receive greater compensation than might be available from a different creditor, unless the loan is actually in the borrower's interest. For such actions to constitute steering, however, the consumer must actually consummate the transaction in question.

In order to facilitate compliance, the rule creates what is referred to as a **safe harbor** by setting specific requirements for providing loan options to consumers.

To stay within the safe harbor, a MLO must obtain loan options from a significant number of the creditors—three or more—with which the originator regularly does business, and the MLO must have a good faith belief that the options presented to the consumer are loans for which the consumer likely qualifies. For each type of transaction in which the consumer has expressed an interest, a MLO must present loan options that include the following:

- Lowest interest rate
- Lowest interest rate without risky features, i.e., prepayment penalties, negative amortization, interest-only payments, balloon payments in the first seven years of the loan, a demand feature, shared equity or shared appreciation; or, in the case of a reverse mortgage, a loan without a prepayment penalty or shared equity or appreciation
- Lowest total dollar amount for origination fees and discount points

The term "type of transaction" refers to the following types of loans:

- One with an annual percentage rate that cannot increase after consummation
- One with an annual percentage rate that may increase after consummation
- A reverse mortgage

It does not apply to a home equity line of credit or a loan secured by a consumer's interest in a timeshare plan.

For each type of transaction, if a mortgage loan originator presents to the consumer *more than three loans*, the MLO must highlight the loans that satisfy the criteria specified in the rule. The MLO can present *fewer than three loans* and satisfy the safe harbor if the loan(s) otherwise meet the criteria in the rule.

A violation of this steering prohibition may provide a borrower with an affirmative defense in a foreclosure proceeding, and note that the Dodd-Frank Act ensures that such a defense is not subject to the statute of limitations that normally impact private action for damages.

For more information, see Title 12: Banks and Banking, Part 226 Regulation Z, Supplement I to Part 226—Official Staff Interpretations at: http://ecfr.gpoacess.gov

Mortgage Loan Originator Licensing

The SAFE Act

The **Housing and Economic Recovery Act of 2008 (HERA)** is a major housing law designed to assist with the recovery and the revitalization of America's residential housing market (Pub.L. 110-289). HERA has multiple purposes: The modernization of the Federal Housing Administration, foreclosure prevention, and the enhancement of consumer protections.

Title V, the **Secure and Fair Enforcement for Mortgage Licensing Act** or **SAFE Act**, is a key component of HERA. It is designed to enhance consumer protection and reduce fraud by requiring national minimum standards for mortgage training, including prelicensing education and annual continuing education. Furthermore, under the SAFE Act, all mortgage loan originators (MLOs) must be either state-licensed or federally registered. All mortgage loan originators seeking state-licensure—or currently holding a state license—are required to pass the SAFE Mortgage Loan Originator Test, which includes a national component and may have a state-specific component.

The SAFE Act requires all states to implement a mortgage loan originator (MLO) licensing process that meets certain standards through the **Nationwide Mortgage Licensing System & Registry (NMLS).** The NMLS, which was started in 2004 by the Conference of State Bank Supervisors (CSBS) and the American Association of Residential Mortgage Regulators (AARMR), is responsible for providing a centralized and standardized system for mortgage licensing that accommodates both the regulatory agencies and the mortgage industry. The NMLS website contains valuable comprehensive information for all mortgage loan originators, including specific details about the steps necessary to set up an account, schedule a test appointment, and access state-specific requirements.

Objectives of the SAFE Act

Among the objectives of the SAFE Act are to:

- Provide uniform license applications and reporting requirements for state-licensed mortgage loan originators.
- Provide a comprehensive licensing and supervisory database.
- Aggregate and improve the flow of information to and between regulators.
- Provide increased accountability and tracking of mortgage loan originators.
- Streamline the licensing process and reduce regulatory burden.
- Enhance consumer protections and support anti-fraud measures.
- Provide consumers with free, easy-to-access information about a mortgage loan originator's employment history and any public disciplinary and enforcement actions.
- Establish a means by which residential mortgage loan originators are required to act in the best interests of the consumer.
- Facilitate responsible behavior in the subprime mortgage market place.
- Provide comprehensive training and examination requirements related to nontraditional mortgage products.
- Facilitate the collection and disbursement of consumer complaints on behalf of state mortgage regulators.

Fulfilling the Mandates of the SAFE Act

With the enactment of the SAFE Act, the **Conference of State Bank Supervisors** (CSBS) and the **American Association of Residential Mortgage Regulators** (AARMR) worked with the Department of Housing and Urban Development (HUD) to fulfill the mandates of the Act, including the requirements that states establish minimum standards for the licensing or registration of all mortgage loan originators. To that end, CSBS and AARMR developed a model state law that met the minimum standards in the SAFE Act, including definitions, education and testing requirements, and financial responsibility and criminal background standards for mortgage loan originators. HUD reviewed the model legislation and determined that it did indeed meet the requirements of the SAFE Act. Therefore, any state legislation that follows the model has also met the applicable minimum requirements of the SAFE Act.

Loan Originator Defined

The SAFE Act defines a loan originator (Sec. 1503) as an individual who:

(A) Takes a residential mortgage loan application.

(B) Offers or negotiates terms of a residential mortgage loan for compensation or gain.

An individual "assists a consumer in obtaining or applying to obtain a residential mortgage loan" by, among other things, advising on loan terms (including rates, fees, other costs), preparing loan packages, or collecting information on behalf of the consumer with regard to a residential mortgage loan.

The definition does **not** include:

- Any individual who performs purely administrative or clerical tasks on behalf of a licensee.
- A person or entity that only performs real estate brokerage activities and is licensed or registered in accordance with applicable state law, unless the person or entity is compensated by a lender, a mortgage broker, or other mortgage loan originator or by any agent of such lender, mortgage broker, or other mortgage loan originator.
- A person or entity solely involved in extensions of credit relating to timeshare plans.

A **loan processor** or **underwriter** who does *not* represent to the public, through advertising or other means of communicating or providing information (including the use of business cards, stationery, brochures, signs, rate lists, or other promotional items), that he or she can or will perform any of the activities of a loan originator shall not be required to be a state-licensed mortgage loan originator.

An **independent contractor** may not engage in residential mortgage loan origination activities as a loan processor or underwriter unless such independent contractor is a state-licensed mortgage loan originator.

The SAFE Act requires all residential mortgage loan originators to be identified by a unique NMLS identifier number as either:

- **Federally registered**—any mortgage loan originator employed by a depository institution, a subsidiary that is owned and controlled by a depository institution and regulated by a federal banking agency, or an institution regulated by the Farm Credit Administration.
- **State-licensed**—all other mortgage loan originators, without exception.

Other Definitions

Administrative or Clerical Tasks. The receipt, collection, and distribution of information common for the processing or underwriting of a loan in the mortgage industry and communication with a consumer to obtain information necessary for the processing or underwriting of a residential mortgage loan.

Depository Institution. Has the same meaning as in section 3 of the Federal Deposit Insurance Act (i.e., any bank or savings association) and includes any credit union.

Federal Banking Agencies. The Board of Governors of the Federal Reserve System, the Comptroller of the Currency, the Director of the Office of Thrift Supervision, the National Credit Union Administration, and the Federal Deposit Insurance Corporation.

Loan Processor or Underwriter. In general, an individual who performs clerical or support duties at the direction of and subject to the supervision and instruction of:

- A state-licensed mortgage loan originator; or
- A registered mortgage loan originator.

"Clerical or support duties" may include:

- The receipt, collection, distribution, and analysis of information common for the processing or underwriting of a residential mortgage loan; and
- Communicating with a consumer to obtain the information necessary for the processing or underwriting of a loan, to the extent that such communication does not include offering or negotiating loan rates or terms, or counseling consumers about residential mortgage loan rates or terms.

Nontraditional Mortgage Product. Any mortgage product other than a 30-year fixed rate mortgage.

Real Estate Brokerage Activity. Any activity that involves offering or providing real estate brokerage services to the public, including:

- Acting as a real estate agent or real estate broker for a buyer, seller, lessor, or lessee of real property;
- Bringing together parties interested in the sale, purchase, lease, rental, or exchange of real property;
- Negotiating, on behalf of any party, any portion of a contract relating to the sale, purchase, lease, rental, or exchange of real property (other than in connection with providing financing with respect to any such transaction);
- Engaging in any activity for which a person engaged in the activity is required to be registered or licensed as a real estate agent or real estate broker under any applicable law; and
- Offering to engage in any activity, or act in any capacity described above.

Registered Loan Originator. Any individual who:

(A) meets the definition of loan originator and is an employee of:

(i) a depository institution;

(ii) a subsidiary that is

(I) owned and controlled by a depository institution; and

(II) regulated by a Federal banking agency; or

(iii) an institution regulated by the Farm Credit Administration; and (B) is registered with, and maintains a unique identifier through, the Nationwide Mortgage Licensing System and Registry.

Residential Mortgage Loan. Any loan primarily for personal, family, or household use that is secured by a mortgage, deed of trust, or other equivalent consensual security interest on a dwelling (as defined in section 103(v) of the Truth in Lending Act) or residential real estate upon which is constructed or intended to be constructed a dwelling (as so defined).

State-Licensed Loan Originator. Any individual who:

(A) is a loan originator;

(B) is not an employee of:

(i) a depository institution;

(ii) a subsidiary that is

(I) owned and controlled by a depository institution; and

(II) regulated by a Federal banking agency; or

(iii) an institution regulated by the Farm Credit Administration; and

(C) is licensed by a state or by the Secretary under section 1508 and registered as a loan originator with, and maintains a unique identifier through, the Nationwide Mortgage Licensing System and Registry.

Unique Identifier. In general, a number or other identifier that:

- Permanently identifies a loan originator;
- Is assigned by protocols established by the Nationwide Mortgage Licensing System and Registry and the Federal banking agencies to facilitate electronic tracking of loan originators and uniform identification of, and public access to, the employment history of and the publicly adjudicated disciplinary and enforcement actions against loan originators; and
- Shall not be used for purposes other than those set forth under the SAFE Act.

To the greatest extent possible and to accomplish the purpose of the SAFE Act, states shall use unique identifiers in lieu of Social Security numbers.

The NMLS unique identifier is required on all marketing materials, applications, required disclosures, and business cards. If the marketing materials are referencing the company only, the company's unique identifier must be used. If the marketing materials and business cards are issued in the name of the mortgage loan originator, then the marketing materials and business cards require the MLO's unique identifier. All disclosures require the MLO's unique identifier.

SAFE Act Licensing Requirements (Sec. 1505-1506)

To meet its objectives, the SAFE Act requires that applicants for a mortgage loan originator license must:

- Submit to a background check (including fingerprints, state and national criminal check).
- Provide personal history and experience.
- Provide authorization to obtain an independent credit report, and information relative to any administrative, civil, or criminal findings.
- Never had a mortgage loan originator license revoked in any government jurisdiction (a subsequent formal vacation of such revocation is not considered a revocation).
- Not have been convicted of or pled guilty or nolo contendere to, a felony in a domestic, foreign, or military court during **the seven-year period preceding** the date of the application for licensing and registration or at **any time preceding** such date of application, if such felony involved an act of fraud, dishonesty, or a breach of trust, or money laundering (any pardon of a conviction is not considered a conviction).

Character and Fitness

The model state language of the SAFE Act indicates that an applicant must demonstrate financial responsibility, character, and general fitness such as to command the confidence of the community and to warrant a determination that the mortgage loan originator will operate honestly, fairly, and efficiently within the purposes of this Act.

A person has shown that he or she is not financially responsible when he or she has shown a disregard in the management of his or her own financial condition. A determination that an individual has not shown financial responsibility may include, but not be limited to:

- Current outstanding judgments, except judgments solely as a result of medical expenses.
- Current outstanding tax liens or other government liens and filings.
- Foreclosures within the past three years.
- A pattern of seriously delinquent accounts within the past three years.

Prelicensing Education Requirements

To become a state-licensed mortgage loan originator, applicants must complete **at least twenty (20) hours** of approved prelicensing education which includes:

- Federal law and regulation (3 hours)
- Ethics, including fraud, consumer protection, and fair lending (3 hours)

- Nontraditional mortgage products, which the SAFE Act defines as anything other than 30-year fixed rate loan (2 hours)
- Elective topics (12 hours)

It is up to each state to determine whether or not to also require state-specific topics, either as part of the 12 hours of electives or in addition to the 20 hours required. .

Mortgage Loan Originator Exam

The SAFE Act mandates that all applicants for a state mortgage loan originator license pass the SAFE Mortgage Loan Originator Test, which is comprised of two parts:

- National component
- State component, which is specific to each jurisdiction in which the MLO chooses to be licensed

The national component covers these topics:

- Federal mortgage-related laws (35%)
- General mortgage knowledge (25%)
- Mortgage loan origination activities (25%)
- Ethics (15%)

The state-specific component covers topics as mandated by each particular jurisdiction.

According to the U.S. Department of Housing and Urban Development (HUD) final rule implementing the SAFE Act, any candidate for licensure who enrolls to take a test may only take and fail the national or a state component of the SAFE MLO Test **three consecutive times**. After the third failure, that candidate must wait at least **six (6) months** before taking the test again.

License Renewal Requirements

State-licensed mortgage loan originators must complete **at least eight (8) hours of continuing education every year, including these topics:**

- Federal law and regulation (3 hours)
- Ethics, including fraud, consumer protection, and fair lending (2 hours)
- Nontraditional mortgage products (2 hours)
- Elective (1 hour)

Each state may impose additional continuing education requirements. Mortgage loan originators cannot get credit for the same continuing education class twice in consecutive years.

Chapter 4 Summary

Requiring Financial Disclosures		
Federal Law	Highlights	Disclosures/Notices
Truth in Lending Act (Regulation Z, TILA) 1968; amended by Mortgage Disclosure Improvement Act (MDIA) 2009 Enforced by Board of Governors of the Federal Reserve System (until transfer to the Consumer Financial Protection Bureau)	• Promotes the informed use of credit by disclosing costs in a uniform manner • Applies to loans with more than four installments • Provides right of rescission for three business days after loan consummation on refinance of owner-occupied property • Completed application requires use of TIL Statement (credit terms, including APR and total finance charges, payment amounts, and due dates) • Imposes a prescribed tolerance between TIL APR and final APR • 3/7/3 Rule – initial disclosure within 3 business days; earliest close 7th business day after initial disclosure; 3 business-day waiting period before consummation if redisclosure required	Within 3 Business Days of Completed Application: • TIL disclosure statement / guide to TIL Statement • When Home is on the Line *(home equity loans)* • CHARM booklet *(ARM loans)* At Settlement (for loans on primary residence): • Notice of right to *rescind (2 copies)* General • Disclosure of APR in advertising with certain triggering terms
Real Estate Settlement Procedures Act (Regulation X, RESPA) 1974 Enforced by Board of Governors of the Federal Reserve System/ Implemented by U. S. Department of Housing and Urban Development (until transfer to the Consumer Financial Protection Bureau)	• Helps consumers compare settlement services and eliminate unnecessary increases in the costs of certain settlement services • Covers loans secured with a mortgage placed on a one- to four-family residential property • Prohibits kickbacks, fee-splitting, and unearned fees • Sets limits on escrow accounts • Prohibits sellers from requiring home buyers to use a particular title insurance company • Requires Good Faith Estimate (GFE) showing amount of settlement charges the borrower is likely to pay; includes tools for consumers to compare • Requires use of HUD-1 or HUD-1A Settlement Statement to clearly show all charges imposed on borrowers and sellers in connection with the settlement (except for open-end home equity)	Within 3 Business Days of Completed Application: • Good Faith Estimate • Mortgage Servicing Disclosure • HUD Booklet on Settlement Costs Before Settlement: • Affiliated Business Arrangement Disclosure • HUD-1 Settlement Statement (within 1 business day of settlement if requested) At Settlement: • HUD-1 Settlement Statement • Initial Escrow Statement After Settlement: • Annual Escrow Statement • Servicing Transfer Statement
Homeowners Protection Act (HPA) 1998 Enforced by Board of Governors of the Federal Reserve System	• Applies to single-family residential dwellings • Allows borrowers to request PMI cancellation when LTV reaches 80% • Automatically terminates PMI when LTV reaches 78% if borrower is not delinquent • Allows borrowers to accelerate the cancellation date by making additional payments that bring the LTV to 80%	• Initial disclosure of HPA provisions with annual reminders • Disclosure of cancellation and automatic termination dates for fixed rate loans

Privacy and Consumer Identification		
Federal Law	Highlights	Disclosures/Notices
Fair Credit Reporting Act (Regulation V, FCRA) 1968 Enforced by Federal Trade Commission (until transfer to the Consumer Financial Protection Bureau)	• Gives consumers access to the same information about themselves that lenders use when making credit decisions • Entitles consumers to free credit report upon adverse action or identity theft • Allows consumers to dispute credit report • Provides additional rights for identity theft victims and active duty military personnel	• One-time written notice of derogatory information, separate from Truth in Lending disclosures
Fair and Accurate Credit Transaction Act of 2003 (FACT Act) Enforced by Federal Trade Commission (until transfer to the Consumer Financial Protection Bureau)	• Amends the Fair Credit Reporting Act to help consumers fight identity theft • Mandates limits on information sharing • Entitles consumers to annual free credit report • Allows consumers to place fraud alerts and credit freezes • Requires businesses to truncate credit/debit card numbers on receipts • Mandates businesses to secure and properly dispose of sensitive personal information in a consumer's credit report • Red Flag Rules require financial institutions and creditors to implement a written identity theft prevention program	When Applying for Credit: • Home Loan Applicant Credit Score Information Disclosure
Gramm-Leach-Bliley Act or Financial Services Modernization Act of 1999 (The Privacy Act) Enforced by Federal Trade Commission	Financial Privacy Rule: • Restricts when and under what circumstances personal financial information may be disclosed to non-affiliated third parties • Allows consumers to opt out of allowing information to be shared Safeguards Rule: • Requires all financial institutions to design, implement, and maintain safeguards to protect customer information while it is in the custody and control of the institution and its agents and in the transfer of such information Pretexting Provisions: • Protects consumers from those who obtain personal information under false, fictitious, or fraudulent pretenses	Before Disclosing Information to Non-Affiliated Third Parties: • Consumer Privacy Policy (and annually to customers as long as the relationship continues)
National Do Not Call Registry Enforced by Federal Trade Commission	• Allows consumers to put phone numbers on a national Do Not Call list • Applies to any plan, program, or campaign to sell goods or services through interstate phone calls • Requires companies to maintain national and internal lists of customers and prospects and keep them updated regularly • Allows business to call a consumer with whom it has an established business relationship (EBR) for up to 18 months after the consumer's last purchase, delivery, or payment; or up to 90 days after an inquiry • Imposes fines of up to $16,000 per violation	None

Privacy and Consumer Identification		
Federal Law	Highlights	Disclosures/Notices
U.S. Patriot Act (Uniting and Strengthening America by Providing Appropriate Tools Required to Intercept and Obstruct Terrorism Act) 2001	• Requires lenders and banks to create and maintain customer identification programs (CIPs) to verify identity of customers entering into a "formal relationship" • Mortgage brokers must also perform the lender's CIP	Patriot Act Information Disclosure
Prohibiting Discrimination		
Federal Law	Highlights	Disclosures/Notices
Civil Rights Act 1866	• Prohibits all racial discrimination, private or public, in the sale and rental of property • Allows someone claiming unlawful discrimination to sue only in federal district court	None
Fair Housing Act 1968	• Prohibits any discrimination in the sale, lease, or loan terms for residential property based on race, color, religion, sex, national origin, disability, or familial status • Allows someone claiming discrimination to file a written complaint to the nearest HUD office within one year of the alleged violation	• Fair/Equal Housing/Lending posters and logos • Post availability of information in lobby (depository institutions)
Equal Credit Opportunity Act (Regulation B, ECOA) 1974 Enforced by Federal Trade Commission (each financial institution under authority of its regulatory agency) (until transfer to the Consumer Financial Protection Bureau)	• Prohibits discrimination in granting credit to people based on sex, age (if at least 18), marital status, race, color, religion, national origin, receipt of public assistance, or exercised rights under the Consumer Credit Protection Act • Requires credit bureaus to keep separate files on married spouses, if requested • Prohibits creditors from refusing to consider or discounting income from alimony, child support, maintenance if borrower chooses to disclose it • Allows borrowers to request copy of appraisal report used in credit decision within 90 days	• ECOA statement of rights, including right to receive a copy of appraisal report • Notification of credit decision within 30 days of application (statement of adverse action if declined, incomplete, or change of terms offered)
Home Mortgage Disclosure Act (Federal Reserve Board's Regulation C, HMDA) 1975 Enforced by Board of Governors of the Federal Reserve System (until transfer to the Consumer Financial Protection Bureau)	• Determines if financial institutions are serving the housing needs of their communities • Applies to financial institutions and non-depository institutions with assets in excess of $10 million or who originate more than 100 loans/year • Identifies possible discriminatory lending patterns through the collection and disclosure of data about applicant and borrower characteristics	Loan/Application Register (LAR): Report to supervisory agencies on a loan-by-loan and application-by-application basis every March
Community Reinvestment Act (CRA) 1977	• Encourage financial institutions to help meet the credit needs of the communities in which they operate. • Requires periodic examinations by federal agencies responsible for supervising depository institutions	None

Against Predatory Lending		
Federal Law	**Highlights**	**Disclosures/Notices**
Home Ownership and Equity Protection Act (HOEPA) 1994 Enforced by Board of Governors of the Federal Reserve System (until transfer to the Consumer Financial Protection Bureau)	• Amends Regulation Z (Section 32) to prohibit deceptive and unfair practices in lending • Establishes additional disclosure requirements for high cost loans • Defines high cost loan as: The APR exceeds the rates on Treasury securities of comparable maturity by more than eight percentage points for a first mortgage or more than ten percentage points for a second mortgage; or the total points and fees exceed 8% of the loan amount, or total dollar amount exceeds $611 for 2012 • Uses some different criteria to define total finance charges, e.g., counts optional credit insurance premiums • Prohibits balloon payments (on loans of less than 5 years), negative amortization, demand clauses • Limits prepayment penalties • Allows three business-day right of rescission for HOEPA loans	Section 32 disclosures include: • Notice that consumer is not required to complete the transaction • Warning that the lender will have a mortgage on the home and the borrower could lose it and equity if in default • The annual percentage rate (APR) • The regular payment amount (including any balloon payment where the law permits balloon payments) • The loan amount • Credit insurance premiums, if applicable • For variable rate loans, the amount of the maximum monthly payment and the fact that the rate and monthly payment may increase
Higher-Priced Loans – Regulation Z § 226.35 as amended by Housing and Economic Recovery Act of 2008 Enforced by Board of Governors of the Federal Reserve System (until transfer to the Consumer Financial Protection Bureau)	• Closed-end mortgage loan secured by borrower's principal dwelling where APR exceeds applicable average prime offer rate by at least 1.5% for first lien loans or 3.5% for junior lien loans • Creditors obligated to verify repayment ability • Prepayment penalties generally prohibited • Escrow account must be established for property taxes and mortgage-related insurance premiums required by creditor	None
MLO Compensation Rule –Regulation Z § 226.36 Enforced by Board of Governors of the Federal Reserve System (until transfer to the Consumer Financial Protection Bureau)	• Amends Regulation Z (§ 226.36) • Prohibits compensation based on loan interest rates or other terms/conditions other than loan amount • Prohibits dual compensation (borrower paid and lender paid) to MLOs • Prohibits steering consumers to specific lenders to gain greater compensation unless loan is in borrower's interest • Sets safe harbor rules for presenting loan options to consumers	Present loan options from significant number of creditors

MLO Licensing		
Federal Law	Highlights	Disclosures/Notices
The Secure and Fair Enforcement for Mortgage Licensing Act of 2008 (SAFE Act, Title V of Housing and Economic Recovery Act) To be enforced by the Consumer Financial Protection Bureau	• Establishes minimum standards for the licensing of state-licensed mortgage loan originators and registered mortgage loan originators • Provides for the establishment and maintenance of a Nationwide Mortgage Licensing System and Registry for the residential mortgage industry • Requires 20 hours of prelicensing education for state-licensed MLO applicants • Requires background checks for applicants • Requires passage of national NMLS exam (which may include state/territory component) • Requires at least 8 hours of annual continuing education for state-licensed MLOs • Requires contractor loan processors and underwriters to have MLO license	• Display of license • Use of NMLS unique ID on applications and other documents

Chapter 4 Quiz

1. ***Which law requires mortgage loan originators to provide borrowers with a Good Faith Estimate of closing costs?***
   A. FCRA
   B. HMDA
   C. RESPA
   D. TILA

2. ***The most important disclosure requirement under the Truth in Lending Act is the***
   A. amount of index.
   B. amount of the loan origination fee.
   C. APR.
   D. name of the secondary market purchaser.

3. ***How many business days after closing does the consumer have the right to rescind a refinance of his personal residence?***
   A. 2
   B. 3
   C. 5
   D. There is no right of rescission.

4. ***Which will trigger the required disclosures of the Truth in Lending Act if included in an advertisement for credit?***
   A. "Affordable Financing"
   B. "Easy Monthly Payments"
   C. "FHA Financing Available"
   D. "Only 360 Monthly Payments"

5. ***If an advertisement discloses only the APR, what additional disclosures are required?***
   A. amount of any finance charges
   B. percentage of down payment
   C. terms of repayment
   D. no additional disclosures are required

6. ***Which act requires mortgage lenders to give consumers information about obtaining their credit report when they are turned down for a loan?***
   A. ECOA
   B. FCRA
   C. RESPA
   D. TILA

7. ***Under what circumstances does RESPA allow a sale to be conditioned on the use of a particular escrow company chosen by the seller?***
   A. if full disclosure is made
   B. if no kickbacks are involved
   C. if no unearned fees are involved
   D. under no circumstances

8. ***Which regulation mandates the use of the HUD-1 Settlement Statement?***
   A. Regulation B
   B. Regulation C
   C. Regulation X
   D. Regulation Z

9. ***For how many months after a loan closes may a mortgage loan originator call a customer whose phone number is on the National Do Not Call Registry to solicit new business?***
   A. 3 months
   B. 6 months
   C. 18 months
   D. No calls can be made to a number on the registry.

10. ***Which law includes Red Flag Rules that require financial institutions and creditors to implement procedures to protect customer identity?***
   A. Fair and Accurate Credit Transaction Act
   B. Fair Credit Reporting Act
   C. Gramm-Leach-Bliley Act (The Privacy Act)
   D. Homeowners Protection Act

11. ***The SAFE Act requires state-licensed originators to have a minimum of how many hours of approved prelicensing education?***
   A. 8
   B. 12
   C. 20
   D. 24

12. ***The Home Ownership and Equity Protection Act***
   A. amends the Homeowners Protection Act.
   B. does not consider optional credit insurance as a finance charge.
   C. gives borrowers with high-cost loans three business days to rescind the loan.
   D. permits negative amortization only for the first five years of a loan.

13. ***According to the Homeowners Protection Act, borrowers may request cancellation of their mortgage insurance premiums when the LTV reaches***

A. 75%.
B. 78%.
C. 80%.
D. 82%.

14. ***As a result of the Mortgage Disclosure Improvement Act, how soon can a residential loan close?***

A. the next business day
B. after three business days for a refinance or home equity loan
C. within three business days of applying
D. on the seventh business day after delivery of required disclosures

15. ***Which fee can be collected prior to delivery of a Truth in Lending Statement and a Good Faith Estimate?***

A. appraisal fee
B. credit report fee
C. origination fee
D. No fees can be collected prior to delivery of these disclosures.

16. ***A mortgage broker rents office space from a title company at a discount in exchange for referring customers for settlement services. Which federal law does this arrangement violate?***

A. RESPA
B. SAFE Act
C. TILA
D. It does not violate any federal law.

17. ***The APR on an initial TIL for a 30-year fixed rate loan is 6.25%, and the APR on the final TIL is 6.5%. After redisclosure, how long must the borrower wait to close the loan?***

A. 1 business day
B. three business days after redisclosure
C. seven business days after redislcosure
D. There is no waiting required since the difference is within the acceptable tolerance.

18. ***A "higher-priced loan" is one that has***

A. an APR that exceeds the applicable average prime offer rate by at least 1.5% for a first lien loan.
B. an APR that exceeds the rates on Treasury securities of comparable maturity by more than 8%.
C. total points and fees greater than 8% of the loan amount.
D. total points and fees greater than 10% of the loan amount for junior liens.

19. ***Which statement about loan origination fees on a GFE is FALSE?***

A. The fee cannot change unless there is a changed circumstance.
B. The fee includes services performed by or on behalf of the mortgage loan originator.
C. Lender and mortgage broker fees for the same transaction must be itemized.
D. Origination fees must be expressed as lump sum.

20. ***According to the SAFE Act, which incident from 10 years ago would NOT automatically disqualify an applicant for a mortgage loan originator license?***

A. conviction for felony assault
B. conviction for felony fraud
C. conviction for felony money laundering
D. revocation by the state of a mortgage broker's license

21. ***Which of these circumstances would NOT be an acceptable reason to provide a revised GFE to a borrower?***

A. The borrower lost the income from a part-time job and so was no longer eligible for the specific loan terms identified in the GFE.
B. The borrower requested to change the loan term from 15 to 30 years.
C. The mortgage loan originator regretted overlooking certain liabilities in order to qualify the borrower for a better interest rate.
D. The title company discovered a junior lien on the property that was not considered when preparing the GFE.

22. ***A 10% tolerance is allowed between the amount shown on the GFE and the actual amount due at closing for which of these charges?***

A. charge for the interest rate chosen when locked
B. government recording charges
C. origination fee
D. transfer taxes

5

Chapter 5

Real Estate Finance Instruments

In This Chapter

Whether you work for a bank, a mortgage company, a mortgage broker, or other type of primary lender, or for an agency that is active in the secondary market, you must know some of the various forms, reports, and other documents you will encounter in your work. The "instruments" discussed in this chapter focus on the more common legal documents you will encounter as part of real estate transactions that are used to establish the rights and duties of the parties involved. These include legal instruments, such as promissory notes, security instruments, trust deeds, and mortgages. We'll also discuss types and features of mortgages, as well as typical clauses found in these instruments.

At the end of this chapter, you will be able to:

- Contrast a financing instrument from a security instrument.
- Discuss advantages and disadvantages of trust deeds.
- Discuss advantages and disadvantages of mortgages.
- Define the purpose of different types of mortgages.
- Identify typical mortgage clauses.

Key Terms

Acceleration Clause
Alienation Clause
Balloon Payment
Construction Loan
Equitable Right of Redemption
Equitable Title
Hypothecate
Judicial Foreclosure
Mortgage
Negotiable Instrument
Non-Judicial Foreclosure
Note Rate
Promissory Note
Security Instrument
Subordination Agreement
Trust Deed (or Deed of Trust)

Promissory Notes

Promissory notes are *financing instruments that evidence a promise to pay a specific amount of money to a specific person within a specific time frame.* Simply stated, a promissory note is a written promise to pay money. Before a lender will finance the purchase of a house, the borrower must promise to repay the funds. The *one promising to pay the money* is called the **maker** of the note, usually the borrower. The *one to whom payment is promised* is called the **payee**, usually the lender, which could also be the seller. Promissory notes are basic evidence of debt, showing who owes how much to whom. A typical promissory note includes:

- Date
- Names of the parties
- Amount of the debt, including the interest rate used to amortize the debt, known as the **note rate**
- How and when the money is to be paid
- What happens in the event of default
- Signature of the maker

Most promissory notes used in real estate are **negotiable instruments**, which means that they are *freely transferable from one party to another.* When a note is freely transferable, the lender or other creditor can obtain immediate cash by selling the note, for example, when a lender sells real estate notes to the secondary market.

Types of Notes

The four types of notes usually used in real estate transactions are:

- **Straight Note or Interest Only Note.** Calls for payments of interest-only during the term of the note, with a balloon payment at the end of the loan term to pay off the principal amount; usually a short-term loan.
- **Installment Note.** Calls for payments of principal and/or interest at designated intervals, (in reality, a balloon payment may be required).
- **Partially Amortizing Installment Note** or **Installment Note with Balloon.** Calls for periodic payments of principal and interest during the loan term with a balloon payment at the end of the term to pay off the balance due.
- **Fully Amortizing Installment Note.** Calls for regular payment of principal and interest, calculated to pay off the entire balance by the end of loan term.

Security Instruments

In almost all real estate financing transactions, a promissory note is accompanied by a **security instrument.** A security instrument requires a debtor to **hypothecate** his or her property as a condition of a loan, which means that *a debtor pledges personal or real property as security for a debt, typically without giving up possession of it.*

A security instrument serves as protection for the creditor, and motivation for the debtor, to make sure that the terms of the note are fulfilled and the note is repaid as agreed. Keep in mind, though, that a security instrument just describes collateral for a note. Even without a security instrument, the debtor is still obligated to pay the note. Failure to repay the debt according to the terms of the agreement could result in foreclosure. When the debt is repaid, the note and the security instrument are cancelled.

The two main types of security instruments used in real estate transactions are trust deeds and mortgages.

NOTE

__________________________, ________ __________________________, _____________

[Date] [City] [State]

____

[Property Address]

1. BORROWER'S PROMISE TO PAY

In return for a loan that I have received, I promise to pay U.S. $____________________ (this amount is called "Principal"), plus interest, to the order of the Lender. The Lender is ____. I will make all payments under this Note in the form of cash, check or money order.

I understand that the Lender may transfer this Note. The Lender or anyone who takes this Note by transfer and who is entitled to receive payments under this Note is called the "Note Holder."

2. INTEREST

Interest will be charged on unpaid principal until the full amount of Principal has been paid. I will pay interest at a yearly rate of _______________%.

The interest rate required by this Section 2 is the rate I will pay both before and after any default described in Section 6(B) of this Note.

3. PAYMENTS

(A) Time and Place of Payments

I will pay principal and interest by making a payment every month.

I will make my monthly payment on the _________ day of each month beginning on ____________________, _____. I will make these payments every month until I have paid all of the principal and interest and any other charges described below that I may owe under this Note. Each monthly payment will be applied as of its scheduled due date and will be applied to interest before Principal. If, on _________________________________, 20____, I still owe amounts under this Note, I will pay those amounts in full on that date, which is called the "Maturity Date."

I will make my monthly payments at ____ or at a different place if required by the Note Holder.

(B) Amount of Monthly Payments

My monthly payment will be in the amount of U.S. $_______________________________.

4. BORROWER'S RIGHT TO PREPAY

I have the right to make payments of Principal at any time before they are due. A payment of Principal only is known as a "Prepayment." When I make a Prepayment, I will tell the Note Holder in writing that I am doing so. I may not designate a payment as a Prepayment if I have not made all the monthly payments due under the Note.

I may make a full Prepayment or partial Prepayments without paying a Prepayment charge. The Note Holder will use my Prepayments to reduce the amount of Principal that I owe under this Note. However, the Note Holder may apply my Prepayment to the accrued and unpaid interest on the Prepayment amount, before applying my Prepayment to reduce the Principal amount of the Note. If I make a partial Prepayment, there will be no changes in the due date or in the amount of my monthly payment unless the Note Holder agrees in writing to those changes.

5. LOAN CHARGES

If a law, which applies to this loan and which sets maximum loan charges, is finally interpreted so that the interest or other loan charges collected or to be collected in connection with this loan exceed the permitted limits, then: (a) any such loan charge shall be reduced by the amount necessary to reduce the charge to the permitted limit; and (b) any sums already collected from me which exceeded permitted limits will be refunded to me. The Note Holder may choose to make this refund by reducing the Principal I owe under this Note or by making a direct payment to me. If a refund reduces Principal, the reduction will be treated as a partial Prepayment.

MULTISTATE FIXED RATE NOTE—Single Family—**Fannie Mae/Freddie Mac UNIFORM INSTRUMENT** **Form 3200 1/01** *(page 1 of 3 pages)*

Sample Promissory Note

6. BORROWER'S FAILURE TO PAY AS REQUIRED

(A) Late Charge for Overdue Payments

If the Note Holder has not received the full amount of any monthly payment by the end of ___________ calendar days after the date it is due, I will pay a late charge to the Note Holder. The amount of the charge will be _____% of my overdue payment of principal and interest. I will pay this late charge promptly but only once on each late payment.

(B) Default

If I do not pay the full amount of each monthly payment on the date it is due, I will be in default.

(C) Notice of Default

If I am in default, the Note Holder may send me a written notice telling me that if I do not pay the overdue amount by a certain date, the Note Holder may require me to pay immediately the full amount of Principal which has not been paid and all the interest that I owe on that amount. That date must be at least 30 days after the date on which the notice is mailed to me or delivered by other means.

(D) No Waiver By Note Holder

Even if, at a time when I am in default, the Note Holder does not require me to pay immediately in full as described above, the Note Holder will still have the right to do so if I am in default at a later time.

(E) Payment of Note Holder's Costs and Expenses

If the Note Holder has required me to pay immediately in full as described above, the Note Holder will have the right to be paid back by me for all of its costs and expenses in enforcing this Note to the extent not prohibited by applicable law. Those expenses include, for example, reasonable attorneys' fees.

7. GIVING OF NOTICES

Unless applicable law requires a different method, any notice that must be given to me under this Note will be given by delivering it or by mailing it by first class mail to me at the Property Address above or at a different address if I give the Note Holder a notice of my different address.

Any notice that must be given to the Note Holder under this Note will be given by delivering it or by mailing it by first class mail to the Note Holder at the address stated in Section 3(A) above or at a different address if I am given a notice of that different address.

8. OBLIGATIONS OF PERSONS UNDER THIS NOTE

If more than one person signs this Note, each person is fully and personally obligated to keep all of the promises made in this Note, including the promise to pay the full amount owed. Any person who is a guarantor, surety or endorser of this Note is also obligated to do these things. Any person who takes over these obligations, including the obligations of a guarantor, surety or endorser of this Note, is also obligated to keep all of the promises made in this Note. The Note Holder may enforce its rights under this Note against each person individually or against all of us together. This means that any one of us may be required to pay all of the amounts owed under this Note.

9. WAIVERS

I and any other person who has obligations under this Note waive the rights of Presentment and Notice of Dishonor. "Presentment" means the right to require the Note Holder to demand payment of amounts due. "Notice of Dishonor" means the right to require the Note Holder to give notice to other persons that amounts due have not been paid.

10. UNIFORM SECURED NOTE

This Note is a uniform instrument with limited variations in some jurisdictions. In addition to the protections given to the Note Holder under this Note, a Mortgage, Deed of Trust, or Security Deed (the "Security Instrument"), dated the same date as this Note, protects the Note Holder from possible losses which might result if I do not keep the promises which I make in this Note. That Security Instrument describes how and under what conditions I may be required to make immediate payment in full of all amounts I owe under this Note. Some of those conditions are described as follows:

> If all or any part of the Property or any Interest in the Property is sold or transferred (or if Borrower is not a natural person and a beneficial interest in Borrower is sold or transferred) without Lender's prior written consent, Lender may require immediate payment in full of all sums secured by this Security Instrument. However, this option shall not be exercised by Lender if such exercise is prohibited by Applicable Law.

MULTISTATE FIXED RATE NOTE—Single Family—**Fannie Mae/Freddie Mac UNIFORM INSTRUMENT** **Form 3200 1/01** *(page 2 of 3 pages)*

Sample Promissory Note

If Lender exercises this option, Lender shall give Borrower notice of acceleration. The notice shall provide a period of not less than 30 days from the date the notice is given in accordance with Section 15 within which Borrower must pay all sums secured by this Security Instrument. If Borrower fails to pay these sums prior to the expiration of this period, Lender may invoke any remedies permitted by this Security Instrument without further notice or demand on Borrower.

WITNESS THE HAND(S) AND SEAL(S) OF THE UNDERSIGNED.

_______________________________________(Seal)
- Borrower

_______________________________________(Seal)
- Borrower

_______________________________________(Seal)
- Borrower

[Sign Original Only]

MULTISTATE FIXED RATE NOTE—Single Family—**Fannie Mae/Freddie Mac UNIFORM INSTRUMENT** **Form 3200 1/01** *(page 3 of 3 pages)*

Sample Promissory Note

Trust Deeds

Trust deeds, or deeds of trust, are instruments *placing a specific financial interest in the title to real property into the hands of a disinterested third party as security for the payment of a note.* With a trust deed, the borrower is called the **trustor**; the lender is the **beneficiary** who retains both the note and the deed of trust; and the **trustee** who holds legal title to the security property described in the deed of trust subject to the terms of the trust for the benefit of the lender. Who is eligible to be a trustee varies from state to state; it could be an attorney, for example, or a title company that provides trustee services. With a trust deed, the borrower has possession of and **equitable title** to the property. When the loan is paid, the note and the deed of trust are cancelled and both legal title and equitable title are then vested in the borrower.

Another distinguishing characteristic of trust deeds is that the trustee has the authority under the terms of the trust to commence a **non-judicial foreclosure action** when the lender has declared the loan to be in default. Such action would not be taken, however, until after the trustee has notified the borrower of the default and given the borrower the opportunity to cure.

Mortgages

A **mortgage** is the *conveyance of an interest in real property to a lender as security for the payment of a note.* A mortgage is a type of security instrument where the borrower (the mortgagor) conveys an interest property to the lender (the mortgagee) as collateral for the debt, creating a **voluntary lien** on the property. When a borrower defaults on a mortgage, the lender may commence a **judicial foreclosure action**.

Lien Theory and Title Theory

Some states follow what is called lien theory, while others follow what is called title theory.

wisconsin

Generally speaking, in **lien theory** states, the *security instrument creates a lien against the property which must be repaid by the debtor*. The property serves as collateral that is hypothecated to the lender as security for the debt, but the mortgagor holds the title to the property (or equitable title if a deed of trust is used). The lender may be required to go through a judicial foreclosure proceeding to obtain title and possession in the event of default.

In **title theory** states, the *security instrument gives actual title to the property to the lender while the debt is outstanding*, with the borrower retaining only equitable title and possession of the land. Once the mortgage amount has been repaid, legal title reverts or is conveyed to the borrower. The lender does not have possession or use of the property, and would have to go through a foreclosure proceeding to gain possession in the event of default, although it may be possible to avoid the lengthy judicial foreclosure proceeding and gain possession through non-judicial or strict foreclosure.

Some lien theory states allow only mortgages to be recorded; some title theory states allow only trust deeds to be recorded; and some states will allow either type of security instrument to be recorded. Make certain that you understand how mortgages and deeds of trust are handled in the states in which you practice.

After Recording Return To:
____
____
____
____

____________________ **[Space Above This Line For Recording Data]** ____________________

MORTGAGE

DEFINITIONS

Words used in multiple sections of this document are defined below and other words are defined in Sections 3, 11, 13, 18, 20 and 21. Certain rules regarding the usage of words used in this document are also provided in Section 16.

(A) "Security Instrument" means this document, which is dated ___________________________, ________, together with all Riders to this document.
(B) "Borrower" is ____. Borrower is the mortgagor under this Security Instrument.
(C) "Lender" is ____. Lender is a __________________________ organized and existing under the laws of ________________________. Lender's address is __________________________________. Lender is the mortgagee under this Security Instrument.
(D) "Note" means the promissory note signed by Borrower and dated ____________________, _____. The Note states that Borrower owes Lender ______________________________________ Dollars (U.S. $_________________) plus interest. Borrower has promised to pay this debt in regular Periodic Payments and to pay the debt in full not later than ___________________________________.
(E) "Property" means the property that is described below under the heading "Transfer of Rights in the Property."
(F) "Loan" means the debt evidenced by the Note, plus interest, any prepayment charges and late charges due under the Note, and all sums due under this Security Instrument, plus interest.
(G) "Riders" means all Riders to this Security Instrument that are executed by Borrower. The following Riders are to be executed by Borrower [check box as applicable]:

☐ Adjustable Rate Rider ☐ Condominium Rider ☐ Second Home Rider
☐ Balloon Rider ☐ Planned Unit Development Rider ☐ Other(s) [specify]_________
☐ 1-4 Family Rider ☐ Biweekly Payment Rider

(H) "Applicable Law" means all controlling applicable federal, state and local statutes, regulations, ordinances and administrative rules and orders (that have the effect of law) as well as all applicable final, non-appealable judicial opinions.
(I) "Community Association Dues, Fees, and Assessments" means all dues, fees, assessments and other charges that are imposed on Borrower or the Property by a condominium association, homeowners association or similar organization.
(J) "Electronic Funds Transfer" means any transfer of funds, other than a transaction originated by check, draft, or similar paper instrument, which is initiated through an electronic terminal, telephonic instrument, computer, or magnetic tape so as to order, instruct, or authorize a financial institution to debit or credit an account. Such term includes, but is not limited to, point-of-sale transfers, automated teller machine transactions, transfers initiated by telephone, wire transfers, and automated clearinghouse transfers.

OHIO--Single Family--**Fannie Mae/Freddie Mac UNIFORM INSTRUMENT** **Form 3036 1/01** (page 1 of 16 pages)

Sample Mortgage

(K) "Escrow Items" means those items that are described in Section 3.
(L) "Miscellaneous Proceeds" means any compensation, settlement, award of damages, or proceeds paid by any third party (other than insurance proceeds paid under the coverages described in Section 5) for: (i) damage to, or destruction of, the Property; (ii) condemnation or other taking of all or any part of the Property; (iii) conveyance in lieu of condemnation; or (iv) misrepresentations of, or omissions as to, the value and/or condition of the Property.
(M) "Mortgage Insurance" means insurance protecting Lender against the nonpayment of, or default on, the Loan.
(N) "Periodic Payment" means the regularly scheduled amount due for (i) principal and interest under the Note, plus (ii) any amounts under Section 3 of this Security Instrument.
(O) "RESPA" means the Real Estate Settlement Procedures Act (12 U.S.C. §2601 et seq.) and its implementing regulation, Regulation X (24 C.F.R. Part 3500), as they might be amended from time to time, or any additional or successor legislation or regulation that governs the same subject matter. As used in this Security Instrument, "RESPA" refers to all requirements and restrictions that are imposed in regard to a "federally related mortgage loan" even if the Loan does not qualify as a "federally related mortgage loan" under RESPA.
(P) "Successor in Interest of Borrower" means any party that has taken title to the Property, whether or not that party has assumed Borrower's obligations under the Note and/or this Security Instrument.

TRANSFER OF RIGHTS IN THE PROPERTY

This Security Instrument secures to Lender: (i) the repayment of the Loan, and all renewals, extensions and modifications of the Note; and (ii) the performance of Borrower's covenants and agreements under this Security Instrument and the Note. For this purpose, Borrower does hereby mortgage, grant and convey to Lender the following described property located in the ______________________________ of ______________________________:
[Type of Recording Jurisdiction] [Name of Recording Jurisdiction]

which currently has the address of ____
[Street]
______________________________, Ohio ____________("Property Address"):
[City] [Zip Code]

TOGETHER WITH all the improvements now or hereafter erected on the property, and all easements, appurtenances, and fixtures now or hereafter a part of the property. All replacements and additions shall also be covered by this Security Instrument. All of the foregoing is referred to in this Security Instrument as the "Property."

BORROWER COVENANTS that Borrower is lawfully seised of the estate hereby conveyed and has the right to mortgage, grant and convey the Property and that the Property is unencumbered, except for encumbrances of record. Borrower warrants and will defend generally the title to the Property against all claims and demands, subject to any encumbrances of record.

THIS SECURITY INSTRUMENT combines uniform covenants for national use and non-uniform covenants with limited variations by jurisdiction to constitute a uniform security instrument covering real property.

OHIO--Single Family--**Fannie Mae/Freddie Mac UNIFORM INSTRUMENT** **Form 3036 1/01** *(page 2 of 16 pages)*

Sample Mortgage

UNIFORM COVENANTS. Borrower and Lender covenant and agree as follows:

1. Payment of Principal, Interest, Escrow Items, Prepayment Charges, and Late Charges. Borrower shall pay when due the principal of, and interest on, the debt evidenced by the Note and any prepayment charges and late charges due under the Note. Borrower shall also pay funds for Escrow Items pursuant to Section 3. Payments due under the Note and this Security Instrument shall be made in U.S. currency. However, if any check or other instrument received by Lender as payment under the Note or this Security Instrument is returned to Lender unpaid, Lender may require that any or all subsequent payments due under the Note and this Security Instrument be made in one or more of the following forms, as selected by Lender: (a) cash; (b) money order; (c) certified check, bank check, treasurer's check or cashier's check, provided any such check is drawn upon an institution whose deposits are insured by a federal agency, instrumentality, or entity; or (d) Electronic Funds Transfer.

Payments are deemed received by Lender when received at the location designated in the Note or at such other location as may be designated by Lender in accordance with the notice provisions in Section 15. Lender may return any payment or partial payment if the payment or partial payments are insufficient to bring the Loan current. Lender may accept any payment or partial payment insufficient to bring the Loan current, without waiver of any rights hereunder or prejudice to its rights to refuse such payment or partial payments in the future, but Lender is not obligated to apply such payments at the time such payments are accepted. If each Periodic Payment is applied as of its scheduled due date, then Lender need not pay interest on unapplied funds. Lender may hold such unapplied funds until Borrower makes payment to bring the Loan current. If Borrower does not do so within a reasonable period of time, Lender shall either apply such funds or return them to Borrower. If not applied earlier, such funds will be applied to the outstanding principal balance under the Note immediately prior to foreclosure. No offset or claim which Borrower might have now or in the future against Lender shall relieve Borrower from making payments due under the Note and this Security Instrument or performing the covenants and agreements secured by this Security Instrument.

2. Application of Payments or Proceeds. Except as otherwise described in this Section 2, all payments accepted and applied by Lender shall be applied in the following order of priority: (a) interest due under the Note; (b) principal due under the Note; (c) amounts due under Section 3. Such payments shall be applied to each Periodic Payment in the order in which it became due. Any remaining amounts shall be applied first to late charges, second to any other amounts due under this Security Instrument, and then to reduce the principal balance of the Note.

If Lender receives a payment from Borrower for a delinquent Periodic Payment which includes a sufficient amount to pay any late charge due, the payment may be applied to the delinquent payment and the late charge. If more than one Periodic Payment is outstanding, Lender may apply any payment received from Borrower to the repayment of the Periodic Payments if, and to the extent that, each payment can be paid in full. To the extent that any excess exists after the payment is applied to the full payment of one or more Periodic Payments, such excess may be applied to any late charges due. Voluntary prepayments shall be applied first to any prepayment charges and then as described in the Note.

Any application of payments, insurance proceeds, or Miscellaneous Proceeds to principal due under the Note shall not extend or postpone the due date, or change the amount, of the Periodic Payments.

3. Funds for Escrow Items. Borrower shall pay to Lender on the day Periodic Payments are due under the Note, until the Note is paid in full, a sum (the "Funds") to provide for payment of amounts due for: (a) taxes and assessments and other items which can attain priority over this Security Instrument as a lien or encumbrance on the Property; (b) leasehold payments or ground rents on the Property, if any; (c) premiums for any and all insurance required by Lender under Section 5; and (d) Mortgage Insurance premiums, if any, or any sums payable by Borrower to Lender in lieu of the payment of Mortgage Insurance premiums in accordance with the provisions of Section 10. These items are called "Escrow Items." At origination or at any time during the term of the Loan, Lender may require that Community Association Dues, Fees, and Assessments, if any be escrowed by Borrower, and such dues, fees and assessments shall be an Escrow Item. Borrower shall promptly furnish to Lender all notices of amounts to be paid under this Section. Borrower shall pay Lender the Funds for Escrow Items unless Lender waives Borrower's obligation to pay the Funds for any or all Escrow Items. Lender may waive Borrower's obligation to pay to Lender Funds for any or all Escrow Items at any time. Any such waiver may only be in writing. In the event of such waiver, Borrower shall pay directly, when and where payable, the amounts due for any Escrow Items for which payment of Funds has been waived by Lender and, if Lender requires, shall furnish to Lender receipts evidencing such payment within such time period as Lender may require. Borrower's obligation to make such payments and to provide receipts shall for all purposes be deemed to be a covenant and agreement contained in this Security Instrument, as the phrase "covenant and agreement" is used in Section 9. If Borrower is obligated to pay Escrow Items directly, pursuant to a waiver, and Borrower fails to pay the amount due

OHIO--Single Family--**Fannie Mae/Freddie Mac UNIFORM INSTRUMENT** **Form 3036 1/01** *(page 3 of 16 pages)*

Sample Mortgage

for an Escrow Item, Lender may exercise its rights under Section 9 and pay such amount and Borrower shall then be obligated under Section 9 to repay to Lender any such amount. Lender may revoke the waiver as to any or all Escrow Items at any time by a notice given in accordance with Section 15 and, upon such revocation, Borrower shall pay to Lender all Funds, and in such amounts, that are then required under this Section 3.

Lender may, at any time, collect and hold Funds in an amount (a) sufficient to permit Lender to apply the Funds at the time specified under RESPA, and (b) not to exceed the maximum amount a lender can require under RESPA. Lender shall estimate the amount of Funds due on the basis of current data and reasonable estimates of expenditures of future Escrow Items or otherwise in accordance with Applicable Law.

The Funds shall be held in an institution whose deposits are insured by a federal agency, instrumentality, or entity (including Lender, if Lender is an institution whose deposits are so insured) or in any Federal Home Loan Bank. Lender shall apply the Funds to pay the Escrow Items no later than the time specified under RESPA. Lender shall not charge Borrower for holding and applying the Funds, annually analyzing the escrow account, or verifying the Escrow Items, unless Lender pays Borrower interest on the Funds and Applicable Law permits Lender to make such a charge. Unless an agreement is made in writing or Applicable Law requires interest to be paid on the Funds, Lender shall not be required to pay Borrower any interest or earnings on the Funds. Borrower and Lender can agree in writing, however, that interest shall be paid on the Funds. Lender shall give to Borrower, without charge, an annual accounting of the Funds as required by RESPA.

If there is a surplus of Funds held in escrow, as defined under RESPA, Lender shall account to Borrower for the excess funds in accordance with RESPA. If there is a shortage of Funds held in escrow, as defined under RESPA, Lender shall notify Borrower as required by RESPA, and Borrower shall pay to Lender the amount necessary to make up the shortage in accordance with RESPA, but in no more than 12 monthly payments. If there is a deficiency of Funds held in escrow, as defined under RESPA, Lender shall notify Borrower as required by RESPA, and Borrower shall pay to Lender the amount necessary to make up the deficiency in accordance with RESPA, but in no more than 12 monthly payments.

Upon payment in full of all sums secured by this Security Instrument, Lender shall promptly refund to Borrower any Funds held by Lender.

4. Charges; Liens. Borrower shall pay all taxes, assessments, charges, fines, and impositions attributable to the Property which can attain priority over this Security Instrument, leasehold payments or ground rents on the Property, if any, and Community Association Dues, Fees, and Assessments, if any. To the extent that these items are Escrow Items, Borrower shall pay them in the manner provided in Section 3.

Borrower shall promptly discharge any lien which has priority over this Security Instrument unless Borrower: (a) agrees in writing to the payment of the obligation secured by the lien in a manner acceptable to Lender, but only so long as Borrower is performing such agreement; (b) contests the lien in good faith by, or defends against enforcement of the lien in, legal proceedings which in Lender's opinion operate to prevent the enforcement of the lien while those proceedings are pending, but only until such proceedings are concluded; or (c) secures from the holder of the lien an agreement satisfactory to Lender subordinating the lien to this Security Instrument. If Lender determines that any part of the Property is subject to a lien which can attain priority over this Security Instrument, Lender may give Borrower a notice identifying the lien. Within 10 days of the date on which that notice is given, Borrower shall satisfy the lien or take one or more of the actions set forth above in this Section 4.

Lender may require Borrower to pay a one-time charge for a real estate tax verification and/or reporting service used by Lender in connection with this Loan.

5. Property Insurance. Borrower shall keep the improvements now existing or hereafter erected on the Property insured against loss by fire, hazards included within the term "extended coverage," and any other hazards including, but not limited to, earthquakes and floods, for which Lender requires insurance. This insurance shall be maintained in the amounts (including deductible levels) and for the periods that Lender requires. What Lender requires pursuant to the preceding sentences can change during the term of the Loan. The insurance carrier providing the insurance shall be chosen by Borrower subject to Lender's right to disapprove Borrower's choice, which right shall not be exercised unreasonably. Lender may require Borrower to pay, in connection with this Loan, either: (a) a one-time charge for flood zone determination, certification and tracking services; or (b) a one-time charge for flood zone determination and certification services and subsequent charges each time remappings or similar changes occur which reasonably might affect such determination or certification. Borrower shall also be responsible for the payment of any fees imposed by the Federal Emergency Management Agency in connection with the review of any flood zone determination resulting from an objection by Borrower.

OHIO--Single Family--**Fannie Mae/Freddie Mac UNIFORM INSTRUMENT** **Form 3036 1/01** *(page 4 of 16 pages)*

Sample Mortgage

If Borrower fails to maintain any of the coverages described above, Lender may obtain insurance coverage, at Lender's option and Borrower's expense. Lender is under no obligation to purchase any particular type or amount of coverage. Therefore, such coverage shall cover Lender, but might or might not protect Borrower, Borrower's equity in the Property, or the contents of the Property, against any risk, hazard or liability and might provide greater or lesser coverage than was previously in effect. Borrower acknowledges that the cost of the insurance coverage so obtained might significantly exceed the cost of insurance that Borrower could have obtained. Any amounts disbursed by Lender under this Section 5 shall become additional debt of Borrower secured by this Security Instrument. These amounts shall bear interest at the Note rate from the date of disbursement and shall be payable, with such interest, upon notice from Lender to Borrower requesting payment.

All insurance policies required by Lender and renewals of such policies shall be subject to Lender's right to disapprove such policies, shall include a standard mortgage clause, and shall name Lender as mortgagee and/or as an additional loss payee. Lender shall have the right to hold the policies and renewal certificates. If Lender requires, Borrower shall promptly give to Lender all receipts of paid premiums and renewal notices. If Borrower obtains any form of insurance coverage, not otherwise required by Lender, for damage to, or destruction of, the Property, such policy shall include a standard mortgage clause and shall name Lender as mortgagee and/or as an additional loss payee.

In the event of loss, Borrower shall give prompt notice to the insurance carrier and Lender. Lender may make proof of loss if not made promptly by Borrower. Unless Lender and Borrower otherwise agree in writing, any insurance proceeds, whether or not the underlying insurance was required by Lender, shall be applied to restoration or repair of the Property, if the restoration or repair is economically feasible and Lender's security is not lessened. During such repair and restoration period, Lender shall have the right to hold such insurance proceeds until Lender has had an opportunity to inspect such Property to ensure the work has been completed to Lender's satisfaction, provided that such inspection shall be undertaken promptly. Lender may disburse proceeds for the repairs and restoration in a single payment or in a series of progress payments as the work is completed. Unless an agreement is made in writing or Applicable Law requires interest to be paid on such insurance proceeds, Lender shall not be required to pay Borrower any interest or earnings on such proceeds. Fees for public adjusters, or other third parties, retained by Borrower shall not be paid out of the insurance proceeds and shall be the sole obligation of Borrower. If the restoration or repair is not economically feasible or Lender's security would be lessened, the insurance proceeds shall be applied to the sums secured by this Security Instrument, whether or not then due, with the excess, if any, paid to Borrower. Such insurance proceeds shall be applied in the order provided for in Section 2.

If Borrower abandons the Property, Lender may file, negotiate and settle any available insurance claim and related matters. If Borrower does not respond within 30 days to a notice from Lender that the insurance carrier has offered to settle a claim, then Lender may negotiate and settle the claim. The 30-day period will begin when the notice is given. In either event, or if Lender acquires the Property under Section 22 or otherwise, Borrower hereby assigns to Lender (a) Borrower's rights to any insurance proceeds in an amount not to exceed the amounts unpaid under the Note or this Security Instrument, and (b) any other of Borrower's rights (other than the right to any refund of unearned premiums paid by Borrower) under all insurance policies covering the Property, insofar as such rights are applicable to the coverage of the Property. Lender may use the insurance proceeds either to repair or restore the Property or to pay amounts unpaid under the Note or this Security Instrument, whether or not then due.

6. Occupancy. Borrower shall occupy, establish, and use the Property as Borrower's principal residence within 60 days after the execution of this Security Instrument and shall continue to occupy the Property as Borrower's principal residence for at least one year after the date of occupancy, unless Lender otherwise agrees in writing, which consent shall not be unreasonably withheld, or unless extenuating circumstances exist which are beyond Borrower's control.

7. Preservation, Maintenance and Protection of the Property; Inspections. Borrower shall not destroy, damage or impair the Property, allow the Property to deteriorate or commit waste on the Property. Whether or not Borrower is residing in the Property, Borrower shall maintain the Property in order to prevent the Property from deteriorating or decreasing in value due to its condition. Unless it is determined pursuant to Section 5 that repair or restoration is not economically feasible, Borrower shall promptly repair the Property if damaged to avoid further deterioration or damage. If insurance or condemnation proceeds are paid in connection with damage to, or the taking of, the Property, Borrower shall be responsible for repairing or restoring the Property only if Lender has released proceeds for such purposes. Lender may disburse proceeds for the repairs and restoration in a single payment or in a series of progress payments as the work is completed. If the insurance or condemnation proceeds are not sufficient

Sample Mortgage

to repair or restore the Property, Borrower is not relieved of Borrower's obligation for the completion of such repair or restoration.

Lender or its agent may make reasonable entries upon and inspections of the Property. If it has reasonable cause, Lender may inspect the interior of the improvements on the Property. Lender shall give Borrower notice at the time of or prior to such an interior inspection specifying such reasonable cause.

8. Borrower's Loan Application. Borrower shall be in default if, during the Loan application process, Borrower or any persons or entities acting at the direction of Borrower or with Borrower's knowledge or consent gave materially false, misleading, or inaccurate information or statements to Lender (or failed to provide Lender with material information) in connection with the Loan. Material representations include, but are not limited to, representations concerning Borrower's occupancy of the Property as Borrower's principal residence.

9. Protection of Lender's Interest in the Property and Rights Under this Security Instrument. If (a) Borrower fails to perform the covenants and agreements contained in this Security Instrument, (b) there is a legal proceeding that might significantly affect Lender's interest in the Property and/or rights under this Security Instrument (such as a proceeding in bankruptcy, probate, for condemnation or forfeiture, for enforcement of a lien which may attain priority over this Security Instrument or to enforce laws or regulations), or (c) Borrower has abandoned the Property, then Lender may do and pay for whatever is reasonable or appropriate to protect Lender's interest in the Property and rights under this Security Instrument, including protecting and/or assessing the value of the Property, and securing and/or repairing the Property. Lender's actions can include, but are not limited to: (a) paying any sums secured by a lien which has priority over this Security Instrument; (b) appearing in court; and (c) paying reasonable attorneys' fees to protect its interest in the Property and/or rights under this Security Instrument, including its secured position in a bankruptcy proceeding. Securing the Property includes, but is not limited to, entering the Property to make repairs, change locks, replace or board up doors and windows, drain water from pipes, eliminate building or other code violations or dangerous conditions, and have utilities turned on or off. Although Lender may take action under this Section 9, Lender does not have to do so and is not under any duty or obligation to do so. It is agreed that Lender incurs no liability for not taking any or all actions authorized under this Section 9.

Any amounts disbursed by Lender under this Section 9 shall become additional debt of Borrower secured by this Security Instrument. These amounts shall bear interest at the Note rate from the date of disbursement and shall be payable, with such interest, upon notice from Lender to Borrower requesting payment.

If this Security Instrument is on a leasehold, Borrower shall comply with all the provisions of the lease. If Borrower acquires fee title to the Property, the leasehold and the fee title shall not merge unless Lender agrees to the merger in writing.

10. Mortgage Insurance. If Lender required Mortgage Insurance as a condition of making the Loan, Borrower shall pay the premiums required to maintain the Mortgage Insurance in effect. If, for any reason, the Mortgage Insurance coverage required by Lender ceases to be available from the mortgage insurer that previously provided such insurance and Borrower was required to make separately designated payments toward the premiums for Mortgage Insurance, Borrower shall pay the premiums required to obtain coverage substantially equivalent to the Mortgage Insurance previously in effect, at a cost substantially equivalent to the cost to Borrower of the Mortgage Insurance previously in effect, from an alternate mortgage insurer selected by Lender. If substantially equivalent Mortgage Insurance coverage is not available, Borrower shall continue to pay to Lender the amount of the separately designated payments that were due when the insurance coverage ceased to be in effect. Lender will accept, use and retain these payments as a non-refundable loss reserve in lieu of Mortgage Insurance. Such loss reserve shall be non-refundable, notwithstanding the fact that the Loan is ultimately paid in full, and Lender shall not be required to pay Borrower any interest or earnings on such loss reserve. Lender can no longer require loss reserve payments if Mortgage Insurance coverage (in the amount and for the period that Lender requires) provided by an insurer selected by Lender again becomes available, is obtained, and Lender requires separately designated payments toward the premiums for Mortgage Insurance. If Lender required Mortgage Insurance as a condition of making the Loan and Borrower was required to make separately designated payments toward the premiums for Mortgage Insurance, Borrower shall pay the premiums required to maintain Mortgage Insurance in effect, or to provide a non-refundable loss reserve, until Lender's requirement for Mortgage Insurance ends in accordance with any written agreement between Borrower and Lender providing for such termination or until termination is required by Applicable Law. Nothing in this Section 10 affects Borrower's obligation to pay interest at the rate provided in the Note.

Mortgage Insurance reimburses Lender (or any entity that purchases the Note) for certain losses it may incur if Borrower does not repay the Loan as agreed. Borrower is not a party to the Mortgage Insurance.

OHIO--Single Family--**Fannie Mae/Freddie Mac UNIFORM INSTRUMENT** **Form 3036 1/01** *(page 6 of 16 pages)*

Sample Mortgage

Mortgage insurers evaluate their total risk on all such insurance in force from time to time, and may enter into agreements with other parties that share or modify their risk, or reduce losses. These agreements are on terms and conditions that are satisfactory to the mortgage insurer and the other party (or parties) to these agreements. These agreements may require the mortgage insurer to make payments using any source of funds that the mortgage insurer may have available (which may include funds obtained from Mortgage Insurance premiums).

As a result of these agreements, Lender, any purchaser of the Note, another insurer, any reinsurer, any other entity, or any affiliate of any of the foregoing, may receive (directly or indirectly) amounts that derive from (or might be characterized as) a portion of Borrower's payments for Mortgage Insurance, in exchange for sharing or modifying the mortgage insurer's risk, or reducing losses. If such agreement provides that an affiliate of Lender takes a share of the insurer's risk in exchange for a share of the premiums paid to the insurer, the arrangement is often termed "captive reinsurance." Further:

(a) Any such agreements will not affect the amounts that Borrower has agreed to pay for Mortgage Insurance, or any other terms of the Loan. Such agreements will not increase the amount Borrower will owe for Mortgage Insurance, and they will not entitle Borrower to any refund.

(b) Any such agreements will not affect the rights Borrower has – if any – with respect to the Mortgage Insurance under the Homeowners Protection Act of 1998 or any other law. These rights may include the right to receive certain disclosures, to request and obtain cancellation of the Mortgage Insurance, to have the Mortgage Insurance terminated automatically, and/or to receive a refund of any Mortgage Insurance premiums that were unearned at the time of such cancellation or termination.

11. Assignment of Miscellaneous Proceeds; Forfeiture. All Miscellaneous Proceeds are hereby assigned to and shall be paid to Lender.

If the Property is damaged, such Miscellaneous Proceeds shall be applied to restoration or repair of the Property, if the restoration or repair is economically feasible and Lender's security is not lessened. During such repair and restoration period, Lender shall have the right to hold such Miscellaneous Proceeds until Lender has had an opportunity to inspect such Property to ensure the work has been completed to Lender's satisfaction, provided that such inspection shall be undertaken promptly. Lender may pay for the repairs and restoration in a single disbursement or in a series of progress payments as the work is completed. Unless an agreement is made in writing or Applicable Law requires interest to be paid on such Miscellaneous Proceeds, Lender shall not be required to pay Borrower any interest or earnings on such Miscellaneous Proceeds. If the restoration or repair is not economically feasible or Lender's security would be lessened, the Miscellaneous Proceeds shall be applied to the sums secured by this Security Instrument, whether or not then due, with the excess, if any, paid to Borrower. Such Miscellaneous Proceeds shall be applied in the order provided for in Section 2.

In the event of a total taking, destruction, or loss in value of the Property, the Miscellaneous Proceeds shall be applied to the sums secured by this Security Instrument, whether or not then due, with the excess, if any, paid to Borrower.

In the event of a partial taking, destruction, or loss in value of the Property in which the fair market value of the Property immediately before the partial taking, destruction, or loss in value is equal to or greater than the amount of the sums secured by this Security Instrument immediately before the partial taking, destruction, or loss in value, unless Borrower and Lender otherwise agree in writing, the sums secured by this Security Instrument shall be reduced by the amount of the Miscellaneous Proceeds multiplied by the following fraction: (a) the total amount of the sums secured immediately before the partial taking, destruction, or loss in value divided by (b) the fair market value of the Property immediately before the partial taking, destruction, or loss in value. Any balance shall be paid to Borrower.

In the event of a partial taking, destruction, or loss in value of the Property in which the fair market value of the Property immediately before the partial taking, destruction, or loss in value is less than the amount of the sums secured immediately before the partial taking, destruction, or loss in value, unless Borrower and Lender otherwise agree in writing, the Miscellaneous Proceeds shall be applied to the sums secured by this Security Instrument whether or not the sums are then due.

If the Property is abandoned by Borrower, or if, after notice by Lender to Borrower that the Opposing Party (as defined in the next sentence) offers to make an award to settle a claim for damages, Borrower fails to respond to Lender within 30 days after the date the notice is given, Lender is authorized to collect and apply the Miscellaneous Proceeds either to restoration or repair of the Property or to the sums secured by this Security Instrument, whether or not then due. "Opposing Party" means the third party that owes Borrower Miscellaneous Proceeds or the party against whom Borrower has a right of action in regard to Miscellaneous Proceeds.

OHIO--Single Family--**Fannie Mae/Freddie Mac UNIFORM INSTRUMENT** **Form 3036 1/01** *(page 7 of 16 pages)*

Sample Mortgage

Borrower shall be in default if any action or proceeding, whether civil or criminal, is begun that, in Lender's judgment, could result in forfeiture of the Property or other material impairment of Lender's interest in the Property or rights under this Security Instrument. Borrower can cure such a default and, if acceleration has occurred, reinstate as provided in Section 19, by causing the action or proceeding to be dismissed with a ruling that, in Lender's judgment, precludes forfeiture of the Property or other material impairment of Lender's interest in the Property or rights under this Security Instrument. The proceeds of any award or claim for damages that are attributable to the impairment of Lender's interest in the Property are hereby assigned and shall be paid to Lender.

All Miscellaneous Proceeds that are not applied to restoration or repair of the Property shall be applied in the order provided for in Section 2.

12. Borrower Not Released; Forbearance By Lender Not a Waiver. Extension of the time for payment or modification of amortization of the sums secured by this Security Instrument granted by Lender to Borrower or any Successor in Interest of Borrower shall not operate to release the liability of Borrower or any Successors in Interest of Borrower. Lender shall not be required to commence proceedings against any Successor in Interest of Borrower or to refuse to extend time for payment or otherwise modify amortization of the sums secured by this Security Instrument by reason of any demand made by the original Borrower or any Successors in Interest of Borrower. Any forbearance by Lender in exercising any right or remedy including, without limitation, Lender's acceptance of payments from third persons, entities or Successors in Interest of Borrower or in amounts less than the amount then due, shall not be a waiver of or preclude the exercise of any right or remedy.

13. Joint and Several Liability; Co-signers; Successors and Assigns Bound. Borrower covenants and agrees that Borrower's obligations and liability shall be joint and several. However, any Borrower who co-signs this Security Instrument but does not execute the Note (a "co-signer"): (a) is co-signing this Security Instrument only to mortgage, grant and convey the co-signer's interest in the Property under the terms of this Security Instrument; (b) is not personally obligated to pay the sums secured by this Security Instrument; and (c) agrees that Lender and any other Borrower can agree to extend, modify, forbear or make any accommodations with regard to the terms of this Security Instrument or the Note without the co-signer's consent.

Subject to the provisions of Section 18, any Successor in Interest of Borrower who assumes Borrower's obligations under this Security Instrument in writing, and is approved by Lender, shall obtain all of Borrower's rights and benefits under this Security Instrument. Borrower shall not be released from Borrower's obligations and liability under this Security Instrument unless Lender agrees to such release in writing. The covenants and agreements of this Security Instrument shall bind (except as provided in Section 20) and benefit the successors and assigns of Lender.

14. Loan Charges. Lender may charge Borrower fees for services performed in connection with Borrower's default, for the purpose of protecting Lender's interest in the Property and rights under this Security Instrument, including, but not limited to, attorneys' fees, property inspection and valuation fees. In regard to any other fees, the absence of express authority in this Security Instrument to charge a specific fee to Borrower shall not be construed as a prohibition on the charging of such fee. Lender may not charge fees that are expressly prohibited by this Security Instrument or by Applicable Law.

If the Loan is subject to a law which sets maximum loan charges, and that law is finally interpreted so that the interest or other loan charges collected or to be collected in connection with the Loan exceed the permitted limits, then: (a) any such loan charge shall be reduced by the amount necessary to reduce the charge to the permitted limit; and (b) any sums already collected from Borrower which exceeded permitted limits will be refunded to Borrower. Lender may choose to make this refund by reducing the principal owed under the Note or by making a direct payment to Borrower. If a refund reduces principal, the reduction will be treated as a partial prepayment without any prepayment charge (whether or not a prepayment charge is provided for under the Note). Borrower's acceptance of any such refund made by direct payment to Borrower will constitute a waiver of any right of action Borrower might have arising out of such overcharge.

15. Notices. All notices given by Borrower or Lender in connection with this Security Instrument must be in writing. Any notice to Borrower in connection with this Security Instrument shall be deemed to have been given to Borrower when mailed by first class mail or when actually delivered to Borrower's notice address if sent by other means. Notice to any one Borrower shall constitute notice to all Borrowers unless Applicable Law expressly requires otherwise. The notice address shall be the Property Address unless Borrower has designated a substitute notice address by notice to Lender. Borrower shall promptly notify Lender of Borrower's change of address. If Lender specifies a procedure for reporting Borrower's change of address, then Borrower shall only report a change of address through that specified procedure. There may be only one designated notice address under this Security Instrument at any one time. Any notice to Lender shall be given by delivering it or by mailing it by first class mail to Lender's address stated herein unless

OHIO--Single Family--**Fannie Mae/Freddie Mac UNIFORM INSTRUMENT** **Form 3036 1/01** *(page 8 of 16 pages)*

Sample Mortgage

Lender has designated another address by notice to Borrower. Any notice in connection with this Security Instrument shall not be deemed to have been given to Lender until actually received by Lender. If any notice required by this Security Instrument is also required under Applicable Law, the Applicable Law requirement will satisfy the corresponding requirement under this Security Instrument.

16. Governing Law; Severability; Rules of Construction. This Security Instrument shall be governed by federal law and the law of the jurisdiction in which the Property is located. All rights and obligations contained in this Security Instrument are subject to any requirements and limitations of Applicable Law. Applicable Law might explicitly or implicitly allow the parties to agree by contract or it might be silent, but such silence shall not be construed as a prohibition against agreement by contract. In the event that any provision or clause of this Security Instrument or the Note conflicts with Applicable Law, such conflict shall not affect other provisions of this Security Instrument or the Note which can be given effect without the conflicting provision.

As used in this Security Instrument: (a) words of the masculine gender shall mean and include corresponding neuter words or words of the feminine gender; (b) words in the singular shall mean and include the plural and vice versa; and (c) the word "may" gives sole discretion without any obligation to take any action.

17. Borrower's Copy. Borrower shall be given one copy of the Note and of this Security Instrument.

18. Transfer of the Property or a Beneficial Interest in Borrower. As used in this Section 18, "Interest in the Property" means any legal or beneficial interest in the Property, including, but not limited to, those beneficial interests transferred in a bond for deed, contract for deed, installment sales contract or escrow agreement, the intent of which is the transfer of title by Borrower at a future date to a purchaser.

If all or any part of the Property or any Interest in the Property is sold or transferred (or if Borrower is not a natural person and a beneficial interest in Borrower is sold or transferred) without Lender's prior written consent, Lender may require immediate payment in full of all sums secured by this Security Instrument. However, this option shall not be exercised by Lender if such exercise is prohibited by Applicable Law.

If Lender exercises this option, Lender shall give Borrower notice of acceleration. The notice shall provide a period of not less than 30 days from the date the notice is given in accordance with Section 15 within which Borrower must pay all sums secured by this Security Instrument. If Borrower fails to pay these sums prior to the expiration of this period, Lender may invoke any remedies permitted by this Security Instrument without further notice or demand on Borrower.

19. Borrower's Right to Reinstate After Acceleration. If Borrower meets certain conditions, Borrower shall have the right to have enforcement of this Security Instrument discontinued at any time prior to the earliest of: (a) five days before sale of the Property pursuant to any power of sale contained in this Security Instrument; (b) such other period as Applicable Law might specify for the termination of Borrower's right to reinstate; or (c) entry of a judgment enforcing this Security Instrument. Those conditions are that Borrower: (a) pays Lender all sums which then would be due under this Security Instrument and the Note as if no acceleration had occurred; (b) cures any default of any other covenants or agreements; (c) pays all expenses incurred in enforcing this Security Instrument, including, but not limited to, reasonable attorneys' fees, property inspection and valuation fees, and other fees incurred for the purpose of protecting Lender's interest in the Property and rights under this Security Instrument; and (d) takes such action as Lender may reasonably require to assure that Lender's interest in the Property and rights under this Security Instrument, and Borrower's obligation to pay the sums secured by this Security Instrument, shall continue unchanged. Lender may require that Borrower pay such reinstatement sums and expenses in one or more of the following forms, as selected by Lender: (a) cash; (b) money order; (c) certified check, bank check, treasurer's check or cashier's check, provided any such check is drawn upon an institution whose deposits are insured by a federal agency, instrumentality or entity; or (d) Electronic Funds Transfer. Upon reinstatement by Borrower, this Security Instrument and obligations secured hereby shall remain fully effective as if no acceleration had occurred. However, this right to reinstate shall not apply in the case of acceleration under Section 18.

20. Sale of Note; Change of Loan Servicer; Notice of Grievance. The Note or a partial interest in the Note (together with this Security Instrument) can be sold one or more times without prior notice to Borrower. A sale might result in a change in the entity (known as the "Loan Servicer") that collects Periodic Payments due under the Note and this Security Instrument and performs other mortgage loan servicing obligations under the Note, this Security Instrument, and Applicable Law. There also might be one or more changes of the Loan Servicer unrelated to a sale of the Note. If there is a change of the Loan Servicer, Borrower will be given written notice of the change which will state the name and address of the new Loan Servicer, the address to which payments should be made and any other information RESPA requires in connection with a notice of transfer of servicing. If the Note is sold and thereafter the Loan is serviced by a Loan Servicer other than the purchaser of the Note, the mortgage loan servicing obligations to

OHIO--Single Family--**Fannie Mae/Freddie Mac UNIFORM INSTRUMENT** **Form 3036 1/01** *(page 9 of 16 pages)*

Sample Mortgage

Borrower will remain with the Loan Servicer or be transferred to a successor Loan Servicer and are not assumed by the Note purchaser unless otherwise provided by the Note purchaser.

Neither Borrower nor Lender may commence, join, or be joined to any judicial action (as either an individual litigant or the member of a class) that arises from the other party's actions pursuant to this Security Instrument or that alleges that the other party has breached any provision of, or any duty owed by reason of, this Security Instrument, until such Borrower or Lender has notified the other party (with such notice given in compliance with the requirements of Section 15) of such alleged breach and afforded the other party hereto a reasonable period after the giving of such notice to take corrective action. If Applicable Law provides a time period which must elapse before certain action can be taken, that time period will be deemed to be reasonable for purposes of this paragraph. The notice of acceleration and opportunity to cure given to Borrower pursuant to Section 22 and the notice of acceleration given to Borrower pursuant to Section 18 shall be deemed to satisfy the notice and opportunity to take corrective action provisions of this Section 20.

21. Hazardous Substances. As used in this Section 21: (a) "Hazardous Substances" are those substances defined as toxic or hazardous substances, pollutants, or wastes by Environmental Law and the following substances: gasoline, kerosene, other flammable or toxic petroleum products, toxic pesticides and herbicides, volatile solvents, materials containing asbestos or formaldehyde, and radioactive materials; (b) "Environmental Law" means federal laws and laws of the jurisdiction where the Property is located that relate to health, safety or environmental protection; (c) "Environmental Cleanup" includes any response action, remedial action, or removal action, as defined in Environmental Law; and (d) an "Environmental Condition" means a condition that can cause, contribute to, or otherwise trigger an Environmental Cleanup.

Borrower shall not cause or permit the presence, use, disposal, storage, or release of any Hazardous Substances, or threaten to release any Hazardous Substances, on or in the Property. Borrower shall not do, nor allow anyone else to do, anything affecting the Property (a) that is in violation of any Environmental Law, (b) which creates an Environmental Condition, or (c) which, due to the presence, use, or release of a Hazardous Substance, creates a condition that adversely affects the value of the Property. The preceding two sentences shall not apply to the presence, use, or storage on the Property of small quantities of Hazardous Substances that are generally recognized to be appropriate to normal residential uses and to maintenance of the Property (including, but not limited to, hazardous substances in consumer products).

Borrower shall promptly give Lender written notice of (a) any investigation, claim, demand, lawsuit or other action by any governmental or regulatory agency or private party involving the Property and any Hazardous Substance or Environmental Law of which Borrower has actual knowledge, (b) any Environmental Condition, including but not limited to, any spilling, leaking, discharge, release or threat of release of any Hazardous Substance, and (c) any condition caused by the presence, use or release of a Hazardous Substance which adversely affects the value of the Property. If Borrower learns, or is notified by any governmental or regulatory authority, or any private party, that any removal or other remediation of any Hazardous Substance affecting the Property is necessary, Borrower shall promptly take all necessary remedial actions in accordance with Environmental Law. Nothing herein shall create any obligation on Lender for an Environmental Cleanup.

NON-UNIFORM COVENANTS. Borrower and Lender further covenant and agree as follows:

22. Acceleration; Remedies. Lender shall give notice to Borrower prior to acceleration following Borrower's breach of any covenant or agreement in this Security Instrument (but not prior to acceleration under Section 18 unless Applicable Law provides otherwise). The notice shall specify: (a) the default; (b) the action required to cure the default; (c) a date, not less than 30 days from the date the notice is given to Borrower, by which the default must be cured; and (d) that failure to cure the default on or before the date specified in the notice may result in acceleration of the sums secured by this Security Instrument, foreclosure by judicial proceeding and sale of the Property. The notice shall further inform Borrower of the right to reinstate after acceleration and the right to assert in the foreclosure proceeding the non-existence of a default or any other defense of Borrower to acceleration and foreclosure. If the default is not cured on or before the date specified in the notice, Lender at its option may require immediate payment in full of all sums secured by this Security Instrument without further demand and may foreclose this Security Instrument by judicial proceeding. Lender shall be entitled to collect all expenses incurred in pursuing the remedies provided in this Section 22, including, but not limited to, costs of title evidence.

23. Release. Upon payment of all sums secured by this Security Instrument, Lender shall discharge this Security Instrument. Borrower shall pay any recordation costs. Lender may charge
Borrower a fee for releasing this Security Instrument, but only if the fee is paid to a third party for services rendered and the charging of the fee is permitted under Applicable Law.

OHIO--Single Family--**Fannie Mae/Freddie Mac UNIFORM INSTRUMENT** **Form 3036 1/01** *(page 10 of 16 pages)*

Sample Mortgage

24. Certain Other Advances. In addition to any other sum secured hereby, this Security Instrument shall also secure the unpaid principal balance of, plus accrued interest on, any amount of money loaned, advanced or paid by Lender to or for the account and benefit of Borrower, after this Security Instrument is delivered to and filed with the Recorder's Office, ________ County, Ohio, for recording. Lender may make such advances in order to pay any real estate taxes and assessments, insurance premiums plus all other costs and expenses incurred in connection with the operation, protection or preservation of the Property, including to cure Borrower's defaults by making any such payments which Borrower should have paid as provided in this Security Instrument, it being intended by this Section 24 to acknowledge, affirm and comply with the provision of § 5301.233 of the Revised Code of Ohio.

BY SIGNING BELOW, Borrower accepts and agrees to the terms and covenants contained in this Security Instrument and in any Rider executed by Borrower and recorded with it.

Witnesses:

____________________ ____________________(Seal)
- Borrower

____________________ ____________________(Seal)
- Borrower

____________ **[Space Below This Line For Acknowledgment]** ____________

Sample Mortgage

Judicial Foreclosure Procedure

When a borrower is in **default** on a loan, the lender *accelerates the due date of the debt to the present and gives the debtor notice of default, demanding the full loan balance be paid at once.* If the debtor fails to do so, the lender files a lawsuit, called a foreclosure action, in a court of jurisdiction where the land is located. There are some differences in how foreclosure proceedings progress, depending on the state and county in which the action takes place. We'll look at one scenario that's typical of foreclosure proceedings, but keep in mind there may be variations in your jurisdiction.

Under a **foreclosure action**, the *court determines whether the lender is rightfully owed the money and the debtor is in default.* If the court finds in favor of the creditor, the creditor takes ownership and a judge will issue an order of execution directing an officer of the court, usually the county sheriff, to seize the property. If the creditor chooses to sell, the public is notified of the place and date of the sale via advertising that runs for a specified number of weeks in a newspaper circulated in the county. On the sale date, a public auction is held at the courthouse where anyone can bid on the property. The minimum bid is generally a set percentage of the appraised value (two-thirds is a common figure), as determined by three disinterested appraisers. (The minimum bid requirement is set by law to protect whatever equity the debtor may have in the property, since a bidder can't simply get a bargain by paying just the mortgage balance.) The property is sold to the highest bidder, with proceeds used to pay costs of the sale and to pay off the mortgages and liens. Any **overages** remaining after all debts, liens, expenses, and costs related to the property are paid go to the debtor.

If the property does not bring enough money at the sale to pay off the mortgage, the creditor may be able to obtain a **deficiency judgment**, which is *a court order stating that the debtor owes money to the creditor when the collateral property does not bring enough at a foreclosure sale to cover the entire loan amount, accrued interest, and other costs.* The deficiency judgment is a personal judgment against the debtor that creates a general, involuntary lien against all real and personal property.

While this was a simple example, note that in today's marketplace, foreclosure procedures are undergoing challenges and modifications by both state governments and federal agencies. Make sure that you stay current with the practices and legal issues in the jurisdictions where you do business.

Redemption

Debtors may be able to redeem (save) their property from the time a *notice of a pending legal action*, called a **lis pendens**, is filed until the confirmation of the foreclosure sale. This is done by paying the court what is due, which may include court costs and attorneys' fees. In some states, this right to *save or redeem the property prior to the confirmation of sale* is called the **equitable right of redemption.** Some other states use the **statutory right of redemption,** which allows debtors to redeem themselves *after the final sale.* Once the redemption is made, the court will set aside the sale, pay the parties, and the debtor gains title to the property again.

One other option debtors have to avoid foreclosure is to make a voluntary conveyance, also called **deed in lieu of foreclosure**. With this action, *debtors still lose the property, but by conveying it voluntarily before final court action, they avoid having a foreclosure on their credit record.* After confirmation of sale, however, it is too late. Note that a lender is not obligated to accept a deed in lieu of foreclosure as full satisfaction of the debt and could still pursue a deficiency judgment.

Mortgage Lien Position

Lien position establishes the *order in which liens are paid off out of the proceeds of a foreclosure sale.* By law, real estate tax liens always have the highest priority and get paid first, followed by the first recorded lien. Then if there's money left, the second lien gets paid, and so on. Once the funds are exhausted, liens in a later position get nothing.

A **first mortgage** is a *security instrument with a first lien position.* As such, a first mortgage almost always has priority over all other mortgages, meaning the first mortgage holder is paid first in the event of a foreclosure sale.

A **second mortgage** is a *security instrument in a second lien position.* A second mortgage may be used to help buy the property (e.g., a small loan from the seller), or a second mortgage might be taken out later (e.g., a home equity loan) to generate additional funds from the owner's accumulated equity in the property for repairs, college tuition, or for some other purpose. Although property is still used as security, the second mortgage lender is in a riskier position because a first mortgage gets paid first out of foreclosure proceedings. If nothing is left, the second mortgage holder gets nothing.

Generally speaking, *any mortgage in a higher lien position* is said to be a **senior mortgage**, so a first mortgage is always a senior mortgage. A **junior mortgage** is *any mortgage with a lower lien position than another.* Thus, a second mortgage is a junior mortgage to a first mortgage, but a second mortgage is a senior mortgage to a third mortgage.

It's important to note that a mortgage would not necessarily be the first recorded lien on a property, however. For example, if someone purchases a new home from a builder who did not pay all of the subcontractors or suppliers prior to the borrower purchasing the home, any lawsuit for collection from the builder may relate back to when the work was commenced, which puts the mechanic's or materialman's lien ahead of the lender.

Subordination Agreement

In some situations, the parties may desire that a later recorded instrument have priority over an earlier recorded instrument. This is common in construction financing, for example. Because of the high-risk nature of construction loans, construction lenders frequently refuse to lend any money unless they can be assured of a first lien position. Since the developer, in many cases, has already purchased the land on some sort of deferred payment plan, there is often a security instrument (mortgage, trust deed, or land contract) that has already been recorded. For the later construction loan mortgage to take priority over the earlier recorded mortgage instrument on the land, the first lender would file a **subordination agreement** in the public record that permits the second lien holder to be in first lien position.

Another example is where a property owner has a junior mortgage, such as a home equity line of credit, and wants to refinance his first mortgage but keep the line of credit open. The holder of the junior mortgage would file a subordination agreement that gives the new mortgage priority, even though it was recorded later.

Typical Clauses in Finance Instruments

Various clauses are used in mortgages to give certain rights to the lender or borrower. Many of these clauses can be found in the promissory note or security instrument, and often they appear in both.

Acceleration Clause

An **acceleration clause** *gives the lender the right to declare the entire loan balance due immediately because of borrower default or for violation of other contract provisions.* Most promissory notes, mortgages, trust deeds, and land contracts contain an acceleration clause allowing the lender to accelerate the debt upon default as defined in the contract. This is important to lenders because, upon default, they want to be able to make all payments due without having to file a separate action for each missed payment.

The actions that constitute default are defined in the contract. A debtor who misses one payment may discover next month that, not just two payments are due but rather, the entire loan balance is due because of the missed payment. Most lenders, though, will wait until payments are delinquent at least 90 days before enforcing an acceleration clause that appears in the mortgage or note.

Alienation Clause

An **alienation clause** in a contract *gives the lender certain stated rights when there's a transfer of ownership in the property.* It may also be referred to as a **due on sale clause**. This is designed to limit the debtor's right to transfer property without the creditor's permission. Depending on the actual wording of the clause (that's why lawyers are important), alienation may be triggered by a transfer of title, by transfer of a significant interest in the property, or even by abandonment of the property. Transfer of a significant interest can be construed as an obvious long-term lease, but often is also interpreted to cover a lease with an option to buy or a land contract.

On sale or transfer of a significant interest in the property, the lender will often have the right to accelerate the debt (here called a due on sale clause), change the interest rate, or charge a hefty assumption fee. Adjustable rate mortgage (ARM) loans seldom have an alienation clause that calls for an interest rate change since the rate can already be adjusted under the original contract. An ARM loan may have other alienation provisions, however, such as an assumption fee. The lender may choose which, if any, options stated in the contract it chooses to enforce. This is true for most conventional loans. Although FHA and VA loans cannot, technically, have alienation clauses, they still attempt to restrict transfers in other ways, such as by reserving the right to approve a new debtor who will take over an FHA or VA loan.

Defeasance Clause

A **defeasance clause** is a *clause in a legal document that states that in the event a stated condition has been fulfilled, the document becomes null and void.* This clause can appear in contracts or mortgages. With a mortgage, for example, once the borrower has repaid the debt, the mortgage is cancelled and the mortgagor can redeem title to the property. This clause is more likely to be found in title theory states where title is transferred to the lender until the debt is repaid.

Partial Release, Satisfaction, or Reconveyance Clause

A **partial release, satisfaction, or reconveyance clause** in a contract *obligates the creditor to release part of the property from lien and convey title to that part back to the debtor once certain provisions of the note or mortgage have been satisfied.* Usually, this occurs after a certain percentage of the mortgage balance has been paid. This is an important clause that appears in many blanket mortgages and some construction mortgages so the developer or builder can sell off completed homes with clear title before having to pay back the entire amount borrowed for the entire development project. Also, if the land is bought with a mortgage, construction financing is much easier to obtain later when the builder owns part of the land free of liens.

Case in Point

A builder bought five acres of land with a contract that had a partial release clause. As per the contract, one acre of land would be released with clear title to the builder for each 20% of the note amount that was paid. This would allow the builder to build a house on this one-acre parcel and sell it free and clear.

Prepayment Clause

A **prepayment clause** in a contract *gives the lender the right to charge the borrower a penalty for paying off the loan early,* such as when refinancing a loan. While the time periods and amount of the penalty may vary considerably, the basic effect of a prepayment clause is to charge the debtor extra money to make up for the interest income the lender loses when the debtor pays the loan early. An example might be a prepayment clause that calls for the debtor to pay an additional 3% of the loan amount if more than 20% of the principal is repaid during the first five years of the loan. This type of clause may be seen in a conventional loan, but it is prohibited in FHA or VA loans.

Title XIV of the Dodd-Frank Wall Street Reform and Consumer Protection Act of 2010, designated as the Mortgage Reform and Anti-Predatory Lending Act, prohibits prepayment penalties on residential mortgage loans other than "qualified mortgages," which are those with points and fees that do not exceed 3% of the loan amount or that do not have adjustable rates and do not result in negative amortization (§ 1414).

Other Mortgage Covenants

In addition to the typical clauses discussed that appear frequently in real estate mortgages, there are also a number of covenants. **Covenants**, simply, are *promises.* Covenants can appear in deeds, mortgages, or any other document. Typical covenants can compel or prevent certain actions by the property owner or uses for the property.

Typical covenants in mortgages that the property owner must sign include provisions protecting the lender's security interests in the property. These covenants include such things as the property owner promising to keep the property in good condition and repair; not committing **waste**, which is damaging or diminishing the value of the property in any way; promising to keep fire, hazard, and flood insurance in force on the property; and agreeing to pay taxes and other assessments on time. Failure to keep any of these promises or covenants can be cited in the mortgage or note as causing the borrower to be in default.

There are, of course, a number of other clauses and covenants important to typical mortgages. Borrowers should make sure they understand them, and should be encouraged to consult legal counsel before entering into a mortgage.

Types and Features of Mortgages

There are actually many different types of mortgages, and they all share many characteristics and have the same origins. The history of the actual word "mortgage" is very interesting. "Mort"—from the Latin—means "death," while "gage" means something deposited as a pledge of performance. So the word mortgage literally means a "dead pledge" in that the property is forfeit or dead to the borrower if the loan isn't repaid, and the pledge or conveyance is dead once the loan is repaid.

Although mortgages are primarily security devices used to collateralize real estate loans, the word mortgage is often prefaced with adjectives that describe the particular function the mortgage is serving, or the nature of the circumstances surrounding its use. For example, a construction mortgage is a mortgage used to secure a construction loan; a blanket mortgage secures a loan with two or more parcels of land as collateral, etc.

√ ***Note:*** Some mortgage loans can be more than one type of mortgage loan at the same time, plus some share many different mortgage features. For example, a borrower can have a conventional mortgage loan that is a first mortgage (and thus a senior mortgage), and this same mortgage can also be an adjustable rate mortgage that is a construction mortgage. Of course, some of the mortgage types and features are mutually exclusive—a construction mortgage can't also be a reverse equity mortgage.

Purchase Money Mortgage

The term **purchase money mortgage** generally describes *any mortgage given by a buyer to a lender or a seller to secure part or all of the money that's borrowed to purchase property.* When a seller takes part of the purchase price as a mortgage to help the sale, it may also be known as a **soft money loan**, because the borrower receives credit toward the purchase instead of actual cash. A purchase money mortgage can be a first mortgage or a junior mortgage, depending on its lien priority.

Refinance Mortgage

A **refinance mortgage** is one *where the borrower replaces the current mortgage with a new loan.* This can be a way for a borrower to simply get a better interest rate or other terms on a new loan compared to the original mortgage, for example, to lower the interest rate, change an adjustable rate to a fixed rate, change a 30-year loan to a 15-year loan, combine multiple mortgages into one, or remove private mortgage insurance. This transaction could be a no cash-out refinance or a cash-out refinance. With any refinance, the mortgage loan originator should be able to show a net tangible benefit to the borrower.

Home Equity Loan, Home Equity Line of Credit

A home equity loan or home equity line of credit (HELOC) is a loan *secured by a mortgage on one's principal residence.* A **home equity loan** is typically a **closed-end** loan that offers a fixed amount of money that can be repaid with regular payments over a fixed term. A **home equity line of credit** is a type of **open-end** loan in which a borrower is granted a specific credit limit from which he or she can draw and pay back principal only as it is used. As the balance is paid down, the principal is available to be used again. HELOCs usually have two phases: A draw period during which borrowers commonly pay interest only, and a repayment period during which payments are generally amortized. Usually, these financing vehicles attach a junior mortgage to the property.

Blanket Mortgage

A **blanket mortgage** *covers more than one parcel of land or lot, and is usually used to finance subdivision developments.* These loans usually have a **partial release clause**, allowing the borrower to pay a certain amount to release some of the lots with the mortgage continuing to cover the remaining lots. Using a subdivision example, a builder may initially have one mortgage covering the entire acreage but, by paying down a certain percentage of the loan, the builder can sell off completed home lots.

Bridge Mortgage

A **bridge mortgage** occurs *between the termination of one mortgage and the beginning of the next.* When the next mortgage is taken out, the bridge mortgage is repaid. Bridge mortgages are designed to be temporary, and are used most commonly for construction financing. A less common use for a bridge mortgage is for someone buying a new home before selling the old one.

Open-End Mortgage

An **open-end mortgage** *allows the borrower to request additional funds from the lender, usually up to a certain pre-defined limit.* In most cases, lenders will not advance funds in excess of the original principal balance of the loan or that exceed a predetermined loan-to-value. As an example, a borrower obtains an open-end mortgage to buy a home. Under the terms of the mortgage, he may borrow additional funds over the term of the loan as long as the unpaid principal does not exceed 80% of the appraised value of the property used as collateral. An example of another type of open-end loan is a home equity line of credit, in which a borrower can borrow, repay, and borrow again up to the pre-defined limit.

Don't confuse an open-end mortgage with an **open mortgage**, which is a term used to describe a mortgage that may be repaid at any time without penalty.

Package Mortgage

A **package mortgage** *includes personal property, like appliances, in the property sale and all are financed together in one contract.* With package mortgages, the personal property also serves as collateral for the loan. A common use for this type of mortgage is to buy a furnished condominium, where the loan and mortgage documents may also recite appliances and/or furniture as part of the transaction. More commonly, lenders obtain a separate financing statement or UCC filing to claim covered personal property as collateral.

Reverse Mortgage

A **reverse mortgage** *allows qualified homeowners age 62 or older to convert equity in the home into a monthly cash stream or line of credit that may be used by the borrower for investment, repairs, payment of debt, or other purposes as the borrower sees fit.* The borrower must have a substantial amount of equity in the home to make this option viable. Unlike a conventional mortgage, the borrower is not required to make payments against a reverse mortgage during the life of the loan. In most cases, the mortgage must be repaid when the home is sold, the borrower does not occupy the home for 12 consecutive months, or the borrower dies. The borrower may also pay off a reverse mortgage at any time or refinance it.

Equity Participation Mortgage

An **equity participation mortgage** *permits the lender to share part of the earnings, income, or profits from a real estate project.* This is usually in addition to collecting principal and interest payments on the loan. For example, the lender may receive 5% of gross rents. This is done mostly for commercial real estate projects.

Wraparound Mortgage

The term **wraparound mortgage** is used to describe a financing arrangement in which *an existing loan on a property is retained while the lender gives the borrower another, larger loan.* For example, this arrangement could be used in lieu of traditional refinancing where a lender makes a second loan to a borrower, leaving the first loan intact. The borrower pays the wraparound lender a single payment on the combined principal. If the wraparound lender is not the original lender, then the wraparound lender makes payments on the original mortgage to the first mortgage lender. For example, a homeowner wants to borrow $40,000. He has an existing mortgage with a balance of $20,000 at 4%. A second lender gives him a wraparound mortgage for $60,000 at 5%. The borrower makes payments on the $60,000 loan to the second lender, who must make payments to the first lender for the $20,000 balance of the first loan. The benefit for the second lender in this arrangement is that it earns a return not only on the money it advanced at 5%, but also on the difference between the rate it is charging the borrower and the rate at which it is repaying the first mortgage. While such an arrangement may be more convenient for the borrower, it can place him at greater risk, since he must depend on the second lender to make timely payments to the first lender. Failure of the second lender to do so could trigger a default and foreclosure action.

Construction Mortgage

A **construction mortgage,** also called an interim loan, is *a temporary loan used to finance the construction of improvements and buildings on land.* Generally, an appraiser will value the property for a construction loan by evaluating the building plans and specifications, completing a "subject to" appraisal. When construction is complete, the appraiser verifies that plans and specifications have been met and the original opinion of value is valid; then the loan is replaced by a permanent amortizing loan, called a **take out loan**. New construction can take as long as a year to complete; therefore, some contracts may include **extended rate locks**.

Construction loans can be profitable, but lenders regard them as risky. Thus, not only do they charge high interest rates and loan fees on construction loans, they also closely supervise the disbursement of funds to ensure that projects are completed. There's always the danger that a borrower will overspend and exhaust the loan funds before construction is complete. If the borrower doesn't have money to finish a project, the lender is left with a partially completed project that can't be sold easily in its existing state—with a very real possibility of foreclosure. To protect themselves against this problem, lenders use plans for **disbursing construction loan proceeds** to guard against overspending by the borrower. Three common disbursement plans are fixed disbursement plan, voucher system, and warrant system.

Disbursement

A **fixed disbursement plan** *pays a percentage of funds at a set time.* A series of predetermined disbursements, called **obligatory advances,** are paid out at various stages of construction. For example, the loan agreement may state that the lender will release only 10% of the funds when a project is 20% complete, with future draws of 20% each time construction progresses 20% more toward completion.

First Release/Draw	10% of Loan	Project 20% complete
Second Release/Draw	20% of Loan	Project 40% complete
Third Release/Draw	20% of Loan	Project 60% complete
Fourth Release/Draw	20% of Loan	Project 80% complete
Fifth Release/Draw	20% of Loan	Project 100% complete

Lenders often hold the final 10% (or more) of the loan proceeds until the lien period has expired to protect against unpaid mechanic's liens, which could affect the marketability of the property. If a valid mechanic's lien is recorded, the construction loan agreement usually allows lenders to pay it from the part of the loan not disbursed.

- **Voucher System.** The contractor or borrower must pay his or her own bills, and then submit the receipts to the lender for reimbursement.
- **Warrant System.** The lender directly pays bills presented by the various suppliers and laborers on a project.

Permanent Construction Loan

A **permanent construction loan** is a *special type of construction loan where there is only one loan and one closing, with no take out loan.* There is a fixed disbursement schedule for loan funds, and the loan automatically converts to a permanent first mortgage when construction is finished.

Graduated Payment Mortgage (GPM)

A **graduated payment mortgage** (GPM) is actually a **specialized payment structure** that *allows the borrower to make smaller payments in the early years of a mortgage.* The lower payments in the early years of a mortgage structured in the note as a GPM are not sufficient to cover the interest due on the loan, and so the unpaid interest is added to the loan balance, resulting in a scheduled period of **negative amortization**. At a predetermined point in the loan term, the payments escalate on a scheduled basis until they eventually reach the point in which they are sufficient to fully amortize the loan over the remainder of its term.

Chapter 5 Summary

1. **Finance instruments** are written documents establishing rights and duties of the parties in a transaction. **Promissory notes** are written promises to pay money. They're **negotiable instruments** and are freely transferable. The one promising to pay is called the **maker** of the note, usually the borrower. The one to whom payment is promised is called the **payee** (usually the lender), or payee's order, or to the order of the payee. There are four common note types: Straight note, installment note, installment note with balloon, and fully amortizing note. The rate that is used to amortize the mortgage loan and determine the monthly loan payments is known as the **note rate**.
2. **Security instruments** give a creditor the right to take ownership of collateral to satisfy the debt if the debtor doesn't pay as agreed; they require a debtor to **hypothecate** the property, which means to pledge it as collateral without giving up possession. Two types are trust deeds and mortgages.
3. **Trust deeds** (or deeds of trust) place legal title interest in the property into the hands of a third party as security for the payment of a note; they allow for non-judicial foreclosure in the event of default.
4. **Mortgages** create liens against property as security for debt. If in default, **judicial foreclosure** ensues: Notice of default; foreclosure action filed; creditor takes ownership; if selling, order of execution has sheriff sell property; advertising; and public auction (minimum bid based on percentage of appraised value, confirmation of sale to highest bidder, sheriff's deed issued.) Debtor has **equitable right of redemption** to regain property until confirmation of sale. Process is slow and expensive, but has court authority. The order of mortgage is important: A **senior mortgage** is any mortgage in a higher lien position; a **junior mortgage** is in a lower lien position. Property tax liens are always paid first.
5. Many clauses are common in real estate financing contracts. An **acceleration** clause lets the lender call the loan balance due if in default. A **prepayment** clause lets lenders charge a penalty for paying off a loan early. An **alienation** clause gives lenders some stated rights if the property is transferred (also called due on sale clause). A **defeasance** clause cancels a mortgage when it has been repaid. **Subordination** lets a later-recorded mortgage take priority over an earlier one. A ***partial* release** is when a part of property is released from the lien upon payment of part of the balance.
6. Mortgages are often prefaced by words describing its type or function. **Purchase money** mortgage—Seller or lender takes mortgage for part of purchase price. **Soft money** mortgage—Borrower gets credit instead of cash. **Hard money** mortgage—Borrower gets actual cash (e.g., cash-out refinance). **Bridge** mortgage—Temporary mortgage between two others and repaid with a later mortgage or proceeds from sale of security property. **Package** mortgage—Includes personal property. **Blanket** mortgage—For more than one land parcel. Construction mortgage—Temporary loan to finance construction of building improvements.

Chapter 5 Quiz

1. ***A promissory note calling only for payment of interest during its term is a(n)***
   A. amortizing note.
   B. installment note.
   C. negotiated note.
   D. straight note.

2. ***The clause that permits a lender to declare the entire unpaid balance on a loan due and payable at once on default of the borrower is a(n)***
   A. acceleration clause.
   B. defeasance clause.
   C. escalation clause.
   D. forfeiture clause.

3. ***A clause that permits the lender to call the outstanding balance due and payable should the property be sold by the borrower is a(n)***
   A. acceleration clause.
   B. alienation clause.
   C. balloon payment clause.
   D. exculpatory clause.

4. ***Which document accompanies the mortgage?***
   A. abstract of title
   B. contract of sale
   C. deed
   D. promissory note

5. ***To foreclose a mortgage, the creditor***
   A. files an attachment in the amount of the debt.
   B. files a court action.
   C. notifies the debtor of the default, waits ten days, publishes a notice of default in the paper, then claims a forfeiture.
   D. notifies the trustee of default.

6. ***A mortgage under which the debtor may re-borrow up to the original note amount under the same document is a(n)***
   A. amortizing mortgage.
   B. hypothecated mortgage.
   C. open-end mortgage.
   D. package mortgage.

7. ***The type of mortgage that may provide the borrower with a monthly check instead of the borrower paying a monthly payment is known as a(n)***
   A. blanket mortgage.
   B. graduated payment mortgage.
   C. interest only mortgage.
   D. reverse mortgage.

8. ***A builder finances the construction of an apartment building through a local bank. If money is released to the builder at various stages of construction, these payments are called***
   A. acceleration advances.
   B. obligatory advances.
   C. release payments.
   D. site drafts.

9. ***The term "take out loan" is most closely associated with***
   A. construction loans.
   B. junior loans.
   C. loans against the land.
   D. Truth in Lending requirements.

10. ***Which term describes the process by which a borrower pledges property as security for a loan without giving up possession of it?***
    A. defeasance
    B. hypothecation
    C. redemption
    D. subordination

6

Chapter 6

Conventional Financing

In This Chapter

Today, nearly half of all residential real estate lending is completed with conventional financing programs, and there are various financing tools available that have expanded the usefulness of these programs. In this chapter, we'll look at different types of conventional loans (e.g., 15-year, 30-year, conforming, nonconforming). In addition, we'll examine how private mortgage insurance and secondary financing options have expanded the availability of conventional lending. Government financing and nontraditional financing tools are covered in the following chapters.

At the end of this chapter, you will be able to:

- Identify the characteristics of a conventional loan.
- Define amortization.
- Identify different types of conventional loans.
- Discuss the use of private mortgage insurance.
- Contrast conforming and nonconforming loans.
- Discuss methods of secondary financing.

Key Terms

Amortization
Conforming Loan
Conventional Loan
Declining Market
Fixed Rate Loan
Jumbo Loan
Loan-to-Value Ratio (LTV)
Negative Amortization
Private Mortgage Insurance (PMI)
Secondary Financing
Self-Liquidating

Conventional Loans

Conventional financing refers to real estate that is paid for or financed with a **conventional loan**—one that is usually made by a bank or institutional lender and that is *not insured or guaranteed by a government entity or agency, such as FHA or VA*. Most conventional loans are, however, written to guidelines set by government-sponsored entities (GSEs), such as Freddie Mac and Fannie Mae, so that they may be sold in the secondary market. When a loan meets the criteria necessary to be sold in the secondary market, it is considered a **conforming** loan. Conventional loans may be conforming loans or nonconforming loans.

Since Fannie Mae and Freddie Mac are now under the conservatorship of the Federal Housing Finance Agency, you might be tempted to say that even conventional loans are "insured" by a government entity. However, for the purpose of this discussion, we will refer to conventional loans in the traditional sense. Just under half of all residential mortgages are handled as conventional financing. That percentage can certainly change depending on market conditions and consumer trends.

Traditional Conventional Loans

Traditional conventional loans are typically **long-term, fully amortizing, fixed rate real estate loans**. This is the type of loan with which borrowers are most familiar. According to the SAFE Act, any loan with terms other than 30-year fixed is defined as **nontraditional.**

Long-Term

Long-term real estate loans generally have total payments spread out over **25 to 30 years,** and even **40-year terms** are offered. While the long-term nature of conventional loans seems natural today, before the Federal Housing Administration (FHA) was formed in 1934, home loans were typically done for terms of five, seven, or ten years. Payments were often high with short loan terms, which required balloon payments to pay off the balance at the end of the loan term. This meant people had to refinance their loans frequently, posing problems for those who could not deliver the required balloon payment or whose qualifying situation may have changed at an inopportune time. Long-term loans give borrowers today a reasonable payment, and the security of a long-term loan that they can choose to refinance if and when the time is right.

Fully Amortizing

Amortization is the *reduction of the balance of the loan by paying back some of the principal owed on a regular basis*. Amortizing loans have payments applied to principal and interest (as opposed to interest-only loans with payments only applied to the interest on the loan). A **fully amortizing loan** is one for which *total payments over the life of a loan pay off the entire balance of principal and interest due at the end of the term*. This is also known as **self-liquidating**. Regular periodic payments reduce the loan by the end of the term, although different amounts are applied to interest and principal out of each regular payment.

Example: $100,000 loan @ 6%, 30-year term (figures approximate)

Pymt. No.	Principal Balance	Total Pymt.	Interest Portion	Principal Portion	Ending Balance
1	$100,000.00	$599.55	$500.00	$99.55	$99,900.45
2	$99,900.45	$599.55	$499.50	$100.05	$99,800.40
3	$99,800.40	$599.55	$499.00	$100.55	$99,699.85
4	$99,699.85	$599.55	$498.50	$101.05	$99,598.80
5	$99,598.80	$599.55	$497.99	$101.56	$99,497.24

NOTE: A complete sample amortization schedule appears in the Appendix.

FIGURE 6.1: Amortization of $100,000 30-Year Loan at 6%.

This is very different from how mortgage loans were repaid before FHA, when loans were only partially amortizing or non-amortizing.

Negative amortization occurs anytime the monthly payment is not sufficient to cover the accrued interest from the previous month.

Fixed Rate

Fixed rate loans have *interest rates that remain constant for the duration of the loan.* This is both good and bad for the borrower and the lender. Of course, the biggest advantage is that a borrower doesn't need to worry that rates will increase. If rates decrease enough, the borrower can refinance. From the lender's perspective, there's a guaranteed rate of return, but the rate is locked in for 30 years, which benefits the borrower when rates go up.

15-Year Mortgage Loans

Lenders will often give a borrower a better interest rate on a 15-year mortgage because the shorter term means less risk for the lender. Over the life of the mortgage, the **total interest** paid on a 15-year, fixed rate mortgage is about **one-third less** than a 30-year mortgage at the same interest rate. An added benefit is that the borrower can attain full ownership in half the time it takes to pay off a 30-year mortgage.

Of course, there are *disadvantages* to 15-year mortgages:

- Payments are higher.
- Higher payments consume financial resources that might be invested other ways and earn a higher return than the interest rate paid on the mortgage.
- The borrower's income tax deduction declines more quickly because less interest is paid each year as the principal is paid sooner.

One way to get some of the benefits of 15-year mortgages (saving interest and paying less over the life of the mortgage) without the legal obligation is for the borrowers to get a 30-year mortgage and make additional principal payments each month. Of course, this takes discipline, but most mortgages allow it. A borrower can retire the debt earlier and save interest without having to worry about the contractual burden of higher payments.

15-YEAR MORTGAGE TO 30-YEAR MORTGAGE COMPARISON OF INTEREST PAID

Loan Amount	Term	Interest Rate	Monthly Payment	Total Interest Paid
$50,000 MORTGAGE	15YR	7%	$449.41	$30,894.54
	30YR	7%	$332.65	$69,754.45
$100,000 MORTGAGE	15YR	7%	$898.83	$61,789.09
	30YR	7%	$665.30	$139,508.90
$150,000 MORTGAGE	15YR	7%	$1,348.24	$92,683.63
	30YR	7%	$997.95	$209,263.35

Note: Typically, rates for a 15-year mortgage is lower than rates for a 30-year mortgage. The same rate was used here for both to illustrate a direct comparison of total interest paid.

FIGURE 6.2: 15-Year to 30-Year Mortgage Comparison.

Bi-Weekly Payment Plan

A mortgage with a **bi-weekly** payment plan is a version of a *fixed rate mortgage set up like a standard 30-year conventional loan calling for regular monthly payments determined by a monthly payment amortization schedule but on which payments are made every two weeks instead of every month*. This alternative payment plan can help a borrower reach a goal of paying off a mortgage earlier and saving interest, since 26 payments are made each year—equal to one extra monthly payment. Loans with bi-weekly payment structures are usually paid off in about 22.3 years, instead of 30 years. For example, with a $70,000 loan at 10.5% fixed-rate loan with 30-year amortization:

SCHEDULE	PAYMENT	# of PAYMENTS	TOTAL AMOUNT PAID
Monthly	$640.32	360	$230,515.20
Bi-Weekly	$320.21	532	$170,351.72

Bi-weekly payment structures do require more servicing for lenders. Most loans today do not have pre-payment penalties so lenders may also allow borrowers to make voluntary extra payments in lieu of a formal payment structure. Borrowers must review the terms of their note to see if partial principal reductions are permitted, how excess funds are applied, and whether or not there are any prepayment penalties.

Conforming versus Nonconforming Loans

Conforming loans *meet Fannie Mae/Freddie Mac standards, and therefore can be sold on the secondary market.* Lenders try to make as many of their loans as possible conforming loans, because they like the option of being able to **liquidate** (sell for cash) their real estate loans on the secondary market if they need more funds. In an earlier chapter, you learned that conforming conventional financing has traditionally used the following qualifying guidelines:

- **28%** total housing expense ratio
- **36%** total debt-to-income ratio

Remember that a borrower must typically qualify under **both** ratios. In addition, note that borrowers should have **5% of their own funds** for a down payment and **two months of reserves on deposit.** For some lenders, however, these guidelines may be less rigid when automated underwriting is used. For example, conventional loans underwritten through Desktop Underwriter® put greater emphasis on the back end, or debt-to-income, ratio to evaluate potential payment shock.

Nonconforming loans, on the other hand, do *not* meet these standards, and therefore *cannot be sold to Fannie Mae or Freddie Mac.* There are other secondary markets where nonconforming loans can be sold, however, and lenders that have the option of keeping loans in their own portfolio (mostly banks and S & Ls) can, within the limits of the law, deviate from the standards set by secondary markets.

There are two main reasons why a loan would be classified as nonconforming:

- **Size of the Loan.** So-called **jumbo loans** *exceed the maximum loan amount established by Fannie Mae and Freddie Mac for conforming mortgage loans.* In 2012, the single-family home conforming loan maximum is $417,000 ($625,500 for most locations in Alaska, Hawaii, Guam, and U.S. Virgin Islands). In addition, the conforming loan maximum can be even higher in specific counties or metropolitan statistical areas. For example, in Washington D.C. and surrounding counties, the maximum conforming loan for a single-family home is $729,750.
- **Credit Quality of Borrower.** You may see a borrower who does not meet the minimum standards established by Fannie Mae/Freddie Mac classified as a **B or C borrower.** This might be someone who has had a credit problem in the past, such as bankruptcy within the past seven to ten years, medical bills, or someone whose credit scores are low because he or she owns multiple investment properties or has been self-employed for too short a period of time. Lenders, such as neighborhood banks, may still offer loans to these borrowers, but the loans cannot be sold to Fannie Mae or Freddie Mac.

A-Minus Conventional Loans

In order to meet the increasing consumer demand and limit the loss of market share to the nonconforming lenders, many lenders instituted an **A-minus conventional loan** program. This loan program allows a borrower with less than perfect credit history, limited money for down payments, or higher debt-to-income ratio to get a loan that could be sold on the secondary market. With this loan, a borrower may be able to benefit from a variety of financing alternatives in order to obtain an interest rate that is much closer to conventional conforming rates. In the past, the only option for these consumers would have been much costlier financing terms, if they would have been able to get a loan at all.

It is important to note that final interest rate and fees are determined on basis of the risk factors present in the loan. So when working with this type of mortgage, mortgage loan originators need to double check the interest rate and all the fees charged so they quote the correct information.

Conventional Loan Programs

Conventional loan programs can be classified by the **percentage of down payment** that the borrower pays to get the loan. The conditions and standards presented here are the most typical, but keep in mind that there are many variations of these loan programs. Lenders are constantly offering innovative loan products and programs to meet the needs of customers and to attract business in a competitive environment. As these "typical" loan programs and "typical" down payments with private mortgage insurance (PMI) are reviewed, remember that some lenders offer high LTV loans where PMI is not necessary, but fees may be higher, or conditions and standards imposed.

80% LTV Conventional Loan

The **loan-to-value ratio** (LTV) refers to *the amount of money borrowed (the loan amount of a first mortgage) compared to the value of the property.* Lenders use LTV to determine how much they are willing to loan on a given property based on its value. The lender will always use the *lower* of the appraised value or the sale price in order to protect its interest. The lower the LTV, the higher the borrower's down payment, which means the loan is more secure.

For example, for years, the **80% conventional loan** was the standard conventional loan, so for a house with a sale price of $200,000, the most a borrower could borrow would be:

$200,000 x 0.8 = $160,000 loan amount

Subtracting the loan amount from the sale price indicates that the borrower would need a down payment of $40,000.

Class Activity: 80% Conventional Loan

Review the following scenario and discuss your responses with the class.

Bill wants to buy a house that is selling for $160,000, and the lender has approved him for an 80% conventional loan.

How much can Bill borrow?

What would be the required down payment?

If the house appraises for $150,000, how much can Bill borrow?

What other options does he have?

Higher LTV Loans

A borrower who does not have enough money for a 20% down payment but still wants a conventional loan can try to get a 90% conventional loan with a 10% down payment, a 95% conventional loan with a 5% down payment, or even a 100% conventional loan. Loans with a LTV higher than 80% are possible because of PMI and secondary financing, which will be covered later in this chapter.

The qualifying standards for higher LTV loans tend to be more stringent, and lenders adhere to those standards more strictly even if the loan is insured through private mortgage insurance (PMI). These loans may also have a higher interest rate, call for higher loan origination fees, or impose additional conditions and standards.

Lender and agency requirements determine if the property must be **owner-occupied** as a condition for obtaining the loan. Most conventional loans over 80%, as well as all FHA and VA loans, require the property to be owner-occupied. There may be exceptions to these guidelines for specific programs or investors.

90% Conventional Loan

For a **90% LTV loan**, at least half of the 10% payment (5%) must be made from personal cash reserves. The remainder of the down payment may be a gift from a family member, equity in other property traded to the seller, or credit for rent already paid under a lease/purchase.

95% Conventional Loan

A **95% LTV loan** requires owner occupancy of the property and the down payment must be made from personal cash reserves, without using secondary (owner) financing or gifts.

Loans for Special Needs

While there are loan products for people who have small down payments but excellent credit, there are people in the opposite situation: They can't pass a stringent credit review, but have a larger down payment. Or perhaps their credit is good, but they have a hard time proving the stability of their income because they are self-employed. To address issues related to prospective borrowers who are either unable or unwilling to supply the normal income documentation, lenders designed various types of mortgage products. These may be referred to as stated-income, no-ratio, low-doc, no-doc, NINA (no income/no asset verification), or "easy qualifier" mortgages.

Although these loans are rare in today's marketplace, lenders who do make these loans modify their qualifying standards or loan criteria based on the customer's needs. For example, lenders may require the same documentation as other conventional loans, but relax qualifying standards due to the increased equity the borrower is putting into the home. Or, the lender may relax income verification standards for borrowers with good credit and a down payment of at least 20%. While higher down payment loans tend to be less expensive, that is not always the case with these types of loans as lenders must look at other factors to determine the interest rate and, possibly, the fees charged.

Current market conditions will drive the availability of such loans. An increase in foreclosures and a stagnant real estate market, for example, tends to limit the number of lenders willing to offer these types of loans.

Private Mortgage Insurance (PMI)

Private mortgage insurance (PMI) is *offered by private companies to insure a lender against default on a loan by a borrower.* Prior to the advent of PMI, lenders would only lend 80% of the value of a property, assuming that the 20% down payment was the incentive needed for the borrower to keep mortgage payments current. Lenders also felt comfortable that, in the event of default, a foreclosure sale would yield 80% of the original sale price (or appraised value) and recover the loan amount.

PMI evolved to compensate the lender for the reduced borrower equity, thus making loans easier for borrowers and safer for lenders. Both Fannie Mae and Freddie Mac also require mortgage insurance—whether lender-paid or third party—on home loans with less than 20% down.

How Mortgage Insurance Works

When insuring a loan, the mortgage insurance company shares the lender's risk, but only *part of the risk.* The insurer does *not* insure the entire loan amount but rather the *upper portion of the loan* that exceeds the standard 80% LTV. The amount of coverage can vary, but is typically 20% to 25% of the loan amount.

Example: 20% coverage on a 90% loan

$100,000	Total Sale Price
x .90	LTV
$ 90,000	90% Loan
x .20	Amount of Coverage
$ 18,000	Amount of Policy

TOTAL SALE PRICE		
	10%	Down payment
	18%	Coverage (20% of loan amount)
	72%	Exposure (80% of loan amount)

FIGURE 6.3: PMI Coverage Example.

Here, $18,000 is the maximum amount a lender can claim as a loss and collect from the private mortgage insurance company.

In the event of default, the insurer and the lender will negotiate how best to proceed in order to mitigate losses. For example, the insurer could purchase the loan for face value or some reduced value, then foreclose or allow the lender to foreclose. If the proceeds from the foreclosure action do not fully reimburse the lender for the principal balance, the lender will be able to make a claim against the insurer up to the policy limit. In this case, the insurer would probably require the lender to assign the note to the insurer. If the foreclosure sale does not yield enough to pay the outstanding loan balance and the cost of the foreclosure and sale, the holder of the note (either the lender or the insurer) may commence a proceeding to obtain a deficiency judgment against the borrower, co-borrower, and any other obligors.

PMI Premiums

There are actually three different ways that a borrower can pay for private mortgage insurance, each with advantages and disadvantages:

- First year's premium at closing and monthly escrow for the renewal premium
- One-time PMI premium
- Lender-Paid Mortgage Insurance (LPMI) through a higher interest rate on the loan throughout its life

Fee at Closing and Renewal Premium

The traditional way that private mortgage insurance companies charge for PMI is with a one time non-refundable fee at closing when the loan is made and a recurring fee, called a renewal premium, that's added to the borrower's monthly mortgage payment. These charges are often referred to as simply PMI. Each company that offers private mortgage insurance will provide rate cards that are used to determine the monthly PMI premium, as in this very simple example.

MONTHLY PMI PREMIUM		FIXED		TEMPORARY BUYDOWNS		ARMs	
		30-yr	15-yr	30-yr	15-yr	30-yr	15-yr
Base LTV	PMI Coverage	1st month and renewal to Yr 10		1st month and renewal to Yr 10		1st month and renewal to Yr 10	
95% to 90.01%	35%	1.06%	0.83%	1.21%	1.10%	1.25%	1.13%
	30%	0.94	0.81	1.04	0.92	1.08	0.95
	25%	0.84	0.70	0.90	0.77	0.94	0.81
90% to 85.01%	30%	0.69	0.54	0.84	0.71	0.89	0.77
	25%	0.62	0.48	0.73	0.60	0.78	0.65
	17%	0.49	0.33	0.56	0.36	0.61	0.44
85% & under	17%	0.43	0.30	0.44	0.30	0.49	0.36
	12%	0.38	0.26	0.39	0.27	0.44	0.31
	6%	0.34	0.24	0.36	0.25	0.40	0.28

FIGURE 6.4: Sample PMI Rate Card.

Class Activity: Mortgage Insurance

Walk through the following scenario and discuss your responses with the class.

If the sales price of a home is $100,000, on a 90% LTV 30-year fixed mortgage, we can calculate the PMI using the sample rate card. Let's use the Fannie Mae/Freddie Mac required 25% coverage, giving us a rate of 0.62%.

What is the loan amount?

What is the fee due at closing?

How much will be added to the borrower's monthly mortgage payment?

One-Time PMI Premium

Some private mortgage insurance companies offer a one-time mortgage insurance premium, with no renewal fee. Combining the initial premium and renewal premiums into one payment allows the borrower to finance the PMI premium. When the PMI premium is financed, monthly payments may still be lower than if the renewal premiums are added to the regular mortgage payment.

Lender Paid Mortgage Insurance (LPMI)

Lender paid mortgage insurance (LPMI) is actually *an interest rate adjustment made at the time of closing in exchange for the lender agreeing to "insure" the home loan themselves.* Basically, the borrower pays the lender a higher interest rate on the higher-risk loan. An advantage for the borrower is that this extra payment is treated like any other interest payment for the purpose of income tax deductions. However, unlike more traditional PMI, this higher payment will be in effect for the life of the loan; there is no cancellation.

PMI Cancellation

Lenders require mortgage insurance on high LTV, low down payment loans as protection against borrower default. Once the increased risk of loss from borrower default has been reduced (when the loan-to-value ratio is reduced to 80% or less), mortgage insurance has fulfilled its purpose. In the past, many lenders didn't cancel PMI even when the risk was reduced. The **Homeowners Protection Act of 1998 (HPA)** requires lenders to automatically cancel PMI when a home has been paid down to **78% of its original value**, assuming the borrower is not delinquent.

The law has some exceptions, such as for multi-family units, non-owner-occupied homes, mortgages on second homes, and second mortgages. As is often the case, though, the law sets a minimum, but the market moves the bar higher. For example, Fannie Mae and Freddie Mac:

- Have adopted rules that apply the 78% cancellation rule to *all* of their mortgages, even those closed before HPA's mandated date of July 1999.
- Have expanded the rules to cover investment properties and second homes.
- Will consider the *present value* of the home, not just the original value as required by the law. This effectively cancels PMI more quickly, assuming the home appreciates. Most lenders also now follow these guidelines.

The law also says that for loans closed *after July 29, 1999,* lenders must drop PMI coverage at a borrower's request if these conditions are met:

- A new lender-approved appraisal shows that the loan has been paid down to 80% or less of the home's original value, and
- The borrower shows a history of timely repayment over the past 12 months.
- Certification that the equity of the mortgagor in the residence securing the mortgage is unencumbered by a subordinate lien.

Again, Fannie Mae and Freddie Mac have gone a step further, allowing borrowers to use 80% of the home's current value if no payments have been more than 30 days late in the prior 12 months for fixed rate loans (or 24 months for ARMs). Fannie Mae and Freddie Mac also apply these rules to all loans, but can require up to five years of seasoning (outstanding age) on the loan before the rules apply.

Whether through automatic or borrower-requested cancellation, when PMI is terminated, the lender cancels the policy and reduces the monthly mortgage payment by the PMI amount. Note that the law and Fannie Mae/Freddie Mac rules do *not* apply to any upfront or one-time PMI premium paid.

Hot Topic: Underwriting PMI in Declining Markets

In recent years, most private mortgage insurance companies have added guidelines for considering the risks of insuring loans in markets where property values are declining. Many factors could go into determining whether or not a market area is declining. For example, the nation's leading provider of private mortgage insurance, Mortgage Guaranty Insurance Corporation (MGIC), has designated a number of urban areas and certain states as "restricted markets" by using objective data to evaluate home prices, changes in median home prices, and home price projections. While it may seem reasonable to be more cautious about standards in markets where property values are in decline, the label can create problems. For example, if an entire metropolitan area is labeled as "declining," it cannot account for specific neighborhoods where properties may be, for whatever reason, highly desirable.

While every company has its own standards for defining a declining market, the result is often that the loan is put in jeopardy. Some PMI providers may simply refuse to offer mortgage insurance in these markets, forcing the borrower to come up with a 20% down payment, for example. Or the insurer may raise the premiums for PMI in those markets, which could make the loan too expensive for the borrower.

Secondary Financing

Secondary financing is when *a buyer borrows money from another source to pay part of the purchase price or closing costs.* This is another way a borrower can get a conventional loan without a 20% down payment. With secondary financing, it may be the **seller** who carries the extra financing. In effect, the seller extends credit to the borrower, just as if the money had been borrowed from a finance company. When underwriting a loan that will have secondary financing, the primary lender will include that payment as part of the borrower's monthly housing expense and consider the total amount borrowed when determining the combined loan-to-value.

It's important to recognize that subordinate financing can be more than simply a second mortgage. Borrowers may have additional **junior liens**, such as with a down payment assistance program or even a third or fourth mortgage.

Combined Loan-to-Value (CLTV)

The **combined loan-to-value** (CLTV) is *the percentage of the property value borrowed through a combination of more than one loan,* such as a first mortgage and a second mortgage home equity loan. When a borrower chooses to use subordinate financing, this loan amount would also be included in the CLTV. The CLTV is calculated by adding all loan amounts and dividing by the home's appraised value or purchase price, whichever is lower. For example, a buyer purchases property valued at $100,000, taking out two loans: A first mortgage for $80,000 and a second for $10,000.

$$\frac{\$80{,}000 + \$10{,}000}{\$100{,}000} = 90\% \text{ CLTV}$$

But, remember that the **loan-to-value ratio** considers *only that first mortgage* and would therefore be just 80%: $80,000 / $100,000. That means that this borrower would *not* need to have private mortgage insurance. Both loan-to-value (LTV) and combined loan-to-value (CLTV) can be used to determine the amount of home equity a borrower has. So, that borrower with 90% CLTV has 10% equity in the property.

Conditions

For conventional loans, the primary lender will often insist on certain conditions with secondary financing from any source. Although individual lenders may impose additional or different specific conditions, the following are some typical examples:

- **Down Payment.** Borrower must make a **5%** down payment. For owner-occupied property, the CLTV must not exceed 95% of the appraised value or sale price, whichever is less. The borrower must pay the remaining 5% of the purchase price with personal funds. The first mortgage can't exceed 80% LTV.
- **Loan Terms.** Term of the second loan cannot exceed 30 years, or be less than 5 years. The term of the loan is the repayment period. The rationale is that a second mortgage should not take longer to pay off than the first mortgage.
- **Interest Rate.** The interest rate on a second mortgage could be fixed or adjustable. Note, however, that a borrower cannot have an adjustable rate on both the first mortgage and the second mortgage.
- **No Prepayment Penalty.** The second mortgage must be payable in full or in part at any time, without penalizing the borrower for paying the debt early.
- **Regularly Scheduled Payments.** Although payments must be due on a regular basis, they do not have to be monthly. Secondary finance payments can be monthly, quarterly, semi-annually, or any other regular schedule. Payments can fully or partially amortize the debt, or pay interest only.
- **No Negative Amortization.** The payments on the second mortgage must, at least, equal the interest on the loan. Loan balances cannot grow because of deferred interest.
- **Ability to Qualify.** Borrower must be able to afford payments on first and second mortgages. This means that the primary lender on the first mortgage will count both mortgages when qualifying the borrower for the mortgage debt.
- **Subordination Clause.** Most primary lenders require secondary financing to have a subordination clause to insure that the primary lender's lien will take priority, even if the second mortgage is recorded first.

Case in Point

Here's how secondary financing might work on a $120,000 home:

	$90,000	**75%**	**First Mortgage (primary lender)**
	$18,000	**15%**	**Second Mortgage (from seller)**
+	**$12,000**	**10%**	**Down Payment (from borrower)**
	$120,000	**100%**	**Total Sales Price**

Lender First and Lender Second

Keep in mind that it's *not always the seller* that carries a second mortgage. A second mortgage can be carried by any lender, investor, or financial institution. In fact, sometimes the same lender may finance the first and second mortgage. For example, one such arrangement is a so-called **conventional 80/20 loans** (essentially a 100% loan, as the same lender does both loans), which can be sold to Fannie Mae and Freddie Mac on the secondary market if the loans meet all standards and criteria. This allows the lender to charge a higher interest rate on the second mortgage—for example, the 80% first mortgage at 5.5% interest, and the 20% second mortgage at 9.25% interest—to reflect the riskier nature of the upper end of the loan amount. An 80/20 loan gives the lender, who will usually charge a fee for both loans, a better yield for taking on the increased risk. The advantage to a borrower is that this avoids both a down payment and PMI. When the upper portion of the loan represented by the second mortgage is paid off, the risk is gone and the borrower still has a first mortgage at a lower interest rate. In today's marketplace, such 80/20 loans are much less common than in years past.

The repayment plan is a matter of agreement between borrower and lender. As with any loan, there are various ways in which a second mortgage can be repaid:

- Fully amortizing
- Partially amortizing
- Interest only

Repayment Method Scenarios

The following example will be used to illustrate three repayment methods:

- A house costs $66,667. The buyer:
- Makes a $6,667 (10%) down payment.
- Gets a $50,000 (75%) first mortgage for 30 years at 6%.
- Gets a $10,000 (15%) second mortgage for five years at 7 7/8%.

Fully Amortizing Second Mortgage

A **fully amortizing** loan is one with the *total payments over the life of a loan paying off the entire balance of principal and interest due at the end of the term.* The shorter the term, the higher the payments. Using the example above:

	$ 299.78	**Payment on First Mortgage ($50,000, 6%, 30 yrs., fully amortizing)**
+	**202.17**	**Payment on Second Mortgage ($10,000, 7 7/8%, 5 yrs., fully amortizing)**
	$ 501.95	**Total Housing Expense (principal and interest only)**

After five years, the second mortgage is paid in full. The total monthly payment for the next 25 years is $299.78 on the first mortgage.

Partially Amortizing Second Mortgage

A **partially amortizing** loan has *payments applied to principal and interest, but the payments do* ***not*** *retire the debt when the agreed upon loan term expires.* Thus, a **balloon payment** is required as a *final payment at the end of the loan term* to pay off the entire remaining balance of principal and interest not covered by payments during the loan term.

To keep the payments low, the lender and borrower calculate the monthly payment *as if the borrower were going to pay off the entire debt over a longer period of time.* For example, the payments may be calculated as if the second mortgage would be repaid over 30 years, but the borrower agrees to make a balloon payment of the loan balance after five years. Using the example, the borrower's housing expense will be:

	$ 299.78	**Payment on First Mortgage ($50,000, 6%, 30 yrs., fully amortizing)**
+	**72.51**	**Payment on Second Mortgage ($10,000, 7 7/8%, amortized as 30 yrs.)**
	$372.29	**Total Housing Expense (principal and interest only)**

The smaller monthly payment makes the total housing expense less and, therefore, easier for the borrower to qualify for a loan. However, after five years, payments based on a 30-year amortization will have only reduced the original loan balance by a relatively small amount. If the second mortgage is to be paid at that time, there will be a substantial balloon payment due or the loan will have to be refinanced.

The following chart illustrates how a $10,000 second mortgage steadily declines over 30 years, if allowed to do so. It also shows the balloon payment due after five years. If all monthly payments are made on time, a 30-year, $10,000 loan at 7 7/8% will have a balance of about $9,496 after five years.

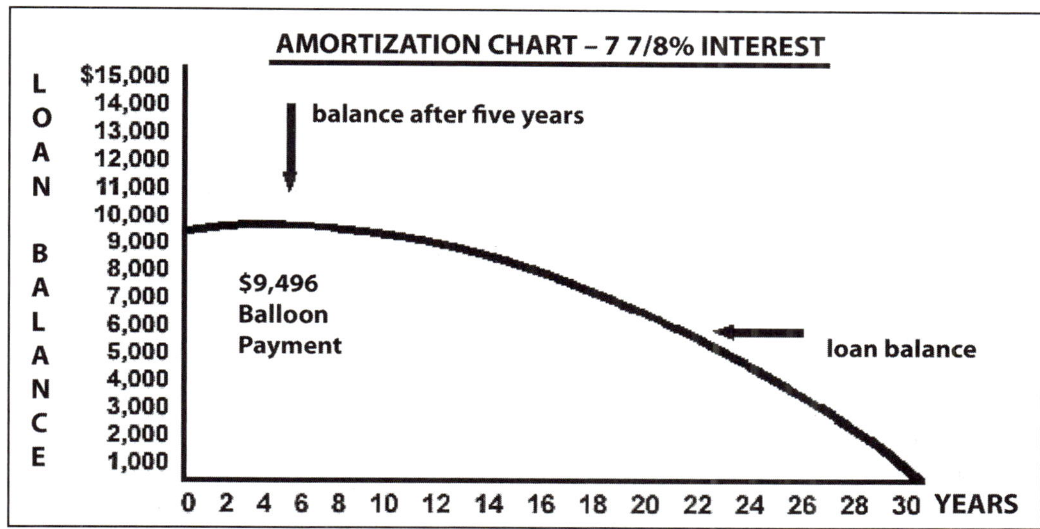

FIGURE 6.5: Partial Amortization Schedule.

Interest Only Second Mortgage

An **interest only loan** is one with *scheduled payments that pay only accrued interest, and not any portion of principal.* This reduces monthly payments even more. With interest only loans, no amortization occurs. A simple way to see how this works is to take the loan amount, multiply by the interest rate, then divide by 12 (months). In this case, the borrower's housing expense will be:

	$ 299.78	**Payment on First Mortgage ($50,000, 6%, 30 yrs., fully amortizing)**
+	**65.63**	**Payment on Second Mortgage ($10,000 x 0.07875 ÷ 12)**
	$ 365.41	**Total Housing Expense (principal and interest only)**

Comparing all of our examples, interest only gives the borrower the lowest housing expense. Of course, if no principal is paid during the loan term, the balloon payment will be the original amount borrowed (in this example, $10,000).

This example determined the payment on an interest only loan by evenly dividing the annual interest over 12 months. With some loans, for example, an open-end loan such as a home equity line of credit, lenders typically calculate the monthly payment of interest due using a daily rate, based on either a 360-day year or a 365-day year. The daily rate is multiplied by the number of days in the month to determine the payment. The terms of how interest is calculated can be found in the note.

Assumption of Conventional Loans

Assumption means that *one party takes over primary liability for the loan of another party, usually implying no change in loan terms.* When a buyer assumes the seller's mortgage, the seller remains secondarily liable unless the lender provides a release. Loan assumption is not always an option with loans written today as lenders try to protect their interests by being able to approve a new buyer. A new loan allows a lender to change interest rates, charge fees, or change loan terms for a new party.

A lender has several options in response to an assumption request:

- Accept the assumption and leave the loan terms intact
- Accept the assumption, but charge an assumption fee and/or increase the loan's interest rate
- Allow the assumption, but keep the original holder (seller) secondarily liable if the new owner defaults
- Not allow the assumption and exercise a call provision (i.e., demand full payment of the loan immediately); would need to be stated in the note or mortgage

Mortgage Exercise 6-1

A potential borrower is applying for a conventional loan to purchase a primary residence. Currently he pays $500 in rent, $420 for an auto loan, $170 toward his VISA bill, and $300 on a student loan each month. His gross monthly income totals $4,900, and his take-home pay after taxes is $3,700. *See the Appendix for answers to check your work.*

1. What is the maximum house payment—including principal, interest, taxes, and insurance—for which the borrower will qualify?

Mortgage Exercise 6-2

A borrower is seeking a fixed rate, conventional loan to purchase a home. The sale price is $189,500 and the property has been appraised at $191,500. The buyer will make a 10% down payment and finance the balance with a 75% conventional first mortgage at 6% interest for 30 years and a 15% second mortgage. The second mortgage bears interest at 11% and calls for a balloon payment after five years (amortized on the basis of a 30-year schedule). There will be a 1.5% loan fee on the first mortgage. To complete this exercise, refer to the Payment Rate Chart found in the Appendix. Note that the numbers there are rounded to the nearest cent. For a more precise total, you can use a financial calculator. *See the Appendix for answers to check your work.*

1. What will the loan amounts for the first and second loans be? What are the LTV and the CLTV?

2. How much will the buyer pay at closing for down payment and loan fees?

3. What is the monthly payment on the first mortgage, including principal and interest?

4. What is the total monthly payment for both loans?

5. The review appraisal just came back at $185,000. What happens now?

Chapter 6 Summary

1. **Conventional** loans are not insured or guaranteed by a government agency. Traditional conventional loans are long-term, fully amortizing, and have a fixed rate. An amortizing loan has payments that applied both to principal and interest. A **fixed rate, fully amortizing** loan has regular payments that are substantially equal in amount so as to fully retire the debt at the end of the term. Conventional loans may be 15- or 30-year, conforming or nonconforming. A **15-year** loan retires sooner and saves interest, but requires higher payments. A **bi-weekly** payment structure allows borrower to make equivalent of one extra monthly payment each year so balance is paid faster, saves interest. **Conforming** loans meet Fannie Mae/Freddie Mac standards and can be sold on the secondary market. Qualifying standards are **28%** for housing expense and **36%** for total debt-to-income. **Nonconforming** loans do not meet these standards and cannot be sold to Fannie Mae/Freddie Mac, but may be sold on the secondary market to other buyers. Nonconforming can be due to credit quality or loan size (jumbo loans exceed Fannie Mae/Freddie Mac maximum loan amount).

2. Conventional loan programs include 80%, 90%, 95% and some loans for special needs. For example, an 80% conventional loan means the **loan-to-value ratio** (LTV) is 80% of the appraised value or sale price of property, whichever is less. For an 80% loan, the borrower must make a 20% down payment; for a 90% loan, the borrower must make a 10% down payment with 5% from personal cash reserves (no gifts, loans, etc.); for a 95% loan, the borrower must make a 5% down payment, all from personal monies. Interest rates and fees may be higher on higher LTVs and PMI is required. Loans with LTV above 80% generally require the property to be owner-occupied.

3. **Private mortgage insurance (PMI)** insures lenders against borrower default, compensating lenders for lower borrower equity, and shares partial risk (upper part) with the lender. PMI can be fee paid at closing and as a renewal premium, one-time PMI premium, or no PMI premium but with a higher interest rate. Federal law says that loans after July 1999 must drop PMI when LTV is **78%** of original property value and the borrower is not delinquent, or if the borrower requests and the appraisal is **80%** of original property value. Fannie Mae/Freddie Mac rules require a drop of PMI if LTV is 78% (or borrower-paid appraisal is 80%) of property's current value.

4. **Secondary financing** is when the buyer borrows money for part of the purchase price or closing costs. To determine the **combined loan-to-value ratio** (CLTV) when there is more than one loan, add all loan amounts and divide by the home's appraised value or purchase price, whichever is lower. Typical conditions for secondary financing: 1. Borrower must make a 5% down payment; 2. Term of second loan must be five to 30 years; 3. No prepayment penalty; 4. Scheduled payments due on a regular basis; 5. No negative amortization; 6. Borrower must be able to afford payments on first and second mortgages; and 7. Required subordination clause.

5. A second mortgage can be **fully amortizing, partially amortizing** with a balloon payment, or **interest only** with a balloon payment. Partial amortization is when payments are scheduled as if the loan term is longer (e.g., 30 years), but the balance is due sooner (e.g., in 5 years). Partially amortizing and interest only loans have smaller payments than fully amortizing loans, so they may help a borrower qualify. Such loans generally have payments that are regular and equal (if fixed) or recomputed regularly (if adjustable) with a final, larger balloon payment at the end of the term that will fully retire the debt. One lender can provide both loans at different interest rates.

6. **Assumption** means that one party (buyer) takes over primary liability for the loan of another party (seller). When trying to assume a loan: 1. Lender can accept assumption and leave loan terms intact; 2. Lender can accept assumption and charge a fee or increase the interest rate; or 3. Lender will not allow assumption and call the note payable immediately. Always consult the original lender or a lawyer concerning assumptions.

Chapter 6 Quiz

1. ***What is the term that describes a second mortgage holder agreeing to accept a second position in a refinance transaction?***
   A. alienation
   B. assumption
   C. subordination
   D. subrogation

2. ***A loan that is repaid with periodic payments of both principal and interest so that the entire loan amount is paid in full at the end of the loan term is a(n)***
   A. annualized loan.
   B. conventional loan.
   C. fully amortizing loan.
   D. partially amortizing loan.

3. ***Which statement about 15-year mortgages is FALSE?***
   A. There's an earlier loss of interest deduction for income tax purposes.
   B. Higher interest rates are usually charged.
   C. They have higher monthly payments.
   D. They result in less interest owed.

4. ***You are pre-qualifying a buyer for a conventional loan on a house with the purchase price of $160,000. She states she does not want to pay PMI on the loan. In that case, what is the maximum loan amount she can receive (assuming no lender-paid PMI)?***
   A. $32,000
   B. $128,000
   C. $136,000
   D. $144,000

5. ***Which type of mortgage is traditionally defined as NOT being insured or guaranteed by the government?***
   A. conventional mortgage
   B. FHA mortgage
   C. rural home mortgage
   D. VA mortgage

6. ***When seeking an 80% conventional loan with the seller taking back a second mortgage, the buyer***
   A. can expect to pay a higher interest rate than with a 90% loan.
   B. may choose which mortgage (first or second) will have lien priority.
   C. must make at least a 5% down payment from personal funds.
   D. must make at least a 20% down payment from personal funds.

7. ***Which would likely have the highest PMI cost?***
   A. 80% loan
   B. 90% loan
   C. 95% loan
   D. house purchased for cash

8. ***PMI must be cancelled***
   A. anytime the borrower requests it.
   B. only if the lender is satisfied that the borrower is no longer a credit risk.
   C. when a home has been paid down to 78% of its original value and the borrower is current.
   D. whenever a new appraisal is ordered, regardless of the value.

9. ***Lenders are often willing to charge lower interest rates for 15-year mortgages because the***
   A. borrower is always a better risk.
   B. interest rate is fixed for a longer period of time.
   C. loan funds will be repaid more quickly.
   D. loan qualifications are much more stringent.

10. ***A buyer is paying $200,000 for a house. He makes a $30,000 down payment, gets a first mortgage for $160,000, and a second mortgage to cover the balance. What is his CLTV?***
    A. 70%
    B. 80%
    C. 85%
    D. 90%

7

Chapter 7
Introduction to Government Agency Loan Programs

In This Chapter

The federal government plays a key role in the national real estate market, and its influence seems to grow every year. In addition to passing legislation that affects mortgage lending in general, one of the most direct ways in which the government can impact a specific borrower is through government agency loan programs that help borrowers purchase or refinance residential real estate. (Don't confuse these programs with government-sponsored entities and their involvement in the secondary mortgage markets.) The two most common programs are **FHA-insured loans**, under the authority of the Department of Housing and Urban Development (HUD), and **VA-guaranteed loans**, under the authority of the Department of Veterans Affairs (VA). Other specialized loan programs exist as well, which will also be briefly discussed in this chapter. This chapter provides an ***introduction*** to these programs; it is not intended to be a comprehensive lesson on underwriting FHA and VA loans.

At the end of this chapter, you will be able to:

- Identify basic qualifying standards for FHA-insured loans.
- Define the use of upfront mortgage insurance premiums.
- Recognize different loan programs available through the FHA.
- Identify basic qualifying standards for VA-guaranteed loans.
- Define eligibility and entitlement for veterans.
- Describe other government agency loan options.

Key Terms

Area Median Income (AMI)
Automatic Endorsers
CAIVRS
Department of Veterans Affairs (VA)
Direct Endorsers
Federal Housing Administration (FHA)
Funding Fee
Mortgage Insurance Premium (MIP)
Rural Development
TOTAL Scorecard

Federal Housing Administration (FHA) Insured Loans

To begin, let's clear up some possible misconceptions: The Federal Housing Administration (FHA) rarely provides mortgage funds directly to borrowers; the FHA does *not* build houses, nor does the FHA set interest rates. Instead, the Federal Housing Administration **insures** loans for single family and multifamily homes made by approved lenders. Mortgage insurance, you'll recall, provides lenders with protection against losses when borrowers default.

Another common misconception about FHA loans is that they are targeted to lower-income borrowers or first-time homebuyers only, but this is not the case. The Federal Housing Administration does *not* have income limits to determine who is eligible for FHA loans. Anyone who is a U.S. citizen, permanent resident, or non-permanent resident with a qualifying work visa, and who meets the lending guidelines may qualify for a FHA-insured loan. The FHA does, however, set a *maximum mortgage amount* that it will insure, as you'll see.

The FHA is part of the Department of Housing and Urban Development (HUD). Oversight of FHA loan programs is through HUD's Office of Housing, which has three business areas related to real estate transactions:

- Single Family Housing
- Multifamily Housing
- Regulatory Programs, which includes the Real Estate Settlement Procedures Act (RESPA) and the Secure and Fair Enforcement for Mortgage Licensing Act (SAFE Act)

HUD issues regulations and establishes guidelines for approving lenders authorized to make FHA loans. Its regulations have the force and effect of law. FHA defines the loan programs and sets guidelines for the programs in accordance with HUD's regulations.

Approved Lenders

Lending institutions that make FHA-insured loans must first be **approved**. If approved as an unconditional **Direct Endorser** (DE), the lender may then underwrite and close mortgage loans without prior FHA review or approval. This includes all aspects of the mortgage loan application, the property analysis, and borrower underwriting. The purpose of the Direct Endorsement program, as authorized under § 203(b) of the National Housing Act (12 U.S.C. 1709 (b), (I)), is to simplify and expedite the process by which mortgagees can obtain mortgage insurance endorsements from HUD.

HUD Homeownership Centers

Four regional Homeownership Centers process FHA loans and oversee the selling of HUD-owned homes acquired through foreclosure or through deed in lieu of foreclosure. Homeownership Centers are organized to serve specific states:

Philadelphia, PA	Connecticut, Delaware, District of Columbia, Maine, Maryland, Massachusetts, Michigan, New Hampshire, New Jersey, New York, Ohio, Pennsylvania, Rhode Island, Vermont, Virginia, West Virginia
Atlanta, GA	Alabama, Florida, Georgia, Kentucky, Illinois, Indiana, Mississippi, North Carolina, South Carolina, Tennessee
Denver, CO	Arkansas, Colorado, Iowa, Kansas, Louisiana, Missouri, Minnesota, Montana, Nebraska, New Mexico, North Dakota, Oklahoma, South Dakota, Texas, Wisconsin, Utah
Santa Ana, CA	Alaska, Arizona, California, Hawaii, Idaho, Nevada, Oregon, Washington

HUD is further organized in 10 regions, each of which is managed by a regional administrator who also oversees the regional office. Within each region are a number of local field offices that offer various support services.

Limited Denial of Participation (LPD)

A **Limited Denial of Participation** (LDP) is an action taken by a HUD Field Office or the Deputy Assistant Secretary for Single Family or Multifamily Housing that excludes a person or company who fails to comply with HUD program standards from further participation in a HUD program area. LDPs are effective nationwide unless otherwise noted and generally expire in one year. Parties who have been issued an LDP should be prevented from new participation in the HUD program; therefore, mortgage loan originators need to check the LPD list before attempting to process an FHA loan application.

In addition to the LDP list, the General Services Administration's (GSA) **Lists of Parties Excluded from Federal Procurement or Nonprocurement Programs** must be checked to determine if individuals or companies are suspended or debarred from further participation in HUD programs.

Underwriting Standards for FHA Loans

When evaluating an application for an FHA loan, underwriters or lenders consider FHA's "4 Cs of Underwriting":

- Credit history of the borrower, which indicates the borrower's willingness to repay debt
- Capacity to repay the loan, which includes income and employment history
- Cash assets available to close the mortgage
- Collateral, which evaluates the value of the home

Although an underwriter likes to see a stellar **credit history**, some prior credit issues might not be a problem. As with other mortgages, however, court-ordered judgments must be paid off first. In addition, a borrower who has defaulted on a student loan or is delinquent or in default on any federal debt would *not* qualify for an FHA loan. This is confirmed through the **Credit Alert Verification Reporting System**—CAIVRS—a federal database of delinquent federal debtors that allows federal agencies to reduce the risk to federal loan and loan guarantee programs. CAIVRS alerts participating federal lending agencies when an applicant for credit benefits, or for a position of trust in support of the administration of a federal credit program, has a federal lien, judgment, or a federal loan that is currently in default or foreclosure, or has had a claim paid by a reporting agency.

FHA is less stringent when it comes to a borrower's level of **income**. While no minimum or maximum income is required for an FHA loan, the borrower must have sufficient income to service the debt on the home mortgage and all other credit obligations. This is determined by housing expense and total debt-to-income ratios, which are slightly more liberal than those allowed for conventional loans.

FHA Underwriting Guidance

HUD Housing Handbooks provide detailed underwriting guidance on FHA loan programs. In particular, MLOs making single family FHA loans will likely become very familiar with these handbooks:

- Mortgage Credit Analysis (4155.1)
- Lender's Guide to the Single Family Mortgage Insurance Process (4155.2)

These are available online from the FHA Handbook page on this website:

www.fhaoutreach.gov/FHAHandbook/prod/index.asp

FHA Underwriting Guidance (continued)

In addition, HUD regularly publishes **Mortgagee Letters** as a way to communicate program changes, commentary on regulations, and other critical information to lenders and mortgage loan originators. Current and past Letters, numbered sequentially by year, can be found on this HUD website:

www.hud.gov/offices/adm/hudclips/letters/mortgagee

Note that the following guidelines discussed in this chapter generally apply to standard **FHA 203(b)** loans on **single family homes**. Other FHA loan types may have different guidelines or additional criteria.

FHA TOTAL Scorecard

The **Technology Open to Approved Lenders** (TOTAL) Mortgage Scorecard was developed by HUD to evaluate the credit risk of FHA loans that are submitted to an automated underwriting system (e.g., Desktop Underwriter® or Loan Prospector®). TOTAL evaluates the overall creditworthiness of the applicants based on a number of variables:

- Credit score
- Monthly housing expense
- Number of monthly payments in reserve
- Loan-to-value ratio
- Loan term

When combined with the functionalities of the AUS, TOTAL indicates a recommended level of underwriting and documentation to determine a loan's eligibility for insurance by FHA:

- **Accept/Approve**, which means that the loan is eligible for FHA endorsement
- **Refer**, which will require the lender to manually underwrite the loan

It is FHA's policy that no borrower will be denied an FHA insured mortgage loan solely on the basis of a risk assessment generated by the TOTAL Scorecard.

Mortgage Payment Expense to Effective Income Ratio

A borrower's mortgage payment expense to effective income ratio, more commonly referred to as the **housing expense ratio**, is *the relationship of the borrower's total monthly housing expense to income, expressed as a percentage*. FHA considers a borrower's income adequate for a loan if the proposed total mortgage payment does not exceed **31%** of gross stable monthly income. As with conventional loans, FHA's maximum mortgage payment includes **principal, interest, taxes, and insurance (PITI)**, as well as any required monthly homeowners association dues.

When you know a borrower's stable monthly income, you can multiply that by the housing expense ratio to determine the maximum monthly housing expense the borrower can afford. For example, if a borrower has a stable monthly income of $3,200, the maximum housing expense on an FHA loan would be $992 ($3,200 x .31).

Here's another way to use this ratio. When you know the total housing expense, you can determine whether the borrower's income is sufficient to qualify under the loan guidelines.

Class Activity: FHA Loan Qualifying (Part 1)

Mary wants an FHA loan to buy a house. She would have these monthly expenses:

	$536.82	Principal and Interest ($100,000 at 5% for 360 months)
	$ 53.00	Property Taxes
	$ 25.00	Homeowners Insurance
	$ 95.83	MIP (FHA Mortgage Insurance Premium based on 96% LTV)
+	$ 90.00	Homeowners Association Dues
	$800.65	Total Housing Expense (PITI)

What would be Mary's required stable monthly gross income in order to qualify for this loan?

Total Debt-to-Income Ratio

A borrower's **total debt-to-income ratio** is *the relationship of the borrower's total monthly debt obligations (including housing and other long-term debts that will not be cancelled) to income, expressed as a percentage.* This back end ratio is given primary consideration by TOTAL Scorecard, looking to ensure the borrower's total expenses do not exceed **43%** of monthly income.

Class Activity: FHA Loan Qualifying (Part 2)

	$800.65	Housing Expense (from previous example)
	$192.65	Auto Payment
+	$ 40.00	Revolving Credit Account
	$1,033.30	Total Debt

Based on her debt, what would be Mary's required stable monthly gross income in order to qualify for this loan using the total debt-to-income ratio?

Compensating Factors

If a loan applicant exceeds either or both of the permissible ratios of 31/43, the lender must document compensating factors that mitigate the risk:

Compensating Factor	Comments
Housing expense ratio	The borrower has successfully demonstrated the ability to pay housing expenses greater than or equal to the proposed monthly housing expenses for the new mortgage over the past 12-24 months.
Down payment	The borrower makes a large down payment of 10 percent or higher toward the purchase of the property.
Accumulated savings	The borrower has demonstrated an ability to accumulate savings and a conservative attitude toward using credit.
Previous credit history	A borrower's previous credit history shows that he/she has the ability to devote a greater portion of income to housing expenses.
Compensation or income not reflected in effective income	The borrower receives documented compensation or income that is not reflected on the 1003, but may affect his/her ability to pay the mortgage.
Minimal housing expense increase	There is only a minimal increase in the borrower's housing expense.
Substantial cash reserves	The borrower has substantial documented cash reserves (at least three months worth) after closing.
Substantial non-taxable income	The borrower has non-taxable income that is not included in on the 1003.
Potential for increased earnings	The borrower has a potential for increased earnings, as indicated by job training or education in his/her profession.
Primary wage-earner relocation	The home is being purchased because the primary wage-earner is relocating, and the secondary wage-earner has an established employment history, is expected to return to work, and has reasonable prospects for securing employment in a similar occupation in the new area.

Property Guidelines for FHA Loans

Among the important property guidelines for FHA loan approval are the **eligibility** of the property, the **condition** of the property, **maximum mortgage amount** permitted where the property is located, and **occupancy**.

Property Eligibility

Eligible one- to four-family dwellings include:

- Detached or semi-detached dwellings (with additional requirements for dwellings that are not detached)
- Row houses
- Multiplex dwellings
- Individual condominium units (approved)
- Some manufactured housing

Additionally, HUD guidelines indicate that utilities and other facilities should be independent for each unit and must include:

- A continuing supply of safe, potable water
- Sanitary facilities and a safe method of sewage disposal
- Heating adequate for health and comfort
- Domestic hot water
- Electricity for lighting and equipment

Property Conditions

At a minimum, the site conditions of a property must be free of health and safety hazards. FHA Handbooks provide **minimum property standards** (MPS) for new construction and **minimum property requirements** (MPR) for existing properties. An appraiser will note any issues and make recommendations about the need to engage qualified property inspectors as necessary to ensure that the property complies with FHA's MPR, or MPS, together with the estimated cost to cure. Typical conditions that would require further inspection or testing by qualified individuals or entities include:

- Infestation/evidence of termites
- Inoperative or inadequate plumbing, heating, or electrical systems
- Structural failure in framing members
- Leaking or worn-out roofs
- Cracked masonry or foundation damage
- Drainage problems

The lender determines which repairs for existing properties must be made for the property to be eligible for FHA-insured financing. Required repairs include those that are necessary to:

- Protect the health and safety of the occupants.
- Protect the security of the property.
- Correct physical deficiencies or conditions affecting structural integrity.

Occupancy

Borrowers with FHA loans are required to establish bona fide occupancy of the property as their principal residence **within 60 days** of signing a security instrument (e.g., mortgage, trust deed). Furthermore, they are required to live in the house for **at least one year**. Generally, a borrower may have only one FHA loan at a time, although some exceptions may be made.

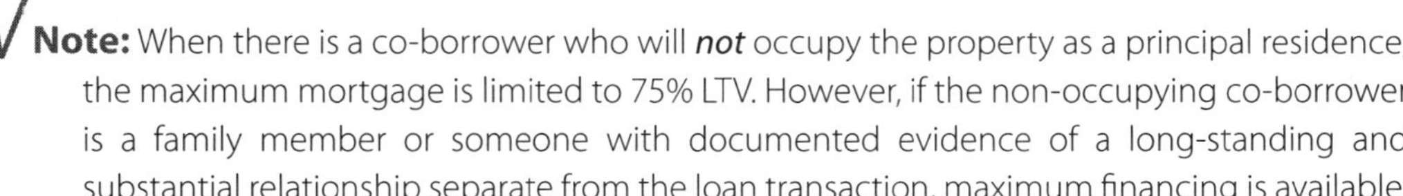

√ **Note:** When there is a co-borrower who will ***not*** occupy the property as a principal residence, the maximum mortgage is limited to 75% LTV. However, if the non-occupying co-borrower is a family member or someone with documented evidence of a long-standing and substantial relationship separate from the loan transaction, maximum financing is available.

Maximum Mortgage Amount

Although there are no income limits with FHA loans, HUD limits the maximum loan amount—sometimes called a **loan ceiling** or **base**—that may be insured in a given community. When determining limits, boundaries may be based on county, zip code, or metropolitan statistical areas (MSAs). The loan amounts are reviewed every three years. For example, the 2011 limits for most single family homes is $271,050 (there are different loan ceilings for one-, two-, three-, and four-family dwellings). High cost area limits are subject to a ceiling based on a percent of the Freddie Mac loan limits. Section 214 of the National Housing Act provides that mortgage limits for Alaska, Guam, Hawaii, and the Virgin Islands may be adjusted up to 150 percent of the ceilings.

A current schedule of maximum FHA loan limits may be accessed from this website:

https://entp.hud.gov/idapp/html/hicostlook.cfm

Loan Regulations

Other important regulations for FHA loans are summarized here.

Required Minimum Investment

A borrower seeking an FHA loan must make a minimum required investment of at least **3.5%** of the home's purchase price or appraised value, *whichever is less* (i.e., maximum LTV of 96.5%) from an acceptable source. This assumes that the borrower has a credit score of **at least 580**. HUD indicates that borrowers applying for an FHA mortgage loan who have a credit score between 500 and 579 require a **10%** down payment, while those whose credit scores fall below 500 are *not* eligible for FHA-insured financing regardless of the down payment. Note that lenders may choose to impose higher standards than HUD in order to protect themselves from losses and have the ability to sell the mortgages on the secondary markets.

Closing costs (closing costs, pre-paid expenses, and discount points) may *not* be used to help meet the required minimum investment. A borrower may qualify for a **down payment assistance** grant from a state or municipal agency, non-profit organization, etc., however.

Gifts

The entire required minimum investment can be a non-repayable **gift** from a relative, an employer or labor union, a charitable organization, or a close friend with a clearly defined and documented interest in the borrower.

The gift donor may *not* be a person or entity with an interest in the sale of the property, such as the seller, a real estate agent or broker, or a builder/associated entity. Gifts from these sources are considered inducements to purchase, and *must* be subtracted from the sales price.

A lender must document any borrower gift funds through a **gift letter**, signed by the donor and borrower, that shows the donor's name and contact information; specifies the dollar amount of the gift; and states the nature of the relationship to the borrower and that no repayment is required.

Secondary Financing

FHA will insure first mortgage transactions that also include secondary financing if:

- The second mortgage or lien is by a federal, state, or local government agency or an approved nonprofit agency, and
- The monthly payment under the insured mortgage and second lien, plus housing expense and other recurring charges, does not exceed the borrowers' ability to pay.

With advance approval, FHA will insure a first mortgage loan on a property that has a second mortgage or lien held by an individual or company, provided that:

- The secondary financing is disclosed at the time of application,
- The required minimum cash investment is *not* financed,
- The first and second mortgage together do *not* exceed FHA mortgage limits,
- The borrower can afford the total amount of the payments,
- Any periodic payments are level and monthly,
- There is no balloon payment during the first ten years, and
- There is no prepayment penalty.

FHA reserves the right to refuse to insure the first mortgage if there is any secondary financing that does not serve the needs of the intended borrower or where the costs to participants outweighs the benefits derived by the borrower.

Seller/Third Party Contribution Limits

The seller and/or third party may contribute up to **6%** of the *lesser of* the property's sales price or the appraised value toward the buyer's closing costs, prepaid expenses, discount points, and other financing concessions. This limit also includes:

- Third party payment for permanent and temporary interest rate buydowns, and other payment supplements (note that borrowers must qualify at the note rate on temporary buydowns)
- Payments of mortgage interest for fixed rate mortgages
- Mortgage payment protection insurance
- Payment of the upfront mortgage insurance premium (UFMIP)

Such contributions *cannot* be used to reduce the borrower's required minimum investment, however.

Payment of real estate commissions or fees, typically paid by the seller under local or state law or local custom, is not considered an interested third party contribution. Contributions exceeding 6% are considered **inducements to purchase**, which requires that each dollar over the 6% limit must be subtracted from the property's sales price before applying the appropriate LTV factor.

√ **Note:** HUD has indicated its intention to reduce allowable seller contributions on FHA loans from 6% to only **3%**. This change is intended to reduce the risk of creating incentives to inflate appraised value. Final approval of this change is pending.

Loan Assumption

Most FHA loans made prior to December 15, 1989, are fully assumable—for a nominal handling fee—since they do not have alienation (due on sale) clauses. Recall that an **alienation clause** would *allow the lender to exercise certain rights upon the sale or transfer of an interest in the property*, for example, to call the note due, change the interest rate, or charge an assumption fee. However, it's important to note that the original borrower is NOT released from liability unless FHA agrees to the assumption.

FHA loans endorsed on or after December 15, 1989, may include an alienation clause. Such loans may be assumable, however, the lender will require a creditworthiness review of the new borrower as well as a fee. With these loans, assumptions without credit approval may be grounds for acceleration of the mortgage. Therefore, any offers involving mortgage assumptions must be investigated thoroughly with the lender, who must supply a specific release of liability, and perhaps even with legal counsel.

Prepayment Penalties

HUD regulations prohibit prepayment penalties in FHA loans. A borrower may prepay a mortgage, in whole or in part, on the first of any month. If the payment is received *after* the first of the month, however, the lender may, at its discretion, collect the remainder of the month's interest.

Mortgage Insurance Premium

A **mortgage insurance premium** (MIP)—not to be confused with PMI for conventional loans—is required for all FHA loans, regardless of the down payment. There is an initial premium—called the **upfront mortgage insurance premium** (UFMIP)—and an **annual premium**, which is based on the annual average outstanding loan balance divided into 12 monthly payments.

The UFMIP on 15- and 30-year purchase and refinance transactions for case numbers assigned on or after October 4, 2010, is **1%** of the loan amount. This policy lowers the UFMIP from 2.25%, which only went into effect as of April 5, 2010. UFMIP for Hope for Homeowners and Home Equity Conversion Loans is 2.00%.

The monthly premium reflects the type of loan and loan-to-value. For example, the annual MIP on a 30-year loan is 1.10% if the LTV is 95% or less and 1.15% if the LTV is greater than 95% for case numbers assigned on or after 4/18/11. On a 15-year loan, it is 0.25% for loans with a 90% LTV or less, and .50% for loans with LTV over 90%.

Financing MIP

If the UFMIP for 15-year or 30-year loans is paid in cash at closing, it may be paid by the borrower or by the seller or other third party (within limits). It is most commonly financed into the loan itself, however. The Housing and Economic Recovery Act of 2008 limits the total FHA-insured first mortgage to 100% of the lesser of the sales price or appraised value, which would include the financing of the upfront mortgage insurance premium (UFMIP) within that limit.

Cancellation

For loans made after January 1, 2001, the MIP is automatically cancelled when the LTV reaches **78%** of the original value (for 30-year mortgages, the annual MIP must have also been paid for at least five years). Borrowers may be able to make additional or early payments of principal to reduce the LTV to that 78% threshold where MIP is automatically cancelled. Financed MIP cannot be cancelled.

Real Success

As you review the regulations discussed here or as you encounter others, be aware that laws regulating FHA loans continually evolve. Any changes to program details—for example, product availability, mortgage insurance premiums, seller contribution limits, credit score requirements, down payments, etc.—are communicated through **Mortgagee Letters**.

See: http://www.hud.gov/offices/adm/hudclips/letters/mortgagee/

FHA Loan Programs

There are many FHA loan programs authorized under the federal statute that created the Federal Housing Administration. Most of these loan programs are referred to by the section number that describes them in the federal statute. For example, the most common type of loan is called a Section 203(b) loan after the statute section and paragraph that explains the requirements. Several programs are summarized here. More details on each of the specific FHA loan programs can be found in the HUD Handbooks.

FHA Loan Program	Description	Conditions
Section 203(b) Home Mortgage Insurance	• Basic owner-occupied loan for one- to four-family dwelling • Any term up to 30 years, fixed	• Required minimum investment of 3.5% with credit score of at least 580; 10% with credit score of 500-579 • Maximum loan origination fee of 1% • Requires UFMIP (1%) and monthly MIP up to 1.15% of loan balance (as of 4/18/11) • Maximum loan amounts range from $271,050 to $729,750 depending on geographic location
Section 203(k) Rehabilitation Home Mortgage Insurance and Streamlined Limited Repair Program	• Purchase and rehabilitate an existing one- to four-family dwelling • Loan for existing debt + repaid costs • Allows 110% LTV • Must bring the property into compliance with FHA standards • Repairs may include such items as: • Structural/additions (not on Streamline) • Siding/roofing • Plumbing/electrical • Heating/AC • Flooring/carpet	Section 203(k) • Must be able to occupy within six months • Minimum repair=$5,000 / Maximum repair=None Section 203(k) Streamline • Must be able to occupy within 30 days • Minimum repair=None / Maximum repair=$35,000
Section 234(c) Condominiums	Available for condo projects approved by FHA based on owner-occupancy and other criteria	Same eligibility as 203(b)
Section 251 Adjustable Rate Mortgages	• Available for 1- to 4-family dwelling or condominium • Allows for variable interest rate to reflect weekly average yield on U.S. Treasury Securities + margin • 1-, 3-, and 5-year ARMs allow: • 1% annual interest rate adjustment after the initial fixed interest rate period • 5% lifetime interest rate cap • 7- and 10-year ARMs allow: • 2% annual interest rate adjustment after the initial fixed interest rate period • 6% lifetime interest rate cap	• Only 30-year terms are allowed • Requires additional disclosures • Borrower must qualify at second year interest rate
Section 255 Home Equity Conversion Mortgage (HECM)	• Allows homeowners age 62 or older to convert equity in home to a monthly stream of income or line of credit	• Requires UFMIP (2.00%) and monthly premium (.5%) • Loan must be repaid when borrower sells, dies, or does not live in house for 12 consecutive months
Section 184 Indian Home Loan Guarantee Program	• Specifically for American Indian and Alaska Native families, tribes, Alaska Villages, or tribally designated housing entities	• 2.25% down payment requirement for loans over $50,000 • 1.25% down payment requirement for loans under $50,000 • No monthly mortgage insurance • A one-time, 1% loan guarantee fee
Energy Efficient Mortgage Program	• Allows borrowers to finance the cost of adding energy efficient improvements into a new home purchase or the refinancing of existing housing • May be used with the 203(k) Rehabilitation program	Same eligibility as 203(b)
Good Neighbors Next Door Program (GNND)	• Qualified civil servants, including firefighters, police officers, and teachers	• Assists public servants to purchase FHA foreclosures • Purchase price as low as 50% of the loan balance • Down payments as low as $100 • Requires occupancy as sole residence; borrower cannot own any other residential real property

Required Documentation

When making an FHA loan, the following documentation and disclosures are required to be given to applicants (in addition to the standard disclosures required in the loan origination process):

Disclosure	Purchase	Refinance
Amendatory Clause (to be included in the sales contract when the borrower has not been informed of the appraised value; provides the borrower with an "escape" clause if the property does not appraise for at least the sales price)	X	
Real Estate Certification (borrower, seller, and selling real estate licensee must certify that the terms and conditions of the sales contract are true to the best of their knowledge)	X	
Important Notice to Homebuyers (HUD 92900-B)	X	X
For Your Protection, Get a Home Inspection (HUD-92564-CN)	X	
Informed Consumer Choice Disclosure (compares terms of FHA loan with conventional financing or other available loan; must be made no later than 3 business days after receipt of the initial mortgage loan application)	X	X
FHA ARM Disclosure (for adjustable rate mortgages as applicable)	X	X
Release of Liability (for loan assumptions)	X	X
FHA Borrower Authorization (allows lender to verify borrower financial and employment information)	X	X
Identity of Interest Certification (identifies any relationship to the seller)	X	
92900 A FHA/VA Addendum (application for mortgage insurance)	X	X
HUD 92561 Hotel/Transient Usage (borrower certification that property will not be used for rentals of less than 30 days or if occupants receive customary hotel services)	X	X
FHA Social Security Number Verification Form	X	X

Important Notice to Homebuyers

U.S. Department of Housing and Urban Development
Office of Housing - Federal Housing Commissioner

OMB Approval No. 2502-0059
(Expires 11/30/2010)

You must read this entire document at the time you apply for the loan.
Return one copy to lender as proof of notification and keep one copy for your records.

Condition of Property

The property you are buying is not HUD/FHA approved and HUD/FHA does not warrant the condition or the value of the property. An appraisal will be performed to estimate the value of the property, but this appraisal does not guarantee that the house is free of defects. You should inspect the property yourself very carefully or hire a professional inspection service to inspect the property for you.

Interest Rate and Discount Points

HUD does not regulate the interest rate or the discount points that may be paid by you or the seller or other third party. You should shop around to be sure you are satisfied with the loan terms offered and with the service reputation of the lender you have chosen.

The interest rate, any discount points and the length of time the lender will honor the loan terms are all negotiated between you and the lender.

The seller can pay the discount points, or a portion thereof, if you and the seller agree to such an arrangement.

Lenders may agree to guarantee or "lock-in" the loan terms for a definite period of time (i.e., 15, 30, 60 days, etc.) or may permit your loan to be determined by future market conditions, also known as "floating". Lenders may require a fee to lock in the interest rate or the terms of the loan, but must provide a written agreement covering a minimum of 15 days before the anticipated closing. Your agreement with the lender will determine the degree, if any, that the interest rate and discount points may rise before closing.

If the lender determines you are eligible for the mortgage, your agreement with the seller may require you to complete the transaction or lose your deposit on the property.

Don't Commit Loan Fraud

It is important for you to understand that you are required to provide complete and accurate information when applying for a mortgage loan.

Do not falsify information about your income or assets.

Disclose all loans and debts (including money that may have been borrowed to make the downpayment).

Do not provide false letters-of-credit, cash-on-hand statements, gift letters or sweat equity letters.

Do not accept funds to be used for your downpayment from any other party (seller, real estate salesperson, builder, etc.).

Do not falsely certify that a property will be used for your primary residence when you are actually going to use it as a rental property.

Do not act as a "strawbuyer" (somebody who purchases a property for another person and then transfers title of the property to that person), nor should you give that person personal or credit information for them to use in any such scheme.

Do not apply for a loan by assuming the identity of another person.

Do not sign an incomplete or blank document; that is, one missing the name and address of the recipient and/or other important identifying information.

Penalties for Loan Fraud: Federal laws provide severe penalties for fraud, misrepresentation, or conspiracy to influence wrongly the issuance of mortgage insurance by HUD. You can be subject to a possible prison term and fine of up to $10,000 for providing false information. Additionally, you could be prohibited from obtaining a HUD-insured loan for an indefinite period.

Report Loan Fraud: If you are aware of any fraud in HUD programs or if an individual tries to persuade you to make false statements on a loan application, you should report the matter by calling your nearest HUD office or the HUD Regional Inspector General, or call the HUD Hotline on 1 (800) 347-3735.

Warning: It is a crime to knowingly make false statements to the United States Government on this or any similar form. Penalties upon conviction can include a fine and imprisonment. For details see: Title 18 U.S. Code Section 1001 and Section 1010.

Discrimination

If you believe you have been subject to discrimination because of race, color, religion, sex, handicap, familial status, or national origin, you should call HUD's Fair Housing & Equal Opportunity Complaint Hotline: 1 (800) 669-9777.

Previous editions are obsolete — Page 1 of 2 — form **HUD-92900-B** (12/2004) ref. Handbooks 4150.1 & 4155.1

Sample HUD Notice for Homebuyers

About Prepayment

This notice is to advise you of the requirements that must be followed to accomplish a prepayment of your mortgage, and to prevent accrual of any interest after the date of prepayment.

You may prepay any or all of the outstanding indebtedness due under your mortgage at any time, without penalty. However, to avoid the accrual of interest on any prepayment, the prepayment must be received on the installment due date (the first day of the month) if the lender stated this policy in its response to a request for a payoff figure.

Otherwise, you may be required to pay interest on the amount prepaid through the end of the month. The lender can refuse to accept prepayment on any date other than the installment due date.

FHA Mortgage Insurance Information

Who may be eligible for a refund?

Premium Refund: You may be eligible for a refund of a portion of the insurance premium if you paid an upfront mortgage insurance premium at settlement and are refinancing with another FHA mortgage.

Review your settlement papers or check with your mortgage company to determine if you paid an upfront premium.

Exceptions:

Assumptions: When a FHA insured loan is assumed the insurance remains in force (the seller receives no refund). The owner(s) of the property at the time the insurance is terminated is entitled to any refund.

FHA-to-FHA Refinance: When a FHA insured loan is refinanced, the refund from the old premium may be applied toward the upfront premium required for the new loan.

How are Refunds Determined?

The FHA Commissioner determines how much of the upfront premium is refunded when loans are terminated. Refunds are based on the number of months the loan is insured.

Monthly Insurance Premiums

If you paid an upfront mortgage insurance premium, you will also be charged a monthly mortgage insurance premium until the loan-to-value of your mortgage reaches 78 percent of the initial sales price or appraised value of your home, whichever was lower (provided that premiums are paid for at least five years). You will reach the 78 percent loan-to-value threshold in one of two ways: Through normal amortization as you make your monthly payments, or by paying additional principal on the mortgage. Your lender can advise you on when the mortgage will reach the 78 percent loan-to-value threshold. If you were not charged an upfront premium, you will pay the monthly premium for the life of the mortgage.

Important: The rules governing the eligibility for premium refunds are based on the financial status of the FHA insurance fund and are subject to change.

SI USTED HABLA ESPANOL Y TIENE DIFICULTAD LEYENDO O HABLANDO INGLES, POR FAVOR LLAME A ESTE NUMERO TELEFONICO 800.697.6967.

You, the borrower(s), must be certain that you understand the transaction. Seek professional advice if you are uncertain.

Acknowledgment: I acknowledge that I have read and received a copy of this notice at the time of loan application. This notice does not constitute a contract or binding agreement. It is designed to provide current HUD/FHA policy regarding refunds.

Signature & Date:	Signature & Date:
X________________	X________________
Signature & Date:	Signature & Date:
X________________	X________________

Previous editions are obsolete — Page 2 of 2 — form **HUD-92900-B** (12/2004) ref. Handbooks 4150.1 & 4155.1

Sample HUD Notice for Homebuyers

Mortgage Exercise 7-1

Borrower Stu wants to get an FHA loan for a home priced at $253,500 and appraised for $257,000. The monthly PITI payment on this house would be $1,780. He has a 680 credit score, gross monthly income of $6,850, other monthly recurring debts of $850, and $75 monthly electric bill. Stu will finance the 1% UFMIP into the loan. Assume that the FHA maximum loan amount for the county is $271,050. *See the Appendix for answers to check your work.*

1. What is borrower Stu's debt-to-income ratio? Based on the information provided, do you think this loan can be made? Why or why not?

2. What is the required minimum investment Stu must make to buy this home? What is the total loan amount? (Round to the nearest dollar.)

3. Would Stu be allowed to obtain secondary financing on this home to make the down payment?

4. What would be the prepayment penalty if Stu pays off the loan early?

VA-Guaranteed Loans

VA-guaranteed loans are *guaranteed by the federal government through the Veterans Benefits Administration*, which is part of the **Department of Veterans Affairs**. The VA's main purpose in guaranteeing loans is to help meet the housing needs of eligible veterans who have served or are currently serving on active duty in the U.S. Armed Forces, which includes: Army, Navy, Air Force, Marine Corps, Coast Guard, Reserves, or National Guard. VA loans are available to eligible veterans for the purchase of owner-occupied single family homes and for multifamily dwellings up to four units if the veteran intends to occupy one of the units as the primary residence.

The VA rarely loans money directly to borrowers. It may do so in isolated rural areas where financing isn't readily available, but usually a veteran must borrow money from a VA-approved lender. Lenders may also apply to become **Automatic Endorsers**, which gives them the authority to close VA-guaranteed loans without the prior approval of VA (except for certain types of loans—such as loans secured by a junior lien—

that must be submitted to VA for prior approval by all lenders). VA Automatic Endorsers are responsible for supervising the entire mortgage process through closing, performing underwriting functions (credit examination, appraisal review, etc.) then submitting the loan to the VA after closing for guaranty.

The VA provides access to an online **Lender's Handbook**—as well as other valuable resources—from their website:

www.homeloans.va.gov

Eligibility

Although the lender will examine the borrower's credit history, amount of income, and other factors before approving the loan, the primary requirement to be approved for a VA loan is the borrower's military **eligibility**, which is based on a person's length of continuous active service and other factors, such as when they enlisted and whether they served during war time. Spouses of veterans who died on active duty from service-related causes or who were MIA or a POW may also be eligible for a VA loan.

A current list of eligibility requirements is available from this VA website:

www.homeloans.va.gov/elig2.htm

Documentation

Lenders may not process or close a VA loan without verifying the eligibility of the borrower with a **Certificate of Eligibility** (COE) issued by the VA. Either the lender or the borrower may apply for a COE online (www.homeloans.va.gov/eligibility.htm). They may also apply for a COE through the mail using VA Form 26-1880, Request for a Certificate of Eligibility.

In order to receive a COE, the veteran must first be able to document his or her service:

- **Discharged veterans who served in a regular component of the Armed Forces.** Certificate of Release or Discharge from Active Duty, or **DD-214**, issued by the Department of Defense to identify the character of service and reason for discharge (honorable, dishonorable, etc,)
- **Discharged members of the Army or Air National Guard never activated.** NGB Form 22 (Report of Separation and Record of Service) or NGB Form 23 (Retirement Points Accounting) and proof of character of service
- **Veterans on active duty or individuals who are still members of the Reserve/Guard.** A statement of service signed by, or by the direction of, the adjutant, personnel office, or commander of the unit or higher headquarters to which they are attached

Maximum Loan Limit

The VA doesn't limit the price a veteran can pay for a house (as long as the house will appraise for the loan amount), but the VA does limit the amount it will guarantee in case of default to **25%** of the purchase price or the established reasonable value, whichever is less. A veteran's maximum guaranty amount, known as **entitlement**, represents the portion of the loan that the VA guarantees in the event of default by the borrowing veteran. Therefore, veterans can generally purchase a home priced up to **four times** the amount of their entitlement with no down payment.

All eligible veterans receive **$36,000 of basic entitlement**. Since the VA requires a minimum 25% of guaranty to meet secondary market requirements, the maximum loan amount a veteran would be eligible for using just basic entitlement would be $144,000 ($36,000 x 4 = $144,000). To account for the rise in the cost of homes, however, the Veteran's Benefits Improvement Act of 2008 provided that every eligible veteran receive a **bonus entitlement** that equals **25%** of the annual loan limit for single family homes in the **county where the property is located**.

In 2010, the single family home loan maximum for most counties is $417,000. This limit is significantly higher in some counties; for example, the 2010 loan limit in Marin County, CA, which is just north of San Francisco, is $962,500. A list of VA annual loan limits by county may be accessed from this website:

www.homeloans.va.gov/loan_limits.htm

The veteran's current eligible entitlement will be documented in the **Certificate of Eligibility** (COE). If the veteran's entitlement is insufficient—or if the purchase price/appraised value of the home exceeds the current VA loan limit for that county—the veteran can make a cash down payment so that the combination of entitlement and down payment equals the required guaranty of 25%. (Equity can also contribute to the 25% guaranty requirement for refinance loans.)

Restoring Entitlement

It is possible for a veteran to use some of his or her entitlement on a previous purchase, and have partial entitlement available for another purchase. Some or all of a veteran's entitlement previously used in connection with a VA home loan may be restored and used again for another VA loan under either of these circumstances:

- The property which secured the VA-guaranteed loan has been sold *and* that loan has been paid in full.
- An eligible veteran has agreed to assume the outstanding balance on a VA loan and substitute his or her entitlement for the same amount originally used on the loan. The assuming veteran must also meet occupancy, income, and credit requirements.

Case in Point

Let's look at some examples to illustrate. Assume each veteran is buying a home in a county where the current conforming loan limit for a single family home is **$417,000**, making the maximum guaranty **$104,250** ($417,000 x .25).

Example 1: Veteran Bob has full entitlement available and is purchasing a home for $350,000.

$350,000	Purchase Price
x .25	
$87,500	Guaranty Required

Since Bob has his entire entitlement of $104,250 available, he can purchase this house without a down payment. Even though he still has $16,750 in available entitlement, however, the loan-to-value on this purchase cannot exceed 100%.

Example 2: Veteran Ann wants to buy a house for $320,000. She has already used $27,500 of her entitlement on a prior loan, which has not been restored.

$ 104,250	Maximum Entitlement
- 27,500	Used Entitlement
76,750	Available Entitlement
$ 320,000	Purchase Price
x .25	
80,000	Guaranty Required
- 76,750	Available Entitlement
$ 3,250	Down Payment

If Ann wants to buy this house, she must convince the seller to lower the price, restore some of her entitlement, or make a down payment of $3,250.

Class Activity: Entitlement

Veteran Dave wants to buy a house for $480,000. He has his full entitlement of $104,250 available.

To buy this house, how much of a cash down payment must Dave make?

Borrower Qualifying Standards

Once a veteran's eligibility is confirmed, underwriters making VA loans must qualify the borrower to ensure that he or she is a satisfactory credit risk and has the means to repay loan. This is accomplished by looking at both the borrower's debt-to-income ratio and the residual income. If legally married, a spouse's income may also be considered for qualification purposes. A non-married co-borrower, however, is *not* allowed on a VA-guaranteed loan unless he or she is also an eligible veteran who will occupy the home as a primary residence.

Total Debt-to-Income Ratio

One difference from conventional underwriting is that underwriters on VA loans do not generally consider the housing expense ratio, also called the front end ratio. Instead, underwriters start with the total debt-to-income ratio, or back end ratio, when evaluating a potential borrower. In general, they also have more latitude than with conventional loans, generally looking for a total DTI that does not exceed **41%.**

√ **Note:** Tax-free income may be "grossed up" for purposes of calculating the debt-to-income ratio only, using current income tax withholding tables to determine an appropriate adjustment. Tax-free income generally includes certain military allowances, child support payments, workers' compensation benefits, disability retirement payments, and certain types of public assistance payments.

Class Activity: VA Loan Qualifying

A veteran with a family of three who lives in the Midwest is applying for $114,000 loan and has the following income and debts:

Gross Monthly Income:

$1,950	Primary Employment
+ 640	Part-time Employment
$2,590	Total Income

Expenses:

$ 706.42	Expected Housing Expense (PITI)
209.00	Car Payment
122.65	Student Loan
+ 52.09	Revolving Credit Account
$1,090.16	Total Expenses

What is the total debt-to-income ratio?

Residual Income

In addition to the debt-to-income ratio, an underwriter must ensure that an eligible borrower has the appropriate balance of cash flow remaining for family support. This is determined by looking at **residual income**, which is *the amount of income remaining after subtracting taxes, housing expenses, and all recurring debts and obligations.* Residual income uses **net effective income** in its calculation, not gross income. This analysis also takes the **size of the veteran's family** into consideration when determining whether the residual income meets the VA's minimum requirements. These figures are determined **regionally**, based on loan amount. The values shown in Figure 7.1 are simply for illustration purposes. VA alerts mortgage loan originators when income values are adjusted.

	Loan amounts $79,999 and below			
Family Size *	**Northeast**	**Midwest**	**South**	**West**
1	$390	$382	$382	$425
2	654	641	641	713
3	788	772	772	859
4	888	868	868	967
5	921	902	902	1,004

* Add $75 for each additional member up to a family of seven.

	Loan amounts $80,000 and above			
Family Size *	**Northeast**	**Midwest**	**South**	**West**
1	$450	$441	$441	$491
2	755	738	738	823
3	909	889	889	990
4	1,025	1,003	1,003	1,117
5	1,062	1,039	1,039	1,158

* Add $80 for each additional member up to a family of seven.

Figure 7.1: Residual Incomes by Region.

Class Activity: Residual Income

Let's say, that based on VA guidelines, a veteran with a family of three who lives in the Midwest applying for a $114,000 loan should have residual income of at least $889 in order to qualify:

$2,590.00	Gross Monthly Income
- $ 432.70	Income Tax Withheld
$2,157.30	Effective Net Income
- $1,090.16	Total Expenses
$1,067.14	Balance for Family Support (Residual Income)

While this borrower meets the residual income standard, recall that his total DTI was 42%. One way for a VA loan underwriter to justify approving a loan when the total DTI ratio exceeds 41% is if a borrower's residual income is at least 20% above the minimum standard established by the VA.

Does this family meet the income qualifications required for approval?

Other Factors to Consider

In addition to residual income and total debt-to-income, other factors an underwriter considers when evaluating a VA loan application include:

- Borrower's demonstrated ability to accumulate cash or other liquid assets, such as stocks or bonds
- Borrower's demonstrated ability to use credit wisely and to avoid incurring an excessive amount of debt
- Relationship between the housing expense for the property being acquired and what the borrower is accustomed to paying
- Number and ages of the borrower's dependents

- Location and general economic level of the subject property's neighborhood
- Likelihood that the borrower's income will increase or decrease
- Borrower's employment history and work experience
- Borrower's demonstrated ability and willingness to make payments on time
- Amount of any down payment made
- Borrower's available cash after paying all closing costs and any other prepaid items related to the purchase of the property

Property Guidelines for VA Loans

An existing home which has either been previously owner-occupied or had all onsite and offsite improvements fully completed for one year or more is eligible for a VA loan. Newly completed properties (completed less than one year and never owner-occupied) are eligible if covered by a one-year VA builder's warranty, enrolled in a HUD-accepted ten-year insured protection plan, or have been built by a veteran, as the general contractor, for his/her own occupancy. Some manufactured homes may also be eligible.

VA's minimum property requirements (MPRs) provide general acceptability criteria for properties that will become the security for VA-guaranteed loans.

Establishing the Reasonable Value

As with any mortgage loan, the value of the collateral being used to secure the note is critical. An appraisal is required to help ensure that any property that will become the security for a VA-guaranteed loan has a value of at least as much as the loan amount and that it is in a condition acceptable to the VA.

Every appraisal made for VA purposes must be reviewed either by the lender's VA-authorized staff appraisal reviewer or a VA staff appraiser, who then issues a **Notice of Value** (NOV) or a **Certificate of Reasonable Value** (CRV). Every NOV or CRV issued in conjunction with an appraisal review must include a list of any conditions and requirements that must be satisfied for the property to be eligible for VA loan guaranty.

The **established reasonable value** (or the sales price, whichever is less) defines the maximum mortgage amount a veteran may have on a VA-guaranteed loan for that property. If the price of the property exceeds the established reasonable value, the veteran must contribute the difference in cash to buy that property. The loan amount cannot exceed the established reasonable value, except to finance the required funding fee.

Occupancy

The law requires a veteran obtaining a VA-guaranteed loan to certify that he or she intends to personally occupy the property as his or her home. As of the date of certification, the veteran must either:

- Personally live in the property as his or her home, or
- Intend, upon completion of the loan and acquisition of the dwelling, to personally move into the property and use it as his or her home within a reasonable time, which generally means **within 60 days** after the loan closing.

Single or married service members, while deployed from their permanent duty station, are considered to be in a temporary duty status and able to meet the occupancy requirement.

VA Loan Regulations

Many terms of a VA loan, such as the interest rate, may be negotiated between the veteran borrower and the lender. However, VA does impose certain requirements and restrictions on loans that it guarantees, some of which are covered here.

Variable Funding Fee

While there is no upfront or monthly mortgage insurance premiums required for VA loans, borrowers must pay a non-refundable one-time **variable funding fee** at closing for guaranteeing the loan. The variable funding fee is waived for disabled veterans and surviving spouses of veterans who died in service or from service-connected disabilities.

The funding fee may be financed or paid in cash. If financed, the funding fee percentage must be applied to the loan amount. The fee is based on the veteran's status, the number of times the veteran has used the program, and the amount of any down payment:

VA Variable Funding Fees *(% of loan amount on purchase, new construction)*			
	Down Payment	1st Use	Subsequent Use
Regular Military	No down payment *	2.15 %	3.30 %
	Up to 9.9% down	1.50 %	1.75 %
	More than 10% down	1.25 %	1.50 %
National Guard and Reservists	No down payment *	2.40 %	3.30 %
	Up to 9.9% down	1.75 %	1.75 %
	More than 10% down	1.50 %	1.50 %
Interest Rate Reduction Refinancing Loans		.50 %	

* Also apply to cash-out refinancing loans

Figure 7.2: VA Variable Funding Fees.

Closing Costs

The veteran can pay a maximum of reasonable and customary amounts for any or all of the itemized fees and charges designated by VA, for example:

- Initial appraisals (VA certificate of reasonable value)
- Inspections
- Credit report
- Recording fees
- Insurance
- Title examination

Whenever the charge relates to services performed by a third party, the amount paid by the borrower must be limited to the actual charge of that third party.

In addition to the itemized charges, the lender may charge a **flat fee not to exceed 1% of the loan amount** to cover the lender's costs and services for originating the loan. If the loan does not close for any reason, the lender must refund this 1% flat fee.

Veteran borrowers cannot be charged commissions, brokerage fees, or buyer broker fees. In addition, VA will not allow the veteran to pay certain other "closing" fees, for example:

- Interest rate lock-in fees
- Tax service fee
- Notary fee
- Escrow fee

The seller, lender, or any other party may pay these fees and charges, including discount points, on behalf of the borrower. VA regulations do not limit the payment of such fees and charges by other parties.

Seller Concessions

A **seller concession** is *anything of value added to the transaction* by the builder or seller for which the buyer pays nothing additional and which the seller is *not* customarily expected or required to pay or provide, for example:

- Payment of the VA funding fee

- Prepayment of property taxes and/or insurance
- Gifts of personal property
- Payment of extra points to provide permanent interest rate buydowns
- Provision of escrowed funds to provide temporary interest rate buydowns
- Payoff of credit balances or judgments on behalf of the buyer

Payment of the buyer's closing costs or points that are appropriate to the market are *not* considered seller concessions.

Any seller concession or combination of concessions which **exceeds 4% of the established reasonable value** of the property is considered excessive, and unacceptable for VA-guaranteed loans. The reason for this restriction is to prevent concessions from enticing unwary and unqualified veterans into home mortgages they cannot afford.

Secondary Financing

The VA permits secondary financing simultaneous with a VA-guaranteed first loan for a variety of purposes, for example, closing costs or a down payment (unless the down payment is required to cover an excess purchase price beyond the VA's established reasonable value). The following conditions must be met:

- The veteran cannot be placed in a substantially worse position than if the entire amount borrowed had been guaranteed by VA.
- The second loan must be subordinated to the VA-guaranteed loan.
- There can be no cash-back to the veteran.
- The veteran must qualify for the second mortgage, which is underwritten as an additional recurring monthly obligation.
- The interest rate on the second mortgage may not exceed the rate on industry standards for second mortgage.
- The second mortgage should not restrict the veteran's ability to sell the property any more than the VA first mortgage (assumable).

Loan Assumption

All VA loans committed or closed prior to March 1, 1988, are freely assumable, meaning that the veteran may sell the property and allow the loan to be assumed without the approval of VA or the loan holder. The veteran still remains liable for any loss associated with the VA loan should the borrower assuming the loan fail to meet the mortgage obligations, however.

For VA loans committed and closed on or after March 1, 1988, VA loan assumptions are *not* allowed unless the veteran first has the assumption **approved** by the Department of Veterans Affairs or its authorized agent (i.e., the loan holder). If an assumption is approved by VA or the loan holder, the veteran is released of liability in the event the assumer defaults on the loan resulting in a loss to VA.

Entitlement associated with an assumption may only be restored to the veteran if these conditions are met:

- The assumer is an eligible veteran.
- The assumption has been approved by the loan holder or VA.
- The assumer-veteran agrees to substitute his or her VA home loan entitlement for the original veteran and occupies the property as his or her principal residence.

Prepayment Penalties

The VA does not allow clauses for prepayment penalties to be included in VA loans. VA loans may be paid off early without additional charges or penalties of any kind. (But the VA may allow these clauses for secondary financing.)

VA Loan Programs

VA Loan Program	Description	Conditions
Purchase Loans	• 100% financing for one- to four-family dwellings • Loan terms negotiated with lender • Repayment plans generally include: • Fixed • Traditional ARM • Hybrid ARM • Graduated payment • Growing equity	• Requires certification that veteran intends to occupy as primary residence • Veteran must have sufficient available entitlement, down payment, and/or equity for 25% guaranty • Requires non-refundable funding fee • Limits lender fee to flat 1% of loan amount
Interest Rate Reduction Refinance Loan (IRRRL or VA Streamline)	• VA-to-VA loan (vet re-uses entitlement) • Available to an original veteran who still owns the home, a surviving spouse of a deceased veteran, an original veteran with a new spouse, or a new veteran who has substituted entitlement • Must be used to lower interest rate, shorten the term of loan, or to change an ARM loan to a fixed rate of an existing VA-guaranty loan	• Requires only certification of prior residency • May add up to $6,000 of energy efficiency improvements to loan • Loan may not exceed sum of outstanding balance of existing loan (no cash-out) except for allowable closing costs, fees, and up to 2 discount points
Cash-Out Refinancing	• A refinance loan where proceeds may be used to pay off other liens or taken as cash for any purpose acceptable to the lender • Can be used to convert a non-VA loan to a VA loan • Veteran must have sufficient available entitlement	• Requires certification that veteran intends to occupy as primary residence • Must be secured by a first lien on the property • Maximum loan amount is 100% of appraised value + any energy efficiency improvements + VA funding fee

OMB Control No. 2900-0523
Respondent Burden: 30 minutes

Department of Veterans Affairs	LOAN ANALYSIS	LOAN NUMBER

PRIVACY ACT INFORMATION: The VA will not disclose information collected on this form to any source other than what has been authorized under the Privacy Act of 1974 or Title 5, Code of Federal Regulations 1.526 for routine uses as (i.e., the record of an individual who is covered by this system may be disclosed to a member of Congress or staff person acting for the member when the request is made on behalf of the individual) identified in the VA system of records, 55VA26, Loan Guaranty Home, Condominium and Manufactured Home Loan Applicant Records, Specially Adapted Housing Applicant Records, and Vendee Loan Applicant Records - VA, published in the Federal Register. Your obligation to respond is required in order to determine the veteran's qualifications for the loan.

RESPONDENT BURDEN: This information is needed to help determine a veteran's qualifications for a VA guaranteed loan. Title 38, USC, section 3710 authorizes collection of this information. We estimate that you will need an average of 30 minutes to review the instructions, find the information, and complete this form. VA cannot conduct or sponsor a collection of information unless a valid OMB control number is displayed. You are not required to respond to a collection of information if this number is not displayed. Valid OMB control numbers can be located on the OMB Internet Page at: **www.whitehouse.gov/omb/library/OMBINV.VA.EPA.html#VA.** If desired, you can call 1-800-827-1000 to get information on where to send comments or suggestions about this form.

SECTION A - LOAN DATA

1. NAME OF BORROWER	2. AMOUNT OF LOAN	3. CASH DOWN PAYMENT ON PURCHASE PRICE
	$	$

SECTION B - BORROWER'S PERSONAL AND FINANCIAL STATUS

4. APPLICANT'S AGE	5. OCCUPATION OF APPLICANT	6. NUMBER OF YEARS AT PRESENT EMPLOYMENT	7. LIQUID ASSETS *(Cash, savings, bonds, etc.)* $	8. CURRENT MONTHLY HOUSING EXPENSE $
9. UTILITIES INCLUDED ☐ YES ☐ NO	10. SPOUSE'S AGE	11. OCCUPATION OF SPOUSE	12. NUMBER OF YEARS AT PRESENT EMPLOYMENT	13. AGE OF DEPENDENTS

NOTE: ROUND ALL DOLLAR AMOUNTS BELOW TO NEAREST WHOLE DOLLAR

SECTION C- ESTIMATED MONTHLY SHELTER EXPENSES *(This Property)*

SECTION D - DEBTS AND OBLIGATIONS *(Itemize and indicate by (✓) which debts considered in Section E, Line 40) (If additional space is needed please use reverse or attach a separate sheet)*

	ITEMS	AMOUNT		ITEMS	(✓)	MO. PAYMENT	UNPAID BAL.
14.	TERM OF LOAN: YRS.		22.			$	$
15.	MORTGAGE PAYMENT (Principal and Interest) @ ________ %	$	23.				
			24.				
16.	REALTY TAXES		25.				
17.	HAZARD INSURANCE		26.				
18.	SPECIAL ASSESSMENTS		27.				
19.	MAINTENANCE & UTILITIES		28.				
20.	OTHER *(HOA, Condo fees, etc.)*		29.	JOB RELATED EXPENSE *(e.g., child care)*			
21.	TOTAL	$	30.	TOTAL		$	$

SECTION E - MONTHLY INCOME AND DEDUCTIONS

	ITEMS		SPOUSE	BORROWER	TOTAL
31.	GROSS SALARY OR EARNINGS FROM EMPLOYMENT				$
32.	DEDUCTIONS	FEDERAL INCOME TAX	$	$	
33.		STATE INCOME TAX			
34.		RETIREMENT OR SOCIAL SECURITY			
35.		OTHER *(Specify)*			
36.		TOTAL DEDUCTIONS	$	$	$
37.	NET TAKE-HOME PAY				
38.	PENSION, COMPENSATION OR OTHER NET INCOME *(Specify)*				
39.	TOTAL *(Sum of lines 37 and 38)*		$	$	$
40.	LESS THOSE OBLIGATIONS LISTED IN SECTION D WHICH SHOULD BE DEDUCTED FROM INCOME				
41.	TOTAL NET EFFECTIVE INCOME				$
42.	LESS ESTIMATED MONTHLY SHELTER EXPENSE *(Line 21)*				
43.	BALANCE AVAILABLE FOR FAMILY SUPPORT			GUIDELINE $	$
44.	RATIO *(Sum of Items 15, 16, 17, 18, 20 and 40 ÷ sum of Items 31 and 38)*				%

45. PAST CREDIT RECORD ☐ SATISFACTORY ☐ UNSATISFACTORY	46. DOES LOAN MEET VA CREDIT STANDARDS? *(Give reasons for decision under "Remarks," if necessary, e.g., borderline case)* ☐ YES ☐ NO

47. REMARKS *(Use reverse or attach a separate sheet, if necessary)*

CRV DATA (VA USE)

48A. VALUE	48B. EXPIRATION DATE	48C. ECONOMIC LIFE YRS.

SECTION F - DISPOSITION OF APPLICATION AND UNDERWRITER CERTIFICATION

☐ Recommend that the application be approved since it meets all requirements of Chapter 37, Title 38, U.S. Code and applicable VA Regulations and directives.

☐ Recommend that the application be disapproved for the reasons stated under "Remarks" above.

The undersigned underwriter certifies that he/she personally reviewed and approved this loan. *(Loan was closed on the automatic basis.)*

49. DATE	50. SIGNATURE OF EXAMINER/UNDERWRITER	
51. FINAL ACTION ☐ APPROVE APPLICATION ☐ REJECT APPLICATION	52. DATE	53. SIGNATURE AND TITLE OF APPROVING OFFICIAL

VA FORM SEP 2006 **26-6393** EXISTING STOCKS OF VA FORM 26-6393, OCT 2005, WILL BE USED.

Sample VA 26-6393 Summary

Mortgage Exercise 7-2

Borrower Nan wants a VA loan to buy her first home. The home is priced at $114,900, and the estimate of reasonable value is $115,000. Nan has stable income, few debts, excellent credit history, but little cash on hand for a down payment. Nan has her COE and her DD-214 showing that she was honorably discharged from regular service in the U.S. Navy. *See the Appendix for answers to check your work.*

1. Do you think this loan can be made? Why or why not? If so, how much would the borrower have to pay at closing as a down payment?

2. What's the maximum flat fee the lender can charge on this loan? How much is the variable funding fee? Can either of these be financed into the loan? If so, what is the total loan amount? (Round to the nearest dollar.)

3. How much of her entitlement did Nan use on this loan?

4. Three years later, Nan wants to move to a bigger home. Can someone assume her mortgage? If so, under what circumstances will Nan be able to restore her entitlement?

Comparison of FHA and VA Qualifying Standards

FHA and VA qualifying standards tend to be more liberal than those for conventional loans. A borrower considered marginal by Fannie Mae and Freddie Mac may qualify more easily for an FHA or VA loan.

	FHA	VA
Borrower: Eligibility	Any qualified borrower	Eligible veteran only (COE and DD-214 or equivalent)
Property: Units Owner-Occupant Only	1-4 Yes (move in within 60 days)	1-4 Yes (move in within 60 days)
Maximum Loan (Neither can exceed appraisal)	Can't exceed maximum for geographic location	No limits
Borrower Qualifying Standards	Housing Expense Ratio: 31% Total Debt-to-Income: 43%	Residual income guidelines Total Debt-to-Income: 41%
Lender Protection	Insured to full extent of losses from default	Maximum guaranty amount = 25% loan limit/county
Maximum Interest Rate	Negotiated between borrower and lender	Negotiated between borrower and lender
Minimum Required Investment/Down Payment?	3.5% if credit score 580 or above 10% if between 500-579	None unless loan amount is greater than 4 times entitlement on COE
Fee/Insurance Premium Required	UFMIP 1%; monthly MIP up to 1.15% of annual average loan balance (as of 4/18/11)	Variable funding fee 1.25% to 3.30% (unless disabled); no insurance premium required
Fee Financed?	Yes (UFMIP only, not monthly)	Yes
Closing Costs Financed?	No	No
Seller Contribution Limit?	Yes, 6 points (proposed reduction to 3 points)	Discount points: No limit (if reasonable) Seller concessions: 4 points
Secondary Financing?	Yes, except minimum down payment	Yes
Assumable Loan?	Not without FHA creditworthiness check	Not without VA/lender approval
Prepayment Penalty?	No	No

Figure 7.3: Comparison of FHA and VA Loans.

USDA Rural Development Programs

In 1994, the U.S. Department of Agriculture (USDA) was reorganized under the Federal Crop Insurance Reform and Department of Agriculture Reorganization Act. Under that Act, **USDA Rural Development** was created to administer the former Farmers Home Administration's (FmHA) non-farm financial programs for rural housing, community facilities, water and waste disposal, and rural businesses.

The opportunities available through the Rural Development **Housing and Community Facilities Programs** (HCFP) are extensive. For example, the USDA makes grants and loans to rural communities for essential facilities and services such as health clinics, schools, and fire and rescue stations. On the housing front, Rural Development has programs to assist with single family and multifamily housing, site preparation, rental assistance, water and waste, and repair and rehabilitation.

Although one mission of Rural Development is to provide financial support to low-income homebuyers in rural communities, the definition of "rural" may be broader than one might think. It can include small towns up to 20,000 people, even those in areas that may be in close proximity to larger metropolitan areas. In addition, the USDA could determine that particular areas are temporarily eligible for their programs in response to certain conditions or natural disasters such as a flood or hurricane. For this reason, a loan officer needs to verify whether the property is located in designated areas for specific programs.

Section 502 Loans

In the remainder of this chapter, we'll look at **Section 502 loans** for single family homes. The Section 502 loan program either **guarantees loans** made by approved private lenders or **makes direct loans** if no local lender is available. Section 502 loans can be used to:

- Purchase an existing home.
- Construct a new home.
- Renovate or repair an existing home.
- Relocate an existing home.
- Purchase and prepare a site for a home, including sewage and water facilities.

Under the Section 502 programs, eligible houses must be modest in size, design, and cost—defined as having a market value that does not exceed the applicable area loan limit and does not contain certain prohibited features.

Applicants for Section 502 loans—guaranteed and direct—must meet certain income requirements based on the **area median income** (AMI). Assuming that the applicant meets the income eligibility and the house is in an approved area, the borrower may receive **100% financing**, based on the appraised value or acquisition cost, whichever is less. Unlike FHA loans, these USDA loans do **not** require mortgage insurance of any kind, even with loans above 80% LTV. The terms of the loan will be different depending on whether it is a guaranteed loan or a direct loan.

To check property eligibility and income limits for Section 502 Direct and Guaranteed loans, visit the USDA website:

http://eligibility.sc.egov.usda.gov/eligibility/

Guaranteed Rural Housing (GRH) Loans

The USDA guarantees loans made by approved lenders through the Section 502 Guaranteed Rural Housing Loan program. Approved lenders may be state housing agencies, any Farm Credit System institution with direct lending authority, or lenders approved by the VA, FHA, Fannie Mae, Freddie Mac, or Ginnie Mae. With these loans, the promissory note rate is set *by the lender.*

Lenders may require borrowers to pay an upfront guarantee fee of 2% when they take out the loan, but borrowers may be able to finance that fee under certain circumstances, allowing them up to **102% LTV**. Even with the guarantee fee, a USDA loan is still less expensive than an FHA loan with a mortgage insurance premium, making it extremely attractive to qualified borrowers in designated rural areas. Loan terms are fixed rate up to **30 years**.

Applicants for Section 502 guaranteed loans may have an income of up to **115%** of the area median income (AMI).

Homeownership Direct Loans

Mortgages obtained through the Direct Loan program are funded by the USDA. Promissory note rates for these direct loans are set by the Housing and Community Facilities Program based on the government's cost of money. The interest rate that the borrower actually pays may be modified by a payment assistance subsidy that could reduce the interest paid on the mortgage to as little as 1%.

Loan terms are up to **33 years** or up to **38 years** for those with incomes below 60% of AMI who cannot afford 33-year terms (limited to 30 years for manufactured housing).

Applicants for Section 502 direct loans must have **very low** or **low** incomes. Very low income is defined as **below 50%** of the area median income (AMI); low income is **between 50% and 80%** of AMI. With direct loans, payment subsidy is available to applicants to enhance repayment ability.

Chapter 7 Summary

1. For the purposes of this chapter, government agency financing refers to real estate loans that have been traditionally insured or guaranteed by government programs. This occurs at the federal level and should not be confused with government sponsored enterprises active in secondary markets. Government agency programs include FHA-insured, VA-guaranteed, and USDA Rural Development guaranteed and direct loans.

2. **FHA-insured** loans are for owner-occupied single family and multifamily dwellings of 4 or fewer units, made by approved lenders. FHA loans require lower down payments and less stringent qualifying standards than conventional loans. Direct Endorsers can underwrite FHA loans. The FHA sets a maximum mortgage amount, depending on the geographic area. HUD issues regulations for FHA loans, including: 1. Required minimum investment of **3.5%** of lesser of purchase price or appraised value with 580 credit score; 10% with 500-579 credit score; 2. UFMIP required (**1%** for most purchase and refinance; monthly MIP on annual average loan balance up to 1.15%; may be cancelled when original value reaches 78% LTV; 3. Assumable only with lender approval for loans on or after December 15, 1989; 4. Prepayment penalty not allowed, but lender can require pay off be made on due date or collect an extra month's interest; 5. Items paid by seller are negotiable, but seller contribution limited to 6 points (proposed reduction to 3 points). MLOs can stay current on FHA loan programs via Mortgagee Letters.

3. **VA-guaranteed** loans help eligible veterans buy homes often with no down payment. Veteran must occupy the home. VA doesn't limit home price, but limits guaranty amount that the lender can recover for default to 25% of maximum loan limit in county where property is located. VA loan rules include: 1. Borrower needs **DD-214** (discharge papers) and **COE** (Certificate of Eligibility); 2. VA issues **Notice of Value** (NOV) or **Certificate of Reasonable Value** (CRV) based on appraisal; if price exceeds estimate of reasonable value, veteran must make up difference with down payment/equity; 3. Secondary financing may be permitted; 4. Required variable **funding fee**—paid in cash or financed (waived for disabled veterans); Lender flat fee limited to 1% of loan amount. 5. No limit on seller contribution to closing costs; 4% limit on seller concessions; 6. Assumable by eligible veterans only with VA approval (for loans after March, 1, 1988); 7. Prepayment penalty not allowed; 8. Veteran may restore entitlement if loan is paid off, home is sold and mortgage assumed by eligible veteran.

4. **Rural Development** is an agency under the U.S. Department of Agriculture (USDA) that offers various assistance programs for both businesses and homebuyers in rural communities, which can include small towns and areas hit by natural disasters. The Rural Development's Housing and Community Facilities Programs **Section 502** loans for single family homes either **guarantees** loans made by private lenders or makes **direct loans** if no local lender is available. Eligible borrowers can get **100% financing** without any mortgage insurance. Applicants for Section 502 Guaranteed Loans may have an income of up to **115%** of the area median income (AMI). Applicants for Section 502 Direct Loans must have **very low** (below 50% AMI) or **low** (between 50% and 80% of AMI) incomes.

Chapter 7 Quiz

1. ***A borrower with a FICO score of 700 applies for an FHA loan on a house with an appraised value of $100,000 and a purchase price of $96,000. What is the required minimum investment?***
   A. $3,000
   B. $3,360
   C. $3,500
   D. $4,800

2. ***An upfront mortgage insurance premium is required***
   A. on all FHA loans.
   B. only when the buyer cannot pay the required down payment in cash.
   C. only when the LTV exceeds 80%.
   D. on y when the LTV exceeds 90%.

3. ***Which statement about FHA-insured loans is FALSE?***
   A. FHA loans are intended for low-income first-time homebuyers.
   B. FHA loans have less stringent qualifying standards.
   C. FHA loans require low down payments.
   D. FHA offers an adjustable rate mortgage.

4. ***To qualify for an FHA loan, a borrower should have a maximum housing expense ratio of _____and a total debt-to-income ratio of_____***
   A. 28%; 36%.
   B. 29%; 36%.
   C. 29%; 41%.
   D. 31%; 43%.

5. ***FHA-insured loans are funded by***
   A. approved lenders.
   B. the Department of Housing and Urban Development.
   C. the Federal Deposit Insurance Corporation.
   D. the Federal Housing Administration.

6. ***The VA provides guaranty on eligible home loans for up to ______ of the loan amount.***
   A. 10%
   B. 25%
   C. 50%
   D. 100%

7. ***A veteran's entitlement for a VA loans is specified in what document?***
   A. COE
   B. CRV
   C. DD-214
   D. NOV

8. ***What is the maximum flat fee that a lender may charge on a VA loan?***
   A. 3.5%
   B. 2%
   C. 1%
   D. There is no limit; the fee is negotiable.

9. ***Full VA entitlement can generally be restored to a veteran***
   A. if any disabled veteran assumes the loan.
   B. if an eligible veteran substitutes his entitlement for the seller's.
   C. when the loan is paid down to below 50% LTV.
   D. under no circumstances.

10. ***The VA may use what document to determine the maximum loan amount on the property being used as collateral?***
    A. county tax assessment roll
    B. DD-214
    C. notice of value
    D. sales contract

11. ***Section 502 home loans are administered by which federal agency?***
    A. Department of Housing and Urban Development
    B. Federal Housing Administration
    C. Federal Housing Finance Agency
    D. U.S. Department of Agriculture

12. ***A buyer wishes to purchase a home in a designated rural community where the area median income is $50,000. What is the maximum LTV allowed for a Rural Development Section 502 guaranteed loan?***
    A. 80%
    B. 90%
    C. 95%
    D. 100%

8

Chapter 8

Nontraditional Mortgage Products

In This Chapter

Even with all of the mortgage products that lenders offer, some borrowers may still require assistance in order to purchase a home. Fortunately, a variety of nontraditional mortgage products offering different financing options have been developed to meet the needs of these borrowers. A **nontraditional mortgage**, as defined by the **SAFE Act**, is *anything other than a 30-year fixed rate mortgage.* The **Interagency Guidance on Nontraditional Mortgage Product Risks**, on the other hand, defines nontraditional mortgage products as ***mortgage products that allow borrowers to defer principal and, sometimes, interest.***

When used properly, these products can help borrowers achieve their goals of qualifying for a loan, getting a lower interest rate, having a lower monthly payment, or buying a bigger house. In this chapter, we'll look closely at two financing tools: Buydowns (or discounts) and adjustable rate mortgages (ARMs). Other financing products include subprime loans, structured mortgages, homebuyer assistance programs, and seller financing, including land contracts.

At the end of this chapter, you will be able to:

- Describe the advantages and disadvantages of buydown plans.
- Identify the elements that make up an adjustable rate mortgage.
- Identify characteristics of a reverse mortgage.
- Identify factors that define a subprime loan.
- Discuss agency guidelines on lending and subprime loans.
- Contrast various types of alternative financing.

Key Terms

Adjustable Rate Mortgage (ARM)
Buydown
Caps
Equity Exchange
Estoppel
Index
Land Contract
Lease/Option
Lease/Purchase
Margin
Option
Participation Plan
Points
Rate Adjustment Period
Reverse Mortgage
Subprime Loan
Teaser Rate

The Use of Nontraditional Mortgage Products

Just as there are many different borrower's' goals, there are also many financing tools to help them achieve those goals. With the wide variety of nontraditional mortgage products available in today's real estate market, it's important to understand how they work so you can help customers reach their goals. For example, if the goal is to lower the monthly payment, the borrower can prepay some of the interest at closing as **discount points** to the lender, which buys down the interest rate and, therefore, lowers the required monthly payment.

Another option for a borrower to decrease the initial interest rate on a loan (thereby decreasing monthly payments) is by agreeing to **assume part of the lender's interest rate risk** with an **adjustable rate mortgage**, or ARM. Since the lender is not locked into a fixed interest rate for the loan term, the lender can offer the borrower a lower interest rate as a start rate.

Other times, loans may be structured differently to achieve a borrower's specific goals, for example:

- **Growth Equity Mortgage (GEM).** A **growth equity mortgage** or growing equity mortgage (GEM) is a *fixed rate mortgage set up like a 30-year conventional loan, but payments increase regularly.* With this type of loan, the total monthly payments increase over time with predictable and scheduled escalation. This type of loan allows a borrower to have lower monthly payments early in the loan and is recommended for a borrower whose income is expected to increase simultaneously with the increase in the payment amount. The fixed interest rate allows 100% of the scheduled payment increases to reduce the principal balance.
- **Reduction Option Mortgage.** A **reduction option mortgage** is a *fixed rate loan that gives a borrower a limited opportunity to reduce the interest rate without paying refinancing costs.* For example, the borrower may get a 30-year, fixed rate loan and pay a fee for the option of reducing the interest rate once during the early years of the loan if market interest rates decline a certain percentage. This allows the borrower to take advantage of a drop in interest rates while avoiding certain refinancing costs, such as for an appraisal.
- **Shared Appreciation Mortgage (SAM).** A **shared appreciation mortgage** (SAM) is one for which *the lender charges below-market interest in exchange for a share of the gains the borrower realizes when the property is eventually sold.* This can help a lender or borrower achieve various goals, including shared risks/rewards on commercial projects.

At the other end of the spectrum is a borrower with less-than-perfect credit or some other risk factor that prevents him from qualifying for a conventional loan. The borrower wants to purchase a home and accepts the lender's offer of an interest rate above that for typical conventional mortgages to achieve this goal. This type of financing is referred to as a **subprime loan**. Subprime loans are rarely available in today's market.

Buydown Plans

Recall from an earlier chapter that a **point** is simply *one percent of the loan amount.* Points may be charged for a variety of reasons, such as to cover the costs of processing or servicing a loan. **Discount points** are *additional funds paid to a lender at the beginning of a loan to lower the note interest rate and, therefore, the monthly payments.* Such a **buydown** could make it easier for a borrower to qualify for the loan.

A buydown can be paid for by the borrower, the seller, an interested third party such as a builder/developer, or even another party such as an employer to help facilitate the move of an employee being transferred. Typically, a borrower pays for a buydown by simply prepaying some interest at closing. Therefore, a buydown in the form of discount points appears on a Good Faith Estimate as a **charge** to the borrower.

Advantages to a buydown plan include:

- The borrower's monthly payment is lower.
- The lender *may* evaluate the borrower for loan qualification on the basis of the reduced payment after the buydown.

While a permanent buydown plan may allow a borrower to lower monthly payments, borrowers must weigh their monthly savings over the life of the loan against what they're paying in upfront points at closing to buy down the interest rate. To determine how many months it would take to recoup those upfront points, divide the payment difference between the two interest rates into the cost of the discount points.

Case in Point

Let's first see how a buydown can help the borrower afford the home. Suppose that a borrower financing $180,000 was quoted an interest rate of 6.5% for a 30-year conventional loan. The payments on that loan would be $1,137.72 per month. At 6.25% for the same $180,000 30-year loan, the payments would be $1,108.29. So by paying discount points up front to buy down the interest rate 1/4%, the borrower pays $29.43 per month less. This may help the borrower qualify for the home loan and make the mortgage payments more attractive.

However, when you consider that a discount point is typically quoted as 1 point per 1/8 rate reduction, the borrower would have likely paid an additional $3,600 at closing to get this interest rate (2 points at $1,800 per point). That means the borrower must stay in the mortgage for at least 123 months ($3,600 / $29.43 = 122.3) to realize the advantages of the buydown. If the borrower refinances or sells the house in the first 10 years of that loan, therefore, he will not recapture what he paid for the upfront discount points.

Another option is for the seller or other interested third party to pay discount points to buy down the interest rate for the borrower. While this means less money in the seller's pocket, it may be necessary to make the deal. The lender determines what the buydown amount is and subtracts that amount from the loan proceeds paid to the seller for the property, reflected on the HUD-1 settlement statement as a charge to the seller. The borrower, however, still signs a note for the full amount but will receive a lower interest rate over the life of the mortgage. The seller just agrees to receive less.

Permanent Buydown

Buydowns can be paid to reduce the borrower's payments early in the loan (temporary buydown) or throughout the life of the loan (permanent buydown).

A **permanent buydown** is when points are paid to a lender to reduce the interest rate and loan payments *for the entire life of the loan.* When a buyer's interest rate is reduced for the life of the loan, the lender will write that lower interest rate into the promissory note. Thus, the nominal rate (or coupon rate) stated in the note will be the actual reduced interest rate.

Temporary Buydown

Here's one way to think of a **temporary buydown**: Whoever pays for the buydown—often the seller or developer, sometimes the borrower—is depositing funds at closing with the lender that will be used to supplement the borrower's reduced monthly out-of-pocket payment. The supplemental funds allow the lender to receive the full payment during the months of the temporary buydown when the borrower's monthly payments are less than what is called for in the note. Once the "deposited" funds run out, in other words, the specified temporary buydown period ends, the borrower must make the full required monthly payment out-of-pocket.

Although the starting interest rate paid by the borrower early in the loan may be discounted, when qualifying a borrower who is using a temporary buydown, underwriters will consider the payments using the **fully indexed rate**, *not* the starting note rate.

Temporary buydown plans can take two forms:

- Level payment
- Graduated payment

Level Payment

A **level payment buydown** is a plan with the *payment reduction remaining constant throughout the buydown period.* For example, the lender makes a 30-year loan for $165,000 at 9% interest rate. The seller agrees to buy down the buyer's interest rate to 7% for three years. The borrower's monthly out-of-pocket payment is less for those three years, but due to the seller's subsidy, the lender still receives 9% interest as specified in the note during the buydown period (and thereafter).

LEVEL PAYMENT EXAMPLE							
Year	Note Interest Rate	Buydown %	Effective Interest Rate	Monthly Payment at 9%	Actual Monthly Payment	Monthly Subsidy	Annual Subsidy
1	9%	2%	7%	$1,328	$1.098	$230	$2,760
2	9%	2%	7%	$1,328	$1.098	$230	$2,760
3	9%	2%	7%	$1,328	$1.098	$230	$2,760
4	9%	-0-	9%	$1,328	$1.328	-0-	-0-
					TOTAL BUYDOWN: $8,280		

FIGURE 8.1: Level Payment Example.

Graduated Payment

A **graduated payment buydown** is a plan for which *payment subsidies in the early years keep payments low, but payments increase each year as indicated in the note.* Usually there's a definite structure to the loan such that the subsidy may last for only two or three years. Two common types of graduated payment buydown plans are often referred to as 2-1 buydowns and 3-2-1 buydowns.

- **2-1 buydown** is a graduated payment buydown with the payments subsidized for only two years—for example 2.5% below the interest rate in the first year and 1.5% the second year.
- **3-2-1 buydown** is a graduated payment buydown with the payments subsidized for three years—for example, 2.5% below the interest rate the first year, 2% the second year, and 1.5% the third year.

The subsidies for graduated payment buydowns may be a borrower's upfront escrow deposit of extra cash that earns interest, or the subsidy may be from a seller or builder trying to help a buyer with lower payments early in the loan.

For example, the lender makes a 30-year loan for $170,000 at 8.75% interest rate. The builder agrees to do a 3-2-1 buydown of the buyer's interest rate. The lender is still earning 8.75% interest, but the borrower is able to take advantage of the subsidy and pay less out-of-pocket each month for the first three years of the loan.

GRADUATED PAYMENT EXAMPLE							
Year	Note Interest Rate	Buydown %	Effective Interest Rate	Monthly Payment at 8.75%	Actual Monthly Payment	Monthly Subsidy	Annual Subsidy
1	8.75%	3%	5.75%	$1,337	$ 992	$345	$4,140
2	8.75%	2%	6.75%	$1,337	$1,103	$234	$2,808
3	8.75%	1%	7.75%	$1,337	$1,218	$119	$1,428
4	8.75%	-0-	8.75%	$1,337	$1,337	-0-	-0-
					TOTAL BUYDOWN: $8,376		

FIGURE 8.2: Graduated Payment Example.

Real Success

The best way to be completely accurate when determining buydown rates is to prepare a lender's quote. There are many variables lenders consider when determining the relationship between discount points and the interest rate. However, as a rough guide, 3-2-1 buydowns generally cost about 5 points, and 2-1 buydowns generally cost about 2.5 points.

Remember that even though the buyer has smaller payments at the beginning, payments increase later in the loan. Careful consideration is needed to determine whether this may pose a problem. Also remember with 3-2-1 buydowns, the lender may only let the borrower qualify at an interest rate up to 2% below the current market rate, not at the full 3% buydown.

Limits on Interested Party Contributions and Other Considerations

Fannie Mae, Freddie Mac, and the FHA limit points and other **interested party contributions** (IPCs) that can be paid. An interested party may be anyone other than the buyer who has a financial interest in, or can influence the terms and the sale or transfer of, the subject property. Limits are placed on these items so buyers aren't induced into a property they can't afford to keep later.

Fannie Mae/Freddie Mac

Fannie Mae and Freddie Mac guidelines impose limits on discounts, buydowns, and other forms of interested party contributions to help buyers get into homes. These other contributions include finance costs, such as prepaid interest, and escrows for property taxes, hazard insurance, and mortgage insurance. Contributions by sellers or other interested parties are limited to a percentage of the sale price of a property or its appraised value, *whichever is less.* If the contributions *exceed* Fannie Mae and Freddie Mac guidelines, the contribution amount must be *deducted* from the value or sale price of the property before determining the maximum loan amount. These maximum contributions are based on the type of property and the loan-to-value:

Property Type	LTV/CLTV Ratio	Maximum Contribution
Investment Property	All CLTV ratios	2%
Principal Residence or Second Home	Greater than 90%	3%
	75.01% - 90%	6%
	75% or less	9%

This example reflects FNMA/FHLMC guidelines. Other investors may impose other standards.

√ **Note:** Contributions made by employers or immediate family members usually are ***not*** subject to these limits.

FHA and VA

FHA guidelines also impose limits on discounts points, buydowns, and other forms of seller/interested party contributions to help buyers purchase homes.

FHA does *not* permit underwriting at a temporary buydown rate on fixed rate mortgages. While builders and sellers may offer temporary buydowns, unless the buydown is permanent, the borrower must qualify at the **note rate**. Furthermore, the buydown must not result in a reduction of more than two percentage points below the interest rate on the note.

FHA allows maximum IPCs of 6% (FHA has proposed a reduction to **3%**). If the contribution is more than the allowable limit, FHA, like Fannie Mae and Freddie Mac, deducts the excess from the maximum loan amount. For this rule, remember that seller-paid contributions include any items normally paid by the buyer. Family and employer contributions are excluded here also.

The VA has no set limits.

Mortgage Exercise 8-1

A borrower wants to buy a $150,000 home, and is going to make a $15,000 down payment. The borrower is seeking a conventional loan, but doesn't want to pay more than 6 1/2% interest. The lender agrees to 6 1/2% interest if the loan has three discount points and the loan origination fee is 2%. *See the Appendix for answers to check your work.*

1. What's the total amount of points (in dollars and percentage) that the lender will receive for making this loan?

150,000 − 15,000 = 135,000 x 5 % = 6,750

2. If the seller agrees to pay the discount points, how much will the seller net from the transaction? (Assume the seller pays no other costs.)

150,000 − 4,050 = $145,950

3. What will the borrower's note state as the interest rate on the loan? What dollar amount will the note say was borrowed?

4. Can the lender sell this loan to Fannie Mae or Freddie Mac on the secondary market? Why or why not?

Yes the lender because it is less then the

Adjustable Rate Mortgages (ARMs)

An **adjustable rate mortgage** (ARM) frees lenders from being locked into a fixed interest rate for the entire life a loan, as interest rates may adjust, according to the terms in the note, to reflect the current cost of money. ARMs are popular alternative financing tools as they may help borrowers qualify more easily for a home loan or for a more expensive home. Many lenders like ARMs because they can pass the risk of fluctuating interest rates on to borrowers.

Because ARMs shift the risk of interest rate fluctuations to the borrower, lenders normally charge a lower start rate for an ARM than for a fixed rate loan. Although the majority of borrowers prefer the security of a fixed rate (provided the rate is not too high), ARMs have maintained a place in the market despite comparatively low mortgage rates. Of course, as interest rates rise, so does ARM popularity.

Terms, rate changes, and many other aspects of ARMs are regulated by several agencies, depending on the type of lender. Any applicable guidelines or requirements of Fannie Mae, Freddie Mac, the FHA, and/or private mortgage insurers must be followed as well.

How ARMs Work

There are several elements to an adjustable rate mortgage:

- Index
- Margin
- Rate adjustment period
- Mortgage payment adjustment period
- Interest rate cap/floor (if any)
- Mortgage payment cap (if any)
- Negative amortization cap (if any)
- Conversion option (if any)

The borrower's interest rate is determined initially by the cost of money when the loan is made. Once the initial interest rate for the loan is set, the rate of the loan is tied to a widely recognized and published index.

Index

When discussing ARMs, the **index** is *a statistic that a consumer can easily examine, such as a published report, that is a generally reliable indicator of the approximate cost of money.* Thus, future interest rate adjustments for ARM loans are based on the up and down movements of the index.

At the time a loan is made, the index preferred by the borrower is selected. Because of market forces, the index fluctuates during the term of the loan, causing the borrower's actual interest rate to increase and decrease. That is why the index is referred to as the variable part of an ARM. The following are among commonly used indexes for adjustable rate mortgage loans:

- **Average One-Year Treasury Constant Maturity Index (TCM).** Average of the 12 most recently published monthly yields on United States Treasury securities, adjusted to a constant maturity of one year; issued monthly.
- **Cost of Funds Index (COFI).** Monthly weighted average cost of funds for savings institutions that are members of the Federal Home Loan Bank System, most often the Eleventh District (the "Bank"). COFI consists of the monthly weighted average cost of savings, borrowings, and bank advances. COFI is becoming more widely used since Fannie Mae uses this when purchasing ARMs.
- **London InterBank Offered Rate (LIBOR).** A reference rate that is computed and published daily, indicating the average rate at which a lending institution can obtain unsecured funding for a given currency. It is also referred to as the British Banker's Association London InterBank Offered Rate (BBALIBOR).
- **Lender's Prime Rate.** At one time, the lender's prime rate was a common index, although now used infrequently and only for commercial and investment property loans.

All of these indexes move in step with other short-term interest rate debt instruments. From the borrower's perspective, it's not as important which index is chosen as long as it is one the lender can't manipulate. The index should be one that is determined and affected by market conditions, and regularly listed in a major publication, such as The Wall Street Journal. Once selected, the index written into the note cannot change, unless for some reason it is no longer available, at which point, a similar type index may be substituted.

Margin

A margin, which is also sometimes referred to as a spread, is the difference between the index value and the interest rate charged on an ARM. The lender adds a margin to the index to ensure sufficient income for administrative expenses and profit. The selected margin remains fixed or constant for the duration of the loan, and is not impacted by the movement of interest rates or other factors in the financial markets.

The index plus the margin equals the adjustable interest rate or fully indexed rate the borrower pays on the loan. For example:

4.25% Current Index Value

\+ 2.00% Margin

6.25% Fully Indexed Rate

From the borrower's perspective, this is where comparisons can make a difference. Different lenders have different requirements for the amount of margin charged. While margins for ARMs are usually 2% to 3%, they can vary greatly from one lender to the next, and may even be very different from the same lender, depending on the loan program or the credit risk of the borrower.

In this hypothetical example, a borrower chose Treasury Securities as the index. The loan interest rate runs roughly parallel to the Treasury Securities index, but always a few percentage points above it. This is the margin the lender added to the index.

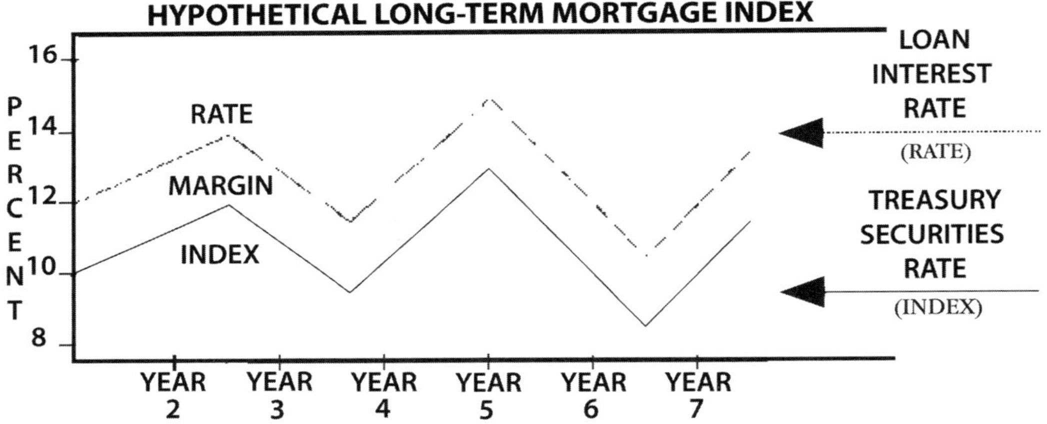

FIGURE 8.3: Hypothetical Long-Term Mortgage Index.

Rate Adjustment Period

The rate adjustment period is the length of time between interest rate changes with ARMs. This interval can range from a few months up to seven years. The most common rate adjustment periods are every six months or one year. ARMs are typically identified by their adjustment period, such as a 1-year ARM or a 3-year ARM. So, for example, with a 1-year ARM, the first adjustment would be made one year after the loan term started, and then every year after that. (In contrast, there are loan products called hybrid ARMs that have a fixed rate for a period of time before the rate adjustment periods begin. These are covered later in this chapter.)

After checking movement in the selected index, the lender will notify the borrower, in writing, of any increase or decrease in the rate. Such notification to the borrower is generally made 45 days prior to the next change.

Mortgage Payment Adjustment Period

The mortgage payment adjustment period is the length of time between payment adjustments with ARMs. Like the rate adjustment period, this payment adjustment interval can range from a period of months up to several years. There are two ways the rate and payment adjustments can be handled:

The lender can adjust the rate periodically, as called for in the loan agreement, and then adjust the mortgage payment to reflect the rate change. In this case, the payments will parallel the index and continue to amortize the loan during the repayment period.

If allowed in the note, the lender can adjust the rate more frequently than the mortgage payment is adjusted. In this case, the two adjustments do not coincide and so the payments will not parallel the index. If the interest rate is adjusted upward before the payment is adjusted, the borrower's payment may be insufficient to cover the accrued interest from the previous month, resulting in negative amortization. If the interest rate is adjusted downward before the payment is adjusted, the borrower will pay more than enough to cover accrued interest, in which case, the excess may be applied to principal.

Teaser Rates

When the initial rate on an ARM, also known as the start rate, is less than the fully indexed rate, it is considered a discounted index rate, sometimes referred to as a teaser rate. Lenders offer teaser rates to make ARMs more attractive to borrowers. The downside to a teaser rate is that it has the potential for a much higher first payment adjustment. Initially, teaser rates were offered without any caps, but industry leaders, especially secondary market investors, began demanding caps on ARMs as a means of protecting borrowers from payment shock, and themselves from portfolio shock—having loans that borrowers no longer had the ability to pay.

Interest Rate Cap

Interest rate caps are used with ARMs to limit the number of percentage points an interest rate can be increased during the term of a loan, helping to eliminate large fluctuations in mortgage payments. More uniform ARM lending practices and a period of self-regulation have resulted in most ARMs having some kind of cap. Rate caps are often shown as two numbers, for example 2/6:

The first number indicates the maximum amount the interest rate can increase (or potentially decrease) from one adjustment period to the next.

The second number indicates the maximum amount the interest rate can increase during the life of the loan.

Some ARMs allow for a higher rate change at the first adjustment, and then apply a periodic adjustment cap to future adjustments. These ARMs are usually identified with three numbers, where the first number is the interest rate cap for the first adjustment, followed by the period adjustment and lifetime interest rate caps. If you see a rate cap described as 5/2/6, for example, the interest rate cannot increase more than:

5% at the first adjustment,

2% for subsequent adjustment periods, and

6% total over the life of the loan.

Note: Just as an ARM may have caps that limit how high an interest rate or payment may increase, some adjustable rate mortgages also have a floor that limits how low an interest rate or payment may decrease. For example, a common floor for an ARM might be the margin indicated in the loan documents. In that case, even if a particular index were to be 0%, the actual rate to the lender would be the margin originally set, providing some risk protection for the lender. Some ARMS may also have a carryover feature, which means that an increase in the rate—not imposed because the rate cap—may be carried over to future rate adjustments. Such interest rate adjustments may also be effective and used for payment adjustment limits (either up or down), if provided for in the note.

Class Activity: ARM Interest Rates

Consider this hypothetical example to illustrate the relationship between interest rate caps and the borrower's interest rate. Let's say that a borrower gets a 1-year ARM loan for $100,000 for 30 years. It has a **5/2/6 interest rate cap**. The current index rate is 4.5%; the margin is 3%; and the discounted start rate is 4%.

As a class, complete the missing data for this particular adjustable rate mortgage example:

	Start / Year 1	Year 2	Year 3	Year 4	Year 5
Index	4.5%	6.5%	4%	7%	8%
Fully Indexed Rate (Index + 3%)	7.5%	9.5%	7%	10%	11%
Borrower' Interest Rate w/ Caps	4% (start)				
Monthly Payment (P&I only)	$536.82	$804.62	$665.30	$804.62	$877.57

Fannie Mae and Freddie Mac Interest Rate Caps. Both Fannie Mae and Freddie Mac have guidelines on ARM interest rate caps. ARMs purchased by Fannie Mae are limited to rate increases of **2%** per year and **6%** over the life of the loan. Freddie Mac rate adjustment guidelines limit rate increases to **2%** per year and **5%** over the life of the loan. While these guidelines do not take the form of regulations, most lenders include these, or even stricter, caps in their loans (particularly if they want to sell them on the secondary market).

FHA Interest Rate Caps. FHA rate adjustment increases are limited to **1%** per year and **5%** over the life of the loan.

VA Interest Rate Caps. VA rate adjustments are limited to 1% annually/5% lifetime on traditional ARMs (adjusts annually), and 2% annually/6% lifetime for their hybrid ARM (fixed for at least five years).

Mortgage Payment Cap

Mortgage payment caps are used with ARMs to *protect a borrower from large payment increases.* This is another way lenders limit the magnitude of payment changes that occur with interest rate adjustments. When there are no limits on the amount mortgage payments can be increased, borrowers are vulnerable to extreme changes in the cost of money. Inevitably, unrestricted increases create hardships for many borrowers. Some lenders only use interest rate caps to limit payment increases; others use both rate and payment caps. Regardless of which policy a lender uses, the objective is the same: To keep payment adjustments within a manageable range for the borrower. Note that if the current interest on the loan exceeds the payment cap, there is a chance for negative amortization.

Negative Amortization Cap

Negative amortization is *when a loan balance grows because payments don't cover the accrued interest due on the loan.* Negative amortization is most likely to occur when there are frequent rate changes (e.g., every six months) and less frequent payment adjustments (e.g., every three years).

A primary motivation for setting a negative amortization cap is to limit the growth of the loan balance beyond a certain point so that the loan-to-value ratio does not exceed the tolerances established by the lender. While negative amortization caps do *not* stop a loan from accruing negative amortization, when the cap is reached, the note usually calls for the lender to adjust, sometimes referred to as **recast**, the monthly payments to prevent any further negative amortization.

The cap is especially important for higher initial LTV loans. One approach is to set the negative amortization cap limit at 110%–125% of the initial loan balance. Another is to set the negative amortization cap limit at 100% of the initial appraised value. Either way, this means that a larger down payment can delay higher payments from re-amortization because it will take longer to reach the negative amortization cap.

Conversion Option

A **conversion option** in an ARM *gives the borrower the right to convert from an adjustable rate loan to a fixed rate loan.* ARMs with a conversion option normally identify the following factors in the note:

- Interest rate (often, the initial rate and converted rate are higher)
- Limited time to convert (e.g., between the first and fifth year)
- Conversion fee (typically about 1%)

For example, a Fannie Mae convertible ARM program may be converted between the 13th and 60th month for a small processing fee paid to the lender. The initial rate on the ARM loan is the same as for other Fannie Mae ARMs but, if converted, the fixed rate is 1/8% higher than the standard fixed rate at the time of conversion. Note that if an ARM is sold to the secondary market, the terms of any built-in conversion option would have to be honored by the secondary market purchaser.

ARM Standardization

The widespread acceptance of ARMs represented a major evolutionary phase in the housing industry. Initially, it was estimated that there were more than 200 different adjustable rate plans. But sharp criticism from confused customers, threats of government regulation, increased dangers of foreclosure, and refusal of secondary markets to buy ARMs led lenders to standardize most ARM programs.

Previously, most lenders underwrote ARMs based on their own standards and kept them as portfolio loans. Now, lenders usually follow secondary market guidelines so they can sell ARMs just as they do fixed rate loans. With uniform ARM underwriting standards, secondary market agencies, such as Freddie Mac, purchase large volumes of ARMs that follow their guidelines.

Loan-to-Value Ratios

ARM loans with loan-to-value ratios (LTVs) of 80%, 90%, and 95% may be available, depending on current conditions in the local market. Loans with higher LTVs, though, are often subject to some restrictions. For example, many lenders refuse to make 90% or 95% ARM loans if there's a possibility of negative amortization. Furthermore, in most cases where borrowers are seeking 90% or 95% ARMs, they're required to occupy the property. Fannie Mae and Freddie Mac have established stricter LTV guidelines for ARMs than for fixed rate loans. Loan-to-value ratios may not exceed 95% for ARMs purchased by Fannie Mae and Freddie Mac. The loan-to-value requirements are based on the potential risk from higher payments when the interest rate is adjusted. Fannie Mae and Freddie Mac also require owner occupancy for all ARMs, since they're considered better risks than non-occupant borrowers. In addition to new LTV restrictions, another recent change has been a tightening of FICO risk scores for some ARM programs, further narrowing the pool of qualified borrowers.

Appraisals on ARM Properties

As an ARM loan already carries some inherent risk, the appraisal is a focal point of any good underwriter. Lenders must insist that the appraisal report accurately reflects an estimate of the true value of the property, uninfluenced by discount rates, subsidy buydowns, or other financing concessions. The terms of the sale must be clearly communicated to the appraiser and identified—preferably in the appraisal report—and the effect of any financing concessions on the value of the property must be fully explained. When underwriting ARMs, the underwriter will carefully review the appraisal report to determine if the appraiser has performed this analysis satisfactorily. If not, the appraisal will be considered deficient because underwriters may subtract the value of any favorable financing from the appraised value in determining the maximum loan for a given LTV.

ARM Qualifying

With the potential risk of an increase in payments that comes with ARM loans, lenders are often stricter in qualifying borrowers to be sure they have sufficient income in the event their payments increase. To do this, lenders often use smaller housing expense and debt-to-income ratios with ARMs, to be conservative, allowing a smaller portion of a borrower's income to count in qualifying for the loan. If payments do increase later, there's less financial strain on a borrower to pay the loan (and less risk for the lender).

Certain ARMs have features (e.g., no rate or payment caps) that increase the likelihood of mortgage payments increasing to dangerous levels after the first rate adjustment. Likewise, loans with teaser rates or subsidy buydowns that exceed 2% add to the chances of significant payment shock. If an ARM is made with these characteristics, secondary market investors and many private mortgage insurance companies will insist that the traditional income ratios of 28% (for total housing expense) and 36% (for total debt-to-income) be disregarded in favor of lower, more conservative ratios.

ARM Disclosures

Lenders offering residential financing, including ARMs, must comply with federal guidelines under Regulation Z of the Truth in Lending Act that require certain disclosures to borrowers. A lender is required to give the loan applicant the **Consumer Handbook on Adjustable Rate Mortgages** (CHARM), prepared by the Federal Reserve Board, within three business days of loan application. The rules also require making certain specific disclosures if relevant to the specific ARM program and disclosing the annual percentage rate (APR).

The following disclosures must be provided to the borrower within three business days of a completed loan application (as appropriate):

- Index used to determine the interest rate
- Location where the borrower may find the index
- Explanation of how the interest rate and payment are determined
- Suggestion that the borrower asks the lender about the current margin and interest rate
- Disclosure of the fact that the initial rate is discounted and a suggestion that the borrower inquire as to the amount of the discount
- Rate and payment adjustment periods
- Rate and payment caps
- Statement that payment caps may result in negative amortization
- Statement that the loan has a demand or call provision
- Description of the information that will be contained in the adjustment notice and when such notices will be provided
- Statement that disclosure forms are available for lender's other ARM loans
- Maximum interest rate and payment
- Initial interest rate and payment
- Conversion option details
- An example, based on a $10,000 loan, showing how the payments and loan balance will be affected by changes in the index used

The lender or servicer must comply with all of the terms of the loan as indicated in the note, including any changes that occur during the life of the loan to the index, the rate, the payment, etc. The note will also indicate specific requirements for disclosing pending changes to the borrower.

Real Success

Mortgage loan originators working with consumers on an adjustable rate mortgage should **never** use the term "fixed rate," even when discussing the period between adjustments during which that interest rate remains unchanged. A consumer will hear "fixed," and that perception could create certain expectations about the loan that are false. Complete disclosure of how an ARM really works and the impact on the borrower is required by law and is simply the ethical behavior expected from all mortgage professionals.

Annual Percentage Rate (APR)

The **annual percentage rate** (APR) is *the relationship between the cost of borrowing money and the total amount financed, represented as a percentage.* Regulation Z disclosures regarding the APR cannot be made based solely on an ARM's initial rate. For an adjustable rate loan, the disclosure of the APR in the federal box on the Truth in Lending Statement (TIL) must reflect the finance charges and fees as well as the **composite annual percentage rate**, which is based on the initial payment rate and the fully indexed rate that could exist for the remaining years on the loan term.

For example, if the initial rate on a 30-year loan is 6% for one year, but then adjusts to COFI (for illustration purposes, let's say it's at 3%) plus 5%, the lender's disclosed payment schedule should reflect a composite APR based on 6% for 12 payments and 8% (3% + 5%) for the remaining 348 payments. The main point is that a lender must disclose more than the low initial rate. A required disclosure under Regulation Z, the APR composite rate is designed to let consumers comparison shop for rates among lenders, since all lenders must calculate APR the same way.

ARM Programs

Lenders may offer multiple types of adjustable rate mortgage programs.

Payment Option ARM

A payment option ARM, sometimes called a "pick-a-payment" loan, is an adjustable rate mortgage that allows borrowers to choose among several payment options each month. The options typically include:

- A **traditional payment of principal and interest**, which reduces the amount owed. Payments are based on a set loan term, such as a 15-, 30-, or 40-year payment schedule.
- An **interest only payment**, which pays the interest due but does not reduce the principal amount owed on the mortgage.
- A **minimum (or limited) payment** that may be less than the amount of interest due that month and may not reduce the amount owed. If a borrower chooses this option, the amount of any interest not paid is added to the principal of the loan, increasing the amount owed, future monthly payments, and the amount of interest paid over the life of the loan. In addition, if a borrower pays only the minimum payment in the last few years of the loan, a balloon payment may be required at the end of the loan term.

Payment option ARMs have a built-in recalculation period, usually every five years (again, lenders may use the term **recast**) and within the same period thereafter. At each recast, the new minimum payment will be a fully amortizing payment and any payment cap ceases to be in force during the current adjustment point, though it may remain in effect at other adjustment points.

Note: This type of loan has been the focus of much discussion in relation to the current foreclosure crisis. As undisciplined borrowers opted for the lower monthly payment and housing values fell, borrowers quickly owed more than their homes were worth. Additionally, these loans often result in negative amortization, which MLOs are specifically cautioned against under the Interagency Guidance on Nontraditional Mortgage Product Risks. Today, few, if any, lenders offer this type of ARM. When the market recovers, payment option ARMs may become available again.

Hybrid ARMs

A **hybrid mortgage** is a *combination of fixed and adjustable rates,* meaning that the loan has a fixed rate for a specified number of years, and then the interest rate adjusts regularly for the remainder of the loan term according to the terms of the note. A hybrid loan may be used as a "band-aid" or two-step type of loan, meaning that the borrower intends to either refinance or sell before the end of the fixed rate period. These types of loans may be used by subprime lenders to get borrowers into a home at a lower rate and payment upfront. Once borrowers have had a chance to establish more credit or repair their credit, they can look into qualifying for a mortgage with a better fixed rate. Hybrid mortgages may be designated by the number of years fixed and adjustable, for example:

2/28 Adjustable Rate Mortgage. A 2/28 ARM is a mortgage that has a fixed rate for the first two years, and then the interest rate adjusts at some predetermined interval as indicated in the note—for example, every month, every six months, annually—for the next 28 years.

3/27 Adjustable Rate Mortgage. A 3/27 ARM is a mortgage that has a fixed rate for the first three years, and then the interest rate adjusts at some predetermined interval as indicated in the note—for example, every month, every six months, annually—for the next 27 years. The 3/27 mortgage gives a longer period of fixed payments but would likely come with a slightly higher rate than a 2/28 ARM would, such as 0.1% to 0.25% higher.

Other hybrid ARMs are designated by the fixed period followed by the adjustment period, for example:

3/1, 5/1, 7/1, or 10/1 ARMs. The fixed period on these hybrids is for either three, five, seven, or ten years, and then the interest rate adjusts annually for the remainder of the loan term.

Again, MLOs need to be careful about how they discuss these loans so that consumers aren't confused by the term "fixed."

Mortgage Exercise 8-2

A borrower received a 30-year ARM mortgage loan for $120,000. The start rate was 3.50% and the loan adjusts every 12 months for the life of the mortgage. Rate caps are 3/2/6. The index used for this mortgage is the LIBOR. For this exercise, let's say it was 3.00% at the start of the loan, 5.00% at the end of the first year, and 4.50% at the end of the second year. The margin on the loan is 3.00%. *See the Appendix for answers to check your work.*

1. What is the borrower's interest rate after the first year?

2. What is the fully indexed rate after the second year?

3. What is the borrower's interest rate after the second year?

4. What is the maximum interest rate this loan could have?

5. What would the LIBOR have to be to obtain that interest rate?

Real Success

You should always be prepared to answer questions about ARM financing. Ultimately, the answers to these questions will be found in the specific terms of the note. When responding to generic questions about ARMs from potential customers, these points may be helpful:

1. What will my interest rate be?

   Be sure you know the initial ARM interest rates. Monitor local rates because they change regularly. The rates are usually published by lending sources, and be sure to compare these rates with those quoted in the business or home section of the local Sunday newspaper. At first, borrowers will be more concerned with the total rate but, as the home purchase gets closer, a borrower may be interested in more specific information.
2. How often will my interest rate change?

   Rate adjustments will be detailed in the loan papers and disclosures. Depending on the index used, rate changes will occur every six months, once a year, every three years, five years, etc. Six-month or one-year intervals are most common.
3. How often will my payment change?

   To provide an accurate answer, you must be familiar with terms offered by the funding source.
4. Is there any limit to how much my interest rate can be increased?

   Most ARMs have interest rate caps. The most common are 1% to 2%; the most common life-of-the-loan caps are the 5% and 6% limits set by Freddie Mac and Fannie Mae.
5. Is there any limit to how much payments can be increased at any one time?

   Some ARMs have payment caps, while others keep payment increases under control with interest rate caps. If there are payment caps, they're usually in the range of 7 1/2% to 15% of the payment amount—equal to about a 1% to 2% interest rate change.
6. What is the probability of runaway negative amortization?

   Not very likely. Interest rate caps, negative amortization caps, and re-amortization requirements protect both the borrower and lender in this regard. Of course, if interest rates sharply and rapidly increase, there's always a possibility of negative amortization. But with the changing nature of money markets, interest rates have not seen huge increases. They rise and fall, so the borrower's rate will be increased at one interval and reduced at another. If, at one point, there's negative amortization when interest due exceeds interest paid, there's a good chance that index declines will result in accelerated amortization at some point. This up and down pattern, though unpredictable, should continue through the life of the loan.
7. Can my ARM be converted to a fixed rate loan?

   Many ARMs have conversion options allowing borrowers to convert to fixed rate loans, for a fee, at certain periods or points in the loan term. ARMs with conversion options often have higher interest rates than those without. The options would be spelled out in the loan documents and disclosures.

Class Activity: ARM Advantages and Disadvantages

As a class, discuss some of the advantages and disadvantages of adjustable rate mortgages, and list them in the appropriate column:

Advantages	Disadvantages

Subprime Loans

Prime loans are loans made to good customers—the ones with good credit. For prime loans, borrowers can usually get the advertised interest rates. **Subprime loans**, on the other hand, have more *risks than are allowed in the conforming loan market.* The rates, fees, and down payment requirements are a reflection of risks associated with the borrower and the property. Such added risk can come from a variety of sources, for example:

- A borrower who has credit, income, debt, or down payment challenges. Such loans may be referenced as B-C credit loans.
- A borrower who has an acceptable credit score and/or assets but is unable, or reluctant, to provide sufficient documentation. Such loans may be referenced as low-doc, no-doc, SISA (stated income/stated assets), or NINA (no income/no asset verification) loans.

These loans—rare in today's market—filled a niche for certain borrowers for whom a conforming loan was not possible.

When considering risk on residential mortgage loans, lenders look at several factors. The cost of money (long-term), other competing investments, expected inflation rates, length of loan commitment, and other risk factors all impact a lender's computation of mortgage interest rates. Even in the prime market, conventional interest rates are risk based and factors such as property type, occupancy type, down payment, and credit scores are considered. To underwrite a subprime loan, the lender is examining *where* the borrower belongs on the risk scale. Credit scoring is helpful in making this determination, as well as the down payment. Subprime loans, to compensate for riskier credit, rely on the equity in the property, making appraisals very important, as the property may be the lender's only recourse in case of default. It takes an experienced underwriter to evaluate the risk factors and select a rate. Most lenders have developed some sort of risk grade matrix that considers all of the factors to determine the rate.

Some lenders and investors are willing to make these riskier loans because they can get higher interest rates and fees than they can with other real estate loans. Many banks and mortgage companies offer loan programs or have separate divisions that specialize in helping people with bad credit obtain a mortgage via subprime loans.

Alt-A Loans versus A-Minus Loans

Alt-A loans, also called alternative documentation loans, are loans that hold borrowers with good credit to different documentation standards than traditional loans. It's possible that a borrower with excellent credit and a large down payment will not be required to furnish as much documentation as a borrower with average scores and average down payment. The automated underwriting system (AUS) will recognize a good credit risk, and may require a reduced list of documentation, for example, only verbal verification of employment as opposed to two years of W-2s.

A-minus loans, on the other hand, are for borrowers who may have credit record blemishes, such as being 30 days late one or two times over the past year, limited funds for a down payment, high debt-to-income ratio, or a record of bankruptcy and/or foreclosure. These are riskier than prime mortgages, but not as risky as subprime mortgages. The approval can be obtained through an automated underwriting system (AUS). Since the loan is riskier, the interest rate will be higher.

Assessing Risk

A subprime borrower is matched to a series of risk profiles the lender has developed based on past lender and industry experience. For example, an "A" borrower may have good credit, but high debt ratios; or the borrower may have minor delinquencies that are explainable, or perhaps a good previous mortgage track record but other slow debts. A "B" borrower may have only average credit, but can explain lateness to the lender's satisfaction. A "C" borrower may have fair credit with high debt ratios, both of which could be due to health or job problems. Willingness and ability to repay are important here. A "D" borrower may have poor credit and high debt ratios, with little chance of improving either the credit or debt ratios.

These risk profiles are just examples. With subprime lending, criteria for who gets approved—and at what interest rate—vary greatly. Sometimes, larger down payments or secondary financing are required by lenders who want to be sure the collateral can cover the first mortgage loan amount. But for some people, it's the only way they are able to buy a house and re-establish their credit. Once borrowers have proven that they can make their mortgage payments for a given period of time, subprime lenders may offer them a chance to refinance their loans at lower interest rates, assuming their general credit and financial situation will allow them to qualify.

Interagency Guidelines

The federal financial regulatory agencies occasionally issue guidelines, recommendations, and policy statements for their member institutions. We will look at two such communications that were jointly published by the following agencies:

- The Office of the Comptroller of the Currency (OCC)
- The Board of Governors of the Federal Reserve System (Board)
- The Federal Deposit Insurance Corporation (FDIC)
- The Office of Thrift Supervision (OTS)
- The National Credit Union Administration (NCUA)

The final versions of these statements reflect the comments and input from financial institutions, trade associations, consumer and community organizations, state and financial regulatory organizations, and other members of the public.

Guidance on Nontraditional Mortgage Product Risks

In 2006, the federal financial regulatory agencies published the **Interagency Guidance on Nontraditional Mortgage Product Risks.** This Guidance applies to **nontraditional mortgage products**, which they define as *mortgage products that allow borrowers to defer principal and, sometimes, interest.* This includes products with an interest only (IO) feature and products with the potential for negative amortization (including those with flexible payment options). The agencies are primarily concerned about payment shock, competitive pressures, and ceding underwriting standards to third-party originations. While the Interagency Guidance may not explicitly pertain to subprime mortgage lending, it does outline prudent underwriting and consumer protection principles that institutions also should consider, including several guiding principles.

Qualification Standards

An institution's qualifying standards should recognize the potential impact of payment shock and should recognize that nontraditional mortgage loans often are not appropriate for borrowers with high loan-to-value (LTV), high debt-to-income ratios, and low credit scores. The analysis of borrowers' repayment capacity should include an evaluation of their ability to repay the debt by final maturity at the fully indexed rate and should avoid "over-reliance" on credit scores.

Collateral-Dependent Loans. Acknowledging that loans to borrowers who do not show capacity to repay the loan from sources other than the collateral are unsafe and unsound, institutions should avoid loan terms that rely on property sale or refinancing once amortization begins.

Risk Layering. Risk layering features—such as low- or no-document loans or simultaneous seconds—should be compensated with risk mitigating features, such as high credit scores, lower LTV, lower debt-to-income ratios, credit enhancements, and mortgage insurance.

Reduced Documentation. While the Statement indicates that lenders should generally be able to readily document income by means such as paystubs, W-2s, or tax returns, it also states that the use of any reduced documentation features should be governed by clear guidelines and accepted only if there are other risk mitigating factors, such as lower LTV.

Simultaneous Second Lien Loans. Loans with minimal owner equity should generally not have a payment structure that allows for delayed or negative amortization.

Introductory Interest Rates. In setting introductory interest rates, institutions should consider ways to minimize the probability of disruptive early recastings or extraordinary payment shock.

Underwriting Standards

The Guidance indicates that mortgage loan underwriting standards should address the effect of a substantial payment increase on the borrower's capacity to repay a nontraditional mortgage loan when amortization begins. For example:

Interest Only. For mortgage loans with an interest only feature, an analysis of a borrower's repayment capacity should include an evaluation of the borrower's ability to repay the debt by final maturity at the fully indexed rate (if adjustable rate) or note rate (if fixed rate), assuming a **fully amortizing repayment schedule** based on the term of the mortgage. The fully indexed rate generally equals the index value prevailing at the time of underwriting plus the applicable margin that will apply after the expiration of any introductory interest rate period.

Negative Amortization. For mortgage loans with a negative amortization feature, the repayment analysis should be based upon the initial loan amount plus any balance increase that may accrue from the negative amortization provision. The balance that may accrue from the negative amortization provision may be calculated by taking the lesser of the negative amortization cap per the mortgage note (the highest percent the loan amount can increase through negative amortization), or the maximum negative amortization percentage that the loan may accrue based on the spread between the introductory or "teaser" rate and the accrual rate before the end of the initial payment option period.

Statement on Subprime Mortgage Lending

In 2007, a **Statement on Subprime Mortgage Lending** was issued by the financial regulatory agencies. The purpose of this interagency statement was to promote consumer protection standards that lenders should follow to ensure that borrowers only obtain loans that they can afford to repay. The statement includes guidelines for defining predatory lending, underwriting standards, establishing control systems, and consumer protection. In particular, the standards are concerned with certain adjustable rate mortgage (ARM) products, typically offered to subprime borrowers, that have one or more of the following characteristics:

- Low initial payments based on a fixed introductory rate that expires after a short period and then adjusts to a variable index rate plus a margin for the remaining term of the loan
- Very high or no limits on how much the payment amount or the interest rate may increase ("payment or rate caps") on reset date
- Limited or no documentation of borrowers' income
- Product features likely to result in frequent refinancing to maintain an affordable monthly payment
- Substantial prepayment penalties and/or prepayment penalties that extend beyond the initial fixed interest rate period

Consumer Protection

The Statement urges lenders to give consumers the facts necessary to understand material terms, costs, and risks of loan products while the consumer is selecting a loan product and before a loan is closed. According to the Statement, MLOs should inform consumers of:

- **Payment Shock.** Potential payment increases, including how the new payment will be calculated when the introductory fixed rate expires
- **Prepayment Penalties.** The existence of any prepayment penalty, how it will be calculated, and when it may be imposed
- **Balloon Payments.** The existence of any balloon payment
- **Cost of Reduced Documentation Loans.** Whether there is a pricing premium attached to a reduced documentation or stated income loan program
- **Responsibility for Taxes and Insurance.** The requirement to make payments for real estate taxes and insurance in addition to their loan payments, if not escrowed, and the fact that taxes and insurance costs can be substantial

Predatory Lending

The Statement defines predatory lending as a loan involving at least one of the following elements:

- Making loans based predominantly on the foreclosure or liquidation value of a borrower's collateral rather than on the borrower's ability to repay the mortgage according to its terms
- Inducing a borrower to repeatedly refinance a loan in order to charge high points and fees each time the loan is refinanced (known as "loan flipping" or "equity skimming")
- Engaging in fraud or deception to conceal the true nature of the mortgage loan obligation, or ancillary products, from an unsuspecting or unsophisticated borrower

Reverse Mortgage

Another type of nontraditional mortgage is the **reverse mortgage**. The purpose of a reverse mortgage is to provide a vehicle for a borrower who has substantial equity in a property to convert that accumulated equity—at a cost—to cash and additional debt without selling the property and without making payments to the lender. Seniors, those adults age 62 or older, can use the equity in their home for any use, including, but not limited to, health care, home repairs and upkeep, and/or to maintain a lifestyle that is otherwise unaffordable. A reverse mortgage may also be called a reverse equity mortgage or a reverse annuity mortgage. The most popular reverse mortgage program is FHA's **Home Equity Conversion Mortgage**, or HECM.

To contrast, with a traditional, fully amortizing "forward" mortgage for a purchase, a homebuyer makes a down payment and borrows the rest of the money needed to purchase the home. They then pay off the loan every month over the course of many years. During the life of the loan, the debt decreases, and the home equity increases. Once the final mortgage payment is made, the homeowner owes nothing and, in theory, the home equity equals the value of the home. You can think of this as a "falling debt, rising equity" scenario.

On the other hand, with a typical reverse mortgage, the balance of the loan rises as the borrower receives money from the lender and incurs interest to the outstanding loan balance. Since the borrower is not making any payments, by the time a reverse mortgage becomes due, the borrower may owe a lot of money and have a small amount of equity. It's even possible, depending on the length of the loan and other factors, that there is no equity left when the loan becomes due. For most reverse mortgages, the amount owed grows and the equity shrinks, which creates a "rising debt, falling equity" scenario.

Eligibility Requirements

Reverse mortgages have some very specific requirements, and some less stringent requirements.

Income

With a traditional mortgage, the income of the borrower is critical in determining the terms of the loan, the amount that can be borrowed, etc. A reverse mortgage, on the other hand, has no income requirements to qualify. The lender will, however, consider the borrower's ability to meet continued obligations to pay property taxes, insurance premiums, homeowners association fees (if applicable), and to maintain the property.

Age

In order to qualify for a reverse mortgage, **all persons who have an ownership interest** in the security property must be at least **62 years of age**. If one of the owners does not satisfy this age requirement, the only way to secure a reverse mortgage loan on the property is for the younger owner to relinquish all ownerships interests in the property. This strategy, while solving the age requirement issue, could create other issues related to ownership and survivorship, and so should be taken with caution. Borrowers should always be advised to seek legal advice on such issues.

Home

Although the specific type of reverse mortgage may impose different standards, in general, single-family, one-unit dwellings are considered eligible properties for a reverse mortgage. Depending on the program, condominiums, planned unit developments (PUDs), and manufactured homes may be acceptable. Mobile home and cooperative units are *not* generally eligible, although HUD may approve some types of mobile homes.

Note that, as with a traditional mortgage, the lender will require that the borrower maintain a **homeowners insurance** policy that is sufficient to cover the replacement value of the collateral property. This protects the lender's interest in the event of damage that causes a loss of value, such as a fire, tornado, etc. The lender may also require a separate flood insurance policy. Since borrowers obtaining a reverse mortgage may have had the same insurance policy in place for years, they are urged to review the policy to ensure that the insurance in place provides adequate coverage.

Ownership

To be eligible for a reverse mortgage, the home must be the principal residence, and any debt on the home should be paid off. A borrower is not necessarily prevented from getting a reverse mortgage if there is debt on the home, however, since funds from the reverse mortgage may be used to pay off any remaining debt on the home.

Meeting with a Counselor

Most reverse mortgage programs impose an additional condition on prospective borrowers by requiring them to participate in a consumer counseling session given by an approved counselor. The counselor will be able to explain the costs of the loan and the financial implications, as well as provide guidance and advice in selecting a program and/or a lender. A lender cannot submit an application for an FHA-insured reverse mortgage until the applicant provides proof that this required counseling session took place.

This unbiased, independent counselor can help guide the borrower through what can be a confusing process and a lot of difficult decisions. And at the end of the session, the counselor must provide any required certification of counseling. A counselor may even point the homeowner to other programs or assistance that might be a better solution than a reverse mortgage.

Amount Available with a Reverse Mortgage

Many factors determine how much money a homeowner can receive with a reverse mortgage. For example, a required appraisal will determine the value of the home. The more the home is worth, the more cash that can borrowed with the reverse mortgage. Other factors that could impact the amount of money available include the amount of equity that has been built up, the payment options, the interest rates, the program costs and/or loan financing fees. And of course, the specific program selected has much to do with determining the impact of these factors. For example, since FHA's HECM is the major reverse mortgage product, the location of the home is critical as that will determine FHA's lending limits.

Age of the Homeowner

Another important factor that figures into the determination of the amount of money available is the **age** of the homeowner. Typically, an older homeowner would have a higher dollar amount available with a reverse mortgage than a younger homeowner since an older person has a shorter life expectancy and, therefore, the loan would be for a shorter term.

For example, Margaret (age 65), Thomas (age 75), and Laura (age 85) own their homes, each of which is valued at $100,000. All three have qualified for a reverse mortgage loan at an interest rate of 8%. All other things being equal, Margaret might be able to borrow only 58% of her home's value; Thomas might be able to borrow up to 70% of his home's value; while Laura might be able to borrow as much as 80% of her home's value.

Note that when the reverse mortgage is in more than one name, it is the age of the youngest that factors into the amount of money available.

Payment Options

The homeowner who takes out a reverse mortgage generally gets to decide how to receive the money. The payment options include:

- **Fixed monthly payments** for either a predetermined period or for as long as the homeowner remains in the home
- A **lump sum** payment up front
- A **line of credit** that allows the homeowner to have access to funds on an "as-needed" basis

A homeowner may also choose to receive some **combination** of these options. However, the payment option that a homeowner chooses could affect the amount of cash they may be eligible to receive from the loan.

Spending Options

Typically, the homeowner who takes out a reverse mortgage also gets to determine how to **spend** the money. It may be that the majority of those who get reverse mortgages do so primarily to supplement a fixed retirement income, cover the costs of healthcare, or make much-needed improvements to their home. But the funds from a reverse mortgage can be used for virtually anything. A homeowner may choose to make that lifelong vacation dream a reality. Another could choose to start a small business, pay off credit card debt, or contribute to a grandchild's college tuition.

Tax Implications

For the most part, the funds paid out with a reverse mortgage are not considered income by the IRS, and so they are not taxed. And unlike a typical house mortgage, the interest that the lender charges on the reverse mortgage can be deducted only at the conclusion of the loan when the loan principal and the interest are repaid. As with anything in life, there are exceptions.

Although the funds paid out from a reverse mortgage are *generally* tax-free, homeowners should get advice from a qualified reverse mortgage counselor and/or attorney to determine whether or not the income received could in any way affect their eligibility for any needs-based public assistance benefits such as Medicaid or Supplemental Social Security.

Repayment

Assuming the borrower upholds the terms of the contract, a typical reverse mortgage becomes due when the last surviving borrower:

- Dies,
- Sells the home, or
- Ceases to live in the home for 12 consecutive months.

At that point, the homeowner or the homeowner's heirs must repay the total loan amount, which includes the money that was paid out as well as any interest, insurance, closing costs, or other fees as stipulated in the terms of the loan.

Of course, it is often the case that the proceeds from the sale of the home are used to repay the reverse mortgage. Any remaining equity belongs to the estate (in event of death) or the homeowner (if they sold or moved).

Non-Recourse Loans

Generally, a lender cannot force a borrower out of his or her home during the life of the loan. Nor can the lender simply sell the home when a reverse mortgage comes due. Usually the lender will allow up to 12 months for payment in the event of death. If the home is not sold or is not deeded to the lender, a formal foreclosure process may be started in the county where the home is located, depending on the terms of the note.

A reverse mortgage is considered a "non-recourse" loan, and so even in the rare instance that the amount of money distributed over the life of the reverse mortgage exceeds the value of the home, the borrower or the borrower's heirs cannot owe more than fair market sale price of the home, minus reasonable sales expenses. The lender has no claims on any other assets that may be held by the borrower or the borrower's heirs.

Accelerating Repayment

As with any mortgage situation, however, there are some circumstances that might cause the lender to require immediate repayment, for example:

- The homeowner fails to make necessary repairs to the property.
- The property is condemned.
- The homeowner does not pay the mandatory property taxes.
- The homeowner ceases to pay the appropriate homeowners insurance premiums.
- A government entity claims eminent domain over the property.
- The borrower ceases to live in the property or it is discovered the property is no longer the borrower's principal residence.

Seller Financing and Other Creative Alternatives

This section presents a brief overview of seller financing and some other forms of creative financing in use today. While the types of transactions discussed here do not require the services of a licensed mortgage loan originator, an awareness of these financing options can be beneficial for the well-rounded MLO.

Alienation Clause

It is imperative that anyone considering any form of seller financing confirm whether any existing mortgage has an **alienation clause**. This clause, sometimes called a **due on sale clause**, gives the lender the *right to exercise certain rights upon transfer of the property.* Most alienation clauses are worded so that the borrower's transfer of ***any ownership interest*** in the property securing the loan without the lender's knowledge or consent would be a **default** under the mortgage. So, for example, the clause would be triggered by the transfer of title, or even by transfer of a significant interest in the property such as with a long-term lease.

An alienation clause may give the lender the right to declare the entire loan balance immediately due and payable (hence, referred to as a due on sale clause), the right to raise the interest rate on the loan, the right to charge an assumption fee, or the right to exercise other rights stated in the contract. Thus, an alienation clause may place the borrower in jeopardy of triggering the acceleration of the loan and possible foreclosure.

It's critical, therefore, in any transaction with an existing mortgage being left in place, to obtain the lender's written consent to the proposed transaction. This may not be necessary if there's no alienation clause in the security instrument (e.g., with some FHA and VA loans). If there is an alienation clause in the mortgage, though, most lenders will insist on renegotiating the loan's interest rate, or demand that the loan be paid off entirely. Only occasionally will a lender consent to a sale without any change in the existing mortgage.

Seller Financing

Seller financing is when a seller extends credit to a buyer to finance the purchase of the property. This can be instead of or in addition to the buyer obtaining a loan from a third party, such as an institutional lender. A seller may help with financing for several reasons, for example, the buyer:

- May be unable to afford the cash necessary for the required down payment for a conventional mortgage.
- May want to take advantage of the low interest rate on the seller's existing mortgage.
- Is not able to qualify for a loan from a lender for various reasons.

In tight money markets, sometimes the only way sellers can make a deal is to finance part of the purchase price themselves. Mortgage money from traditional lenders may be too costly in terms of interest rates or it may be simply unavailable. In any case, sellers can often enhance the salability of their properties by offering complete or partial financing.

Seller financing should not be undertaken without checking the laws of the state in which the property is located. It may be necessary to seek legal advice, as many states have limitations as to the recourse a seller may have if the purchaser defaults, for example.

Purchase Money Mortgage

The term **purchase money mortgage** may be used to describe a *mortgage given by the buyer to the seller for the purchase of real estate.* You may also see this referred to as simply a **seller held mortgage.** The central advantage of this arrangement is that sellers are not bound by institutional policies regarding loan ratios, interest rates, or qualifying standards. To make the sale, a seller may charge a below-market interest rate, or may offer financing to a buyer who is considered a credit risk by institutional lenders. Whether the seller finances all or part of the purchase, the seller is taking a risk; but the risk may be justified if it allows the sale to proceed or enables the seller to get a higher price for the home. Purchase money financing may take any of the many forms discussed earlier, such as variable interest rates, graduated payments, or partial amortization with balloon payment. It could be in a first lien position or, if the seller is financing only part of the purchase price, it could be a junior lien. The parties must be sure not to violate any laws, such as usury laws limiting the maximum interest rate that can be charged.

Assumption

Assumption of a loan means *one party agrees to take over payments of another party's debt, with terms of the note staying unchanged.* FHA and VA loans permit assumptions (with a credit check of buyers); some conventional mortgages also allow assumptions because they don't have an enforceable alienation clause. (Borrowers should always consult the original lender or a lawyer.) The property is still security for the loan, but the buyer becomes primarily liable for repayment. In the event of foreclosure, the lender may still have recourse against the original party (seller) if the debt isn't fully satisfied. To be relieved of liability, the seller must get a **release** from the lender, which is a document in which a legal right is given up. Here, the lender gives a release, accepting the buyer as the new mortgagor and releasing the seller from all mortgage obligations. If a release is signed by the lender, the lender's only recourse is against the buyer who assumed the loan.

Seller-Sponsored Wraparound Financing

In this situation, *the seller offers the wraparound mortgage, retaining an existing loan on the property while giving the buyer a second loan.* This new total loan is treated as one obligation by the buyer, who makes one payment to the seller for the entire (combined) debt. The seller, in turn, pays the original mortgage lender and keeps the excess. By using a wraparound mortgage sales contract, the seller can extend the benefit of an existing loan at lower-than-market interest rates, even if the buyer is unwilling or unable to assume the loan directly. For wraparound financing to be proper and legal, however, there must be an assumable mortgage with bank approval or no alienation clause in the original mortgage.

Land Contracts

Land contracts are another instrument used to finance the purchase of real estate. A **land contract** is a *real estate installment agreement where the buyer makes payments to the seller in exchange for the right to occupy and use the property, but no deed or title is transferred until all, or a specified portion, of the payments have been made.* Land contracts—also called land installment contracts, installment sales contracts, land sales contracts, real estate contracts, and other names, are much different than mortgages or trust deeds, where the debtor takes possession of the property while the creditor holds a mortgage or trust deed as a security lien against the property. Under a land contract, the seller (**vendor**) actually holds title to the property as security, not just a mortgage lien. The buyer/debtor (**vendee**) has the right to possess and enjoy the land, but is *not* the legal owner. The seller retains legal title to the subject property, while the buyer is only an owner in fact, having possession and **equitable title**, but no actual title and no deed.

Land contracts are a popular form of seller financing in some parts of the country. Land contracts may be structured subject to an existing mortgage or structured to allow the vendee to assume the vendor's mortgage. But this type of financing has many of the same advantages as any other form of seller financing, such as freedom from institutional loan qualifying standards and flexibility of terms. The main disadvantage is that land contracts can't be resold to Fannie Mae, although a few private secondary market investors may be willing to buy land contracts. Because the laws governing land contracts can vary by state, it is important for anyone contemplating a land contract to consult the laws in the jurisdiction where the property is located.

Land contracts usually require the vendor to give the vendee a statement, at least once a year or as requested, showing the amount of payments that have been credited to principal and interest, and the balance due under the contract.

For the vendor, the advantage of a land contract is the right to hold title as security. This lack of ownership is, conversely, the main disadvantage for a vendee since it makes it difficult to later obtain financing based on the equity built up or for improvements, as banks are reluctant to lend to a person without actual legal title to the property.

Estoppel Letter

Estoppel is *a basic legal doctrine that prevents a person (or artificial person such as a lender or company) from asserting rights or facts inconsistent with earlier actions or statements when he or she failed to object (or attempt to stop) another person's actions*. Here's one example of the doctrine of estoppel: When a party to a land contract sends an estoppel letter to the lender about a land contract arrangement, the lender must object immediately or the lender is estopped (legally prevented) from objecting later. The lender, though, will almost always respond. An estoppel letter, therefore, becomes a lender's written consent to a sale, acknowledging the transfer and waiving any right to accelerate the loan because of the sale.

Other Forms of Creative Financing

These financing alternatives provide additional opportunities for motivated sellers and purchasers to close a transaction.

Lease/Option

A **lease/option** is *when a seller leases property to someone for a specific term, with an option to buy the property at a predetermined price during the lease term.* The lease/option plan is comprised of two elements—a lease and an option. A **lease** is a *contract where one party pays the other rent in exchange for possession of real estate.* An **option** is a *contract giving one party the right to do something within a designated time period, without obligation to do so.* Obviously, the lease/option is *not* the equivalent of a sale, but there exists a good possibility that a sale will take place under its terms. The prospective purchaser is referred to as the **optionee**; the property owner is the **optionor**. Consideration is given by the optionee to the optionor in return for a commitment to sell the property to the optionee at some time in the future. An optionor and optioneer may agree to credit any portion of the rent that is **above the established market rent** for a comparable property toward the down payment, loan amount, or sales price, thus reducing the cost and making it easier to buy the property later.

Lease/Purchase

A **lease/purchase** is *when a seller leases property to someone for a specific term, with the tenant agreeing to buy the property at a set price during or following the lease term.* The lease/purchase plan is comprised of two elements: A lease and a purchase contract. Both contracts must conform to all laws governing real estate contracts. The lease/purchase is the equivalent of a sale, but there are additional considerations to take into account because the sale is delayed until a later date. The purchase agreement locks in a predetermined price for the property and sets a date for the sale transaction to be completed on or by. Here, the buyer is committing to purchasing the property, but can't buy it until certain problems are resolved or other events take place.

Equity Exchanges

An **equity exchange** is *value in one property being traded for value in another property.* This is also called a tax-deferred exchange, tax-free exchange, like-kind exchange, or Section 1031 (from the section number of IRS law). In order to make a tax-deferred equity exchange of real estate, the properties must be like-kind property (real estate for real estate) and the properties must be held for use in a trade or business, or held by the party as an investment. When property is exchanged as part of an equity exchange, the seller defers paying taxes until a capital gain (profit) is actually realized from the transaction. Usually, this means when the property is sold in the future. If the transaction does qualify for tax-free exchange treatment, any gain that is purely a result of the exchange is deferred. **Professional tax advice and legal counsel should always be consulted for any deal involving equity exchanges or tax deferral.**

Participation Plans

In a **participation plan**, also known as an **equity participation mortgage** or a **shared equity plan,** *a borrower and an investor enter into an agreement through which the investor* (who may be the seller, a bank, or any private investor) provides cash for the purchase. Instead of charging interest, the investor in a participation plan receives a percentage of the equity (the difference between the property's value and the indebtedness secured by the property). The buyer, though, must generally still make principal payments, although these may be deferred. Different investors will have varying requirements as to the percentage of equity to be shared and method of repaying the investment. These issues are a matter of institutional policy or negotiation between buyer and investor. Participation plans can be fairly complex when compared with other creative financing methods, and so a real estate lawyer experienced in participation plans should always be consulted.

Homebuyer Assistance Programs

Homebuyer assistance programs can be down payment assistance programs (sometimes referred to collectively as DAP programs), subsidized mortgage interest rates, help with closing costs, or a combination. These programs may be offered by government or non-profit organizations to promote home ownership, or by lenders as part of their obligation under the Community Reinvestment Act.

Some programs allow people to buy homes with lower down payments than conventional loans, often 3% or less. This may be offered by cities, counties, or the state, and the money may be targeted to specific neighborhoods. Often a portion or all of the required down payment is paid on behalf of the buyer. Money for these programs is usually limited and administered on a first-come, first-served basis. Various bond issues or levies may replenish the funding for the program, but it is hard to predict when money will become available. Some non-profit organizations also provide grants, gifts, or otherwise arrange money for down payment assistance.

Interest rate subsidies may also be obtained from a variety of sources. Bond money is available from time to time, whereby the state issues bonds and uses the funds to subsidize the interest rate paid on mortgages by low-income families. Underwriting requirements may be the same as for FHA loans, but the interest rate is lower than an FHA loan because of the subsidy. Some such programs may even offer both down payment assistance and interest rate subsidies through various agencies.

First Time Homebuyer Loans or **Community Homebuyer Programs** are some of the generic names for the various programs that lenders have created that allow them to offer more flexible financing than that for conforming loans with regard to credit, income, and down payment as a means of supporting the community. The law does not require lenders to make high-risk loans, but loans in the community should be made whenever possible while maintaining the safety of the institution. Borrowers with poor credit may have to complete a course on financial responsibility to qualify for a loan.

All of these government and private sector programs have numerous rules that must be followed for borrowers to qualify for the assistance programs. Nevertheless, the maze of regulations and paperwork can offer hope to some who might not otherwise be able to buy a home on their own. Supporters of these programs applaud the fact that they help more people buy homes; detractors worry about high potential default rates for people with little money to put down on a home or spend on upkeep.

Chapter 8 Summary

1. **Nontraditional mortgage products** are defined by the SAFE Act as anything *other than* 30-year fixed rate loans. The Interagency Guidance on Nontraditional Mortgage Product Risks defines nontraditional mortgage products as mortgage products that allow borrowers to defer principal and, sometimes, interest. Such products can help buyers qualify for larger loans or help them reach other financial goals.

2. **Buydowns** are additional money (discount points) paid to the lender at the start of a loan to lower interest rate and payments. Discount points are paid to the lender to make up the difference between the market interest rate and the rate a borrower gets in the note. A permanent buydown (for life of loan) has a reduced rate stated in the note. A temporary buydown (early in loan) can be level payment or graduated payment. With buydowns, the lowest a buyer can qualify is 2% below market rate. FHA requires buyers to qualify at the note rate, not the buydown rate. Fannie Mae, Freddie Mac, and the FHA limit points and other interested party contributions (IPCs) that can be paid.

3. **Adjustable rate mortgages** (ARMs) have interest rates that may adjust up or down according to the terms of the note. Borrowers select an **index** (statistical report reflecting cost of money), lenders add a **margin** (spread), and this is the **fully indexed rate** paid on the loan. Loan documents must state: Rate, index, margin, and payment adjustment period; caps (if any) on rate, payments or negative amortization; conversion option (if any). Rates that change more frequently than payments may create **negative amortization** (payments insufficient to cover interest due). **Caps** keep loans from growing out of control. Lenders periodically **readjust** or **recast** the loan by recalculating payments based on the loan balance at specific interval. **Conversion options** allow buyers to convert to fixed rate. MLOs must provide CHARM booklet to borrower in addition to other mandated disclosures, including the **annual percentage rate** (APR). For ARMs, it is a composite rate that reflects the lower rate for certain number of years and the higher rate for later years. Lenders cannot disclose only initial low rates.

4. Proceeds from a **reverse mortgage** may be disbursed to eligible borrowers aged 62 or older as a monthly payment, a lump sum of cash, or a line of credit, based on the equity in their homes. Among the events that trigger loan repayment are when the borrower dies, moves out of the house for 12 months, or sells the house.

5. **Structured mortgages** help borrowers reach other financial goals. **Growth equity**: Fixed rate, but payments increase regularly as indicated in the note. **Reduction option**: Buyer can reduce rate one time, with fewer refinancing costs. **Shared appreciation**: Lender shares equity in commercial project.

6. **Subprime** loans (B-C loans, low-doc, SISA, NINA) have more risk than what is allowed by the conventional market. Borrower risk factors determine interest rate and terms. A-minus loans are riskier than prime loans, less risky than subprime loans.

7. **Seller financing** is when seller extends credit to buyer to finance the purchase of property. Seller can extend all or partial credit. This can help a buyer who doesn't have enough cash to buy a property, can't qualify for a conventional loan, or wants or needs a lower-than-market interest rate. Seller gets the benefit of a home that's easier to sell, and often a better price by offering terms. A **purchase money mortgage** or **seller-held mortgage** is given by buyer to seller to secure part or all of the money borrowed to purchase property. Unencumbered property with no liens is best for this transaction; encumbered property with liens needs assumption or wraparound. **Assumption** has the buyer take responsibility for the mortgage, but the seller must get a release from the lender. A **seller-wraparound mortgage** has the seller retain existing mortgage (the buyer makes one larger payment; the seller pays the lender and keeps difference).

8. A **land contract** is a real estate installment agreement. Buyer (vendee) makes payments to seller (vendor) for right to occupy land, but no title is transferred until all, or part of, payments are made. Buyer has **equitable title** under a land contract. States differ in how they treat land contracts. Problems

for the buyer include difficulty in borrowing against equity with a land contract and protecting equity if land contract is not recorded. A lender may consent to the deal using an **estoppel** letter.

9. A **lease/option** has the seller (optionee) lease to a tenant (optionor) who has the right (but not the obligation) to buy the property at a set price within a certain time. An option can be used for profit, speculation, investment, comparison, or to give the optionor time to acquire cash, to qualify, or credit rent toward purchase price. A **lease/purchase** combines a lease with a purchase contract. An **equity exchange** (tax-deferred exchange, Section 1031) is property traded for value in other property. Properties must be exchanged (or delayed exchange), like kind, and held for trade, business, or investment. Capital gains tax is deferred, but boot (unlike property added to balance value) is taxed. Tax-free exchanges are not available for residential property. **Participation plans** have investors/lenders share equity in the property instead of or in addition to receiving interest.

10. **Homebuyer assistance programs** can be down payment assistance programs (DAP), subsidized mortgage interest rates, help with closing costs, or combination. Programs can be offered by government or non-profit groups, or by lenders.

Chapter 8 Quiz

1. ***A borrower is purchasing a home for $100,000. The LTV on the loan is 80%. If the borrower pays a total of 6 points on the loan, how much will the points cost him?***
   A. $2,400
   B. $3,400
   C. $4,800
   D. $6,000

2. ***A buydown plan can reduce the borrower's payments***
   A. early in the loan only, but requires a large balloon payment.
   B. early in the loan or for the entire life of the loan.
   C. for the entire life of a loan, but with an automatic prepayment penalty.
   D. with gradual payment decreases throughout the life of the loan.

3. ***Which statement is true about interest rate buydowns on FHA loans?***
   A. Borrowers may qualify at the buydown rate.
   B. Borrowers must qualify at the note rate.
   C. FHA does not allow builder-paid buydowns.
   D. FHA does not allow seller-paid buydowns.

4. ***Which of the following is NOT an element of an ARM?***
   A. index
   B. margin
   C. positive amortization cap
   D. rate

5. ***What is the adjustable number used to compute the interest rate on an ARM called?***
   A. cap
   B. index
   C. margin
   D. prepayment

6. ***With an ARM, the index is added to the ______ to determine the __________ .***
   A. APR / cost of funds
   B. home value / amount borrowed
   C. margin / interest rate charged
   D. qualifying ratio / maximum monthly mortgage payment

7. ***Negative amortization occurs when***
   A. a borrower suffers payment shock.
   B. each mortgage payment is adjusted more frequently than is the interest rate.
   C. the payment made does not cover the interest due for that period.
   D. all of the above

8. ***How are subprime loans different from conforming loans?***
   A. They allow for lower interest rates.
   B. They allow for more risk.
   C. They are only offered by banks.
   D. They are sold in the secondary market.

9. ***Which scenario best describes a land contract?***
   A. A buyer makes payments to the seller in exchange for the right to occupy, use, and enjoy the property, but no deed or title transfers until a specified portion of payments have been made.
   B. A buyer takes over primary liability for the loan of a seller, usually implying no change in loan terms.
   C. A seller keeps the existing loan and continues to pay on it while giving the buyer another loan.
   D. A seller leases the property with the provision that part of the rent payments be applied to the sale price if the tenant decides to purchase before the lease expires.

10. ***An equity exchange may be treated as a tax-free exchange when property is***
    A. for profit and of like kind.
    B. held for sale by a dealer only.
    C. owner-occupied.
    D. rental only.

11. ***In which federal law would you find the definition of a nontraditional loan?***
    A. Homeowners Equity Protection Act
    B. Real Estate Settlement Procedures Act
    C. Secure and Fair Enforcement for Mortgage Licensing Act
    D. Truth in Lending Act

12. ***During the life of a typical reverse mortgage, which of the following factors is decreased?***

    A. debt
    B. equity
    C. interest
    D. monthly payments

13. ***According to the Interagency Guidance on Nontraditional Mortgage Product Risks, nontraditional mortgage loans may be LEAST risky for borrowers with***

    A. high debt-to-income ratios.
    B. high loan-to-value.
    C. low credit scores.
    D. low debt-to-income ratios.

14. ***Each of these are characteristics that could make a loan nontraditional EXCEPT***

    A. 15-year term.
    B. adjustable rate.
    C. fixed rate.
    D. temporary buydown.

15. ***A borrower has a ARM with a 5/2/6 interest rate cap. The start rate is 4%, the current index is 3%, and the margin is 3%. What is the borrower's interest rate if the index rises to 5% at the time of the first adjustment?***

    A. 5%
    B. 6%
    C. 8%
    D. 9%

9

Chapter 9

Legal Concepts in Real Estate

In This Chapter

A general understanding of basic civil law and other legal concepts is important in the real estate and mortgage industries. These concepts detail legal relationships between the parties and also affect property value. This chapter explains the distinction between real property and personal property, with an in-depth discussion of the rights of ownership that go with real property. These rules are important to everyone involved in the sale of real estate because they determine exactly what is being sold—and what is being mortgaged. We will also discuss public and private restrictions on property and how those and other interferences with property rights may affect value.

At the end of this chapter, you will be able to:

- Identify the essential elements of a valid contract.
- Contrast real property and personal property.
- Identify the bundle of real property rights.
- Identify public and private restrictions on real property.

Key Terms

Annexation
Appurtenances
Attachments
Bundle of Rights
Contract
Deed Restrictions
Easement
Eminent Domain
Encroachment
Escheat
Fixtures
Improvement
Location Survey
Nuisance
Personal Property
Police Power
Real Property
Trade Fixtures
Trespass
Waste

Basic Civil Law Concepts

Civil law is the *body of law concerned with the rights and liabilities of one individual in relation to another.* A person who fails to live up to a legal duty or to respect another's legal right may cause harm to another person or property. These rights, responsibilities, and remedies can be summed up in the three fundamental categories of civil law: Contracts, torts, and property.

Contracts

A **contract** is an *agreement between two or more parties to do, or not do, a certain thing.* A contract is a legally binding promise. When two people enter into a contractual relationship, they voluntarily take on legal duties toward one another. There is an entire body of rules that governs legal relationships based on contracts. These rules apply to any kind of contract, whether it concerns employment, the sale of a condominium, or commercial shipping. These basic rules also apply to contracts concerning real property, including real estate purchase contracts, leases, promissory notes, mortgages, and others. In the most general sense, for a contract to be binding, it must have these essential elements:

- Competent parties; each side must have the capacity to enter into a contract (which in many states requires the legal age of majority)
- Consideration, such as money or services to be performed
- Mutual agreement, also known as meeting of the minds, which requires offer and acceptance of the terms of the contract

Torts

A **tort** is a *breach of the standards of reasonable conduct imposed by law that causes harm to another person.* Unlike contract law, these legal duties are not voluntarily assumed. Rather, law requires everyone to take reasonable care to avoid injuring another person or damaging another's property. Tort law concerns the duties of reasonable conduct imposed by law. For example: Running desperately through the station to catch a train, Ann accidentally knocks down Bob. Bob's arm is broken in the fall. Ann has breached the legal duty to use reasonable care in passing through a public place. In other words, Ann has committed a tort against Bob.

Property

Property is *something that is owned—real or personal—and includes the rights of ownership.* The rights of ownership allow the owner to use, possess, transfer, or encumber the property owned. Property law includes rules about acquiring ownership and losing ownership, and about the rights and duties that ownership carries with it.

Class Activity: Legal Issues

Contract, tort, and property issues can be entwined in a single legal problem. Suppose two neighbors have a dispute about where their property boundary is, and each claims to own a particular strip of land. One neighbor's tenant slips and breaks her collarbone. It's not clear whose property she was on when she slipped because of the boundary dispute. To determine which of the neighbors, if any, must compensate her for her injury, the lawyers will have to sort out several issues.

As a class, discuss what some of those issues may include.

√ ***Note:*** The rest of this chapter deals with a more basic legal property issue: What exactly is owned when a person owns property? This is an important concept because it has significant implications for buyers and sellers, mortgagors and mortgagees. This goes right to the core of value.

Legal Concepts Affecting Property Value

There are many legal distinctions that can impact property value. Of course, **you should never give legal advice unless you are a lawyer**, but it is helpful to understand these concepts and how they may affect the value of real estate. Certain things are included with property: Real property and personal property, attachments and improvements, real property rights, and appurtenances. These are important concepts affecting real property value.

Real Property or Personal Property

The law classifies all property as either real property or personal property:

- **Real property** is defined as *the physical land and everything attached to it, plus the rights of ownership (bundle of rights) in real estate.* Real property is also called **realty**.
- **Personal property** is defined as *tangible items not permanently attached to, or part of, real estate.* Personal property is also called **personalty** or **chattel**.

People tend to think of the land itself when they hear the term "real property." The term refers to much more than rocks and dirt, however. It also encompasses items attached to the land (attachments or improvements), rights that go with ownership of the land (appurtenances), and limitations on the use of land (public and private restrictions). These are important because mortgage professionals must be aware of real property issues and distinctions that may impact value for property being considered as collateral for a loan.

The distinction between real property and personal property becomes important whenever the ownership or possession of land is transferred. Unless otherwise agreed, the law says that all of the real property is included in the transfer, but personal property that happens to be on the land—but is not permanently attached to the land—is *not* included. Because of this legal doctrine, buyers and sellers, landlords and tenants, and owners and foreclosing lenders often disagree about whether something is real property or personal property. Determining what is personal property and what is real property can sometimes lead to serious disputes and court battles.

Case in Point

A built-in dishwasher would be considered part of the real property; a refrigerator would more likely be considered personal property. Built-in bookcases are considered real property; a sofa is personal property. An in-ground pool is real property, but an above ground pool is personal property. Lenders must be aware of this because the presence or absence of built-in items might affect the value of the property; but personal property items should not influence value.

One less clear-cut example to contemplate is a chandelier. A light fixture that is attached to the ceiling would normally be considered part of the real property. It's not uncommon, however, for homeowners to want to take such items with them when they move. Fixtures may be detached from real property through the process of **severance**, becoming personal property again. As you can imagine, this can create serious disputes in a real estate transaction, even if the seller replaces the chandelier with some other light fixture before closing. When one person considers an item to be personal property and another person thinks it is real property, trouble arises. To avoid this, the purchase contract should specifically list any questionable items to make sure everyone knows what is and isn't intended to be part of the sale.

Attachments

Attachments are *things connected to the land, whether natural or man-made.* All attachments are generally considered real property. Attachments both grow on the land (trees and shrubs) and are built on the land (houses and fences). Natural attachments that grow on the land are treated essentially the same way, whether naturally occurring or planted. Both types of natural attachments are ordinarily considered part of the real property while they're growing, but when they are severed from the land, they become personal property. For example, timber growing in a wooded area of the land is part of the real property. Once the timber has been cut down, however, it's personal property. The same concept applies to crops: Apple trees are real property; harvested apples are personal property.

Fixtures

Fixtures are *man-made attachments.* They include any item of personal property attached to or closely associated with real property in such a way that it has legally become part of the real property. For instance, an air conditioner is personal property, but it becomes a fixture when it's permanently installed in a building. A window air conditioner, on the other hand, is more likely to be personal property. A pile of lumber is personal property, but it's turned into a fixture when it's used to build a barn. A *major fixture that impacts the value of the property (such as a building)* is commonly called an **improvement**. When present, an improvement becomes the focal point of an appraisal.

Trade Fixtures

Trade fixtures are *any equipment or personal property a tenant installs for business purposes.* Generally, a tenant is allowed to remove trade fixtures before a lease ends (unless a written document, such as the lease, forbids it). Thus, a tenant who opens a pizza shop can remove the ovens, even though they're attached to the floor, but the tenant must repair any damage caused by the removal.

Annexation

Annexation is the *legal term for attaching or affixing personal property to real property.* Since fixtures and improvements are part of the land, they generally need not be mentioned in the purchase agreement. They are included by implication in the description of the real estate. Trouble can arise, however, when one encounters questionable items that could be classified different ways depending on who is asked and the interests of the parties involved.

Legal Considerations

The legal aspects of what makes something real property versus personal property can be distilled down to two basic questions which most courts consider:

1. What was the intention of the annexer?
2. What was the purpose of the annexation?

The **annexer** is *the person who owned the item as personal property and brought it onto the real property.* Did the annexer intend for the disputed item to become part of the real property, or to remain personal property? Did the annexer acquire the item to improve the real property, or just for personal use?

In answering these questions, the court will look for objective evidence of the annexer's intent. It's not enough for the annexer to claim that he or she always intended to remove the item. The court looks at the nature of the item and the manner of annexation as objective evidence of intent. For example, embedding a birdbath in concrete shows intent to make it a fixture; simply setting one out on the lawn does not.

The original rule was that if the item was securely attached to the real property (e.g., nailed down), then it was considered a fixture. If it wasn't securely attached, then it wasn't a fixture. This test isn't rigidly applied today. Physical attachment is still taken into account, but it isn't decisive. Consider a rug in the foyer of a home. Even if the owner tacked it down to keep it from sliding, it could still be considered personal property if the owner never meant for the rug to stay with the house.

At the other end of the spectrum are personal property items that are so closely associated with the house they become real property items, even though they may not be physically attached to the house. Some examples include the keys to the house and garage door openers. Another unusual circumstance may be a built-in appliance that is at the repair shop on the day of closing. The buyer still takes possession of the built-in item even if it is not physically in the house at the time of closing.

When disputes arise, the courts also take into account the relationship of the parties involved. Buyers are generally favored over sellers (because the item may have induced the buyer to make the purchase), lenders over borrowers (so as not to diminish the value of the lender's collateral), but tenants over landlords (because courts recognize that personal property items are installed for personal or business use rather than for the benefit of the property).

The Uniform Commercial Code

The **Uniform Commercial Code (UCC)** is a *comprehensive code governing, among other things, transactions involving personal and real property.* The UCC is a model code that has been enacted in some form or another by all 50 states. It supports the concept that personal property becomes realty when any of the criteria for fixtures is met. Therefore, the UCC and its procedures may be able to protect the vendor of the personal property, the new owner of the property, the lender, and the seller, by fixing the rights of each at the time of the sale regarding the item to be affixed.

Suppose, for example, someone purchases a home with a new furnace. It is clear from any test that this furnace is a fixture, that is, part of the house. At one time, however, it stood on a showroom floor or was crated in a box in a warehouse as personal property. Let's assume that at the time the furnace was purchased, the owner entered into an installment contract to pay for the furnace, and that it was not completely paid off when that person sold the home. The seller of the home assumes that the new buyer will have to pay for the furnace, since the buyer bought the furnace as part of the real estate. The vendor's contract, however, is with the seller. But the seller has moved and, perhaps, is no longer in the area.

The vendor could decide to file suit to seek satisfaction from the seller or from the buyer. Depending on the laws of his state, the vendor might instead be able to file a mechanic's or materialman's lien against the property, which would also burden the new homeowner.

The UCC addresses situations like this by requiring vendors to file a financing statement with the county recorder where the property is located when installing fixtures such as a furnace. This fixture filing is intended to make the resolution less contentious because it would include a legal description of the land as well as the name and address of the landowner. The homebuyer would, therefore, be on notice of the debt, and the seller might not be able to convey marketable title without first paying for the furnace. It makes it more likely that the vendor will not have to chase the parties in litigation. This also gives the lender public notice of any potential disputes. Vendors who fail to file in a timely manner could lose their rights against the owner in cases like the one just described.

Real Success

As a mortgage professional, you must be aware of potential areas of dispute as they may impact the value of the collateral property, especially when foreclosure is necessary. If items are to be included or excluded, that fact should be clearly stated in the purchase contract. While the inclusion of personal property items (such as appliances) would likely not increase the value of real property, any real property items that are being excluded may have a negative impact on valuation, for example, built-in bookcases removed by the seller.

If a dispute arises, the courts will look at some of the criteria just mentioned in deciding the case. One criterion that is rarely considered, though, is the value of the item. Furthermore, a written agreement between the parties, such as a purchase contract, will almost always be enforced by the courts.

Real Property Rights

Real property rights are defined in terms of a bundle of rights. The **bundle of rights** refers to *all real property rights conferred with ownership.* These rights include, but are not limited to these:

- The **right of possession** gives the owner the right to physically occupy the land and to use the land and make it productive. Owners can use the land in any way they want—as long as it is legal and does not interfere with other people's rights (or government restrictions).
- The **right of enjoyment** confers upon the owner the freedom to use the land without undue interference from the outside. This also includes the responsibility to ensure that neighbors' enjoyment of their land is not adversely affected.
- The **right of disposal** confers upon the owner the ability to transfer all or some of the bundle of rights to others. A landowner normally has the right to sell the land, divide and retain part while selling the rest, lease the land, give it away, bequeath it upon death, or dispose of the land in some other way.
- The **right of exclusion** allows the owner to stop others from using the property or even from entering the property.
- The **right of control** allows the owner to *physically alter or change the property.* For example, a property owner can build a garage, tear down a fence, put in a swimming pool, etc. (Of course, there could be zoning issues related to this.)

If someone secures the entire bundle of rights, that person is said to be the owner. This type of ownership is called fee simple. **Fee simple** is the *greatest estate one can have in real property.* It is freely transferable and inheritable—and of indefinite duration—with no conditions on the title.

Appurtenances

Appurtenances are *rights that go with real property.* When real property is sold, appurtenant rights are ordinarily sold along with it. They can, however, be sold separately, and may be limited by past transactions. In addition to knowing the boundaries of the land and which items are considered part of the real property, lenders also need to understand which rights are being transferred along with that parcel of real estate.

Fee simple ownership includes such appurtenances as *access rights, surface rights, subsurface rights, mineral rights, some water rights, and limited air rights.* One way to understand the rights that accompany real property is to imagine the property as an inverted pyramid, with its tip at the center of the earth and its base extending out into the sky. An owner has rights to the surface of the land within the property's boundaries, plus everything under or over the surface within the pyramid. This includes oil and mineral rights below the surface, and certain water and air rights. (States differ in how they confer water rights; air rights are limited to allow for air traffic.)

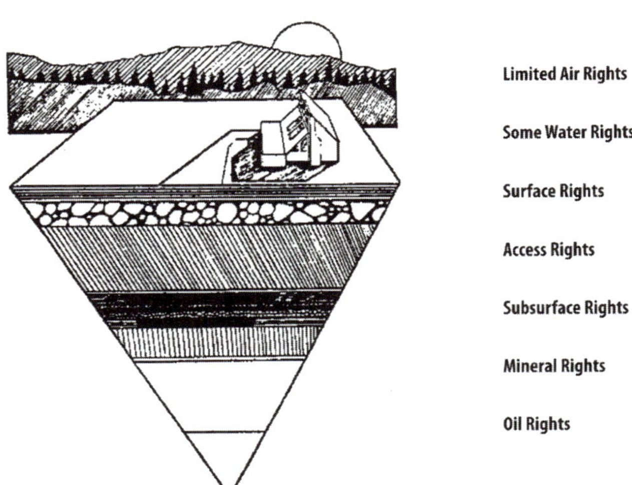

Figure 9.1: The Inverted Pyramid: A Summary of Appurtenances.

It's possible, though, for the owner to transfer only some of the rights of ownership to another person. For example, a property owner may sell the mineral rights to a piece of property, but keep ownership of the farm. Later, when the land is sold, the mineral rights will most likely stay with the mining company (depending on the wording of the contract involved), even though the rest of the bundle of rights in the land is transferred to the new owner. The new owner is limited by the past transaction of the previous owner, and may not sell these mineral rights to another party, nor transfer them in a future sale of the land.

A lender must know if the entire bundle of rights is being transferred (fee simple) or if there are restrictions or past transactions that may limit the current transfer of ownership in any way. This is important because it may have a great effect on the value of the real property. Transfer of access rights for a sidewalk to be placed across the front of a subdivision lot generally would not have a significant impact on the value of a piece of land. Transfer of mineral rights to a mining company, as in the previous example, likely would impact the value.

Public and Private Restrictions

We have discussed real property rights as a bundle of rights conferred with ownership. If one secures the entire bundle of rights, then that person is said to be the owner. It's important to realize, though, that these rights are not absolute. We talked about the owner's ability to sell some of these rights separately. In this section, we'll discuss other ways that those real property rights can be restricted—voluntarily or involuntarily—by government and the private sector. These restrictions may or may not have an impact on real property value.

Public Restrictions

Public restrictions on land use are imposed by government in a variety of ways, and for a variety of reasons. These government restrictions can have a serious impact on land's value. Governments have four powers (remember P E T E):

- Police power
- Eminent domain
- Taxation
- Escheat

Police Power

Police power is *the constitutional power of state (and local) governments to enact and enforce laws that protect the public's health, safety, morals, and general welfare.* From the lender's standpoint, the most important restrictions that government can place on land come from its police power, which can take the form of land use controls (primarily zoning laws and building codes) and environmental protection laws.

- **Zoning Laws.** Zoning laws are local ordinances dividing a city, county, etc., into zones, allowing different types of land use in different areas. Zoning and other laws restricting land usage (e.g., building codes) are passed to protect the health, safety, and welfare of the community. Land use controls have an impact on real estate since they may limit development, thus affecting property values. Land may be more valuable with an office building instead of a house, but zoning laws may not permit that land use. Other zoning ordinances may also restrict how and where the building may be constructed on the property, minimum lot size, building height limits, setback and side yard rules, permitted building density, off-street parking requirements, and other things that a local government may feel are necessary. Exceptions to zoning laws are possible, but often not easily obtained.
- **Building Codes.** Building codes set construction standards, requiring builders to use particular methods and materials. A local government usually has many building codes including fire, plumbing, electrical, etc. In most states, minimum building standards are set by state law, but a local government can require additional, stricter standards. The lender must consider whether the proposed highest and best use for the property can be achieved economically, given the applicable building code regulations that must be followed. For example, putting a large commercial building on a property located in a flood plain may require additional foundation support or superstructure reinforcement to keep the building in compliance with state and local building codes. This will add to development costs.

- **Environmental Protection Laws.** Land use controls at state and federal levels are increasing as a means of protecting the environment. Regulations can involve blocking or restricting land use where environmental concerns exist. Sometimes, this conflicts with landowners' usage. For example, land can't be used for a hazardous waste site (or some industrial uses) without government approval. The government also controls land use in protecting wildlife, endangered species, and wetlands. Federal agencies may deem land a safe haven or protected area that can't be developed.

Eminent Domain

Eminent domain is *the government's constitutional power (right) to take (or appropriate or condemn) private property for public use, as long as the owner is paid just compensation.* Eminent domain affects real estate because of government involvement in fair market pricing, and by making adjacent land more or less valuable, depending on a proposed use (e.g., freeway interchange, landfill). Remember, eminent domain is the *right*; **condemnation** is the *action*.

Taxation

Taxation is *the process of government levying a charge on people or items.* Here we are specifically talking about **property taxes** (called *ad valorem* taxes). Low taxes might encourage real estate activity in a certain area, whereas high taxes could have the opposite effect. Similar to the authority to tax, **special assessments** are *charges that may be levied by a government entity only against specific properties that benefit from a public improvement* (e.g., new sewer line, street lights). Although the property benefits, the extra charge could cause buyers to favor other properties that do not have to pay the charge. All of these have the potential to affect the value of real estate in the marketplace.

Escheat

Escheat is *when property reverts to the state after a person dies without leaving a valid will and without heirs or creditors.* (Property also reverts to the state after abandonment.) The reasoning behind this is that since the rights of property ownership are derived from the government, those rights should revert to the state if they aren't assigned to someone else by the owner, or if there are no heirs. The value of real estate in an area can be affected by the actions of the government in disposing of the land or utilizing it in ways that are either beneficial or detrimental to other properties in the area.

Private Restrictions

Private restrictions on land can be imposed by a former owner or developer. These restrictions may or may not have an impact on land value, depending on their purpose and severity. The two main types of private restrictions that we will focus on are deed restrictions and easements.

Deed Restrictions

Deed restrictions are *limitations on real property use, imposed by a former owner through language included in the deed.* These may also be called **restrictive covenants**, especially if they are recorded in a later document. Deed restrictions and restrictive covenants that are recorded **run with the land** and are thus *enforceable against future property owners.* Note, however, that deed restrictions and restrictive covenants must touch and concern the land to be legal and binding on future transfers.

Usually these restrictions make a new owner promise not to use property in a particular way. For example, suppose a fast food restaurant decides to build a new location a few doors down from its current location instead of remodeling the existing restaurant. When the land is sold, the company might include a deed restriction prohibiting another fast food restaurant from using that location in a competitive manner. This type of restriction may or may not have a negative impact on value, depending on the dynamics of the marketplace.

CC&Rs

A **declaration of covenants, conditions, and restrictions** (CC&Rs) is often placed in the deed by the original subdivider of land or condominium developer, although it can also be added later. The purpose of CC&Rs is to *keep the subdivision attractive and protect the market value of properties.* Examples include deed restrictions setting a minimum or maximum house size that can be built on the land or prohibitions against certain types of fences. These types of deed restrictions can have a positive impact on value because they promote conformity in the neighborhood. Severe restrictions, on the other hand, can hurt property value, although this is usually not the case with subdivision CC&Rs.

Easements

An **easement** is *a right to use another person's real property for a particular purpose.* Easements can be public (e.g., for a sidewalk) or private (e.g., for access to a landlocked parcel). It's important to understand that easements restrict how a parcel of land may be used because, usually, a structure cannot be put on an easement. The easement creates limited rights for the easement holder.

Easements can be put into a deed before a transfer of property occurs or created separately as an agreement between the parties. A recorded easement (either in a deed or as a separate document) gives notice to third parties and usually causes the easement to transfer with the property. When put into a deed, the easement becomes a restriction, often granting the previous owner or other parties an easement for access across the piece of land being transferred. An easement that *grants access* is referred to as a **right of way** (ROW). Often, an easement across the front of land is held by the government for future road widening or by utility companies for access to power lines. In either case, easements may have a negative impact on value if they severely limit buildable site area.

Interference with Property Rights

Certain activities interfere with a property owner's bundle of rights. To the extent that they are unlawful, the owner may take steps to stop their occurrence. In extreme cases, the lender may also step in to prevent abuse to preserve the property value when it serves as collateral for a mortgage loan.

Trespass

Trespass is defined as *a physical invasion of the land by another person who has no lawful right to enter the land.* Trespass interferes with the owner's possessory interest in the land, diminishing the owner's rights of use and enjoyment, since during the trespass, the landowner has less than full possession of it. For an action in trespass to ensue, however, the act of trespass must cause direct, rather than consequential, damage.

Encroachment

Encroachment occurs *when a physical object intrudes onto neighboring property,* often due to a mistake regarding the boundary. Encroachment is a legal synonym for trespass, but the term is only used in reference to objects, such as buildings, whereas trespass refers to people. Thus, if a neighbor's building is built over your property line, that neighbor's building encroaches on your land. Legal steps can be taken to either force the encroaching landowner to remove the encroachment by tearing down the building, or buy the land on which the encroachment sits.

Real Success

One way that lenders try to preempt trouble created by encroachments is to find out about them before the loan is made. A **location survey** simply *determines whether the property's buildings encroach onto adjoining property, or any adjoining property's buildings encroach on the subject property.* The exact boundaries of the property aren't certified by a location survey, but this type of survey is often required for the secondary mortgage market. If an encroachment is found, then the lender might request a written easement be executed and filed as a condition of granting the mortgage loan. (A location survey is different from a traditional survey or pin survey, which is a much more expensive process of physically determining the size and/or boundaries of property.)

Nuisance

Nuisance involves *interference with the quiet enjoyment of the land from the outside, so it does not interfere with possessory rights.* This, by definition, requires that the nuisance originate from another person's property. You cannot be a nuisance to yourself, only to neighbors. And *a nuisance that is more or less permanent* is referred to as **external obsolescence**, and can affect property values in the entire neighborhood, such as noise from an airport or the stench from a factory or farm. Both would tend to hurt property values by making property less desirable, less valuable, and contribute to the decline of a neighborhood. Further, implicit in the definition of a nuisance is that it cannot contribute to a neighborhood or property values in a positive way.

To be actionable, a nuisance must be more than a single occurrence. It must be a condition that constitutes an unreasonable use of the land by the offending landowner over a period of time. Should the complaining landowner prevail in court, he or she may collect damages as well as enjoin (stop) the unreasonable use of the land through an injunction.

Normally, courts take a dim view of actions in nuisance where the offended landowner moved into the area with knowledge of the nuisance. Thus, a landowner offended by the smells of the stockyards situated a few blocks away will find it hard to sustain an action in nuisance. Furthermore, where the common good would be served better by not disturbing the offending use, the offended landowner may not win in court. A factory built in an area of high unemployment would probably be protected against landowners claiming that the smoke is a nuisance.

Waste

Waste is *use or abuse of property in any way that would permanently damage or reduce its market value.* Typically, the property owner is contractually obligated in the mortgage to take steps to preserve the property and prevent waste. The mortgage clause that explicitly states this contains many other provisions, such as a promise to maintain adequate insurance coverage for the property. There are similar legal obligations in place to preserve property when more than one person or entity has an interest in the property.

Chapter 9 Summary

1. **Civil law** is the body of law concerned with the rights and liabilities of one individual in relation to another. Contracts, torts, and property are the fundamental concepts of civil law. A contract is an agreement between two or more parties to do, or not do, a certain thing. **Contract** law concerns voluntarily assumed duties. A **tort** is a breach of the standards of reasonable conduct imposed by law that causes harm to another person. Tort law concerns the duties of reasonable conduct imposed by law. **Property** is something that is owned, real or personal, and includes the rights of ownership in that thing. The rights of ownership allow the owner to use, possess, transfer, or encumber the property owned. Property law concerns the rights and duties inherent in ownership.
2. **Real property** is land and everything attached or appurtenant to it. Real property rights are defined in terms of a bundle of rights that are conferred by ownership. These rights are the right of use, the right of enjoyment, the right of disposal, and the right of exclusion. If one secures the entire bundle of rights from another, that person is said to be the owner.
3. **Attachments** to real property are part of the real property. The two types of attachments are natural attachments, such as plants and trees, and man-made attachments, such as fences or buildings. Man-made attachments are called **fixtures**. A major fixture, such as a building, is called an **improvement**. Unless otherwise agreed, attachments are transferred along with the land; personal property is not. Difficulties can arise over what is considered real property and what is considered personal property.
4. A **fixture** is an item of personal property that has been attached to or closely associated with real property in such a way that it has legally become part of the real property. In deciding whether an item is a fixture, a court tries to determine the intention of the annexer, the nature of the item, the manner of annexation, the purpose for which it was annexed, the relationship of the parties, and any written agreement. Written agreements always take precedence. **Trade fixtures** are an exception to the general fixture rules. Since they are installed by a tenant for use in business, trade fixtures generally may be removed when the lease period is over.
5. Public and private restrictions on land can affect value. Public restrictions include four powers of government: **Police power, eminent domain, taxation**, and **escheat** (P E T E). Government restrictions via police power that can impact land value include zoning, building codes, and environmental laws. Private restrictions on ownership are deed restrictions (restrictive covenants, CC&Rs) and easements. They are often used by the original subdivider, but can also be added later.
6. An **appurtenance** is a right that goes along with or relates to real property, including air, water, mineral, and support rights. These rights are ordinarily transferred with the land, but they may be severed from it and sold separately. Trespass, encroachment, and nuisance are three kinds of interference with these rights. **Waste** is use or abuse of property in any way that would permanently damage it or reduce its market value. This will likely be limited by the lender in the mortgage documents.

Chapter 9 Quiz

1. ***Which is NOT a primary focus of civil law?***
   A. compensating a tort victim
   B. determining ownership rights
   C. enforcing a contract
   D. punishing a criminal

2. ***In determining whether an item is a fixture, the most important test is the***
   A. intention of the annexer.
   B. physical attachment to realty.
   C. relationship of the parties.
   D. size of the item.

3. ***Trade fixtures***
   A. are considered the landlord's personal property.
   B. are considered real property and can't be removed by the tenant.
   C. can be removed by the tenant before the lease expires.
   D. can't be removed unless the lease specifically states they are personal property.

4. ***Which is NOT included in the bundle of real property rights?***
   A. disposal
   B. enjoyment.
   C. escheat
   D. exclusion

5. ***Which is NOT a police power of government?***
   A. building codes
   B. environmental laws
   C. restrictive covenants
   D. zoning laws

6. ***The government's constitutional power to take private property for public use, so long as the owner is paid just compensation, is called***
   A. condemnation.
   B. confiscation.
   C. eminent domain.
   D. immediate possession.

7. ***Private restrictions on land can include all of the following EXCEPT***
   A. deed restrictions.
   B. easements.
   C. property tax liens.
   D. restrictive covenants.

8. ***An easement granting access to property may be referred to as a***
   A. DHA.
   B. FHA.
   C. POW.
   D. ROW.

9. ***In looking for encroachments, a lender is most likely to order a(n)***
   A. appraisal.
   B. location survey.
   C. survey.
   D. title search.

10. ***A(n) ____________ is something that occurs outside of the property.***
    A. encroachment
    B. nuisance
    C. trespass
    D. waste

10

Chapter 10

Interests in Real Property

In This Chapter

A person who has a property right or a claim against property is said to have an interest in the property. Ownership is just one of many ways that parties can have an interest in real estate. For most of these interests, various legal documents outline the relationships and responsibilities of the parties. An ownership interest is evidenced by a deed, a right to use the land may be shown by an easement, and a lender's financial claim against the title is protected by a mortgage. There are actually many other interests that one can have in real property. This chapter explores various types of real property interests, how they're created and terminated, documents that show their existence, and how they affect property.

At the end of this chapter, you will be able to:

- Distinguish among the different forms of deeds.
- Discuss the purpose of the public records system and the significance of a marketable title.
- Describe the purpose of title insurance.
- Identify alternate ways people can take ownership of real property.
- Contrast freehold and leasehold estates.
- Discuss various types of liens and easements and their impact on property.

Key Terms

Abstractor
Acknowledgment
Adverse Possession
Chain of Title
Clouds on the Title
Co-ownership
Condominium
Cooperative
Deed
Dower
Easement
Encumbrance
Estate
Fee Simple
Freehold Estate
Leasehold Estate
Lien
Life Estate
Marketable Title Record
Possessory Interest
Quitclaim Deed
Recording
Root of Title
Severalty
Title
Undivided Interest
Warranty Deeds

Deeds

A **deed** is *an instrument that conveys a grantor's interest, if any, in real property.* The deed is the document used by the owner of real property to transfer all or part of his interests in the property to another. The deed serves as evidence of title.

Title is *the actual lawful ownership of real property.* Title refers to holding the bundle of rights conveyed. Title is not a document, but rather a concept or theory of ownership. The deed is written proof of the rights conveyed to the owner, but having title to the land is what must be held to actually "own" it. **Equitable title** is an *interest in property created on the execution of a valid sales contract, whereby actual title will be transferred by deed at a future date,* such as at the closing. Having equitable title is *not* the same as having actual title, but the person who holds equitable title still enjoys certain rights and privileges.

Real Success

Much of the discussion about ownership options and deeds involves the practice of law and, thus, is not an area about which you can advise clients or customers, unless you are also licensed to practice law. Still, it's necessary for your professional development and overall knowledge to understand these concepts, since a real estate transaction culminates in delivery and acceptance of a properly drafted deed.

However, it's important to remember that this chapter is intended to be an overview. It should NOT be used as the basis for personal action and is NOT intended as a substitute for competent professional legal advice.

Requirements of a Valid Deed

For a deed to be valid in most states, it must be *in writing* and contain necessary information on its face. In most states, basic requirements for a valid deed are:

1. Competent **grantor**(s),
2. Identifiable **grantee** to whom title will pass, named in such a way so as to reasonably separate this person from all others,
3. Words of **conveyance** stating the grantor's intent to convey the land,
4. Legal **description** of the property being conveyed, adequate enough to distinguish it from all other parcels of land,
5. **Consideration** recited to prove that a sale of land took place, and
6. Acknowledgment **signature** of the grantor, usually before a notary public, stating that the sale of land is a free and voluntary act.

Once the deed is valid, **delivery and acceptance** of the deed, during the grantor's life, will transfer the title from the grantor to the grantee.

Warranty Deeds

A **warranty** deed, in the general sense, is a *deed that carries certain guarantees related to title and the grantor's right to convey title.* Warranties may be very broad or very limited. When a warranty is breached, the grantee has the right to sue the grantor for compensation.

WARRANTY DEED 2922 PAGE 561 FUTURE TAX BILLS TO THE CALHRSA P. ... CO.

COLUMBUS BLANK BOOK CO., COL., O.
FORM NO. L12-9

Know all Men by these Presents

That Ralph B. S. Mowery, Widower 19096

5. Consideration

of the City of Columbus, County of Franklin and State of Ohio Grantor, in consideration of the sum of One Dollar ($1.00) and other good and valuable considerations to him paid by William A. Thompson and Helen Thompson

2. Grantee

of the City of Columbus, County of Franklin and State of Ohio Grantees, the receipt whereof is hereby acknowledged, does hereby **grant, bargain, sell and convey** to the said Grantees William A. Thompson and Helen Thompson

3. Words of Conveyance

their heirs and assigns forever, the following **Real Estate** situated in the County of Franklin in the State of Ohio, and in the City of Columbus and bounded and described as follows:

4. Description

Being Lot Number Eighty-five (85) of CHARLES R. CORNELL'S SUBDIVISION in the said City of Columbus, Ohio, as the same is numbered and delineated upon the recorded plat thereof, of record in Plat Book No. 5, page 48, Recorder's Office, Franklin County, Ohio.

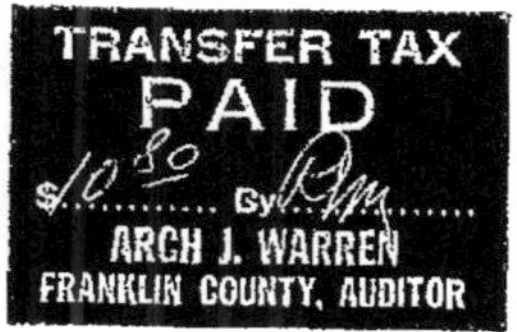

Last Transfer: Deed Record Volume 734, Page 67

To have and to hold said premises, with all the privileges and appurtenances thereunto belonging, to the said Grantees their heirs and assigns forever.

And the said Grantor for himself and his heirs, does hereby covenant with the said Grantees their heirs and assigns, that he is lawfully seized of the premises aforesaid; that the said premises are **Free and Clear from all Incumbrances whatsoever** Except taxes and assessments due and payable hereafter and all conditions, easements and restrictions of record.

Example of a General Warranty Deed. Note that in addition to being a written document, this example contains 6 of the 7 requirements for a valid deed; delivery and acceptance cannot be illustrated here.

VOL. PAGE

and that he will forever **Warrant and Defend** the same, with the appurtenances, unto the said Grantees their heirs and assigns against the lawful claims of all persons whomsoever

In Witness Whereof the said Grantor Ralph B. S. Mowery, Widower has hereunto set his hand, this 27th day of August in the year of our Lord one thousand nine hundred and sixty-eight (1968)

Signed and acknowledged in presence of

C. Richard O'Neil
Robert H. Moore

Ralph B. S. Mowery
Ralph B. S. Mowery

1. Grantors' Signatures

The State of OHIO FRANKLIN **County** ss.

Be it Remembered That on this 27th day of August, A.D. 1968, before me, the subscriber, a Notary Public in and for said county, personally came the above named Ralph B. S. Mowery the Grantor in the foregoing Deed, and acknowledged the signing of the same to be his voluntary act and deed, for the uses and purposes therein mentioned.

6. Acknowledgment

In Testimony Whereof, I have hereunto subscribed my name and affixed my official seal on the day and year last aforesaid.

C. Richard O'Neil
C. RICHARD O'NEIL
ATTORNEY-AT-LAW
NOTARY PUBLIC, STATE OF OHIO

This instrument was prepared by C. RICHARD O'NEIL
ATTORNEY-AT-LAW
2346 N. HIGH ST.
COLUMBUS 2, OHIO

Warranty Deed 19096

MAIL TO

Transferred 19

COUNTY AUDITOR

STATE OF OHIO
COUNTY OF FRANKLIN SS
RECEIVED FOR RECORD ON THE AUG 28 1968 19
day of at o'clock M
and RECORDED AUG 30 1968 19 in
DEED BOOK PAGE
James A. Schaefer
COUNTY RECORDER
RECORDERS FEE $ 2.50

General Warranty Deeds

General warranty deeds are *deeds in which a grantor warrants title against defects that may have arisen before or during the grantor's ownership*. (Also called standard warranty deeds or, sometimes, simply warranty deeds.) A general warranty deed gives the grantee the greatest possible protection. General warranty deeds are the most common for property transfers. Grantor guarantees typically include the following covenants:

- **Covenant of Seizin.** The grantor owns the estate and has the right to convey it.
- **Covenant Against Encumbrances.** The property is free of encumbrances not recited as exceptions in the deed.
- **Covenant of Quiet Enjoyment.** The grantee can possess the land without claims of title from others.
- **Covenant of Warranty Forever.** The grantor will defend the grantee's interest against all lawful claims of title.

Limited Warranty Deeds

Limited warranty deeds are *deeds with which the grantor warrants title only against defects arising from the time the grantor owned the land, but makes no further warranties.* These types of deeds, which may also be called **special warranty deeds**, are common when foreclosed property is transferred to a new owner. With these, the grantor only:

- Guarantees there are no encumbrances that he or she created.
- Promises to defend title against anyone claiming under grantor.

Deeds without Warranties

Deeds without warranties can also transfer title to real property but, with them, the grantor makes no warranties regarding title, nor does the grantor guarantee that he even has the right to convey title.

Quitclaim Deeds

Quitclaim deeds are deeds that convey any interest in a piece of real property that the grantor has at the time the deed is executed. A quitclaim deed makes no warranties whatsoever regarding the title, if any, held by the grantor. It conveys whatever right, title, or interest the grantor holds in the property without representation that there is any interest at all. Often, quitclaims are used to clear up title problems (e.g., a spouse may use a quitclaim deed to release dower interest not conveyed). It may also be used, in the case of a life estate, to deed the remainder interest to a life tenant, creating marketable title by merger.

Bargain and Sale Deeds

Bargain and sale deeds imply that the grantor owns the property and has a right to convey it, but there are no warranties that go with it.

Fiduciary Deeds

Fiduciary deeds, also called **judicial deeds**, are *executed by a trustee, executor, or other fiduciary, conveying property the fiduciary doesn't own but is authorized to manage.* A fiduciary is one in an appointed position of trust and acting on another's behalf. The fiduciary cannot give general warranty provisions, since the fiduciary is acting on behalf of someone else. The only warranties fiduciaries can give, by law, involve their role as fiduciaries, not the condition of title to land. Fiduciaries warrant that they've been duly appointed by a court of competent jurisdiction as fiduciaries, and that the act of selling the land falls within their duties as a fiduciary.

Evidence of Marketable Title

When conveying real property, the seller is generally expected to deliver a **marketable title**, *a title that is free and clear from undisclosed encumbrances or other defects that would expose a purchaser to litigation or impede a purchaser's ability to enjoy the property or to later sell the property easily.* A **title search** of the public records, also known as a title examination, is necessary to *determine ownership and the quality of the title prior to conveyance.* If a marketable title cannot be produced, a closing may have to be postponed.

Public Records

Recording is *the act of filing a document in the county where the property is located so that it will be placed in the public record.* The public records system is a way to provide **notice** so that the public is able to determine who holds an interest in any piece of property. Recording a document is a simple process and requires a fee to the county recorder's office. In most counties, the document is placed in the public record by being electronically copied to a database, but is sometimes photographed onto microfilm. Anyone can view these documents and request a copy. The documents are recorded in the order they are filed. This is very important, since deed priority or lien priority often depends on when the documents were filed. Each document is numbered so it can be located easily.

Recording documents allows property owners to defend their estate, right, or interest against third parties claiming a subsequent interest. Although there is no legal requirement to record a real estate document, such as a deed or title, an unrecorded document is likely to be unenforceable against a third party claiming a subsequent right or interest in the property. In most states, a recorded deed takes precedence over any prior unrecorded deed, and so it is in all parties' best interests to record deeds.

Notice

The concept of *constructive notice* provides this protection. A person is considered to have **constructive notice** of something when *it should be known,* even if it is not. Since the public records are available for anyone's inspection, *everyone is considered to have constructive notice of the contents of recorded documents.* The burden of discovery rests with the general public. Furthermore, the law expects a buyer or lender to search the public record for his or her own protection. This results in **actual notice,** which exists *when individuals have actual knowledge of a fact.* Actual notice includes what someone personally saw, heard, read, or observed.

In addition to actual notice and constructive notice, there's **inquiry notice**. A person has inquiry notice when there's *an indication of a claim or other situation that would alert a reasonable person to a possible problem, causing further inquiry about the title.* If you don't find a claim because you fail to look further, you may still be held to have inquiry notice of a claim. Also, when someone is in possession of land, a buyer is held to have inquiry notice of the possessor's claim, even if the buyer never visited the land, which is why land should not be purchased sight unseen.

Class Activity: Notice

Property owner Mary grants an easement across her land to Bill, so Bill records the easement document. Mary then sells her land to Joe. Joe claims he doesn't have to honor the easement since he couldn't tell it existed by looking at the land, and Mary never told him about it.

Is this a valid easement?

Abstract of Title

To perform a title search, a **title abstractor** will examine the public records for deeds, taxes, special assessments, liens, judgments, mortgages, and other encumbrances that have ever affected the property, even if the encumbrance has been removed or satisfied. The resulting **abstract of title** is *a chronological history of title to a property, listing all recorded documents that affect the title, as well as all public records searched, or not searched.*

An abstract of title does *not* ensure the validity of the title, and there is no guarantee associated with this type of title evidence, so the homeowner or lender does not have any recourse if title defects are discovered later.

Chain of Title

The **chain of title** is a *clear and unbroken chronological record of the ownership of a specific piece of property.* Tracing the chain of title simply means tracing the successive conveyances of title, starting with the current deed and going back a suitable number of years. Each owner is linked to the *previous* owner and the *subsequent* owner through deeds, forming a chain of title as disclosed in the public records.

A *gap or flaw in the chain of title* creates uncertainty, which is referred to as a **cloud on the title.** A cloud on the title could be something simple. For example, Sue Jones buys a house; she gets married and is now Sue Smith. When she sells the house, the grantor name on the deed is Sue Smith. This creates an ambiguity in the title.

A **suit to quiet title**, also called a quiet title action, may be required to close any missing links and remove the cloud on the title. This is a *lawsuit filed to determine and resolve problems of instruments conveying a particular piece of land.* The purpose of this suit is to clear a particular known claim, title defect, or perceived defect. To close the gap and clear the cloud on the title, the court may issue a quitclaim deed or a judicial deed.

A *deed that falls outside of the chain of title* is said to be a **wild deed**. Buyers and lenders are not generally held to have constructive notice of wild deeds.

Class Activity: Recording Deeds

Ann buys a house and records her deed. Later she sells the house to Bob, who does not record his deed. Bob sells the land to Curt, and Curt records his deed promptly. Now there's a break in the chain of title—the record shows only Ann's deed and Curt's deed, but the link between them (Bob's deed) is missing.

Whose deed, if anyone's, is wild? Curt's deed wild

Ann is aware that Bob never recorded his deed and decides to sell the same property a second time. This time she sells it to Dan. Dan doesn't know about Bob or Curt, so he has no reason to look up those names in the grantee/grantor index. He looks up Ann's name in the index, and as far as he can tell from the record, she still owns the property. So, Dan buys the house.

Does Dan have constructive notice of Curt's interest?

Dan does not

Marketable Title Act

About half of the states have some equivalent of a **marketable title act**, a law which is *intended to improve the marketability of title and simplify the title search process by extinguishing certain old claims against a title.* Generally speaking, a marketable title act is designed to assure a title searcher who has found a chain of title starting with a document at least 40 years old that he need search no further back in the record to establish **marketable record title.** The **root of title** is the deed or other title transaction in the chain of title which was the *most recent to be recorded as of a date 40 years before the time marketability is being determined.*

Class Activity: Marketable Title

For example, a title researcher in 2011 finds six recorded deeds on a particular parcel of land:

July 12, 1889:	Grantor, U.S. Land Office	>	Grantee, Robert Brown
March 5. 1934:	Grantor, Robert Brown	>	Grantee, Lyle Baxter
June 21, 1956:	Grantor, Lyle Baxter	>	Grantee, Peter Jones
April 4, 1989:	Grantor, Peter Jones	>	Grantee, Margaret Headley
June 14, 2005:	Grantor, Margaret Headley	>	Grantee, Denise Russell

Which is the root of title?

Does Denise have marketable record title?

√ ***Note:*** The marketable title act in some states may not use a 40-year benchmark and could require either less or even a farther look back. Regardless of the state law, many attorneys prefer a title search of 60 years or more.

The Torrens System

Some states use the **Torrens System** of title registration, which is *an alternative to the recording system*. To use the Torrens System, an owner registers land with the state Torrens registrar. A careful title search and survey of the land are performed, and a Torrens certificate is issued. The original certificate is kept in the registrar's office, and the property owner receives a duplicate. When the owner sells the property, the duplicate certificate must be surrendered to the registrar.

Once land has been "Torrenized," no deed, mortgage, lien, easement, or other encumbrance has any legal effect unless it's registered with a Torrens registrar. If a lien is recorded and not registered, the lien has no effect. A buyer or lender can check title status with the Torrens register, with no need to search public records. Despite its convenience, the Torrens System is rarely used because it is expensive.

Title Insurance

Title insurance *protects lenders (and sometimes property owners) against loss due to disputes over ownership of a property and defects in the title not found in the search of the public record.* Further, title insurance protects lenders and property owners from claimants not listed in the insurance policy, including defects in the public record such as forged documents, improper deeds, undisclosed heirs, errors in a property's legal description, and other mistakes. Title insurance does not generally cure defects, although a title company could potentially purchase the property and fix the problem. More commonly, it simply insures against losses (up to the coverage amount specified in the policy) due to title defects *other than those specifically excluded.* It may require the title company to go to court if necessary and defend its policyholder against any claim against the ownership of the land.

When considering title insurance, the abstract, chain of title, and any pertinent documents may be examined by the title company or perhaps by an attorney who issues a **letter of opinion** regarding the quality of the title. This process is to identify any encumbrances that must be removed, liens that must be paid, or other issues clarified, in order to deliver good title. Once all of the issues have been resolved, and a check of the public records ensures that outstanding encumbrances have been cancelled, the insurer can issue a policy.

Types of Title Insurance Policies

A title insurance policy, generally paid for with a one-time premium, may have different insureds.

Mortgagee's Policies

The mortgagee (lender) will have a policy to protect its interests in the property. Sometimes called a lender's loan policy, the mortgagee's policy is for the loan amount outstanding at the time a claim is paid. The owner's policies and the mortgagee's policies typically coincide, so the title insurance issuer is not paying twice on the same claim. The existence of a mortgagee's policy helps facilitate the sale of the mortgage to the secondary market.

Owner's Policies

Owner's fee title insurance policies are issued in the name of the property owner. It may be paid for by the buyer or seller as indicated in the sales contract. An owner's policy insures that the title to the property is free from liens, encumbrances, and defects except for those listed as exceptions. It also generally covers losses and damages if the title is unmarketable or if there is no right of access to the property (this does not necessarily mean simply vehicular access; it could include pedestrian access, water access, etc.). Coverage runs from the time of purchase for as long as the policyholder owns the property, usually with no additional premium. When the property is sold, the new buyer must purchase a new policy and be named beneficiary to collect on a claim from a title defect. An owner's policy does continue to protect the owner who has given a warranty deed, however, if a problem is later discovered which the owner did not cause and about which the purchaser is attempting to sue for damage.

Other Policy Types

- **Leasehold Policies.** A less common type of title insurance is the leasehold policy. Lessees typically obtain this type of insurance when a substantial amount of money is invested in a property, such as for a building owned on leased land.
- **Easement Policies.** Another less common type of title insurance is the easement policy, which *protects an easement owner's interests across another's property.*

American Land Title Association (ALTA)

The **American Land Title Association** (ALTA), founded in 1907, is the national trade association and voice of the abstract and title insurance industry. ALTA members *search, review, and insure land titles to protect home buyers and mortgage lenders who invest in real estate.* ALTA members are in business in most counties across the nation, and most title insurance companies—in addition to abstractors and title agents—hold ALTA membership. Associate members of ALTA may include attorneys, builders, developers, lenders, real estate brokers, surveyors, consultants, educational institutions, computer services firms, and related national trade associations.

The typical ALTA form that is used throughout the country for one- to four-family residences insures against these losses:

1. The title to the property on which the mortgage is being made is either not in the mortgagor's name; is subject to defects, liens, or encumbrances; or is unmarketable,
2. There is no right of access to the land (vehicular, pedestrian, or otherwise), and
3. The lien created by the mortgage is invalid or unenforceable; is not prior to any other lien existing on the property on the date the policy is written; or is subject to mechanic's liens under certain circumstances.

ALTA policy forms also cover the cost of defending the insured against challenges.

MERS

ALTA, along with other participants in the mortgage industry, helped to fund the development of the **Mortgage Electronic Registrations System** (MERS), which registers and tracks mortgage loans electronically. MERS, a privately-held company, asserts that it streamlines the mortgage process by naming MERS as the original mortgagee, thereby eliminating the need to prepare and record loan assignments (*See: www.mersinc.org*). One intended benefit of MERS is to enable settlement agents to obtain timely, accurate, and reliable pay-off amounts and terms without the typical "telephone tag" or the costly and time-consuming FAXing back and forth.

Acquisition of Title

Generally speaking, ownership or title to property can be **acquired and conveyed** through any of these methods:

- **Deed**, which is *a document that transfers ownership of real property*, as when someone sells a house to someone else.
- **Devise**, which is *when real property is transferred after the death of the owner because of a will.*
- **Descent**, which is an operation of law *when real property is transferred to an heir after the death of the owner who leaves no will.*

Title to any single piece of property may be conveyed through any combination of these methods over time. Consider this example: A couple acquires title to property they purchased through the granting of a deed by the seller. When one spouse dies, the surviving spouse owns the property in severalty as an operation of law. When the surviving spouse dies, the heirs acquire title to the property either by devise or descent.

Forms of Ownership

Since deeds transfer ownership, the next logical step is to look at how ownership can be held. Ownership can be divided into two primary forms that describe how the property is held: Ownership in severalty and co-ownership.

Ownership in Severalty

Ownership in severalty, the simplest form of ownership, is a sole form of ownership, meaning that *only one person or legal entity holds the title to that property.* A "person" could involve a single "real" person, or a single legal "non-living" entity, such as a corporation. With ownership in severalty, the owner's interest has been *severed from the interests of all others.*

Co-Ownership

Co-ownership, also known as concurrent ownership, is *any form of ownership where two or more persons share title to real property, with each person having an undivided interest in the property.* **Undivided interest** gives *each co-owner the right to possession of the whole property, not just part of it.* Under the law, any number of persons may join in the co-ownership of real property.

There are three forms of co-ownership: Tenancy in common, joint tenancy, and tenancy by the entirety. A key distinguishing factor is the method in which the ownership interest is passed. The **right of survivorship** means that *the property passes automatically to other co-owners when one co-owner dies.*

Additionally, the presence of several conditions, known as **unities**, will define the form of co-ownership:

- **Unity of Possession.** *All co-owners hold the same undivided right to possess the whole property* (as opposed to a designated portion of that property).
- **Unity of Interest.** *All co-owners hold equal ownership interests.*
- **Unity of Time.** *All co-owners acquired their interests at the same time.*
- **Unity of Title.** *All co-owners acquired their interests by the same deed or will.*

Most states have specific laws that define the forms of co-ownership and how property may be held or conveyed. Make sure that you understand the laws in the states in which you conduct business.

Tenancy in Common

Tenancy in common is a form of co-ownership with *two or more persons having an undivided interest in the entire land, but no right of survivorship.* Tenancy in common is the most common form of co-ownership and requires **only the unity of possession.** Tenancy in common is the only co-ownership that can be owned in unequal portions. When a tenant in common dies, his interest in the property passes to his heirs.

For example, Mike, Dan, and Sam own a farm. Mike has a 50% interest in the property; Dan and Sam each have a 25% interest in the property. Sam can sell his 25% interest to Mary if he wants. When Mike dies, his 50% interest goes to his heirs, not to Dan and Mary.

If language in a deed does not specify a different type of co-ownership, or if the co-owners are not married to each other, tenancy in common is assumed. If the deed is silent as to the interests of the parties, the shares will be equal.

Joint Tenancy

Joint tenancy exists when *each co-owner has an equal undivided interest in the land with right of survivorship.* Joint tenancy requires **all four unities**: Possession, interest, time, and title. A main feature of joint tenancy is that it allows co-owners to take ownership shares of a deceased co-owner automatically. Since survivors take ownership equally and simultaneously, a person can't will or inherit a survivorship estate. For example, Ann, Bob, and Curt take title to property as joint tenants. Each owns a one-third interest in the property. When Ann dies, her interest passes to Bob and Curt automatically, who each now own a half interest.

Generally speaking, when a joint tenant *conveys* an interest, the joint tenancy—and the right of survivorship—ends and the new form of ownership is tenancy in common. For example, Dan, Ed, and Fran co-own a property as joint tenants. Fran sells her share to Gary. Dan, Ed, and Gary are now tenants in common. If Dan dies, his interest goes now goes to his heirs.

Tenancy by the Entirety

Tenancy by the entirety is a *form of co-ownership that involves only owners who are husband and wife with each having an equal and undivided share of the property.* This form of ownership includes the right of survivorship, with property automatically going to the surviving spouse. Tenancy by the entirety requires all **four unities**—possession, interest, time, and title—as well as the **unity of person**, since spouses are considered a single, indivisible legal person. In most states, husband and wife ownership is assumed to be tenancy by the entirety unless specified otherwise in the deed.

This type of ownership can be terminated if:

- Either spouse dies, at which point the surviving spouse becomes owner in severalty.
- Both parties agree to end this type of ownership and both sign a new deed.
- The couple divorces. In most states, after a divorce, the couple owns the property as tenants in common.

Adverse Possession

Adverse possession is a process by which someone may be able to *acquire title to someone else's real property without compensation by possession of it.* Adverse possession laws are designed to encourage productive use of land, with the rationale that it's better to give title to someone who actively uses the land, instead of someone who ignores it.

Acquiring title through the courts to land by adverse possession requires open and notorious, hostile and adverse, and exclusive and continuous use of another's land for a number of years (as specified by state law). These requirements are similar to those for easement by prescription, but the adverse possessor's use must be exclusive (not so for an easement). And an adverse possessor may actually be able to acquire title to the property, not just an easement. Most property can be adversely possessed, except land owned by federal or state governments, municipal streets, and Torrens system registered land.

Possessory Interests in Property

A person with a *property right or a claim against property* is said to have an **interest** in the property. An interest may be an ownership right, a right to use the land, or a financial claim against the title. An **estate** is a *possessory interest in real property*, which entitles the holder to possess the property now (a present interest) or sometime later (a future interest). In addition to being classified as to the time of enjoyment, present or future, interests are also classified as a freehold or leasehold estate.

Freehold Estates

A **freehold estate** is a *possessory interest of uncertain duration*; it may end, but no one knows when. Some events that will end a freehold estate include the transfer of the property to someone else, the death of the owner, foreclosure, and confiscation for back taxes. There are different types of freehold estates: Fee simple, qualified fee, fee on condition, and life estates.

Fee Simple Estate

A **fee simple estate** is the *fullest freehold estate interest that exists in real property.* It is also called fee title or fee simple absolute. A person referred to as the "owner" of land usually holds a fee simple absolute interest. The owner of a fee simple absolute has all the bundle of legal rights. Since the fee simple estate is absolute, this implies there are *no conditions on the title*. It is perpetual, inheritable, and transferable. When a fee simple absolute owner deeds an interest in property to someone else, it is presumed the entire estate is transferred, unless the deed language specifies otherwise.

Qualified Fee Estate

A **qualified fee estate** means that *a grantor puts a condition or requirement in the deed that terminates the estate automatically if the condition or requirement is not met and reverts the title back to the grantor or the grantor's heirs.* This may also be called **fee simple defeasible**. For example, deed language may transfer Ann's land to Bob, as long as the land is used as a park. If Bob uses the land for another purpose, the title to the property reverts back to Ann (or Ann's heirs).

Fee on Condition

A **fee on condition estate** means that *a grantor puts a condition or requirement in the deed that gives the grantor the "right of reentry" if the condition or requirement is not met.* In this type of estate, the grantor (or heirs) has the right to terminate the estate, but this does not happen automatically. For example, deed language may transfer Ann's land to Bob, but if Bob builds a bar, Ann may go to court to regain possession.

Life Estates

A **life estate** is a *freehold estate that lasts only as long as a specified person, the "measuring life," lives.* For example, if Ann owns property in fee simple, she could deed it to Bob for life. Bob then has the right to occupy and use the property for the rest of his life. But when Bob dies, the life estate ends. Life estates are created for a variety of reasons, such as to simplify property division in a will or so property won't have to be probated after death.

The *holder of a life estate* is called a **life tenant**. In a **conventional** life estate, when Ann grants property to Bob for life, the life estate's duration is measured by the lifetime of the life tenant, Bob. A life estate may also be *based on another person's life.* For example, a grantor could deed property to Bob for the life of Curt. Bob's life estate would end when Curt died. This is called a life estate **pur autre vie** (for another's life). Curt is the measuring life.

A life tenant owns an interest in land that can be sold, mortgaged, or leased. But a person can only transfer the interest that he owns. Someone who buys a life tenant's interest only has a life estate; the buyer's interest ends when the measuring life dies. Also, a mortgage signed by a life tenant becomes an invalid lien when the life estate ends, and a lease signed by a life tenant ends when the life estate ends.

A life tenant may not commit an **act of waste** to the property, which means *using the property in a way that damages it or reduces its market value.* Thus, a life tenant has restricted rights of use that are transferred with the life estate.

Dower Rights or Community Property

In some states, **dower** is *a special real property interest the law gives to a spouse as a statutory life estate when a married person owns real property.* Dower rights—usually referencing the wife's rights—attach with marriage for property brought into the marriage or acquired during the marriage. The common law equivalent of dower rights for husbands is called **curtsy** rights, or curtesy rights. These define the rights that a husband has to the property that his deceased wife owned. As long as the married person owns the property, or remains alive, the spouse's dower or curtsy rights are inchoate (pronounced in-KOE-it), meaning contingent, inactive, or incomplete. These inchoate rights aren't possessory, only potentially possessory. Dower and curtsy rights are terminated by divorce, and can't be willed to heirs since this is a life estate interest. Dower and curtsy rights become choate (active or complete) when the owner spouse sells the property without benefit of release, and/or the owner spouse dies before the other spouse. Dower and curtsy must be released in almost all real estate transactions involving married sellers. There's a serious issue of marketable title if there's no release. Even if there's a pre-nuptial agreement, title companies still often require a spouse to release dower or curtsy as there's always a chance the agreement could be declared void in the future. Note that many states have officially abolished curtsy and dower.

In **community property** states, *two people in a marriage are equal but separate partners.* Any property acquired during the marriage is owned equally. Any property or assets acquired *before* the marriage are separate and belong only to that individual. There are some exceptions, such as for property inherited or gifted during the marriage which may belong only to the individual who inherited it. However, keep in mind that there are no two community property states with exactly the same laws on how community property is determined.

Leasehold Estates

A **leasehold estate** is an interest in real estate that *gives the holder a temporary right to possession, without conveying title.* The *holder of a leasehold estate* is known as a **tenant** or **lessee**. The *property owner* is known as the **landlord** or **lessor**. Leasehold estates are created by lease agreements that provide contractual rights and obligations to all parties involved. A leasehold interest is reversionary, meaning that once the lease ends, *possession of the property reverts to the landlord.* There are several types of leasehold estates.

Estate for Years

An **estate for years** is a leasehold estate *set to last for a specific period, after which it automatically terminates.* It is also known as a **term tenancy**. Duration of an estate for years can be any amount of time, even just for one day. An estate for years terminates automatically at the end of the specified rental period and does not require either party to give notice. Unless someone breaches the terms of the lease, neither the landlord nor the tenant can terminate a term tenancy sooner than what is stated in the contract, unless both parties agree. *Ending a lease by mutual consent* is called **surrender**. An estate for years is *not* terminated by the death of either party or by the sale of the property.

Periodic Estate

A **periodic estate** (or **periodic tenancy**) is a *leasehold estate that continues for successive equal periods of length until terminated by proper notice from either the lessor or the lessee.* The term of a periodic estate may be any length of time agreed to—such as week-to-week, month-to-month, or year-to-year—and the tenancy automatically renews itself at the end of each period until one party terminates it. A periodic estate is *not* terminated by the death of either party or by the sale of the property.

Estate at Will

An **estate at will** (or **tenancy at will**) is a *leasehold estate that does not have a lease to specify the termination date and rental period.* Sometimes no rent is paid (e.g., resident apartment superintendent), or the rent owed has no reference to time periods (e.g., "35% of gross profits"). A common example of an estate at will is someone who rents to a family member who occasionally pays rent, but there is no lease agreement. Either party can end an estate at will at any time with proper notice. Unlike the estate for years or the periodic estate, an estate at will *automatically terminates* when either the landlord or tenant dies. Tenancy at will is not recognized in some states.

Tenancy at Sufferance

Tenancy at sufferance describes *possession of property by a tenant who came into possession of the property under a valid lease, but stays on after the lease expires without the landlord's permission.* This so-called **holdover tenant** is not much different from a trespasser, except that he originally had a right to be there. A tenancy at sufferance is ***not a leasehold estate***; however, most leases will contain provisions that address such a situation. For example, the landlord may allow the tenant to remain but at an increased rent. Remember that landlords cannot use force to regain possession of the property; in most states, only a sheriff can physically remove a holdover tenant.

Eviction

If a tenant breaches the lease contract, an owner can choose to terminate the contract by evicting the tenant. **Eviction** is *the forced removal, by legal means, of a tenant and the tenant's belongings from a leased premise.* The key word in this definition is *legal.* This process is known as **actual eviction.** Although the process may be different from state to state, the steps to legally evict a tenant usually involve:

1. A **notice to vacate**, in which the landlord demands the tenant to vacate.
2. A **forcible entry and detainer lawsuit**, which is filed by a landlord to evict the tenant.
3. A **writ of execution**, which is a court order directing a public officer (often the sheriff or marshal) to seize and/or sell property to regain possession for the owner and/or satisfy a debt.

Note that this is essentially the same process that would be followed by the new owner of property acquired through foreclosure if the previous owner refuses to vacate the property.

Ownership by Organizations

Ownership in severalty and co-ownership can be further categorized into ownership by business entities, which include nonprofit groups and other organizations. Depending on its form, a business association may be a legal entity separate from its members or owners.

Sole Proprietorship

A **sole proprietorship** is a *business owned by a single individual (or a husband and wife for tax purposes) in severalty.* With this, the owner is personally responsible for any business debts, and personal assets could be attached in the event of default (except for property that is owned with a spouse as tenants by the entirety). A sole proprietorship can operate under the sole proprietor's name or under an assumed or fictitious name, if registered with the state; for example, Joe Smith doing business as (dba) Smith Realty or Patsy Davis also known as (aka) Patsy Cakes.

Partnerships

A **partnership** is *an association of two or more individuals as co-owners of a business, as specified in the partnership agreement.* For title to real property to be held in the partnership's name, a business name certificate must be recorded in the county where the partnership's principal office is located, and also in the county where the real property is located. The certificate lists the names and addresses of all partners. The partnership agreement will indicate the authority that individual partners may have to convey or mortgage property held by the partnership. The type of partnership determines how much control and liability each individual will bear.

General Partnership

A **general partnership** is *an association of two or more individuals as co-owners of a business where all partners share in the financial liability, both individually and as a member of the partnership.* It doesn't have to be formally organized like a corporation. A group of people running a business may be a partnership without even realizing it. For most purposes, the law doesn't recognize a general partnership as an entity independent from the individual partners, thus for example, all partners share in the financial liability for actions of the other partners.

Limited Partnership

A **limited partnership** is an *association of two or more persons as co-owners of a business with one or more general partners and one or more limited partners.* The rights and duties of general partners in a limited partnership are the same as in a general partnership, but limited partners have no say in partnership matters. Further, the partners' liability is limited to their original investment.

Corporations

A **corporation** is a *legal entity that is created and operated according to the laws of each state.* A corporation could be public (cities, counties, school districts, etc.), private for profit, or private nonprofit. It is regarded by the law as a legal person *separate from the individual stockholders*, and therefore shareholders are not personally liable for the corporation's debts. Within a corporation, property is owned *in severalty* as the legal person. The corporation must pass a resolution authorizing the sale or purchase of real estate. The most common types of corporations are:

- A **C Corporation** must pay corporate income tax. Then when profits are distributed to the shareholders, the shareholders pay income tax on the dividends as well, which leads to a situation of double-taxation.
- A **subchapter S Corporation** functions as a corporation, but like a partnership, it does not pay any corporate income taxes. Instead, the corporation's income or losses are divided among and passed through to its shareholders. The shareholders must then report the income or loss on their own individual income tax returns.

Condominiums, Cooperatives, and Townhomes

Condominiums and other housing alternatives physically and legally combine individual ownership with co-ownership.

Condominiums

Condominiums are *properties developed for co-ownership where each co-owner has a separate fee simple interest in the interior airspace of an individual unit and an undivided interest in the common areas of the property,* which usually includes the land on which the condominium sits; condominium owners generally have no exclusive ownership interest in the actual land beneath their individual units. Common areas are areas of the development that all residents use and own as tenants in common, such as the parking lot, hallways, and recreational facilities. Condominium owners must follow the declarations and by laws set forth by the condominium founder, and maintained and enforced by the owners association. A condominium may be for residential or commercial use.

Each owner may give a lender a mortgage on his or her unit and undivided interest in common areas. Each owner's creditors can claim a lien against that unit and undivided interest. If a lien holder forecloses, only that unit and its undivided interest are affected without jeopardizing the entire condominium. Property taxes are also levied against each unit separately, and thus don't affect the whole property. Owners association levies to pay for common area expenses are divided among unit owners, and can also result in a lien on an individual unit if unpaid. Hazard insurance on the building and the common areas is also paid with the owners association fees, although failure by the owners association to pay the insurance could have negative consequences for the entire development. Individual unit owners must insure the contents of their units, similar to renter's insurance.

When a condominium unit is sold, an undivided interest in common areas and membership in the owners association are automatically transferred, too.

Cooperatives

Cooperatives (or co-ops) *are buildings owned by corporations, with the residents as shareholders who each receive a proprietary lease on the interior of an individual unit and the right to use common areas.* The title to the cooperative building is held by a corporation formed for that purpose. A person who wants to live in the building buys shares in the corporation, instead of renting or buying a unit, and is given a proprietary lease for a unit in the building. **Proprietary leases** have *longer terms than ordinary leases and give the shareholder more rights than an ordinary tenant.*

A cooperative shareholder pays a prorated share of the building's expenses, including property taxes and hazard insurance for the building. If a resident doesn't pay his or her share of expenses, the entire cooperative may be threatened with foreclosure. So, an agreement may provide that a shareholder can't transfer an interest without the other shareholders' consent. To transfer a cooperative interest, a shareholder conveys his or her stock and assigns the proprietary lease to the new shareholder.

Planned Unit Developments (PUDs)

The term **planned unit development (PUD)** is often used to define a *special type of subdivision that may combine nonresidential uses—for example, commercial or recreational—with residential uses, which could be single-family homes or some form of co-owned property.* PUDs may depart from ordinary zoning and subdivision regulations. For example, the homes in a PUD may be clustered together on smaller lots than generally allowed in order to maximize common green space. Unlike condominium owners, property owners in a PUD generally own the land beneath their individual units. PUDs generally have an association funded by fees from the owners that is responsible for upkeep and maintenance, as well as declarations and bylaws that owners must follow.

Townhomes

Townhomes are *properties developed for co-ownership where each co-owner has a separate fee simple interest in an individual unit, including its roof and basement, as well as the land directly beneath the unit, and an undivided interest in the common areas of the property.* Many townhomes share a common wall. The fee simple ownership may extend to a small patio or lawn outside of the unit.

Townhomes, like condominiums and PUDs, generally have owners associations that propagate declarations and by laws and that assess fees for the maintenance of common areas and other association benefits.

Non-Possessory Interests: Easements

Non-possessory interests are also called **encumbrances**, since they *encumber (or burden) a real property owner's title.* Someone who holds a non-possessory interest has a claim or right concerning the real property, but does not have the right to possess the property. Two types of non-possessory interests detailed here are easements and liens. (Restrictive covenants, which were discussed in a previous chapter, also create non-possessory interests.)

An **easement** is a *right to use another person's real property for a particular purpose.* An easement creates limited rights for the easement holder related to the land surface, its airspace, or subsurface. An *easement that grants access to property* is commonly referred to as a **right of way** (ROW).

Types of Easements

Easements can be **public** (e.g., for power lines) or **private** (e.g., for access to a landlocked parcel) and can be put into a deed before a transfer of property occurs or created separately as an agreement between the parties. Easements are classified according to how the land is burdened and who benefits.

Easements Appurtenant

An **easement appurtenant** involves *two separately deeded parcels that are owned by different parties. This type of easement burdens one piece of land for the benefit of the other piece of land.* Appurtenances are rights that go with real property (e.g., air rights), so an easement appurtenant is a *right that goes with land ownership.* A recorded easement (either in a deed or as a separate document) gives notice to third parties, and so usually causes the easement to transfer with the property, which means the easement *runs with the land.* When title is transferred, the new owner owns the easement or takes title subject to the burden of the easement.

Easements in Gross

An **easement in gross** involves a *specific parcel of land and benefits a person or company* (called the **dominant tenant**), *not a piece of land.* The *burdened land* is called a **servient tenement.** Easements in gross are most commonly held by the government and public utilities for commercial purposes; for example, a utility easement that a power company has to place power lines over someone's property or that a municipality has to place sewer lines under the surface. Easements in gross that belong to companies can be assigned to others. For example, if Phone Company A has an easement in gross to place underground lines, they could assign or sell the easement rights to Cable Company B. Easements in gross can also be granted for noncommercial purposes, for example, an easement that allows access to a public beach.

License or Easement

A **license** is *a temporary, revocable, non-assignable permission to enter another's land for a particular purpose.* A license is *similar* to an easement because it grants permission to use another's property and may be granted for a specific purpose and duration. Unlike an easement, a license does ***not*** create an interest in property and is not considered an encumbrance. Some other differences are:

- While an easement could be for a specified duration, easements are often for an indefinite period of time, while licenses are often temporary.
- Easements are created by written agreement or action of law, but licenses may be created by oral contract.
- Easements run with the land, but licenses do not have to.
- Easements cannot be revoked, whereas licenses may be revoked at any time, except where the licensee makes a substantial financial commitment in reliance on the license.
- A license cannot be assigned and becomes invalid if the licensee dies.

Creation of Easements

Easements can be created many ways, voluntarily or involuntarily. Easements created by agreement of the parties involved must be in writing to be valid. A document granting an easement should be drawn up and signed just like a deed, and should be recorded to ensure that anyone who buys the land has notice of the easement. If the buyer doesn't have notice, the easement probably won't run with the land. Easements can be created a number of ways:

- **Easement by Express Grant.** A *landowner sells land and includes deed language that creates an easement across the land.* This can also be part of the deed transfer or be in a separate document conveying only the easement.
- **Easement by Implication.** *Created by law when land is divided, and there is a long-standing apparent use reasonably necessary for the enjoyment of the land.* This is also called an implied easement. Generally, easement by implication arises when a tract of land was originally held by one owner and divided into two or more parcels. The original owner would keep an ingress or egress, which is a means to enter or exit property.
- **Easement by Necessity.** A *special easement that arises if land would be completely useless without the easement, even if there is no long-standing apparent use.* An example is a **landlocked** property with no access. For a court to assign an easement by necessity, the claimant must prove an easement is strictly necessary (not just reasonably necessary) to use the land; if there is another way to access the land, easement by necessity will not be assigned. This type of easement is not automatic and usually not granted to owners of vacant land.
- **Easement by Prescription.** *Created by open and notorious, hostile and adverse use of another person's land for a specific time, as indicated by state law.* **Open and notorious** use of the land means the use must be obvious and unconcealed, so if the landowner is kept reasonably informed about the property, she would be aware of the use. **Hostile and adverse** is use without the owner's permission and against his interests. If the owner gives permission, there is no easement by prescription. **Continuous use** for specified period of years is required by state law.
- **Easement by Condemnation.** *Occurs through the government's power of eminent domain.* Just as the power of eminent domain allows the government to take title to private property for a public use, the same power allows government entities to impose easements upon private property. These easements are usually for the purpose of future rights of way, visibility, safety, and expansion of existing roadways or utilities and require payment of just compensation to the servient tenant.
- **Party Wall Easement.** *When a wall is shared between two connected properties.* The ownership of the wall is split between the two, and each has an appurtenant easement in the other half of the wall. An agreement should be expressed in writing outlining the ownership of the wall between the two parties. Each owner shares in the building and maintenance costs of the wall.

Terminating Easements

Easements can be terminated in several ways:

- **Release.** A document *the easement holder signs releasing the easement holder's interest in the property.* Easement releases should always be recorded.
- **Merger.** *Uniting two or more separate properties by transferring ownership of all properties to one person.* If one person owns the property, both the dominant tenement and the servient tenement, the easement is terminated by merger. If the land is later divided again, the easement no longer exists and must be recreated if desired.
- **Abandonment.** The failure *to occupy and use property, which may result in a loss of rights.* An easement ceases to exist if the owner abandons it. Non-use alone, however, is not enough for abandonment. There must be an act or statement that clearly expresses the owner's intention to abandon the easement.
- **Prescription.** Loss of easement by prescription occurs after a certain number of years as specified by each state. If an easement owner does not use the property within that timeframe, it can be lost by prescription.
- **Failure or Expiration of Purpose.** An easement terminates when *the purpose for which it was created no longer exists.*

Encroachment or Encumbrance

An **encroachment** is *a physical object intruding onto a neighbor's property.* A driveway that extends two feet over a property line is an example of an encroachment. Another common example is a tree limb that extends over a property line. Although most encroachments are unintentional, they are a form of trespassing in the eyes of the law. If a neighbor sues, the court can order removal of the encroachment or payment of damages to the neighbor by the encroacher, but the owner of the encroached upon property does ***not*** have the right to destroy the encroachment.

An encroachment is ***not*** an encumbrance because it is not a right or interest that is held. However, the encroacher could get an easement from the neighbor to allow the encroachment.

Financial Encumbrances: Liens

A **lien** is not only *a financial interest in property; it is also a financial encumbrance.* Liens are typically security for a debt that gives the creditor, or lien holder, the right to foreclose on the debtor's property if the debt is not paid. In **foreclosure**, the *property is sold and the lien holder collects the amount of the debt from the proceeds of the foreclosure sale.*

Liens against property don't prevent its transfer, but the liens still exist. The buyer takes the property subject to the liens. This means that the buyer takes the property along with the liens, but without being personally liable. The buyer must keep paying the liens to keep the property, but only loses equity in the event of default. The creditor can't go after the new owner personally for these debts because the new owner did not assume the debts. In most real estate transactions, though, the seller must clear the title of liens at closing by paying off the debts. A lien can be:

- **General**, which means it attaches *to all property, personal and real, owned in the county by the debtor,* or
- **Specific**, which means it *attaches only to specific property.*

Liens may also be either voluntary or involuntary.

Voluntary Liens: Mortgages

Voluntary liens are *liens placed against property with consent of the owner.* The most common form is a mortgage or, similarly, a home equity line of credit. **Mortgages** are *written instruments that use specific real property to secure payment of a debt.* Without a debt, there can be no mortgage. A **note**, or promissory note, is *a written, legally binding promise to repay a debt.* The note creates the debt and the mortgage secures payment. A mortgage is a powerful incentive for an owner to pay, since it represents a potential transfer of title to the mortgagee in case of default. **Default** is *the failure to fulfill an obligation, duty, or promise, as when a borrower fails to make payments.* The mortgage instrument itself defines what constitutes default. The most common reason for default is not making payments by the due date, but other factors (e.g., failing to pay property taxes) may also result in default.

The lender is a **secured creditor**, *a creditor with a lien on specific property*, in this case holding the mortgage as security. If default occurs, the lender can pursue judicial foreclosure. **Judicial foreclosure** under a mortgage *may result in a court-ordered sheriff's sale of the property to repay the debt.* If the foreclosure sale doesn't yield enough to pay the debt, a deficiency judgment could result. A **deficiency judgment** is *granted by the courts, and allows the creditor to go after other property owned by the debtor.* It is enforceable and collectable in the same manner as any other judgment at law.

Involuntary Liens

Involuntary liens, also referred to as statutory liens, *arise by operation of law without consent of the property owner.* These liens are created to protect creditors of the landowner. These liens can be general or specific. A general lien attaches to all property owned in the county by the debtor. A specific lien attaches to specific property.

Mechanic's and Materialman's Liens

Mechanic's liens and **materialman's liens** are liens *claimed by someone who performed work on real property and was not paid.* The property serves as security for payment if the property owner does not pay contractors, subcontractors, laborers, or materialmen for improvements to their property. If a property owner does not pay the bills, the holder of this lien can go to court and force the sale of the property to collect the debt from the proceeds according to the particular laws of the state.

Tax Liens

Tax liens are *liens on property to secure the payment of taxes.* **Property taxes** create an *involuntary, specific* lien against real estate. A property tax lien could result from ad valorem taxes assessed by local entities such as municipalities and school districts to raise revenue, or special assessment taxes to pay for specific improvements that only affect specific property owners. Unpaid **federal income taxes** also create liens on real property. Income tax liens are *involuntary, general* liens, and so unlike other tax liens, these can be attached to personal property as well.

Judgment Liens

Judgment liens are liens *against a person's property through court action.* At the end of a lawsuit, if it is determined that one party owes the other money, a judgment is entered. The winner of the lawsuit (judgment creditor) may claim a lien against the other party's (judgment debtor) real property.

To claim a lien, the judgment creditor obtains a certificate of judgment from the court issuing the judgment and files it in the county where the judgment debtor owns real property. A judgment lien attaches to all of a debtor's real property in each county where the certificate is recorded. It is valid for ten years from the judgment date and renewable for ten more years. Judgment liens are *involuntary, general* liens.

Attachment Liens

Attachment liens are liens intended *to prevent transfer of property pending the outcome of litigation.* When a plaintiff files a lawsuit, there is a danger that before a judgment is entered, the defendant may sell all property, making a judgment worthless. To prevent this, at the outset of a lawsuit, a plaintiff can ask the court to issue an order of attachment. The order directs the sheriff to seize personal property or to create an *involuntary lien against real and/or personal property*. A notice of a pending suit, called a **lis pendens**, may also be recorded. Although this is not a lien, it can *serve notice to potential buyers that there is a lawsuit pending*, and the outcome may affect the title to the subject property.

Real Success

Many states have a form of **commercial broker lien law**. With such a law, a broker in a commercial transaction has an automatic lien against a property that is the subject of a contract, for the contracted commission amount. This is enforceable, however, only when the contract is fulfilled and the broker files a lien affidavit in the recorder's office in the county where the property is located. Many states also have laws that dictate the process by which residential real estate brokers may go about enforcing a commission payment. Make sure you know the laws in the states in which you practice.

Lien Priority

It is not unusual for real estate to have several liens against it at the same time (e.g., mortgage, mechanic's lien, and property tax lien). Sometimes, the total owed for the liens is more than the land will bring at a sale, so there is an order of priority for paying off liens after foreclosure. Generally, liens are paid in the order they were attached to the land. An important exception is a **property tax lien**, which is *superior to all other liens*. If the sale of the property does not produce enough money to pay off all of the lien holders, later lien holders may get nothing.

Sometimes a lender is willing to change its order of priority with a **subordination agreement**. With this contract, a *lender voluntarily puts its lien in a lower order of priority*. This is usually done if the lender is sure the property is worth enough to pay off the additional liens *and* the mortgage.

Class Activity: Lien Classification

Individually or as a class, classify each type of lien:

Type of Lien	Voluntary	Involuntary	General	Specific
Property Tax Lien				
Income Tax Lien				
Mortgage Lien				
Mechanic's Lien				
Judgment Lien				
Attachment Lien				

Homestead Laws

Most states have homestead laws that give owner-occupied residences some protection from lien foreclosure, by exempting some of a homeowner's equity in real estate. In some states, homestead protection is limited by statute to a set amount. The exemption may apply only to attachment or judgment liens. (A special homestead exemption may also result in a lower assessed property value for tax purposes for homeowners age 65 or older with limited income.)

Chapter 10 Summary

1. **Deeds** are instruments that convey ownership in real property. **Title** is the holding of rights conveyed. Deed is evidence of title; title is actual ownership. Title is not a document, but a concept or theory of ownership. Seller is the grantor; buyer is the grantee. Valid deeds must be written and have competent grantor's signature, identifiable grantee, words of conveyance, description of property, consideration, acknowledgment, and delivery and acceptance.

2. **General warranty deeds** obligate the grantor to defend the grantee from claims against the title, give the grantee the best possible protection, and are most often used for real estate transfers. Most common deeds without warranty are **quitclaim deeds,** where the grantor conveys only the interest he may have in the property, without warranty that he or she has an interest. Quitclaim deeds are mostly used to clear up clouds on title.

3. **Title insurance** protects lenders and sometimes property owners against loss up to the coverage amount in the policy due to disputes over ownership of a property and defects in the title not found in a public record search. The **American Land Title Association** (ALTA) is a national trade association that provides standardized policy forms used throughout the country for one- to four-family residences insured against title-related losses.

4. Recording documents gives notice of ownership or rights. **Actual notice** is a known fact. One has **constructive notice** of all filings in public records. People have a duty to check public records for real property filings. Many states have a **marketable title act:** Unbroken chain of title back a specified number of years finds the root of title, establishes marketable title. Easements and other rights must be recorded or put specifically in deeds to preserve the rights. **Torrens System** must be recorded with the registrar to be valid (rare).

5. Ownership can be held **in severalty** (one person), or co-owned by two or more persons with each having **undivided interest**: Each co-owner may possess the whole property, not just part of it. Forms of co-ownership are **tenancy in common, joint tenancy**, or **tenancy by the entirety.** Title to real property can be held by associations of individuals: Corporations, general and limited partnerships. **Condominium** units are owned in severalty; owner has undivided interest in common areas. **Cooperatives** are owned by corporation; each shareholder has proprietary lease for one unit. **Adverse possession** is acquiring title to other's real property by open and hostile possession for a specified time.

6. **Estates** are possessory interests in real property, either now or in the future. Freehold estates are of uncertain duration. They are **fee simple** (inheritable, transferable, and perpetual ownership) or **life estates** (possession as long as specified person lives). Fee simple absolute is fullest interest in property. **Defeasible** or **conditional** fee estates can be undone if conditions aren't met. **Dower** or **curtsy** is an interest held by married persons in each other's real property as recognized in some states. **Leasehold estates** give tenants a temporary possessory interest, but they don't hold title. An **estate for years** can be any fixed period of time. **Actual eviction** is the legal removal of a tenant from the property.

7. **Easements** are a non-possessory right to use another's land for a certain purpose. They're appurtenant or in gross; created by express grant, reservation, implication, necessity, or prescription. **Liens** are also non-possessory interests, which are financial encumbrances. Lien holders can **foreclose** on property in the event of default, forcing it to be sold so the unpaid debt can be paid from the sale proceeds. The most common liens are mortgages, tax liens, mechanics' liens, and judgment liens. Usually liens are prioritized (and thus paid out in foreclosure) in the order they are recorded, but property tax liens always have priority. Later recorded liens may not be paid if no money remains after sale. **Lis pendens** is a recorded notice stating that a lawsuit is pending, which may affect title to property.

Chapter 10 Quiz

1. ***A deed is***
   A. actual ownership to real estate rights.
   B. better than title.
   C. a document that must be recorded.
   D. evidence of title.

2. ***A grantor acknowledges a deed before a***
   A. federal official.
   B. lender representative.
   C. notary public.
   D. witness.

3. ***Requirements for a valid deed include all EXCEPT***
   A. an acknowledgment before a notary public.
   B. an adequate description of the property conveyed.
   C. delivery and acceptance of the deed.
   D. the signature of a competent grantee.

4. ***Alice and Conrad bought a house and received a general warranty deed. Later, they discover that the previous owner's wife didn't release dower. What's the best way to correct this?***
   A. The previous owner executes a quitclaim deed.
   B. The previous owner and spouse execute another general warranty deed.
   C. The previous owner and spouse issue a wild deed.
   D. The wife of the previous owner executes a quitclaim deed.

5. ***Documents are recorded to give***
   A. actual notice.
   B. constructive notice.
   C. inquiry notice.
   D. legal notice.

6. ***A Marketable Title Act says that proper title is established by***
   A. adequately searching the public records.
   B. buying adequate title insurance.
   C. making sure that no wild deeds exist.
   D. an unbroken chain of title back a specified number of years to the root of title.

7. ***How many persons may share ownership in severalty?***
   A. one
   B. two, as long as they are married to each other
   C. two or more, as long as there is unity of title
   D. any number, regardless of unity of title

8. ***Which rights are NOT transferred with real property?***
   A. disposal rights
   B. easements
   C. encroachments
   D. surface rights

9. ***Which is NOT an encumbrance on real property?***
   A. appurtenant easement
   B. judgment lien
   C. personal license
   D. restrictive covenant

10. ***In deciding who gets paid from a foreclosure sale, which lien has priority?***
    A. first lien recorded
    B. lien for delinquent property taxes
    C. mechanics or materialmen who file a timely notice after commencing work on the property
    D. mortgagee or original lender

11. ***A non-possessory interest in real property is also called a(n)***
    A. encumbrance.
    B. leasehold estate.
    C. license.
    D. servient tenement.

12. ***Which condition of use is NOT required for adverse possession?***
    A. continuous use for a number of years, as specified by state law
    B. hostile and adverse
    C. open and notorious
    D. permission of the owner

Chapter 11

The Value of Real Estate

In This Chapter

To fully understand real estate valuation, there are several definitions and concepts that are important to know. The seven characteristics of real estate include four value characteristics that all items must have, as well as three physical characteristics that are unique to real estate. This chapter also discusses broad market factors and property-specific factors that can affect real property value. That's followed by the difference between value, price, and cost, before defining market value and the required elements of an arm's length transaction. Finally, assemblage, plottage, subdividing, and frontage as they relate to increasing the value of land are discussed.

At the end of this chapter, you will be able to:

- Describe how several broad factors and specific principles impact the value of property.
- Contrast value, price, and cost.
- Define the necessary factors for an arm's length transaction.
- Identify factors related to subdividing land that impact its value.

Key Terms

Arm's Length Transaction
Assemblage
Conformity
Contribution
Demand
Depreciation
Effective Demand
External Obsolescence
Frontage
Functional Obsolescence
Highest and Best Use
Immobility
Indestructibility
Law of Decreasing Returns
Law of Increasing Returns
Market Value
Plottage
Price

Characteristics of Real Estate

Mortgage professionals possess a broad base of knowledge. Since mortgage loans depend on the value of the real estate as the underlying collateral for the loan, a basic understanding of value and how it applies to real estate is useful. There are seven characteristics of real estate: Four value characteristics and three physical characteristics. All of these are important to real estate value. As we review the seven characteristics of real estate, note that the four value characteristics apply to all products and services, not just land. These must be present in any item for it to have value. On the other hand, the three physical characteristics are unique to real estate. These physical characteristics are what make land inherently valuable.

Value Characteristics

Value is *the amount of goods or services offered in the marketplace in exchange for something else.* For anything to have value, certain value characteristics must be present and perceived by the user and other potential users of the property. All four of these characteristics must be present and in harmony for the item to achieve maximum value. The four value characteristics are demand, utility, scarcity, and transferability (remember D U S T).

Demand

Demand is *the need or desire for a specific good or service,* and is an essential ingredient in creating value. Without demand, any amount of supply is meaningless. Sometimes though, demand can be created simply by lowering the price.

On the other hand, prices can be raised too high even when there appears to be strong demand. High prices cause some people to look for alternatives in the marketplace. This is known as the theory of substitution, which is discussed later.

One final element of demand to consider is a person's ability to pay for an item. **Effective demand**, or purchase ability, means a prospective buyer has enough disposable income available to satisfy her needs or desires. A person may want a million-dollar home, but if she can't afford to buy it, then that person's demand doesn't count.

Utility

Utility is *the ability of a good or service to satisfy human wants, needs, or desires.* Utility is the degree of usefulness to prospective users. For example, there can be demand for housing, but your house must be perceived as useful (e.g., enough bedrooms) to someone interested in buying a house for it to have value to that potential buyer.

Furthermore, if there's no perceived use for something, then there's no perceived value. This is why public and private restrictions on land can impact value. For example, government restrictions on the size and placement of buildings may mean that a certain type of building can't be built on a lot. Any such restrictions can impact the utility, and hence the value, of land.

Scarcity

Scarcity is *the perceived supply of a good or service relative to the demand for the item.* If there's an unlimited supply of something, then it's perceived to have little value. Of course, the scarce item must also be useful (have utility). Scarcity and utility must both be present. Things that are scarce but not useful have little value (e.g., common fossils), just as things may have little value if they happen to be plentiful, even if useful (e.g., air or an abundant source of water).

People generally perceive land to be valuable because there's a limited supply of it. This notion of scarcity feeds the anticipation of real estate buyers who feel they're buying property as an investment that will increase in value. Value is also derived from scarcity due to uniqueness; for example, the fact that there's only one of a particular house in a given location. If people really desire a certain home in a certain location, then more value may be created.

Transferability

Transferability is *the ability to freely buy, sell, encumber, or dispose of property in any way that the owner sees fit.* Property value is derived from the freedom to transfer title readily from one person to another. The fewer restrictions there are on property, the more perceived value it has in the marketplace. If there are conditions on title to land, which restrict its future transfer, a buyer would likely not pay as much for the land (given that ready substitutes exist in the marketplace). Again, public and private restrictions are a factor. If there are any restrictions imposed on transferability, they may decrease the perceived value to potential buyers.

Finally, there's the added requirement that the person receiving the property must have the ability to pay for it. We referred to this earlier as effective demand or purchase ability. Without this, desires and demands go unfulfilled because property won't be transferred to the person who desires it.

Physical Characteristics

Real estate has three physical characteristics that give land some inherent value. These unique characteristics are not present as a group in other types of property. Only real estate has this combination of physical attributes and, as a result, they have the ability to affect value. As we discuss the three physical characteristics of real estate, note how they often intertwine with the four value characteristics.

Uniqueness

Uniqueness is a physical characteristic of real estate referring to the fact that *each piece of land, each building, and each house is said to be a different piece of real estate.* No two are exactly the same (also called non-homogeneity). Even if two houses or two buildings look the same, they are said to be different because of their location. Since more land cannot be created in a given location, this uniqueness leads potential buyers to view land as a scarce commodity. When people want to build in a certain area, they must compete with others for the limited supply of land in that area. Value is derived from this perceived scarcity due to uniqueness.

Immobility

Immobility is a physical characteristic of real estate referring to the fact that *it can't be moved from one place to another.* This is an equal benefit or detriment to all parcels of real estate in the same general area. This immobility of land helps its value in a good market, since other land can't be moved in to take away potential customers (as can be done with other products), but it can also hurt land value in a bad market. Note that customers are somewhat immobile as well. It's impossible to move a house and land from Boston to Chicago where there's a buyer, and usually a person in Denver won't buy a house in Atlanta if that person's job can't move too.

Indestructibility

Indestructibility is a physical characteristic of real estate referring to the concept that *it can't be destroyed.* Thus, real estate is said to always have some minimum value by virtue of its existence. Land is not consumed, nor does it wear out like other goods. But the actual and perceived utility of land can be affected by the marketplace or other forces. Land always has the potential to be useful, but its usefulness, and hence its value, can change over time.

However, the land itself can move or change shape by natural forces, for example:

- Erosion, which is the wearing away of soil due to the action of wind, water, or other forces
- Accretion, which is the addition to land, such as through deposits by water of sand or silt

Property-Specific Factors Affecting Real Estate Value

There are additional factors to consider when valuing a specific piece of property. More or less in their order of importance, these are: Highest and best use, location, substitution, conformity, contribution, and depreciation.

Highest and Best Use

Highest and best use is *the use that is physically possible, legally permissible, most economically feasible, and maximally profitable or productive.* To expand on this:

- **Physically possible** means that any potential use must conform to the size, topography, shape, and other physical characteristics of the subject property.
- **Legally permissible** refers to uses that are not forbidden by zoning or other government regulations as well as uses that are not prohibited by any deed restrictions or other covenants.
- **Economically feasible** refers to the ability to get the best dollar return out of the property without overspending on acquisition and improvements.

Highest and best use may be the most important property-specific factor that an appraiser considers before making a determination of value. As you can see from the comprehensive definition, a number of factors contribute to this determination. Of course, with most houses this isn't necessary since they're in the middle of residential neighborhoods. Highest and best use becomes a vital consideration, though, when examining vacant land or land that has changed zoning since the original structure on it was built.

Highest and best use is such an important and complex topic that entire real estate and appraisal courses are taught on it. For our purposes here, it's important to understand the basic concept. If a house sits on a widened street and is surrounded by commercial buildings, it's very likely that land would be more valuable if it were also put to a commercial use. We must consider other parts of the definition, as well. That is, the zoning laws must permit the intended use and the owner must be able to build the proposed structure on the land. All of these factors must be considered when valuing a piece of real estate.

Location

Location is *the exact position of a piece of real estate.* Location can be talked about with respect to a given neighborhood, and even within the neighborhood itself. It's easy to understand that homes in a growing, popular, and prosperous neighborhood are more highly sought after and valued than those in other neighborhoods. It's also important to recognize, though, that each individual home's location within that neighborhood affects its value. A home on a corner lot, next to the park, or on a cul-de-sac would usually have a higher value than that same home sitting next to a railroad track.

"Best" and "Worst" Homes

An important corollary to the concept of location is the **effect of surrounding homes** on valuation. There are technical terms often used to describe this concept, but you only need to understand the theory. Basically, the theory is that *the value of the "worst" home in a given area is increased by the other homes in the area.* The value of this theoretical "worst" home can only go so low, because the desirability of the other homes in the neighborhood keeps it from falling too far. Conversely, *the value of the "best" home in a given area is decreased by the other homes in the area.* The value of this theoretical "best" home can only go so high, because if the other homes in the neighborhood are less expensive, people that can afford this "best" home will be attracted to other neighborhoods.

For example, if each of the homes in a neighborhood average $200,000, a run-down home in that area, that may only command $120,000 in another area, is helped by the fact that people will pay more than that in this particular neighborhood. The reason being is that they anticipate a higher value for the investment they make by improving the property. Conversely, in another neighborhood where the average home price is $180,000, a much larger-than-average home with a swimming pool and other amenities, that would command $300,000 in another area, is hurt by the fact that people who can afford this home probably want to live in a neighborhood with homes closer to that average price, and they may fear a lower future resale value in the less expensive area.

Substitution

Substitution says that *an informed buyer will not pay more for a home than a comparable substitute.* Although each home is said to be unique, there's a price point beyond which a buyer won't select a particular home. Of course, no one really knows what that point is until trying to sell a home for too much, with no resulting sale. The theory of substitution can also be applied to items within a home. When an appraiser determines the value of a fireplace in an area where most homes don't have one, the appraiser must take into account that a buyer is not going to pay more for that home than for a similar home plus the cost of adding a fireplace. In other words, if a fireplace costs $2,500 to add to a typical home in the area, an appraiser can't justify adding much more than that to the value of a home.

Conformity

Conformity says that *a particular home achieves its maximum value when surrounded by homes of similar style and function.* This applies to neighborhoods as well. Neighborhoods as a whole are more desirable when there is a general similarity in utility and value for all homes in it. This relates to our best/worst home scenario. Most people want to live in areas with like homes. A home that stands out as being too different from the rest is worth less than that same home would be if it were in a different, more homogeneous neighborhood. If too many homes stand out as different, the neighborhood's desirability is hurt, as well.

Contribution

Contribution says that *a particular item or feature of a home is only worth what it actually contributes in value to that piece of property.* Thus, if a five-bedroom home is not desirable, putting an addition onto a house to add a fifth bedroom doesn't increase the value of the home that much. The owner of the house may want or need a fifth bedroom, but he should not expect it to add significantly to the value of the home when it's sold. The value of an item or improvement is only equal to what a prospective buyer is willing to pay for it, not what it actually cost the owner to install or construct it. This is an important value concept for mortgage professionals, especially when evaluating requests for home improvement loans or lines of credit.

Laws of Decreasing and Increasing Returns

It's important to understand the **law of decreasing returns**, which says that *beyond a certain point, the added value of an additional feature, addition, repair, etc., is less than the actual cost of that item.* This is also called the law of diminishing returns. In other words, you can add too much to a property and not be able to increase the price enough to recoup the money you've invested. You may still want or need to do something to the property, just don't expect to get the full cost of the labor and materials back when you sell.

The corollary to this is the **law of increasing returns,** which says that *the added value of an additional feature, repair, etc., is more than the actual cost of that item.* Consider the example of a house in such need of repair that doing anything would have a dramatic increase in its value. Of course you can go too far, and beyond a certain point, you'll be back at the law of decreasing returns.

Depreciation

Depreciation is the *loss in value to property for any reason.* Factors contributing to depreciation can be classified as **curable**, which means that they can be *remedied at a reasonable cost*, or **incurable**, which means that the *cost to remedy the issue would exceed what it contributes to the value of the property.* Depreciation is usually attributed to one of three causes:

- **Physical Deterioration.** *Actual wear and tear due to age, the elements, unrepaired damage, or other forces.* While physical deterioration is usually curable (e.g., replacing a roof, painting), it could be incurable (e.g., severe structural damage due to a flood or fire). Regular maintenance can slow the process of normal physical deterioration.
- **Functional Obsolescence.** Describes a building that is less desirable because of something *inherent in the structure itself,* such as a house with an outdated style, inadequate fixtures, impractical floor plan, etc. This too may be curable or incurable. For example, if adding a second bathroom to a house with five bedrooms results in an increase in value that is greater than the cost of the improvement, it is curable functional obsolescence.

- **External Obsolescence.** Also known as economic obsolescence, occurs when something *outside the control of the property* makes it less desirable. Some examples are the general decline of a neighborhood, loss of an area's economic base, a nearby landfill, or the construction of a new highway that creates noise or re-routes traffic. Other examples could be high tension power lines too close to the property, a railroad adjacent to the property, or perhaps air traffic noises caused by proximity to an airport. External obsolescence is always considered incurable since the property owner cannot remedy it.

Economic Factors Affecting Real Estate Value

When considering broad economic factors, the law of **supply and demand** says that for all products, goods, and services, *when supply exceeds demand, prices will fall and when demand exceeds supply, prices will rise.* This has a very important role in real estate because of the inherent difficulties in adjusting supply and demand. Because of the lag time for market forces (e.g., construction companies) to respond to supply and demand situations, there are often buyer's markets and seller's markets.

Buyer's Markets

A **buyer's market** is a situation in the housing market when *buyers have a large selection of properties from which to choose.* This may be due to population shifts away from an area, overbuilding by construction companies, or bad economic conditions like a plant closing. A buyer's market can be neutralized if some sellers pull their homes off the market. But a glut is a glut, and usually there's downward pressure on real estate values. When more homes are available, the increased supply tends to keep home values lower. Often, in this situation, a buyer is in a position to negotiate for a lower price or more favorable terms of sale.

Seller's Markets

A **seller's market** is a situation in the housing market when *sellers can choose from a large number of buyers who are looking for houses in a particular area.* This may be due to people moving into an area, little building by the construction industry in response to a prior oversupply, high construction costs for labor or materials, good economic conditions like a new plant opening, or lower interest rates. When fewer properties are available, the lower supply (relative to the demand) tends to keep home values higher. Often in this situation, a seller is in a position to stay closer to the original asking price or negotiate favorable terms.

During the lag time for market forces to respond, a supply and demand imbalance can have a real impact on the value of a house, positively or negatively. If the subject home's value is higher than expected because of a housing shortage in the area, this would likely be mentioned in the appraisal. Conversely, an appraiser may have to justify lowering a home's appraisal value because of a temporary glut in the market due to, for example, the closing of a major company that has hurt the economic base of an area.

The real estate market is said to be in **balance** when there are *slightly more homes available than buyers.* This keeps real estate prices in check and curtails the impact of people putting their homes for sale at a higher price to test the market. In fact, the market will determine if the price is too high.

Defining Market Value

Although at times the term "value" seems to be synonymous with "price," these two words actually have very different meanings. **Value** is *what a typical person would pay for something*; **price** is *what one person actually paid.* Price is a fact. Of course, both value and price may have nothing to do with cost. **Cost** is *the dollars needed to develop, produce, or build something.* The value of a piece of real estate should never be confused with its price.

Most residential appraisals completed for mortgage professionals are to determine the **market value** of property. Market value is *the most probable price that a property should bring in a competitive and open market under all conditions requisite to a fair sale.* This is the accepted definition of market value by Fannie Mae and most others in the secondary mortgage market. In fact, Fannie Mae guidelines state that the final value entered on the Uniform Residential Appraisal Report (URAR) should represent the appraiser's opinion of market value.

This is important because lenders can't rely on the hope of future appreciation to secure their current investment. Buyers can do this, though, because they expect to live in the home for a period of time; lenders can't, because they must consider the possibility of foreclosure as a contingency that could occur at any time. If a property must be foreclosed on, lenders want to know what value they can reasonably expect to get from the property. The best estimate for this figure can be derived by analyzing comparable properties that have recently sold in the same area. Recent marketplace activity is the best objective evidence of what a typical buyer would do or pay.

Arm's Length Transaction

The definition of market value talks about a "competitive and open market." This assumes that property is part of a typical "arm's length" transaction. An **arm's length transaction** is *a transaction that occurred under typical conditions in the marketplace with each party acting in his own best interest.* Those "typical" conditions are:

- The buyer paid cash for the property at closing or obtained a conventional mortgage through a lender so as to pay the seller the agreed upon price at closing.
- The seller did not grant any unusual payment concessions, such as owner financing or other payment terms.
- The buyer and seller are not related in any way.
- The buyer and seller are both acting in their own best interests.
- The buyer and seller are not acting out of undue haste or duress.
- The buyer and seller are both reasonably informed about all aspects of the property, its potential uses, market value, and market conditions.
- The property has been available on the market for a reasonable period of time.

All of these factors should be considered when evaluating comparable properties to use when determining a property's value. If the seller was forced to sell because of a lost job, this would tend to lower the selling price of the subject home. Or, if the seller agreed to some type of owner financing, this may contribute to a higher selling price. When such properties are used as comparable sales, an appraiser must take these factors into consideration when making adjustments. A good appraiser makes a serious effort to research all of these factors, takes them into account, and describes any relevant impact on value in the final appraisal report. This is important for determining what a typical buyer would do in a typical transaction.

Making Land More Valuable

Although the focal point of a real estate appraisal is the improvement or structure on the land, the land itself has some inherent value derived from its location and scarcity. This inherent value, though, is only changed by market conditions. Improvements to raw land to make it into a site can add some value to the land, but the inherent value of the land is still the same. And if buildings are added, the value of the real estate is increased, but not the inherent value of the land. About the only way to increase the value of land without waiting for market appreciation is to have more of it.

Assemblage and Plottage

Assemblage is *combining two or more parcels of land into one larger parcel.* This is typically done to increase the usefulness of the land. By allowing one larger building to be constructed on the larger parcel than could have been built on the smaller individual parcels, the value of the land has also increased. In fact, this one large parcel is likely worth more than the sum total of the smaller parcels. This is referred to as plottage. **Plottage** is *an increase in value (over the cost of acquiring the parcels) by successful assemblage, usually due to a change in use.* By creating a larger parcel with more utility and higher and better use than the individual sites, the owner has successfully achieved an increase in the inherent value of the land. Actually, individual landowners can benefit as well.

Let's look at an example.

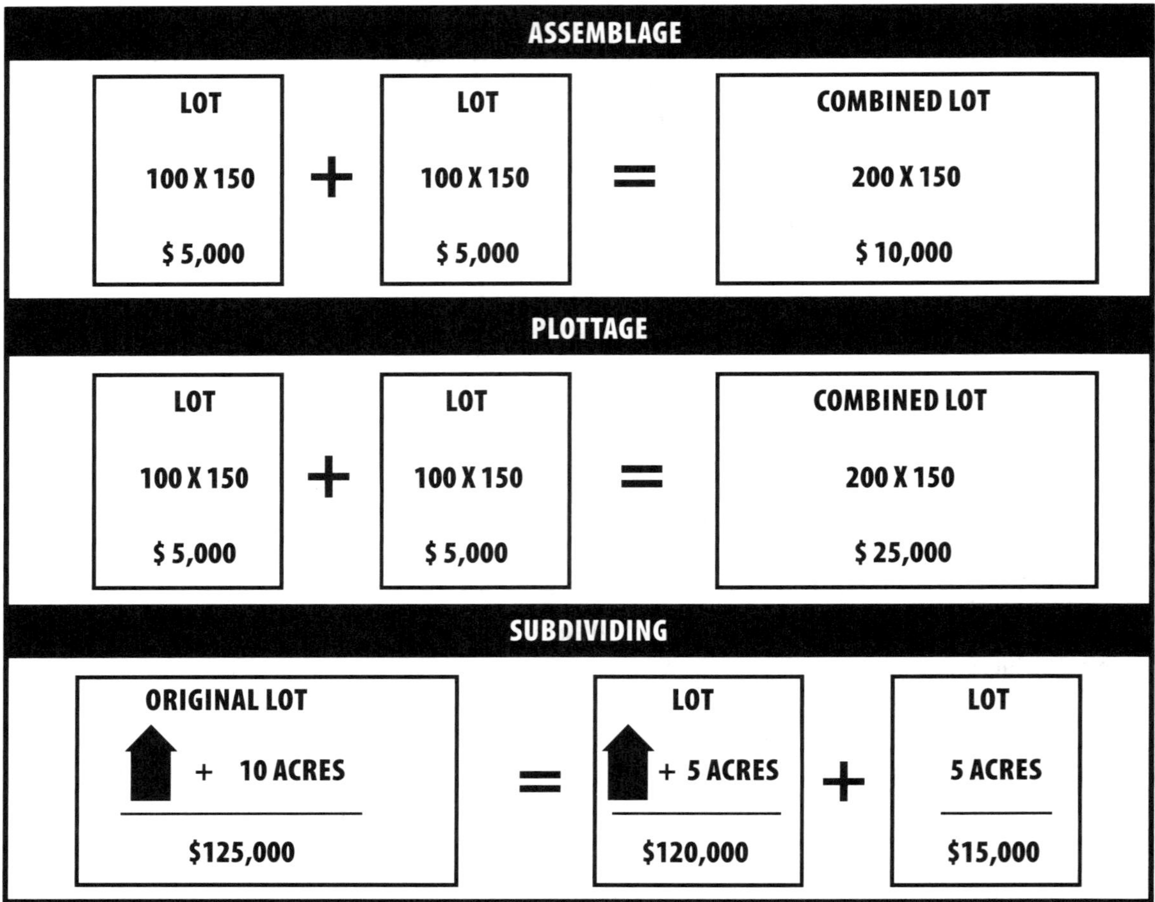

Figure 11.1: Examples of Assemblage, Plottage, and Subdividing.

Class Activity: Assemblage

Mega Company wants to build a new shopping center. They've selected an ideal location where ten homes now sit. Each of those homes is worth about $100,000. Mega knows, though, that the value of all ten parcels together is $2,000,000. Instead of trying to buy each home for only $100,000, Mega is likely to offer the owners, say, $120,000 as an incentive for them to sell. If every home was purchased for $120,000, Mega's total cost would be $1,200,000—much less than the total value of the combined larger parcel.

What are some of the potential pitfalls with this strategy for Mega? For the homeowners? Discuss your thoughts with the class.

Subdividing

There are times when **subdividing** property by *splitting it into multiple smaller parcels* can increase value. Suppose a house sits on 10 acres of land. If the property is not being used for farming or another specialized use that requires that much land, the owner might want to consider splitting it into two parcels: One parcel of five acres with the house and another, separate five-acre parcel. Of course, the specific property and market would need to be analyzed, but it's very likely that the value of the house and five acres would not be worth much less than the house and 10 acres. But now the owner has an additional parcel of land to sell or develop, thus increasing the total maximum productivity and profitability of the land. (Zoning may allow subdividing the land into smaller lots, but many areas require platting and place restrictions on lots of less than five acres, hence this example.)

Value of Frontage

As a correlation to assemblage and plottage, it's important to understand that the addition of some land is more valuable than other land. This is especially true for commercial property, which is compared by the front foot. Adding more **frontage**, which is *the dimension across the access side of a property*, makes land more valuable than adding more depth, even if the total amount of land added is the same. When giving the size of a lot, frontage is expected to be the first number. Let's explain. If a lot is 200 feet by 100 feet, and a person buys another lot that's 100 feet by 200 feet, both lots have the same total area (20,000 square feet). However, the first lot would be worth more because it has greater frontage—and, therefore, access along the road—rather than depth.

Real Success

With commercial properties, frontage is valued more since it is more useful for business purposes. Adding depth still increases the value of the lot, but as the depth of a lot increases, the value per front foot increases at a decreasing rate. If a lot is 100 feet wide and 10,000 feet deep, how much would someone be willing to pay to make the lot 10,005 feet deep? Not much. The total value increase to the lot would be small.

Now consider this, how much would someone be willing to pay for a few more feet of road frontage to that lot that is 100 feet wide and 10,000 feet deep? More than someone would pay for more depth! Remember, our examples are primarily concerned with commercial properties.

Generally, the marketplace does not make the same distinction for frontage when valuing residential properties. An increase in lot size (whether frontage or depth), generally contributes the same amount of extra value to a lot based on the total size of the lot. When comparing two lots that are not the same size, the marketplace ultimately determines how much additional lot area is sufficient to warrant an increase in value. A sales comparison of comparable properties in the market is the best way to determine if a larger lot is worth more, how much more the larger lot is worth, and what amount of additional land is needed for an increase in value.

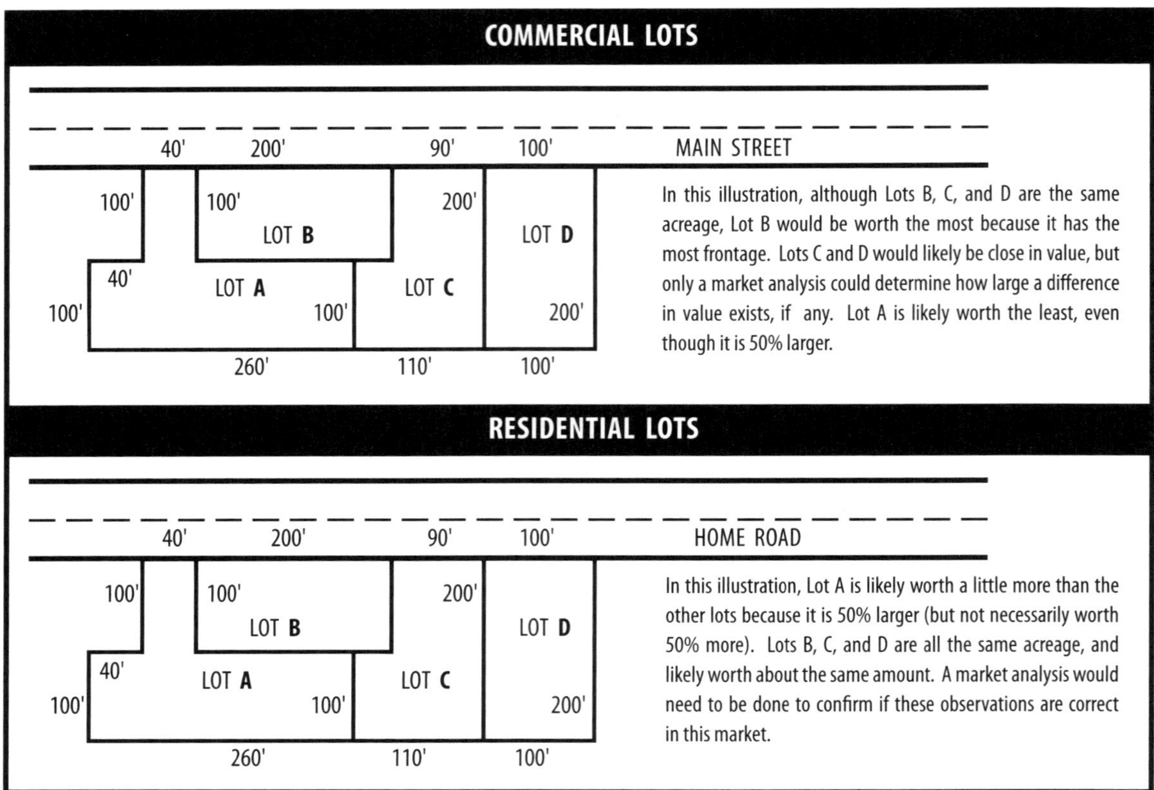

Figure 11.2: Lot Value Examples.

Chapter 11 Summary

1. **Value** is the amount of goods or services offered in the marketplace in exchange for something. There are seven characteristics of real estate. Maximizing value requires all four value characteristics—demand, utility, scarcity, transferability (DUST)—plus the three physical characteristics—immobility, indestructibility, uniqueness. Buyers must want a site, feel it's useful to satisfy needs, perceive limited supply, and be free to transfer the site later. To have value, scarcity must be coupled with utility. Without demand, supply is meaningless, but a person must also have an ability to purchase (effective demand).

2. Factors that affect the value of a particular piece of real estate include many of the same economic, governmental, and social factors that influence the broad real estate market. Some of the most relevant broad market factors that influence the value of a particular piece of real estate include **supply and demand**, **uniqueness**, and **scarcity**. Property-specific factors include **highest and best use, location, substitution, conformity,** and **contribution**.

3. **Market value** is the theoretical price that a piece of real estate is most likely to bring in a typical transaction, not to be confused with market **price**, which is the actual price paid for a piece of real estate. A typical real estate transaction is often referred to as an **arm's length transaction,** meaning the transaction occurred under typical conditions in the marketplace. Typical conditions are buyer paying cash or getting a mortgage, seller not offering financing or unusual terms, buyer and seller are not related, buyer and seller acting in their own best interests, buyer and seller not acting out of undue haste or duress, both are reasonably informed about the property, and the property has been on the market for a reasonable period of time.

4. Inherent value of land can be increased through assemblage or subdivision. **Assemblage** is combining two or more parcels of land into one larger parcel, increasing the usefulness of the site. If the larger parcel is worth more than the sum total of the smaller parcels, this is called **plottage**. **Subdividing** a larger parcel of land can also result in more utility and more value. **Frontage** is the dimension across the access side of a parcel of land. With commercial property, frontage is usually more valuable than depth. The first number in a lot size is always the frontage. With residential land, usually, only total size is compared. In both cases, a market study must be done to determine any amount of value difference.

Chapter 11 Quiz

1. ***The amount that one particular person paid for property is its***
   A. cost.
   B. market value.
   C. price.
   D. value.

2. ***What are the value characteristics that properties must have in harmony to maximize value?***
   A. demand, utility, scarcity, transferability
   B. supply and demand
   C. uniqueness, immobility, indestructibility
   D. utility and scarcity, coupled with a lack of purchasing power

3. ***Land has inherent value because of***
   A. immobility.
   B. indestructibility.
   C. uniqueness.
   D. all of the above

4. ***Which is an example of real estate put to its highest and best use?***
   A. a flat, paved parking lot in downtown Boston
   B. a house in a residential subdivision
   C. an old house on a major highway surrounded by commercial buildings
   D. a vacant lot

5. ***Which house will hold its value best?***
   A. "best" house in the "worst" neighborhood
   B. "worst" house in the "best" neighborhood
   C. $50,000 house that overlooks a huge landfill
   D. $500,000 house in an area of apartment complexes

6. ***Which is NOT a characteristic of an arm's length transaction?***
   A. Buyer and seller are not related.
   B. Each party acts in its own best interest.
   C. Neither party is acting under duress.
   D. Seller offers financing concessions.

7. ***Someone buys two adjacent parcels of land for $20,000 each. An appraisal shows that the combined larger parcel is now worth $40,000. What has occurred?***
   A. assemblage
   B. frontage
   C. plottage
   D. subdividing

8. ***Someone buys two adjacent parcels of land for $20,000 each. An appraisal shows that the combined larger parcel is now worth $50,000. What has occurred?***
   A. assemblage
   B. frontage
   C. plottage
   D. subdividing

9. ***Someone buys one large parcel of land for $200,000 with plans to sell it later as 10 separate lots for $25,000 each. The owner would be increasing the value of the land through***
   A. assemblage.
   B. frontage.
   C. plottage.
   D. subdividing.

10. ***A fast food chain is looking for a new location. Assuming the cost of the lot is less of a concern than customer convenience of entering and exiting the property, which of these lots would the restaurant likely choose?***
    A. 100' x 200'
    B. 125' x 150'
    C. 150' x 125'
    D. 200' x 100'

12

Chapter 12

Understanding Appraisals

In This Chapter

As a mortgage professional, it is important to understand how to read and use appraisals. Appraisal reports document an opinion of market value for a property based on objective data. The Uniform Residential Appraisal Report (URAR) is the primary appraisal form used by lenders for residential property. The sales comparison approach to value is an important process for determining an opinion of market value. This chapter defines the concept and key terms, and then reviews the procedure. After a brief discussion of selecting comparable sales, the chapter focuses on the rules and procedures for making adjustments. Next addressed is researching the sale and transfer history of properties, as required on the URAR. Finally, some points are made about the reconciliation process and developing a final opinion of value.

At the end of this chapter, you will be able to:

- Identify the steps necessary to complete a real estate appraisal.
- Contrast the three appraisal approaches used to arrive at an opinion of value.
- Identify the elements recorded on a Uniform Residential Appraisal Report (URAR).
- Describe how adjustments are made to comparable properties.
- Discuss the impact of rules on appraisal independence.

Key Terms

Appraisal
Appraisal Management Company (AMC)
Automated Valuation Model (AVM)
Comparables
Contributory Value
Drive-by Appraisal
Gross Living Area (GLA)
Indicated Value Range
Market Value
Matched Pair Analysis
Neighborhood
Recertification of Value
Reconciliation
Sales Comparison Approach
Subject Property
Substitution
URAR
USPAP

Real Estate Appraisal

An **appraisal** is an *estimate or opinion of value as of a certain date that is supported by objective data.* There are many important concepts in that short definition. First, an appraisal is only an **estimate** or **opinion**; it is not a guarantee of value. While it is an opinion of value, however, it must be supportable and based on facts. The other equally important part of the definition of appraisal is that the estimate of value is as of a **certain date**. Change is constantly occurring, and so value is also subject to constant change. This is why an appraisal is only valid as of its effective date, which establishes terms, conditions, and economic circumstances upon which the value is estimated. Appraisals may be performed for a variety of reasons.

Appraisal Approaches

Appraisers value properties using three different approaches. Each approach is independent of the others and is performed separately to arrive at an opinion of value. Many factors can drive the appraiser's choice in the application of the approaches, such as the type of property being appraised and the type and extent of research and analysis needed in an assignment. As a result, the appraiser could elect to use one, two, or all three approaches.

- **Sales Comparison Approach.** Develops an opinion of value of real property by comparing the property being appraised with other similar properties, called comparables or comps, which have sold recently in the same market area as the subject property.
- **Cost Approach.** Develops an opinion of value for a property by calculating the cost of the land, site improvements, the cost to build the structure on the land, and the cost of any depreciation to the property. The cost approach to value is best for relatively new construction or for unusual or special purpose properties that have few or no comparables and do not produce income, such as hospitals, schools, or churches.
- **Income Approach.** Sometimes called the capitalization approach, it estimates the value of real estate by analyzing the revenue, or income, the property currently generates or could generate often comparing it to other similar properties. This approach is most widely used with commercial or investment properties.

Uniform Standards of Professional Appraisal Practice (USPAP)

The **Uniform Standards of Professional Appraisal Practice (USPAP)**, established and promoted by the Appraisal Foundation, dictates a number of standards, rules, and guidelines that licensed appraisers must follow when completing an appraisal report. Many of these rules relate directly to the appraisal report itself. For example, whenever an appraiser undertakes an assignment to develop an opinion of value, it is unethical for the appraiser to accept compensation contingent upon the reporting of a predetermined value, a direction in value that favors the client, etc. Any interest the appraiser may have in the subject property or the outcome of the appraisal must be clearly documented in the appraisal report.

A written report, such as the Uniform Residential Appraisal Report (URAR), must also adhere to certain standards regarding the amount of research and work that must be performed. Under USPAP rules, the appraiser must also prepare a complete workfile for each assignment that includes, among other things, all data and documentation necessary to support the appraiser's opinions and conclusions in the report. Other USPAP rules are highlighted as they become relevant to this discussion.

The Uniform Residential Appraisal Report (URAR)

The **Uniform Residential Appraisal Report (URAR)** is the predominant appraisal report form you will likely see and use as a residential mortgage professional. The URAR is referred to as Fannie Mae Form 1004 or Freddie Mac Form 70. The URAR is used for single-family homes, individual units in a planned unit development (PUD), or other one-family properties. This form is *not* designed for appraising condominiums (Form 1073), multi-family investment properties (Form 1025), or manufactured homes (Form 1004C).

The URAR form is based on the appraiser performing **both an interior and exterior inspection** of the subject property. Additionally, the appraiser is to inspect the exterior of the comparable sales used to support the conclusion of value. This exterior inspection from the street verifies that the comparable's condition in relation to the subject generally conforms to the neighborhood and otherwise represents a comparable property.

Keep in mind that the URAR is used not only to report a final opinion of value for the subject property, but also as a means of communicating with the client and anyone else authorized to read the appraisal report. The lender is considered an authorized user of the report regardless of who orders or who pays for the appraisal. Note that a lender generally will only consider and use appraisals that are addressed to the lender from an appraiser on its approved list or from an approved appraisal management company.

The appraiser's report should be clear and concise, logical and consistent, but it must also be supported and documented with market evidence in defense of the conclusions reached. The appraiser's opinions must be supported by analytical data to ensure the integrity of the appraisal process. The reader should be led to the same conclusion the appraiser reached in evaluating the available data. The URAR form can offer a process, but it does not substitute the standards for compliance as set forth by USPAP.

The Sales Comparison Approach

The **sales comparison approach** compares the subject property with other recently sold properties in the same location as the subject in order to assign value. The **subject property** is *the property being appraised or for which a value opinion is sought.* The *properties used to support the opinion of value* are the **comparables**, also called comps. For residential appraisals, USPAP rules state that when the sales comparison approach is applicable, an appraiser must analyze as many comparable sales as are necessary. The URAR form is designed for inclusion of three comparables, but additional sheets can be used if more comparables are needed to support the appraisal conclusions.

The sales comparison approach is considered the most useful and accurate of the three appraisal methods because it's rooted in actual market activity. It is also sometimes referred to as the **market data approach**. This approach, however, only considers *past sales that have actually closed.* Properties currently for sale are not used as comparables since their final selling price hasn't been determined. Appraisers must look at past sales for the objective evidence to support their analyses of property value based on what a typical buyer would pay without undue influence. This is implied in the Fannie Mae definition of **market value** as *the most probable price that a property should bring in a competitive and open market.* With a truly objective appraisal, another buyer should agree with the value and be willing to pay the same price for the property. By looking at enough comparable sales, the assumption is made that the resulting appraisal analysis reflects the actions of typical real estate buyers in the marketplace.

Substitution and the Typical Buyer

The integrity of the appraisal process depends on basing property value on the actions of a **typical buyer,** *one acting in his or her own best interest, without undue pressure, influence, or emotional attachment, and who would rationally and readily accept a less expensive substitute if available.* The theory of **substitution** says that *an informed buyer will not pay more for a home (or a feature in a home) than a comparable substitute.* Appraisers must take this into account as it limits a property's worth in the marketplace.

But a buyer who employs the theory of substitution considers *all* properties currently for sale, not just those already closed, as the appraiser does. Acknowledging this inherent limitation to the sales comparison approach, the URAR form has a place (at the top of the Sales Comparison section) for information on comparable properties currently for sale and all comparable properties that have sold within the past 12 months. This ensures these figures are considered when determining whether the subject property should be at the high or low end of the indicated value range.

Finding Comparable Sales

The sales comparison approach typically uses between three and five comparable sales to arrive at a value figure in a residential appraisal. A **minimum of three** comparables is required by most secondary market lenders to ensure an accurate appraisal from sufficient data. Comparables should be **recent sales**, usually *within six months prior to the date of the appraisal.* If any comparables used are older than six months, the appraiser must comment on the reasons for using them as supporting data and make any necessary value adjustments to reflect any differences in market conditions.

There are	7	comparable properties currently offered for sale in the subject neighborhood ranging in price from $	174,900	to $ 192,500	.
There are	12	comparable sales in the subject neighborhood within the past twelve months ranging in sale price from $	168,500	to $ 191,000	.

FIGURE 12.1: Top lines of a sample Sales Comparison Approach from the URAR Form.

Same Market Area

The ideal situation is to use recently sold comparables in the same market area as the subject property. Defining the neighborhood is one part of the process, but this is often more than just physical boundaries, such as roads. Neighborhood boundaries can also be defined by price range, demographics, or government services. In fact, almost anything can be used to define a neighborhood, except those things prohibited by fair housing laws.

If there aren't enough properties that have recently sold in a given area, other similar areas may be researched. The appraiser must use knowledge and judgment to select the best areas for comparably valued properties, and make appropriate price adjustments, along with clear explanations as to why they were necessary to use.

While physical location is important, any comparable property must be close in style and other features to the subject property. Similarity in use and other externalities ensures that a typical buyer would see the properties as ready substitutes for one another.

Same Transfer of Rights

The subject property and the comparables chosen for comparisons should involve the same transfer of rights. Most often, the subject of a residential appraisal will involve a fee simple transfer, in which the entire bundle of rights is sold to the new owner. The appraiser should verify that the comparables used in the appraisal report were also a fee simple transfer. When part of the bundle of rights (e.g., mineral rights) is sold separately, it is best that the subject and the comparables involve the same transfer of rights to avoid potentially complex calculations that may or may not be a true measure of market value impact in that particular area. If the appraisal assignment calls for the valuation of some partial interest in the subject property (e.g., equitable title), then the comparables chosen should also involve the same transfer of partial interests.

Part of an Arm's Length Transaction

The comparables used as the basis for comparisons must have been part of an **arm's length transaction** that occurred *under typical conditions in the marketplace, with each party acting in his or her own best interests.* The transaction should have involved payment for the property in cash or with a mortgage through a lender, where the seller did not make any unusual payment concessions or owner financing. Comparables with related parties, that sold as part of a liquidation sale (e.g., foreclosure), or with other unusual terms or concessions, should be eliminated.

Adjusting Comparable Sales

Since it may be difficult to find properties that are the same as the subject property in all respects, the sales comparison approach allows for adjustments. **Adjusting properties** is *the process of making chosen comparables come as close as possible in features to the subject so that meaningful price comparisons can be made.* The rules for adjusting properties are simple:

1. The subject property is the starting point and *never changes.*
2. If the comparable is missing a feature that the subject has, the appraiser *adds* to the comparable to make the properties equal.
3. If the comparable has a feature that the subject property does not, the appraiser *subtracts* from the comparable to make them equal.

Class Activity: Adjustment

Let's say that the value of a garage is determined to be $5,000. Individually or as a class, fill in the blanks in this simple example of adjusting comparable sales and discuss a reasonable value for the subject property:

	Subject Property	Comparable 1	Comparable 2	Comparable 3
Feature	1-car garage	No garage	1-car garage	2-car garage
Adjustment Needed	Never adjust!			
Pre-adjustment Value	--	$91,000	$100,000	$110,000
Final Value	$100,000			

This process is repeated for each significant feature that is different between the subject property and the comparables ***on the day they were sold.*** After all adjustments are made, an appraiser can reconcile the adjusted prices of the comparables to estimate the value of the subject property, weighting the comparables as appropriate—**never averaging them**.

Adjustments as of Sale Date

Adjustments are made to comparables for differences between the subject property and the comparables, *only as of the day the comparables were sold.* Changes to the comparables after they sold don't count because they would not be reflected in the price. If an appraiser is considering a comparable, but then learns it needed extensive repair or rehabilitation work when sold, it's not a good choice unless the subject property also needs similar work.

Significant Features

Adjustments are only made to comparables for significant features, generally physical features, but they can also be *features of the transaction,* such as when a sale occurred or financing terms. Some features are objective, such as the number of bedrooms, while other features are subjective, such as the condition. Also, significant features can change from area to area; for example, a view of the golf course in a golf course community or access to a waterway for riverfront property. Every feature doesn't need to be considered every time, since the object is to find comparables that are already as close as possible to the subject.

If differences in features between the comparables did *not* result in differences in sale prices, then only those features that appeared to contribute to any price differences should be noted. For example, if two similar comparables sold for almost exactly the same price, even though one has central air conditioning and one has a heat pump, one could conclude that the presence of central air or a heat pump did not have a significant effect on the price. Therefore, this is not a significant feature.

Limits on Adjustments

Total adjustments that may be made to comparables are limited by Fannie Mae and others in the secondary market. The reason for limitations is to provide some sort of benchmark as to how close the comparables actually are to the subject property. If they are too dissimilar, this will result in excessive adjustments. When making adjustments, Fannie Mae prefers the comparables to fall within the following guidelines unless there's an appropriate explanation and justification. As a guideline, note that any **individual line adjustment** to the comparables sales price should not exceed **10%**. For example, if the comparable sale price was $100,000, no individual line adjustment should exceed $10,000.

Total Net Should Not Exceed 15%

The total net value of all adjustments should not exceed **15%** of the comparable sale price. With this guideline, all adjustments must be added or subtracted together, following the sign of the adjustment. So, all positive adjustments (for missing features) are added together, and all negative adjustments (for additional features) are subtracted from that total. This final figure generally should not exceed the 15% limit.

Total Gross Should Not Exceed 25%

The total gross (absolute) value of all adjustments should not exceed 25% of the comparable sale price. With this guideline, all adjustments are added together, but without regard to their sign; it doesn't matter if adjustments are positive or negative. Total adjustments generally should not exceed 25%.

Class Activity: Adjustment Limit

Property #1:

A comparable sold for $85,000. It had positive adjustments for a garage (+$3,000) and a half bath (+$1,500), and a negative adjustment for a basement (-$2,500).

What is net adjustment, and is it within acceptable parameters?

Property #2:

A comparable sold for $55,000. It had a positive adjustment for a half bath (+$1,500), and negative adjustments for owner financing (-10% = -$5,500), basement (-$2,500) and garage (-$3,000).

What is the net adjustment, and is it within acceptable parameters?

Property #3:

A comparable sold for $55,000. It had positive adjustments for a garage (+$3,000) and half bath (+$1,500) and negative adjustments for owner financing (-$5,500), a basement (-$2,500), and bedroom (-$2,000).

What is the gross adjustment, and is it within acceptable parameters?

Property #4:

A comparable sold for $95,000. It had positive adjustments for a basement (+$2,500) and bedroom (+$2,000) and negative adjustment for a garage (-$3,000).

What is the gross adjustment, and is it within acceptable parameters?

Sequence of Adjustments

All adjustments made are based on an analysis of market data for the various elements of comparison. The sequence of adjustments is important to follow so all values are adjusted consistently. The sequence of adjustments, in order of priority, is:

1. Property rights conveyed
2. Financing terms
3. Conditions of sale
4. Market conditions (date of sale)
5. Location
6. Physical characteristics

Furthermore, some adjustments must be made first because they are adjusted as a *percentage of the comparable's sales price, rather than a set dollar amount.* The rationale is to make adjustments for features affecting the overall property before adjusting for individual features. With percentage adjustments, the appraiser extracts the difference in a dollar figure from market data and converts it to a percentage that is applied to the comparable sale. When applying percentage adjustments, property rights, financing, condition of sale, and market conditions are adjusted *individually and in sequence.* Then, all other adjustments may be combined. Of course, it is not necessary to make adjustments to every feature every time, since the objective is to find comparables that are already as close to the subject as possible.

Element of Comparison	Market Indicated Adjustment	Adjustment to Comparable
Sale Price	—	$136,000
Property Rights Conveyed	+5%	+ $6,800
Adjusted Price	—	$142,800
Financing Terms	-3%	- $4,284
Adjusted Price	—	$138,516
Market Conditions	+7%	+ $9,696
Adjusted Price	—	$148,212
Location	+11,000	+ 11,000
Physical Characteristics	-$7,500	- $7,500
Value Indication		$151,712

FIGURE 12.3: Elements of Comparable Adjustment.

Property Rights Conveyed

Most residential transactions involve **fee simple interest**, meaning that *all property rights typically transferred with real property in the market are being conveyed.* A rare exception might be when the property interest is subject to a **leasehold interest**, such as when the improvements are constructed on lands subject to ground rent. When a property is appraised subject to a leasehold interest, a detailed analysis is required. Comparable properties are preferred that reflect similar leasehold scenarios. However, if necessary, comparable properties sold in fee simple could be utilized with appropriate percentage adjustments.

Financing Terms

According to Fannie Mae guidelines, financing concessions include:

- Interest rate buydowns
- Below market rate financing
- Loan discount points
- Fees or closing costs paid by the seller (if customarily paid by the buyer)
- Refunds or credits for borrower's expenses
- The inclusion of non-realty items

Other items considered are assumptions and owner/seller financing. In fact, any type of sale concession the seller may have made to sell the home should be considered, such as paying for inspections or repairs. Any or all of these items might need to be adjusted by the appraiser if the concessions are not typical for the market and may have influenced the transaction.

After an adjustment is made for financing concessions, the result is what's referred to as the (sale price adjusted to) cash equivalency.

Percentage Adjustment. With financing terms, straight dollar amounts do not yield accurate adjustment figures. For example, if the seller carried a small second mortgage that resulted in a $10,000 increase in the sale price on a $100,000 home, this would not indicate a $10,000 adjustment in the price of any home where the seller carried a second mortgage. It would be inaccurate to apply this same dollar figure of appreciation to a $50,000 home. Instead, a 10% adjustment is reasonable for the $50,000 home (since $10,000 is 10% of the $100,000 home price), provided the appraiser determines that this reflects market conditions for the sales examined.

Fannie Mae Guidelines. When contemplating adjustments for financing terms, Fannie Mae has several points to consider. First, the actual dollar amount of sales or financing concessions paid by the seller must appear somewhere in an explanation on the form, whenever that information is available. The appraiser has a responsibility to obtain this information from reliable and verifiable sources, such as publicly recorded documents or a party to the transaction. Second, Fannie Mae does not want the final adjustment amount to simply repeat the cash equivalency of the seller concession. Instead, Fannie Mae expects the appraiser to enter an adjustment amount equal to the actual influence the amount had on the sale price.

And third, Fannie Mae states that positive adjustments for sale/financing concessions are not acceptable. In other words, if most sales in a neighborhood had the seller paying points, but one of the comparables sold without the seller paying points, Fannie Mae does not want to see any adjustment for this reflected in the appraisal. The actual sale price of the property should be used and treated as a cash equivalency price in that situation.

Market Conditions (Date of Sale)

The date that a sale took place is always a consideration. The appraiser should select comparables that sold as recently as possible to avoid making adjustments for date of sale. Since market conditions are always changing, an older sale may have fluctuated due to market conditions related to supply, demand, economic trends, interest rates, etc. Some think of market conditions as a direct relationship to time, which might not necessarily be true. Looking back at a 12-month period, property may have appreciated 3% during the first six months of the year but then decreased 2% in the most recent six months when interest rates rose sharply. In actuality, this would represent a 1% upward adjustment to a one-year-old comparable. However, if a six-month-old comparable were being used, a 2% downward adjustment would be warranted. In most circumstances, though, without unusual volatility in the market, it could be concluded that using older transactions will most likely require adjustments. This is why the secondary market prefers comparables that are not older than six months. However, in some markets and market segments, it is necessary to use comparable sales that exceed this guideline. The appraiser must always survey the market to consider whether an adjustment is warranted.

Percentage Adjustment. Property values, whether increasing or decreasing, do so in percentages, not whole dollar amounts. If a $100,000 home went up $10,000 in the past year, then a similar adjustment of 10% is reasonable for other homes, provided this reflects market conditions in the area.

Here too, the percentage adjustment is made to the market rather than to the actual comparable. Thus, differences between the comparables and other properties on the market dictate the adjustment, and not the specific difference the comparable has versus the subject property. The objective is to normalize the values across a theoretical market that is devoid of time differences. Again, the matched pair analysis method is used, with the dollar figure converted to a percentage of the home's value.

Fannie Mae Guidelines. Fannie Mae requires **at least three comparables** that have actually closed be used for the sales comparison approach. The appraiser must comment on any comparables used that were sold *more than six months prior to the appraisal,* and provide a reasonable explanation for why this had to be done. Beyond the three required comparables, the appraiser may use older sales, pending sales, or even a prior sale of the subject property if it can be shown in the appraisal report why the information provides additional support to the conclusion of value.

Location

The location of the comparables relative to the subject is an important value factor and encompasses several aspects. The two primary aspects the appraiser considers are the market area where the comparable is located, and the exact position within a neighborhood. In most situations, the appraiser should try not to use comparables from different market areas. For established neighborhoods, the appraiser should use comparables from within the same subdivision (or PUD project) because they are the best indicator of value. Newer subdivisions may require the appraiser to use at least one comparable from a similar subdivision to support value if there are not enough sales without builder financing and subsidies. Rural properties can pose a challenge to appraisers because the only comparables available may be a significant distance from the subject. When no other comparables are available, the appraiser may use some from the nearest similar market area with an appropriate explanation and any necessary value adjustments. Underwriting requirements may vary as to whether such deviations in market area may disqualify the property for approval of a mortgage loan. Position differences within a neighborhood are usually handled as part of the adjustment process for physical differences. The appraiser checks to see if there is any discernible value difference for properties based on lot position in a particular market, and then determines an appropriate adjustment based on a matched pair analysis.

Dollar Value Adjustments. The matched pair analysis method produces a dollar value for location differences that is applied dollar-for-dollar to the home's value. The value applied to the comparables can be derived from other sales data, not necessarily from the comparables used in the appraisal. In fact, appraisers gather matched pair data on a regular basis, and store that information for future use. If a significant difference is noted between the comparables and the subject, the appraiser often refers to stored data to determine an appropriate value adjustment to apply.

Fannie Mae Guidelines. The description used for the location of the comparables relative to the subject should be very specific. On the Proximity to Subject line of the URAR form, Fannie Mae is looking for details, such as "1/2 mile south" or "two blocks east." The appraiser must include an explanation or comment if the distance would seem excessive to someone not familiar with the market area. On the Location line of the URAR form, Fannie Mae is looking for specific information that might distinguish the value of the comparables and the subject. Even if no value adjustment is needed for the relevant location features in a particular market, Fannie Mae still wants to see specifics, such as "corner lot" or "cul-de-sac." Furthermore, the appraiser may use this space to indicate any adjustment value for Proximity to Subject, if warranted, based on market data.

Physical Characteristics

The rest of the sales comparison grid on the URAR form focuses on various physical differences that may or may not warrant an adjustment. At the end of the features and amenities listed, there are additional blank spaces where more items can be inserted if other elements of comparison are responsible for value differences between a comparable and the subject. Ideally, only comparables that need as few adjustments as possible should be chosen. Those needing only adjustments for physical differences are preferable.

When entering descriptions for items that are not quantifiable, for example, quality of construction, appraisers rate them as excellent, good, average, fair, or poor.

Dollar Value Adjustments. The matched pair analysis produces a dollar value for physical differences that is applied dollar-for-dollar to the home's value. Deriving the adjustment value from actual sales is the best reflection of market value of a feature or amenity. Many items do not add market value equal to their cost to install. In colder climate areas, an in-ground swimming pool is a great example of this.

Fannie Mae Guidelines. One area of concern is over-improvement. An **over-improvement** is *a property or feature with a cost exceeding its market value.* Such a property may be rejected by a typical buyer and could create a problem for Fannie Mae in the event of foreclosure. If the value of the property is still within the neighborhood range, it is likely acceptable. Fannie Mae urges additional scrutiny when over-improvements are involved, asking the appraiser to ensure that only the actual contributory value of the feature is included. The appraiser must also make appropriate comments or explanation in the appraisal report.

Fannie Mae also reminds appraisers that below grade areas should be considered separately from the gross living area of the house. **Gross living area** (GLA) is *residential space that's finished, heated, and above grade.*

Garages, finished basements, and storage areas don't count in GLA. Even areas partially below grade should not count as part of the gross living area. Instead, finished areas below grade must be considered as separate items, and adjusted according to their presence or absence in the comparables and the subject. Also, room counts do not include bathrooms or foyers, and bedrooms must have a closet. Other considerations may be customary in the local market. Room count and square footage of the gross living area should be similar between the subject and the comparables. The market will dictate when to make adjustments and the amount of adjustment to be applied.

FEATURE	SUBJECT	COMPARABLE SALE # 1		COMPARABLE SALE # 2		COMPARABLE SALE # 3	
Address	22 OAKWOOD DRIVE WESTERVILLE, OH 43081	21 VALLEYVIEW COURT WESTERVILLE, OHIO		337 CHRIS COURT WESTERVILLE, OHIO		321 PEARSON DRIVE WESTERVILLE, OHIO	
Proximity to Subject		0.37 MILE NORTHEAST		0.33 MILE NORTH		0.62 MILE SOUTHEAST	
Sale Price	$ $178,000		$ 180,000		$ 185,000		$ 172,000
Sale Price/Gross Liv. Area	$ 91.19 sq.ft.	$ 89.82 sq.ft.		$ 97.16 sq.ft.		$ 99.48 sq.ft.	
Data Source(s)		FRANKLIN CO. AUDITOR		FRANKLIN CO. AUDITOR		FRANKLIN CO. AUDITOR	
Verification Source(s)		COLS. MLS, BROKER		COLS. MLS, BROKER		COLS. MLS, BROKER	
VALUE ADJUSTMENTS	DESCRIPTION	DESCRIPTION	+(-) $ Adjustment	DESCRIPTION	+(-) $ Adjustment	DESCRIPTION	+(-) $ Adjustment
Sales or Financing Concessions		CONV NONE		CONV SELLER PAID	-5,000	CONV NONE	
Date of Sale/Time		4/30/2005		3/5/2005		5/14/2005	
Location	INSIDE LOT	INSIDE LOT		INSIDE LOT		INSIDE LOT	
Leasehold/Fee Simple	FEE SIMPLE	FEE SIMPLE		FEE SIMPLE		FEE SIMPLE	
Site	16,500 SQ.FT.	17,200 SQ. FT.		15,740 SQ. FT		13,650 SQ. FT.	
View	RES/AVG	RES/AVG		PARK/GOOD	-2,500	RES/AVG	
Design (Style)	COLONIAL/2ST	COLONIAL/2ST		COLONIAL/2ST		COLONIAL/2ST	
Quality of Construction	AVERAGE	AVERAGE		AVERAGE		AVERAGE	
Actual Age	6 YEARS	5 YEARS		6 YEARS		8 YEARS	
Condition	GOOD	GOOD		GOOD		AVERAGE	+2,500
Above Grade	Total / Bdrms. / Baths	Total / Bdrms. / Baths		Total / Bdrms. / Baths		Total / Bdrms. / Baths	
Room Count	7 / 3 / 2.1	6 / 3 / 2.1		8 / 3 / 2.1		7 / 3 / 2	+500
Gross Living Area	1,952 sq.ft.	2,004 sq.ft.	-1,250	1,904 sq.ft.	+1,250	1,729 sq.ft.	+5,500
Basement & Finished Rooms Below Grade	642 Sq.Ft. 2 RMS, F BA	1,002 SQ. FT. UNFINISHED	-2,000 +3,000	700 SQ. FT. 1 RM. FIN	+2,000	600 SQ. FT. 2 RMS, F BA	
Functional Utility	AVERAGE	AVERAGE		AVERAGE		AVERAGE	
Heating/Cooling	GFA/CENTRAL	GFA/CENTRAL		GFA/CENTRAL		GFA/CENTRAL	
Energy Efficient Items	TYPICAL	TYPICAL		TYPICAL		TYPICAL	
Garage/Carport	2-C ATT GAR	2-C ATT GAR		2-C ATT GAR		2-C ATT GAR	
Porch/Patio/Deck	PORCH, PATIO	PORCH, DECK		PORCH, PATIO		PORCH,DECK	
	B-I SPA	NONE	+500	IN-GRD POOL	-500	B-I SPA	
	WD PRIV FNC	WD PRIV FNC		WD PRIV FNC		NONE	+500
	FIREPLACE	FIREPLACE		2 FIREPLACES	-1,000	FIREPLACE	
Net Adjustment (Total)		☒ + ☐ -	$ 250	☐ + ☒ -	$ -5,750	☒ + ☐ -	$ 9,000
Adjusted Sale Price of Comparables		Net Adj. 0.1 % Gross Adj. 3.8 %	$ 180,250	Net Adj. 3.1 % Gross Adj. 6.6 %	$ 179,250	Net Adj. 5.2% Gross Adj. 5.2%	$ 181,000

FIGURE 12.4: Data Grid Portion of the Sales Comparison Approach section from a URAR Form.

Researching the Sale and Transfer of Properties

An important step to ensure the integrity of the appraisal process is research, verification, and analysis of the **transfer history** of the properties. This applies to the subject as well as the comparables. Analysis of the purchase contract normally only shows price and financing concessions. Determining the current owner of the property is important, as well as recent sales history. The appraiser is trying to ascertain whether the transactions represent *bona fide transfers at market value.* If not, the comparables should *not* be used to support value. If there are questions about the subject, the appraiser has an obligation to alert the lender or client to any potential irregularities and their effect on value.

Transfer History of the Subject

USPAP requires the appraiser to analyze the purchase contract, current listing, and recent prior sales for the *past three years.* As well, the URAR form asks for research of the subject's transfers from three years prior to the effective date of the appraisal. The source of the data must be entered on the form, as well as the effective date of the data sources (essentially, how recent the information is and/or when the source was last updated).

This is designed to give the lender or client a complete picture of the subject property value. It may also lead the appraiser or lender to seek more information or data on the subject property. For example, if the subject property was transferred just two months ago for half of the current contract price, the appraiser would need to research this to determine if the current sale price represents true market value. The property could have been sold in a distressed situation, there may have been legitimate repairs done that can be documented with receipts, or the property could be part of a property-flipping scheme.

Property Flipping

Property flipping is defined by Fannie Mae as *the process of purchasing existing properties with the intention of immediately reselling them for a profit.* While property flipping is not automatically illegal, it has gained a bad reputation because of the amount of fraud associated with it. The fraud occurs when a property's value is inflated and the final purchaser pays more than the property is worth. Appraisers can get caught in the scheme wittingly or unwittingly. Researching the transfer history of the property is one way for the unsuspecting appraiser to become aware of any possible fraud and alert others. Frequent transfers with escalating values in a short period of time are one red flag that merits further investigation. Even distressed properties can be subject to fraud if repairs were done poorly or not performed at all. The appraiser is ***not*** a home inspector, but the lender or client is relying on the appraiser as a collector and conveyor of information. The appraisal report must be carefully and thoroughly prepared to avoid misleading the lender or client with an inflated property value.

Again, property flipping is not illegal by definition, but if the seller has held the property for an unusually short period of time—or has not even taken title to the property—then there must be some justification and documentation for the increase in value. The appraiser and the lender/client must be satisfied that the current contract is legitimate and that the current price represents the true market value of the property.

Fannie Mae Guidelines

Fannie Mae expects the appraisal report to include an analysis of the sales contract, property listing, and the sales history of the subject when the information is "reasonably available." This presumably means the appraiser must thoroughly search public records. If the appraiser does not have the data resources or expertise in the market area as expected by Fannie Mae, then Fannie Mae expects the appraiser to reject those appraisal assignments.

One of Fannie Mae's goals is to reduce and eliminate instances of fraud where predatory transactions cause an uninformed buyer to pay more for a property than it is worth. Fannie Mae's position is that the likelihood of fraud and misrepresentation increases when the seller is not the owner of record for a property. Furthermore, reviewing and analyzing the prior sales of the subject property as compared to the sale price trends in the area can help confirm the current value for the subject property is reasonable and representative of true market value.

Transfer History of the Comparables

The URAR form asks for information on comparable transfer activity for one year prior to the comparable's sale date. The goal for researching them is the same as for researching the subject property—to determine if the transfer price is an accurate reflection of market value. If the property has been transferred several times in a short period of time with escalating values, then the comparable should be investigated further or discarded. There are other things you can learn from the transfer history of a property that may influence its choice as a comparable sale. For example, if a lender is shown as the prior owner, this might indicate that the comparable is a distressed property with a transfer value that did not reflect market value.

Fannie Mae Guidelines

Just as with the transfer history of the subject, Fannie Mae also expects appraisers to analyze the transfer history of the comparables when the information is "reasonably available."

In an effort to reduce fraud, Fannie Mae recommends rejecting comparables if the prior transfer involved "back-to-back," "simultaneous," or "double" transaction closings where the price increased from one transaction to the next. Such comparables are problematic and should be discarded early in the data collection process.

I [X] did [ ] did not research the sale or transfer history of the subject property and comparable sales. If not, explain

My research [ ] did [X] did not reveal any prior sales or transfers of the subject property for the three years prior to the effective date of this appraisal.
Data Source(s) FRANKLIN COUNTY AUDITOR
My research [X] did [ ] did not reveal any prior sales or transfers of the comparable sales for the year prior to the date of sale of the comparable sale.
Data Source(s) FRANKLIN COUNTY AUDITOR
Report the results of the research and analysis of the prior sale or transfer history of the subject property and comparable sales (report additional prior sales on page 3).

ITEM	SUBJECT	COMPARABLE SALE #1	COMPARABLE SALE #2	COMPARABLE SALE #3
Date of Prior Sale/Transfer	NONE IN 36 MONTHS	9/23/2004	NONE IN 12 MONTHS	NONE IN 12 MONTHS
Price of Prior Sale/Transfer		$155,000		
Data Source(s)		FRANKLIN CO AUDITOR		
Effective Date of Data Source(s)		6/3/2005		

Analysis of prior sale or transfer history of the subject property and comparable sales RESEARCH REVEALED THAT SALE #1 TRANSFERRED ON 9/23/2004 FOR $155,000. FURTHER INQUIRY WITH THE SELLER IN THE MOST RECENT TRANSACTION REVEALED THAT THE PURCHASE WAS VIA SHERRIFF'S AUCTION. COSMETIC RENOVATIONS WERE PERFORMED PRIOR TO THE PROPERTY BEING RE-MARKETED.

FIGURE 12.5: Transfer history part of the Sales Comparison Approach section from URAR Form.

Reconciliation and Indicated Value

Reconciliation is *the appraisal process of analyzing the values derived from the different appraisal approaches to arrive at a final value opinion.* Fannie Mae guidelines point out that reconciliation is actually an ongoing process the appraiser should consider throughout the entire appraisal.

Sales Comparison Opinion of Value

The final step in the sales comparison approach is to reconcile the values of the comparables to reflect an opinion of value for the subject. This is important because it is rare for the adjusted values of all comparables to be equal. An appraiser considers each comparable and gives the most weight to the one that is most similar to the subject property as indicated by the fewest adjustments. The final values are **never averaged** in this step.

Fannie Mae Guidelines. The appraiser must present a brief narrative that accurately describes the thought process that went into the final indicated value. This includes any special notes about the subject or comparables, any relevant items in the prior transfer history of the properties, and an explanation of the reconciliation process, including which comparables were given the most weight and why.

Determining a Value Range

The appraiser develops an indicated value range for the appraisal as a result of the data analysis performed. Determining the acceptable value range for a property is one of the appraiser's most challenging tasks. Since all aspects of the marketplace are constantly subject to change, the appraiser must perform a thorough analysis of all market factors and verify all available data. During this process, the appraiser gives the most consideration to comparables most similar to the subject, taking into account the condition of the properties, circumstances of the sales, and other factors. Under normal market conditions, the appraiser would likely choose the highest value-adjusted comparable as the upper end of the value range, and the lowest value-adjusted one as the lower end of the value range.

In markets experiencing growth or decline, however, the appraiser might also consider pending offers or competitive listings to examine trends and confirm the market's direction. The lender or client is also interested in these properties because they tend to represent the upper limit of value in the marketplace as of the appraisal date. This is why data on the price range of current offerings and comparable sales over the past 12 months are included on the appraisal form. Although the data are superficial and incomplete, they can reveal trends and help determine value limits in the marketplace.

Summary of Sales Comparison Approach THE SALES REFLECT A REASONABLE VALUE RANGE. ALL SALES ARE FROM THE IMMEDIATE MARKET AREA. CORRELATION IS TOWARD THE UPPER PART OF THE VALUE RANGE, WITH TWO OF THE THREE SALES INDICATING THAT DIRECTION. THESE SALES ARE THE MOST RECENT AND REQUIRE THE FEWEST NET ADJUSTMENTS.

Indicated Value by Sales Comparison Approach $ 178,000

FIGURE 12.6: Summary portion of the Sales Comparison Approach section from the URAR Form.

Real Success

It is against USPAP rules for the appraiser to steer a value to a target price. The appraiser must see the purchase contract for the subject property because any special terms or conditions may affect the appraisal, but the appraiser cannot ethically appraise the property to the target contract price. Only if the contract price falls within the appraiser's developed value range, and the transaction of the subject is concluded to be an arm's length transaction, is it then acceptable for the final value to equal the contract sales price.

Final Reconciliation on the URAR Form

Estimates of value derived from the various appraisal approaches (sales comparison, cost, income) must be reconciled to arrive at a final opinion of value for the subject property. This is the appraiser's opportunity to bring together all the data collected, verified, and analyzed during the appraisal process.

After the appraiser decides which appraisal approach should be given the most consideration, he must explain the reasoning that went into reaching the final opinion of value in the appraisal report. Although the appraiser's final reconciliation statement is broken down into only a few sentences, this belies the amount of thought and experience that goes into these statements.

The Reconciliation section of the URAR form is brief but powerful. In it, the appraiser sums up the entire appraisal process and provides a final opinion of value for the lender or client. The Reconciliation section that appears in Figure 12.6 was developed from various analyses performed by the appraiser.

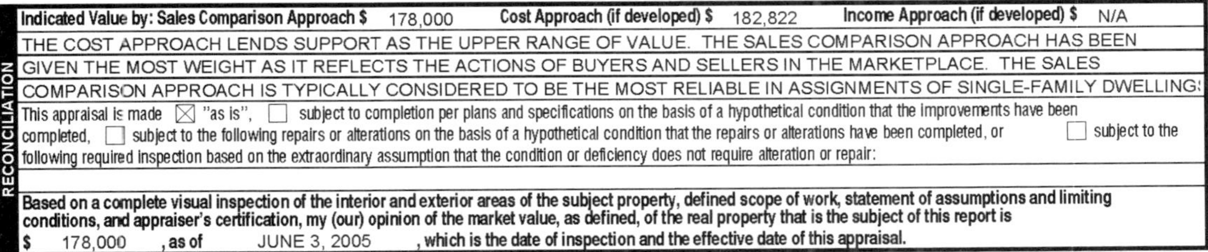

RECONCILIATION

Indicated Value by: Sales Comparison Approach $ 178,000 Cost Approach (if developed) $ 182,822 Income Approach (if developed) $ N/A

THE COST APPROACH LENDS SUPPORT AS THE UPPER RANGE OF VALUE. THE SALES COMPARISON APPROACH HAS BEEN GIVEN THE MOST WEIGHT AS IT REFLECTS THE ACTIONS OF BUYERS AND SELLERS IN THE MARKETPLACE. THE SALES COMPARISON APPROACH IS TYPICALLY CONSIDERED TO BE THE MOST RELIABLE IN ASSIGNMENTS OF SINGLE-FAMILY DWELLING!

This appraisal is made ☒ "as is", ☐ subject to completion per plans and specifications on the basis of a hypothetical condition that the improvements have been completed, ☐ subject to the following repairs or alterations on the basis of a hypothetical condition that the repairs or alterations have been completed, or ☐ subject to the following required inspection based on the extraordinary assumption that the condition or deficiency does not require alteration or repair:

Based on a complete visual inspection of the interior and exterior areas of the subject property, defined scope of work, statement of assumptions and limiting conditions, and appraiser's certification, my (our) opinion of the market value, as defined, of the real property that is the subject of this report is $ 178,000 **, as of** JUNE 3, 2005 **, which is the date of inspection and the effective date of this appraisal.**

FIGURE 12.7: Sample Reconciliation section from the URAR Form.

When appraising residential homes using the URAR report, the sales comparison approach is usually given the most weight. If this is not the case, then there must be an appropriate explanation. For example, if the subject is a newly built home in an area with insufficient sales or market activity, it might be reasonable to give the cost approach the most weight in developing a final opinion of value. The explanation is important here so the lender or client understands the process and reasoning involved. Fannie Mae, however, will not accept any appraisals where the cost approach is used as the only indicator of value because cost alone is not deemed to be a reflection of true market value.

Market Value

Fannie Mae guidelines state that the final value entered on the URAR report should represent the appraiser's opinion of market value, as defined in the appraisal report itself: *"Market value is the most probable price which a property should bring in a competitive and open market under all conditions requisite to a fair sale, the buyer and seller, each acting prudently, knowledgeably and assuming the price is not affected by undue stimulus."*

Fannie Mae wants the final indicated value to represent true market value as much as possible, and thus the comprehensive explanation of market value in the URAR form is designed to ensure uniform treatment of adjustments across all properties. Special attention is paid to sales and financing concessions because they have the greatest potential to alter the price paid for property. Fannie Mae is interested in the appraiser using his or her best judgment in determining the market's reaction to these concessions.

Indicated Value Range

Analysis of the adjusted sales data results in an indicated value range. Depending on the scope of work, the entire range could be used as a value conclusion or the opinion could reflect a relationship to a benchmark, such as the mid-point of the range. However, the URAR form and other forms require the value opinion to be stated as a single number. It is unethical for the appraiser to simply value a property at the target value the client requests or that is stated in the purchase contract. But if the appraiser can justify that number based on the data, and that value falls within the appraiser's indicated value range, then it may be acceptable to place that number on the final report.

"As Is"

An important part of the Reconciliation section is the indication of whether the appraisal was performed "as is," or subject to other hypothetical conditions or extraordinary assumptions. A typical appraisal is done "as is," meaning the property value was determined based on a complete and thorough examination of the subject property as it currently sits and in its present condition.

Updating or Recertifying an Appraisal

Sometimes it may be necessary to **readdress** an appraisal, such as when a new lender evaluates an application. While it may seem to be a simple request from a lender's perspective, an appraiser is obligated to abide by the standards set forth in USPAP, which considers a request to readdress—or update—an appraisal as a *new assignment*. This makes sense when you recall that an appraiser's opinion of value is technically valid only as of the date of the appraisal, so if the lender is looking for a more current value, a new appraisal is required.

A **recertification of value** (recert) may be necessary to confirm whether or not certain conditions in the original appraisal have been met, such as when the property was "subject to" some repair or renovation or when the appraisal was performed on a property under construction. A recert, also called a **completion report**, does *not* change the effective date of the valuation. It simply verifies that the "subject to" conditions of the original appraisal have been met and that the original opinion of value is valid.

If a lot of time has passed between an original appraisal that was "subject to" some condition and the actual completion of the improvements, it may be necessary to have *both* a recertification to remove the condition and an update to get a more current date for the value.

Automated Valuation Models (AVMs)

Automated underwriting can reduce the time and costs necessary to close a loan, providing a streamlined process of document submission, underwriting, and loan approval. With automated underwriting, the value of the property is initially determined using an **automated valuation model** (AVM). AVMs are able to *provide a probable value range for properties by performing a statistical analysis of available data.* This is far from a perfect system. AVMs tend to put values in the middle of the range as they often do not factor in trends. Thus, it can be difficult to approve values at the high end of the range. Still, AVMs are popular because they provide an inexpensive, fast, and predictable means for valuing properties.

AVMs are not true appraisals because they do not provide an opinion of value. The numbers that AVMs produce are a raw interpretation of data. There is no mechanism for considering subjective circumstances, obtaining better data that may be outside the program's parameters, or assessing quality and condition of properties. AVMs work for typical homes, but they are not useful in all situations. For example, homes in less-than-average condition may get higher AVM valuations than they would from a traditional appraisal, whereas nicer-than-average homes might receive lower AVM values. Also, distressed sales and sales with financing concessions are factored in with the same weight as traditional sales. In short, AVMs are a tool, not a replacement. In actual practice, appraisers still have a role in many AVM scenarios.

The AVM component of Fannie Mae's automated underwriting system—**Desktop Underwriter®** (DU®)—uses public information, such as tax records, to determine the reasonableness of the sale price, and whether the property is adequate collateral for the loan. If everything appears within normal parameters, DU® recommends the use of Form 2075.

Form 2075

Form 2075 is Desktop Underwriter's® Property Inspection Report. The 2075 is a "drive-by" form used by appraisers, but it technically is not an appraisal because there is no value reported on the form. In this case, the value is being established through an AVM. When DU® recommends the 2075, the lender must get an exterior-only inspection of the subject property from the street by a state-licensed or state-certified appraiser. No estimate of market value for the property is included in the report, but the appraiser must still attach the required exhibits of a street map showing the location and a photograph showing the front of the subject property. The general market analysis portion of the report may include a similar amount of effort and work by the appraiser as when actually performing an appraisal. The amount of work and data required for the appraiser's report, as well as the type and format for the reporting form, are based on the scope of work determined by the appraiser with input from the client at the time of accepting the assignment, not the minimum form chosen to report the conclusions by the Desktop Underwriter®.

The appraiser has the sole responsibility to determine whether the scope of work and the reporting form are appropriate and/or adequate based on the relevant property characteristics. If the property conforms to the neighborhood, no physical deficiencies are noted, and no adverse conditions exist, then DU® relies on the value produced by the AVM and no property appraisal is required for the transaction. If problems or conditions are noted on the 2075, or in instances where AVMs produce numbers that do not fit within the framework that the lender (or other client) expects, then the lender is required to upgrade to a complete appraisal.

Appraiser Independence

The **Home Valuation Code of Conduct (HVCC)** went into effect in 2009 with the intention of setting standards on solicitation, selection, compensation, conflicts of interest, and appraiser independence with a primary goal of ensuring that real estate appraisers are not coerced *in any way* into establishing a pre-determined or desired valuation on a property. As originally written, HVCC prohibited mortgage broker or staff from having any role in selecting, retaining, or compensating an appraiser, even if from an **authorized appraisal management company** (AMC). While HVCC was not a federal law, it applied to every mortgage on **one- to four-family homes** from any lender in the country who intends to sell the loan on the secondary market to Fannie Mae or Freddie Mac. HVCC did not apply to FHA, VA, or USDA loans as originally implemented. Under HVCC, only a lender or any third-party specifically authorized by the lender (including, but not limited to, appraisal management companies and correspondent lenders) was allowed to select, retain, and compensate an appraiser. Under HVCC, mortgage brokers could initiate the appraisal process on the lender's behalf if directed to submit a loan application to a specifically authorized AMC previously arranged by the lender.

Rules on Valuation Independence

The goals of the Home Valuation Code of Conduct may have been commendable, but HVCC came under considerable criticism within the industry. The Dodd-Frank Wall Street Reform and Consumer Protection Act of 2010 (Pub.L. 111-201, H.R. 4173) includes provisions in Subtitle F of Title XIV, designated as the Mortgage Reform and Anti-Predatory Lending Act, related to upgrading the federal oversight of appraisal activities. The Act required an evaluation of the Home Valuation Code of Conduct to determine whether or not to replace it with new rules on valuation accuracy and independence. In response, an interim final rule amending Regulation Z (12 C.F.R. § 226.42) was released by the Federal Reserve Board of Governors in October 2010, effective April, 2011.

The rule prohibits **coercion** in connection with a covered transaction in any way (including extortion, inducement, bribery, intimidation of, compensation of, or instruction to) of a person who prepares valuations or performs valuation management functions. Examples include:

- Seeking to influence a person who prepares a valuation to report a minimum or maximum value for the consumer's principal dwelling.
- Withholding or threatening to withhold timely payment to a person who prepares a valuation or performs valuation management functions because the person does not value the consumer's principal dwelling at or above a certain amount.
- Implying to a person who prepares valuations that current or future retention of the person depends on the amount at which the person estimates the value of the consumer's principal dwelling.
- Excluding a person who prepares a valuation from consideration for future engagement because the person reports a value for the consumer's principal dwelling that does not meet or exceed a predetermined threshold.
- Conditioning the compensation paid to a person who prepares a valuation on consummation of the covered transaction.

However, it is permissible to ask a person preparing a valuation to:

- Consider additional, appropriate property information.
- Provide additional details or explanation about his or her conclusions.
- Correct errors in a valuation.

It is also acceptable to obtain multiple valuations and select the most reliable, or to withhold compensation due to breach of contract or substandard performance of services. In addition, the interim final rule:

- Prohibits **materially misrepresenting** the value of the consumer's principal dwelling.
- Prohibits someone performing a valuation from having a direct or indirect **conflict of interest**, financial or otherwise, in the property.
- Prohibits creditors from **extending credit** when the creditor knows, at or before consummation, that of a violation of this rule occurred.
- Requires the payment of **reasonable and customary compensation** to appraisers who are not employees of the creditors or of the appraisal management companies hired by the creditors.
- Requires any covered person who reasonably believes an appraiser has not complied with the Uniform Standards of Professional Appraisal Practice or ethical or professional requirements for appraisers under applicable state or federal statutes or regulations to **report** the matter to the appropriate state agency if the failure to comply is material.

C. Patrick McAllister Associates, Inc.

Uniform Residential Appraisal Report

815
File # 18988

The purpose of this summary appraisal report is to provide the lender/client with an accurate, and adequately supported, opinion of the market value of the subject property.

SUBJECT

Property Address 22 OAKWOOD DRIVE | City WESTERVILLE | State OH | Zip Code 43081
Borrower CHRISTOPHER S. JONES | Owner of Public Record JAMES R. & MARIA S. HOLDER | County FRANKLIN
Legal Description LOT #27, PHASE II, LAKE RIDGE SUBDIVISION
Assessor's Parcel # 62-42316000 | Tax Year 2004 | R.E. Taxes $ 4,397.00
Neighborhood Name LAKE RIDGE SUBDIVISION | Map Reference 45 P40 | Census Tract 0071.93
Occupant ☒ Owner ☐ Tenant ☐ Vacant | Special Assessments $ NONE | ☐ PUD | HOA $ N/A | ☐ per year ☐ per month
Property Rights Appraised ☒ Fee Simple ☐ Leasehold ☐ Other (describe)
Assignment Type ☒ Purchase Transaction ☐ Refinance Transaction ☐ Other (describe)
Lender/Client SECOND FEDERAL MORTGAGE | Address 2723 NORTH MAIN STREET, HILLIARD, OHIO
Is the subject property currently offered for sale or has it been offered for sale in the twelve months prior to the effective date of this appraisal? ☒ Yes ☐ No
Report data source(s) used, offering price(s), and date(s). THE SUBJECT HAS BEEN LISTED THROUGH THE COLUMBUS MULTIPLE LISTING SERVICE FOR $179,900. THE PROPERTY HAS BEEN LISTED APPROXIMATELY 35 +/- DAYS.

CONTRACT

I ☒ did ☐ did not analyze the contract for sale for the subject purchase transaction. Explain the results of the analysis of the contract for sale or why the analysis was not performed. THE CURRENT AGREEMENT TO PURCHASE INCLUDES THE FOLLOWING PERSONALTIES: RANGE, REFRIGERATOR AND MISCELLANEOUS WINDOW COVERINGS. NONE ARE CONSIDERED TO CONTRIBUTE SIGNIFICANT VALUE TO THE TRANSACTION.
Contract Price $ $178,000 | Date of Contract 6/1/2005 | Is the property seller the owner of public record? ☒ Yes ☐ No | Data Source(s) FRANKLIN CO. REC.
Is there any financial assistance (loan charges, sale concessions, gift or downpayment assistance, etc.) to be paid by any party on behalf of the borrower? ☒ Yes ☐ No
If Yes, report the total dollar amount and describe the items to be paid. $3,000.00 THE SELLER IS PAYING UP TO $3,000 TOWARD THE PURCHASER'S POINTS AND/OR CLOSING COSTS.

NEIGHBORHOOD

Note: Race and the racial composition of the neighborhood are not appraisal factors.

Neighborhood Characteristics				One-Unit Housing Trends				One-Unit Housing			Present Land Use %	
Location	☐ Urban	☒ Suburban	☐ Rural	Property Values	☒ Increasing	☐ Stable	☐ Declining	PRICE		AGE	One-Unit	90 %
Built-Up	☐ Over 75%	☒ 25-75%	☐ Under 25%	Demand/Supply	☐ Shortage	☒ In Balance	☐ Over Supply	$ (000)		(yrs)	2-4 Unit	0 %
Growth	☒ Rapid	☐ Stable	☐ Slow	Marketing Time	☒ Under 3 mths	☐ 3-6 mths	☐ Over 6 mths	155	Low	2	Multi-Family	0 %
								279	High	9	Commercial	0 %
								180	Pred.	5	Other	10 %

Neighborhood Boundaries SPRINGHILL DRIVE TO THE NORTH, STONERIDGE DRIVE TO THE EAST, FLOWER AVENUE TO THE SOUTH, CUSTER DRIVE TO THE WEST.
Neighborhood Description THE IMMEDIATE MARKET AREA IS PREDOMINATELY SINGLE-FAMILY HOUSING OF VARIOUS STYLES WITH SCATTERED UPPER-MID RANGE CUSTOM CONSTRUCTION. PROXIMITY TO SERVICES, EMPLOYMENT, AND RECREATION IS CONSIDERED AVERAGE. OTHER LAND USE IS THE INFLUENCE OF A PUBLIC PARK WITHIN THE DEFINED NEIGHBORHOOD.
Market Conditions (including support for the above conclusions) INTEREST RATES APPEAR TO BE STABLE AND REMAIN FAVORABLE, WITH MANY FINANCING AVENUES AVAILABLE. ONGOING NEW CONSTRUCTION SUPPORTS STEADY TO RAPID GROWTH PATTERN OF THE OVERALL MARKET. EXISTING HOUSING RESALES COUPLED WITH NEW CONSTRUCTION MAINTAIN SUPPLY/DEMAND IN BALANCE.

SITE

Dimensions 110' X 150' | Area 16,500 SQ.FT. | Shape RECTANGULAR | View RESID. HOUSING
Specific Zoning Classification R-4 | Zoning Description LOW DENSITY RESIDENTIAL DISTRICT
Zoning Compliance ☒ Legal ☐ Legal Nonconforming (Grandfathered Use) ☐ No Zoning ☐ Illegal (describe)
Is the highest and best use of subject property as improved (or as proposed per plans and specifications) the present use? ☒ Yes ☐ No If No, describe

Utilities	Public	Other (describe)		Public	Other (describe)	Off-site Improvements - Type	Public	Private
Electricity	☒	☐	Water	☒	☐	Street ASPHALT	☒	☐
Gas	☒	☐	Sanitary Sewer	☒	☐	Alley NONE	☐	☐

FEMA Special Flood Hazard Area ☐ Yes ☒ No | FEMA Flood Zone X | FEMA Map # 39049C0069H | FEMA Map Date 4/21/1999
Are the utilities and off-site improvements typical for the market area? ☒ Yes ☐ No If No, describe
Are there any adverse site conditions or external factors (easements, encroachments, environmental conditions, land uses, etc.)? ☐ Yes ☒ No If Yes, describe
NO ADVERSE SITE CONDITIONS OR ENCROACHMENTS HAVE BEEN NOTED. FLOOD INFORMATION IS PER FLOODSOURCE FLOOD MAPPING SERVICE, AND IS NOT TO BE RELIED UPON FOR FLOOD INSURANCE DETERMINATION. THE CLIENT SHOULD RELY UPON THEIR FLOOD CERTIFICATION SOURCE FOR FINAL DETERMINATION.

IMPROVEMENTS

General Description	Foundation	Exterior Description materials/condition	Interior materials/condition
Units ☒ One ☐ One with Accessory Unit	☐ Concrete Slab ☒ Crawl Space	Foundation Walls POURED CONC.	Floors WOOD/CRPT/CER
# of Stories 2	☐ Full Basement ☒ Partial Basement	Exterior Walls VINYL/BRICK	Walls DRYWALL
Type ☒ Det. ☐ Att. ☐ S-Det./End Unit	Basement Area 642 sq.ft.	Roof Surface DIM. SHINGLE	Trim/Finish STND. OAK
☒ Existing ☐ Proposed ☐ Under Const.	Basement Finish 75 %	Gutters & Downspouts ALUMINUM	Bath Floor CERAMIC
Design (Style) COLONIAL/2ST	☐ Outside Entry/Exit ☒ Sump Pump	Window Type DOUBLE HUNG	Bath Wainscot CERAMIC
Year Built 1999	Evidence of ☐ Infestation	Storm Sash/Insulated INSULATED	Car Storage ☐ None
Effective Age (Yrs) 3 YEARS	☐ Dampness ☐ Settlement	Screens YES	☒ Driveway # of Cars 2
Attic ☐ None	Heating ☒ FWA ☐ HWBB ☐ Radiant	Amenities ☐ Woodstove(s) #	Driveway Surface CONCRETE
☐ Drop Stair ☐ Stairs	☐ Other Fuel NAT. GAS	☒ Fireplace(s) # 1 ☒ Fence WD. PRIV.	☒ Garage # of Cars 2
☐ Floor ☒ Scuttle	Cooling ☒ Central Air Conditioning	☒ Patio/Deck REAR ☒ Porch FRONT	☐ Carport # of Cars
☐ Finished ☐ Heated	☐ Individual ☐ Other	☐ Pool ☒ Other B-I SPA	☒ Att. ☐ Det. ☐ Built-in

Appliances P Refrigerator P Range/Oven ☒ Dishwasher ☒ Disposal ☒ Microwave ☐ Washer/Dryer ☒ Other (describe) TRASH COMPACTOR
Finished area **above** grade contains: 7 Rooms 3 Bedrooms 2.1 Bath(s) 1,952 Square Feet of Gross Living Area Above Grade
Additional features (special energy efficient items, etc.). MONITORED SECURITY AND FIRE ALARM SYSTEM. GARAGE HAS FINISHED INTERIOR, 2 ELECTRIC DOOR OPENERS AND BUILT-IN STORAGE AREA.
Describe the condition of the property (including needed repairs, deterioration, renovations, remodeling, etc.). THE SUBJECT WAS FOUND TO BE IN OVERALL ABOVE AVERAGE CONDITION AND REASONABLY MAINTAINED. THE EFFECTIVE AGE IS SLIGHTLY LESS THAN ACTUAL DUE TO OVERALL CONDITION.
Are there any physical deficiencies or adverse conditions that affect the livability, soundness, or structural integrity of the property? ☐ Yes ☒ No If Yes, describe
Does the property generally conform to the neighborhood (functional utility, style, condition, use, construction, etc.)? ☒ Yes ☐ No If No, describe

Freddie Mac Form 70 March 2005 | Fannie Mae Form 1004 March 2005

Uniform Residential Appraisal Report - Page 1 of 3

Uniform Residential Appraisal Report

815
File # 18988

There are 7 comparable properties currently offered for sale in the subject neighborhood ranging in price from $ 174,900 to $ 192,500 .

There are 12 comparable sales in the subject neighborhood within the past twelve months ranging in sale price from $ 168,500 to $ 191,000 .

SALES COMPARISON APPROACH

FEATURE	SUBJECT	COMPARABLE SALE # 1		COMPARABLE SALE # 2		COMPARABLE SALE # 3	
Address	22 OAKWOOD DRIVE WESTERVILLE, OH 43081	21 VALLEYVIEW COURT WESTERVILLE, OHIO		337 CHRIS COURT WESTERVILLE, OHIO		321 PEARSON DRIVE WESTERVILLE, OHIO	
Proximity to Subject		0.37 MILE NORTHEAST		0.33 MILE NORTH		0.62 MILE SOUTHEAST	
Sale Price	$ $178,000		$ 180,000		$ 185,000		$ 172,000
Sale Price/Gross Liv. Area	$ 91.19 sq.ft.	$ 89.82 sq.ft.		$ 97.16 sq.ft.		$ 99.48 sq.ft.	
Data Source(s)		FRANKLIN CO. AUDITOR		FRANKLIN CO. AUDITOR		FRANKLIN CO. AUDITOR	
Verification Source(s)		COLS. MLS, BROKER		COLS. MLS, BROKER		COLS. MLS, BROKER	
VALUE ADJUSTMENTS	DESCRIPTION	DESCRIPTION	+(-) $ Adjustment	DESCRIPTION	+(-) $ Adjustment	DESCRIPTION	+(-) $ Adjustment
Sales or Financing Concessions		CONV NONE		CONV SELLER PAID	-5,000	CONV NONE	
Date of Sale/Time		4/30/2005		3/5/2005		5/14/2005	
Location	INSIDE LOT	INSIDE LOT		INSIDE LOT		INSIDE LOT	
Leasehold/Fee Simple	FEE SIMPLE	FEE SIMPLE		FEE SIMPLE		FEE SIMPLE	
Site	16,500 SQ.FT.	17,200 SQ. FT.		15,740 SQ. FT		13,650 SQ. FT.	
View	RES/AVG	RES/AVG		PARK/GOOD	-2,500	RES/AVG	
Design (Style)	COLONIAL/2ST	COLONIAL/2ST		COLONIAL/2ST		COLONIAL/2ST	
Quality of Construction	AVERAGE	AVERAGE		AVERAGE		AVERAGE	
Actual Age	6 YEARS	5 YEARS		6 YEARS		8 YEARS	
Condition	GOOD	GOOD		GOOD		AVERAGE	+2,500
Above Grade Room Count	Total 7 / Bdrms. 3 / Baths 2.1	Total 6 / Bdrms. 3 / Baths 2.1		Total 8 / Bdrms. 3 / Baths 2.1		Total 7 / Bdrms. 3 / Baths 2	+500
Gross Living Area	1,952 sq.ft.	2,004 sq.ft.	-1,250	1,904 sq.ft.	+1,250	1,729 sq.ft.	+5,500
Basement & Finished	642 Sq.Ft.	1,002 SQ. FT.	-2,000	700 SQ. FT.		600 SQ. FT.	
Rooms Below Grade	2 RMS, F BA	UNFINISHED	+3,000	1 RM. FIN	+2,000	2 RMS, F BA	
Functional Utility	AVERAGE	AVERAGE		AVERAGE		AVERAGE	
Heating/Cooling	GFA/CENTRAL	GFA/CENTRAL		GFA/CENTRAL		GFA/CENTRAL	
Energy Efficient Items	TYPICAL	TYPICAL		TYPICAL		TYPICAL	
Garage/Carport	2-C ATT GAR	2-C ATT GAR		2-C ATT GAR		2-C ATT GAR	
Porch/Patio/Deck	PORCH, PATIO	PORCH, DECK		PORCH, PATIO		PORCH,DECK	
	B-I SPA	NONE	+500	IN-GRD POOL	-500	B-I SPA	
	WD PRIV FNC	WD PRIV FNC		WD PRIV FNC		NONE	+500
	FIREPLACE	FIREPLACE		2 FIREPLACES	-1,000	FIREPLACE	
Net Adjustment (Total)		☒ + ☐ -	$ 250	☐ + ☒ -	$ -5,750	☒ + ☐ -	$ 9,000
Adjusted Sale Price of Comparables		Net Adj. 0.1 % Gross Adj. 3.8 %	$ 180,250	Net Adj. 3.1 % Gross Adj. 6.6 %	$ 179,250	Net Adj. 5.2% Gross Adj. 5.2%	$ 181,000

I ☒ did ☐ did not research the sale or transfer history of the subject property and comparable sales. If not, explain

My research ☐ did ☒ did not reveal any prior sales or transfers of the subject property for the three years prior to the effective date of this appraisal.

Data Source(s) FRANKLIN COUNTY AUDITOR

My research ☒ did ☐ did not reveal any prior sales or transfers of the comparable sales for the year prior to the date of sale of the comparable sale.

Data Source(s) FRANKLIN COUNTY AUDITOR

Report the results of the research and analysis of the prior sale or transfer history of the subject property and comparable sales (report additional prior sales on page 3).

ITEM	SUBJECT	COMPARABLE SALE #1	COMPARABLE SALE #2	COMPARABLE SALE #3
Date of Prior Sale/Transfer	NONE IN 36 MONTHS	9/23/2004	NONE IN 12 MONTHS	NONE IN 12 MONTHS
Price of Prior Sale/Transfer		$155,000		
Data Source(s)		FRANKLIN CO AUDITOR		
Effective Date of Data Source(s)		6/3/2005		

Analysis of prior sale or transfer history of the subject property and comparable sales RESEARCH REVEALED THAT SALE #1 TRANSFERRED ON 9/23/2004 FOR $155,000. FURTHER INQUIRY WITH THE SELLER IN THE MOST RECENT TRANSACTION REVEALED THAT THE PURCHASE WAS VIA SHERRIFF'S AUCTION. COSMETIC RENOVATIONS WERE PERFORMED PRIOR TO THE PROPERTY BEING RE-MARKETED.

Summary of Sales Comparison Approach THE SALES REFLECT A REASONABLE VALUE RANGE. ALL SALES ARE FROM THE IMMEDIATE MARKET AREA. CORRELATION IS TOWARD THE UPPER PART OF THE VALUE RANGE, WITH TWO OF THE THREE SALES INDICATING THAT DIRECTION. THESE SALES ARE THE MOST RECENT AND REQUIRE THE FEWEST NET ADJUSTMENTS.

Indicated Value by Sales Comparison Approach $ 178,000

RECONCILIATION

Indicated Value by: Sales Comparison Approach $ 178,000 **Cost Approach (if developed) $** 182,822 **Income Approach (if developed) $** N/A

THE COST APPROACH LENDS SUPPORT AS THE UPPER RANGE OF VALUE. THE SALES COMPARISON APPROACH HAS BEEN GIVEN THE MOST WEIGHT AS IT REFLECTS THE ACTIONS OF BUYERS AND SELLERS IN THE MARKETPLACE. THE SALES COMPARISON APPROACH IS TYPICALLY CONSIDERED TO BE THE MOST RELIABLE IN ASSIGNMENTS OF SINGLE-FAMILY DWELLINGS.

This appraisal is made ☒ "as is", ☐ subject to completion per plans and specifications on the basis of a hypothetical condition that the improvements have been completed, ☐ subject to the following repairs or alterations on the basis of a hypothetical condition that the repairs or alterations have been completed, or ☐ subject to the following required inspection based on the extraordinary assumption that the condition or deficiency does not require alteration or repair:

Based on a complete visual inspection of the interior and exterior areas of the subject property, defined scope of work, statement of assumptions and limiting conditions, and appraiser's certification, my (our) opinion of the market value, as defined, of the real property that is the subject of this report is $ 178,000 **, as of** JUNE 3, 2005 **, which is the date of inspection and the effective date of this appraisal.**

Freddie Mac Form 70 March 2005 Fannie Mae Form 1004 March 2005

Uniform Residential Appraisal Report - Page 2 of 3

Uniform Residential Appraisal Report

815
File # 18988

ADDITIONAL COMMENTS

COST APPROACH TO VALUE (not required by Fannie Mae)

Provide adequate information for the lender/client to replicate the below cost figures and calculations.

Support for the opinion of site value (summary of comparable land sales or other methods for estimating site value) ESTIMATED SITE VALUE IS DERIVED FROM A SALES COMPARISON ANALYSIS OF LOT SALES WITHIN THE SUBJECT'S SUBDIVISION. THIS ANALYSIS IS CONTAINED IN THE APPRAISER'S WORKFILE.

ESTIMATED ☐ REPRODUCTION OR ☒ REPLACEMENT COST NEW

Source of cost data MARSHALL SWIFT COSTING SERVICE

Quality rating from cost service AVG Effective date of cost data 3/1/2005

Comments on Cost Approach (gross living area calculations, depreciation, etc.)

GROSS LIVING AREA HAS BEEN DETERMINED FROM EXTERIOR DIMENSIONS. LOCAL COST DATA CONTAINED IN THE APPRAISER'S FILES HAS ALSO BEEN RESEARCHED. DEPRECIATION HAS BEEN CALCULATED USING THE AGE/LIFE METHOD.

OPINION OF SITE VALUE			=$	35,000
DWELLING	1,952 Sq.Ft. @ $	67.40	=$	131,565
FOUNDATION	642 Sq.Ft. @ $	12.00	=$	7,704
			=$	
Garage/Carport	528 Sq.Ft. @ $	18.00	=$	9,504
Total Estimate of Cost-New			=$	148,773
Less Depreciation	Physical 5,951	Functional	External =$(	5,951)
Depreciated Cost of Improvements			=$	142,822
"As-is" Value of Site Improvements			=$	5,000
INDICATED VALUE BY COST APPROACH			**=$**	182,822

Estimated Remaining Economic Life (HUD and VA only) 72 Years

INCOME APPROACH TO VALUE (not required by Fannie Mae)

Estimated Monthly Market Rent $ N/A X Gross Rent Multiplier N/A = $ N/A Indicated Value by Income Approach

Summary of Income Approach (including support for market rent and GRM) THE INCOME APPROACH HAS NOT BEEN PROCESSED DUE TO A LACK OF COMPARABLE MARKET DATA. THE MARKET IS PRIMARILY OWNER-OCCUPIED.

PROJECT INFORMATION FOR PUDs (if applicable)

Is the developer/builder in control of the Homeowners' Association (HOA)? ☐ Yes ☐ No Unit type(s) ☐ Detached ☐ Attached

Provide the following information for PUDs ONLY if the developer/builder is in control of the HOA and the subject property is an attached dwelling unit.

Legal Name of Project

Total number of phases Total number of units Total number of units sold

Total number of units rented Total number of units for sale Data source(s)

Was the project created by the conversion of existing building(s) into a PUD? ☐ Yes ☐ No If Yes, date of conversion.

Does the project contain any multi-dwelling units? ☐ Yes ☐ No Data Source

Are the units, common elements, and recreation facilities complete? ☐ Yes ☐ No If No, describe the status of completion.

Are the common elements leased to or by the Homeowners' Association? ☐ Yes ☐ No If Yes, describe the rental terms and options.

Describe common elements and recreational facilities.

Freddie Mac Form 70 March 2005 Fannie Mae Form 1004 March 2005

Uniform Residential Appraisal Report - Page 3 of 3

Chapter 12 Summary

1. An **appraisal** is an opinion of value of property, as of a specified date, supportable by objective data. Appraisers follow a well-defined process to value properties using three different methods: Sales comparison approach, cost approach, and income approach. **Uniform Standards of Professional Appraisal Practice** (USPAP) rules and guidelines must be followed so work is seen as complete, accurate, and unbiased. The result of an appraisal is an appraisal report, which communicates the opinion of value and the supporting data. The **Uniform Residential Appraisal Report (URAR)** is the primary form used by lenders for residential property appraisal.
2. The **sales comparison approach** estimates property value by comparing the subject property with other recently sold comparable properties in the same market area. Fannie Mae requires that no less than three comparables be analyzed in the process, but additional comparables may be used for added support. Only past sales are used since they are objective evidence. Fannie Mae's definition of **market value** is the most probable price a property should bring in a competitive and open market. Typical buyers, acting in their own best interest, won't pay more for a home or feature than a comparable substitute.
3. **Comparables** must be similar to the subject, recent sales, and in the same market area. **Adjustments** are made to comparables for differences; the subject never changes. If a comparable lacks something the subject has, add value to it to make it like the subject; if a comparable has something extra, subtract value from it. Adjustments are only made for features present or absent as of the day a comparable was sold; adjustments are only made for significant features.
4. Elements of comparison are any aspects of property that cause a difference in value. The **sequence** of adjustments is: (1) property rights conveyed, (2) financing terms, (3) conditions of sale, (4) market conditions (date of sale), (5) location, and (6) physical characteristics. Adjusting for financing terms is a percentage adjustment. Fannie Mae wants to see actual dollar amounts, but only wants the adjustment to equal the concession's actual effect on sale price. No positive adjustments are permitted. Date of sale adjustment is also a percentage. Adjustments for location and physical features are done as dollar amounts. Total adjustments made to comparables are limited by the secondary market. Accepted adjustment guidelines are that line adjustments should not exceed 10% of the comparable sales price; the total **net** adjustments should not exceed **15%** of comparable's price; and total **gross** adjustments should not exceed **25%** of comparable's price.
5. The URAR form asks for the subject's **transfer history** for the past three years to check for inflated prices. Property flipping is buying property and quickly reselling it for a profit. While not illegal, fraud can occur if the property value is inflated. Frequent transfers with escalating values in a short time period are warning signs. The URAR form also asks for comparable transfer history for the year prior to the date of transfer to determine if the transfer price actually reflects market value. If a comparable was transferred many times with escalating values, or was involved in "back-to-back," "simultaneous," or "double" transaction closings, it should be discarded.
6. **Reconciliation** is the process of analyzing values derived from different appraisal approaches to arrive at a final opinion of value. Values of the different approaches are never averaged to reach a final value. The reconciliation section also indicates if the appraisal was performed "as is" or is subject to other conditions or assumptions, which require additional explanation.
7. With automated underwriting, the value of the property is initially determined using an **automated valuation model** (AVM). AVMs are able to provide a probable value range for properties by performing a statistical analysis of available data.
8. If an appraisal must be updated or readdressed, as when a lender evaluates an application, it must be considered a new assignment by the appraiser. A **recertification of value** (recert) may be necessary to confirm whether or not certain conditions in the original appraisal have been met without changing the effective date of the valuation.
9. The Federal Reserve Board of Governors released an interim final rule on valuation independence, effective April of 2011, that sets standards on compensation, conflicts of interest, and appraiser independence with a goal of ensuring that real estate appraisers are not coerced *in any way* into establishing a pre-determined or desired valuation on a property.

Chapter 12 Quiz

1. ***Which form is used most frequently for residential appraisals?***
   A. FNMA
   B. HVCC
   C. URAR
   D. USFAP

2. ***Jack has been contracted to determine the value of a large apartment building for a potential investor. Which appraisal method is probably the most useful for this situation?***
   A. competitive market analysis
   B. cost approach
   C. income approach
   D. sales comparison approach

3. ***Which of the following is a correct adjustment?***
   A. The comparable has an extra bathroom, so $3,000 is added to the subject price.
   B. The comparable has an extra bathroom, so $3,000 is subtracted from the subject price.
   C. The subject has an extra bathroom, so $3,000 is added to the comparable price.
   D. The subject has an extra bathroom, so $3,000 is subtracted from the comparable price.

4. ***Two homes are similar in every respect except one has air conditioning and the other has a heat pump. Both sold for $125,000. What can we conclude?***
   A. Air conditioning is more desirable than a heat pump.
   B. A heat pump is more desirable than air conditioning.
   C. Neither a heat pump nor air conditioning is a significant feature.
   D. There must be some information missing from the question because air conditioning is always worth more.

5. ***Which is considered first in the sequence of adjustments?***
   A. date of sale
   B. location
   C. physical differences
   D. property rights conveyed

6. ***When a percentage adjustment is made for a sale concession, what is the result?***
   A. The comparable price is now the cash equivalency.
   B. The comparable price is now the time-adjusted normal sale price.
   C. The subject is adjusted to the market.
   D. Nothing, because sales concessions are never percentage adjustments.

7. ***Why are there guidelines on adjustment limits?***
   A. because lenders wanted to limit the number of loans being made
   B. so appraisers do not adjust the subject too much
   C. to gauge how close a comparable approximates the subject
   D. to test which appraisers are more adept at math skills

8. ***On the URAR form, the transfer history for the subject must be reported for***
   A. any suspicious transfers in the public record.
   B. the past three years.
   C. the past year.
   D. The past six months.

9. ***A recert does NOT***
   A. address issues in a "subject to" appraisal.
   B. change the effective date of the valuation.
   C. confirm the validity of the original opinion of value.
   D. verify that conditions stated in the original appraisal have been met.

10. ***Under the provisions of the interim final rule on valuation independence, which would NOT be prohibited?***
   A. asking an appraiser to report a specific property value
   B. conditioning compensation to an appraiser based on consummation of the transaction
   C. obtaining multiple valuations and selecting the most reliable
   D. refusing to use an appraiser who provided a lower than expected valuation on a previous engagement

13

Chapter 13

Ethics in the Mortgage Lending Profession

In This Chapter

Ethics and fair lending are two of the most important issues you will face in your mortgage career. Although ethics, as a philosophical discipline, is a vast topic, in the simplest sense, ethical behavior can be thought of as nothing more than doing the right thing, behaving with integrity, treating people fairly, evaluating a situation and choosing the moral path even if that path is not the easiest one to follow. When considering ethics, it's important to note that unethical behavior may not necessarily be illegal, but once you begin to consider only the legality of your actions, you may have passed the point of giving appropriate consideration to the ethical issues at hand. Still, every person must make choices about how to conduct his or her business and personal life, and while a mortgage professional who always strives to do the right thing is in little danger of violating the law, the law does provide us with a common standard by which to evaluate behavior. Therefore, some important legal points are reviewed in this chapter as we look at conduct that violates anti-discrimination laws, as well as conduct that may be evidence of deception, mortgage fraud, or predatory lending.

At the end of this chapter, you will be able to:

- Define ethics and discuss the purpose of codes of ethics.
- Recognize material facts in an advertisement.
- Define the bait and switch advertising strategy.
- List classes that are protected from illegal discrimination.
- Identify scenarios that violate RESPA's prohibition against kickbacks.
- Recognize indicators of mortgage fraud.
- Identify the participants and their roles in mortgage fraud schemes.
- Identify predatory lending practices.

Key Terms

Bait and Switch
Blockbusting
Civil Rights
Community Reinvestment Act
Equal Credit Opportunity Act (ECOA) / Regulation B
Fair Housing Act
Familial Status
Flipping
Fraud
Home Mortgage Disclosure Act
Kickback
Material Fact
Negligence
Predatory Lending
Redlining
Steering
Straw Buyer

Ethical and Legal Considerations

Ethics in the mortgage industry may seem like a complex issue, but it really boils down to a few simple points:

- Treat everyone equally.
- Be honest.
- Give full disclosure.
- Don't take advantage of people.
- Keep good documentation.

If you do these things, follow the law, and adhere to a code of ethics put forth by your state or local mortgage board and other industry groups, then you shouldn't have any problems.

In an earlier chapter, you learned about federal laws related to consumer rights, and disclosure obligations. In this chapter, you'll look at laws related to fair lending. The laws are the *minimum* duty required of every mortgage professional. You should always strive to fulfill not only the letter of the law, but also its intent. You will also learn about mortgage fraud, predatory lending, and deceptive advertising practices. There are many sources from which a mortgage professional can obtain ethical guidance. The Better Business Bureau (BBB) and the attorney general's office in your state can provide guidance. Also, it is crucial to respond to consumer complaints filed with those agencies. Many training and educational organizations offer business ethics training for mortgage professionals and their support staff.

Code of Ethics

The **National Association of Mortgage Professionals** (which was known previously as NAMB or the National Association of Mortgage Brokers) has promulgated a **Code of Ethics**.

Honesty and Integrity

Mortgage professionals should conduct business in a manner reflecting honesty, honor, and integrity. Obviously, honesty and integrity are the very heart of ethical behavior. You have a basic obligation to protect consumers, to act in accordance with standard practices, and to follow the law. Not only must you act with integrity, but you should insist that those with whom you do business act with integrity as well. What good is it if you are fair and honest, yet you accept an appraisal from someone who has the reputation for hitting a requested value whether it is there or not? The "Golden Rule" you learned as a child still applies: Treat others as you would like to be treated.

Professional Conduct

Reasonable care and skill must always be used when acting on behalf of a customer. Mortgage professionals should be working to find a fair and workable solution for their customers. Within that framework, you will be viewed as a professional and an expert. A form filled out incorrectly or a misunderstood law could cause problems. If a customer loses money due to your incompetence or carelessness, you may be held liable for **negligence**, which is an unintentional breach of a legal duty.

Also, never take on tasks beyond your ability or claim expertise where you have no special training or skills. If you're not qualified in an area, you must tell a client to seek advice from an accountant, appraiser, attorney, or other expert to protect yourself from liability. For example, during the loan process, customers may raise legal questions. Mortgage professionals need to remember that if they aren't licensed to practice law, they **should never give legal advice** or perform any acts that require a lawyer's expertise. Nor should they perform activities reserved for a real estate licensee in any private party transaction by completing a purchase agreement, lease, land contract, or other occupancy, usage, or transfer agreement, or provide the forms and documents required to create such contracts.

In addition, a mortgage professional should never pressure any provider of services, goods, or facilities to circumvent industry professional standards. Nor should they respond to any pressure placed upon them.

Honesty in Advertising

Often, the primary source of information that a consumer has about a particular mortgage loan originator, lender, or loan product comes from advertising, whether it's in print, on the radio, on television, or on the Internet. Mortgage professionals should strive to be truthful in all advertisements and other solicitations for business that they make. For example, this means that you should:

- Clearly state that loan terms and conditions can change if they can or are likely to.
- Advertise only loan terms and conditions that are likely to be available at the time the loan closes.

Confidentiality

As a mortgage professional, you are privy to your customers' personal information. You know about their jobs, their finances, their bank accounts, their credit scores, etc. To keep from destroying the integrity of the process, such information given by the customer or gained from other sources must be kept confidential.

You can use such information only for the business purpose for which it was intended and you cannot share it with anyone outside of your office—including family and friends—or even with co-workers if they don't need that information to complete tasks related to that transaction.

This ethical responsibility to maintain confidential information also means that you cannot take advantage of confidential information for personal benefit. Furthermore, confidential information learned in the course of a transaction should remain confidential, even after the transaction is closed.

Maintaining confidential information goes beyond simply not talking about customers and clients with those who are not a party to the transaction. The financial industry must put procedures in place that ensure the protection of such confidential information. For example, it's important to have a strategy for safely storing and securing documents; it's also necessary to have a strategy for destroying personal papers or documents that contain confidential information.

Compliance with the Law

It goes without saying that you should obey the law, but it may seem sometimes like the law is a moving target. The mortgage industry is highly regulated, as you know, and has been in a genuine state of transition for a couple of years now. The changes are likely to continue for some time. Not only are you obligated to know and understand the law, you have a duty to stay current with changes to the law. You owe it yourself, your employer, the lenders you deal with, and especially your customers, to make a habit of:

- Staying abreast of local and national news regarding trends and issues that affect the financial and mortgage industries.
- Reading industry publications.
- Attending relevant seminars and workshops.
- Keeping up with your continuing education requirements.
- Reviewing program and guideline change announcements.

Disclosure of Financial Interests

You are expected to avoid all situations that might lead to a real or apparent conflict between your self-interest and your duty as a mortgage professional. This means you are not to use your position for personal gain or benefit, or in any manner that could reflect unfavorably on you or your employer. When you have any equity or financial interest in a property being offered as collateral to secure a loan, you must disclose your professional status and your financial interests. To avoid real and apparent conflicts of interest, a mortgage loan originator should disclose, for example:

- Outside business relationships or employment with any party to a transaction.
- Personal or family relationship with any party to the transaction.
- Any equity or financial interest in the collateral offered to secure a loan.
- Prior employer relations that may have included a non-compete, confidentiality, or other agreement that could restrict you from performing your duties.

Title X of the Dodd-Frank Wall Street Reform and Consumer Protection Act of 2010, designated as the Consumer Financial Protection Act, gives the Consumer Financial Protection Bureau authority in § 1031 to prevent its regulated institutions from engaging in unfair, deceptive, or abusive practices. Section 1412 of Title XIV defines an **abusive act** as one that materially interferes with a consumer's ability to understand the product or service or that takes unreasonable advantage of the consumer's lack of understanding, inability to protect his or her interests, or reasonable reliance on a creditor or mortgage loan originator to act in the interests of the consumer. Every mortgage loan originator is responsible for staying current with the rules and regulations implementing these reforms as they become effective.

Class Activity: Ethical Discussion #1

Joyce walks in to MLO Roger's office and asks to complete a loan application. He takes Joyce's personal information, discusses qualification standards, loan options, rates, etc. Then he asks her if she has a specific property in mind. She says she made an offer of $210,000 on a house at 123 Oak Street. Roger recognizes that as the house that he has always wanted to own. As soon as Joyce leaves, Roger finds the phone number of the real estate broker listing the house. He tells her that he wants to make an offer of $215,000 on the house, and that he can guarantee he'll get the loan closed within seven days.

Were Roger's actions ethical? Why or why not? Discuss your responses with the class.

Penalties for Unethical Behavior

When a mortgage loan originator behaves in an unethical manner or otherwise breaches his or her professional obligations, there are a number of possible consequences:

- Action by the state licensing authority,
- Civil lawsuits filed by injured parties,
- Disciplinary action by professional associations, and, in very serious cases,
- The filing of criminal charges.

Ethics in Advertising

In your career, you will spend hours every day dealing with the intricacies of the industry. But most consumers are significantly less informed, and buying or refinancing a home is usually a stressful and confusing undertaking. According to the Better Business Bureau, many consumers begin their search for a mortgage by reviewing printed advertisements in newspapers or magazines. Television and radio commercials—as well as the internet—are also being used more frequently as a means of advertising mortgages and other loan products. According to § 226.2 of Regulation Z, an advertisement is a **commercial message in *any medium* that promotes, directly or indirectly, a credit transaction**.

While there are obviously many laws that have been put in place to protect consumers—the Truth in Lending Act and the Wall Street Reform and Consumer Protection Act of 2010 certainly come to mind—consumers generally rely on the honesty and integrity of those mortgage professional with whom they deal.

The **Federal Trade Commission** has the authority to act in the interest of all consumers to prevent deceptive and unfair acts or practices. Section 5 of the Federal Trade Commission Act (Title 15 U.S.C. 41-58) prohibits unfair or deceptive practices of any kind, which would include advertising in any medium. Therefore, advertising must tell the truth and not mislead consumers. A claim can be misleading if relevant information is left out or if the claim implies something that's not true. For example, an advertisement for a loan that promotes "$0 Down" may be misleading if significant and undisclosed charges are due at closing.

To comply with the mandate to be truthful and fair, advertising should not:

- Misrepresent **material facts** or make **false promises** likely to influence, persuade, or induce an applicant for a mortgage loan or mortgagor to take a mortgage loan.
- **Conceal** any material factors, terms, or conditions of a transaction to which he is a party, including the receipt of payment from a third party, pertinent to an applicant for a mortgage loan or a mortgagor.

Misrepresentation and Material Facts

Misrepresentation is more than mere "**puffing**," which is an opinion that is not necessarily intended as a representation of fact, such as "best customer service in town!" When a misrepresentation is made to a consumer with the intent to deceive, it is a form a fraud and can result in prosecution. Note that written disclosures or fine print in an ad may not be sufficient to correct a misleading representation.

Sometimes, a misrepresentation may be made unintentionally or through **negligence**. While not necessarily actionable fraud, obviously a mortgage professional has an obligation to consumers to be factually accurate in all communication. Either way, misrepresentation is serious, especially when it involves material facts.

When claiming fraud or deception, it may not be necessary to prove that the person to which the deliberate misstatement, misrepresentation, or omission was made was harmed financially in the transaction or relied upon such misstatement, misrepresentation, or omission to make a decision in the transaction. This brings us to the next key concept: What is a "**material fact**"? A material fact is generally defined as one that, if known, might have caused a reasonable consumer to make a different decision. For example, when offering a mortgage loan, material facts may include:

- Annual percentage rate
- Length of loan term
- Fixed or adjustable interest rate
- Origination fees or other closing costs
- Prepayment penalties

From a legal perspective, the misrepresentation of a material fact *could possibly* give a consumer grounds to rescind a contract. Because the terms of a mortgage loan constitute material facts, however, federal law requires significant disclosures that inform and protect the consumer.

Bait and Switch

When discussing advertising, you may hear the term **bait and switch.** This is a tactic of luring consumers in with promises of low rates and specific products, and then **steering** otherwise qualified buyers to other terms so that the mortgage loan originator can earn a higher fee. The Federal Trade Commission Act addresses the practice of bait and switch in Title 16, Part 238. According to § 238.0:

> *Bait advertising is an alluring but insincere offer to sell a product or service which the advertiser in truth does not intend or want to sell. Its purpose is to switch consumers from buying the advertised merchandise, in order to sell something else, usually at a higher price or on a basis more advantageous to the advertiser. The primary aim of a bait advertisement is to obtain leads as to persons interested in buying merchandise of the type so advertised.*

So, for example, mortgage loan originator Jack advertises refinance loans with 0 points and 3.8% APR just to get prospective borrowers in the door. Then, he tells them that such terms are not available to them because of their debt, or their income, or any other such factor. In reality, Jack had no intention of placing any loan on those terms.

Jack baited consumers with his advertisement, which is violation of 16 C.F.R. 238 § 238.1:

> *No advertisement containing an offer to sell a product should be published when the offer is not a bona fide effort to sell the advertised product.*

Bona Fide Offer

Furthermore, it is a violation of 16 C.F.R. 238 to *discourage* the purchase of the advertised merchandise as part of a bait scheme to sell other merchandise. When determining whether or not the initial offer was a bona fide offer, these points would be considered:

- The refusal of the advertiser to show, demonstrate, or sell the product offered in accordance with the terms of the offer
- The disparagement by acts or words of the advertised product or the disparagement of the guarantee, credit terms, availability of service, repairs or parts, or in any other respect, in connection with it
- The failure to have available at all outlets listed in the advertisement a sufficient quantity of the advertised product to meet reasonably anticipated demands, unless the advertisement clearly and adequately discloses that supply is limited and/or the merchandise is available only at designated outlets
- The refusal to take orders for the advertised merchandise to be delivered within a reasonable period of time
- The showing or demonstrating of a product which is defective, unusable, or impractical for the purpose represented or implied in the advertisement
- Use of a sales plan or method of compensation for salesmen or penalizing salesmen, designed to prevent or discourage them from selling the advertised product

While some of these points may seem more relevant to personal property such as appliances or automobiles, you should certainly be able to see how they could apply to mortgage products and services as well.

Switch After Sale

Section 238.4 of the FTC Act indicates that no practice should be pursued by an advertiser, in the event of sale of the advertised product, of "unselling" with the intent and purpose of selling other merchandise in its stead. Among acts or practices which will be considered in determining if the initial sale was in good faith, and not a stratagem to sell other merchandise, are these:

- Accepting a deposit for the advertised product, then switching the purchaser to a higher-priced product
- Failure to make delivery of the advertised product within a reasonable time or to make a refund
- Disparagement by acts or words of the advertised product, or the disparagement of the guarantee, credit terms, availability of service, repairs, or in any other respect, in connection with it
- The delivery of the advertised product which is defective, unusable or impractical for the purpose represented or implied in the advertisement

But what if the consumer decided to accept different terms and apply for the loan anyway? According to 16 C.F.R. Part 238, even though the true facts are subsequently made known to the buyer, the law is violated if the first contact or interview is secured by deception.

Class Activity: Mortgage Advertising

You may wonder how bait and switch relates to advertising mortgage loans, but consider these examples and discuss your thoughts with the class.

Scenario1: MLO Jane advertises what she calls "5 for 5" mortgage loans: 5% down and 5% fixed rate interest for 30 years. A qualified borrower comes in and starts the loan process, paying for a credit report, and completing a loan application. But Jane does not lock in that interest rate. She knows that rates are going up, so she sits on the application for an extra week, and then tells the borrower that the best she can do is 5 3/4%.

Would this be considered an example of a bait and switch tactic? Why or why not?

Scenario 2: MLO Alex advertises that he will close loans in 14 business days, even though he knows that his average close takes 47 days. His ad brings in 100 new customers, and he works extra hard to close a few of those loans in 14 days so that his advertisement remains legitimate.

Would this be considered an example of a bait and switch tactic? Why or why not?

Unfair and Deceptive

When determining whether or not an advertisement or practice is likely to be deceptive, the FTC will examine it from the perspective of a consumer acting reasonably in the circumstances, examining the entire advertisement, transaction, or course of dealing in determining how reasonable consumers are likely to respond. Rather than focusing on certain words, the FTC indicates that it looks at the ad in context—including words, phrases, and images—to determine what it conveys to consumers.

If the representation or practice affects or is directed primarily to a particular group, such as the elderly, the FTC examines reasonableness from the perspective of that group.

For example, think about the advertisements you see on television for reverse mortgages, which are marketed for homeowners age 62 or older as a way to take advantage of the equity in their homes. These ads often employ well-known actors telling potential borrowers about the benefits of this particular loan product, but do not necessarily explain all the details. While there are certainly many regulations in place to protect elderly borrowers—such as required counseling—when considering advertisements, the FTC would examine the ad's message from the perspective of an elderly homeowner.

To assist consumers in determining whether advertisements for mortgage products are fair, the Federal Trade Commission distributed a consumer alert entitled **Deceptive Mortgage Ads: What They Say; What They Leave Out.** The main points are summarized below:

- Consumers should be able to understand all the terms and conditions of a proposed loan. They are advised to learn to read what's between the lines as well as what's emphatically stated in the ad.
- Some ads—whether on the internet, on television, in the paper, fax, or mail—may look tempting, but are flawed if they don't disclose the true terms.
- The annual percentage rate is a critical factor in comparing mortgage offers from different lenders; sometimes the APR is hidden in the fine print or buried deep in a website.

- Important payment information is often excluded from an ad; consumers should be prepared to ask about payments, terms, escrow, penalties, etc.
- Consumers are advised to consider shopping with several lenders to compare all of the fees they charge and encouraged to ask MLOs to see a list of mortgage rates.
- Consumers are reminded that negotiating is acceptable.

(See: http://www.ftc.gov/bcp/edu/pubs/consumer/alerts/alt023.shtm)

Evaluating Buzzwords

The FTC consumer alert on mortgage advertising also advises consumers to look for certain buzzwords that often appear in ads. Though these are not deceptive in and of themselves, when preparing an advertisement, you should consider whether or not the use of such words or terms is fair, accurate, and complete within the context of your advertisement. Taking time to evaluate such language will help you remain in compliance with state and federal laws prohibiting deception. Look at these examples:

- **Low "Fixed" Rate.** If an ad indicates availability of a "fixed" rate, it should also indicate how long it will be "fixed."
- **Very Low Rates.** Is the ad referring to a low "payment" rate or a low interest rate? There's a big difference, and it should be clear to the consumer. Also, does the rate apply only for an introductory period? Ads with teaser rates don't often disclose that a rate or payment is for a very short introductory period. Consumers must be informed of all the details in order to avoid payment shock when the rate and payment increase dramatically.
- **Very Low Payment Amounts.** Such ads should tell the whole story. Is it an interest-only loan? Does it cover the interest due? Is it an adjustable rate loan?

The FTC alert also provides examples of solicitation and advertising tactics that are intended to deceive consumers, such as mailers that have information about their mortgage that are not actually from their lender or mailings with official-looking stamps, envelopes, forms, etc., that appear to be from a government agency. Sadly, there are people and organizations out there who are willing to walk a fine line when it comes to deceptive advertising, and consumers must be on their guard.

The Internet

Obviously, the world today is different place today because of the internet. As consumers, we comparison shop, we play games, we socialize, all without leaving our living rooms. As members of the mortgage business community, we advertise, we provide guidance and counseling, we accept loan applications. The internet has become indispensible, and the power of the internet to reach potential consumers for our products and services seems virtually limitless. It's critical to understand, though, that the same laws that regulate print and broadcast media apply equally to advertising, promotion, and marketing on the internet. In a nutshell:

- Advertising must be truthful and not misleading.
- Advertisers must have evidence to back up their claims.
- Advertisements cannot be unfair.

An unfair or deceptive message will be unfair or deceptive wherever the consumer views or hears it. Additionally, required disclosures are as important online as anywhere else, and you must comply with all laws related to disclosures. The mandate that disclosures be "clear and conspicuous" applies here as well.

When considering the idea of clear and conspicuous disclosures in online ads, placement and proximity are critical. The FTC's **Dot Com Disclosures: Information about Online Advertising** paper provides some valuable guidance on making disclosures clear and conspicuous:

- Place disclosures **near**, and when possible, on the same screen as the triggering claim.
- Use text or visual **cues** to encourage consumers to scroll down a Web page when it is necessary to view a disclosure.
- If using hyperlinks to lead to disclosures, make the link **obvious**, label the hyperlink appropriately to convey the importance of the information it leads to, and take consumers directly to the disclosure (note that it might not be possible to meet the letter of the law by burying disclosures in a link).

- **Prominently** display disclosures so they are noticeable to consumers, and evaluate the size, color and graphic treatment of the disclosure in relation to other parts of the page.
- Review the entire ad to ensure that other elements—text, graphics, hyperlinks or sound—**do not distract** consumers' attention from the disclosure.
- **Repeat** disclosures, as needed, on lengthy web sites and in connection with repeated claims.
- Display visual disclosures for a **duration** sufficient for consumers to notice, read, and understand them.
- Use **clear language** and syntax so that consumers understand the disclosures.

(See: http://www.ftc.gov/opa/2000/05/dotcom.shtm)

And with the advent of emerging technology of social media, such as Facebook, LinkedIn, and Twitter, the need for clear and conspicuous disclosure to avoid even unintentional deception is an ongoing challenge.

Advertising Guidance

The Better Business Bureau also offers some general guidance related to advertising ethics. When creating advertisements, consider these questions:

- Does your advertising make your customers satisfied that they do business with you? Your advertising is just another outlet through which you can promote good will and customer loyalty.
- Are you avoiding impossible promises and guarantees? When using the term "guarantee," you should include a statement that explains complete details are available at the store, or, in the case of mail or telephone sales, are available free upon written request.
- Are your advertised merchandise or programs readily available?
- Do you mean to sell what you advertise? Do not participate in **bait and switch** tactics that involve advertising a low-priced item to bring in customers, then persuading them to buy similar, but higher-priced items.
- Do your ads avoid misleading inferences? Misleading advertising is considered a questionable business practice that should be avoided.
- Do your advertised terms agree with the facts? An advertisement as a whole may be misleading even if every sentence separately considered is literally true.
- Is your advertising easy to understand without asterisks and fine print? Asterisks should not be used as a means of contradicting or substantially changing the meaning of an advertising statement.
- Do you believe your own comparatives? You should be able to substantiate all claims made in the ad.
- Would you be attracted by what your ad says? If it is not attractive to you, it most likely will not be attractive to your customers.

Finally, you must, of course, follow all federal and state laws and regulations related to advertising, such as the requirement to include your NMLS unique identifier and Equal Housing Lender logo/slogan as applicable, and the disclosure requirements found in the Truth in Lending Act and Regulation Z (explained in detail in Chapter 4).

Illegal Discrimination

Fair and equitable treatment in housing and real estate transactions is a right by law. The two federal anti-discrimination statutes that have the greatest impact on real estate transactions are the **Civil Rights Act of 1866** and Title VIII of the Civil Rights Act of 1968, commonly referred to as the **Fair Housing Act**. In addition, these laws also affect the granting of credit by real estate lenders:

- The Equal Credit Opportunity Act (ECOA)
- The Community Reinvestment Act (CRA)
- The Home Mortgage Disclosure Act (HMDA)

Real Success

All mortgage industry professionals are required to observe these federal laws, as well as the anti-discrimination statutes and laws passed by their state and local governments. If you are accepting a mortgage application and the property is in another state other than where you normally do business, it is your responsibility to research any specific laws and regulations for that state. Also, know the licensing requirements in that state.

Civil Rights Act of 1866

The **Civil Rights Act of 1866**, codified in Title 42, Section 1981(a) of the U.S. Code, prohibits public and private racial discrimination in any property transaction in the United States. The Act states:

> *"All citizens of the United States shall have the same right, in every State and Territory, as is enjoyed by white citizens thereof to inherit, purchase, lease, sell, hold, and convey real and personal property."*

The 1866 Civil Rights Act applies to all property—real or personal, residential or commercial, improved or unimproved. The Act prohibits any discrimination based on race or ancestry, and was upheld in 1968 by the United States Supreme Court in the landmark case of *Jones v. Mayer.* The court ruled that the 1866 federal law "prohibits all racial discrimination, private or public, in the sale and rental of property" and is constitutional based on the 13th Amendment to the U.S. Constitution, which prohibits slavery.

Enforcement

A person who has been unlawfully discriminated against under the 1866 Act can sue only in federal district court. The court fashions the remedies it finds necessary, which may include **injunctions** (court orders requiring the defendant to do or refrain from doing a particular act), **compensatory damages** (reimbursement for expenses caused by the discrimination and/or for emotional distress), and **punitive damages** (to punish the wrongdoer if the acts are deliberate or egregious). Depending on the circumstances, these remedies may be instead of or in addition to those available to parties under other federal and state statutes.

Fair Housing Act

Title VIII of the Civil Rights Act of 1968 is commonly called the **Fair Housing Act**. The Fair Housing Act expanded on the 1866 Act, making it illegal to discriminate in the sale or lease of residential property, including vacant land intended for residential housing. The Act has been amended several times and now extends protection against discrimination based on:

- Race
- Color
- Religion
- Sex
- National origin
- Disability
- Familial status

Although the federal Fair Housing Act prohibits discrimination in housing against the disabled, Congress further expanded protection with the more comprehensive **Americans with Disabilities Act (ADA)**, which was signed into law in 1990.

Fair Housing Act Exemptions

The Fair Housing Act covers the majority of residential transactions in the U.S., although there are specific exemptions:

- The rental of a room or unit in a dwelling with no more than four independent units provided that the owner occupies one unit as a residence
- Single-family home sold or rented by a private owner without the use of a broker
- Housing operated by organizations
- Housing operated by private clubs

Fair Housing Violations

The following discriminatory practices and activities violate the Fair Housing Act (42 U.S.C. §§ 3604-3605) if they are based on a person's membership in a protected class:

Violation	Example
Refusing to rent or sell residential property after receiving a good faith offer	A homeowner decides not to accept the offer after learning that the buyer is Jewish.
Refusing to negotiate for the sale or rental of residential property	A listing agent follows his seller's instructions to not show the house to any Asians.
Taking any action that would otherwise make residential property unavailable or deny it to any person	A minority couple tells an agent what they're looking for in a home. Six listings in the MLS match their criteria, but the agent tells them about only the three that are in neighborhoods with a high population of minorities.
Using discriminatory advertising or any other notice that indicates a limitation or preference or intent to make any limitation, preference, or discrimination	A landlord includes the phrase "no children" in an advertisement for an apartment.
Making any representation that property is not available for inspection, sale, or rent when it is, in fact, available	A landlord tells a potential tenant who has a Hispanic accent that the apartment is already rented, but shows the unit to a white man.
Coercing, intimidating, threatening, or interfering with anyone because of his enjoyment, attempt to enjoy, or encouragement and assistance to others in their enjoyment of the rights granted by the Fair Housing Act	A landlord threatens to evict a tenant who files a fair housing complaint.
Discriminating in the terms or conditions of any sale or rental of residential property or in providing any services or facilities in connection with such property	A landlord requires applicants to include a deposit, but the property manager does not tell male applicants about the requirement, so their applications are not processed.

In addition, it is illegal for anyone to threaten, coerce, intimidate, or interfere with anyone exercising a fair housing right or assisting others who exercise that right.

Discrimination in Mortgage Lending

From the perspective of a mortgage professional, no one may take any of the following actions if they are based on a person's membership in a protected class:

- Refusing to make a mortgage loan
- Refusing to provide information regarding loans
- Imposing different terms or conditions on a loan, such as different interest rates, points, or fees
- Discriminating in the appraisal of property
- Refusing to purchase a loan
- Setting different terms or conditions for purchasing a loan, for example, a bank charging a higher interest rate to a creditworthy borrower who wants to buy a house in a minority neighborhood than is charged for an equally creditworthy borrower in a different neighborhood

Discriminatory Practices

Most discussions on fair housing include these illegal acts:

Blockbusting. Blockbusting is *trying to induce owners to sell their homes by suggesting that the ethnic or racial composition of the neighborhood is changing, with the implication that property values will decline.* This practice is also called **panic selling**. The person making the prediction buys the properties from the owners and then resells them for a profit.

Steering. Steering is *channeling prospective real estate buyers or tenants to particular neighborhoods based on their race, religion, or ethnic background.* This may never be done in order to maintain or change the character of those neighborhoods.

Redlining. Redlining is a refusal to make loans—or making loans on less favorable terms—on property located in a particular neighborhood for discriminatory reasons. In the past, many lenders assumed that an integrated or predominantly minority neighborhood was automatically a place where property values declined. Based on that assumption, they refused to make loans in these neighborhoods. Since it was almost impossible to obtain purchase or renovation loans, it was extremely difficult to market, maintain, or improve homes, which caused neighborhood values to decline even further, a cycle from which few neighborhoods could recover.

Lenders may still deny loans in neighborhoods where property values are declining, but this must be based on objective criteria regarding the condition and value of the property or area. A lender may not simply equate integrated or minority neighborhoods with declining property values.

Advertising Provisions

The Fair Housing Act also prohibits discrimination in advertising, real estate brokerage, lending, and some other services associated with residential transactions. To comply with this Act, lenders are required to:

- Include the "equal housing lender" slogan in any broadcast advertisement,
- Display the Equal Housing Opportunity poster in every branch where mortgage loans are made, and
- Display the Equal Housing Opportunity logo on all printed promotional material.

Enforcement

A person who has been discriminated against in violation of the Fair Housing Act may file a written complaint to the nearest HUD office within **one year** of the alleged violation (42 U.S.C. § 3610). Complaints are investigated by the Office of Fair Housing and Equal Opportunity (FHEO). HUD may refer complaints to the state or local agency that has similar responsibilities (for example, a state Civil Rights Commission), or HUD itself may investigate the incident. HUD tries to obtain voluntary compliance with the Fair Housing Act.

The parties involved in the discrimination may choose to have the dispute decided in a civil lawsuit instead, either in U.S. District Court or another court that has jurisdiction. The court may grant an injunction, compensatory damages, punitive damages, and attorney's fees. In addition, the U.S. Attorney General may bring a civil suit in federal district court against anyone engaged in an ongoing pattern or practice of discriminatory activities, referred to as "pattern or practice lawsuits."

THE HOUSING FINANCIAL DISCRIMINATION ACT OF 1977
FAIR LENDING NOTICE

DATE: COMPANY: *[INSERT COMPANY NAME]*
APPLICATION NO: *[INSERT ADDRESS]*
PROPERTY ADDRESS:

It is illegal to discriminate in the provisions of or in the availability of financial assistance because of the consideration of:

1. Trends, characteristics or conditions in the neighborhood or geographic area surrounding a housing accommodation, unless the financial institution can demonstrate in the particular case that such consideration is required to avoid am unsafe and unsound business practice; or
2. Race, color, religion, sex, marital status, national origin or ancestry.

It is illegal to consider the racial ethnic, religious or national origin composition of a neighborhood or geographic area surrounding a housing accommodation or whether or not such composition is undergoing change, or is expected to undergo change, in appraising a housing accommodation or in determining whether or not, or under what terms and conditions, to provide financial assistance.

These provisions govern financial assistance for the purpose of the purchase, construction, rehabilitation or refinancing of a one-to-four unit family residence occupied by the owner and for the purpose of the home improvement of any one-to-four unit family residence.

If you have any questions about your rights, or if you wish to file a complaint, contact the management of this financial institution or the agency noted below:

[INSERT APPROPRIATE ENFORCEMENT AGENCY NAME/ADDRESS HERE]

I/We received a copy of this notice

(Date) (Date)

Sample Fair Lending Notice

The Equal Credit Opportunity Act

The **Equal Credit Opportunity Act** (15 U.S.C. § 1691) is a federal law that *ensures that all consumers are given an equal chance to obtain credit.* The **Equal Credit Opportunity Act** requires anyone who grants credit or sets the terms of that credit must never discriminate based on the basis of:

- Race,
- Color,
- Religion,
- National origin,
- Age (provided applicant has the capacity to contract, i.e., 18 years old),
- Sex,
- Marital status,
- Receipt of income from public assistance programs, or
- Exercised rights under the Consumer Credit Protection Act.

As a matter of fact, the law indicates that someone cannot even be **discouraged from applying for credit** based on any of these factors.

The law protects a borrower against any creditor who regularly extends credit, including banks, small loan and finance companies, retail and department stores, credit card companies, and credit unions. Anyone involved in granting credit, such as real estate brokers and mortgage brokers who arrange financing, is covered by the law. Businesses applying for credit also are protected by the law. ECOA, implemented by **Regulation B** of the Board of Governors of the Federal Reserve System, must be followed when:

- Taking loan applications.
- Evaluating an application.
- Approving or denying a loan.

The law was originally passed in 1974 to prohibit lending discrimination on the basis of sex or marital status. This law led to, among other things, the requirement that credit bureaus maintain separate credit files on married spouses, if so requested. The law ensured that women received the same consideration by lenders when applying for credit. The law was expanded in 1976 to include all of the protected classes listed above. Most notable among the law's revisions is prohibiting the discrimination against a potential borrower on public assistance.

Note the provision in this Act that protects a borrower who is on public assistance. As long as the borrower's income from public assistance is stable (or permanent), the lender or mortgage broker must consider this income as valid as any other qualifying income. The adequacy and stability of a borrower's income should be considered and *not* its source. Lenders and mortgage brokers must therefore:

- Consider reliable public assistance income the same way as other income.
- Consider reliable income from part-time employment, Social Security, pensions, and annuities.
- Consider reliable alimony, child support, or separate maintenance payments if the borrower chooses to provide this information (lenders may ask for proof).
- Accept someone other than a spouse as a co-signer, if one is needed.

While the Equal Credit Opportunity Act clearly indicates that a lender or mortgage broker must consider reliable alimony, child support, or separate maintenance payments as income, the applicant is **not required to disclose** such income. Furthermore, a mortgage loan originator may not discriminate against an applicant who exercises his or her good faith rights of nondisclosure of those sources of income.

EQUAL CREDIT OPPORTUNITY ACT

APPLICATION NO:

PROPERTY ADDRESS:

The Federal Equal Credit Opportunity Act prohibits creditors from discriminating against credit applicants on the basis of race, color, religion, national origin, sex, marital status, age (provided the applicant has the capacity to enter into a binding contract); because all or part of the applicant's income derives from any public assistance program; or because the applicant has in good faith exercised any right under the Consumer Credit Protection Act. The Federal Agency that administers compliance with this law concerning the company is *[INSERT APPROPRIATE FEDERAL AGENCY HERE]*.

We are required to disclose to you that you need not disclose income from alimony, child support or separate maintenance payment if you choose not to do so.

Having made this disclosure to you, we are permitted to inquire of any of the income shown on your application is derived from such a source and to consider the likelihood of consistent payment as we do with any income on which you are relying to qualify for the loan for which you are applying.

____________________ (Applicant) (Date) ____________________ (Applicant) (Date)

____________________ (Applicant) (Date) ____________________ (Applicant) (Date)

Sample Equal Credit Opportunity Notice

Real Success

To comply with ECOA, you usually may not ask interested borrowers of their marital status. Nor can you ask someone about their spouse unless it is a joint application and the spouse will use the account or be contractually liable, or if the applicant is relying on their spouse's income or alimony, or child support from a former spouse to qualify for the loan. When the loan is secured by property—as with a mortgage—you *may* ask about a spouse, since in many states, certain rights and benefits exist for spouses. If, for example, a lender must foreclose on a property, it may be necessary for the spouse to legally relinquish those rights.

When permitted to ask about marital status, you may not ask the applicant if he or she is widowed or divorced, however. You may use only these terms:

- Married
- Unmarried (which includes single, divorced, or widowed)
- Separated

Additionally, you cannot ask an applicant about any plans for having or raising children, but you can ask questions about expenses related to any dependents.

In states that recognize **dower or curtesy rights** of spouses, it is acceptable to ask about marital status even if only one person is applying for the loan. In such states, the non-borrowing spouse must consent, since the non-borrowing spouse has an interest in the security instrument.

Loan Application

It is permissible to ask someone applying for a loan to purchase or refinance a principal residence for certain information for the use of the federal government in monitoring lender compliance with equal credit and equal housing laws. Section X of the Uniform Residential Loan Application asks the borrower to supply the following data:

- Ethnicity (Hispanic or Latino/Not Hispanic or Latino)
- Race (American Indian or Alaska Native, Native Hawaiian or Other Pacific Islander, Asian, White, Black or African American)
- Sex (Male or Female)

The application clearly states that applicants may refuse to furnish this information, and that a lender cannot discriminate based on either the information supplied or on the applicant's refusal. If the applicant does refuse, the interviewer is required to note the information on the basis of visual observation and surname when the application is made in person.

Considering Income

When evaluating a potential borrower's gross income, a creditor may consider the amount and probability of any income continuing. A creditor may NOT:

- Refuse to consider public assistance income the same way as other income.
- Discount income because of sex or marital status.
- Discount or refuse to consider income because it comes from part-time employment or pension, annuity, or retirement benefits programs.
- Refuse to consider regular alimony, child support, or separate maintenance payments.

While the Equal Credit Opportunity Act clearly indicates a lender must consider reliable alimony, child support, or separate maintenance payments as income, the applicant is **not required to disclose** such income. Furthermore, a mortgage loan originator may not discriminate against applicants who exercise their good faith rights of nondisclosure of those sources of income.

Age of Applicant

Creditors can consider the age of an applicant for credit under these circumstances:

- The applicant is too young to sign contracts, generally under age 18.
- The creditor would favor applicants age 62 and older.
- It is used to determine the meaning of other factors important to creditworthiness, such as to determine if an applicant's income might drop because of pending retirement.
- It may be used in a valid credit scoring system that favors applicants depending on their age.

Enforcement

ECOA is enforced by the **Federal Trade Commission**; however, each financial institution further falls under the authority of its respective regulatory agency. Consumers who apply for credit and feel that they've been unjustly discriminated against may file a complaint with the same bodies as they would for other types of discrimination claims. Any creditor that fails to comply with a requirement imposed by ECOA is subject to civil liability for actual and punitive damages in individual or class actions. Liability for punitive damages can apply only to nongovernmental entities and is limited to $10,000 in individual actions and the lesser of $500,000 or 1% of the creditor's net worth in class actions. A civil action may be brought in the appropriate United States district court within **two years** after the date of the occurrence of the violation.

Community Reinvestment Act (CRA)

Congress enacted the **Community Reinvestment Act** (12 U.S.C. § 2901 et seq.) in 1977 to encourage financial institutions to help meet the credit needs of the communities in which they operate, including low- and moderate-income neighborhoods, consistent with safe and sound lending practices.

The CRA requires that each insured depository institution's record in helping meet the credit needs of its entire community be evaluated periodically. That record is taken into account in considering an institution's application for deposit facilities, including mergers and acquisitions. CRA examinations are conducted by the federal agencies that are responsible for supervising depository institutions: The Board of Governors of the Federal Reserve System (FRB), the Federal Deposit Insurance Corporation (FDIC), the Office of the Comptroller of the Currency (OCC), and the Office of Thrift Supervision (OTS).

In some states, the requirements of CRA have been extended to mortgage lenders. Make sure you know the laws of the states in which you conduct business.

Home Mortgage Disclosure Act of 1975 (HMDA)

The **Home Mortgage Disclosure Act** (12 U.S.C. § 2801-2810), enacted by Congress in 1975, is enforced by the Federal Reserve Board's **Regulation C** and applies to certain financial institutions, including banks, savings associations, credit unions, and other mortgage lending institutions or non-depository institutions with assets in excess of $10 million or who originate more than 100 mortgage loans per year. HMDA provides loan data that can be used by the public to assist in:

- Determining whether financial institutions are serving the housing needs of their communities.
- Aiding public officials in distribution of public-sector investment in order to attract private investment where needed.
- Identifying possible discriminatory lending patterns through the collection and disclosure of data about applicant and borrower characteristics.

As the name implies, the Home Mortgage Disclosure Act is a disclosure law that relies upon public scrutiny for its effectiveness. It does not prohibit any specific activity of lenders, and it does not establish a quota system of mortgage loans to be made in any metropolitan statistical area (MSA) or other geographic area as defined by the Office of Management and Budget.

Covered Properties

The provisions of HMDA affect applications for residential loans, including:

- Home purchase,
- Home improvement,
- Refinancing, and
- Subordinate financing.

It does *not* apply to loans on vacant land, new construction, or on loans that are sold as part of a pool for servicing.

Data Reporting

Regulation C requires financial institutions to submit a report—called a **Loan/Application Register** or LAR—to their supervisory agencies on a loan-by-loan and application-by-application basis every March. Data for the LAR is collected on loan originations, applications, and loan purchases, as well as requests under a pre-approval program, if the pre-approval request is denied or results in the origination of a home purchase loan.

These reports can be used to discover discriminatory practices, including redlining, by analyzing whether an institution turns down a disproportionate percentage of applications by race, gender, or ethnicity or by certain neighborhoods. The application, lending, and denial data that lending institutions subject to HMDA are required to report for all borrowers includes:

- Loan type, amount, and purpose
- Rate spread (the difference between the annual percentage rate and the rate on Treasury securities of comparable maturity) only if above designated thresholds
- Property type and occupancy
- Ethnicity, race, and sex of applicant and co-applicants
- Applicant gross income
- Loan decision, including denial reason(s)
- Population and the percentage of which is minority (census tract)
- Whether or not the loan is subject to the Home Ownership and Equity Protection Act (HOEPA) controls related to predatory lending
- The type of purchaser for mortgage loans that they sell

The loan application register information must be maintained and made available upon request for **three years.**

Additional Data

Title X of the Dodd-Frank Wall Street Reform and Consumer Protection Act of 2010, which is designated the Consumer Financial Protection Act, includes provisions that, when implemented via regulation, will also require MLOs to collect the following data about mortgage loan applicants in order to comply with HMDA:

- Age
- Credit score
- Total points and fees
- Loan term and pricing
- Prepayment penalty information

- Loan-to-value
- Period of any introductory interest rate
- Interest-only or negative amortization information
- Channel of origination

Role of the FFIEC

Supervisory agencies, through the **Federal Financial Institutions Examination Council** (FFIEC), compile HMDA data in the form of individual disclosure statements for each institution, and in the form of aggregate reports for all covered institutions within each MSA. In addition, the FFIEC produces other aggregate reports that show lending patterns by median age of homes and by the central city or non-central city location of the property. The analysis of this data is a critical component to determine if there is compliance with ECOA as well as fair lending laws.

Regulation C requires a lending institution to post a general notice about the availability of HMDA data in the lobby of its home office and of each branch office located in a metropolitan area. The suggested, not mandated, wording is as follows:

HOME MORTGAGE DISCLOSURE ACT NOTICE

The HMDA data about our residential mortgage lending are available for review. The data show geographic distribution of loans and applications; ethnicity, race, sex, and income of applicants and borrowers; and information about loan approvals and denials. Inquire at this office regarding the locations where HMDA data may be inspected. To receive a copy of these data send a written request to [INSERT ADDRESS OF LENDER/BROKER].

Real Success

ECOA requires you to ask the applicant for the information needed for the Loan/Application Register whether the application is taken in person, by mail or telephone, or on the Internet—but you cannot require the applicant to provide it. If the applicant declines to answer these questions or fails to provide the information on an application taken by mail or telephone or on the Internet, the data need not be provided. If the applicant chooses not to provide the information for an application taken in person, however, you must note this fact on the form and then note the applicant's ethnicity, race, and sex on the basis of visual observation and surname, to the extent possible.

Other Types of Discrimination

Blatant discrimination still exists, but it is less common today. Instead, there are more subtle ways—both intentional and unintentional—that may amount to discrimination. If you are ever in doubt about what qualifies as discrimination, talk with your employer or an experienced mortgage professional.

Discrimination in Municipal Actions

Exclusionary zoning laws are defined as *any laws that have the effect of denying housing to minorities or other protected classes.* The clause "make otherwise unavailable or deny" in anti-discrimination legislation has been interpreted to prohibit such exclusionary zoning. Since it's currently unlikely that a municipality would enact an openly racist ordinance, these cases usually involve arguments based on the concept of **disparate impact.** A law with disparate impact *may be neutral on its face, but it has a discriminatory effect since it has a greater adverse impact on one group than on others.*

Exclusionary zoning cases usually involve ordinances that prohibit or unreasonably restrict multifamily or low-income housing. Statistics show in comparison to the white population, members of minority groups are more likely to be considered low-income. As a result, it has been successfully argued in a number of cases that ordinances limiting low-cost housing have a disparate impact on minority groups, in effect excluding them from certain communities.

Discrimination in Advertising

Words carry great power. The use of certain words can influence, inform, and sometimes, mislead consumers, and the misuse of words, even if unintentional, can create problems. For example, certain phrases used in residential mortgage advertising could convey either overt or tacit discriminatory preferences or limitations.

In addition to outlawing discrimination in housing, the federal Fair Housing Act restricts the publication of any real estate advertising that indicates a limitation, preference, or intent to discriminate based on race or other protected class. Specifically, §804(c) of the Fair Housing Act states that it is:

> *"... unlawful to make, print, or publish, or cause to be made, printed, or published, any notice, statement, or advertisement, with respect to the sale or rental of a dwelling, that indicates any preference, limitation, or discrimination because of race, color, religion, sex, handicap, familial status, or national origin, or an intention to make any such preference, limitation, or discrimination. However, the prohibitions of the Act regarding familial status do not apply with respect to housing for older persons..."*

These provisions apply to advertisements for residential mortgage loans as well. Under certain circumstances, even the newspapers chosen for advertising may be held to have the effect of racial steering. MLOs should choose their words very carefully and should measure whether advertising content could be construed as being in violation of the federal Fair Housing Act

Discriminatory advertising may be subtle. In today's world of "politically correct" language, words carry great power, and the misuse of words, even if unintentional, can create problems. Seemingly innocent statements are sometimes intended or interpreted as discriminatory. Certain phrases used in advertising could convey either overt or tacit discriminatory preferences or limitations.

And it's not just the words. An appendix to the Fair Housing Act indicates that human models in photographs, drawings, or other graphic techniques may not be used to indicate exclusiveness because of race, color, religion, sex, handicap, familial status, or national origin. If models are used in display advertising campaigns, the models should be clearly definable as reasonably representing majority and minority groups in the metropolitan area, both sexes, and, when appropriate, families with children. Models, if used, should portray persons in an equal social setting and indicate to the general public that the housing is open to all without regard to race, color, religion, sex, handicap, familial status, or national origin, and is not for the exclusive use of one such group.

Class Activity: Illegal Discrimination

Read through the following scenarios and consider whether or not they could be examples of illegal discrimination. Discuss your responses with the class.

Scenario 1: Mortgage broker Lou has been extremely busy lately. To add to his hectic situation, one of his employees just quit. Since Lou is too busy to answer the phone, he sets aside time at the end of each day to check the messages on his voice mail, responding only to calls from those who sound like they have the best chance to get approved. He manages his time in the office similarly, asking his secretary to screen out potential borrowers who receive public assistance, since they will be wasting their time and his by applying for a mortgage.

Could Lou be violating laws against illegal discrimination or is he simply practicing good time management?

Scenario 2: A large real estate brokerage in a diverse city advertised its listed properties in two newspapers distributed over the entire metropolitan area, a number of smaller newspapers circulated primarily in certain neighborhoods, and a weekly newspaper circulated mainly in African American neighborhoods. Whenever the brokerage took a listing in one of the "changing areas" of the city (a neighborhood becoming more integrated or becoming predominantly African American), its standard practice was to advertise that home in the African American newspaper and not in the newspapers of general circulation.

Is this an example of illegal discrimination or just smart use of limited marketing dollars?

Kickbacks and Referral Fees

Recall that the **Real Estate Settlement Procedures Act (RESPA)** of 1974 requires mortgage lenders, mortgage brokers, or servicers of home loans to *provide borrowers with pertinent and timely disclosures of the nature and costs of the real estate settlement process.* Its purpose is to regulate settlement and closing procedures and to protect borrowers.

Section 8 of RESPA prohibits anyone from giving *or* accepting a fee, kickback, or anything of value in exchange for referrals of settlement service providers involving a federally-related mortgage loan. RESPA also prohibits fee splitting and receiving unearned fees for settlement services not actually performed.

Key terms related to these provisions include "thing of value" and "referral." RESPA defines a **thing of value** to include *any payment, advance, funds, loan, service, or other consideration.* A **referral** includes *any oral or written action directed to a person which has the effect of affirmatively influencing the selection of a settlement services provider.* A referral also occurs when a borrower is required to use a particular provider of settlement services.

Allowable Fees

Fees, salaries, compensation, or other payments for services *actually rendered* and that are *not based on a referral* do **not** violate RESPA. This includes:

- A payment to an attorney at law for services actually rendered
- A payment by a title company to its duly appointed agent for services actually performed in the issuance of a policy of title insurance
- A payment by a lender to its duly appointed agent or contractor for services actually performed in the origination, processing, or funding of a loan
- A payment to any person of a *bona fide* salary or compensation or other payment for goods or facilities actually furnished or for services actually performed
- A payment pursuant to cooperative brokerage and referral arrangements or agreements between real estate agents and real estate brokers (this does *not* apply to any fee arrangements between real estate brokers and mortgage brokers or between mortgage brokers)
- Normal promotional and educational activities that are not conditioned on the referral of business and that do not involve the defraying of expenses that otherwise would be incurred by persons in a position to refer settlement services or business
- An employer's payment to its own employees for any referral activities

Multiple Services

When a person in a position to refer settlement service providers—such as an attorney, mortgage loan originator, real estate broker or agent, or developer or builder—receives a payment for providing additional settlement services as part of a real estate transaction, such payment must be for services that are actual, necessary, and distinct from the primary services provided by such person.

"Required Use"

According to RESPA definitions, a "required use" occurs when a consumer paying for a settlement service is required to use a particular provider of that settlement service. While RESPA makes clear that the use of both economic incentives and disincentives to improperly influence a consumer's choice of settlement service providers are prohibited, this provision does not prohibit **legitimate** discounts on services to consumers.

RESPA provides that settlement service providers can offer **legitimate discounts** to consumers by offering **a combination of settlement services** at a total price lower than the sum of the individual settlement services. This combination of services will **not** be considered a prohibited "required use" if:

1. The use of any such combination is *optional* to the purchaser, and
2. The lower price for the combination is not made up by higher costs elsewhere in the settlement process.

Violations

Violations of Section 8's anti-kickback, referral fees, and unearned fees provisions of RESPA are subject to criminal and civil penalties. In a criminal case, a person who violates Section 8 may be fined **up to $10,000** and/or be imprisoned up to **one year**. In a civil lawsuit, a person who violates Section 8 may be liable to the person charged for the settlement service an amount equal to **three times** the amount of the charge paid for the service.

Class Activity: RESPA Violations

Read through these scenarios and consider who—if anyone—is in violation of RESPA. Discuss your responses with the class.

Scenario 1: XYZ Mortgage encourages borrowers who receive federally-related mortgage loans from them to employ attorney Bob to perform title searches and related settlement services in connection with their transaction. XYZ and Bob have an understanding that in return for the referral of this business, Bob provides legal services to XYZ's officers or employees at abnormally low rates or for no charge.

Since the borrower is not required to use the attorney, is anyone in violation of RESPA?

Scenario 2: ABC Credit Reporting Bureau places a computer in the office of TOP Mortgage so that TOP can easily transmit requests for credit reports and ABC can respond. ABC supplies the computer for free to any mortgage office that orders a specific number of credit reports each month.

Is anyone in violation of RESPA?

Mortgage Fraud

Being honest with everyone means you should avoid fraud—intentional or unintentional—at all times. Either may lead to civil, and even criminal, penalties. **Negligence** is *an unintentional breach of a legal duty.* It's a tort if it causes harm, though, and you can be sued for it. **Fraud** is *intentional or negligent misrepresentation or concealment of material facts.* Failing to disclose information you're required to disclose can be a form of fraud. Fraud also includes actively concealing information and making false or misleading statements.

- **Actual Fraud.** Actual fraud is *an intentional misrepresentation or concealment of a material fact.* Actual fraud occurs when a person actively hides information, or makes statements known to be false or misleading. When any of these is done with intent to deceive, they constitute actual fraud. (This is also called deceit or intentional misrepresentation).
- **Constructive Fraud.** Constructive fraud is *a negligent misrepresentation or concealment of a material fact.* When information is not disclosed or false statements are made unintentionally, it may be considered constructive fraud. Here, the false statements or failure to disclose are the result of carelessness or negligence, rather than an intent to deceive. (This is also called negligent misrepresentation.)

Mortgage fraud involves any misrepresentation or concealment used in an attempt to obtain a mortgage loan. It can generally be divided into two main categories: Fraud for **profit**, which is usually perpetrated by industry insiders, and fraud for **property**, which is usually perpetrated by borrowers. This is a serious federal crime when done for any federally related loan (which includes most loans, since HUD, Fannie Mae, or a federally chartered bank are involved at some point in the process).

Common ways in which fraud may be committed include:

- **Material misrepresentations**, such as altered paycheck stubs and tax returns.
- **Material misstatements**, such as the intent to occupy a home as a primary residence when it really is intended to be used as a rental.
- **Omission**, such as failing to mention the borrower is taking an early retirement in six weeks.

The fraud can be perpetrated by borrowers who lie on applications, by an appraiser who provides an inflated property value, or by a mortgage broker who ignores derogatory information to get a loan approved. This also includes not reporting all items on the HUD closing statement accurately, creating phantom documents for verification, or concealing the true nature of a borrower's down payment.

Fraud Participants

Since many people are involved in the process of making loans for property, the opportunity for fraud exists on several levels. A fraud scheme could be simply the initiative of a desperate borrower, or it could involve the participation of multiple industry insiders, such as an appraiser who provides an inflated property value or by a mortgage broker who ignores derogatory information to get a loan approved. This also includes not reporting all items on the HUD closing statement accurately, creating phantom documents for verification, or concealing the true nature of a borrower's down payment.

Borrowers

Borrowers who knowingly supply false documents, such as verifications of employment (VOEs) or forged W-2s, or false information on the loan application, commit mortgage fraud, whether or not they're working in partnership with any mortgage professionals. Borrowers who commit fraud typically do so in order to obtain ownership of property. The borrower usually plans to make regular payments and has no plans to default. The purpose of the fraud is to make the mortgage loan happen at desirable terms for the borrower, not to enter into foreclosure or flip a property for profit.

A borrower might also act as a **straw buyer**, which is *someone who allows his name and personal details to be used to obtain a mortgage loan for a property he has no intention of inhabiting*. Sometimes straw buyers are paid for their participation in the scheme, and sometimes a straw buyer has no idea that his personal information was used.

Borrowers can also get involved in **credit enhancement** schemes. In an effort to show the necessary assets or credit to qualify for a loan, borrowers may look for fraudulent ways to enhance their financial situation. For example, they may add their names to the bank accounts of friends or family to show that they have sufficient assets on deposit. Another scheme is where friends, family—or even builders or mortgage loan originators—temporarily park assets into a borrower's account until the underwriter qualifies the borrower and the loan closes. This type of fraud can be very sophisticated, even to the point of borrowers "buying" seasoned credit account lines and creating fraudulent retailer relationships in an effort to improve the borrower's credit history and credit scores.

As home values continue to fall, many homeowners find themselves underwater with their mortgage—owing more than the property is worth. This has led to record foreclosures, of course, as well as homeowners with little or no equity in the property just walking away from the house and the loan. The current mortgage market has led to some "creative" schemes by borrowers to get out from under an unsustainable mortgage payment:

- **Buy and Bail.** Homeowners apply for a mortgage to purchase a similar home that, because of the market, sells for less money. The homeowner may claim that they are renting out the original property, perhaps engaging a family member or friend to claim to be the renter and even supplying a fake lease. Then after getting the new property, the borrower simply walks away from the first home and bails on that mortgage.
- **Short Sale Fraud.** A borrower who is facing default may offer to short sell the property so that the lender will not have to foreclose. With a short sale, the lender agrees to allow the sale of the property to a third party for less than the balance owed and release its lien on the collateral property. A short sale will not bring a sufficient amount to pay off the lender in full, , but the lender would not have to foreclose and title to or market the property, and will get the nonperforming loan off its books. Some lenders even agree to forgive any deficiency between the sale and the balance owed. A short sale is not necessarily fraudulent. However, if a borrower intentionally stopped making mortgage payments to force default, then enlists the assistance of someone else—a straw buyer—to purchase the property at a reduced price, fraud has most likely occurred.
- **Arson.** In order to avoid foreclosure, some homeowners may actually resort to the crime of arson in order to file fraudulent insurance claims.

Lenders and Brokers

Lenders and mortgage brokers commit mortgage fraud by falsifying loan documents, making loans to straw buyers, illegally flipping properties, and through other schemes. Lenders benefit by making loans that should probably never have been made and selling them to the secondary market as quickly as possible. Mortgage brokers benefit by collecting fees and yield spread premiums for putting together fraudulent mortgage packages. Dishonest lenders and mortgage brokers see the opportunity to make a loan resulting in a commission with high profitability. Often, these loans are knowingly made to unqualified buyers, or even straw buyers who will never make a payment on the loan, resulting in foreclosure.

Appraisal Practices Prohibited by Regulation Z

Regulation Z (12 C.F.R. **§ 226.36 (b)**) was amended effective in 2009 to specifically address perceived abuses in the mortgage industry. Lenders, mortgage brokers, and their affiliates are prohibited from coercing, influencing, or encouraging an appraiser to misstate the value of the dwelling. For example, the law specifically prohibits these practices:

- Implying to an appraiser that current or future retention of the appraiser depends on the amount at which the appraiser values a consumer's principal dwelling
- Excluding an appraiser from consideration for future engagement because the appraiser reports a value of a consumer's principal dwelling that does not meet or exceed a minimum threshold
- Telling an appraiser a minimum reported value of a consumer's principal dwelling that is needed to approve the loan
- Failing to compensate an appraiser because the appraiser does not value a consumer's principal dwelling at or above a certain amount
- Conditioning an appraiser's compensation on loan consummation

In addition, a lender cannot extend credit if the lender knows, at or before closing, that improper coercion has occurred by anyone unless the lender can document that it has acted with reasonable diligence to determine that the appraisal does not materially misstate or misrepresent the dwelling's value. It is not a violation to ask an appraiser to consider additional information about the dwelling or comparable properties or to ask an appraiser to correct factual errors. In addition, the following practices are ***not*** prohibited:

- Obtaining multiple appraisals of a consumer's principal dwelling, unless the creditor adheres to a policy of selecting the most reliable appraisal, rather than the appraisal that states the highest value
- Withholding compensation from an appraiser for breach of contract or substandard performance of services as provided by contract

Appraisers

Appraisals are a critical aspect of mortgage lending. An appraisal with inaccurate information—whether completed because of fraud or negligence—can have a serious impact. An **inflated appraisal** scheme occurs when a property is intentionally appraised with a higher-than-market value by an appraiser acting in collusion with a real estate agent, mortgage broker, or lender. Lenders hiring these appraisers use only those who agree to "hit the number," "push the value," or "work with us on the number" regardless of its relationship to actual market value. If the mortgages are part of sales transactions, continued inflation of values in the same neighborhood (with inflated sale prices) can result in continued appraisals at higher-than-market values that appear justified. Even unsuspecting appraisers are caught in this when they unknowingly use the inflated sale prices as comparables.

While inflated appraisals may be the more common type of appraisal fraud, deliberately **understating** the value of a property is also fraud. An appraiser may do this, for example, to allow someone to purchase a foreclosed home or short sale at a lower price. Understated appraisals may also be used to get more favorable terms from a lender with a loan modification.

Other Industry Insiders

- **Attorneys** may prepare bogus deeds and get them duly recorded on public records with the participation of government workers.
- **Accountants** may falsify tax returns, profit and loss statements, and other documentation required by lenders to qualify loans.
- **Title companies** may charge borrowers fees for services never provided at the closing or may complete incorrect title reports that omit valid liens or that create false chains of title.
- **Government workers** may falsify deeds and other records.
- **Real estate agents** may assist in the preparation of false documentation, such as sales contracts or property inspections, and even finding straw buyers for the property. Real estate brokers and agents collude in flipping schemes by finding borrowers for scams and by raising listing prices of homes after a deal is put together to make the over-inflated appraisal value appear valid. Unscrupulous real estate agents may also steer borrowers to a specific lender in exchange for a kickback or other consideration.
- **Rehabbers** and **FSBO (For Sale By Owner) flippers** may use sub-par material, removing materials or fixtures after an appraisal, providing straw buyers, and improperly influencing appraisers, loan officers, and title companies.
- **Investment Property Owners** may falsify occupancy rates on their rent rolls or otherwise misrepresent the condition of rental units or incomplete renovations.

Class Activity: Appraisal Concerns

Read through the following situation and consider the questions about the MLO's options and the potential consequences. Discuss your thoughts with the class.

MLO Marge has worked with Bill for many years, putting together loans for him on a number of properties. Now they are working on cash-out refinance for Bill's vacation home. Since Marge is planning on submitting the loan to a private investor for funding, she goes ahead and orders an appraisal from Hannah, who she's worked with before. When Marge gets Hannah's appraisal report, she's happy to see that the value range is what she expected based on her discussions with Bill. As Marge looks through the appraisal, however, she gets to the last page, where Hannah has included a number of photographs of the property. Marge had not asked photographs when she ordered the appraisal. While the property seems to be in excellent condition, the photographs show rooms emptied of furniture, window coverings, and anything else that might indicate the property is occupied.

1. What do the photographs most likely indicate?

2. Did appraiser Hannah do anything wrong? What should Marge do with the appraisal report?

3. Bill is one of her best customers. Should Marge go through with the loan?

Flipping

One of the most common and well-known mortgage fraud schemes is **property flipping.** Many people are confused by the term "flipping," as it has long been understood to mean that an investor has remodeled a property and quickly sold it for a profit. If the investor bought the property below market, and remodeling has brought it up to true market value, this is the good side of flipping, and is completely legal. It also serves the public well, as it increases property values, improves neighborhoods, and provides housing that otherwise might not be available.

Illegal flipping is something else entirely. Illegal property flipping generally requires collusion between the seller, buyer, appraiser, and lender/broker. An illegal property flipping scheme occurs when a property is purchased at a low price, appraised at an inflated value without any valid reason for the increase, and then resold at a much higher price. It may involve a series of sales and quick re-sales, with one property and a group of sellers and buyers changing ownership among them.

The home in a flipping scheme is typically resold at a new, higher price fairly soon after its initial purchase at the lower price. Statistics show that the criminals involved in these schemes do not wait long time periods, often only weeks, or perhaps a few months at most.

Attributes of Flipping Schemes

Typically, flipping schemes are more prevalent in mixed value areas where higher-priced homes are located near lower-priced homes in poor repair, and home values fluctuate extremely. These neighborhoods often include rental properties and tend to have a higher rate of crime, which can adversely affect property values.

The distressed nature of the properties can include broken pipes, no electrical wiring, or other items in poor condition. Homes involved in flipping schemes are often purchased at low prices because they are in poor condition. If repairs are made after the purchase, they are generally cosmetic or exterior-only repairs.

Another common attribute of illegal flipping is that perpetrators rarely use local entities to handle the loan. If local lenders are not used for the mortgage loan, underwriters who review the loans are not based locally and are unfamiliar with the property and neighborhood.

FHA Response to Flipping Schemes

FHA has responded to the increase in property flipping schemes by requiring sellers to own a property for at least **three months** prior to the new sale. And for resales ranging from 91-180 days, FHA may impose additional requirements, assuming that criminals interested in quick resales are not willing to wait. FHA rules include:

- FHA will not insure any resale properties unless the owner of record is the seller. This prevents thieves from flipping property without ever having legally owned it.
- Resales that take place 91–180 days after the initial sale can be FHA-insured only if there is a **second appraisal** that matches a resale threshold percentage established by HUD.

FHA does occasionally waive this rule. For example, in February of 2010, HUD placed a moratorium on this anti-flipping rule—extended through December 31, 2011—which would allow the sale of homes that have been held for less than 90 days under certain circumstances, such as:

- It must be an arm's length transaction.
- Any seller profit is limited to 20% above the purchase cost unless an independent appraiser confirms that repairs and renovations justify the sale price.

This step was taken in an effort to facilitate the return of repaired and habitable properties to the market in a timely fashion, particularly foreclosed/real estate owned (REO) properties.

Other Types of Mortgage Fraud

Sadly, someone determined to act illegally can dream up any number of schemes. We'll look at a few of them next.

Air Loan

An **air loan** scam involves a loan made on non-existent properties. For example, a broker enlists or creates a straw buyer, identifies fictional properties, opens accounts for payments, and maintains custodial accounts for escrow payments. A bank of telephones in an office may even be set up, with one phone line used for the employer, one for the appraiser, etc., for verification purposes.

Deed Scam

In a **deed scam,** the seller's signature on the deed is forged, meaning the real homeowner is not even aware the property is being fraudulently transferred. The deed is recorded; the thief mortgages the property with cash-out refinancing, then walks away with the money, and walks away from the mortgage without making a payment. And, again, the owner has no idea the property has even been transferred! Often this scheme takes place when an owner owns the property free and clear, the property is vacant, or the owners are having trouble making their mortgage payments.

Double Sold Loans

Double sold loans are instigated in various ways. One method involves the primary mortgage holder who sells the loan on the secondary market. In this instance, the loan is sold to a fraudulent company that, supposedly, will service the loan (and receive the mortgage payments). However, when a payment is received, the fraudulent company simply steals the money. The property will eventually go to foreclosure because the loan payments are never actually applied to the mortgage loan.

Another method of devising a double sold loan is when a borrower signs multiple copies of the same documents and the mortgage loan originator submits each "set" of the loan papers to different lenders. When the loan is approved by more than one lender, the mortgage loan originator forges a duplicate set of closing documents, delivers them to a second lender, and keeps the proceeds.

Unrecorded or Silent Second

In a down market, it's not that unusual for a seller to make concessions in order to entice a buyer. These concessions could even include financing some of the purchase price for the buyer. For example, let's say that the buyer applies for a 75% first mortgage, agrees to pay 5% down, and gives the seller a second mortgage at 20% of the sale price. This second mortgage will not be recorded so that the lender will think that the buyer is actually putting 25% down.

The buyer may have every intention of paying the seller, but this **unrecorded second**—also called a **silent second**—is actually a type of mortgage fraud. And it could be quite a risk for the seller. If the buyer does not pay the loan, the seller would not be able to foreclose to get the property back. And even if the seller does at some point record the mortgage, there may be other liens against the property or the property owner by that time that would have priority over the second mortgage.

Disappearing Second

A more common variation on this scheme is when the buyer has *no intention of paying* the second mortgage. For example, schemers will find uninformed buyers willing to sign a sales contract beyond market prices with such enticements as "seller will help finance." In these cases, the seller holds a second mortgage that they present to the lender as if it were an actual mortgage to induce the bank to loan a higher amount. Once the transaction closes, the seller destroys the mortgage, sometimes even giving it back to the buyer immediately. This is called a **disappearing second**. The lender thinks it has a 80% LTV loan, for example, when it may actually be 100% LTV.

Email/Mail Scams

In these scams, e-mail messages or letters promise to eliminate mortgage loans or get rid of credit card debt in return for paying a fee. The consumer pays the money but gets nothing in return. Consumers desperate to eliminate their crushing debt are most vulnerable to these schemes. The e-mail messages or letters often offer credit counseling or are sent under a name like "American Credit Counseling," implying a legitimate business performing a public service.

Identity Theft

A false identity *is when someone uses another person's identity on a loan application without the knowledge of the rightful property owner;* this is also known as identity theft. An identity can be stolen in a variety of ways, including such common scenarios as applying for a job or from discarded documents.

Many times, a thief needs only one piece of information—a Social Security number—to steal an identity. Today, counterfeit Social Security numbers are relatively easy to obtain. Thieves use retired numbers (due to death), numbers issued to someone else, stolen numbers, or numbers issued before the borrower's birth year. Thieves also use altered employment records, bank statements, and pay stubs to commit identity theft. With this information, they are able to impersonate homebuyers and sellers using actual, verifiable identities that give the mortgage transactions the appearance of legitimacy.

Class Activity: Identity Theft

Read through the following incident of identity theft.

A university student database, which includes Social Security numbers and other personal identifying information, is compromised by a computer hacker. The investigation reveals that the hacker subsequently sold the personal identification information to a third party, who then proceeded to submit falsified mortgage loan applications to numerous financial institutions. Law enforcement stated that the third party, in collusion with a notary, appraiser, and other industry insiders, used the student information to purchase homes owned by the third party and other collaborators at highly inflated prices. In addition to identity theft, the loan files also include misrepresentations of employment, falsified down payments, and inflated appraisals. The end result was approximately $5 million in losses to the financial institutions.

What are some "best practices" that would have helped avoid such mortgage fraud from this incident? Discuss your ideas with the class.

Red Flags of Mortgage Fraud

A red flag is a situation that requires additional scrutiny. According to the **Federal Financial Institutions Examination Council** (FFIEC), one red flag by itself may not be significant; however, multiple red flags may indicate an operating environment that is conducive to fraud. The following are some red flags that could signal mortgage fraud:

- **Steering Buyers to a Specific Lender.** Buyers may choose any lender they want for a purchase transaction. However, it is not unusual for real estate agents to recommend the use of a certain lending institution. Lenders often solicit loans through these real estate agents by forming alliances with them. If a transaction will close only if a certain lender is used, ask questions because it is unlikely that only one lender would offer a buyer certain favorable terms. Unfortunately, in many mortgage fraud scams, the buyer is unsophisticated in seeking financing, and may have credit issues that make lending more challenging. The buyer may be told this is the only chance for a home purchase when, in fact, it is a scam.
- **Stated Income.** Since the inception of no-doc or low-doc loans, the documentation required for the loan may be limited. These loans—rare in today's market—allow the borrower to indicate, without verification, employment history, income, and debt. Be suspicious if a borrower only had to produce minimal documentation to qualify for the loan.
- **No Money Due at Closing.** If a buyer is not required to pay anything at closing, questions should be asked. What this means is the buyer has been able to get around down payment requirements, and the seller is paying all the points and closing costs involved with the buyer's loan. In theory, the sales price may have been inflated to cover these costs. Even with less stringent lending guidelines and requirements, it is unusual for a buyer to need no money for a closing.

- **Sale Subject to the Seller Acquiring Title.** A huge red flag in a transaction is when the seller on the purchase contract is not the owner of record. There could be legitimate reasons for this, like the seller could be the buyer of the property via land contract or the seller could have recently purchased the property at a sheriff's sale and will not gain title until confirmation of the sale. Participants in the sale should ask why the seller is not the owner of record and verify that the reason is legitimate.
- **Difference in Sale Price.** The sales contract is supposed to guide the title agency or closing agent to the terms of the HUD-1 settlement statement, and there should be no discrepancies. Buyers have the right to review their closing statements one business day before closing. They should compare this document to the purchase contract and to the Good Faith Estimate received from the lender.
- **Sale Price Changes to Fit Appraisal.** To carry out this scheme, an appraisal is ordered and completed. The appraiser is then contacted regarding alterations or addendums to the purchase contract, typically made after the lender is told the appraised amount. The new, altered contract now matches the appraisal value. These schemes enable the lender to profit more from the transaction, because more money was available through a higher-than-expected appraisal.
- **Related Parties Involved.** Certainly, there is no law against a mother selling her property to her son or daughter, even at a discounted price. However, mortgage fraud scams often involve family members. So, when the transaction is not an arm's length transaction, full disclosure is imperative. Cases of mortgage fraud involving entire families have been reported. Many times, the straw buyer in a scam is a family member. Purchase contracts between family members should specifically state their relationships so it does not appear intentionally hidden.
- **Funds Paid to Undisclosed Third Parties.** In certain mortgage fraud schemes, unknown third parties who appear to have no relevance to the transaction are paid out of the funds received at the closing. The implication, of course, is there may be debt not revealed in the closing statements. Once again, a closing statement that is not followed to the letter is a red flag to the borrower. It may be prudent to have legal representation to review all the closing paperwork before signing any of the documents.
- **Cash Paid to Seller Outside of Escrow.** The seller receives cash from the sale of the property; however, it is not stated in closing statements or in the purchase contract. The motive, of course, is unstated profits. No paper trail exists to show the payment.
- **Cash Paid to Borrower.** The borrower receives cash when purchasing the property. Usually, in these cases, the borrower does not have a down payment and the purchase contract calls for the seller to pay all loan costs. Although seller-paid costs are becoming more typical in today's economy, schemes in which the borrower receives money from the transaction are not.

Fraud Enforcement

The **Fraud Enforcement and Recovery Act** of 2009 (Pub.L. 111-21), or **FERA,** is a public law in the United States enacted in 2009 that takes a number of steps to enhance criminal enforcement of federal fraud laws, especially regarding financial institutions, mortgage fraud, and securities or commodities fraud. One provision of the Act is that it amends the definition of a *financial institution* for the purposes of federal criminal law to include **mortgage lending businesses**, which are defined as "organizations which finance or refinance any debt secured by an interest in real estate, including private mortgage companies and any subsidiaries of such organizations, and whose activities affect interstate or foreign commerce." This, in effect, makes it a felony to falsify loan documents submitted to a broad range of financial institutions, including mortgage lending businesses. It also includes any other person "that makes in whole or in part a federally related mortgage loan." The amendments assure that private mortgage brokers and companies are held accountable under federal fraud laws. Without the amendments, for example, the financial institution bribery statute would not extend beyond traditional banks and financial institutions

FBI and Suspicious Activity Reports

The Federal Bureau of Investigation (FBI) tracks mortgage fraud through **Suspicious Activity Reports** (SARs) filed by federally insured financial institutions and others, and from reports from the Department of Housing and Urban Development's Office of the Inspector General. The FBI also receives complaints from the mortgage industry at large. The FBI's website indicated that as of 7/31/11, they had received 80,549 Suspicious Activity Reports with more than $3.2 billion in losses! Due to the huge financial losses faced by consumers and lenders on a national scale, the FBI has committed itself to dedicating unprecedented levels of manpower and funding to the investigation of mortgage fraud. Its investigations involve all levels and aspects of the schemes, from undercover work on the "inside" to prosecution of those accused of participating in mortgage fraud. And they continue to be very busy. As of 7/31/11, the FBI indicated 2,872 pending investigations (with 72% involving losses of more than $1 million). Compare this to 3,129 investigations (with 71% involving losses of more than $1 million) in ***all of 2010***. (See: http://www.fbi.gov/about-us/investigate/white_collar/mortgage-fraud/mortgage_fraud)

An eye-opening statement in the 2010 Mortgage Fraud Report is that mortgage fraud continued at elevated levels and that fraud schemes are "**particularly resilient, and they readily adapt to economic changes and modifications in lending practices.**" (See: http://www.fbi.gov/stats-services/publications/mortgage-fraud-2010/2010-mortgage-fraud-report) Unfortunately, it seems as quickly as enforcement agencies identify fraud schemes and put regulations into place, unethical people will hit on new schemes.

One way you can participate in combating fraud and protecting your reputation is by staying current with what's going on in the industry. For example, **Mortgage Asset Research Institute** (MARI) is a private subscription service that gives members access to a database of all fraud and suspected fraud as reported by its members and state and federal regulatory agencies, as well as the actions taken. The service allows those in the industry to check credentials of companies and individuals with whom they work.

√ **Note:** There are also many free websites that document various mortgage fraud scams and the consequences to the participants. It would be a good practice to bookmark some of those sites and make a point of visiting them regularly.

MORTGAGE FRAUD IS INVESTIGATED BY THE FBI

DEPARTMENT OF JUSTICE
FEDERAL BUREAU OF INVESTIGATION
FIDELITY BRAVERY INTEGRITY

Mortgage Fraud is investigated by the Federal Bureau of Investigation and is punishable by up to 30 years in federal prison or $1,000,000 fine, or both. It is illegal for a person to make any false statement regarding income, assets, debt, or matters of identification, or to willfully overvalue any land or property, in a loan and credit application for the purpose of influencing in any way the action of a financial institution.

Some of the applicable Federal criminal statutes which may be charged in connection with Mortgage Fraud include:

18 U.S.C. § 1001 - Statements or entries generally
18 U.S.C. § 1010 - HUD and Federal Housing Administration Transactions
18 U.S.C. § 1014 - Loan and credit applications generally
18 U.S.C. § 1028 - Fraud and related activity in connection with identification documents
18 U.S.C. § 1341 - Frauds and swindles by Mail
18 U.S.C. § 1342 - Fictitious name or address
18 U.S.C. § 1343 - Fraud by wire
18 U.S.C. § 1344 - Bank Fraud
42 U.S.C. § 408(a) - False Social Security Number

Unauthorized use of the FBI seal, name, and initials is subject to prosecution under Sections 701, 709, and 712 of Title 18 of the United States Code. This advisement may not be changed or altered without the specific written consent of the Federal Bureau of Investigation, and is not an endorsement of any product or service.

Mortgage Fraud Warning Poster. Source: Federal Bureau of Investigation (http://www.fbi.gov/about-us/investigate/white_collar/mortgage-fraud/)

Class Activity: Fraud Schemes

Read through the following scenarios and decide what sort of scheme is being perpetrated. Discuss your thoughts with the class.

Scenario 1: Young couple June and Bud really wanted to buy a home, but their debt ratio was too high and they didn't have much for a down payment. June's dad, Jack, decided to help them by applying for a FHA loan himself, with the understanding that June and Bud would make the mortgage payments. Within a year of moving in, they were well behind in their monthly payments, and the lender called Jack. Jack said he had no intention of making the payments, so the lender started foreclosure procedures, and June and Bud moved into Jack's basement.

Scenario 2: MLO Stu is working with Emily, who is planning on buying her cousin Doug's house. Emily is putting 10% down and Doug is willing to hold a 10% purchase money mortgage so that Emily can avoid paying private mortgage insurance. As he's consulting with Doug and Emily to put the deal together, Doug asks Stu if he can just tear the mortgage up after closing, since he doesn't really expect Emily to pay him back.

Scenario 3: Patrick is behind on his mortgage payments and has been threatened with foreclosure. He has his house on the market, and a few people are showing interest in purchasing the property. Patrick contacts his lender and asks whether or not they would consider agreeing to a short sale. Patrick has a number of offers, but does not submit the highest offer to the lender, instead, convincing his friend Joe to purchase the property. The lender agrees to the sale, and once the lien is released, Joe sells the property at market value to the other prospective buyer, and he and Patrick split the $30,000 profit.

Predatory Lending

Along with the advantages of subprime lending, which extends credit to people who might not otherwise qualify for a home mortgage, come some of the inevitable negative by-products—lenders taking advantage of borrowers. **Predatory lending** involves loans that *take advantage of ill-informed consumers through excessively high fees, misrepresented loan terms, frequent refinancing that does not benefit the borrower, and other prohibited acts.* Predatory lending targets borrowers with little knowledge of, or defense against, these practices. New regulations require that complete and clear disclosures be made to borrowers and specifically prohibits certain practices, including:

- Packing a loan with credit insurance and other extra fees.
- Extending credit to people with little or no income and who have little chance of repaying the loan (the lender forecloses on the property and keeps the excess equity to cover costs).
- Refinancing the lender's own high-cost loan with another fee-rich loan in less than a year's time (unless a lender can show that the new loan benefits the borrower).

The motive for predatory lending is profit. The goal of a predatory lender is to take the property or strip its equity, or to profit from the exorbitant fees charged. Undoubtedly, the lender claims to help borrowers achieve the dream of homeownership. Predatory loans are approved without regard for the borrower's ability to repay. Interest rates are higher than the level of risk justifies. And, lenders may bundle unrelated products—such as a life insurance policy—into the mortgage loan to further their profit.

Title XIV of the Dodd-Frank Wall Street Reform and Consumer Protection Act of 2010, designated as the **Mortgage Reform and Anti-Predatory Lending Act**, prohibits mortgage loan originators from steering borrowers to any loan that the borrower lacks the ability to repay or that has predatory characteristics, such as equity stripping, excessive fees, or abusive terms (§1403). Final rules on these steering provisions were adopted by the Federal Reserve Board to amend Regulation Z (§ 226.36 (e)) and became effective as of April 2011. For more on this, see the topic on the **Federal Reserve Mortgage Loan Originator Compensation Rule** in Chapter 4.

Subprime Lenders and Predatory Lending

Legitimate subprime lenders offer loans to low-income and risky borrowers, and must charge higher interest rates to accommodate the risk. The higher-than-typical closing and processing fees allow them to take on that risk. Without these lenders, riskier borrowers could not tap into their home equity or even own a home. Subprime lenders may be mainstream lenders who also offer conventional loans to borrowers or mortgage brokers specializing in working with the "credit impaired" or with borrowers who are unable or unwilling to meet other criteria—such as verification of income or assets—required for a conventional loan. These lenders usually do not make government-backed loans and, therefore, often operate outside of some federally-related loan guidelines.

While many instances of predatory lending involve subprime loans, it's certainly not reasonable to say that all subprime lenders are predatory lenders. Still, it may be difficult for potential borrowers to discern who is legitimate and who is not.

Excessive Fees

Predatory lending costs the borrower in many ways. Although it is understandable a higher-risk borrower would pay higher interest rates than someone with good credit, it still forces borrowers to pay more than they would for a typical transaction. If the terms are difficult to understand, the borrower may be paying exorbitant loan origination, settlement, and servicing fees.

Total fees greater than 4-5% of the loan amount may be considered higher than normal and may be a red flag to look for **junk fees**—multiple fees under a variety of names alleging services done on the borrower's behalf.

Exorbitant **prepayment penalties** may lock borrowers into abusive loans that cannot be easily refinanced when credit scores improve. Prepayment penalties may be tens of thousands of dollars and be enforced for many years into the loan. The reason? To discourage payoff of the highly profitable loan. In reality, the majority of lenders do not charge prepayment penalties or, if they do, only in the first years of the loan.

Documentation

For many borrowers, but particularly those not well informed, loan documents may be difficult to understand. Legal jargon, small print, and page after page of confusing documentation may be presented for immediate signature. Often, the pressure is on finishing the closing with no time allowed to read the documents carefully. What is the solution for the borrower? Borrowers should be advised to have an attorney review all documents before signing or get a credit counselor or other expert to review them.

Equity Skimming

Equity skimming involves lenders making various types of loans knowing the borrowers will not be able to make the monthly payments and thus setting them up for foreclosure. The borrower loses everything—the home and the equity in it. Some common types of equity skimming schemes include:

Loans Exceeding Ability to Repay. Borrowers typically rely on a lender's advice regarding debt-to-income ratio, believing there are reasonable limits in place on what they can borrow. Equity skimming schemes may falsify loan documents so the borrower does not realize the amount being borrowed is too much, with a monthly payment amount that is too high. The lender makes the loan, knowing the borrower will not be able to make those monthly payments, setting them up for foreclosure. The borrower loses everything—the home and the equity in it.

Home Improvement Scams. In these instances, a contractor working in conjunction with a predatory lender recommends repairs to the home, driveway, basement, etc. (Work may or may not actually need to be done.) The quote for the work is typically extremely high, and the contractor indicates arrangements for financing are available. Enter the lender—offering a loan that will strip the equity out of the home, again resulting in possible foreclosure.

Loan Flipping. This involves refinancing over and over again, usually with minimal to no net tangible benefit to the borrower in terms of lowering the interest rate or saving fees. The borrower is promised benefits that never materialize. Since the lender profits every time a loan is made, there is no incentive for the lender to recommend otherwise. Often, the refinancing actually raises the interest rate to the borrower. With higher monthly payments, the borrower may wind up defaulting on the loan, undergoing foreclosure, or being forced to refinance into even more unfavorable terms. Once again, the high-risk borrower takes a hit financially—a price he can ill afford to pay!

Extreme Lending. Some borrowers fall victim to extreme lending. Borrowers with extremely high debt in relationship to income are targets. With typical lending guidelines restricting borrowers to around 30% of income toward the mortgage payment, this extreme lending—often as much as 50% of income going toward the mortgage payment or more—puts borrowers at risk. If this borrower is laid off, loses a job, or experiences unanticipated expenses due to injury or illness, the risk for foreclosure is great because of the high percentage of income going to the mortgage loan.

Foreclosure Rescue Scams

In the current housing market, the number of foreclosures is staggering. Honest homeowners are desperate to save their homes, and unscrupulous schemers are eager to take advantage of their vulnerability. The **Federal Trade Commission** warns borrowers about certain schemes, including:

- **Phony Counseling or Phantom Help**. A scam artist tells homeowners that he can negotiate a deal with their lender to save their homes for an upfront fee. Homeowners may be told not to contact their lenders, lawyers, or credit counselors, and to let the scam artist handle all the details. Once they pay the fee, the scam artist takes off with their money. Sometimes, the scam artist insists that homeowners make all mortgage payments directly to him while he negotiates with the lender. In this instance, the scammer may collect a few months of payments before disappearing.
- **Rent-to-Buy Scheme.** A homeowner is told to surrender the title as part of a deal that allows him to remain in the home as a renter with the intention of buying it back during the next few years. The schemer may tell the homeowner that surrendering the title will permit a different borrower with a better credit rating to secure new financing and prevent the loss of the home. But the terms of these deals usually are so burdensome that buying back the home becomes impossible. The homeowner loses the home, and the scam artist walks off with all or most of the home's equity. Worse yet, when the new borrower defaults on the loan, the original homeowner is evicted. In a variation, the scam artist raises the rent over time to the point that the former homeowner can't afford it. After missing several rent payments, the renter—the former homeowner—is evicted, leaving the "rescuer" free to sell the house.

Foreclosure Rescue Scams (continued)

- **Bait and Switch Scheme.** Recall that the term "bait and switch" usually refers to an advertising tactic where a consumer is enticed with what sounds like a great deal, and then is sold something else, either more expensive or somehow less advantageous to the consumer. Similarly, a rescue scam artist will provide borrowers with loan documents they need to sign to make their mortgage current, but buried in the stack of documents is one that surrenders title to the scammers.

See: http://www.ftc.gov/bcp/edu/pubs/consumer/credit/cre42.shtm

Indicators of Predatory Lending

Changing loan terms at closing was historically one of the most common predatory lending schemes. Borrowers discovered closing documents do not reflect the loan terms and fees originally stated in the Good Faith Estimate, and often feel as though they had no choice but to go through with the loan. A difference between the sale price on the HUD-1 Settlement Statement and the price on the sales contract is a red flag. Of course, it could be an honest mistake, but as the sales contract is supposed to guide the title agency or closing agent to the terms of the HUD-1, and there should be no discrepancies. The 3/7/3 Rule introduced with the Mortgage Disclosure Improvement Act amendments to TILA that requires an additional waiting period of three business days after disclosing changed loan terms helps to address this situation (12 C.F.R. § 226.19 (a)(2)(ii)).

The Department of Housing and Urban Development (HUD) identifies several other predatory schemes used by unscrupulous mortgage loan originators, including the following:

- Encouraging borrowers to lie about their income, expenses, or cash available for down payments in order to get a loan.
- Knowingly lending more money than a borrower can afford to repay.
- Charging high interest rates to borrowers based on their race or national origin and not on their credit history.
- Charging fees for unnecessary or nonexistent products and services.
- Pressuring borrowers to accept higher-risk loans such as balloon loans, interest only payments, and steep prepayment penalties.
- Targeting vulnerable borrowers to cash-out refinances offers when they know borrowers are in need of cash due to medical, unemployment or debt problems.
- Stripping homeowners' equity from their homes by convincing them to refinance again and again when there is no benefit to the borrower.

HUD also indicates that borrowers should be aware of the following red flags that could indicate predatory tactics:

- Lenders tell borrowers that they are the borrower's only chance of getting a loan or owning a home. Borrowers should be able to take their time to shop around and compare prices and houses.
- The house the borrower is buying costs a lot more than other homes in the neighborhood, but isn't any bigger or better.
- Borrowers are asked to sign a sales contract or loan documents that are blank or that contain information which is not true.
- Borrowers are told that the Federal Housing Administration insurance protects them against property defects or loan fraud when it does not.
- The cost or loan terms at closing are not what the borrower agreed to.
- Borrowers are told that refinancing can solve their credit or money problems.

See: http://portal.hud.gov/hudportal/HUD?src=/program_offices/housing/sfh/buying/loanfraud

Class Activity: Predatroy Lending

Read through the following scenarios and decide if they are examples of predatory lending. Discuss the rationale for your conclusions with the class.

Scenario 1: Allen faces possible foreclosure, and contacts a mortgage lender whose ad promises to save his home. At closing, Allen sees that the lender changed the terms of the loan that they had agreed to, but he felt he had no choice but to go ahead with the loan or lose the house.

Scenario 2: Bill takes an application for a cash-out loan from a woman on a fixed income so that she can pay her real estate taxes. Bill does not tell her that she can make sure the new loan collects for real estate taxes, hoping in a few years she will need to get a new loan for the same reason.

Scenario 3: Kara has some credit issues, trying to bounce back from a recent bankruptcy. Still, she is interested in buying a home. She finds a mortgage broker who can secure a loan for her, but only if she will pay 20% down and consent to an interest rate that is higher than that offered to consumers with perfect credit.

Scenario 4: Pamela has applied for a loan with XYZ Mortgage Company. The mortgage loan originator tells her that since she is a single woman, she can only be approved for the loan if she takes out a credit insurance policy to cover the mortgage in the event of her death. The insurance policy requires a significant one-time fee at closing.

Mortgage Assistance Relief Services (MARS) Rule

In October of 2010, the Federal Trade Commission issued final rule that, according to the FTC, addresses many mortgage relief scams that have sprung up recently that take advantages of distressed homeowners. The following are among the provisions of the final rule (16 C.F.R. Part 322):

- A ban on those who provide mortgage foreclosure rescue and loan modification services from collecting fees until homeowners have a written offer from their lender or servicer that they decide is acceptable.
- A requirement that mortgage relief companies disclose key information to consumers to protect them from being misled and to help them make better informed purchasing decisions, for example, the company's fee, the fact that the company is not associated with the government, and that the consumer has the right to discontinue doing business with the company at any time.
- A prohibition against making any false or misleading claims about their services, for example, any guarantees or the amount of money the consumer will save.
- A prohibition barring mortgage relief companies from advising consumers to discontinue communication with their lenders.

See: http://www.ftc.gov/opa/2010/11/mars.shtm

Class Activity: Ethical Discussion #2

Read through the following scenario and think about how you might handle the situation. What are some issues to consider? Discuss your thoughts with the class.

Velma, a 59-year-old minority woman who works as a teacher, contacts you about getting a loan to purchase a condominium. As you're chatting, she indicates that she's hoping to retire from teaching in three years. You take her financial and personal information and see that you should be able to get her the amount she needs to purchase the home, and now you need to discuss terms. You share some loan options with her, and she insists that she's only interested in an adjustable rate mortgage, since she wants the lower monthly payments to start and she's convinced the interest rates will stay low or go down even further.

What should you share with Velma about the ARM loan given her situation? Are you obligated to help her apply for the loan she wants?

Let's say you decide that you will not submit an application for an ARM due to Velma's intention to retire in three years, about the time the monthly payments on the loan could jump beyond her ability to pay on a fixed income. You don't want to seem as though you're pushing through an inappropriate loan. Velma is very unhappy and accuses you of refusing to help her because she's a woman and a minority.

It seems as though your choice is between risking accusations of discrimination or accusations of predatory lending. Now what do you do?

Class Case Study and Discussion

To conclude this chapter, read the following consumer complaint letter, review the mortgage loan originator's notes, and then discuss the scenario with your class. *See the Appendix for some additional discussion.*

January 18, 2012

State Commissioner, Division of Banks

Anytown, USA 10001

Dear Commissioner,

On December 1, 2011, I telephoned the ABCDFG Mortgage Company of Anytown, USA. I spoke to John Doe. On that day, Mr. Doe advised me that his company was one of the most competitive and respected in the state. He informed me that he could refinance my present mortgage for 15 years at 6.625% with 0 points. He also told me that, based upon the information I had given him and my credit report, this would be an easy loan and I would have no problem at all.

A sudden death in my family made it impossible for me to meet with Mr. Doe until December 14. On that morning, I called Mr. Doe to confirm our appointment for later in the day and also to confirm that the rate of 6.625% with no points was still in place. He confirmed this. That evening when Mr. Doe arrived at my home, he informed me that the market changed and the rate would now be 6.75%. We proceeded to complete the application at the 6.75% rate.

Mr. Doe completed the mortgage application, had me sign some documents and disclosures, and assured me that copies would be made for my records of the signed disclosures. He also told me that his processor would mail back my original documents along with some other mortgage papers I would need to sign.

On December 28, I called and emailed John Doe for a status of my mortgage application. He returned my call and said everything was "fine." I had read that interest rates had increased but did not worry because my rate had been locked in for 30 days. I asked Mr. Doe when I would be hearing from the appraiser, and he told me that the appraisal had been ordered but the appraisers were busy. He told me not to worry; he would take care of everything.

On January 15, John Doe called me to let me know my interest rate would be 7.375%. I told him that this was not the rate we had agreed to and wanted my money back. He said that my application fee was already "spent," my interest rate was "floating," and he would forward me a copy of my appraisal. He told me I was not entitled to any refund.

I am enclosing copies of the papers given to me at application. I am disappointed over how my mortgage application was handled—the increase in the interest rate and the loss of my application fee. Because of current interest rates, I have lost the ability to refinance and lower my current interest rate. Is there anything you can do to assist me?

Sincerely,

Jane Consumer

Loan Application Log

ABCDFG Mortgage Company of Anytown

Borrower: Jane Consumer **Loan #: 123456-78**

Address: 123 Elm St. **LO/Proc.: John Doe / Sue Smith**

Anytown, USA 10001

12-14-11	Notes to Processor: Copy attached original documents and return to borrower. Open file and send GFE, TIL and mortgage disclosures. Lock loan at Investor A at 6.625% with 0 points. (JD)
12-15-11	Opened file, ordered appraisal, sent originals back to borrower. (SS)
12-18-11	Sue – lock in fax confirmation to Investor A shows busy, called Stan in secondary marketing dept., he shows NO LOCK!!!! Rates have moved... will have to float. Notice we didn't send the GFE/TIL/disclosures ... backdate disclosures but do not send lock conf. (JD)
12-28-11	Sue – borrower called on appraisal. What is the status? (JD)
12-28-11	John – called appraiser. They let their clerical person go because of mistakes, couldn't find order. Will send out appraiser ASAP and will RUSH. Rates are rising and loan is still not locked. (SS)
1-5-12	Loan submitted to investor. (SS)
1-7-12	Loan approved by investor – rate is floating, need to send commitment letter. (SS)
1-7-12	Send approval out dated January 8 at original rate with 0 points. Will advise borrower that we are unable to close... don't see rate lock in file. (JD)
1-12-12	Advised borrower that investor needed 48 hours notice to close, also that loan had to fund within three-day rescission period. Told the borrower the only option is to wait until original "lock" expires, then get best market price. Will call borrower on 1-15-10. (JD)

1. *If you were the Commissioner of Banks who received that letter from Jane Consumer, what would be your impression of the ABCDFG Mortgage Company?*

2. *Were the mortgage loan originator's actions:*

   ETHICAL *UNETHICAL* *DEBATABLE*

3. *Discuss what bothers you about the actions taken by the mortgage loan originator.*

Real Success

As a mortgage professional, you are deemed to be in a superior position because of your knowledge of the mortgage loan process. This is an advantage that should not be used for personal gain or the gain of your employer at the expense of the general public. The government takes all complaints seriously, especially when consumers feel victimized.

It's important to understand that many borrowers are working with you to complete the single largest transaction they will make in their lives. Most people will be happy and excited, but when people have less experience or knowledge than you, there's always a chance for some to feel they did not come out ahead in the transaction. You may not make everyone happy all the time, but if you follow the same guidelines and procedures for everyone (whether given to you by your employer or created on your own), you should avoid many of the potential pitfalls you could face in your mortgage career—or have the records, reputation, and other tools to help get yourself out of a bad situation if the need arises. And, by treating others ethically, honestly, and with respect, you can strive to earn their respect and repeat business and referrals.

While you may not be legally obligated to keep notes of every substantive conversation you have, it can be your strongest defense to establish that you gave equal professional service. Keep good records of all meetings, phone calls, appointments, and missed appointments. If you find yourself being questioned—or even end up in court—at least you can demonstrate a conscious effort to be fair, open, and honest with everyone. Some organizations require their employees to use a preprinted contact form to document whom they spoke with, what they discussed, etc., as part of their compliance procedures to show that they provided equal service to all and met all disclosure obligations.

Chapter 13 Summary

1. The laws outlined are the minimum duty required of a mortgage loan originator. MLOs, however, should strive to fulfill not only the letter of the law, but also its intent. There are many sources from which a MLO can obtain ethical guidance. The Better Business Bureau (BBB) and your state attorney general's office can provide guidance. The National Association of Mortgage Brokers (NAMB) has promulgated a Code of Ethics.

2. **Bait and switch** advertising is an alluring but insincere offer to sell a product or service which the advertiser in truth does not intend or want to sell in order to switch consumers from buying the advertised merchandise. Every advertisement should be a bona fide offer to sell. **Misrepresentation** is simply false or misleading information that could include documents, misstatements, or omission. A **material fact** is one that, if known, might have caused a reasonable consumer to make a different decision. **The Federal Trade Commission Act** states that advertisements must be truthful and non-deceptive, that advertisers must have evidence to back up their claims, and that advertisements cannot be unfair. An ad is **unfair** if it causes or is likely to cause substantial consumer injury which a consumer could not reasonably avoid and it is not outweighed by the benefit to consumers. An ad is **deceptive** if it contains a statement—or omits information—that is likely to mislead consumers acting reasonably under the circumstances and is material to a consumer's decision to buy or use the product. The same laws that regulate print and broadcast media apply equally to advertising, promotion, and marketing on the internet.

3. Treating everyone equally helps avoid violations of the **Civil Rights Act of 1866** and the federal **Fair Housing Act of 1968** (Title VIII). It is illegal to discriminate based on race, color, religion, sex, national origin, disability, or familial status. **Redlining** is illegally refusing to make loans on property located in a particular neighborhood for discriminatory reasons. The **Home Mortgage Disclosure Act** (HMDA) helps enforce compliance of this by requiring certain lenders and mortgage brokers to file an annual report categorizing the location of loans they made so cases of redlining can be spotted. Exclusionary zoning laws are also discriminatory, especially if they have a disparate impact on a minority group. The courts can step in to remedy these situations. Advertising must also be fair and neutral in its language. The **Equal Credit Opportunity Act** prohibits discrimination in granting credit to people based on sex, age (if at least 18), marital status, race, color, religion, national origin, receipt of public assistance, or exercised rights under the Consumer Credit Protection Act.

4. The **Real Estate Settlement Procedures Act** (RESPA) regulates settlement and closing procedures and requires lenders, mortgage brokers, or servicers of home loans to provide borrowers with pertinent and timely disclosures. Among RESPA requirements is Section 8, which prohibits kickbacks and unearned fees.

5. Being honest with everyone involves avoiding **fraud**—intentional misrepresentation or concealment of a material fact. Mortgage professionals must also steer clear of any situation that can be construed as mortgage fraud because it is a serious crime. The fraud can be perpetrated by borrowers who lie on applications, by an appraiser who provides an inflated property value, or by a mortgage loan originator who ignores derogatory information to get a loan approved. Mortgage fraud also includes not reporting all items on the HUD closing statement accurately, creating phantom documents for verification, or concealing the true nature of the borrower's down payment.

6. **Predatory lending** involves loans that take advantage of ill-informed consumers through excessively high fees, misrepresented loan terms, frequent refinancing that does not benefit the borrower, and other prohibited acts. Predatory lending targets borrowers with little knowledge of, or defense against, these practices. Laws such as the **Home Ownership and Equity Protection Act (HOEPA)** the **Mortgage Disclosure Improvement Act (MDIA)**, and the **Mortgage Reform and Anti-Predatory Lending Act** (Title XIV of the Dodd-Frank Wall Street Reform and Consumer Protection Act of 2010), establish disclosure requirements and prohibit equity stripping and other abusive practices.

Chapter 13 Quiz

1. ***The Civil Rights Act of 1866 prohibits what type of discrimination in property transactions?***
   A. race
   B. religion
   C. sex
   D. all of the above

2. ***The federal Fair Housing Act prohibits discrimination based on race, color, religion, sex, and***
   A. age, national origin, disability/handicap, or familial status.
   B. disability, national origin, or sexual orientation.
   C. marital status, national origin, disability/handicap, or familial status.
   D. national origin, disability/handicap, or familial status.

3. ***Which law requires lenders to document how they are serving the lending needs within the communities in which they do business?***
   A. Equal Credit Opportunity Act
   B. Fair Credit Reporting Act
   C. Fair Housing Act
   D. Home Mortgage Disclosure Act

4. ***Which act specifically prohibits redlining?***
   A. Civil Rights Act of 1866
   B. Equal Credit Opportunity Act
   C. Fair Housing Act
   D. Home Mortgage Disclosure Act

5. ***As mortgage loan originator Sam puts together an ad to attract some new customers, what law should he be most concerned about?***
   A. FACT Act
   B. GLBA
   C. RESPA
   D. TILA

6. ***Mortgage loan originator Dave knows that his customer is losing his job at the end of the month because the plant where he works is closing, but in his eagerness to close the deal, he decided to ignore that fact. This might be considered an example of***
   A. actual fraud.
   B. constructive fraud.
   C. good business.
   D. negligent misrepresentation.

7. ***Mortgage fraud can be committed by***
   A. appraisers only.
   B. borrowers only.
   C. lenders and brokers only.
   D. any party to a mortgage loan.

8. ***Which law prohibits kickbacks?***
   A. Fair Credit Reporting Act
   B. Gramm-Leach-Bliley Act
   C. Regulation Z
   D. RESPA

9. ***Predatory lending involves***
   A. forcing the borrower to refinance a loan with inferior terms.
   B. misrepresenting the loan terms by the lender.
   C. requiring excessively high fees, such as for credit life insurance.
   D. all of the above

10. ***Which situation is LEAST likely to be an example of predatory lending?***
    A. ABC Mortgage Co. offers a subprime loan to Mark, who is coming out of bankruptcy.
    B. Dave shows up at closing and finds that the lender has changed the terms of the loan.
    C. Ellie was 12 days late paying her mortgage, and the lender raised the interest rate 1/4%.
    D. Frank paid off his mortgage loan early with lottery winnings and the lender charged a $12,000 prepayment penalty.

11. ***Which situation does NOT involve a straw buyer?***
    A. Ann revises her pay stubs so she can qualify for a loan to buy her dream house.
    B. Bob uses his twin brother's Social Security number and credit information to apply for a loan.
    C. Dave agrees to secure a loan under his name even though only his sister with bad credit will live in the house.
    D. Tina tells Rob, who is facing foreclosure, that if he deeds the property to her, she will refinance on good terms and let him stay in the house.

12. ***MLO Cindy's customer purposely does not tell her that he just co-signed his nephew's auto loan. The credit report shows neither that loan nor a credit inquiry, and so that debt is not considered when the lender pre-approves him for a larger mortgage than he really should have. Do you think Cindy did anything wrong?***
    A. No, she can't be held responsible if a client withholds information that does not show on his credit report.
    B. Yes, she colluded with the customer to withhold material information.
    C. Yes, she committed actual fraud by approving a purposely false application.
    D. Yes, she committed constructive fraud by not confirming the customer's debts.

13. ***Which of the following is NOT an indicator of predatory lending?***
    A. charging excessive prepayment penalties
    B. falsifying loan documents
    C. increasing interest charges on late loan payments
    D. requiring mortgage insurance

14. ***If an ad mentions the interest rate on a specific loan product, that interest rate must be***
    A. available for at least 10 business days.
    B. given to every applicant.
    C. locked in without a lock-in fee.
    D. made available to a reasonable number of qualified applicants.

15. ***Which statement about a bait and switch advertising strategy is FALSE?***
    A. The advertiser does not intend to sell the offered product.
    B. The consumer is lured in by attractive terms or promises.
    C. The goal is to get interested consumers in the door.
    D. There is no bait and switch if the consumer accepts the new terms.

Appendix

Appendix A

Answers to Chapter Quizzes

Chapter 1 An Overview of Mortgage Lending

1. c	2. d	3. c	4. c
5. a	6. b	7. b	8. d

Chapter 2 The Business of Real Estate

1. b	2. c	3. b	4. b	5. d
6. b	7. d	8. c	9. b	10. d

Chapter 3 The Mortgage Lending Process

1. a	2. d	3. d	4. c	5. c
6. b	7. a	8. b	9. b	10. a

Chapter 4 Federal Mortgage Lending Legislation

1. a	2. d	3. c	4. c	5. b	6. d	7. d	8. b
9. d	10. c	11. d	12. c	13. a	14. c	15. c	16. c
17. d	18. b	19. a	20. b	21. a	22. c	23. a	24. c
25. b							

Chapter 5 Finance Instruments

1. d	2. a	3. b	4. d	5. b
6. c	7. d	8. b	9. a	10. b

Chapter 6 Conventional Financing

1. c	2. c	3. b	4. b	5. a
6. c	7. c	8. c	9. c	10. c

Chapter 7 Introduction to Government Agency Loan Programs

1. b	2. a	3. a	4. d	5. a	6. b
7. a	8. c	9. b	10. c	11. d	12. d

Chapter 8 Nontraditional Mortgage Products

1. c	2. b	3. b	4. c	5. b	6. c
7. c	8. b	9. a	10. a	11. c	12. b
13. d	14. c	15. c			

Chapter 9 Legal Concepts in Real Estate

1. d	2. a	3. c	4. c	5. c
6. c	7. c	8. d	9. b	10. b

Chapter 10 Interests in Real Property

1. d	2. c	3. d	4. d	5. b	6. d
7. a	8. c	9. c	10. b	11. a	12. d

Chapter 11 The Value of Real Estate

1. c	2. a	3. d	4. b	5. b
6. d	7. a	8. c	9. d	10. d

Chapter 12 Understanding Appraisals

1. c	2. c	3. c	4. c	5. d
6. a	7. c	8. b	9. b	10. c

Chapter 13 Ethics in the Mortgage Lending Profession

1. a	2. d	3. d	4. c	5. d
6. a	7. d	8. d	9. d	10. a
11. a	12. a	13. d	14. d	15. d

Answers to Mortgage Exercises

Chapter 3 The Mortgage Lending Process

Mortgage Exercise 3-1

1. $18 hourly wage x 40 hours in a week x 52 weeks = $37,440 annual income

   $37,440 annual income ÷ 12 months = $3,120 Mrs. Zorn's monthly income

   $625 weekly income x 52 weeks = $32,500 annual income

   $32,500 annual income ÷ 12 months = $2,708.33 Mr. Zorn's monthly income

   $3,120 + $2,708.33 = $5,828.33 total stable monthly income

   $5,828.33 x 0.28 = $1,631.93 maximum housing expense

2. $5,828.33 x 0.36 = $2,098.20 maximum debt-to-income allowed

   $2,098.20 - $400 (car loan) = $1,698.20 maximum housing expenses allowed

   Remember to use the lower monthly payment allowable, which is $1,631.93.

3. Yes, although Lisa and Dave have only been at their jobs a short time, Lisa had special training in the Air Force, and Dave is a vocational nurse, which also implies special training.

Mortgage Exercise 3-2

1. $700 weekly income x 52 weeks = $36,400 annual income

   $36,400 annual income ÷ 12 months = $3,033.33 monthly income

   $878 mortgage payment ÷ $3,033.33 monthly income = 0.29 (29% housing expense ratio)

2. $878 mortgage payment + $212 auto payment = $1,090 total debt service

   $1,090 total debt-to-income ÷ $3,033.33 monthly income = 0.36 (36% total debt-to-income ratio)

3. Yes, Mr. Able will have a few problems closing this transaction. The equity in his home ($14,000) plus money in the bank ($3,600) equals only $17,600, but his down payment plus estimated closing costs = $18,400. He must be able to provide documentation that he has two additional months of cash reserves available, and his housing expense ratio of 29% exceeds guidelines.

4. Yes, Mr. Able's Verification of Deposit is a problem because his current balance of $3,600 is significantly higher than his average balance of $1,000. He will need to have a good explanation of where the funds came from so the lender knows that he did not borrow the down payment.

Chapter 6 Conventional Financing

Class Activity: 80% Conventional Loan

For an 80% conventional loan, he can borrow $128,000 and needs to make a 20% down payment, or $32,000. If the house appraises for less than $160,000—say $150,000—then Bill can borrow only 80% of the appraised value ($120,000). Bill has a couple of options if he still wants to buy the home: He can offer the seller the appraised value of $150,000, or he needs to come up with an additional $8,000 as part of his down payment.

Class Activity: Mortgage Insurance

$100,000	Sales price
$90,000	Loan amount (90% LTV)
$558	Fee due at closing (0.0062 rate card factor x $90,000)
$46.50	Month fee ($558.00 / 12 = $46.50)

Note: Although this example was for a fixed rate mortgage, you can see from the sample rate card that private mortgage insurance companies also insure other products, such as ARMs. Again, rates can vary between companies; this example is intended only as an illustration.

Mortgage Exercise 6-1

1. The borrower's monthly debt is $890 (auto loan + VISA + student loan); rent does not count as debt since he will no longer pay that once he's in his house. Conventional qualifying guidelines allow a total housing expense ratio of 28% and a total debt -to-incomeratio of 36%, based on gross monthly income. Under the first ratio, the borrower would qualify for $1,372 ($4,900 x .28). Under the second ratio, the borrower would qualify for $874 ($4,900 x .36 = $1,764; $1,764 - $890 = $874). Remember that you must accept whichever is lower.

Mortgage Exercise 6-2

1.	$189,500 (purchase price) x 0.75 (% of 1st loan)	= $142,125	1st loan amount
	$189,500 x 0.15 (% of 2nd loan)	= $28,425	2nd loan amount
	Loan-to-Value = 75%		
	Combined Loan-to-Value = 90% (75% 1st loan + 15% 2nd loan)		
2.	$189,500 (purchase price) x 0.10 (10% down)	= $18,950	Down payment
	$142,125 (loan amount) x 0.015 (fee %)	= $2,131.88	Loan origination fee
	$18,950 (down) + $2,131.88 (origination fee)	= $21,081.88	Total due at closing

3. ($142,125 / 1,000) x 6.00 payment rate = $852.75 Monthly principal and interest on 1st loan

   (This solution uses the Payment Rate Chart found in the Appendix. Note that the numbers there are rounded to the nearest cent. For a more precise total, you can use a financial calculator.)

4. $189,500 (purchase price) x 0.15 = $28,425 2nd loan

   ($28,425 / 1,000) x 9.53 payment rate) = $270.89 Monthly principal and interest on 2nd loan

   (This solution uses the Payment Rate Chart found in the Appendix. Note that the numbers there are rounded to the nearest cent. For a more precise total, you can use a financial calculator.)

   $852.75 + $270.89 = $1,123.64 total monthly principal and interest payment

5. You must use the lower of the appraised value or the purchase price. The buyer would either need to bring an additional $4,500 to closing, or the purchase price—and therefore the loan amounts—would need to be adjusted accordingly.

Chapter 7 Introduction to Government Agency Loan Programs

Class Activity: FHA Loan Qualifying

- **Part 1:** When you divide the total housing expense by 31%, you see this loan requires a stable monthly income of $2,582.74 ($800.65 / .31 = $2,582.74).
- **Part 2:** FHA allows a maximum total debt-to-income ratio of 43%, so $1,033.30 ÷ 0.43 = $2,403.02, the minimum monthly income needed. Remember, though, a borrower must qualify under both ratios, so $2,403.02 is actually the minimum monthly income Mary would need in order to buy this home (barring other offsetting factors).

Mortgage Exercise 7-1

1. The borrower's total monthly debt is $2,630 ($1,780 + $850). Remember that utilities are not included as part of the debt ratio calculation. Divide that by gross monthly income of $6,850 to give him a total debt-to-income ratio of 38%, which is below the 43% FHA guideline. His credit score is acceptable and the sale price of the home is below the county loan limit, so yes, this loan can probably be made.
2. The minimum investment Stu must make is 3.5% of the sale price or appraised value, whichever is lower, so the minimum down payment is $8,872.50 ($253,500 x 0.035), making the base loan amount $244,628 (rounded up to the nearest dollar). The UFMIP is $2,446.28 ($244,628 x .01). Since he's financing that, add it to the base loan amount for a total loan amount of $247,074.
3. While borrowers can obtain secondary financing on FHA loans, it cannot be used for the required minimum investment. He could use a non-repayable gift for that, however.
4. $0.00; there is no prepayment penalty allowed on FHA loans, though the lender could require Stu to pay interest for the month if the loan is not repaid on the first on the month.

Class Activity: Entitlement

$ 480,000	Purchase Price
x .25	
$ 120,000	Guaranty Required
- 104,250	Available Entitlement
$ 15,750	Down Payment

If Dave wants to buy this house, he must make a cash down payment so that that guaranty amount is 25% of the loan amount.

Class Activity: VA Loan Qualifying

$1,090.16 ÷ $2,590 = 0.42 or 42% total debt-to-income ratio

This is just higher than the recommended 41%, so other offsetting factors would likely be needed for loan approval.

Class Activity: VA Residual Income

The family's residual income is $178.14 more than the $889 minimum guideline, which is just over 20% higher ($889 x .20 = $177.80), so this application should meet the income qualifications needed for approval. However, remember that these are simply guidelines and other factors will be considered.

Mortgage Exercise 7-2

1. Since she is an eligible veteran and this is her first home purchase, we can assume she has her full entitlement. The home's sale price of $114,900 is less than the estimate of reasonable value and well below the county maximum, so with all of these factors, it's likely that this loan can be made with no down payment.
2. The maximum fee the lender can charge is 1% of the loan, or $1,149. This and other closing costs cannot be financed into the loan. The variable fee for first use, regular military with no down payment is 2.15% of the loan, or $2,470. This can be financed into the loan, so the total loan amount is $117,370.
3. VA requires a guaranty of 25% of the loan amount, so Nan used $29,343 of her entitlement to buy this house ($117,370 x 0.25 = $29,342.58).
4. It may be possible for another eligible veteran to assume this loan, if the new borrower is approved by the VA. And if the new borrower agrees to substitute his entitlement, Nan's will be restored.

Chapter 8 Nontraditional Mortgage Products

Mortgage Exercise 8-1

1. Points are based on the loan amount, in this case, $135,000 ($150,000 - $15,000 down payment). The lender is charging a total of 5 points, or 5% of the loan. Discount points total $4,050 ($135,000 x .03) and the loan origination fee is $2,700 ($135,000 x .02). The total the lender will receive in points is $6,750 ($4,050 + $2,700).
2. The seller net is the sale price minus any seller-paid points, so the seller will net $145,950 ($150,000 - $4,050).
3. The loan note rate will be 6.500% since this is not a temporary buydown. The amount on the note equals the loan amount, not the sale price, and does not reflect the seller-paid points. So, it's $135,000 ($150,000 - $15,000).
4. Yes, the lender should be able to sell this loan to Fannie Mae/Freddie Mac on the secondary market because it has less than the 6% seller assistance limit that the programs allow with a 90% LTV.

Class Activity: ARM Interest Rates

Interest Rate with Caps: Year 2=9%; Year 3=7%; Year 4=9%; Year 5=10%

Mortgage Exercise 8-2

1. The start rate is 3.50%. The fully indexed rate after the first year is 8.00% (5.00% index + margin of 3.00% = 8.00%). BUT, the periodic maximum rates caps (in this example, annual) have to be taken in consideration also. In this mortgage, the maximum rate increase the first year is 3.00% (2.00% in all other years). So 3.50% + 3.00% = 6.50%, which will be the interest rate after the first adjustment.
2. The fully indexed rate is 7.50% (LIBOR rate of 4.50% + 3.00% margin).
3. The borrower's interest rate after the first adjustment period was 6.50%. Adding the periodic maximum adjustment cap of 2.00% would be 8.50%. However, the borrower's interest rate would be the LOWER of the two interest rates, which is 7.50%.
4. The maximum interest rate equals the start rate of 3.50% + the life of the loan cap of 6.00%, so the maximum interest rate this loan could have is 9.50%.
5. In order for this loan to get to that rate, the LIBOR would have to increase 2.00% from its current rate of 4.50% to 6.50%: 9.50% (maximum lifetime rate) – 3.00% (margin) = 6.50% (LIBOR)

Class Activity: ARM Advantages and Disadvantages

Advantages of ARMs include:

- Lower initial interest rate and payments
- May be easier to qualify for loan
- Leverage buyer into a higher-priced home
- Payments may decrease over time
- May be converted to a fixed-rate loan
- Good in times of low inflation or for short-term ownership

Disadvantages of ARMs include:

- No interest rate guarantees
- No payment guarantees

- Buyer's financial situation may change
- Buyer may over-leverage
- Possibility of negative amortization
- May have to pay a fee to convert even if you choose not to convert

Note: These are just representative, there may be others

Chapter 9 Legal Concepts in Real Estate

Class Activity: Legal Issues

- Contract issues (What rights and duties did the lease give the tenant?)
- Property issues (Who owned that strip of land?)
- Tort issues (Did she slip because the owner failed to maintain the property in a safe condition or because of her own carelessness?)

Chapter 10 Interests in Real Property

Class Activity: Notice

The easement, however, is still valid because Joe is deemed to have constructive notice of it. Although he didn't have actual notice, he could have found out about the easement granted to Bill by checking the public records.

Class Activity: Recording Deeds

- Curt's deed is a wild deed.
- Dan doesn't have constructive notice of Curt's interest in the property, because Curt's deed was outside the chain of title.

Class Activity: Marketable Title Act

Going back 40 years from 2011, the root of title would be the deed from 1956. Denise Russell, therefore, is considered to have marketable record title. When an owner establishes a marketable record title, claims that arose before the root of title are extinguished. That said, however, certain exceptions—such as mineral reservations, government interests, or railroad and utility easements—may survive from as far back as the original grant or patent on the land. Therefore, a thorough title search should extend beyond the root of title.

Class Activity: Lien Classification

Type of Lien	Voluntary	Involuntary	General	Specific
Property Tax Lien		X		X
Income Tax Lien		X	X	
Mortgage Lien	X			X
Mechanic's Lien		X		X
Judgment Lien	X	X	X	
Attachment Lien		X	X	X

Chapter 11 The Value of Real Estate

Class Activity: Assemblage

This strategy will likely work at first, but become less effective as time goes on and the last few owners learn about it. These last few homes will likely cost Mega more, but the owners have to be careful, too. If they're unrealistic about the worth to Mega's project or how high Mega is willing to go with its offer, they may get nothing. If these owners hold out too long for too much money, Mega may decide to design the project around them.

Chapter 12 Understanding Appraisals

Class Activity: Adjustments

Comp #1 Adjustment: Add $5,000 for final value of $96,000

Comp #2 Adjustment: None needed for final value of $100,000

Comp #3 Adjustment: Subtract $5,000 for final value of $105,000

Adjustment Limit Exercise

- **Property #1:** 3,000 + 1,500 - 2,500 = $2,000. Dividing that by the sales price of $85,000 results in adjustments of 2.4%. Since this is less than 15%, it is well within acceptable parameters.
- **Property #2:** 1,500 - 5,500 - 2,500 - 3,000 = -$9,500. Total net adjustments of $9,500 exceed the 15% limit ($9,500 / $55,000 = 17.3% or $55,000 x 15% = $8,250).
- **Property #3:** 3,000 + 1,500 + 5,500 + 2,500 + 2,000 = $14,500. Total absolute value of all adjustments exceeds 25% limit ($14,500 / $55,000 = 26.4% or $55,000 x 25% = $13,750).
- **Property #4:** 2,500 + 2,000 + 3,000 = $7,500. Total absolute value of all adjustments (without regard to sign) is less than 25% ($7,500 / $95,000 = 7.9% or $95,000 x 25% = $23,750).

Chapter 13 Ethics in the Mortgage Lending Profession

Class Activity: Ethical Discussion #1

There are a number of issues to consider in this scenario. Did Roger breach confidentiality? You might think not, since the address of a home for sale is most likely a matter of public record. But it's not really such a gray area. Roger has a fiduciary obligation to protect the confidentiality of ALL the information his customer furnishes—personal information as well as information related to the purchase contract and the property address. Customer Joyce should never have to be concerned that information she supplies might be used against her. His willingness to use that information for his own advantage should certainly raise some red flags, at the very least. He now has "inside" information that he's using for personal gain, which is highly unethical. Furthermore, it shows a complete lack of character, which really should disqualify him from even holding a MLO license. You might also want to consider the real estate agent's response to such an offer. Agents also have a fiduciary duty to their seller clients to present all offers on the listed property. While Roger may be able to get a loan closed as he promised, he has put the listing agent in an awkward position. Imagine if Roger took it a step further and held up Joyce's loan application or refused to offer her terms that were appropriate to her situation!

Class Activity: Mortgage Advertising

- **Scenario 1:** Yes, if Jane had never intended to close a so-called "5 for 5" loan and just wanted to get prospective borrowers in the door, her offer was not in good faith.
- **Scenario 2:** Yes, even though Alex is closing some of the loans in the timeframe advertised, he still used deception to bring in more customers, since he never intended to achieve that closing timeframe for most loans. This is also an example of bait and switch.

Class Activity: Illegal Discrimination

- **Scenario 1:** If Lou was using voice mail to screen prospects and doesn't reply to members of "protected classes" based on their voice, accent, or dialect, this would certainly be an illegal discriminatory practice. Whenever a definite pattern of unequal or biased treatment in the way a licensee answers the telephone or responds to voicemail is found and documented, a formalized discrimination complaint may be warranted. Such response patterns, called linguistic profiling, may include actions like seldom answering or responding to calls that are assumed to be from "protected class" members or otherwise discouraging those prospects. And if Lou is discouraging potential borrowers who receive some sort of public assistance from applying for a loan, he is also in violation of the Equal Credit Opportunity Act.
- **Scenario 2:** Under certain circumstances, even the newspapers chosen for advertising may be held to have the effect of racial steering. This is actually a real case. Because of the brokerage's advertising policy (and some of its other policies), the U.S. Attorney General filed a pattern and practice lawsuit against the brokerage. The court held that the advertising policy had an impermissible steering effect. It brought homes in the integrated and African American neighborhoods only to the attention of the readers of the African American newspaper, and most of those readers were African American. As a result, the advertising policy was likely to contribute to changing an integrated neighborhood into a predominantly African American neighborhood. That violated the government's policy of fostering integrated neighborhoods and it violated the federal Fair Housing Act. The court ordered the brokerage to maintain the same level of advertising in the African American newspaper, but also advertise those same homes in the two newspapers of general circulation, plus do advertising in smaller community newspapers. U.S. v. Real Estate One, Inc., 433 F. Supp. 1140 (E.D. Mich. 1977).

Class Activity: RESPA Violations

- **Scenario 1:** Both the attorney and the lender are in violation of RESPA since they are rendering of something of value (free services) in exchange for the referral.
- **Scenario 2:** This situation also likely violates Section 8 of RESPA, since the computer is a thing of value that the credit agency is providing in exchange for the referral of business from the lender. So even though the companies may argue that it was done for convenience, it would not be allowed. If, however, the credit agency provided the computer for free without placing any conditions on the lender, there would be no violation of Section 8 of RESPA. An example of a condition that would make this a RESPA violation might be requiring the lender to order a specific number of credit reports each month. What if the computer was used ONLY for ordering credit reports from the agency and not for other business? It might be OK to place the computer and require the lender to order a certain number of credit reports each month in order to have it for free. This provides an opportunity to point out students that sometimes an answer may not be so clear-cut.

Class Activity: Appraisal Concerns

1. Although Bill indicated that this property was his vacation home, even if Bill only used the property as a vacation a week or two a year, it would most likely be furnished with something. The empty rooms indicate that this is more likely an investment property for Bill that currently has no tenant.
2. An appraiser who supplies more information about the subject property than requested hasn't done anything wrong. Since Marge did not order the photographs as part of the appraisal, you might be tempted to think that she can remove the photographs before she sends the appraisal to the underwriter, since an underwriter does not typically care about photographs, and no one will know they were there except the appraiser. Or you might think it would be OK to just order a second appraisal and, if the value range is in line, to submit that instead. Marge can't "unsee" those photographs, however, and she now has additional knowledge about the property. To ignore or remove the photographs could be considered actual fraud.
3. Marge does have a dilemma, since Bill is a long-time customer. But, she cannot ethically push this refinance loan through as originally structured. She should tell Bill that they have to restructure the loan for an investment property, which will likely result in a higher interest rate. Might she lose a good customer over this? Possibly, but to do otherwise would be unethical and fraudulent.

Class Activity: Identity Theft

1. Review credit report for large numbers of recently opened accounts and conflicting information with the application.
2. Obtain valid government identification at the time of application.
3. Use fraud detection software to assist in verification of identity.
4. Check the Social Security Administration's death master index.

Class Activity: Fraud Schemes

- **Scenario 1:** Jack is technically a straw buyer in this situation, since he used his personal information to apply for a loan on a property where he did not intend to live and for which he did not intend to make mortgage payments. Although he may have had pure intentions, since he applied for the loan, Jack was contractually obligated to ensure that the monthly payments were made, whether he lived in the house or not. Additionally, Jack could possibly even be criminally liable for making a fraudulent statement (that he would live in the house, a requirement of an FHA loan) on a matter related to transaction with a federal agency. At the very least, he's got a stain on his credit report, and he no longer has his basement to himself!
- **Scenario 2:** Doug could be on the verge of perpetrating a fraud scheme called a disappearing second. The lender thinks it has a 80% LTV loan, for example, when it may actually be 90% LTV. Stu should be aware that if he goes along with facilitating this deal, he could be guilty of a material omission if he does not inform the lender of seller Doug's plans. Another issue is the fact that the buyer and seller are related. Certainly, there is no law against someone selling his property to a cousin, even at a discounted price. However, mortgage fraud scams often involve family members. So, in these instances, full disclosure is imperative. Purchase contracts between family members should specifically state their relationships so it does not appear intentionally hidden. Stu probably needs to get out of this transaction.
- **Scenario 3:** This is an example of a short sale fraud, and also a flipping scheme. You could even reasonably say that Joe was a straw buyer, since he never intended to make payments on the mortgage loan. In order for the short sale to go through, it's also very likely that Joe and Patrick did not reveal their relationship. Short sales that involve relatives and friends is a large red flag. As the number of foreclosures rise, it's likely that the related fraud schemes will continue to rise as well.

Class Activity: Predatory Lending

- **Scenario 1:** This is an obvious case of predatory lending. The consumer was under duress in this situation, and the lender took advantage of it by changing the loan terms. Furthermore, unless the lender's changes were below the tolerances that require redisclosure of terms, the lender is in violation of the Truth in Lending Act that requires a waiting period of three business days after redisclosure.
- **Scenario 2:** Making loans with a meager tangible benefit that does not resolve the borrower's problem but creates repeat business would be considered predatory lending. More specifically, this is an example of loan flipping, which is a type of equity skimming.
- **Scenario 3:** Borrowers with less than perfect credit may have to pay higher rates in order to secure a loan. That alone would not necessarily be considered predatory. It does depend on the actual terms of the loan, so more information would be needed to make a definitive call on this one.
- **Scenario 4:** Legitimate lenders do not require credit insurance, and in fact, many states forbid it since the loan balance would be paid off when the property was sold out of her estate. This could, therefore, be an example of predatory lending. (This might also be an example of illegal discrimination if such credit insurance is not required of single men.)

Class Activity: Ethical Discussion #2

You need to be very clear that Velma understands all conditions and terms associated with an adjustable rate mortgage. She needs to understand that the interest rate she will pay when adjusted according to the terms in the note will be set based off a standard index over which neither she nor her lender has any control, and it could be lower, but it could also be higher. You are not required to take her loan application, as long as your refusal is not based on Velma's membership in a protected class (race, color, religion, nationality, sex, disability, familial status, source of income). But you might have a hard time proving that. If you submit the loan application, you should take extra special care to confirm that you have made all required disclosures and that she acknowledges the receipt of them.

Class Case Study and Discussion

1. It would seem that there was some confusion and errors on the processing of the loan, if not outright intentional misrepresentation
2. The mortgage loan originator's actions were unethical.
3. The mortgage loan originator delegated rate locking to his processor, who it seems tried to lock the rate, but the FAX failed to make it to the lender. Indeed, the rate lock may not have been processed until four days after requested, if at all. The resulting efforts to cover the tracks of the internal clerical/processing errors—back dating forms, intentionally sending out disclosures with knowingly false information, and, it seems, falsified contact dates in the conversation log about the negative news, never accepting responsibility for the failure to get the rate locked as promised—shows an intent to deceive the borrower.

APPENDIX B

Worksheets and Other Resources

INCOME QUALIFYING — CONVENTIONAL LOANS

Monthly Gross Income:

Base salary	________
Overtime	________
Bonuses	________
Commissions	________
Other	________
Total	________

Long-term Monthly Debt:

Car payment	________
Child support	________
Credit cards	________
Other loans	________
Other debts	________
Total	________

(Consider 5% payments on all revolving charges)

Housing Expense-to-Income Ratio:

________	Stable Monthly Income
x .28	Income Ratio
________	Maximum Mortgage Payment (PITI)

Total Debt Service Ratio:

________	Stable Monthly Income
x .36	Income Ratio
________	Maximum Mortgage Obligations
________	Maximum Monthly Income
–	Monthly Obligations
________	Maximum Mortgage Payment (PITI)

MAXIMUM MORTGAGE PAYMENT (PITI) ________

________	Maximum PITI (less 20% of mortgage payment)
–	(Insurance, taxes, PMI)
________	Maximum Principal and Interest Payment
________	**MAXIMUM LOAN AMOUNT** (using calculator or interest factor tables)

INCOME QUALIFYING — FHA-INSURED LOANS
Income Ratio Method

Monthly Gross Income:

Base salary	________
Overtime	________
Bonuses	________
Commissions	________
Other	________
Total	________

Long-term Monthly Debt:

Car payment	________
Child support	________
Credit cards	________
Other loans	________
Other debts	________
Total	________

(Consider 5% payments on all revolving charges)

Housing Expense-to-Income Ratio: 31%

________	Stable Monthly Income
x .31	Income Ratio
________	Maximum Mortgage Payment (PITI)

Total Debt Service Ratio: 43%

________	Stable Monthly Income
x .43	Income Ratio
________	Maximum Montly Obligations
________	Maximum Monthly Obligation
–	Monthly Obligations
________	Maximum Mortgage Payment (PITI)

MAXIMUM MORTGAGE PAYMENT (PITI) ________

________	Maximum PITI (less 20% of mortgage payment)
–	(Insurance, taxes, PMI)
________	Maximum Principal and Interest Payment
________	**MAXIMUM LOAN AMOUNT** (not to exceed regional mortgage amount limitations)

MAXIMUM HOUSING EXPENSE ________

Total Housing Expenses	________
less 20% (taxes insurance, maintenance, utilities)	–
	________

Maximum Principal & Interest Payment ________

________	**Maximum Loan Amount** (Not to exceed regional mortgage amount limitations)

INCOME QUALIFYING — VA GUARANTEED LOAN

Monthly Gross Income:

Base salary ____________
Overtime ____________
Bonuses ____________
Commissions ____________
Other ____________
Total ____________

Long-term Monthly Debt:

Car payment ____________
Child support ____________
Credit cards ____________
Other loans ____________
Other debts ____________
Total ____________

Less All Taxes:

Federal Income tax ____________
Social Security (7.65%) ____________
State Income Tax ____________
Other Tax ____________
Total ____________

Net Income ____________
less:
long-term debts ____________
required reserves ____________
Total ____________

RESIDUAL INCOMES BY REGION, LOAN AMOUNTS $79,999 AND BELOW

Family*	Northeast	Midwest	South	West
1	$390	$382	$382	$425
2	654	641	641	713
3	788	772	772	859
4	888	868	868	967
5	921	902	902	1,004

*For over 5 family members, add $75 for each up to 7.

RESIDUAL INCOMES BY REGION, LOAN AMOUNTS $80,000 AND ABOVE

Family*	Northeast	Midwest	South	West
1	$450	$441	$441	$491
2	755	738	738	823
3	909	889	889	990
4	1,025	1,003	1,003	1,117
5	1,062	1,039	1,039	1,158

*For over 5 family members, add $80 for each up to 7.

MAXIMUM HOUSING EXPENSE ____________

Total Housing Expenses ____________
less 20% (taxes insurance, maintenance, utilities) ____________
____

Maximum Principal & Interest Payment ____________

____________ **Maximum Loan Amount** (Not to exceed lender limitations)

Total Debt Service Ratio: 41%

____________ Stable Monthly Income
x .41 Income Ratio
____________ Maximum Mortgage Obligations

____________ Maximum Monthly Income
____________ Monthly Obligations
____________ Maximum Mortgage Payment (PITI)

MAXIMUM MORTGAGE PAYMENT (PITI) ____________

____________ Maximum PITI
(less 20% of mortgage payment)
____________ (Insurance, taxes, PMI)
____________ Maximum Principal and Interest Payment

____________ **MAXIMUM LOAN AMOUNT** (not to exceed lender limitations)

ESTIMATED CLOSING COST COMPARISON

	CONV		FHA		VA	
Loan Origination Fee	1.00%	BSL	1.00%	BSL	1.00%	BSL
Loan Discount Points	Varies	BSL	Varies	BSL	Varies	BSL
Appraisal Fee	$450.00	BSL	$450.00	BSL	$450.00	BSL
Credit Report	$50.00	BSL	$50.00	BSL	$50.00	BSL
Settlement Fee	$180.00	BSL	$180.00	BSL	$180.00	SL
Title Insurance	$300.00	BSL	$300.00	BSL	$300.00	BSL
Title Binder	$125.00	BSL	$125.00	BSL	$125.00	BSL
Underwriting Fee	$160.00	BSL				
Processing Fee	$300.00	BSL	$300.00	SL	$300.00	SL
Tax Service Fee	$275.00	BSL	$275.00	SL	$275.00	SL
Document Preparation	$100.00	BSL	$100.00	BSL	$100.00	BSL
Recording Fees	$180.00	BSL	$180.00	BSL	$180.00	BSL
Survey	$140.00	BSL	$140.00	BSL	$140.00	BSL
Flood Certificate	$20.00	BSL	$20.00	BSL	$20.00	BSL
ARM Endorsement	$75.00	BSL	$75.00	BSL		
PREPAIDS						
PMI/MIP/Funding Fee	**	BSL	1.75%	BSLF	***	BSLF
Hazard Insurance	1 Yr.	BSL	1 Yr.	BSL	1 Yr.	BSL
Hazard Insurance Escrow	2 Mo.	BSL	2 Mo.	BSL	2 Mo.	BSL
Property Tax Escrow	2 Mo.	BSL	2 Mo.	BSL	2 Mo.	BSL
Interest (15 Days)		BSL		BSL		BSL

B = Borrower S = Property Seller L=Lender F = Financed

	CONV	FHA	VA
Sellers Contribution	LTV >90.01 3%	6%	4% (+ Disc. Pts.)
	LTV <90.00 6%		
	LTV <75.00 9%		
	Investment Property any LTV = 2%		

** Conventional Mortgage Insurance varies with loan to value.

*** If veteran has never used their entitlement, figure funding fee @ 2.00% with 0% down, 1.50% if between 5-10% down and 1.25% if down payment is at least 10% or greater.

Note: The figures used in this chart are for illustration only. The sample fees will vary depending on the service providers, the lender, the region, and other factors.

Sample Amortization Schedule **Page 1**

Amortization Results

Loan amount:	$100,000.00
Interest rate:	8.5%
Term of loan:	30 Years
Mortgage payment:	$768.91

Year	Loan Balance	Principal	Interest	Total Payments	Total Interest
1	$99,939.42	$60.58	$708.33	$768.91	$708.33
2	$99,178.10	$65.93	$702.98	$9,995.88	$9,173.98
3	$98,349.49	$71.76	$697.15	$19,222.84	$17,572.33
4	$97,447.64	$78.11	$690.81	$28,449.80	$25,897.44
5	$96,466.07	$85.01	$683.90	$37,676.76	$34,142.83
6	$95,397.74	$92.52	$676.39	$46,903.72	$42,301.46
7	$94,234.98	$100.70	$668.21	$56,130.68	$50,365.67
8	$92,969.44	$109.60	$659.31	$65,357.65	$58,327.09
9	$91,592.04	$119.29	$649.62	$74,584.61	$66,176.65
10	$90,092.89	$129.84	$639.08	$83,811.57	$73,904.46
11	$88,461.23	$141.31	$627.60	$93,038.53	$81,499.77
12	$86,685.35	$153.80	$615.11	$102,265.49	$88,950.84
13	$84,752.49	$167.40	$601.52	$111,492.46	$96,244.95
14	$82,648.79	$182.19	$586.72	$120,719.42	$103,368.21
15	$80,359.14	$198.30	$570.62	$129,946.38	$110,305.52
16	$77,867.10	$215.83	$553.09	$139,173.34	$117,040.44
17	$75,154.79	$234.90	$534.01	$148,400.30	$123,555.10
18	$72,202.74	$255.67	$513.25	$157,627.26	$129,830.00
19	$68,989.75	$278.27	$490.65	$166,854.23	$135,843.98
20	$65,492.77	$302.86	$466.05	$176,081.19	$141,573.95
21	$61,686.68	$329.63	$439.28	$185,308.15	$146,994.83
22	$57,544.17	$358.77	$410.15	$194,535.11	$152,079.28
23	$53,035.49	$390.48	$378.43	$203,762.07	$156,797.57
24	$48,128.30	$424.99	$343.92	$212,989.03	$161,117.33
25	$42,787.35	$462.56	$306.35	$222,216.00	$165,003.34
26	$36,974.31	$503.45	$265.47	$231,442.96	$168,417.27
27	$30,647.45	$547.95	$220.97	$240,669.92	$171,317.37
28	$23,761.35	$596.38	$172.53	$249,896.88	$173,658.23
29	$16,266.58	$649.09	$119.82	$259,123.84	$175,390.43
30	$8,109.35	$706.47	$62.45	$268,350.81	$176,460.15
END	$0.00	$763.51	$5.41	$276,039.94	$176,808.85

NOTE: This amortization schedule assumes that all payments were made on time and for the exact payment amounts. Late payments may add additional interest and/or late charges. Early payments or payments larger than the scheduled payments could result in the balance being paid sooner and/or less total interest being paid over the life of the loan.

LOAN PROGRESS CHARTS

Example: $50,000 original loan @ 12¼% for 30 years

PROBLEM: FIND BALANCE AFTER 3 YEARS

Step 1

Choose the **chart** that corresponds to the interest rate of the loan in question.

Step 2

Choose the **column** that corresponds to the original term of the loan. For example, thirty-year loans are found in the farthest right hand column of the chart.

12¼%

AGE OF LOAN	ORIGINAL LOAN TERM 22	23	24	25	26	27	28	29	30	
1	990	992	993	994	994	995	996	996	997	1
2	980	982	984	986	988	989	991	992	993	2
3	968	972	975	978	981	983	985	987	988	3
4	954	959	964	969	972	976	979	981	983	4
5	938	946	952	958	963	968	971	975	978	5

DOLLARS STILL OWED FOR EVERY $1000 BORROWED

Step 3

Choose the **row** that corresponds to the age of the loan. For example, a three-year-old loan would utilize row 3 of the chart.

Step 4

Multiply the number at the intersection by the number of **$1,000 increments** in the original loan.

$988
x 50 ($50,000)
$49,400 present balance

If the original loan amount had been **$50,600,** you would multiply 988 times 50.6.

5 %

ORIGINAL LOAN TERM 5 YR.	10 YR.	15 YR.	20 YR.	25 YR.	30 YR.	AGE OF LOAN
819	921	954	970	979	985	1
630	838	906	939	958	970	2
430	750	855	906	935	953	3
220	659	802	871	911	936	4
0	562	746	835	886	918	5
	461	687	796	859	899	6
	354	625	756	832	880	7
	242	560	714	802	859	8
	124	491	669	772	837	9
	0	419	622	739	813	10
		343	573	705	789	11
		264	521	670	764	12
		180	467	632	737	13
		92	410	593	709	14
		0	350	551	679	15
			287	508	648	16
			220	462	615	17
			150	414	580	18
			77	363	544	19
			0	310	506	20
				254	466	21
				195	424	22
				133	380	23
				68	333	24
				0	285	25
					233	26
					179	27
					122	28
					63	29
					0	30

5¼ %

ORIGINAL LOAN TERM 5 YR.	10 YR.	15 YR.	20 YR.	25 YR.	30 YR.	AGE OF LOAN
820	922	955	971	980	986	1
631	840	908	940	959	971	2
432	753	858	908	937	955	3
222	661	805	874	914	939	4
0	565	749	838	889	922	5
	464	691	801	864	903	6
	357	629	761	836	884	7
	244	564	719	808	864	8
	125	496	675	777	842	9
	0	423	628	745	820	10
		347	579	712	796	11
		267	527	677	771	12
		183	473	639	744	13
		94	415	600	716	14
		0	355	559	687	15
			291	515	656	16
			224	169	623	17
			153	421	589	18
			79	369	553	19
			0	316	515	20
				259	475	21
				199	432	22
				136	388	23
				70	340	24
				0	291	25
					239	26
					184	27
					126	28
					64	29
					0	30

6 %

ORIGINAL LOAN TERM 5 YR.	10 YR.	15 YR.	20 YR.	25 YR.	30 YR.	AGE OF LOAN
823	925	958	973	982	988	1
636	845	913	945	963	975	2
436	760	865	915	943	961	3
225	670	814	883	922	946	4
0	574	760	849	899	931	5
	473	703	813	875	914	6
	365	642	775	850	896	7
	251	578	734	823	878	8
	129	509	691	794	858	9
	0	437	645	764	837	10
		359	597	731	815	11
		277	545	697	791	12
		190	490	660	766	13
		98	432	622	739	14
		0	371	580	711	15
			305	537	680	16
			236	490	648	17
			162	441	614	18
			83	389	578	19
			0	333	540	20
				274	499	21
				212	456	22
				145	410	23
				75	362	24
				0	310	25
					255	26
					197	27
					135	28
					70	29
					0	30

6¼ %

ORIGINAL LOAN TERM 5 YR.	10 YR.	15 YR.	20 YR.	25 YR.	30 YR.	AGE OF LOAN
824	926	958	974	983	988	1
637	847	914	946	965	976	2
438	762	867	917	945	963	3
226	673	817	886	925	948	4
0	577	764	853	903	933	5
	476	707	817	879	917	6
	368	647	779	854	900	7
	253	582	739	828	882	8
	130	514	697	799	863	9
	0	441	651	769	842	10
		363	603	737	821	11
		281	551	703	797	12
		193	496	667	773	13
		100	438	629	746	14
		0	376	588	718	15
			310	544	688	16
			239	497	657	17
			165	448	623	18
			85	395	587	19
			0	339	548	20
				280	508	21
				216	464	22
				149	418	23
				77	369	24
				0	317	25
					261	26
					202	27
					139	28
					71	29
					0	30

6½ %

ORIGINAL LOAN TERM 5 YR.	10 YR.	15 YR.	20 YR.	25 YR.	30 YR.	AGE OF LOAN
825	927	959	975	984	989	1
638	848	916	948	966	977	2
439	765	869	919	947	964	3
227	676	820	889	927	951	4
0	580	767	856	906	936	5
	479	711	821	883	921	6
	371	651	784	858	904	7
	255	587	744	832	887	8
	132	518	702	805	868	9
	0	445	657	775	848	10
		367	608	744	826	11
		284	557	710	804	12
		196	502	674	779	13
		101	444	636	753	14
		0	381	595	726	15
			314	551	696	16
			243	504	665	17
			167	455	631	18
			86	402	595	19
			0	345	557	20
				285	516	21
				220	472	22
				152	426	23
				78	376	24
				0	323	25
					267	26
					206	27
					142	28
					73	29
					0	30

6¾ %

ORIGINAL LOAN TERM 5 YR.	10 YR.	15 YR.	20 YR.	25 YR.	30 YR.	AGE OF LOAN
826	928	960	976	984	989	1
640	950	917	949	967	978	2
441	767	872	921	949	966	3
228	678	823	891	930	953	4
0	583	771	859	909	939	5
	482	715	825	886	924	6
	373	655	788	863	908	7
	257	591	749	837	891	8
	133	523	707	810	872	9
	0	450	662	781	853	10
		371	614	750	832	11
		288	563	716	810	12
		198	508	681	786	13
		102	449	643	760	14
		0	386	602	733	15
			319	558	704	16
			247	511	672	17
			170	462	639	18
			88	408	603	19
			0	351	565	20
				290	524	21
				225	480	22
				155	433	23
				80	383	24
				0	330	25
					272	26
					211	27
					145	28
					75	29
					0	30

7 %

ORIGINAL LOAN TERM 5 YR.	10 YR.	15 YR.	20 YR.	25 YR.	30 YR.	AGE OF LOAN
827	928	961	976	985	990	1
641	852	919	951	968	979	2
442	769	874	923	951	967	3
229	681	826	894	932	955	4
0	586	774	863	912	941	5
	485	719	829	890	927	6
	376	659	793	867	912	7
	259	596	754	842	895	8
	134	527	712	815	877	9
	0	454	668	786	858	10
		375	620	756	838	11
		291	569	723	816	12
		201	514	687	792	13
		104	455	649	767	14
		0	392	609	740	15
			324	565	711	16
			251	518	680	17
			173	468	647	18
			90	415	611	19
			0	357	573	20
				295	532	21
				229	488	22
				158	441	23
				82	390	24
				0	336	25
					278	26
					216	27
					149	28
					77	29
					0	30

7¼ %

ORIGINAL LOAN TERM 5 YR.	10 YR.	15 YR.	20 YR.	25 YR.	30 YR.	AGE OF LOAN
828	929	962	977	985	990	1
643	853	921	952	970	980	2
444	772	876	925	952	969	3
230	684	829	897	934	957	4
0	589	778	866	915	944	5
	488	723	833	893	930	6
	379	664	797	871	915	7
	262	600	759	846	899	8
	136	532	718	820	882	9
	0	458	673	792	863	10
		379	626	762	843	11
		295	575	729	822	12
		203	520	694	799	13
		150	460	656	774	14
		0	397	616	747	15
			329	572	719	16
			255	525	688	17
			176	475	655	18
			91	421	619	19
			0	363	581	20
				300	540	21
				233	496	22
				161	448	23
				83	397	24
				0	343	25
					284	26
					220	27
					152	28
					79	29
					0	30

7½ %

ORIGINAL LOAN TERM 5 YR.	10 YR.	15 YR.	20 YR.	25 YR.	30 YR.	AGE OF LOAN
829	930	963	978	986	991	1
644	855	922	953	971	981	2
445	774	879	927	954	970	3
231	687	832	899	936	959	4
0	592	781	869	917	946	5
	491	726	836	897	933	6
	382	668	801	875	918	7
	264	604	763	851	903	8
	137	536	723	825	886	9
	0	463	679	797	868	10
		383	631	767	849	11
		298	580	735	828	12
		206	525	700	805	13
		107	466	663	781	14
		0	402	623	754	15
			333	579	726	16
			259	532	696	17
			179	482	663	18
			93	427	627	19
			0	369	589	20
				306	548	21
				238	504	22
				164	456	23
				85	404	24
				0	349	25
					289	26
					225	27
					155	28
					81	29
					0	30

7¾ %

ORIGINAL LOAN TERM 5 YR.	10 YR.	15 YR.	20 YR.	25 YR.	30 YR.	AGE OF LOAN
830	931	963	978	986	991	1
646	857	924	955	972	982	2
467	776	881	929	956	972	3
232	689	834	902	939	960	4
0	595	784	872	920	949	5
	494	730	840	900	936	6
	384	672	806	878	922	7
	266	609	768	855	907	8
	138	541	728	830	890	9
	0	467	684	803	873	10
		387	637	773	854	11
		302	586	741	833	12
		209	531	707	811	13
		108	472	670	787	14
		0	407	629	761	15
			338	586	733	16
			263	539	703	17
			182	489	670	18
			95	434	635	19
			0	375	597	20
				311	556	21
				242	511	22
				167	463	23
				87	412	24
				0	355	25
					295	26
					230	27
					159	28
					83	29
					0	30

8 %

ORIGINAL LOAN TERM 5 YR.	10 YR.	15 YR.	20 YR.	25 YR.	30 YR.	AGE OF LOAN
831	932	964	979	987	992	1
647	858	925	956	973	983	2
448	778	883	931	957	973	3
233	692	837	904	941	962	4
0	598	788	875	923	951	5
	497	734	844	903	938	6
	387	676	810	882	925	7
	268	613	773	859	910	8
	139	545	733	834	894	9
	0	471	689	808	877	10
		391	642	779	859	11
		305	592	747	839	12
		211	537	713	817	13
		110	477	676	793	14
		0	412	636	768	15
			343	593	740	16
			267	546	710	17
			185	495	678	18
			96	440	643	19
			0	381	605	20
				316	564	21
				246	519	22
				171	471	23
				89	418	24
				0	362	25
					300	26
					234	27
					162	28
					84	29
					0	30

8¼ %

ORIGINAL LOAN TERM 5 YR.	10 YR.	15 YR.	20 YR.	25 YR.	30 YR.	AGE OF LOAN
832	933	965	980	987	992	1
649	860	927	957	974	983	2
450	781	885	933	959	974	3
234	695	840	907	943	964	4
0	601	791	878	925	953	5
	500	738	847	906	941	6
	390	680	814	886	928	7
	271	618	777	863	914	8
	141	550	738	839	898	9
	0	476	695	813	882	10
		396	648	784	864	11
		309	597	753	844	12
		214	542	719	823	13
		111	483	683	800	14
		0	418	643	774	15
			247	600	747	16
			271	553	718	17
			188	502	685	18
			98	447	650	19
			0	387	613	20
				321	571	21
				251	527	22
				174	478	23
				91	426	24
				0	368	25
					306	26
					239	27
					166	28
					86	29
					0	30

8½ %

ORIGINAL LOAN TERM 5 YR.	10 YR.	15 YR.	20 YR.	25 YR.	30 YR.	AGE OF LOAN
832	934	966	980	988	992	1
650	861	928	958	975	984	2
451	783	887	935	960	975	3
235	697	843	909	945	966	4
0	604	794	881	928	955	5
	503	742	851	909	943	6
	393	684	818	889	931	7
	273	622	782	867	917	8
	142	554	743	844	902	9
	0	480	700	818	886	10
		399	653	789	868	11
		312	603	759	849	12
		217	548	725	828	13
		113	488	689	806	14
		0	423	649	781	15
			352	606	754	16
			275	559	725	17
			191	508	693	18
			99	453	658	19
			0	392	620	20
				327	579	21
				255	534	22
				177	485	23
				92	432	24
				0	375	25
					312	26
					243	27
					169	28
					88	29
					0	30

8¾ %

ORIGINAL LOAN TERM 5 YR.	10 YR.	15 YR.	20 YR.	25 YR.	30 YR.	AGE OF LOAN
833	935	966	981	988	993	1
651	863	929	960	976	985	2
453	785	889	937	962	976	3
236	700	845	912	947	967	4
0	607	798	884	930	957	5
	506	745	854	912	946	6
	396	688	822	893	964	7
	275	626	786	871	920	8
	144	558	747	848	906	9
	0	484	705	823	890	10
		404	659	795	873	11
		315	609	765	854	12
		219	554	731	834	13
		114	494	695	812	14
		0	428	656	787	15
			357	613	761	16
			279	566	732	17
			194	515	700	18
			101	459	665	19
			0	398	628	20
				332	587	21
				260	542	22
				180	493	23
				94	440	24
				0	391	25
					318	26
					248	27
					173	28
					90	29
					0	30

9 %

ORIGINAL LOAN TERM						AGE OF LOAN
5 YR.	10 YR.	15 YR.	20 YR.	25 YR.	30 YR.	
834	935	967	981	989	993	**1**
653	865	931	961	977	986	**2**
454	787	891	938	963	978	**3**
237	703	848	914	949	969	**4**
0	610	801	887	933	959	**5**
	509	749	858	915	948	**6**
	398	692	826	896	936	**7**
	277	630	791	875	924	**8**
	145	563	752	852	910	**9**
	0	489	710	827	894	**10**
		408	664	800	878	**11**
		319	614	770	859	**12**
		222	559	737	839	**13**
		116	499	702	817	**14**
		0	433	662	793	**15**
			361	620	767	**16**
			283	573	738	**17**
			197	522	707	**18**
			103	466	673	**19**
			0	404	635	**20**
				337	594	**21**
				264	549	**22**
				184	500	**23**
				96	446	**24**
				0	388	**25**
					323	**26**
					253	**27**
					176	**28**
					92	**29**
					0	**30**

9¼ %

ORIGINAL LOAN TERM						AGE OF LOAN
5 YR.	10 YR.	15 YR.	20 YR.	25 YR.	30 YR.	
835	936	968	982	989	994	**1**
654	866	932	962	948	986	**2**
446	790	893	940	965	979	**3**
238	705	851	916	951	970	**4**
0	613	804	890	935	961	**5**
	512	753	861	918	950	**6**
	401	696	830	899	939	**7**
	280	635	795	879	927	**8**
	146	567	757	857	913	**9**
	0	493	715	832	898	**10**
		412	670	805	882	**11**
		323	620	776	864	**12**
		225	565	743	844	**13**
		118	505	708	823	**14**
		0	439	669	799	**15**
			366	626	774	**16**
			287	579	745	**17**
			200	528	714	**18**
			105	472	680	**19**
			0	410	643	**20**
				343	602	**21**
				268	557	**22**
				187	507	**23**
				98	453	**24**
				0	394	**25**
					329	**26**
					258	**27**
					180	**28**
					94	**29**
					0	**30**

9½ %

ORIGINAL LOAN TERM						AGE OF LOAN
5 YR.	10 YR.	15 YR.	20 YR.	25 YR.	30 YR.	
836	937	968	982	990	994	**1**
656	868	934	963	978	987	**2**
457	792	895	942	966	980	**3**
239	708	853	918	952	971	**4**
0	616	807	893	937	962	**5**
	515	756	864	921	953	**6**
	404	700	833	903	942	**7**
	282	639	799	883	930	**8**
	148	571	762	861	917	**9**
	0	497	720	837	902	**10**
		416	675	810	886	**11**
		326	625	781	869	**12**
		227	570	749	850	**13**
		119	510	714	828	**14**
		0	444	675	805	**15**
			371	633	780	**16**
			291	586	752	**17**
			203	535	721	**18**
			106	478	687	**19**
			0	416	650	**20**
				348	609	**21**
				273	564	**22**
				190	514	**23**
				100	460	**24**
				0	400	**25**
					335	**26**
					262	**27**
					183	**28**
					96	**29**
					0	**30**

9¾ %

ORIGINAL LOAN TERM						AGE OF LOAN
5 YR.	10 YR.	15 YR.	20 YR.	25 YR.	30 YR.	
837	938	969	983	990	994	**1**
657	869	935	964	979	988	**2**
459	794	897	943	967	981	**3**
241	711	856	921	954	973	**4**
0	619	810	895	940	964	**5**
	518	760	868	924	955	**6**
	407	704	837	906	944	**7**
	284	643	803	886	933	**8**
	149	576	766	865	920	**9**
	0	502	725	841	906	**10**
		420	680	815	890	**11**
		330	631	786	873	**12**
		230	576	755	855	**13**
		121	516	720	834	**14**
		0	449	682	811	**15**
			376	639	786	**16**
			295	592	758	**17**
			206	541	728	**18**
			108	484	694	**19**
			0	422	657	**20**
				353	616	**21**
				277	571	**22**
				194	522	**23**
				102	467	**24**
				0	407	**25**
					340	**26**
					267	**27**
					187	**28**
					98	**29**
					0	**30**

10 %

ORIGINAL LOAN TERM						AGE OF LOAN
5 YR.	10 YR.	15 YR.	20 YR.	25 YR.	30 YR.	
838	939	970	983	991	994	**1**
658	871	936	965	980	988	**2**
460	796	899	945	969	982	**3**
242	713	858	923	956	974	**4**
0	622	813	898	942	966	**5**
	521	763	871	926	957	**6**
	410	708	841	909	946	**7**
	286	647	807	890	935	**8**
	150	580	771	869	923	**9**
	0	506	730	846	909	**10**
		424	685	820	894	**11**
		333	636	792	878	**12**
		233	581	760	859	**13**
		122	521	726	839	**14**
		0	454	688	817	**15**
			380	645	792	**16**
			299	599	765	**17**
			209	547	734	**18**
			110	491	701	**19**
			0	428	664	**20**
				358	623	**21**
				282	578	**22**
				197	529	**23**
				103	474	**24**
				0	413	**25**
					346	**26**
					272	**27**
					190	**28**
					100	**29**
					0	**30**

10¼ %

ORIGINAL LOAN TERM						AGE OF LOAN
5 YR.	10 YR.	15 YR.	20 YR.	25 YR.	30 YR.	
839	940	970	984	991	995	**1**
660	872	938	966	981	989	**2**
462	798	901	947	970	982	**3**
243	716	861	925	957	975	**4**
0	625	816	901	944	967	**5**
	524	767	874	929	959	**6**
	412	712	844	912	949	**7**
	289	652	812	893	938	**8**
	152	584	775	872	926	**9**
	0	510	735	850	913	**10**
		428	691	825	898	**11**
		337	641	797	882	**12**
		236	587	766	864	**13**
		124	526	732	844	**14**
		0	459	694	822	**15**
			385	652	798	**16**
			303	605	771	**17**
			212	554	741	**18**
			112	497	708	**19**
			0	434	671	**20**
				364	630	**21**
				286	585	**22**
				203	536	**23**
				105	480	**24**
				0	419	**25**
					352	**26**
					277	**27**
					194	**28**
					102	**29**
					0	**30**

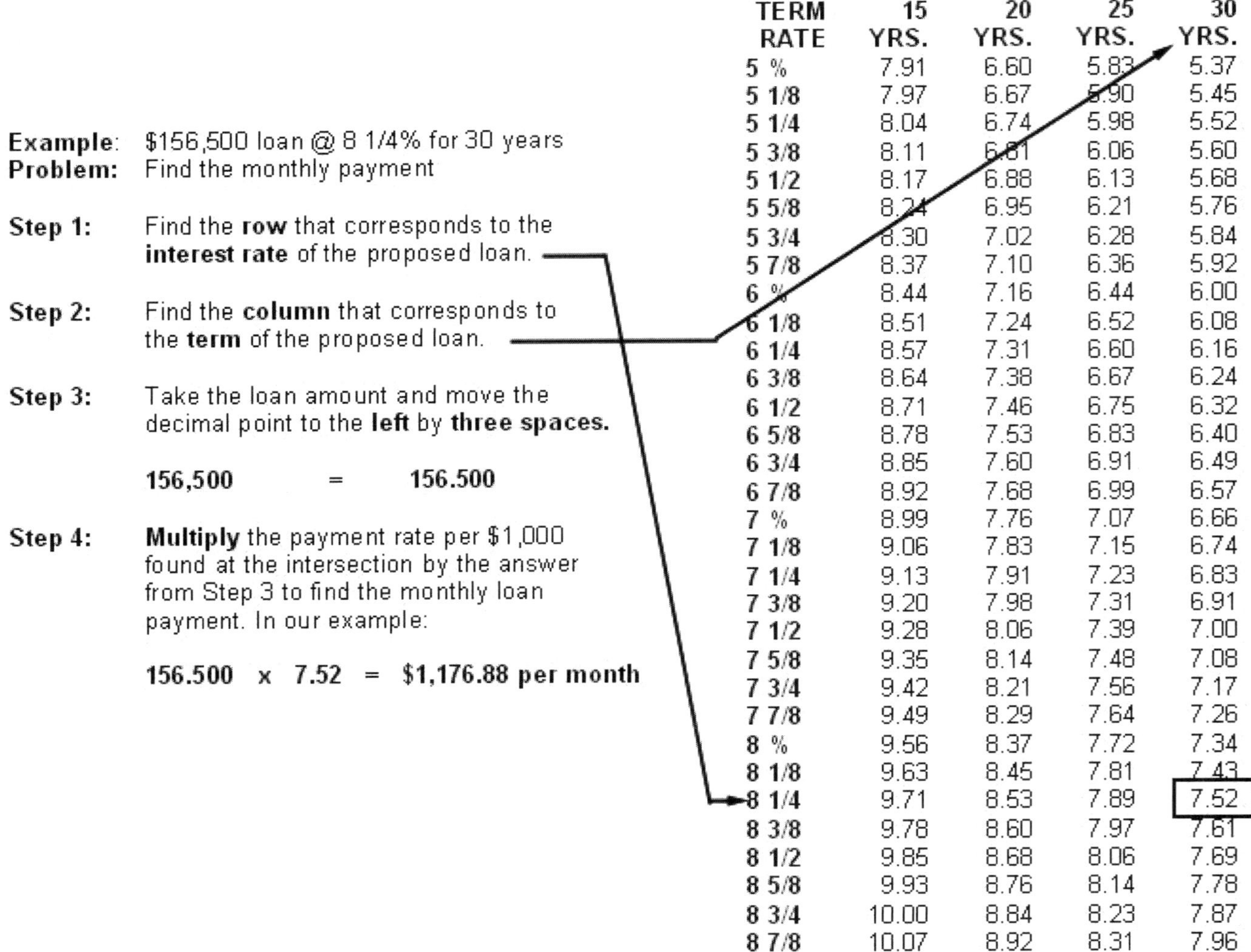

Example: $156,500 loan @ 8 1/4% for 30 years
Problem: Find the monthly payment

Step 1: Find the **row** that corresponds to the **interest rate** of the proposed loan.

Step 2: Find the **column** that corresponds to the **term** of the proposed loan.

Step 3: Take the loan amount and move the decimal point to the **left** by **three spaces.**

156,500 = 156.500

Step 4: **Multiply** the payment rate per $1,000 found at the intersection by the answer from Step 3 to find the monthly loan payment. In our example:

156.500 x 7.52 = $1,176.88 per month

Payment Rate Chart
Equal Monthly Payment Needed to Amortize a Loan of $1,000
(rounded to the nearest cent)

TERM RATE	15 YRS.	20 YRS.	25 YRS.	30 YRS.
5 %	7.91	6.60	5.83	5.37
5 1/8	7.97	6.67	5.90	5.45
5 1/4	8.04	6.74	5.98	5.52
5 3/8	8.11	6.81	6.06	5.60
5 1/2	8.17	6.88	6.13	5.68
5 5/8	8.24	6.95	6.21	5.76
5 3/4	8.30	7.02	6.28	5.84
5 7/8	8.37	7.10	6.36	5.92
6 %	8.44	7.16	6.44	6.00
6 1/8	8.51	7.24	6.52	6.08
6 1/4	8.57	7.31	6.60	6.16
6 3/8	8.64	7.38	6.67	6.24
6 1/2	8.71	7.46	6.75	6.32
6 5/8	8.78	7.53	6.83	6.40
6 3/4	8.85	7.60	6.91	6.49
6 7/8	8.92	7.68	6.99	6.57
7 %	8.99	7.76	7.07	6.66
7 1/8	9.06	7.83	7.15	6.74
7 1/4	9.13	7.91	7.23	6.83
7 3/8	9.20	7.98	7.31	6.91
7 1/2	9.28	8.06	7.39	7.00
7 5/8	9.35	8.14	7.48	7.08
7 3/4	9.42	8.21	7.56	7.17
7 7/8	9.49	8.29	7.64	7.26
8 %	9.56	8.37	7.72	7.34
8 1/8	9.63	8.45	7.81	7.43
8 1/4	9.71	8.53	7.89	7.52
8 3/8	9.78	8.60	7.97	7.61
8 1/2	9.85	8.68	8.06	7.69
8 5/8	9.93	8.76	8.14	7.78
8 3/4	10.00	8.84	8.23	7.87
8 7/8	10.07	8.92	8.31	7.96

Equal Monthly Payment Needed to Amortize a Loan of $1,000

TERM RATE	15 YRS.	20 YRS.	25 YRS.	30 YRS.
5 %	7.91	6.60	5.83	5.37
5 1/8	7.97	6.67	5.90	5.45
5 1/4	8.04	6.74	5.98	5.52
5 3/8	8.11	6.81	6.06	5.60
5 1/2	8.17	6.88	6.13	5.68
5 5/8	8.24	6.95	6.21	5.76
5 3/4	8.30	7.02	6.28	5.84
5 7/8	8.37	7.10	6.36	5.92
6 %	8.44	7.16	6.44	6.00
6 1/8	8.51	7.24	6.52	6.08
6 1/4	8.57	7.31	6.60	6.16
6 3/8	8.64	7.38	6.67	6.24
6 1/2	8.71	7.46	6.75	6.32
6 5/8	8.78	7.53	6.83	6.40
6 3/4	8.85	7.60	6.91	6.49
6 7/8	8.92	7.68	6.99	6.57
7 %	8.99	7.76	7.07	6.66
7 1/8	9.06	7.83	7.15	6.74
7 1/4	9.13	7.91	7.23	6.83
7 3/8	9.20	7.98	7.31	6.91
7 1/2	9.28	8.06	7.39	7.00
7 5/8	9.35	8.14	7.48	7.08
7 3/4	9.42	8.21	7.56	7.17
7 7/8	9.49	8.29	7.64	7.26
8 %	9.56	8.37	7.72	7.34
8 1/8	9.63	8.45	7.81	7.43
8 1/4	9.71	8.53	7.89	7.52
8 3/8	9.78	8.60	7.97	7.61
8 1/2	9.85	8.68	8.06	7.69
8 5/8	9.93	8.76	8.14	7.78
8 3/4	10.00	8.84	8.23	7.87
8 7/8	10.07	8.92	8.31	7.96

TERM RATE	15 YRS.	20 YRS.	25 YRS.	30 YRS.
9 %	10.15	9.00	8.40	8.05
9 1/8	10.22	9.08	8.48	8.14
9 1/4	10.30	9.16	8.57	8.23
9 3/8	10.37	9.24	8.66	8.32
9 1/2	10.45	9.33	8.74	8.41
9 5/8	10.52	9.41	8.83	8.50
9 3/4	10.60	9.49	8.92	8.60
9 7/8	10.67	9.57	9.00	8.69
10 %	10.75	9.66	9.09	8.78
10 1/8	10.83	9.74	9.18	8.87
10 1/4	10.90	9.82	9.27	8.97
10 3/8	10.98	9.90	9.36	9.06
10 1/2	11.06	9.99	9.45	9.15
10 5/8	11.14	10.07	9.54	9.25
10 3/4	11.21	10.16	9.63	9.34
10 7/8	11.29	10.24	9.72	9.43
11 %	11.37	10.33	9.81	9.53
11 1/8	11.45	10.41	9.90	9.62
11 1/4	11.53	10.50	9.99	9.72
11 3/8	11.61	10.58	10.08	9.81
11 1/2	11.69	10.67	10.17	9.91
11 5/8	11.77	10.76	10.26	10.00
11 3/4	11.85	10.84	10.35	10.10
11 7/8	11.93	10.93	10.44	10.20
12 %	12.01	11.02	10.54	10.29
12 1/8	12.09	11.10	10.63	10.39
12 1/4	12.17	11.19	10.72	10.48
12 3/8	12.25	11.28	10.82	10.58
12 1/2	12.33	11.37	10.91	10.68
12 5/8	12.41	11.45	11.00	10.77
12 3/4	12.49	11.54	11.10	10.87
12 7/8	12.58	11.63	11.19	10.97

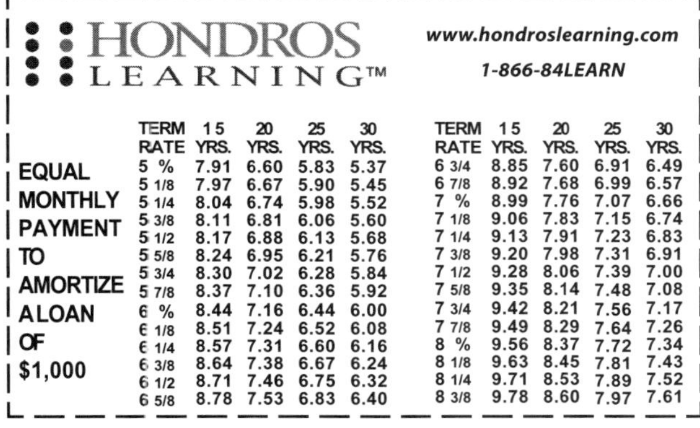

HONDROS LEARNING™

www.hondroslearning.com

1-866-84LEARN

EQUAL MONTHLY PAYMENT TO AMORTIZE A LOAN OF $1,000

TERM RATE	15 YRS.	20 YRS.	25 YRS.	30 YRS.
5 %	7.91	6.60	5.83	5.37
5 1/8	7.97	6.67	5.90	5.45
5 1/4	8.04	6.74	5.98	5.52
5 3/8	8.11	6.81	6.06	5.60
5 1/2	8.17	6.88	6.13	5.68
5 5/8	8.24	6.95	6.21	5.76
5 3/4	8.30	7.02	6.28	5.84
5 7/8	8.37	7.10	6.36	5.92
6 %	8.44	7.16	6.44	6.00
6 1/8	8.51	7.24	6.52	6.08
6 1/4	8.57	7.31	6.60	6.16
6 3/8	8.64	7.38	6.67	6.24
6 1/2	8.71	7.46	6.75	6.32
6 5/8	8.78	7.53	6.83	6.40

TERM RATE	15 YRS.	20 YRS.	25 YRS.	30 YRS.
6 3/4	8.85	7.60	6.91	6.49
6 7/8	8.92	7.68	6.99	6.57
7 %	8.99	7.76	7.07	6.66
7 1/8	9.06	7.83	7.15	6.74
7 1/4	9.13	7.91	7.23	6.83
7 3/8	9.20	7.98	7.31	6.91
7 1/2	9.28	8.06	7.39	7.00
7 5/8	9.35	8.14	7.48	7.08
7 3/4	9.42	8.21	7.56	7.17
7 7/8	9.49	8.29	7.64	7.26
8 %	9.56	8.37	7.72	7.34
8 1/8	9.63	8.45	7.81	7.43
8 1/4	9.71	8.53	7.89	7.52
8 3/8	9.78	8.60	7.97	7.61

Rate Card Courtesy of Hondros Learning.

EQUAL MONTHLY PAYMENT TO AMORTIZE A LOAN OF $1,000

TERM RATE	15 YRS.	20 YRS.	25 YRS.	30 YRS.
8 1/2	9.85	8.68	8.06	7.69
8 5/8	9.93	8.76	8.14	7.78
8 3/4	10.00	8.84	8.23	7.87
8 7/8	10.07	8.92	8.31	7.96
9 %	10.15	9.00	8.40	8.05
9 1/8	10.22	9.08	8.48	8.14
9 1/4	10.30	9.16	8.57	8.23
9 3/8	10.37	9.24	8.66	8.32
9 1/2	10.45	9.33	8.74	8.41
9 5/8	10.52	9.41	8.83	8.50
9 3/4	10.60	9.49	8.92	8.60
9 7/8	10.67	9.57	9.00	8.69
10 %	10.75	9.66	9.09	8.78
10 1/8	10.83	9.74	9.18	8.87
10 1/4	10.90	9.82	9.27	8.97
10 3/8	10.98	9.90	9.36	9.06
10 1/2	11.06	9.99	9.45	9.15
10 5/8	11.14	10.07	9.54	9.25

TERM RATE	15 YRS.	20 YRS.	25 YRS.	30 YRS.
10 3/4	11.21	10.16	9.63	9.34
10 7/8	11.29	10.24	9.72	9.43
11 %	11.37	10.33	9.81	9.53
11 1/8	11.45	10.41	9.90	9.62
11 1/4	11.53	10.50	9.99	9.72
11 3/8	11.61	10.58	10.08	9.81
11 1/2	11.69	10.67	10.17	9.91
11 5/8	11.77	10.76	10.26	10.00
11 3/4	11.85	10.84	10.35	10.10
11 7/8	11.93	10.93	10.44	10.20
12 %	12.01	11.02	10.54	10.29
12 1/8	12.09	11.10	10.63	10.39
12 1/4	12.17	11.19	10.72	10.48
12 3/8	12.25	11.28	10.82	10.58
12 1/2	12.33	11.37	10.91	10.68
12 5/8	12.41	11.45	11.00	10.77
12 3/4	12.49	11.54	11.10	10.87
12 7/8	12.58	11.63	11.19	10.97

Online Resources

Federal Regulation

Consumer Financial Protection Bureau	www.consumerfinance.gov
Department of Housing and Urban Development	www.hud.gov/offices/hsg
Fair Housing	www.hud.gov/offices/fheo/FHLaws/yourrights.cfm
Farm Credit Administration (FCA)	www.fca.gov
Federal Deposit Insurance Corporation (FDIC)	www.fdic.gov/quicklinks/bankers.html
FDIC/Bankers	www.fdic.gov
Federal Financial Institutions Examination Council (FFIEC)	www.ffiec.gov
Federal Housing Administration	www.fha.com
Federal Housing Finance Agency	www.fhfa.gov
Federal Reserve System Board of Governors	www.federalreserve.gov
Federal Trade Commission	www.ftc.gov
FTC Privacy Initiatives	www.ftc.gov/privacy
Internal Revenue Service	www.irs.gov
National Credit Union Association	www.ncua.gov
National Do Not Call Registry	www.donotcall.gov
Office of the Comptroller of the Currency	www.occ.treas.gov
Office of Thrift Supervision	www.ots.treas.gov
Real Estate Settlement Procedures Act (RESPA)	www.hud.gov/settlement
U.S. Treasury Department	www.ustreas.gov

Secondary Markets

Federal National Mortgage Association (Fannie Mae)	www.fanniemae.com www.efanniemae.com
Federal Home Loan Mortgage Corporation (Freddie Mac)	www.freddiemac.com
Government National Mortgage Association (Ginnie Mae)	www.ginniemae.gov

Mortgage Industry

American Association of Residential Mortgage Regulators	www.aarmr.org
National Association of Mortgage Brokers (NAMB)	www.namb.org
Nationwide Mortgage Licensing System (NMLS)	www.stateregulatoryregistry.org/nmls

Loan Programs

FHA Maximum Loans/County	www.fhaloan.com/fha_limits.cfm
HUD/Handbooks and Forms	www.hud.gov/handbooks
HUD/Lender Resources	www.hud.gov/groups/lenders.cfm
USDA Rural Development	www.rurdev.usda.gov/rhs
VA Certificates of Eligibility	www.homeloans.va.gov/eligibility
VA Loan Guaranty Program	www.homeloans.va.gov
Veteran's Administration	www.va.gov

Miscellaneous

American Land Title Association (ALTA)	www.alta.org
Annual Credit Report	www.annualcreditreport.com
The Appraisal Foundation (USPAP)	www.appraisalfoundation.org
Conference of State Bank Supervisors	www.csbs.org
Independent Valuation Protection Institute	www.ivpi.org

Glossary

2-1 Buydown A graduated payment buydown that provides for subsidized payments in the first two years of the loan.

3-2-1 Buydown A graduated payment buydown that provides for subsidized payments in the first three years of the loan.

3/7/3 Rule A provision of the Truth in Lending Act related to required disclosures and waiting periods. Initial disclosure to be delivered within three business days of receipt of a completed application; earliest to close a loan is the seventh business day after disclosures are provided; a three business-day waiting period imposed after borrower receives redisclosures before a loan can close.

A-Minus Loans Loans for borrowers who may have credit record blemishes, limited funds for a down payment, high debt-to-income ratio, or a record of bankruptcy and/or foreclosure; riskier than prime mortgages, but not as risky as subprime mortgages.

Abstract of Title A chronological history of title to a property, listing all recorded documents that affect the title, as well as all public records searched or not searched.

Abstractor A person who prepares a summary (or abstract) of public records relating to title to a specific parcel of land.

Acceleration Clause A contract clause that gives the lender the right to declare the entire loan amount due immediately because of borrower's default or other reasons as stated in the contract.

Acceptance 1. Agreeing to the terms of an offer to enter into a contract, thereby creating a binding contract. 2. Taking delivery of a deed.

Accrued Expenses Items on a settlement statement for which the cost has been incurred, but the expense has not yet been paid.

Acknowledgment A formal declaration from a person who has signed a document to an authorized official (usually a notary public) that he or she signed voluntarily. The official certifies that the signature is voluntary and genuine.

Acquisition Cost The total amount needed to purchase property, including down payment, loan amount, and any allowable buyer-paid closing costs.

Adjustment In appraisal, the process of making chosen comparables come as close as possible in features to the subject so that meaningful price comparisons can be made.

Adjustable Rate Mortgage (ARM) A type of mortgage loan on which the interest rate may be adjusted according to the terms of the note. *May also be called* ***Variable Rate Mortgages (VRMs)*** *or* ***Adjustable Rate Loans (ALMs).***

Adjustment Interval On an adjustable rate mortgage, the time between changes in the interest rate or monthly payment.

Advancement An improvement in one's employment position, given as a reason for changing employers (as opposed to job hopping for no reason).

Adverse Action A decision by creditor that involves either the denial of credit, an offer of less favorable terms than those applied for, or changes to the terms of an existing credit agreement.

Adverse Possession Acquiring title to someone else's real property through open, notorious, and hostile possession of it for the required statutory amount of time.

Advertisement A commercial message in *any medium* that promotes, directly or indirectly, a credit transaction. It must follow guidelines of federal, state, and local fair housing acts, as well as Regulation Z and the Truth in Lending Act.

Advertising, Foreclosure Required notification of foreclosure sale, notifying the public of the date and time of the sale, for the statutory period of time in a general circulation newspaper in the county.

Affiliated Business Arrangement (AfBA or **ABA)** An arrangement in which a person who is in a position to refer business incident to or part of a real estate settlement service involving a federally related mortgage loan—or an associate of that person—has either an affiliate relationship with or a direct or beneficial ownership interest of more than 1% in a provider of settlement services and who then refers business to that provider or in some way influences the selection of that provider.

Alienation The transfer of ownership or an interest in property from one person to another, by any means.

Alienation, Involuntary The transfer of an interest in property against the will of the owner, or without action by the owner, occurring through operation of law, natural processes, or adverse possession.

Alienation, Voluntary The voluntarily transfer of an interest in property to someone else.

Alienation Clause A contract clause that gives the lender certain stated rights when there is a transfer of ownership in property. *Also called a* ***due-on-sale clause***.

Alimony Money paid to an ex-spouse as part of a divorce settlement. Alimony does not have to be revealed as a source of income if it is not counted to help repay the loan, but must be revealed as a debt obligation.

Alt-A Loans Loans that hold borrowers with good credit to different documentation standards than traditional loans. *Also called* ***Alternative Documentation Loans***.

Amortization The decrease of a loan balance due to periodic installments paid on the principal and interest. *Compare to* ***Negative Amortization***. *See* ***Re-Amortization***.

Amortization Schedule A table or chart that shows the periodic payments, interest and principal requirements, and unpaid loan balance for each period of the life of a loan.

Amortize To calculate payments to pay off a debt by periodic installments, with payments going to pay principal and interest.

Amortizing Loan Loan with payments applied to principal and interest. *Compare to* ***Fully Amortizing Loan*** *and* ***Partially Amortizing Loan***.

Annexation The legal term for attaching or affixing personal property to real property.

Annexer The person who owned the item as personal property and brought it onto the real property.

Annual Percentage Rate (APR) The effective interest rate on a loan after taking into account the finance charges associated with the extension of credit.

Appraisal A professional estimate or opinion of the value of a piece of property as of a certain date. *Also called* ***Valuation***.

Appraisal Management Company A business entity that—for a management fee—administers a network of certified and licensed appraisers to fulfill real estate appraisal assignments on behalf of mortgage lending institutions.

Application The submission of a borrower's financial information in anticipation of a credit decision relating to a federally related mortgage loan.

Appreciation An increase in the value of a property due to changes in market conditions or other causes.

Appurtenances Rights that go with real property, for example, access rights, surface rights, subsurface rights, mineral rights, some water rights, and limited air rights.

APR *See* ***Annual Percentage Rate***.

Area Median Income (AMI) Midpoint in the family-income range for a specific statistical area. The figure often is used as a basis to stratify incomes into low, moderate and upper ranges. These figures are adjusted for family size and calculated annually by the U.S. Department of Housing and Urban Development (HUD) for every region in the country.

ARM *See* ***Adjustable Rate Mortgage***.

Arm's Length Transaction A transaction occurring under typical market conditions with each party acting in his or her own best interests.

As Is In an appraisal, the determination of property value based on a complete and thorough examination of the subject property as it currently sits and in its present condition.

Assemblage Combining two or more parcels of land into one larger parcel.

Assessed Value The valuation placed upon property by a public tax assessor for purposes of taxation.

Assessments Taxes levied only against properties that benefit from a public improvement (e.g., new sewer line).

Assets Items that are of value to an owner. *See* ***Liquid Assets***.

Assign 1. To transfer a right or interest to another. 2. When a tenant transfers his or her right of possession, or other interest in leased property, to another person for the entire remainder of the lease term.

Associate In connection to an affiliated business arrangement, one who has one or more of the following relationships with a person in a position to refer settlement business: (A) a spouse, parent, or child of such person; (B) a corporation or business entity that controls, is controlled by, or is under common control with such person; (C) an employer, officer, director, partner, franchisor, or franchisee of such person; or (D) anyone who has an agreement, arrangement, or understanding, with such person, the purpose or substantial effect of which is to enable the person in a position to refer settlement business to benefit financially from the referrals of such business.

Assumable Any loan for which an assumption may be exercised.

Assumption A financing strategy where one party takes over the primary liability for the loan of another party and the terms of the loan or note remain unchanged; usually lender approval is needed; also, a release is needed or original party remains secondarily liable for the loan.)

Attachments Things connected to the land, whether natural or man-made; generally considered to be real property.

Attestation The signing of a legal document by witnesses to affirm that the parties' signatures are real; the act of witnessing the execution of a legal document (such as a deed or will). *Compare to* ***Acknowledgment***.

Automated Underwriting System (AUS) Process where loan applicant information is entered into a computer program and an evaluation comes back within minutes advising the lender to either accept the loan or refer the loan application for further review.

Automated Valuation Models (AVMs) Computer programs that are able to provide a probable value range for properties by performing a statistical analysis of available data.

Automatic Endorsers Lenders authorized to underwrite their own VA loan applications and who are responsible for the entire mortgage process through closing.

Average Prime Offer Rate An annual percentage rate derived from average interest rates, points, and other loan pricing terms that are currently offered to consumers by a representative sample of lenders for mortgage transactions that have low-risk pricing characteristics.

B-C Credit Refers to credit condition of people with less-than-perfect credit or serious blemishes on their credit report; may be used to describe borrowers who do not meet the qualifying standards set by Fannie Mae/ Freddie Mac, making such loans nonconforming. *Also used to refer to* ***Subprime Loans***.

Bait and Switch An alluring but insincere offer to sell a product or service which the advertiser in truth does not intend or want to sell. Its purpose is to switch consumers from buying the advertised merchandise, in order to sell something else, usually at a higher price or on a basis more advantageous to the advertiser.

Balloon Payment A final payment at the end of a loan term to pay off the entire remaining balance of principal and interest not covered by payments during the loan term.

Bankruptcy A court process that cancels debt and provides some relief for creditors; Chapter 7, sometimes called a straight bankruptcy, it is a liquidation proceeding; Chapter 13, sometimes called a reorganization proceeding, is filed by individuals who want to pay off their debts over a period of three to five years.

Basis Point A unit that is equal to 1/100th of 1% and is used to denote the change in a financial instrument, commonly used for calculating changes in interest rates. The relationship can be summarized as 1% change = 100 basis points.

BEACON Score *See* ***FICO Score***.

Beneficiary One who receives a benefit; refers to the lender in a trust deed.

Bill Consolidation Borrowing a larger sum of money to pay off many smaller debts.

Binder A preliminary agreement, usually the equivalent of a commitment, clearly stating conditions and terms.

Blockbusting The illegal practice of inducing owners to sell their homes (often at a deflated price) by suggesting that the ethnic or racial composition of the neighborhood is changing, with implication that property values will decline as a result. *Also called* ***panic selling*** *or* ***panic peddling***.

Board of Governors A seven-member board that controls the Federal Reserve System. *Also called the* ***Federal Reserve Board****, or the* ***Fed***.

Bond-Type Securities Mortgage backed securities issued by Ginnie Mae, which are long-term, pay interest semi-annually, and provide for repayment at a specified date.

Bonuses Money paid to someone in addition to his or her regular salary and may only be counted as income if consistent.

Boot Unlike properties added to a deal to balance the value and are taxable as part of an exchange. *See* ***Equity Exchange***.

Broker Price Opinion Tool that is sometimes used by lenders and mortgage companies to value properties in situations where they believe the expense and delay of an appraisal is not necessary.

Building Codes Rules that set construction standards, requiring builders to use particular methods and materials.

Bundle of Rights All real property rights conferred with ownership, including, but not limited to, the right of use or possession, the right of enjoyment, the right of exclusion, and the right of disposal.

Business Day Generally refers to a day on which a creditor's offices are open to the public for carrying on substantially all of its business functions; however, for purposes of rescission and disclosure under the Truth in Lending Act, the term means all calendar days except Sundays and legal public federal holidays.

Business Cycles General swings in business activity, resulting in expanding or contracting activity during different phases of the cycle.

Buydown Additional funds in the form of points paid to a lender at the beginning of a loan to lower the interest rate and monthly payments.

Buydown, Permanent The payment of points by a borrower to a lender to reduce the interest rate and loan payments for the entire life of the loan.

Buydown, Temporary The payment of points by a borrower to a lender to reduce the interest rate and payments early in a loan, with interest rate and payments rising later. Plans include level payment, where the interest rate reduction, and hence the payment, is constant throughout the buydown period, or graduated payment, where payment subsidies in the early years of a loan keep payments low, but payments increase each year until they are sufficient to fully amortize the loan.

Buyer's Market A situation in the housing market where buyers have a large selection of properties from which to choose.

CAIVRS *See* ***Credit Alert Verification Reporting System***.

Cancellation Terminating an obligation, such as when a note is cancelled after payment, or when PMI is cancelled after certain conditions are met.

Cap, Interest Rate The highest amount of interest that can be charged according to a legal agreement on an adjustable rate mortgage.

Cap, Lifetime A provision of an ARM that limits the highest rate that can occur over the life of the loan.

Cap, Mortgage Payment A limit on the amount that a mortgage payment (principal and interest) may increase on the scheduled adjustment dates of an adjustable rate mortgage.

Cap, Negative Amortization A limit on the amount of negative amortization that can occur with an adjustable rate mortgage.

Cap, Payment A provision of some ARMs limiting the amount by which a borrower's payments may increase regardless of any interest rate increase; may result in negative amortization.

Capital Gain The increased sales price over the purchase price of an asset.

Cash Flow Money available to an individual after subtracting all cash expenses. *See* ***Residual Income***.

Cash Reserve A requirement of some lenders that buyers have sufficient cash remaining after closing to make the first two monthly mortgage payments.

Certificate of Eligibility A certificate issued by the Department of Veteran's Affairs to establish status and amount of a veteran's eligibility to qualify for loan guaranty.

Certificate of Reasonable Value (CRV) A document issued by the VA which establishes the reasonable value of the subject property based on an approved appraisal. The VA loan amount cannot exceed the CRV. *See* ***Notice of Value***.

Chain of Title A clear and unbroken chronological record of the ownership of a specific piece of property.

Character Stability in job and responsibilities such that, even with setbacks, financial obligations will be honored by the borrower.

Child Support Money paid to the parent or guardian of a child as part of a settlement. Child support does not have to be revealed as a source of income if it is not counted to help repay the loan, but it must be revealed as a debt obligation.

Civil Law The body of law concerned with the rights and liabilities of one individual in relation to another.

Civil Rights Fundamental rights guaranteed to all persons by the law. The term is primarily used in reference to constitutional and statutory protections against discrimination based on race, religion, sex, or national origin.

Civil Rights Act of 1866 Federal law prohibiting public and private racial discrimination in any property transaction in the U.S.

Civil Rights Act of 1968 Federal law prohibiting discrimination based on race, color, religion, sex, national origin, disability, or familial status. *Also called* ***Title VIII*** *or* ***Federal Fair Housing Act***.

Clause A paragraph or section of a contract or other document that defines or assigns specific rights and duties to the parties involved.

Clear to Close All of the conditions necessary to make the loan have been satisfied and the lender gives the final approval to schedule the closing.

Clear Title A title that is free of liens or legal questions as to ownership of property. *See also* ***Unencumbered Property***.

Closing The final state in the process of granting a loan as funds are disbursed in accordance with the settlement statement. If the transaction involves the sale of real property, closing also involves transfer of ownership of real property from seller to buyer, according to the terms and conditions in the sales contract or escrow agreement.

Closing Costs Expenses incurred in the transfer of real estate in addition to the purchase price; (e.g., the appraisal fee, title insurance premiums, broker's commission, transfer tax, etc.)

Closing Statement *See* ***Settlement Statement***.

Clouds on the Title Encumbrances or outstanding claims that could affect the owner's title; problems or uncertainties with a title to real property.

Co-Mortgagor A person who signs a mortgage (or other security instrument) with the primary mortgagor and generally receives a share in the encumbered property; a co-mortgagor may or may not accept a joint obligation to repay the loan.

Co-Ownership Any form of ownership which is owned by more than one person who shares title to real property, with each person having an undivided interest in the property.

Co-Signer A person that signs a credit application with another person, agreeing to be equally responsible for the repayment of the loan.

COFI *See* ***Cost of Funds Index***.

Collateral Property pledged as security for a debt. *See* ***Hypothecate***.

Combined Loan-to-Value (CLTV) The percentage of the property value borrowed through a combination of more than one loan, such as a first mortgage and a second mortgage home equity loan.

Commercial Banks Financial institutions that provide a variety of financial services, including loans.

Commercial Real Estate Lenders Lenders who loan money for commercial real estate projects.

Commissions The compensation paid to someone in lieu of, or in addition to, regular salary. Commissions may be a flat rate or percentage of sale price, but can only be counted as income if they are consistent.

Commitment Letter A formal offer by a lender stating the terms under which it agrees to lend money to a home buyer.

Community Property In some states, the recognition that any property acquired during marriage is owned equally.

Community Reinvestment Act (CRA) Federal law emphasizing that regulated financial institutions have a continuing obligation to help meet the credit needs of the local communities in which they operate, especially in low-income neighborhood**Comparables** Other similar properties that have sold recently in a certain area.

Composite Annual Percentage Rate The relationship between the cost of borrowing money and the total amount financed, represented as a percentage and based on the initial payment rate and the fully indexed rate that would exist for the remaining years on the loan term on an adjustable rate mortgage.

Condition 1. A provision in a contract, deed, law, regulation, guideline, etc., that makes the parties' rights and obligations depend on the occurrence, or non-occurrence, of a particular event. *Also called a* ***Contingency Clause***. 2. A provision of a contract, law, regulation, guideline, etc., that allows, or does not allow, something else to occur based on whether or not certain other events occur or do not occur. 3. Other factors that reflect the general state of something as good or bad; (e.g., economic conditions of an area, property condition, etc.).

Condominium A form of property ownership where each co-owner has a separate fee simple interest in the interior of an individual unit, combined with an undivided interest in common areas of the property. *Compare to* ***Cooperative***.

Condominium Loan *See* ***Section 234(c) FHA Loan***.

Confirmation of Sale A document filed by the court finalizing the sale of property at foreclosure, and after which time the equitable right of redemption is no longer available to the original defaulting borrower.

Conforming Loans Loans that meet Fannie Mae/Freddie Mac standards and which can be sold on the secondary market. *Compare to* ***Nonconforming Loans***.

Conformity Value characteristic that says a particular home achieves its maximum value when it is surrounded by homes similar in style and function. Conformity applies to neighborhoods as well.

Consideration Anything of value, such as money, services, goods, or promises, given to induce another to enter into a contract. *Sometimes called* ***valuable consideration***. Consideration for an option is option money.

Consumer An individual who obtains or has obtained a financial product or service from a financial institution for personal, family, or household reasons.

Contingency Clause *See* ***Condition***.

Contingent Interest A term used to describe the lender's share of the appreciation paid on a shared appreciation mortgage (SAM) loan or other participation plan loan.

Contract An agreement between two or more parties to do, or not do, a certain thing. The requirements for an enforceable contract are: capacity, mutual consent, lawful objective, and consideration. In addition, certain contracts must be in writing to be enforceable.

Contract Escrow An approach used to ensure that payments are made on an existing mortgage, whereby an escrow account or servicing agreement is set up. Buyer makes payments into the escrow account; escrow agent then pays the existing mortgage and passes the surplus money to seller. Often used for land contracts with existing mortgages.

Contribution A value theory that says a particular item or feature of a home is only worth what it actually contributes in value to the property.

Contributory Value The actual amount that a particular item or feature of a property actually adds in value.

Conventional Loan A loan that is not insured or guaranteed by the federal government.

Conversion Option A right the borrower has to convert from an adjustable rate mortgage to a fixed rate mortgage one time during the loan term, provided certain conditions are met.

Convertible ARM An adjustable rate mortgage that can be converted to a fixed rate mortgage under specified conditions.

Conveyance The transfer of title to real property from one person to another by means of a written document, such as a deed.

Conveyance, Voluntary The voluntary transfer of property from a debtor to the lender in lieu of foreclosure, applying the value of the property toward the outstanding debt.

Cooperative (Co-op) A building owned by a corporation, with its shareholders each receiving a proprietary lease on an individual unit, the right to use common areas, and an obligation to pay a pro rata portion of the operational expenses of the property. *Compare to **Condominium**.*

Corporation A legal entity that is created and operated according to the laws of each state.

Cost of Funds Index (COFI) An index that reflects the cost of borrowing money as per the 11th District Federal Home Loan Bank. This index is used by Fannie Mae when purchasing ARM loans.

Cost of Money The interest rate people or businesses pay to use another's money for their own purposes.

Coupon Rate The interest rate stated in a note. *Also called **Nominal Rate** or **Note Rate**.*

Covenant A promise in a contract which, if not kept or broken, is a default by the promisor.

Credit 1. The availability of money; the ability to borrow money. 2. A sum of money to be received. *See **Rent Credit**.*

Credit Alert Verification Reporting System (CAIVRS) Federal database of delinquent federal debtors that allows federal agencies to reduce the risk to federal loan and loan guarantee programs.

Credit History A person's record of debt repayment detailing how a person paid credit accounts in the past. Credit history is used as a guide to how likely the borrower is to pay accounts on time and as agreed in the future.

Credit Report A report of an individual's credit history prepared by a credit bureau and used by a lender in determining a loan applicant's creditworthiness.

Credit Scoring An objective means of determining creditworthiness of potential borrowers based on assigning specified numerical values to different aspects of a borrower. *See also **FICO Score**.*

Credit Unions A cooperative financial institution owned and controlled by members in order to pool their deposits together, pay members better interest rates, and loan money to fellow members.

Creditor A person or other entity, such as a bank, who is owed a debt.

CRV *See **Certificate of Reasonable Value**.*

Customer A consumer with a long-term and/or continuing relationship with a financial institution.

Customer Identification Programs (CIPs) Processes that creditors must employ as directed by the U.S. Patriot Act to verify the identity of customers who are entering into a formal relationship, such as taking out a loan or a credit account.

Dealer A person who holds property for the sole purpose of reselling it.

Debit A sum of money that is owed.

Debt Money that is owed. Any recurring monetary obligation that will not be cancelled (e.g., monthly bills) until repaid.

Debt-to-Income Ratio The relationship of a borrower's total monthly debt obligations, including housing and long-term, debts with 10 or more payments remaining, to income, expressed as a percentage (Total Debt ÷ Income = Ratio %). *Also called **DTI**, **total debt service ratio**, or **back end ratio**.*

Debtor A person or other entity who owes money to another.

Declining Market A somewhat vague term used generally to describe areas where home prices are going down, due to any number of factors.

Deed The legal document conveying title to a property.

Deed in Lieu of Foreclosure Deed given by borrower to lender to satisfy a debt, avoiding foreclosure. *Also called **Voluntary Conveyance**.*

Deed of Trust An instrument placing some interest in the property into the hands of a disinterested third party as security for the payment of a note, creating a voluntary lien on real property to secure repayment of a debt. Parties to a deed of trust are grantor or trustor (borrower), beneficiary (lender), and trustee (third party). Unlike a mortgage, a trust deed has a power of sale clause, allowing a trustee to foreclose non-judicially. *Also called a **Trust Deed**. Compare to **Mortgage**.*

Deed Restrictions Limitations on real property use, imposed by a former owner through language included in the deed. *Also called **restrictive covenants**.*

Default Failure to fulfill an obligation, duty, or promise, as when borrower fails to make payments, tenant fails to pay rent, or party fails to perform a contract. Mortgage, note, or other document defines what constitutes default.

Defeasance Clause 1. A clause in a legal document stating that in the event a stated condition has been fulfilled, the document becomes null and void. 2. Used in title theory states, whereby a mortgagee agrees to return title of property to the mortgagor after all contract terms have been performed as agreed.

Deferment Permission to delay fulfillment of an obligation (e.g., paying taxes) until a later date.

Deferred Interest Accrued interest that is not paid by regularly scheduled payments; interest that is accumulated during payment periods but is not paid until a later date. This can be an element of ARMs and may cause negative amortization to occur.

Deficiency Judgment A court order stating the amount of money that a debtor still owes to the creditor because the collateral property did not bring enough at foreclosure sale to cover the entire loan amount, accrued interest, and other costs.

Deficit Spending The situation that occurs when the government spends more money than it takes in from tax revenue.

Delinquency A loan in which a payment is overdue but which has not yet been declared to be in default.

Demand Quantity of a commodity or service wanted at a specified price and time.

Demand Deposits Money that is immediately accessible and a customer may elect to withdraw from the bank at any time.

Department of Veterans Affairs (VA) Federal agency that oversees programs for veterans of the U.S. Armed Services, including the Veterans Benefits Administration and Veterans Health Administration.

Deposit 1. Money offered as an indication of good faith regarding the future performance of a purchase agreement. *Also called* ***earnest money***. 2. A tenant's security deposit.

Depreciate To decline in value.

Depreciation 1. A loss in property value for any reason. 2. For taxes, the expensing of the cost of business or investment property over a set number of years, determined by IRS to be an asset's useful life.

Derogatory Credit Credit history showing previous problems in meeting financial obligations.

Descent An operation of law when real property is transferred to an heir after the death of the owner who leaves no will.

Desktop Underwriter® (DU®) An automated underwriting system that puts lenders in direct contact with Fannie Mae, providing a streamlined process of document submission, underwriting, and loan approval.

Devise The transfer of real property through a will.

Direct Endorsers Lenders authorized to underwrite their own FHA loan applications and who are responsible for the entire loan process through closing.

Disability A physical or mental impairment that substantially limits one or more of the major life activities of such for an individual.

Disability Payments Payments made as a result of an injury, illness, or other infirmary. The payments may be permanent if the disability is permanent, and thus may be counted as part of stable monthly income.

Disclosures Points or facts that must be revealed. For example, the law requires certain financial disclosures, specific disclosures for ARMs, and disclosures under Truth in Lending Act.

Discount The difference between the stated amount of an obligation and the amount paid.

Discount Points Points the borrower chooses to pay at the beginning of a loan for the purpose of reducing the note interest rate charged.

Discount Rate The interest rate charged by the Federal Reserve Banks on loans to member financial institutions for short-term loans of reserves. *Also referred to as the* ***Federal Discount Rate***.

Discrimination Violating civil rights law by treating people unequally because of their race, religion, sex, national origin, age, or some other characteristic of a protected class.

Disintermediation The loss of deposits to competing investments that offer higher returns.

Disparate Impact The adverse consequence a law that is not discriminatory on its face has on a minority group.

Do Not Call Registry National registry managed by the Federal Trade Commission that limits commercial telemarketers from phoning consumers who place their phone numbers on a list.

Dower A special real property interest the law in many states gives as a statutory life estate to a widow when her husband owns/owned real property during their marriage.

Down Payment The amount a buyer pays to obtain a property in addition to the money that the buyer borrows.

Drive-By Appraisal An appraisal performed according to USPAP guidelines, but with only an exterior inspection of the subject property.

Due on Sale Clause A provision in a mortgage allowing the lender to demand repayment in full if the borrower sells the property securing the mortgage. *Also called* ***Alienation Clause***.

Durability The likelihood or probability that a person's source of stable monthly income will continue into the future.

Dwelling Any building, structure, or portion thereof which is occupied as, or designed or intended for occupancy as, a residence by one or more families, and any vacant land which is offered for sale or lease for the construction or location of any such building or structure.

Earnest Money A deposit made by the potential home buyer to show that he or she is serious about buying the house.

Easement A right of way giving persons other than the owner access to or over real property for a particular purpose.

Easy Qualifier Loan A conventional loan with a loan-to-value ratio (LTV) of 75% or less; a loan where lenders require the same documentation as other conventional loans, but relax qualifying standards due to increased equity the borrower is putting into the home; lenders view this loan as less risky since borrower has more to lose and lenders can more easily recoup 75% of a home's value in foreclosure.

ECOA *See* ***Equal Credit Opportunity Act***.

Economic Base The main business or industry that a community uses to support and sustain itself. A good economic base is critical for home values.

Effective Demand The situation that occurs when a prospective buyer has enough disposable income available to satisfy his or her needs or desires. *Also called* ***purchase ability***.

Eminent Domain The government's constitutional power to take (appropriate or condemn) private property for public use, as long as the owner is paid just compensation.

Employment History The stability of a person's job tenure at various companies, used on loan applications to help gauge income durability and reliability.

Encroachment A physical object intruding onto neighboring property, often due to a mistake regarding the boundary.

Encumbered Property Property with mortgages, liens, or other restrictions against it that prevent or restrict its transfer.

Encumbrance A non-possessory interest in property; a lien, easement, or restrictive covenant burdening the property owner's title.

Entitlement The dollar amount of loan guarantee to which an eligible veteran is entitled.

Environmental Impact Statement (EIS) Study required for all federal and federally related projects by the National Environmental Policy Act, which details a development project's impact on energy use, sewage systems, drainage, water facilities, schools, and other environmental, economic, and social areas.

Equal Credit Opportunity Act (ECOA) Federal law that prohibits discrimination in granting credit to people based on sex, age, marital status, race, color, religion, national origin, receipt of public assistance, or rights exercised under the Consumer Credit Protection Act.

Equity The difference between market value of a property and the sum of the mortgages and liens against it.

Equity Exchange When value in a property is traded for value in another property. Properties must be of like kind, held for use in trade or business, or as investment to qualify for tax deferment. An equity exchange can also be a delayed exchange, with a promise to provide a replacement property. To qualify for tax deferment, the replacement property must be located within 45 days and closed within 180 days of the first exchange. *Also called* ***Tax-Deferred Exchange***, ***Tax-Free Exchange***, ***Like Kind Exchange***, *or* ***Section 1031*** *(from the section number of IRS law).*

Equity Skimming Predatory lenders making various types of loans knowing the borrowers will not be able to make the monthly payments and thus setting them up for foreclosure.

Escheat The legal process by which property reverts to the state after a person does not claim it within a specified time or dies without a valid will and without heirs or creditors.

Escrow The system in which things of value, like money or documents, are held on behalf of the parties to a transaction by a disinterested third party, or escrow agent, until specified conditions have all been met. *Compare to* ***Escrows***.

Escrow Closing A closing by a disinterested third party, often an escrow agent.

Escrow Instructions The contract that authorizes an escrow agent to deliver items deposited in escrow once the parties have complied with specified conditions. This can be the purchase contract for real estate or a separate document.

Escrows Prepayable expenses the lender requires a borrower to set aside prior to closing (e.g., property taxes and insurance). *Also called* ***Impounds***.

Established Reasonable Value The maximum mortgage amount a veteran may have on a VA-guaranteed loan for that property as determined by a Certificate of Reasonable Value or a Notice of Value.

Estate A possessory interest in real property.

Estate for Years A leasehold estate set to last for a specific period, after which it automatically terminates. *Also known as a* ***term tenancy***.

Estimated Closing Costs An approximation of the amount of money a borrower will need to buy a particular property. *See* ***Good Faith Estimate***.

Estoppel Legal doctrine that prevents a person (or artificial person such as a lender or company) from asserting rights or facts inconsistent with earlier actions or statements, when he or she failed to object (or attempt to stop) another person's actions.

Estoppel Letter A lender's written consent to a sale acknowledging the transfer and waiving any right to accelerate the loan because of the sale.

Exclusionary Zoning A zoning law that effectively prevents certain groups, such as minorities or the poor, from living in a particular community.

Execute 1. To sign. 2. To perform or complete.

Fair and Accurate Credit Transaction Act (FACT Act or FACTA) Amendment to the federal Fair Credit Reporting Act intended primarily to help consumers fight the growing crime of identity theft; includes provisions for fraud alerts and credit freezes, as well as provisions known as Red Flag Rules.

Fair Credit Reporting Act (FCRA) Federal law dealing with the granting of credit, access to credit information, the rights of debtors, and the responsibilities of creditors.

Fair Housing Act 1968 Act (amended in 1974 and 1988) providing the HUD Secretary with fair housing enforcement and investigation responsibilities. A law that prohibits discrimination in all facets of the homebuying process on the basis of race, color, national origin, religion, sex, familial status, or disability.

Fair Market Value The price a property would sell for on the open market.

Familial Status A protected class under the federal Fair Housing Act and many state civil rights laws, making it illegal to discriminate against a person because he or she is the parent or guardian of a child younger than 18 years of age.

Fannie Mae *See* ***Federal National Mortgage Association***.

FCRA *See* ***Fair Credit Reporting Act***.

FDIC *See* ***Federal Deposit Insurance Corporation***.

Fed, The *See* ***Federal Reserve Board***.

Federal Advisory Council A body of 12 members, with each member elected by one of the 12 Federal Reserve Banks as district representatives. It meets quarterly with the Board of Governors of the Federal Reserve Board to discuss business conditions and make policy recommendations.

Federal Budget Deficit The situation that occurs when the federal government's income is less than its expenditures.

Federal Deposit Insurance Corporation (FDIC) A public corporation, established in 1933, that insures up to $250,000 for each depositor for member commercial banks and S & Ls. FDIC has its own reserves and can also borrow from the U.S. Treasury.

Federal Discount Rate The interest rate charged to banks by the Federal Reserve on loans to member commercial banks.

Federal Funds Rate The Federal Reserve's target for short-term interest rates. *Also called* ***Fed Funds Rate***.

Federal Home Loan Mortgage Corporation (Freddie Mac or FHMLC) Federally chartered institution that functions as buyer and seller of residential mortgages.

Federal Housing Administration (FHA) Provides mortgage insurance on loans made by FHA-approved lenders throughout the United States and its territories since its inception in 1934. FHA insures mortgages on single-family, multifamily, and manufactured homes and hospitals. It is the largest insurer of mortgages in the world.

Federal Housing Finance Agency (FHFA) Government agency into which the powers and regulatory authority of the following entities were merged: Federal Housing Finance Board (FHFB) and the Office of Federal Housing Enterprise Oversight (OFHEO), as well as the GSE mission office at the Department of Housing and Urban Development (HUD); the conservator of Fannie Mae and Freddie Mac.

Federal National Mortgage Association (Fannie Mae or FNMA) As part of the secondary mortgage market, the nation's largest investor in residential mortgages.

Federal Open Market Committee (FOMC) A body that controls the Fed's sale and purchase of government securities. The FOMC consists of the seven members of the Federal Reserve Board, plus the president of the Federal Reserve Bank of New York, and four other Federal Reserve Bank presidents.

Federal Reserve Banks Banks that provide services to financial institutions (e.g., check clearing), which have one main office in each Federal Reserve district. All nationally chartered commercial banks must join the Federal Reserve and buy stock in its district reserve bank.

Federal Reserve Board The body responsible for U.S. monetary policy, maintaining economic stability and regulating commercial banks. *Also referred to as* ***Board of Governors****, but most commonly called* ***the Fed***.

Federal Reserve System Established by the Federal Reserve Act of 1913 with 12 Federal Reserve Banks as a lender of last resort.

Federally Registered Mortgage Loan Originator Any mortgage loan originator who is employed by a depository institution, a subsidiary that is owned and controlled by a depository institution and regulated by a federal banking agency, or an institution regulated by the Farm Credit Administration and registered with the NMLS.

Fee 1. An estate of inheritance; title to real property that can be willed or descend to heirs. 2. Charge made for services rendered.

Fee at Closing Refers to a PMI payment due at closing. *See* ***Private Mortgage Insurance***.

Fee Simple The greatest estate one can have in real property. It is freely transferable and inheritable, and of indefinite duration, with no conditions on the title.

FHA *See* ***Federal Housing Administration***.

FICO Score Credit scoring where a number from 300–850 is assigned to a consumer's credit history. The lower the score, the greater the risk of default. Generally, above 660 is an acceptable risk, 620–660 is a marginal risk, below 620 is a high risk. Another type of credit score is a **BEACON Score**.

Fiduciary Person in a position of trust, held by law to high standards of good faith and loyalty.

Fiduciary Deeds Deeds executed by a trustee, executor, or other fiduciary, conveying property the fiduciary does not own but is authorized to manage.

Finance Charge The cost of consumer credit, interest paid over the life of a loan and upfront fees, expressed as a dollar amount.

Finance Companies Financial institutions that specialize in making higher-risk loans at higher interest rates.

Finance Instrument A written document used in the borrowing or lending of money.

Financial Institutions Reform, Recovery, and Enforcement Act (FIRREA) A federal law passed in 1990 in response to the crisis in the savings and loan industry. It revised the regulation of thrifts (S & Ls) and created several new agencies, such as Office of Thrift Supervision (OTS) and Resolution Trust Corporation (RTC).

Financial Statement A document that shows assets and liabilities of an entity or an individual at a specific point in time, or that shows the profits and losses over a period of time.

Financing Statement A brief document that, when recorded, gives constructive notice of a creditor's security interest in an item of personal property.

Financing Tools Alternative financing methods that can help a borrower get approved for a loan more easily or with less of a down payment.

Finder's Fee A referral fee paid for directing a buyer or seller to a certain company or provider.

FIRREA *See* ***Financial Institutions Reform, Recovery, and Enforcement Act***.

First Lien Position The spot held by the lien with highest priority when there is more than one mortgage or other debt or obligation secured by the property.

Fiscal Policy The government's plan for spending, taxation, and debt management.

Fixed Disbursement Plan A type of construction mortgage payout schedule where a percentage of funds is paid at a set time.

Fixed Rate Loan Loan with a constant interest rate remaining for the duration of the loan.

Fixed Term A period of time with a definite ending date.

Fixtures Man-made attachments.

Flipping Defined by Fannie Mae as the process of purchasing existing properties with the intention of immediately reselling them for a profit.

Flipping, Illegal Property purchased at a low price, appraised at a high value without valid reason, and resold at the higher price.

Float An unlocked interest rate that could change between the time of application and closing.

Floor The maximum amount that an interest rate or payment may decrease on an adjustable rate mortgage.

FOMC *See* ***Federal Open Market Committee***.

Foreclosure The process of causing a property pledged as collateral to be sold so that the net proceeds can be applied to the debt.

Foreclosure, Judicial A lawsuit filed by a lender or other creditor to foreclose on a mortgage or other lien; a court ordered sheriff's sale of the property with the net proceeds to be applied to the debt.

Foreclosure, Non-Judicial Foreclosure by a trustee under the power of sale clause in a deed of trust, without the involvement of a court.

Foreclosure, Strict Foreclosure with a strict deadline, past which a mortgagor can no longer reclaim interest in real property from the foreclosure proceedings by bringing the mortgage current.

Foreclosure Action A lawsuit filed by a creditor to begin foreclosure proceedings.

Forfeiture Loss of a right or something else of value as a result of failure to perform an obligation or condition.

Fraud An intentional or negligent misrepresentation or concealment of a material fact; making statements that a person knows, or should realize, are false or misleading.

Freddie Mac *See* **Federal National Home Mortgage Corporation**.

Freehold Estate A possessory interest of indefinite duration.

Freely Transferable A condition in an agreement or contract that allows a party to freely assign its rights to another. A note that is negotiable allows a lender or creditor to obtain immediate cash by selling it (assigning) it (e.g., when real estate notes are sold to the secondary market).

Frontage The dimension across the access side of a parcel of land. When referring to lot size, frontage is the first number. For example, if a lot size is 150' x 100', the frontage is 150'.

FSLIC The Federal Savings and Loan Insurance Corporation, which formerly provided deposit insurance to S & Ls, but was abolished in 1990 with the passage of FIRREA. S & L deposit insurance is now provided by FDIC.

Fully Amortizing Loans Loans where the total payments over the life of the loan pay off the entire balance of principal and interest due at the end of the loan term.

Funding Fee A fee charged on VA-guaranteed loans in place of mortgage insurance.

Garnishment Legal process by which a creditor gains access to a debtor's personal property or funds in the hands of a third party. If a debtor's wages are garnished, the employer pays part of them directly to the creditor.

General Warranty Deeds A deed in which a grantor warrants title against defects that may have arisen before or during the grantor's ownership.

Gift Letter A statement from someone who is providing funds for a down payment (e.g., friend, relative, employer) indicating that the money is not expected to be repaid.

Good Faith Estimate (GFE) The mortgage loan originator's estimate of closing costs the borrower must pay for a real estate loan. The lender must give this to the borrower within three business days of completed loan application.

Government National Mortgage Association (Ginnie Mae or GNMA) Government-owned corporation that guarantees the timely payment of principal and interest on mortgage-backed securities backed by federally insured or guaranteed loans. Ginnie Mae does not issue MBS nor buy or sell loans.

Government-Sponsored Enterprise (GSE) A group of financial services corporations created by the United States Congress to enhance the flow of credit to targeted sectors of the economy and to make those segments more efficient and transparent.

Gramm-Leach-Bliley Act Also known as the Financial Modernization Act of 1999, includes provisions in Title V to protect and regulate the disclosure of consumers' personal financial information. *See **Privacy Rule**.*

Grantee Person receiving a grant of real property; the purchaser in a typical real estate transaction.

Grantor Person who grants an interest in real property to another; the seller in a typical real estate transaction.

Gross Income Income before taxes and other expenses have been deducted.

Gross Living Area (GLA) Residential space that is finished, heated, and above grade. Garages, finished basements, and storage areas do not count in GLA.

Guardian A person appointed by a court to administer the affairs of a minor or an incompetent person.

Hazard Insurance Insurance coverage that compensates for physical damage to a property from fire, wind, vandalism, or other hazards.

Highest and Best Use The most profitable, legally permitted, feasible, and physically possible use of a piece of property.

HMDA *See **Home Mortgage Disclosure Act**.*

Holder in Due Course One who acquires a negotiable instrument in good faith and for consideration, and thus has certain rights above the original payee.

Home Equity Line of Credit (HELOC) Available money that can be borrowed by a homeowner, secured by a second mortgage on the principal residence. Home equity lines of credit can be accessed at any time up to a predetermined borrowing limit and are often used for non-housing expenditures. *Compare to **Home Equity Loan**.*

Home Equity Loan A loan taken by a homeowner, secured by a second mortgage on the principal residence. Home equity loans are usually a one-time loan for a specific amount of money and obtained for a specific expenditure. *Compare to **Home Equity Line of Credit**.*

Home Mortgage Disclosure Act (HMDA) A law requiring certain institutional mortgage lenders to make annual reports of all mortgage loans made in a given geographic area where they have at least one office. This law is designed to help the government detect patterns of **redlining**.

Home Ownership and Equity Protection Act (HOEPA) 1994 amendment to the Truth in Lending Act establishing disclosure requirements and prohibiting equity stripping and other abusive practices associated with high cost loans.

Home Valuation Code of Conduct (HVCC) Intended to set standards on solicitation, selection, compensation, conflicts of interest, and appraiser independence with a primary goal of ensuring that real estate appraisers are not coerced in any way into establishing a predetermined or desired valuation on a property.

Home Warranty A warranty that covers any problems that occur with a home within a specific amount of time.

Homeowner's Association Fees Charges imposed on a property owner to pay for upkeep, maintenance, and sometimes hazard insurance of common property, for example, a condominium; when required as a condition of ownership, the monthly amount must be added to PITI to get the complete housing expense.

Homeowner's Insurance An insurance policy that combines personal liability coverage and hazard insurance coverage for a dwelling and its contents.

Homeowners Protection Act (HPA) Federal law that requires lenders or servicers to provide certain disclosures and notifications concerning private mortgage insurance on residential loan transactions.

Homestead Protection Limited protection for a debtor against claims of judgment creditors; applies to property of the debtor's residence.

Housing and Economic Recovery Act of 2008 (HERA) Major federal law designed to assist with the revitalization of the U.S. housing market; includes provisions related to foreclosure prevention and consumer protections, as well as establishing minimum standards for licensing and registration of mortgage loan originators. *See the **Secure and Fair Enforcement for Mortgage Licensing Act**.*

Housing Expense Ratio The relationship of a borrower's total monthly housing expense to income, expressed as a percentage (Total Housing Expense ÷ Income = Ratio%). *Also called the **front end ratio**.*

HUD *See **U.S. Department of Housing and Urban Development**.*

HUD Uniform Settlement Statement (HUD-1) A settlement statement, required under RESPA, that details all costs associated with closing a loan, showing how much was paid, to what companies or parties, and for what purpose.

Hypothecation The pledging of real or personal property by a debtor as security for a loan without giving up possession of it, as with a mortgage. *Compare to **Pledge**.*

Immobility A physical characteristic of real estate referring to the fact that it cannot move from one place to another.

Improvement A major fixture that impacts the value of the property, such as a building.

Incapacity A condition that prevents someone from legally being able to sign a note or enter into any other kind of contract (e.g., because of age or mental incompetence).

Income The money one receives from a job, investment, or other use of skills or capital.

Income Qualifying Standards The criteria used to evaluate the quality and durability of a borrower's source of income, in conjunction with an assessment of the borrower's housing expense ratio and total debt-to-income ratio.

Indemnify 1. To protect another against loss or damage. 2. To compensate a party for loss.

Independent Contractors Self-employed individuals paid based on jobs completed rather than hours worked, and who are responsible for setting their own hours and paying their own taxes.

Indestructibility A physical characteristic of real estate referring to the fact that it cannot be destroyed.

Index A statistical report that is generally a reliable indicator of the approximate change in the cost of money. With an adjustable rate mortgage, the borrower's interest rate increases and decreases as the chosen index fluctuates during the term of the loan.

Inflation An increase in the cost of goods or services over a period of time, which impacts a buyer's purchasing power.

Initial Premium The first insurance premium paid for PMI. *See **Private Mortgage Insurance**.*

Installment Note A note that calls for periodic payments of principal and/or interest during the term of the note.

Installment Sales Contract *See **Land Contract**.*

Instrument Any document that transfers title (such as a deed), creates a lien (such as a mortgage), or gives a right to payment (such as a note or contract).

Insurance The indemnification of one party by another against loss resulting from a specified peril or risk.

Insurance Companies Institutions that write contracts to cover specified risks. Such companies generally have large sums of stable, long-term investment capital and look for high return investments, such as long-term commercial real estate projects, or are investors in secondary mortgage markets.

Interest 1. A right or share in something, such as a piece of real estate. 2. A charge a borrower pays to a lender for the use of the lender's money. *Compare to **Principal**.*

Interest Rate The rate which is charged by or paid to a lender for the use of money, generally expressed as a percentage of the principal.

Interested Party Contributions (IPCs) Funds paid on a loan by anyone other than the buyer who has a financial interest in, or can influence the terms and the sale or transfer of, the subject property.

Interest Rate Reduction Refinancing Loan (IRRRL) A VA-guaranteed mortgage loan that allows an eligible owner to refinance an existing loan for a lower interest rate.

Interest Only Loan (I/O) A loan where scheduled payments only pay accrued interest and not any portion of the principal. A balloon payment equal to the entire principal amount of the loan is due at the end of the loan term.

Interest Shortfall Any accumulated interest accrued, but not collected, through regular payments because of the adjustable rate or graduated payment feature of a loan.

Interest Yielding Investments Investments that pay interest to the holder or bearer. These earnings may be counted as stable monthly income if the payments are consistent and do not deplete the principal amount of the investment.

Intermediary A person or institution that originates and/or services loans on behalf of another party (e.g., a mortgage broker).

Invalid Not legally binding or effective; not valid.

Investment A use of capital designed to produce income and/or profit.

Irregular Transaction According to the Truth in Lending Act, a transaction that includes either multiple advances, irregular payment periods, or irregular payment amounts (other than an irregular first period or irregular first and final payment).

Joint Tenancy A form of co-ownership giving each tenant equal, undivided interest and rights in the property, including the right of survivorship.

Judgment Creditor One who has received a judgment for money from a judgment debtor.

Judgment Debtor One against whom a judgment has been issued by a court for money owed.

Jumbo Loans Loans that exceed the maximum loan amount that Fannie Mae/Freddie Mac will buy, which makes them nonconforming.

Junior Mortgage Any mortgage with a lower lien position than another.

Junk Fees Charges assessed to a borrower by a loan originator that serve little if any function and are often hidden in mortgage documents.

Just Compensation Appropriate or fair value for private land taken by the government for public use. *See **Eminent Domain**.*

Kickback Fee or other compensation given for services not performed, but as a means of payment for business referrals. Kickbacks are prohibited by RESPA.

Land Contract A real estate installment agreement where buyer makes payment to seller in exchange for right to occupy and use property, but no deed or title is transferred until all, or a specified portion of, payments have been made. *Also called **installment land contract**, **installment sales contract**, **land sales contract**, **real estate contract**, and other names.*

Land Use Controls Public or private restrictions on how land may be used (e.g., zoning).

Landlord An owner who leases property to a tenant. *Also called the **lessor**.*

Late Charge The penalty a borrower must pay when a payment is made after the due date.

Lease A contract under which one party pays the other rent in exchange for possession of real estate; a conveyance of a leasehold estate from the fee owner to a tenant.

Lease/Option A financing strategy in which a seller leases property for a specific term, giving the tenant an option to buy the property at a predetermined price during the lease term, usually with a portion of the lease payments applied to the purchase price.

Lease/Purchase A financing strategy in which a seller leases property for a specific term, with the tenant agreeing to buy the property at a set price during or following the lease term.

Leasehold Estate An interest that gives the holder a temporary right to possession of the property, without granting title, for the term of the lease. Right of possession generally does not terminate upon the sale of the property.

Lender First and Lender Second A situation in which a lender holds two different mortgages on the same property, often at different interest rates. *May be called a **Piggyback Loan**.*

Lender's Yield The total amount of money the lender makes from a loan in relation to the amount invested, expressed as an annual percentage rate. *Also called **Lender's Return**.*

Lessee A person who leases property from another; a tenant.

Lessor A person who leases property to another; a landlord.

Liabilities Financial obligations or debt. Any money that is owed. *Compare to **Debt**.*

LIBOR *Also called: **BBALIBOR**. See **London InterBank Offered Rate**.*

License A temporary, revocable, non-assignable permission to enter another's land for a particular purpose.

Lien A non-possessory interest in property, giving a lienholder the right to foreclose if the owner does not pay a debt owed to the lienholder; a financial encumbrance on the owner's title.

Lien, Equitable Written contract or court judgment placing a lien on property as collateral for a loan.

Lien, General A lien that attaches to all of the debtor's property.

Lien, Involuntary A lien that arises by operation of law without the consent of the property owner. *Also called a **statutory lien**.*

Lien, Judgment A lien placed against a person's property through court action.

Lien, Materialman's Similar to a mechanic's lien, but based on a debt owed to someone who supplied materials, equipment, or fuel for a project rather than labor.

Lien, Mechanic's A specific lien claimed by someone who performed work on the property (construction, repairs, or improvements) and has not been paid. This term is often used in a general sense, referring to materialman's liens as well as actual mechanics' liens.

Lien, Specific A lien that attaches only to a particular piece of property.

Lien, Tax A lien on real property to secure the payment of taxes.

Lien, Voluntary A lien placed against property with the consent of the owner; a mortgage or a deed of trust.

Lien Priority The order in which liens are paid out of the proceeds of a foreclosure sale. For example, tax liens always have the highest priority and a first mortgage would have the next highest priority.

Lien Theory States States where a mortgagee holds only a lien against property (not actual title) until the loan is repaid. The mortgagor holds the actual title. *Compare to* ***Title Theory States.***

Lienholder, Junior Secured creditor with a lower priority lien than another lien on the same land.

Life Estate A freehold estate that lasts only as long as a specified person, the measuring life, lives.

Life Tenant The holder of a life estate.

Like Kind Property The same type of property (such as real estate for real estate), as a necessary condition for a tax-free exchange.

Limited Denial of Participation (LDP) An action taken by a HUD Field Office or the Deputy Assistant Secretary for Single Family or Multifamily Housing that excludes a person or company who fails to comply with HUD program standards from further participation in a HUD program area.

Line of Credit Available money that a borrower can access at any time up to a predetermined borrowing limit. If the loan is secured by a second mortgage on the borrower's principal residence, it is *referred to as a* ***Home Equity Line of Credit.***

Liquid Assets Cash and any other assets, such as stocks or bonds, that can be converted to cash quickly.

Lis Pendens A recorded notice that a lawsuit concerning real estate has been filed.

Loan/Application Register A record of each loan application taken by a creditor, together with the disposition of that application (closed, denied, withdrawn). This information may be included in a required report submitted by certain financial institutions to supervisory agencies with loan details used to discover possible discriminatory practices in order to comply with the Home Mortgage Disclosure Act.

Loan Fee *See* ***Origination Fee.***

Loan Flipping Refinancing a loan over and over.

Loan Originator One who is responsible for working with a prospective borrower to gather information, assist with completing applications, and otherwise making or initiating a new loan.

Loan Processor One who is responsible for verifying information contained in a prospective borrower's loan file and for coordinating aspects of the loan process.

Loan Prospector® (LP®) An automated underwriting system that puts lenders in direct contact with Freddie Mac, providing a streamlined process of document submission, underwriting, and loan approval.

Loan-to-Value (LTV) The relationship between the unpaid principal balance of the mortgage and the appraised value (or sales price if it is lower) of the property.

Local Market *See* ***Primary Mortgage Market.***

Location Exact position of a piece of real estate.

Location Survey A survey that determines if a property's buildings encroach on adjoining property, or if any adjoining property's buildings encroach on the subject property.

Lock-In A written agreement guaranteeing the homebuyer a specified interest rate provided the loan is closed within a set period of time. The lock-in also usually specifies the number of points to be paid at closing.

London InterBank Offered Rate (LIBOR) A reference rate computed and published daily indicating the average rate at which a lending institution can obtain unsecured funding for a given currency. It may be used as an index by lenders when making adjustable rate mortgage loans. *Also called:* ***BBALIBOR*** *or* ***British Banker's Association London InterBank Offered Rate.***

Long-Term Loans in real estate that have payments spread over 25–30 years.

Lot A parcel of land; a parcel in a subdivision.

LTV *See* ***Loan-to-Value Ratio.***

Maintenance Payments Money paid as part of a divorce settlement. Maintenance payments do not have to be revealed as a source of income if not counted to help repay a loan, but must be revealed as a debt obligation.

Maker One promising to pay money in a note, the borrower.

Margin The agreed to difference between the index value and the interest rate charged to the borrower with an adjustable rate mortgage. *Sometimes referred to as* ***Spread.***

Market Area *See* ***Neighborhood.***

Market Price The price for which a piece of real estate actually sold.

Market Value The most probable price that a property should bring in a competitive and open market, provided that all conditions requisite to a fair sale are present, the buyer and seller are knowledgeable and acting prudently, and the price is not affected by any undue stimulus.

Marketable Record Title Unbroken chain of recorded titles going back a statutory number of years.

Marketable Title Act A law which is intended to improve the marketability of title and simplify the title search process by extinguishing certain old claims against a title.

Matched Pair Analysis The process of determining the value of specific property characteristics or features by comparing pairs of similar properties. *Also called* ***Paired Data Analysis***.

Materialman A person who supplies materials, equipment, etc., for construction projects. *See* ***Lien, Materialman's***. *Compare to* ***Mechanic***.

Maximum Guaranty Amount The maximum amount that can be guaranteed by a VA loan.

Maximum Mortgage Amount The maximum amount that can be financed by an FHA loan.

Mechanic A person who performs work (construction, remodeling, repairs, or demolition) on real property. *Compare to* ***Materialman***. *See* ***Lien, Mechanic's***.

Member Banks The 5,000+ commercial banks across the U.S. that, as members of the Federal Reserve, are subject to the rules and policies implemented by the Fed.

Merger When discussing real property, the uniting of two or more separate properties by transferring ownership of them all to one person.

Metropolitan Statistical Area (MSA) An area with at least one urbanized area of 50,000 or more population, plus adjacent territory that has a high degree of social and economic integration with the core, as measured by commuting ties.

Military Eligibility *See* ***Certificate of Eligibility***.

Minor A person who has not yet reached the age of majority.

MIP *See* ***Mortgage Insurance Premium***.

Misrepresentation A false or misleading statement. *See* ***Fraud***.

Monetary Policy Means by which the government exerts control over the supply and cost of money.

Monthly Income Income received on a monthly basis. *See* ***Income***.

Moral Suasion The attempt to use persuasive influences of authorities on the public so they will behave in a specific way.

Mortgage An instrument that creates a voluntary lien on real property to secure repayment of a debt. The parties to a mortgage are the mortgagor (borrower) and mortgagee (lender).

Mortgage, Balloon A loan with a note that has level monthly payments that would fully amortize it over a stated term, but which provides for a lump-sum payment to be due at the end of an earlier specified term.

Mortgage, Bi-Weekly Payment Plan A payment plan that has a fixed rate mortgage amortized using a month payment schedule but with payments made every two weeks instead of every month, thus making an extra payment each year.

Mortgage, Blanket A mortgage that covers more than one parcel of real estate, usually used to finance entire subdivision developments rather than an individual unit or lot.

Mortgage, Bridge A mortgage that occurs between the termination of one mortgage and the commencement of another. When the next mortgage is taken out, the bridge is repaid.

Mortgage, Cash-Out A mortgage that a borrower gives to a lender in order to get cash for the equity that has built up in property (e.g., a home equity loan taken out for a non-house purpose, or an investor trying to recoup money invested in fixing up a property).

Mortgage, Closed-End A typical real estate loan in which the balance is expected to be repaid—along with any interest and finance changes—by a specified future date.

Mortgage, Construction A temporary loan used to finance the construction of a building on land. Replaced with a takeout loan.

Mortgage, Conventional A loan that is not insured or guaranteed by a government agency.

Mortgage, Equity Participation A mortgage that lets the lender share part of the earnings, income, or profits from a real estate project.

Mortgage, First A security instrument with a first lien position, meaning the first mortgage holder is paid first from a foreclosure sale. One exception is a tax lien on the property, which always takes first lien position.

Mortgage, Graduated Payment (GPM) Specialized payment structure that allows the borrower to make smaller payments in the early years of the mortgage, with payments increasing on a scheduled basis at a predetermined point until they are sufficient to fully amortize the loan over the remainder of its term.

Mortgage, Growth Equity (GEM) A fixed rate mortgage set up like a 30-year conventional loan, but payments increase regularly. *Also called a* ***Rapidly Amortizing Mortgage***.

Mortgage, Hard Money A mortgage that allows a borrower to receive cash instead of credit (e.g., a cash-out mortgage).

Mortgage, Hybrid A loan to purchase a home that combines an adjustable rate mortgage with a fixed rate mortgage.

Mortgage, Open-End A mortgage that allows a borrower to request more funds from the lender, up to a certain pre-defined limit, even re-borrowing part of the debt that has been repaid (at lender's discretion) without having to renegotiate the loan.

Mortgage, Package A mortgage where personal property (e.g., appliances) is included in a real estate sale and financed with one contract.

Mortgage, Purchase Money Generally describes a mortgage used to finance the purchase of property; may specifically refer to a situation where the seller finances all or part of the sale price of a piece of property for the buyer, in which case may be called a **Seller Held Mortgage**.

Mortgage, Reduction Option A fixed rate mortgage that gives the borrower a limited opportunity to reduce the interest rate one time during the course of the loan, provided certain conditions are met.

Mortgage, Refinance A mortgage that a borrower gives to a lender to redo or expand the loan on the property, usually to get a better interest rate or pay off other debts.

Mortgage, Reverse A loan used by qualified homeowners age 62 or older to convert equity in the home into a lump sum, a monthly cash stream, and/or a line of credit; generally repaid when the last surviving borrower dies, sells the home, or ceases to live in the home for 12 consecutive months.

Mortgage, Shared Appreciation (SAM) A mortgage where the lender charges below-market interest rates in exchange for a share of the borrower's equity.

Mortgage, Soft Money A mortgage where the borrower receives credit instead of actual cash, as when a lender pays the seller on a purchase transaction.

Mortgage, Variable Balance (VBM) A mortgage with an adjustable interest rate, but with payments that never change. Instead, as the rate goes up or down and the payments are remitted, the outstanding balance amortizes more slowly or more rapidly depending on the interest rate and the portion of the payment left to apply to the balance.

Mortgage, Wraparound A financing arrangement in which an existing loan on a property is left outstanding while the lender gives the borrower another, larger loan (whose balance encompasses the existing first loan), charges interest on the larger balance, and generally undertakes to make payments on the first loan.

Mortgage-Backed Securities (MBS) Debt obligations that represent claims to the cash flows from pools of mortgage loans.

Mortgage Banker A company, individual, or institution that originates, processes, underwrites, closes/funds, and/or services mortgage loans

Mortgage Banking Company Financial institution that earns a fee for serving as an intermediary between borrowers and lenders, originating mortgage loans, funding mortgage loans, and/or servicing mortgage loans.

Mortgage Broker An individual or company that, for a fee, acts as an intermediary between borrowers and lenders.

Mortgage Disclosure Improvement Act (MDIA) An amendment to the Truth in Lending Act enacted in 2009 that adds additional disclosure requirements, APR tolerances, and waiting periods on closing mortgage loans, as well as limiting fees that can be charged prior to disclosure.

Mortgage Fraud Any misrepresentation or concealment used to obtain a mortgage loan.

Mortgage Insurance Insurance offered by private companies (PMI) or the government through the FHA (MIP) to insure a lender against default on a loan by a borrower. *See* ***Private Mortgage Insurance (PMI)*** *and* ***Mortgage Insurance Premium (MIP)***.

Mortgage Insurance Premium (MIP) The fee charged for FHA mortgage insurance coverage. The initial premium can be financed, and there may be a renewal premium. *Also called* ***Upfront Mortgage Insurance Premium (UFMIP)***.

Mortgage Loan Originator (MLO) As defined by the SAFE Act, an individual who either takes a residential mortgage loan application or offers or negotiates terms of a residential mortgage loan for compensation or gain.

Mortgage Servicing Disclosure Statement Document required by RESPA that discloses to the borrower whether the lender intends to service the loan or transfer service to another lender. It also provides information about complaint resolution.

Mortgagee A lender who accepts a mortgage as security for repayment of the loan.

Mortgagor A person who borrows money and gives a mortgage to the lender as security.

Mrs. Murphy Exemption An exemption to the federal Fair Housing Act, which holds that the rental of a unit or a room in an owner-occupied dwelling containing four units or less is exempt from the Fair Housing Law, provided rental ads are not discriminatory and a real estate agent is not used to locate tenants. Some states do NOT recognize this exemption.

Mutual Mortgage Insurance Fund Government sponsored mortgage insurance administered by the Federal Housing Administration which insures mortgage loans on one- to four-family residential housing; designed to be self-funding,

Mutual Savings Banks Federal or state-chartered banks, located mostly in the northeastern U.S., owned by depositors and operated for their benefit. Usually, a large portion of their assets are mortgages.

National Credit Union Administration (NCUA) Independent federal agency that charters and supervises federal credit unions.

Nationwide Mortgage Licensing System & Registry (NMLS) Organization responsible for providing a centralized and standardized system for mortgage licensing that accommodates both the regulatory agencies and the mortgage industry.

Natural Attachments Plants growing on the land.

Negative Amortization A situation that occurs when the minimum required periodic payment for principal and interest does not cover the accrued interest due for that period, resulting in the unpaid interest being added to the principal balance.

Negligence Unintentional breach of a legal duty; a tort if it causes harm.

Negotiable Instrument Promissory note or other finance instrument that is freely transferable.

Neighborhood Group of houses or properties that shares common characteristics. *Also called a* ***market area***.

Net and Gross Adjustment A means of limiting total adjustments that may be made to comparable sales to determine how closely they resemble the subject when performing the sales comparison approach to appraisal.

Net Income Income after expenses.

Net to Seller An estimate of the money a seller should receive from a real estate transaction, based on a certain selling price after all costs and expenses have been paid.

Net Worth The measure of the financial value of a business or individual, determined by subtracting liabilities from assets.

No Document Loan A loan where a borrower has good credit, but trouble providing income documentation, so the loan is decided on other merits. These loans may be offered at a lower LTV, and the lender may still require tax returns. *Also called* ***Stated Doc*** *or* ***No Ratio***.

Nominal Rate The interest rate stated in a note. *Also called* ***Coupon Rate*** *or* ***Note Rate***.

Nonconforming Loans Residential mortgage transactions that do not meet the qualifying standards required by Fannie Mae/Freddie Mac. *Compare to* ***Conforming Loans***.

Nontraditional Mortgage Product (SAFE Act) Anything other than a 30-year fixed rate loan.

Nontraditional Mortgage Product (Interagency Guidance on Nontraditional Mortgage Product Risks) Mortgage products that allow borrowers to defer principal and, sometimes, interest.

Notary Public An official whose primary function is to witness and certify the acknowledgment made by one signing a legal document.

Note A written, legally binding promise to repay a debt.

Note, Fully Amortizing A note that calls for regular, substantially equal, payments of principal and interest, calculated to pay off the entire balance of the loan by the end of the loan term.

Note, Installment A note that calls for periodic payments of principal and/or interest during the term of the note.

Note, Partially Amortizing A note that calls for regular, substantially equal, payments of principal and/or interest during the loan term, with a balloon payment at the end of loan term to pay off balance due. *Also called* ***Installment Note with Balloon***.

Note, Straight A note that calls for payments of interest only during the term of the note with a balloon payment at the end of the loan term to pay off the principal amount.

Note Rate The interest rate stated in a note. *Also called* ***Coupon Rate*** *or* ***Nominal Rate***.

Notice Knowledge or information about a fact, often used with regard to public documents.

Notice of Default A formal written notice to a borrower that a default has occurred and that legal action may be taken.

Nuisance Interference with the quiet enjoyment of land from the outside.

Obsolescence, External Any influence that falls outside the actual property site and negatively affects a property's value. *Also called* ***Economic Obsolescence***.

Obsolescence, Functional Loss in property value resulting from changes in tastes, preferences, or market standards.

Office of Comptroller of Currency (OCC) Federal government entity that charters, regulates, and supervises all National banks and federal branches/agencies of foreign banks.

Office of Thrift Supervision (OTS) Federal government entity that regulates Savings and Loans in the same manner the Federal Reserve regulates commercial banks.

One-Time Premium The initial fee paid for private mortgage insurance, with no renewal premium. *See* ***Private Mortgage Insurance***.

Open Market Operations When the Federal Reserve Board sells or buys government securities (bonds) as a means of controlling the supply of, and demand for, money. The Fed can also buy and sell U.S. dollars on the international market.

Option A contract giving one party the right to do something within a designated time period, without obligation to do so.

Option Money Cash consideration given for an option contract.

Option to Purchase A contract giving the optionee the right, but not the obligation, to buy property owned by the optionor at an agreed price during a specified period.

Optionee Person to whom an option is given.

Optionor Person who gives an option.

Order of Execution A court order directing a public officer (often the sheriff or marshal) to seize and/or sell property to regain possession for the owner and/or satisfy a debt. *Also called an **Order of Attachment**.*

Origination The process of making or initiating a new loan.

Origination Fee A fee paid to a lender to cover the administrative costs of making and processing a loan, stated as a percentage of the mortgage amount.

OTS *See* **Office of Thrift Supervision**.

Over-Improvement A property or feature for which the cost exceeds market value.

Overtime Money paid to someone for hours worked beyond their normal workday or week. Overtime may only be counted as income if consistent.

Owner Financing A property purchase transaction in which the property seller provides all or part of the financing. *Also called **Seller Financing**.*

Panic Peddling, Panic Selling *See* **Blockbusting**.

Par Rate The rate that lenders offer only to mortgage brokers that does not create an additional charge or provide for a credit for the borrower. *Also known as the **Wholesale Rate**.*

Part-Time Earnings Money paid to someone for a job that is not considered full time. Part-time earnings may only be counted as income if consistent.

Partial Release, Satisfaction, or Conveyance Clause A contract clause that obligates the creditor to release part of the property from lien and convey title to that part back to the debtor once certain provisions of the note or mortgage have been satisfied.

Partially Amortizing Loans Loans for which payments are applied to principal and interest, but the payments do not retire the debt when the agreed upon loan term expires, thus requiring a balloon payment at the end of the loan term.

Participation Plan A loan for which the borrower enters into a partnership with the investor/lender whereby the investor/lender shares in the equity of the property instead of or in addition to earning interest. *Also called a **Shared Equity Plan**.*

Partner, General A partner who has unlimited liability for the obligation of a partnership.

Partnership, General Voluntary association of two or more people as co-owners in a for-profit organization.

Pass-Through Securities A pool of securities backed by a package of assets from which a servicer earns a fee for collecting monthly payments from issuers and passing the payments to the security holders.

Patriot Act Common name of the 2001 Uniting and Strengthening America by Providing Appropriate Tools Required to Intercept and Obstruct Terrorism Act that, among other provisions, requires lenders and banks to create and maintain customer identification programs (CIPs) to verify identity of customers entering into a formal relationship.

Payee The one promised payment in a note.

Pension Funds Sources of large sums of capital looking for high return investments.

Pensions Money paid to someone as part of their retirement benefits. Pensions may only be counted as income if consistent.

Periodic Estate A leasehold estate that continues for successive equal periods of length until terminated by proper notice from either the lessor or the lessee.

Periodic Re-Amortization The recalculation of payments on a loan at a specific time based on the loan balance at that time so the new payments will fully amortize the loan over the remaining loan term.

Permanent Construction Loan A special type of construction loan where there is only one loan and one closing, with no take-out loan.

Personal Property Tangible items that usually are not permanently attached to, or part of, the real estate or intangible items that are representative of value. *Also called **personalty** or **chattel**.*

PITI A typical monthly mortgage payment that includes **p**rinciple, **i**nterest, **t**axes, and **i**nsurance.

Planned Unit Development (PUD) A special type of project or subdivision that may combine nonresidential uses with residential uses, or otherwise depart from ordinary zoning and subdivision regulations.

Pledge The deposit of personal property by a debtor with a creditor as security for a debt.

Plottage An increase in value, over the cost of acquiring the separate parcels, by successful assemblage, usually due to a change in use.

PMI *See **Private Mortgage Insurance**.*

Point One percent of the loan amount. Points are charged for any reason, but are often used for buydowns, where they may also be called discount points. Points are used to increase the lender's yield on a loan.

Police Power The constitutional power of state and local governments to enact and enforce laws that protect the public's health, safety, morals, and general welfare.

Portfolio The collection of mortgages and other securities held by a lender and not sold on the secondary market.

Portfolio Lenders Strategy where financial institutions that make real estate loans keep and service those loans in-house as part of their investment portfolios, instead of selling on the secondary market.

Possessory Interest Entitles holder to possession of property, now or in the future.

Power of Attorney A legal document that gives one person the full legal right and authority to act for another person.

Power of Sale Clause A clause that allows the trustee to sell trust deed property, with or without court supervision, when terms of the trust deed are not kept.

Pre-Approval Process by which a lender determines if potential borrowers can be financed through the lender, and for what amount of money.

Predatory Lending Loans that take advantage of ill-informed consumers through excessively high fees, misrepresented loan terms, frequent refinancing that does not benefit the borrower, and other prohibited acts.

Prepaid Expenses Items on a settlement statement the seller has already paid.

Prepayment Clause A clause in a contract gives the lender the right to charge the borrower a penalty for paying off the loan early.

Prepayment Penalty A fee that may be charged to a borrower who pays off a loan before it is due.

Pre-Qualification The process of determining how much money a prospective borrower might be eligible to borrow; it is not a guarantee.

Price What one person paid for something. *Compare to* ***Value***.

Primary Mortgage Markets The making of mortgage loans from lenders directly to borrowers. *Also referred to simply as* ***Primary Markets***. *Compare to* ***Secondary Mortgage Markets***.

Primary Mortgage Market Lenders Lenders who make loans directly to borrowers (e.g., neighborhood banks).

Prime Rate The lowest interest rate that banks charge their best commercial customers.

Principal 1. With regard to a loan, the amount originally borrowed or the current balance. *Compare to* ***Interest***. 2. A person who grants another person (an agent) authority to represent him or her in dealing with third parties. 3. One of the parties to a transaction (such as the buyer or seller), as opposed to those who are involved as agents or employees (such as a broker or escrow agent).

Privacy Rule Provision of the federal Gramm-Leach-Bliley Act that regulates the handling and disclosure of private financial information of consumers.

Private Mortgage Insurance (PMI) Insurance offered by private companies to insure a lender against default on a loan by a borrower.

Profit The financial gain realized when earned revenue exceeds all of the expenses necessary to maintain or sustain the enterprise.

Promisee A person who has been promised something; a person who is supposed to receive the benefit of a legally binding contractual promise (e.g., with a promissory note).

Promisor A person who has made a contractual promise to another (e.g., in a promissory note).

Promissory Note A financing instrument that serves as evidence of a promise to pay a specific debt; a written, legally binding promise to repay a debt.

Property Something that is owned, real or personal, and includes the rights of ownership in that thing.

Proration The division of expenses between buyer and seller in proportion to the actual usage of the item represented by a particular expense as of the day the loan is funded.

Public Auction An auction where anyone can bid on property that is in foreclosure proceedings.

Purchase Agreement A contract in which a seller promises to convey title to real property to a buyer in exchange for the purchase price. *Also called a* ***purchase and sale agreement***, *a* ***purchase contract***, *or an* ***earnest money agreement***.

Qualifying The process of determining whether or not a borrower is likely to default on a loan and that the property is worth enough to satisfy the debt if the borrower does default.

Qualifying Ratios Guidelines applied by the lenders to determine how large a loan to grant a homebuyer.

Quality Control The secondary mortgage market's effort to standardize mortgages.

Quiet Title Action A lawsuit filed to determine and resolve problems of instruments conveying a particular piece of land; may be required to close any missing links and remove the cloud on the title.

Quitclaim Deeds Deeds that convey any interest in a piece of real property the grantor has at the time the deed is executed. A quitclaim deed makes no warranties regarding the title, if any, held by the grantor.

Racial Discrimination The practice of treating people unequally because of their race, ancestry, or national origin. Such discrimination in a violation of civil rights laws is illegal.

Radon A radioactive gas found in some homes that in sufficient concentrations can cause health problems.

Rate Adjustment Period The length of time between interest rate changes with an adjustable rate mortgage.

Rate Lock A specific fixed interest rate for a specified amount of time that is guaranteed by the mortgage lender.

Re-Amortization The recalculation of payments on a loan so the new payment will fully amortize the loan over the remaining loan term. *Also known as* ***recast***.

Real Estate Contract 1. A purchase agreement. 2. A land contract. 3. Any contract having to do with real property.

Real Estate Cycles General swings in real estate activity, resulting in increasing or decreasing activity, and property values, during different phases of the cycle.

Real Estate Investment Trust (REIT) A real estate investment business with at least 100 investors, organized as a trust.

Real Estate Owned (REO) Property acquired by a lending institution through foreclosure and held in inventory.

Real Estate Settlement Procedures Act (RESPA) Federal consumer protection law dealing with real estate closings that provides specific procedures and guidelines for the disclosure of settlement costs; *promulgated as* ***Regulation X***.

Real Property Physical land and everything attached to it, plus the rights of ownership (bundle of rights) in real estate. *Also called* ***realty***.

Realty Real property.

Recast *See* ***Re-Amortization***.

Recertification of Value (Recert) Action taken to validate that any "subject to" conditions of an original appraisal have been met and that the original opinion of value is still valid; as when construction or renovations are complete. *Also called a* ***Completion Report***.

Reconciliation 1. The determination of how funds are distributed at closing by examining all credits and debuts. 2. The appraisal process of analyzing the values derived from the different appraisal approaches to arrive at a final opinion of value.

Recording The act of filing a document at the county recorder's office so it will be placed in the public record.

Red Flag Rules Section 114 of the Fair and Accurate Credit Transaction Act requiring financial institutions to implement identity theft prevention programs.

Redemption, Equitable Right of The right to save or redeem the property prior to the confirmation of sale in a foreclosure procedure.

Redemption, Statutory Right of The right to save or redeem the property after to the confirmation of sale in a foreclosure procedure.

Redlining The illegal practice of refusing to make loans secured by property in a certain neighborhood because of the racial or ethnic composition of the neighborhood.

Refinancing The process of paying off one loan with the proceeds from a new loan using the same property as security.

Regulation 1. A rule adopted by an administrative agency. 2. Any governmental order having the force of law.

Regulation Z Federal guidelines under the Truth in Lending Act that require full disclosure of all credit terms for consumer loans.

Rehabilitation Loans *See* ***Section 203(k) FHA Loan***.

Release 1. A document in which one gives up a legal right. 2. To give up a legal right.

Renewal Premium Recurring fee to continue an insurance policy, such as PMI.

Rent Consideration paid by a tenant to a landlord in exchange for possession and use of property.

Rent Credit A financing strategy that causes part of a rent payment to be applied against the purchase price of a property, especially with lease/purchase contracts.

Rental Income Money paid to someone for the right to use a property. Rental income may only be counted as income if it is consistent. Only the part of the rental income that is over and above expenses (net rental income) may be counted.

REO *See* ***Real Estate Owned***.

Rescind To take back or withdraw an offer or contract. *See* ***Right to Rescind***.

Reserve Requirements The percentage funds that depository institutions must hold in reserve against specified deposit liabilities in the form of cash or in an account at a Federal Reserve Bank.

Reserves Cash on deposit or other highly liquid assets a borrower must have in order to cover two months of PITI mortgage payments, after they make the cash down payment and pays all closing costs.

Residual Income The income a borrower has left after subtracting taxes, housing expense, and all recurring debts and obligations (used for VA loan qualifying). *Also called* ***Cash Flow Analysis***.

RESPA *See* ***Real Estate Settlement Procedures Act***.

Restrictive Covenants *See* ***Deed Restrictions***.

Retirement Benefits *See* ***Pension***.

Right of Disposal Confers upon the owner the ability to transfer all or some property rights to others.

Right of Enjoyment Confers upon the owner the freedom to use land without undue interference from the outside.

Right of Use Confers upon the owner the right to make the land productive.

Right of Way (ROW) An easement that grants access.

Right to Rescind The right of a consumer to rescind some credit transactions that involve their principal residence as collateral up to midnight of the third business day.

Root of Title The deed or other document of transfer that was the first recorded, going back at least as far as required by state law.

Roundtable Closing A closing conducted with all parties present.

Rural Development A government agency under the Department of Agriculture that guarantees or makes loans to help buyers of homes and farms in rural areas or small towns. Formerly the Farmer's Home Administration. (FmHA)

S & Ls *See* ***Savings and Loan Associations***.

SAFE Act *See* ***Secure and Fair Enforcement for Mortgage Licensing Act.***

Sales Comparison Approach An appraisal method that estimates the value of real property by comparing it with other, recently sold properties in the same area. *Also called* ***Market Approach.***

Satisfaction of Mortgage The document a mortgagee gives the mortgagor when a mortgage debt has been paid in full, acknowledging that the debt has been paid and the mortgage is no longer a lien against the property.

Savings and Loan Associations Institutions that specialize in taking savings deposits and making mortgage loans.

Savings Association Insurance Fund (SAIF) A fund under the control of the Federal Deposit Insurance Corporation (FDIC), which insures deposits in Savings and Loan Associations; replaces the Federal Savings and Loan Insurance Corporation (FSLIC).

Scarcity Physical characteristic of real property referring to the limited supply of real estate; also, the perceived supply of a good or service relative to the demand for the item.

Second Mortgage A mortgage that has a lien position subordinate to the first mortgage.

Secondarily Liable A party who is not the primary obligor on an obligation; thus if the lender cannot recover the loan amount from the new party who assumed primary liability, the original party, who is secondarily liable, may still be pursued if that party has not been released.

Secondary Financing The borrowing of money from another source in addition to the primary lender to pay for part of the purchase price or closing costs.

Secondary Mortgage Markets The private investors and government agencies that buy and sell real estate mortgages. *Compare to* ***Primary Mortgage Markets.***

Section 1031 *See* ***Equity Exchange.***

Section 203(b) FHA Loan The standard FHA-insured loan program. There are no income limits on this type of loan. The borrower must meet all FHA qualifying standards and the property cost must not exceed the maximum FHA mortgage amounts. *Also called the* ***Standard FHA Loan Program.***

Section 203(k) FHA Loan The FHA-insured loan program that allows a buyer to buy property and borrow extra money to repair it. Borrower must meet all FHA qualifying standards and must spend at least $5,000 in rehab costs; property cannot exceed maximum FHA mortgage amounts and must be brought up to FHA standards. *Also called* ***Rehabilitation Loan FHA Loan Program.***

Section 234(c) FHA Loan The FHA-insured loan program for condominiums, available only for FHA qualified, single-family condos. The borrower must meet all FHA qualifying standards and property cost must not exceed the maximum FHA mortgage amounts. *Also called* ***Condominium FHA Loan Program.***

Secure and Fair Enforcement for Mortgage Licensing Act (SAFE Act) A key element of the Housing and Economic Recovery Act of 2008 (HERA) designed to enhance consumer protection and reduce fraud by requiring states to establish minimum standards for the licensing and registration of mortgage loan originators.

Secured Creditor A creditor with a lien on specific property, which enables foreclosures and collection of debt from the sale proceeds, if not otherwise paid.

Securities Instruments that pledge assets as security for a debt (e.g., mortgages and trust deeds), or documents that serve as evidence of ownership (e.g., stocks and bonds).

Securitization Act of pooling mortgages and then selling them as mortgage-backed securities.

Security Instrument An instrument that gives a creditor the right to sell collateral to satisfy a debt if the debtor fails to pay according to the terms of the agreement. *Also called* ***Security Agreement.***

Security Interest The interest a creditor may acquire in the debtor's property to ensure that the debt will be paid.

Self-Employment Income Money someone earns working independently, either doing freelance work, as an independent contractor, or as the owner of a company. Self-employment income may only count as income if it is consistent. Tax returns are usually required proving consistency.

Self-Liquidating Description of a fully amortizing loan for which the total payments over the life of the loan pay off the entire balance by the end of the loan's term.

Seller Concession Anything of value added to the transaction by the builder or seller for which the buyer pays nothing additional and which the seller is not customarily expected or required to pay or provide.

Seller Financing The extension of credit from a seller to a buyer in order to finance the purchase of the property, which can be instead of or in addition to the buyer obtaining a loan from a third party, such as an institutional lender.

Seller-Paid Items Closing costs paid by the seller instead of the buyer. This usually refers to items normally paid by the buyer, but in some instances are paid by the seller to help close the sale. FHA and VA loans limit this.

Seller's Market Situation in the housing market where there are more buyers than sellers. This allows sellers to choose from a large number of buyers looking for property in a specific area.

Senior Mortgage A mortgage that has a higher lien position than another mortgage.

Servicer The person or organization responsible for the ongoing management and maintenance of a loan.

Servicing The process of collecting payments, keeping records, and handling defaults for loans.

Settlement Statement A document that presents detailed accounting for a real estate transaction, listing each party's debits and credits and the amount each will receive or be required to pay at closing. *Also called a **closing statement** or a **HUD-1**.*

Severalty Ownership of real property by one person.

Shared Equity Loan, Plan *See **Participation Plan**.*

Sheriff's Deed A deed issued by the court to a purchaser of property from a foreclosure sale.

Sheriff's Sale A foreclosure sale held after a judicial foreclosure. *Sometimes called an **Execution** or an **Execution Sale**.*

Short Sale Strategy where a lender agrees to allow a mortgagor to sell property, accepting a lesser amount than what is owed and releasing its lien on the collateral property being sold.

Simple Interest Interest calculated as a percentage of the principal only. *Compare to **Compound Interest**.*

Single Family Property A single-unit family residence, detached or attached to other housing structures.

Social Security Income Money one receives from the government under the Social Security program. Social Security payments may be counted as income only if they are consistent.

Sole Proprietorship A business owned by a single individual (or a husband and wife for tax purposes) in severalty.

Speculation Investing or optioning with the anticipation that something will go up in value.

Stable Income Income expected to continue in the future.

Steering Illegal activity of channeling prospective buyers or tenants to particular neighborhoods based on their race, religion, national origin, or ancestry. May also include "steering" potential borrowers to closing service providers for a fee, which is contrary to the Real Estate Settlement Procedures Act.

Step Rate Loan *See **Graduated Payment Buydown**.*

Stipulations Conditions that must be met before a loan can close.

Straw Buyer A person who receives payment for the use of that person's name and credit history to apply for a loan, generally as part of a mortgage fraud scheme.

Subdividing The act of splitting a larger parcel of land into several smaller parcels.

Subject Property The property being appraised or for which a value opinion is being sought.

Subject To The transfer of property to a buyer along with an existing mortgage or lien, but without the buyer accepting personal responsibility for the debt. The buyer must make the payments to keep the property, but only loses his or her equity in the event of default. *Compare to **Assumption**.*

Subordination Agreement An agreement that gives a mortgage recorded at a later date the right to take priority over an earlier recorded mortgage.

Subprime Loans Loans that have more risks than allowed in the conforming market.

Substitution Value characteristic that says an informed buyer will not pay more for a home than a comparable substitute.

Supply and Demand Law of economics that says when supply exceeds demand for all products, goods, and services, prices will fall and when demand exceeds supply, prices will rise.

Survey A drawing or map showing the precise legal boundaries a property, the location of improvements, easements, rights of way encroachments, and other physical features. *Compare **Location Survey**.*

T-Bills *See **Treasury Bills**.*

Table Funding A lending method that involves a mortgage broker closing the loan in its name, then immediately (within one business day) assigning it to the lender who provided the funds.

Take-Out Loan A loan used to pay off a construction loan when construction is complete.

Tax, Property An annual tax levied on the value of real property.

Taxation The process of a government levying a charge on people or things.

Teaser Rates A low initial rate on an adjustable rate mortgage. The rate usually returns to normal at the first adjustment date.

Technology Open to Approved Lenders (TOTAL) Mortgage Scorecard Developed by HUD to evaluate the credit risk of FHA loans that are submitted to an automated underwriting system.

Tenancy by the Entirety A type of joint ownership of property that provides right of survivorship and is available only to a husband and wife.

Tenancy in Common A type of joint ownership in a property without right of survivorship.

Tenant Someone in lawful possession of real property. Someone who is leasing property from the owner. *Also called **Lessee**.*

Term A prescribed period of time; especially, the length of time a borrower has to pay off a loan, or the duration of a lease.

Title Lawful ownership of real property. Also, in informal usage, the deed or other document that is evidence of ownership.

Title Company A company that specializes in examining and insuring titles to real estate.

Title, Equitable An interest created in property upon the execution of a valid sales contract, whereby actual title is transferred by deed at a closing. The buyer's interest in property under a land contract. *Also called an **Equitable Interest**.*

Title VIII Part of the Civil Rights Act of 1968; prohibits discrimination based on race, color, religion, sex, national origin, disability, or familial status. *Also referred to as the federal **Fair Housing Act**.*

Title Insurance Insurance that indemnifies against losses resulting from undiscovered title defects and encumbrances.

Title Search A check of the title records to ensure that the seller is the legal owner of the property and that there are no liens or other claims outstanding.

Title Theory States States where a mortgagee holds actual title to property until the loan is repaid. *Compare to **Lien Theory States**.*

Torrens System A system of title registration that is an alternative to the recording system.

Tort A breach in standards of reasonable conduct imposed by law that causes harm to another person.

Townhomes Properties developed for co-ownership where each co-owner has a separate fee simple interest in an individual unit, including its roof and basement, as well as the land directly beneath the unit, and an undivided interest in the common areas of the property.

Trade Fixtures Any equipment or personal property a tenant installs for business purposes.

Transferability The ability to freely buy, sell, encumber, or dispose of property in any way the owner sees fit.

Transfer Tax State or local tax payable when title passes from one owner to another.

Treasury Constant Maturity (One-Year Index) An index used for ARM loans.

Trespass A physical invasion of land by another person with no lawful right to enter the land.

Trust A legal arrangement in which title to property or funds is vested in one or more trustees, who manage the property or invest the funds on behalf of the trust's beneficiaries, in accordance with instructions set forth in the document establishing the trust.

Trust Deed *See **Deed of Trust**.*

Trustee A person appointed to manage a trust on behalf of the beneficiaries; in a trust deed, an independent third party that holds legal title to the property described in the security agreement.

Trustor The borrower in a trust deed.

Truth in Lending Act (TILA) Federal act that requires lenders to disclose credit costs in order to promote informed use of consumer credit. *Also known as **Regulation Z**.*

Truth in Lending Statement (TIL) Disclosure of the true costs associated with a residential loan, including the annual percentage rate, that is required to be given to prospective borrowers within three business days of a completed loan application.

UCC *See* **Uniform Commercial Code**.

Underwriter Individual who evaluates a loan application to determine its risk level for a lender or investor; final decision maker on a loan application.

Underwriting The process of evaluating and deciding whether to make a new loan and on what terms.

Underwriting Standards The criteria an underwriter uses to determine if a borrower or property qualifies for a loan.

Undivided Interest Legal doctrine that gives co-owners the right to possession of the whole property and not just part of it.

Unemployment Money paid to someone for support, compensation, or temporary income after losing a job. Unemployment compensation may be counted as income only if it is consistent.

Unencumbered Property Property for which the seller has clear title, free of mortgages or other liens.

Uniform Commercial Code Comprehensive code governing, among other things, transactions involving personal and real property; used as a model that has been enacted in some form or another by all 50 states.

Uniform Residential Appraisal Report (URAR) Standard appraisal report form used by lenders and appraisers. The URAR was developed and approved by Fannie Mae (Form 1004) and Freddie Mac (Form 70).

Uniform Standards of Professional Appraisal Practice (USPAP) Professional appraisal standards promulgated by The Appraisal Foundation and recognized throughout the United States as the accepted standards of appraisal practice.

Uniqueness Characteristic of real property that says that every piece of land, every building, and every house is said to be a different piece of real estate. *Also called **non-homogeneity**.*

URAR *See **Uniform Residential Appraisal Report**.*

USPAP *See **Uniform Standards of Professional Appraisal Practice**.*

U.S. Department of Housing and Urban Development (HUD) Established in 1965 to increase homeownership, support community development, and increase access to affordable housing free from discrimination.

U.S. Treasury Department The part of the executive branch of the federal government that is the fiscal manager of the nation; responsible for carrying out the nation's fiscal policy by doing the actual spending, taxing, and debt financing via an account it keeps with the Federal Reserve.

Usury Charging an interest rate that exceeds legal limits.

Utility The ability of a good or service to satisfy human wants, needs, or desires.

VA Guaranty The dollar amount of loan that will be paid by the VA in the event of borrower default.

Valid The legal classification of a contract that is binding and enforceable in a court of law.

Value The amount of goods or services offered in the marketplace in exchange for something else.

Value Range A range of possible values for a property based on the data analyzed by the appraiser.

Variable-Rate Mortgage (VRM) Any loan in which the interest rate may change, whether it is tied to an index or not. VRMs are now obsolete and replaced by adjustable rate mortgages (ARMs).

Vendee A buyer or purchaser; particularly, someone buying property under a land contract.

Vendor A seller; particularly, someone selling property by means of a land contract.

Verification of Deposit (VOD) A process used by creditors to review a borrower's financial accounts for verification of status and account balance.

Verification of Employment (VOE) A process used by creditors to review a borrower's employment history for verification of job stability, income history, etc.

Veteran's Benefits Administration Government agency, part of the U.S. Department of Veteran's Affairs, that guarantees mortgage loans for eligible veterans.

Void Having no legal force or effect.

Voucher System A disbursement plan for construction mortgage payouts whereby the contractor pays his or her own bills and then submits bills to the lender for reimbursement.

Waiver The voluntary relinquishment or surrender of a right.

Warehouse Lending A line of credit extended to a mortgage loan originator by a lender that allows the MLO to fund a loan initially before selling it either to the lender or the secondary market upon closing.

Warrant System A disbursement plan for construction mortgage payouts whereby the lender directly pays bills presented by the various suppliers and laborers on the project.

Warranty Deed A deed that carries certain warranties related to title and the grantor's right to convey title; warranties may be broad or limited.

Waste Use or abuse of property in any way that permanently damages it or reduces its market value.

Welfare Money paid to someone from the government for support. Welfare may only be counted as income if it is consistent or permanent.

Wild Deed A deed outside the chain of title.

Words of Conveyance Deed language that clearly states the grantor's intention to transfer the real property.

Writ of Execution A court order directing a public officer, often the sheriff or marshal, to seize and/or sell property to regain possession for the owner and/or satisfy a debt.

Yield The total amount of money that can be made from an investment.

Yield Spread Premium (YSP) Tool that allows a borrower to accept a slightly higher interest rate in exchange for financing upfront fees and closing costs associated with a loan, thereby reducing cash needed to close.

Zoning The classification of land by types of uses permitted and prohibited in a given district, and by densities permitted and prohibited, including regulations regarding building location on lots.

Zoning Ordinances Local laws dividing a city, county, etc., into zones, allowing different types of land use in different areas, as well as codes that must be followed to ensure safe construction practices.

Index

B

C

M

Q

R